FINANCIAL VALUATION: BUSINESSES AND BUSINESS INTERESTS

JAMES H. ZUKIN
Editor in Chief

JOHN G. MAVREDAKIS
Managing Editor

WARREN GORHAM LAMONT
A Division of Research Institute of America Inc.

Copyright © 1990

RESEARCH INSTITUTE OF AMERICA INC.

ALL RIGHTS RESERVED

No part of this publication may be reproduced in any form, by photostat, microfilm, xerography, or any other means, or incorporated into any information retrieval system, electronic or mechanical, without the written permission of the copyright owner. Inquiries regarding permission for use of material contained in this publication should be addressed to:

WARREN GORHAM LAMONT
210 South Street
Boston, Massachusetts 02111

ISBN 0-13-945023-8

Library of Congress Catalog Card No. 89-26668

This publication is designed to provide accurate and authoritative information in regard to the subject matter covered. In publishing this book, neither the author nor the publisher is engaged in rendering legal, accounting, or other professional service. If legal advice or other expert assistance is required, the services of a competent professional should be sought.

PRINTED IN THE UNITED STATES OF AMERICA

BOARD OF ADVISERS AND CONTRIBUTORS

JAMES H. ZUKIN, Editor in Chief	*Managing Director, Houlihan, Lokey, Howard & Zukin, Inc., Los Angeles, Ca.*
JOHN G. MAVREDAKIS,* Managing Editor	*Managing Director, Houlihan, Lokey, Howard & Zukin, Inc., Los Angeles, CA*
BYRLE ABBIN	*Partner, Arthur Andersen & Co., Washington, D.C.*
RALPH ARNOLD*	*Senior Valuation Analyst, Willamette Management Associates, Portland, OR*
JACK W. BERKA*	*Senior Vice President, Houlihan, Lokey, Howard & Zukin, Inc., Los Angeles, CA*
MICHAEL J. BOLOTSKY*	*Independent Business Consultant, Plainsboro, NJ*
RICHARD S. BRAUN*	*Managing Director, Houlihan, Lokey, Howard & Zukin, Inc., Los Angeles, CA*
MARKO A. BUDGYK*	*Senior Vice President, Houlihan, Lokey, Howard & Zukin, Inc., Los Angeles, CA*
ROGER C. DAVISSON*	*General Partner, Brentwood Associates, Los Angeles, CA*
JAY E. FISHMAN*	*President, Financial Research, Inc., Ardmore, PA*
WALLACE F. FORBES*	*Consultant, Founder, Benchmark Valuation Consultants; Former Principal, KMPG Peat Marwick, New York, NY*
PETER B. FRANK*	*Partner, Price Waterhouse, Los Angeles, CA*

---

* Contributor
** Contributor and Board Member

JAN C. GABRIELSON, ESQ.*	*Shareholder, Walzer & Gabrielson, Los Angeles, CA*
GLENN GARLICK*	*Vice President, Houlihan, Lokey, Howard & Zukin, Inc., Los Angeles, CA*
ROBERT GESKE	*Professor of Finance, Graduate School of Management, University of California at Los Angeles; President, LOR/ Geske Bock Associates, Los Angeles, CA*
KENT V. GRAHAM, ESQ.**	*Partner, O'Melveny & Myers, Los Angeles, CA*
JEFFREY R. GREENE*	*Managing Director, Houlihan, Lokey, Howard & Zukin, Inc., New York, NY*
ALEX W. HOWARD*	*Senior Vice President, Lovett Underwood Neuhaus & Webb, Inc., Houston, TX*
ROBERT F. HOWARD*	*Managing Director, Houlihan, Lokey, Howard & Zukin, Inc., Los Angeles, CA*
DONALD P. JACOBS*	*Manager, KPMG Peat Marwick, New York, NY*
JARED KAPLAN, ESQ.	*Partner, Keck, Mahin & Cate, Chicago, IL*
CHARLES F.G. KUYK*	*Partner, Price Waterhouse, San Francisco, CA*
M. MARK LEE	*Associate Director, Bear Stearns & Co., New York, NY*
MARK S. LEFENFELD, ESQ.*	*Managing Director, Russell Miller, Inc., San Francisco, CA*
O. KIT LOKEY	*Managing Director, Houlihan, Lokey, Howard & Zukin, Inc., Los Angeles, CA*

---

* *Contributor*
** *Contributor and Board Member*

BOARD OF ADVISORS AND CONTRIBUTORS

ALVIN D. LURIE, ESQ.	*Partner, Meyers, Tersigni, Lurie, Feldman & Gray, New York, NY*
RUSSELL R. MILLER*	*Chairman, Russell Miller, Inc., San Francisco, CA*
PHILIP H. OSBORNE	*Senior Vice President, Management Planning, Inc., Princeton, NJ*
SHANNON P. PRATT**	*President, Willamette Management Associates, Inc., Portland, OR*
LORI M. PRICE*	*Vice President, Houlihan, Lokey, Howard & Zukin, Inc., Los Angeles, CA*
WAYNE REID	*Partner, Arthur Andersen & Co., Atlanta, GA*
JAMES H. SCHILT*	*Independent Business Appraiser; Founder and Editor of Business Valuation Review, San Francisco, CA*
MAYER SIEGEL, ESQ.	*Partner, Fried, Frank, Harris, Shriver & Jacobson, New York, NY*
DONALD V. SMITH	*Managing Director, Houlihan, Lokey, Howard & Zukin, Inc., New York, NY*
ROBERT SOCOL*	*Managing Director, Houlihan, Lokey, Howard & Zukin, Inc., Los Angeles, CA*
CHARLES H. STRYKER*	*Senior Manager, KPMG Peat Marwick, New York, NY*
RICHARD M. WISE**	*President, Richard Wise & Associates, Montreal, Canada*
ARTHUR F. WOODARD, ESQ.	*Partner, Kaye Scholer Fierman, Hays & Handler, New York, NY*

---

* *Contributor*
** *Contributor and Board Member*

HOW TO USE THIS BOOK

The valuation needs and activities of the business community are presented in *Financial Valuation: Business and Business Interests* in cogent, pragmatic format. The book is divided into three parts: Valuation Theory and Principles (Chapters 1-7), Valuation for Specific Purposes (Chapters 8-13), and Valuation by Industry (Chapters 14-21). A Summary Table of Contents and a detailed Table of Contents have also been included, enabling users to scan for and locate material with ease.

Each part and each chapter opens with a synopsis of its major coverage. Each chapter is organized in a numbered-paragraph format for easy identification and location of material. The book also includes one appendix (a reprint of the pivotal Revenue Ruling 59-60) and an up-to-date bibliography of financial valuation resources. A table of cases and subject-matter index appear at the end of the book; they are conveniently keyed to the numbered paragraphs in the text.

Regular supplementation of this book is planned to keep users abreast of the rapid changes in the field.

PREFACE

Financial Valuation: Businesses and Business Interests is a response to the growing importance of financial valuation in the business world. This comprehensive volume addresses the most commonly asked valuation questions and presents concepts never before published in book format. An authoritative collection of the research and findings of the leading financial experts, this multiauthored work is the first of its kind and establishes a range of perspectives for professionals who perform valuation services or need access to in-depth valuation policies, practices, and procedures. Its purpose is to bring practitioners—lawyers, financial analysts, accountants, investment bankers, regulators, stockbrokers, bankers, and investors—and business owners/executives—chief financial officers, tax managers, chief executive officers, presidents, and chairmen—directly into the world of financial valuation.

Recognizing the importance of a solid theoretical ground in this complex field, Part I opens with the historical background and general theory of financial valuation, providing complete definitions and description of the valuation methodologies, including a discussion of the distinction between fairness and fair market value. The most important variables encountered by valuation professionals—capitalization rates and discount rates—are discussed in depth. The analytical heart of Part I is a cumulative case study as well as a discussion of options, warrants, the real value of securities, and, more importantly, fixed-income securities. The outgrowth of a massive statistical study, the fixed-income chapter breaks new ground in financial research as applied to fixed income and develops new and important insights.

Part II shows how the theories, methodologies, and procedures outlined in Part I are applied in specific business situations. This part opens with a thorough analysis of employee stock ownership plans, and valuation litigation. From this point, the discussion moves on to valuation of common equity securities, marital dissolutions, and valuation for the purposes of start-ups/initial public offerings/private placements, bankruptcy, and venture capital.

Part III changes the focus from generic business situations to specific industries, many of which require their own peculiar analytical approaches and application principles. There is significant difference, for example, between valuing a financial intermediary and a manufacturing firm. Part III closes with a chapter on financial valuation in Canada where the professional valuation society is well developed and perhaps more advanced than the United States but where differences in procedures and practices are important to those doing business across the border.

The ultimate goal of the valuation expert when performing an evaluation analysis is to balance the theoretical and the empirical. The goal in this volume is to help the reader achieve that critical balance.

This ground-breaking volume is the product of many years of research and work by its authors, who number among the leading experts in the field of financial valuation. In addition, the book has benefited from the expertise and prestige of its board of advisers. Special acknowledgment must also be given to John G. Mavredakis, who is my editorial partner on and the managing editor of this project, Lynne Farris, who helped bring the project to fruition, and to Marie Orsini Rosen, who lent her editorial support.

James H. Zukin
Editor in Chief

SUMMARY TABLE OF CONTENTS

		Page
	HOW TO USE THIS BOOK	vii
	PREFACE	ix

PART I	VALUATION THEORY AND PRINCIPLES	
Chapter 1	Appraisal in Retrospect by James H. Schilt	1-1
Chapter 2	Valuation Terminology and Methodology by Jay E. Fishman	2-1
Chapter 3	Fairness vs. Fair Market Value by Kent V. Graham	3-1
Chapter 4	Ratio Analysis for Evaluating Financial Performance by Robert Socol	4-1
Chapter 5	Capitalization and Discount Rates by Richard S. Braun	5-1
Chapter 6	Valuation Case Study by John G. Mavredakis and Glenn Garlick	6-1
Chapter 7	Valuation of Fixed-Income Securities: Bonds and Preferred Stock by Marko A. Budgyk	7-1

PART II	VALUATION FOR SPECIFIC PURPOSES	
Chapter 8	ESOP Valuations by Richard S. Braun	8-1
Chapter 9	Valuation Litigation by Charles F.G. Kuyk, Robert F. Howard and Peter B. Frank	9-1
Chapter 10	Valuation of Common Equity Securities When Asset Liquidation Is an Alternative by Michael J. Bolotsky	10-1
Chapter 11	Valuation in Marital Dissolutions by Jan C. Gabrielson	11-1
Chapter 12	Valuation of Start-Ups, Initial Public Offerings, and Private Placements by Roger C. Davisson	12-1

Chapter 13	Solvency Analysis in Leveraged Transactions *by Jeffrey R. Greene and Lori M. Price*	13-1
PART III	**VALUATION BY INDUSTRY**	
Chapter 14	Differentiating Approaches by Industry Groups *by Shannon P. Pratt*	14-1
Chapter 15	Manufacturing *by Wallace F. Forbes*	15-1
Chapter 16	Service Companies *by Donald P. Jacobs and Charles H. Stryker* ..	16-1
Chapter 17	Financial Institutions *by Jack W. Berka*	17-1
Chapter 18	Insurance Companies and Agencies *by Russell R. Miller and Mark S. Lefenfeld* ...	18-1
Chapter 19	Natural Resources *by Alex W. Howard*	19-1
Chapter 20	Professional Practices *by Ralph Arnold and Shannon P. Pratt*	20-1
Chapter 21	Canadian Financial Valuation *by Richard M. Wise*	21-1
APPENDIX A	REVENUE RULING 59-60	A-1
	BIBLIOGRAPHY	B-1
	TABLE OF CASES	T-1
	INDEX	I-1

TABLE OF CONTENTS

                                                    Page

How to Use This Book vii
Preface ix

PART I VALUATION THEORY AND PRINCIPLES

Chapter 1
Appraisal in Retrospect

¶ 1.1	Concepts Behind Business Valuation.............	1-2
	[1] Goodwill.................................	1-2
	[2] Fair Market Value........................	1-3
	[3] Organization and Capitalization of Earnings.	1-3
	[4] Capitalization Rates	1-4
	[5] Formula for Determining Loss of Goodwill .	1-4
	[6] Value of Intangibles	1-5
¶ 1.2	Evolution of Appraisal Firms....................	1-5
¶ 1.3	Development of IRS Guides and Manuals	1-7
¶ 1.4	Publication of Recent Standard Texts	1-8
¶ 1.5	Summary of Major Court Decisions	1-9
¶ 1.6	Evolution of Professional Associations...........	1-13

Chapter 2
Valuation Terminology and Methodology

¶ 2.1	Definitions of Value	2-3
	[1] Fair Market Value........................	2-3
	[2] Fair Value	2-3
	[3] Investment Value or Intrinsic Value	2-4
	[4] Going-Concern Value	2-4
	[5] Liquidation Value	2-4
	[6] Book Value	2-5
	[7] Enterprise Value.........................	2-5
¶ 2.2	Description of the Particular Asset	2-5
¶ 2.3	Valuation Date	2-6
¶ 2.4	Equity Valuation	2-6
	[1] Understanding the Subject Enterprise	2-7
	[2] Economic- and Industry-Specific Analysis ...	2-10
¶ 2.5	Financial Statement Analysis and Adjustment....	2-11
	[1] Examining the Financial Statements	2-13
	[2] Income Statement	2-13
	[3] Balance Sheet	2-16

			Page
	[4]	Statement of Changes in Financial Position or Funds Flow Statement	2-17
¶ 2.6		**Common-Size Statements**	2-17
	[1]	Income Statement	2-18
	[2]	Balance Sheet	2-18
	[3]	Financial Ratios	2-19
	[4]	Liquidity	2-20
	[5]	Asset Management	2-20
	[6]	Accounts Receivable Turnover or Average Collection Period	2-21
	[7]	Total Asset Utilization	2-21
	[8]	Debt Management	2-21
	[9]	Profitability	2-22
	[10]	Adjusting Financial Statements	2-23
	[11]	Balance Sheet	2-24
	[12]	Income Statement	2-25
	[13]	Mechanics of Adjusting Financial Statements	2-26
¶ 2.7		**Valuation Methodologies**	2-27
¶ 2.8		**Market Comparison Approach**	2-27
	[1]	Comparative Company Search	2-27
	[2]	Valuation Ratios Derived From Comparatives	2-30
	[3]	Sources of Market Information	2-32
¶ 2.9		**Income Approach**	2-34
	[1]	Defining the Benefit Stream	2-35
	[2]	Time Horizon Used	2-36
	[3]	Concept of Risk and Its Application	2-37
	[4]	Methods for Determining Cost of Equity	2-38
¶ 2.10		**Cost Approach**	2-42
	[1]	Underlying Asset Approach	2-42
	[2]	Excess Earnings Approach	2-44
¶ 2.11		**Discounts and Premiums**	2-45
¶ 2.12		**Summary**	2-46

Chapter 3
Fairness vs. Fair Market Value

¶ 3.1		Basic Distinction Between Fairness and Fair Market Value	3-2
	[1]	When Relevant	3-2
		[a] Mergers and Acquisitions	3-2
		[b] Other Fairness Opinions	3-3
	[2]	Parties Involved	3-3

TABLE OF CONTENTS

Page

¶ 3.2	Director Conduct vs. Shareholder Rights	3-6
	[1] Business Judgment Rule	3-6
	[2] Appraisal Rights	3-7
¶ 3.3	Courts' Concept of Fairness	3-9
	[1] "Entire Fairness"	3-9
	[2] Fair Value	3-11
	[3] Procedural Fairness	3-12
¶ 3.4	Role of Valuation Expert	3-13
	[1] Weight Given to Fairness Opinion	3-16
	[a] Independence	3-16
	[b] Sufficient Time	3-16
	[c] Information Available	3-17
	[d] Disclosure to Third Parties	3-19
	[2] Liability of Valuation Experts	3-19
¶ 3.5	Disclosure Requirements	3-20
	[1] Federal	3-21
	[2] State	3-23

Chapter 4
Ratio Analysis for Evaluating Financial Performance

¶ 4.1	Ratio Analysis and Financial Statements	4-2
¶ 4.2	Financial Ratios	4-6
	[1] Liquidity Ratios	4-6
	[a] Current Ratio	4-6
	[b] Quick (or Acid Test) Ratio	4-7
	[c] Cash Ratio	4-10
	[2] Leverage Ratios	4-10
	[a] Total Debt/Total Assets Ratio	4-11
	[b] Total Interest-Bearing Debt/Equity Ratio	4-12
	[c] Times Interest Earned Ratio	4-12
	[d] Fixed-Charges Coverage Ratio	4-13
	[3] Activity Ratios	4-13
	[a] Inventory Turnover Ratio	4-13
	[b] Average Collection Period Ratio	4-14
	[c] Fixed-Assets Turnover Ratio	4-16
	[d] Working Capital Turnover Ratio	4-16
	[e] Total Assets Turnover Ratio	4-17
	[4] Profitability Ratios	4-17
	[a] Gross Profit Margin/Sales Ratio	4-18
	[b] Profit Margin/Sales Ratio	4-18
	[c] Return on Total Assets Ratio	4-18

			Page
	[d]	Return on Net Worth Ratio	4-19
	[5]	Evaluating the Ratios	4-19
¶ 4.3	Trend Analysis		4-20
¶ 4.4	du Pont System		4-23
¶ 4.5	Financial Leverage		4-23
¶ 4.6	Industry Rates of Return		4-25
¶ 4.7	Comparative Industry Ratios		4-26
¶ 4.8	Security Analysis		4-27
¶ 4.9	Ratio Analysis Limitations		4-27
¶ 4.10	Ratio Analysis Summary		4-28

Chapter 5
Capitalization and Discount Rates

¶ 5.1	Capitalization Rates			5-2
	[1]	Types of Capitalization Rates		5-3
		[a]	Price/Earnings Multiple	5-3
		[b]	Price/Future Earnings Multiple	5-4
		[c]	Price/Cash-Flow Multiple	5-4
		[d]	Price/Debt-Free Earnings Multiple	5-5
		[e]	Price/Debt-Free Cash-Flow Multiple	5-6
		[f]	Other Debt-Free Capitalization Rates	5-6
		[g]	Price/Net Book Value Multiple	5-7
		[h]	Other Multiples	5-7
	[2]	Computation of Capitalization Rates		5-8
		[a]	Numerator Selection	5-8
		[b]	Denominator Selection	5-8
	[3]	Variation in Capitalization Rates		5-9
		[a]	General Economic Conditions	5-9
		[b]	Industry-Specific Factors	5-9
		[c]	Company-Specific Factors	5-10
¶ 5.2	Discount Rates			5-10
	[1]	Concept of Present Value		5-11
	[2]	Comparison With Capitalization Rates		5-11
	[3]	Market Examples		5-12
	[4]	Stated Yields versus Discount Rates		5-13
	[5]	Determination of Proper Discount Rate		5-13
	[6]	Use of Financial Theory		5-14
	[7]	Changing Capital Structures		5-15
¶ 5.3	Summary			5-15

TABLE OF CONTENTS

Page

Chapter 6
Valuation Case Study

¶ 6.1	Purpose...	6-2
¶ 6.2	General Valuation Considerations	6-3
¶ 6.3	Scope of Investigation	6-4
¶ 6.4	Corporate Description	6-5
	[1] Company History...........................	6-5
	[2] Products	6-6
	[3] Customers.................................	6-6
	[4] Marketing	6-7
	[5] Competition	6-7
	[6] Suppliers	6-7
	[7] Personnel	6-7
¶ 6.5	General Economic Overview and Industry Review	6-8
	[1] General Economy	6-8
	[2] Industry Review	6-8
¶ 6.6	Financial Review	6-9
	[1] Financial Condition and Results of Operations	6-9
	[a] Current Assets.......................	6-14
	[b] Current Liabilities	6-15
	[c] Liquidity	6-15
	[d] Gross Profits	6-16
	[e] Operating Income.....................	6-16
	[f] Profitability..........................	6-17
	[2] Projections	6-17
	[3] Industry Comparison	6-18
¶ 6.7	Valuation Methodology Overview	6-20
	[1] Multiple of Earnings and Cash Flow........	6-20
	[2] Capitalization of Dividends.................	6-21
	[3] Market Price to Book Value...............	6-21
	[4] Discounted Future Debt-Free Cash Flow ...	6-21
	[5] Adjusted Book Value	6-21
	[6] Other Indices of Value	6-22
¶ 6.8	Valuation Analysis	6-22
	[1] Selection of Comparative Public Companies .	6-22
	[2] Comparison of Elcon With Comparative Public Companies.........................	6-23
	[3] Market Comparison Approaches............	6-26
	[a] Multiple of Earnings-Price/Earnings Approach	6-26

			Page
	[b]	Multiple of Cash Flow-Price/Cash Flow Approach	6-29
	[c]	Price/EBIT and Price/EBDIT Approaches	6-30
	[d]	Capitalizaiton of Dividends and Price/Net Book Value Approaches	6-31
	[4]	Discounted Future Cash Flows	6-32
	[5]	Adjusted Book Value	6-34
	[6]	Other Indices of Value	6-35
¶ 6.9		**Other Valuation Considerations**	6-37
	[1]	Premium for Controlling Interest	6-38
	[2]	Discount for Minority Interest	6-39
	[3]	Discount for Lack of Marketability	6-39
¶ 6.10		**Valuation Summary**	6-40
	[1]	Reconciliation of Value Indications	6-41
	[2]	Conclusions	6-42

Chapter 7
Valuation of Fixed-Income Securities: Bonds and Preferred Stock

¶ 7.1		**Bonds vs. Preferred Stock**	7-2
¶ 7.2		**Basic Valuation Principles**	7-2
¶ 7.3		**Issue-Specific Risk**	7-3
	[1]	Duration	7-3
	[2]	Dividend and Interest Protection	7-5
	[3]	Asset Protection	7-6
	[4]	Corporate Protection	7-7
		[a] Callability	7-7
		[b] Exchangeability	7-7
¶ 7.4		**Company-Specific Risk**	7-8
	[1]	Nature of Capital Structure	7-8
	[2]	Variability of Operations	7-9
¶ 7.5		**Measuring and Quantifying Risk**	7-9
	[1]	Measures of Risk	7-9
	[2]	Issue-Specific Risk	7-10
		[a] Duration	7-10
		[b] Position in Capital Structure	7-11
		[c] Collateralization	7-12
	[3]	Callability	7-13
	[4]	Company-Specific Risk	7-14
¶ 7.5		**Summary**	7-16

PART II VALUATION FOR SPECIFIC PURPOSES

Chapter 8
ESOP Valuations

		Page
¶ 8.1	What Is an ESOP?	8-2
¶ 8.2	Proposed Adequate Consideration Regulations	8-3
¶ 8.3	Types of ESOPs	8-3
	[1] Nonleveraged ESOPs	8-3
	[a] Stock Contributions	8-4
	[b] Cash Contributions	8-5
	[2] Leveraged ESOPs	8-6
	[a] Stock Purchases	8-6
	[b] Dilution Impact	8-7
	[c] Decline in Value	8-7
¶ 8.4	Quantification of ESOP Benefits	8-8
¶ 8.5	Multi-Investor Equity Allocation Issues	8-9
	[1] Equity Allocation Approaches	8-10
¶ 8.6	Adequate Consideration	8-11
	[1] Fair Market Value	8-11
	[2] Premiums and Marketability	8-12
	[3] Independence	8-13
¶ 8.7	Effective Date of Appraisal	8-14
¶ 8.8	Report Format and Content	8-14
¶ 8.9	Fairness	8-15
¶ 8.10	Conclusion	8-15
Appendix 8-1 DOL Proposed Regulation Relating to the Definition of Adequate Consideration		8-15

Chapter 9
Valuation Litigation

¶ 9.1	The Litigation Setting	9-4
	[1] Common Valuation Litigation	9-5
	[2] Uniqueness of the Legal Context	9-6
	[a] Statutory Law	9-6
	[b] Regulatory and Administrative Law	9-7
	[c] Case Law	9-7
	[d] Rules of Civil Procedure and Evidence	9-8
	[3] The Judicial Process	9-11
	[a] The Complaint	9-11
	[b] The Answer	9-12
	[c] Discovery	9-12

				Page
		[d]	Motions, Stipulations, and Requests for Admission	9-15
		[e]	Pretrial Hearings	9-16
		[f]	Trial	9-17
		[g]	Judge and Jury	9-18
		[h]	The Verdict	9-19
¶ 9.2	**Guidelines for the Expert Witness**			9-19
	[1]	Attributes of the Valuation Expert Witness		9-19
		[a]	Personal Attributes	9-20
		[b]	Professional Attributes	9-21
	[2]	The Litigation Engagement		9-22
		[a]	Expert Witness or Consultant	9-22
		[b]	The Exercise of Professional Judgment	9-24
		[c]	Conflicts of Interest	9-24
		[d]	Inconsistencies With Prior Case Testimony	9-25
		[e]	Engagement Acceptance Considerations	9-26
		[f]	Testimony Evidence Submitted	9-27
		[g]	Reliance Upon Company Financial Statements	9-28
		[h]	What to Expect From the Opposition	9-28
		[i]	What to Expect in the Deposition	9-30
	[3]	The Valuation Report and Expert Testimony		9-31
		[a]	Standards of Report Content	9-31
		[b]	Preparation for Testimony	9-32
		[c]	Conduct in Depositions	9-33
		[d]	Conduct in Trial	9-33
¶ 9.3	**Valuation Litigation by Case Type**			9-35
	[1]	Dissenting Shareholder Statutes		9-35
		[a]	Appraisal Rights	9-35
		[b]	Standard of Value	9-37
		[c]	Entire Fairness	9-39
		[d]	Burden of Proof	9-39
		[e]	Valuation Approaches	9-40
		[f]	Other Factors	9-42
		[g]	The Level of Value	9-42
		[h]	Summary	9-45
	[2]	Corporate or Partnership Dissolution Statutes		9-46
		[a]	Forms of Liquidation	9-46
		[b]	Voluntary vs. Involuntary Dissolution	9-49
		[c]	Partnership Dissolution vs. Corporate Dissolution	9-50

			Page
	[d]	The Valuation Date	9-52
	[e]	Summary	9-52
	[3]	Business Valuations Under Federal Statutes	9-52
¶ 9.4	**Recovery of Damages**		9-54
	[1]	Corporate Damages	9-54
		[a] Origins of Litigation	9-54
		[b] Valuation vs. Damage Determination	9-55
		[c] Legal Theory of Damages	9-57
		[d] Elements of Recovery	9-58
	[2]	Human Capital Valuation	9-62
		[a] Elements of Damage	9-62
		[b] Medical and Funeral Expenses	9-63
		[c] Personal Injury Lost Earnings	9-64
		[d] Wrongful Death/Lost Earnings	9-65
		[e] Assessing the Impact of Inflation	9-72
		[f] Discounting Future Earnings	9-73
Appendix 9-1	**Federal Rules of Evidence—Article VII.**		
	Opinions and Expert Testimony		9-76
Appendix 9-2	**Sample Litigation Retainer Agreement**		9-78

Chapter 10
Valuation of Common Equity Securities When Asset Liquidation Is an Alternative

¶ 10.1	**The Mechanics of Liquidation Analysis**		10-3
	[1]	Determination of "Combined Highest and Best Use"	10-3
		[a] Liquidation vs. Continued Operation	10-4
		[b] The Role of Intangible Assets	10-5
	[2]	Determination of Gross Liquidation Proceeds	10-5
	[3]	Reduction of Gross Proceeds to Net Liquidation Value	10-5
		[a] Reduction for Costs and Taxes and Comparison to Going-Concern Value	10-5
		[b] Reduction to Present Worth and Comparison to Going-Concern Value	10-6
	[4]	Summary	10-7
¶ 10.2	**Examples of Liquidation Analysis**		10-10
	[1]	Liquidation of the Entire Entity	10-10
	[2]	Liquidation of a Portion of the Entity	10-11
¶ 10.3	**Choice of Discount Rate**		10-12
	[1]	Comparison to the Discount Rate for an Operating Company	10-14

			Page
	[2]	Factors to Consider	10-15
	[3]	Quantification of the Factors	10-16
	[4]	Selection of a Discount Rate	10-18
		[a] Low-Risk Scenario	10-18
		[b] High-Risk Scenario	10-19
	[5]	Relative Risk in Liquidation vs. Continued Operation	10-20
¶ 10.4	**Additional Considerations**		10-21
	[1]	Liquidation Value of Assets vs. Liquidation Value of Stock	10-21
	[2]	Liquidation Value of Assets as the "Floor" of Value of the Stock	10-21
	[3]	Intangible Asset Value	10-22
	[4]	Factoring in Both Liquidation and Continued Operation	10-23
	[5]	The Value of Minority Interests	10-23
		[a] When and How to Factor in Liquidation	10-24
		[b] Applicability of a Minority-Interest Discount	10-25
		[c] Fairness Considerations	10-26
		[d] Discount for Lack of Marketability	10-26
	[6]	Shareholder-Level Taxes and the Value of Common Stock	10-27
¶ 10.5	**Summary**		10-30
Appendix 10-1	Detail of Table 10-1 Liquidation Value Computations		10-30

Chapter 11
Valuation in Marital Dissolutions

¶ 11.1	**Valuing Businesses for Purposes of Marital Dissolution**		11-3
¶ 11.2	**The Meaning of Value in the Context of Marital Dissolution**		11-4
	[1]	Market Value	11-4
	[2]	Investment Value	11-5
	[3]	Compulsion Value	11-5
¶ 11.3	**Formulas**		11-5
	[1]	Uses of Formulas	11-6
	[2]	Derivation of Formulas	11-6
		[a] Tax Rulings and Cases	11-6
		[b] "Creative" Appraisal Methods	11-7

		Page
	[c] Problems With Formulas	11-7
¶ 11.4	**Judicial Attitude Toward Valuation Methods**	11-8
	[1] Most Methods Approved on Appeal	11-8
	[2] Mandated Methods	11-8
	[3] Forbidden Methods	11-8
	[a] Price/Earnings Ratio	11-9
	[b] Stock-for-Stock Transactions as Comparable Prices	11-9
	[4] Splitting the Difference	11-9
	[5] Reservation of Jurisdiction Over Contingencies	11-10
¶ 11.5	**Other Factors in Valuation**	11-10
	[1] Buy-Sell Agreements	11-10
	[a] Binding Values	11-11
	[b] Influential Tax Cases	11-11
	[c] Specific Provisions for Marital Dissolutions	11-11
	[d] Legal Issue or Valuation Issue?	11-12
	[2] Potential Tax Liabilities	11-12
¶ 11.6	**Tactical Problems**	11-13
	[1] Concealed Income	11-13
	[2] Assertions of Confidentiality	11-14
	[a] Trade Secrets; Patient and Client Records	11-14
	[b] Privacy of Business Associates	11-14
¶ 11.7	**Components of Value**	11-14
	[1] "Hard" Assets	11-15
	[2] Accounts Receivable	11-15
	[a] Reduction for Taxes	11-15
	[b] Receivables and Alimony: The Double Dip	11-15
	[c] Vanishing Separate Accounts Receivable	11-16
	[3] Goodwill	11-16
	[a] Goodwill as Property in a Marital Dissolution	11-16
	[b] Problems of Valuing Goodwill	11-16
	[c] Discount for Relocating	11-17
	[4] Loans to Shareholders	11-17
	[a] Loan Accounts	11-17
	[b] Handling the Balance at Separation	11-17
	[c] Handling Additions After Separation	11-18
¶ 11.8	**Effect of Separation**	11-18

			Page
	[1]	Earnings Become Nonmarital Property	11-18
	[2]	Effect of Postseparation Work	11-18
	[3]	Restrictions on Earnings History	11-19
		[a] Postseparation Earnings	11-19
		[b] How the Valuation Is Affected	11-19
		[c] Applicability of Rule to Spouse's Earnings	11-20
		[d] Comparing Preseparation Earnings With a Comparable Period	11-20
	[4]	Definition of Separation	11-20
¶ 11.9	**Apportionment of Premarital Property and Marital Property**		11-20
	[1]	Fair Return on Separate Capital Method	11-21
	[2]	Reasonable Compensation Method	11-21
	[3]	Court Discretion to Determine Method	11-21
¶ 11.10	**Date of Valuation**		11-22
	[1]	Statutory and Decisional Provisions	11-22
	[2]	Distinction From Restrictions on Earnings History	11-23
¶ 11.11	**Management and Control Problems That Affect Valuation While Marital Dissolution Is Pending**		11-23
	[1]	One Spouse Working in the Business	11-23
	[2]	Both Spouses Working in the Business	11-24
¶ 11.12	**Professional Practices**		11-24
	[1]	Professional Practices as Assets	11-24
	[2]	Absence of a Market	11-24
	[3]	Income Usually Produced by Current Work	11-25
	[4]	Small Share in a Big Firm	11-25
	[5]	Valuation of License and Education	11-25
¶ 11.13	**Distribution of Business Interests Between the Spouses**		11-26
	[1]	Corporate Stock	11-26
	[2]	Both Spouses in the Same Business	11-26

Chapter 12
Valuation of Start-Ups, Initial Public Offerings, and Private Placements

¶ 12.1	**Start-ups, IPOs, and Private Placements: General Similarities**		12-2
	[1]	Common Element of Financing	12-2
	[2]	Driving Force of the ROI	12-3
	[3]	Key Differences	12-3

	[4] Comparables	12-3
	[5] ROI Analysis	12-4
	[a] Dilution	12-5
	[b] Premoney vs. Postmoney Valuations	12-6
¶ 12.2	**Valuing Start-Ups**	12-6
	[1] Key Determinants	12-6
	[a] Required ROI	12-6
	[b] Valuing What Exists	12-7
	[c] Expected Upside	12-7
	[d] Additional Capital Requirements	12-8
	[e] Risks	12-8
	[2] Rules of Thumb	12-8
¶ 12.3	**Valuing IPOs**	12-9
	[1] Valuation Theory	12-10
	[a] Mathematical Basis	12-10
	[b] Application to IPOs	12-11
	[2] Valuation in Practice	12-12
	[a] Use of Comparables	12-12
	[b] Projections	12-13
	[c] Finding Comparables	12-16
	[d] Practical Example	12-16
	[e] Limitations of Price/Earnings Multiples	12-25
	[f] After-Market Considerations	12-25
¶ 12.4	**Valuing Private Placements**	12-25
	[1] Key Considerations	12-26
	[a] Required ROI	12-26
	[b] Expenditures to Date	12-26
	[c] Expected Upside	12-27
	[d] Need for Additional Capital	12-27
	[e] Remaining Risk	12-27
	[2] Rules of Thumb	12-28
	[a] Performance vs. Promise	12-29
	[3] Calculation Case Study	12-29
¶ 12.5	**Summary**	12-31

Chapter 13
Solvency Analysis in Leveraged Transactions

¶ 13.1	**The Legal Framework of Fraudulent Conveyances**	13-2
	[1] Recent Court Decisions	13-5
	[2] Accountants' Solvency Letters	13-5
¶ 13.2	**Components of a Solvency Analysis**	13-6
	[1] Due Diligence	13-7

			Page
	[2]	Balance Sheet Test	13-8
		[a] Valuing a Company's Assets	13-8
		[b] Valuing Interest-Bearing Debt	13-8
		[c] Valuing Contingent Liabilities	13-9
	[3]	Cash Flow Test	13-10
	[4]	Reasonable Capital Test	13-10
¶ 13.3	Solvency Case Study		13-10
	[1]	Overview of the Company	13-11
	[2]	Balance Sheet Test	13-11
		[a] Historical Financial Summary	13-11
		[b] Normalized Earnings and Cash Flow	13-12
		[c] Market Multiple Selection	13-12
		[d] Discounted Cash Flow Approach	13-17
		[e] Asset Valuation Summary	13-18
		[f] Valuing Liabilities: Guarantee of Subsidiary's Debt	13-19
		[g] Valuing Liabilities: Convertible Subordinated Debt	13-21
		[h] Summary	13-21
	[3]	Cash Flow Test	13-21
	[4]	Reasonable Capital Test	13-24
		[a] Revenue Growth and Margin Sensitivity	13-24
		[b] Volatility of Asset Prices	13-25
		[c] Maturity Structure of Fixed and Contingent Obligations	13-25
¶ 13.4	Summary		13-25

PART III VALUATION BY INDUSTRY

Chapter 14
Differentiating Approaches by Industry Groups

¶ 14.1	Valuation Approach Concerns		14-2
¶ 14.2	The SIC Code System		14-3
	[1]	Classifications	14-3
	[2]	Usefulness	14-4
	[3]	Limitations	14-4
		[a] Method of Classification	14-4
		[b] Obsolescence	14-5
		[c] Trend Away From Homogeneity	14-5
¶ 14.3	Industry Characteristics That Affect Valuation Approaches		14-5
	[1]	Capital Intensity	14-5

	Page
[2] Nature of Assets	14-5
[a] Financial Assets	14-5
[b] Inventory	14-6
[c] Real Estate	14-6
[d] Furniture, Fixtures, Machinery, and Equipment	14-7
[e] Natural Resources	14-8
[3] Extent of Off Balance Sheet Factors	14-8
[4] Regulatory Environment	14-9
[5] Ease of Entry	14-9
[6] Degree of Product or Service Differentiation Among Competitors	14-10
[7] Degree of Industry Homogeneity	14-10
[8] Business Continuity Characteristics	14-11
[9] Owner-Manager Personal Involvement	14-11
[10] Manner in Which Benefits Are Realized by Owners	14-12
[11] Specialized Accounting Practices	14-13
[12] Size of Business Unit	14-13
¶ 14.4 Market Factors That Affect Valuation Approaches	14-15
[1] Supply and Demand Conditions	14-15
[2] Typical Terms of Sale and Types of Consideration Paid	14-15
[a] Notes or Contracts Receivable	14-15
[b] Stock	14-16
[c] Convertible Securities	14-16
[d] Earnout Provisions	14-16
[3] Channels Through Which Industry Units Are Sold	14-16
¶ 14.5 Availability and Nature of Comparative Transaction Data	14-17
[1] Public Market Trading Data	14-17
[2] Merger, Acquisition, and Divestiture Data	14-18
[3] Small Private Company Sales Data	14-18
¶ 14.6 Industry Rule-of-Thumb Valuation Formulas	14-18

Chapter 15
Manufacturing

¶ 15.1	Diversity Within the Manufacturing Industry and Manufacturing Valuations	15-2
	[1] SIC Code Breakdown	15-2
	[2] Defining What Is to Be Valued	15-3

			Page
	[a]	Legal Structure	15-3
	[b]	Type of Interest	15-3
	[c]	Size of Interest	15-4
	[d]	Rights or Restrictions	15-4
	[3]	Purpose of Valuation	15-5
	[4]	Revenue Ruling 59-60	15-5
¶ 15.2	**Company Qualitative Analysis**		15-6
	[1]	Product Line	15-6
	[2]	History and Organization	15-7
	[3]	Raw Materials	15-7
	[4]	Producing the Product	15-8
		[a] Work Force	15-8
		[b] Technology and Research and Development	15-9
	[5]	Marketing, Sales, and Distribution	15-9
	[6]	Other Factors	15-11
	[7]	Management	15-11
¶ 15.3	**Company Financial Analysis**		15-13
	[1]	Historical Income Statements	15-13
	[2]	Historical Balance Sheets	15-16
	[3]	Relating Income Statements to Balance Sheets	15-17
	[4]	Plans and Prospects	15-17
¶ 15.4	**Industry Analysis**		15-17
¶ 15.5	**Valuation Approaches**		15-22
	[1]	The Asset Approach	15-22
	[2]	The Earnings (Discounted Cash Flow) Approach	15-23
	[3]	The Market Approach	15-25
		[a] The Capitalization of Earnings	15-25
		[b] Market/Book Value Relationships	15-26
		[c] Dividend Returns	15-27
	[4]	Other Valuation Approaches	15-27
	[5]	Other Considerations	15-27

Chapter 16
Service Companies

¶ 16.1	**What Is a Service Company?**		16-2
¶ 16.2	**When Are Valuations Needed?**		16-3
	[1]	Tax-Related Needs	16-3
	[2]	ESOPs	16-4
	[3]	Mergers and Acquisitions	16-4

		Page
	[4] Other Purposes	16-5
¶ 16.3	**Information and Sources**	16-6
¶ 16.4	**Intangible Assets**	16-7
	[1] Work Force	16-8
	[2] Customer Contracts	16-8
	[3] Software and Databases	16-8
	[4] Customer Base	16-9
	[5] Employment Contracts and Agreements Not to Compete	16-9
	[6] Trade Names	16-9
	[7] Other Intangibles	16-9
¶ 16.5	**Financial Considerations**	16-10
	[1] Cash vs. Accrual Accounting	16-10
	[2] Deferred Revenues	16-10
	[3] Working Capital	16-11
	[4] Other Financial Factors	16-11
¶ 16.6	**Valuation Approaches**	16-11
	[1] Majority vs. Minority Interests	16-12
	[2] Premises of Fair Market Value for Common Stock	16-12
	[3] Market Approach	16-13
	[4] Earnings Approach	16-18
	[5] Asset Approach	16-18
	[6] Rules of Thumb	16-20
¶ 16.7	**Special Considerations**	16-20
	[1] Hotels and Lodging	16-20
	[2] Personal Services	16-21
	[3] Business Services	16-21
	[4] Automotive Repair and Garage Services	16-21
	[5] Motion Picture Services	16-21
	[6] Amusement and Recreation Services	16-22
	[7] Health Services	16-22
	[8] Legal Services	16-22
	[9] Educational Services	16-22
	[10] Social Services	16-22
	[11] Museums, Art Galleries, Botanical and Zoological Gardens	16-23
¶ 16.8	**Summary**	16-23

Chapter 17
Financial Institutions

			Page
¶ 17.1	Financial Institutions Industry		17-3
	[1] Changes in the 1980s		17-4
		[a] Depository Institutions Deregulation and Monetary Control Act of 1980	17-4
		[b] Garn-St Germain Depository Institutions Act of 1982	17-4
		[c] Nonbank Banks	17-4
		[d] Growth in Secondary Loan Markets and Changing Capital Markets	17-4
		[e] Interstate Banking	17-5
		[f] The Tax Reform Act of 1986	17-5
		[g] Competitive Equality Banking Act of 1987	17-5
		[h] Hostile Takeovers	17-5
		[i] The Financial Institutions Reform, Recovery and Enforcement Act of 1989	17-5
		[j] Future Deregulation	17-5
¶ 17.2	Savings and Loan Analysis		17-6
	[1] Balance Sheet		17-6
		[a] Assets	17-6
		[b] Liabilities	17-10
		[c] Equity	17-10
	[2] Income Statement		17-10
		[a] Operating Income	17-10
		[b] Expenses	17-12
		[c] Nonoperating Income and Expenses	17-12
	[3] Financial Analysis		17-12
		[a] Size	17-15
		[b] Liquidity	17-15
		[c] Deposit Mix	17-18
		[d] Asset Mix	17-18
		[e] Capital Adequacy	17-20
		[f] Profitability	17-20
		[g] Interest Analysis	17-21
		[h] Growth	17-21
	[4] Additional Analysis		17-21
	[5] Summary		17-22
¶ 17.3	Commercial Bank Analysis		17-22
	[1] Balance Sheet		17-22
		[a] Assets	17-22

TABLE OF CONTENTS

			Page
	[b]	Liabilities	17-23
[2]	Income Statement		17-26
[3]	Financial Analysis		17-27
	[a]	Total Interest Expense/Average Earnings Assets	17-28
	[b]	Total Interest Income/Average Earnings Assets	17-30
	[c]	Earnings Asset Yield—Break-Even Yield	17-30
	[d]	Total Interest Expense/Total Interest-Bearing Liabilities	17-30
	[e]	Equity Capital + Capital Notes + Reserve for Loan Losses/Gross Loans	17-30
	[f]	Loan Loss Provision/Average Gross Loans	17-31
	[g]	Net Charge-Offs/Average Gross Loans	17-31
	[h]	Nonperforming Loans/Average Loans	17-31
	[i]	Loan Loss Provisions/Charge-Offs	17-31
[4]	Summary		17-32

¶ 17.4 **Other Valuation Considerations** 17-32
    [1] Off Balance Sheet Assets and Liabilities 17-33
    [2] Public Company Comparables 17-33
    [3] Control Premiums/Discounts for Minority Interest 17-33
    [4] Accounting Issues 17-33
    [5] Management Issues 17-34

¶ 17.5 **Summary** 17-34

Chapter 18
Insurance Companies and Agencies

¶ 18.1 **Valuing Insurance Companies** 18-4
    [1] Reasons for Valuations................... 18-5
        [a] Mergers and Acquisitions 18-5
        [b] Long-Term Planning 18-5
        [c] Initial Public Offerings 18-5
        [d] Employee Stock Ownership Plans 18-5
        [e] Demutualization 18-6
    [2] Steps in the Valuation Process............. 18-6
    [3] Evaluation of Management Practices........ 18-6
        [a] Organizational Structure 18-7
        [b] Internal Controls System 18-7
        [c] Key Personnel and Functions.......... 18-7

			Page
	[d]	Recorded Financial Events	18-7
	[e]	Sources of Anticipated Growth and Profit	18-8
[4]		Analysis of the Business	18-8
	[a]	Business Mix and Products Offered	18-8
	[b]	Forecasting Growth and Profit	18-8
	[c]	Reinsurance Contracts and Reinsurers	18-8
		[i] Contracts Ceding Reinsurance	18-9
		[ii] Contracts of Assured Reinsurance	18-9
	[d]	Underwriting Philosophies	18-10
	[e]	Claims Department Procedures	18-10
	[f]	Procedure for Estimating Incurred But Not Reported Losses	18-10
	[g]	Determining Sufficiency of Loss Reserves	18-11
	[h]	Reviewing Company's Investment Policies	18-11
	[i]	Combined Ratio	18-11
	[j]	Responsiveness	18-12
	[k]	Competition	18-12
	[l]	Price Competitiveness	18-12
	[m]	Quality and Autonomy of Branch Office Network	18-12
	[n]	Geography	18-13
[5]		Financial Report Review	18-13
	[a]	GAAP Statements	18-13
		[i] Annual Reports	18-13
		[ii] Proxy Statement	18-16
		[iii] Form 10-K	18-16
		[iv] Quarterly Reports	18-17
		[v] Form 10-Q	18-17
		[vi] Supplemental Financial Information	18-17
		[vii] Loss and Loss Reserve Actuarial Report	18-18
		[viii] Industry Data	18-18
	[b]	Statutory Convention Statements	18-18
		[i] Balance Sheet	18-19
		[ii] Underwriting and Investment Income Exhibit	18-19
		[iii] Statement of Changes in Financial Position	18-20

			Page
		[iv] Additional Exhibits	18-20
		[v] General Interrogatories	18-20
		[vi] Notes to Financial Statements	18-20
		[vii] Supporting Schedules	18-20
[6]	Valuation Methods		18-21
	[a]	Adjusted Net Book Value Method	18-21
		[i] Appraisals	18-21
		[ii] Intangibles	18-22
		[iii] Valuing Licenses	18-22
		[iv] Valuing Reserves	18-23
		[v] Valuing Unearned Premium Account	18-23
		[vi] Federal Income Tax Effects	18-23
		[vii] Example	18-23
	[b]	Trading Market Method	18-24
		[i] Selecting Comparable Insurance Companies	18-24
		[ii] Adjusting Index	18-25
		[iii] Establishing Sustainable Pretax Income Level	18-25
		[iv] Determining Value	18-25
		[v] Example	18-26
	[c]	Acquisition Value Method	18-26
		[i] Developing Index Ratio	18-26
		[ii] Segmenting Index	18-27
		[iii] Adjusting Index	18-27
		[iv] Determining Value	18-27
		[v] Example	18-28
	[d]	Present Value of Future Profits: Method 1	18-28
		[i] Capitalizing Earnings	18-28
		[ii] Adjusting Capitalization Rate	18-29
		[iii] Using Risk-Free Rates	18-29
		[iv] Determining Value by Capitalization of Earnings	18-29
		[v] Example	18-29
	[e]	Present Value of Future Profits: Method 2	18-30
		[i] Value of Business in Force	18-31
		[ii] Value of New and Renewable Business	18-31
		[iii] Premium Growth Rate	18-31

			Page
	[iv]	Renewal Rate	18-31
	[v]	Loss and Loss Adjustment Expense Ratio	18-31
	[vi]	Expense Ratio	18-32
	[vii]	Loss Reserve Run-Out	18-32
	[viii]	Current Earnings Rate on Investments	18-32
	[ix]	Future Earnings Rate on Investments	18-32
	[x]	Policyholder Surplus	18-32
	[xi]	Alternative Assumptions	18-32
	[xii]	Value Conclusions	18-32
	[xiii]	Example	18-33
[f]	Summary of Methods and Required Factors		18-33
	[i]	Adjusted Net Book Value Method	18-33
	[ii]	Trading Market Method	18-33
	[iii]	Acquisition Value Method	18-34
	[iv]	Present Value of Future Profits Method	18-34
[7]	Tax Reform Act of 1986		18-34
[a]	Unearned Premium Reserve		18-34
[b]	Recapture of Unearned Premium Reserve		18-35
[c]	Dividends and Tax-Exempt Interest		18-35
[d]	Loss Reserve Discounting		18-35
[e]	Life Insurance Company Deduction		18-35
[f]	Corporate Alternative Minimum Tax		18-36
[g]	Impact of the Tax Reform Changes on Valuations		18-36
[8]	Conclusion		18-36
¶ 18.2	**Valuing Insurance Agencies**		**18-36**
[1]	Valuation Myths		18-37
[a]	Commission Multiples		18-37
[b]	Revenue Multiples		18-38
[2]	Valuation Methods		18-38
[a]	Public Company Method		18-39
	[i]	Dilution of Earnings	18-40
	[ii]	Discounting Shares	18-40
	[iii]	Price/Earnings Multiple	18-40
	[iv]	Working Capital Requirement	18-42
	[v]	Tangible Net Worth	18-42

			Page
	[b]	Capitalization of Earnings Method	18-42
		[i] Minimum Risk Investments	18-43
		[ii] Additional Return Required	18-43
	[c]	Wasting Asset Method	18-43
		[i] Present Value Discount Rate	18-45
		[ii] Agency Growth	18-45
[3]	Factors in a Valuation		18-46
	[a]	Income Statement Considerations	18-46
		[i] Pro Forma Adjustments	18-46
		[ii] Revenue and Expense Adjustments	18-46
	[b]	Balance Sheet Considerations	18-47
		[i] Tangible Net Worth	18-47
		[ii] A Public Company's Approach	18-47
		[iii] Amortization of Expirations	18-48
[4]	Conclusion		18-50

Chapter 19
Natural Resources

¶ 19.1	Industry Orientation	19-2
	[1] Basic Valuation Principles	19-3
	[2] Practical Considerations	19-3
	[3] Companies Covered	19-3
¶ 19.2	**Oil and Gas Companies**	19-3
	[1] Ownership Forms	19-3
	[a] Corporations	19-4
	[b] Partnerships	19-4
	[c] Royalty Trusts	19-4
	[2] Financing Methods	19-4
	[a] Industry Deals	19-5
	[b] Drilling Partnerships	19-5
	[3] Operational Data	19-5
	[a] Reserve Production Profile	19-5
	[b] Reserve Changes and Causes	19-6
	[c] Lifting Costs	19-6
	[d] Finding Costs	19-6
	[e] Prospect Generation	19-6
	[f] Undeveloped Acreage	19-6
	[g] Drilling Record	19-6
	[h] Drilling Rigs	19-6
	[i] Government Regulation	19-7
	[j] Contracts	19-7

			Page
[4]	Taxation		19-7
[5]	Accounting		19-8
	[a]	Methods	19-8
	[b]	Adjusting for Comparability	19-9
[6]	Reserves		19-9
	[a]	Petroleum Engineers' Reserve Analysis.	19-9
		[i] Proved Reserves	19-10
		[ii] Probable and Possible Reserves	19-10
	[b]	SEC Method	19-10
		[i] Pricing and Volumes	19-10
		[ii] Discount Rate	19-10
	[c]	Petroleum Engineer's Role	19-10
		[i] Reserve Quantities	19-11
		[ii] Pricing Scenarios	19-11
		[iii] Discount Rate	19-11
[7]	Considerations in Selecting Comparables		19-11
	[a]	Methods of Financing	19-11
	[b]	Ownership Form	19-12
		[i] Corporation	19-12
		[ii] Partnership	19-12
	[c]	Location of Reserves or Exploratory Activity	19-12
	[d]	Composition of Assets and Size	19-12
	[e]	Sources of Information	19-12
[8]	Valuation Methods		19-13
	[a]	Break-Up Value (Appraised Net Worth)	19-13
		[i] Reserves	19-13
		[ii] Undeveloped Leases	19-14
		[iii] Drilling Rigs, Well Service Assets, and Pipeline Assets	19-14
		[iv] Liabilities	19-14
	[b]	Financial and Operating Comparisons	19-14
		[i] Operating Data	19-14
		[ii] Financial Data	19-15
	[c]	Minority vs. Controlling Interests	19-15

¶ 19.3 **Coal Companies** 19-15
    [1] Influencing Factors 19-16
    [2] Valuation Methods 19-16
    [3] Taxation 19-16

¶ 19.4 **Timber Companies** 19-17
    [1] Operating vs. Holding Companies 19-17
        [a] Operating Company 19-17

			Page
	[b]	Holding Company	19-17
	[2]	Partnerships	19-17
	[3]	Taxation	19-18
¶ 19.5	Other Extractive Industries		19-18

Chapter 20
Professional Practices

¶ 20.1	**Distinctive Characteristics**		20-2
	[1]	Cash-Basis Accounting	20-3
	[2]	Unaudited Financial Statements	20-3
	[3]	Personal Nature	20-4
	[4]	Intertwined Practice and Professional Goodwill	20-4
	[5]	Comparative Transaction Data Dependent on Private Sources	20-5
¶ 20.2	**The Balance Sheet**		20-5
	[1]	Accounts Receivable	20-5
		[a] Aging of Receivables	20-6
		[b] Actual Payment History	20-7
	[2]	Work-in-Process Inventory	20-8
		[a] Fees Based on Time	20-8
		[b] Contingent Fees	20-8
	[3]	Supplies	20-9
	[4]	Prepaid Expenses	20-9
	[5]	Equipment	20-9
	[6]	Leasehold Improvements	20-10
	[7]	Actual and Contingent Liabilities	20-10
		[a] Accounts Payable	20-10
		[b] Accrued Liabilities	20-11
		[c] Deferred Liabilities	20-11
		[d] Long-Term Debt	20-12
		[e] Lease Obligations	20-12
		[f] Contingent Liabilities	20-13
¶ 20.3	**Normalized Earnings**		20-13
	[1]	Nonrecurring Income and Expenses	20-13
	[2]	Extraneous Income and Expenses	20-13
	[3]	Change in Outlook for Income and Expenses	20-14
¶ 20.4	**Practice Goodwill and Professional Goodwill**		20-14
	[1]	Practice Goodwill	20-14
	[2]	Professional Goodwill	20-14
¶ 20.5	**Elements of Goodwill in Purchases and Sales**		20-15
	[1]	Expected Future Earnings	20-15

			Page
	[2]	Level of Competition	20-16
	[3]	Referral Base	20-16
	[4]	Types of Patients and Clients	20-16
	[5]	Work Habits of the Practitioner	20-16
	[6]	Fee Schedules	20-17
	[7]	Practice Location	20-17
	[8]	Employees of the Practice	20-17
	[9]	Marketability of the Practice	20-18
¶ 20.6	**Elements of Goodwill in Divorce Valuations**		20-18
	[1]	Practitioner's Age and Health	20-19
	[2]	Demonstrated Past Earning Power	20-19
	[3]	Reputation for Judgment, Skill, and Knowledge	20-19
	[4]	Comparative Professional Success	20-19
	[5]	Nature and Duration of Practice	20-20
¶ 20.7	**Value of the Practice**		20-20
	[1]	Valuation Methods	20-20
		[a] Excess Earnings Method	20-21
		[i] Earnings Levels	20-21
		[ii] Capitalization Rates	20-22
		[b] Capitalization of Earnings Method	20-23
		[c] Multiple of Revenues Method	20-23
	[2]	Complete Value	20-24
¶ 20.8	**Summary**		20-24

Chapter 21
Canadian Financial Valuation

¶ 21.1	**Statutes**		21-3
	[1]	Income Tax Law	21-3
	[2]	Company Law	21-5
	[3]	Securities Regulation	21-6
	[4]	Family Law	21-7
	[5]	Expropriation Law	21-9
	[6]	Bankruptcy Law	21-9
	[7]	Competition Law	21-9
	[8]	Employee Share Ownership Plans	21-11
¶ 21.2	**Commercial Transactions**		21-13
	[1]	Acquisition, Sale, or Merger of a Business	21-13
		[a] Material Contracts/Agreements	21-16
		[b] Contingent and Other Liabilities	21-16
		[c] Economic and Political Climate	21-16
		[d] Taxation	21-16

TABLE OF CONTENTS

			Page
	[2]	Corporate Reorganizations	21-17
	[3]	Fairness Opinions	21-18
	[4]	Going Public	21-19
	[5]	Going Private	21-19
		[a] Compulsory Acquisition Following Take-Over Bid	21-20
		[b] Oppression Remedy	21-20
		[c] Defining Fair Value	21-21
		[d] Valuation Approaches	21-22
		[e] Forcing-Out Premium	21-23
	[6]	Partnership/Shareholder Buy-Sell Agreements	21-24
	[7]	Employee Stock Option Plans	21-25
	[8]	Allocation of Purchase Price	21-25
	[9]	Related-Party Transfers	21-26
	[10]	Financial Solvency Analyses	21-26
	[11]	Government Privatization	21-27
¶ 21.3	**Litigation Support**		21-27
	[1]	Litigious Issues	21-28
		[a] Income Tax	21-28
		[b] Going-Private Transactions	21-30
		[c] Minority Shareholder Oppression	21-32
		[d] Separation and Divorce	21-33
		[e] Expropriation—Business Disturbance, Loss of Goodwill	21-35
		[f] Breach of Contract	21-36
		[g] Torts	21-36
		[h] Personal Injury	21-37
		[i] Insurance Claims	21-38
	[2]	Arbitration	21-38
¶ 21.4	**Valuation Profession**		21-39
	[1]	The Canadian Institute of Chartered Business Valuators	21-39
	[2]	The Canadian Institute of Chartered Accountants	21-40
¶ 21.5	**Valuation Terms**		21-41
¶ 21.6	**Case Law and Regulatory Pronouncements and Practices**		21-41
	[1]	Leading Judicial Decisions	21-41
	[2]	Revenue Canada, Taxation	21-41
	[3]	Ontario Securities Commission	21-43
		[a] Ontario Policy Statement	21-45

		Page
[b]	Decisions Relating to Valuation	21-45
[4]	British Columbia Securities Commission	21-47

Appendix A Revenue Ruling 59-60 ... A-1
Bibliography ... B-1
Table of Cases ... T-1
Index ... I-1

I
VALUATION THEORY AND PRINCIPLES

I
VALUATION THEORY AND PRINCIPLES

Part I Introduction I-3
Appraisal in Retrospect 1-1
Valuation Terminology and Methodology 2-1
Fairness vs. Fair Market Value 3-1
Ratio Analysis for Evaluating Financial Performance 4-1
Capitalization and Discount Rates 5-1
Valuation Case Study 6-1
Valuation of Fixed-Income Securities: Bonds and Preferred Stock 7-1

Part I INTRODUCTION

Financial Valuation: Businesses and Business Interests opens with Part I, "Valuation Theory and Principles." Part I includes seven chapters, which provide both in-depth discussions and practical applications of current valuation theory.

Chapter 1 on "Appraisal in Retrospect" by James H. Schilt acquaints practitioners with the historical background of valuation theory. The history behind such important concepts as goodwill, fair market value, capitalization of earnings, capitalization rates, and the value of intangibles is explored. The discussion then turns to the evolution of appraisal firms and the eventual intervention of the government (especially with Revenue Ruling 59-60) in the valuation process. In addition, the major court decisions impacting on valuation—from the 1928 *Couzens v. Commissioner* case to the most important "Delaware Block Method" cases—are analyzed. The chapter concludes with coverage of professional valuation associations, from the nineteenth century to the present.

Chapter 2 on "Valuation Methodology and Terminology" by Jay E. Fishman continues to set the stage of the rest of Part I. This chapter's broad coverage extends from the definitions of "value" (including "fair market value" and "fair value") to the significance of the valuation date in the valuation process. An explanation of equity valuation then leads to the use of financial statement analysis and of adjustment and common-size statements in the valuation process. The rest of the chapter is devoted to the various valuation methodologies, especially the three basic approaches recognized by the experts: the market comparison approach, the income approach, and the cost approach. The chapter concludes with a discussion of discounts and premiums.

Chapter 3 on "Fairness vs. Fair Market Value" by Kent V. Graham goes to the heart of valuation theory introduced in Chapter 2: the distinction between the financial concept of fair market value and the legal concept of fairness. Many of the cases analyzed focus on the dynamic between director conduct and shareholder rights and have led to the courts' development of the business judgment rule. Most recent judicial decisions have relied on this rule as well as on the concept of "entire fairness" in transactions involving potential conflicts of interest. Such pivotal cases as *Singer v. Magnavox Company*, *Jones v. H.F. Ahmanson & Company*, *Joseph v. Shell Oil Company*, *Weinberger v. UOP, Inc.*, and *Smith v. Van Gorkam*, among others, are analyzed in this regard. Despite these many judicial decisions, the chapter notes, there is some ambiguity about the duty of care owed by valuation analysts in rendering a fairness opinion. To help these analysts, the chapter includes a discussion of the two theories outlining the legal responsibilities of an investment banker to minority shareholders in the valuation process: third-party liability for negligent representation and direct fiduciary duty owed to minority shareholders. The chapter concludes with explanations of disclosure requirements on the federal and state levels.

Chapter 4 on "Ratio Analysis for Evaluating Financial Performance" by Robert Socol explains why ratio analysis is a convenient method for summarizing large quantities of data and for comparing company performance during the valuation process. How financial ratios—liquidity, leverage, activity, and profitability ratios—are used to value a company is illustrated through the activities of a fictitious firm, the Seneca Corporation. Practitioners are shown, step by step, how to determine the company's financial performance by calculating financial ratios and preparing financial statements. This type of ratio analysis in the valuation process can be supplemented with trend analysis, the du Pont System, financial leverage, industry rates of return, and comparative industry ratios, all of which are also covered in the chapter. The chapter concludes with a discussion of how financial ratio analysis can be used in security analysis.

Chapter 5 on "Capitalization and Discount Rates" by Richard S. Braun emphasizes that the valuation process is dependent on the analyst's choices of inputs. Among the most important are the choices of capitalization and discount rates. A series of market examples demonstrates how capitalization rates (including the most common one, the price/earnings multiple) are chosen. The examples show practitioners how to compare these rates and how to apply them to the valuation process. The discussion then moves on to the topic of discount rates, with a particular focus on the concept of present value. The chapter concludes with additional market examples and the use of financial theory, especially the application of the Capital Asset Pricing Model and the weighted average cost of capital (WACC).

Chapter 6 on a "Valuation Case Study" by John G. Mavredakis and Glenn Garlick is a cumulative practical application of the previous five chapters' coverage of valuation theory. This chapter applies valuation analysis to a fictitious company, the Elcon Company, for purposes of estate planning, ESOPs, and the sale of the company. Analysts are taken, again step by step, through the valuation process, starting with a description of the corporation and continuing with a general economic, industry, and financial review. The chapter is replete with models of actual calculations, tables, graphs, and financial statements that take into account the multiple of earnings and cash flow, capitalization of dividends, market price to book value, discounted future debt-free cash flow, and adjusted book value.

Chapter 7 on "Valuation of Fixed-Income Securities: Bonds and Preferred Stock" by Marko A. Budgyk makes a smooth transition from the previous chapter's cumulative case study to an analysis of the differences *and* similarities between the valuation of common stock and the valuation of fixed-income securities. The chapter analyzes, through the use of helpful tables and graphs, both issue-specific risk and company-specific risk. The chapter concludes with coverage of measuring and quantifying risk.

1

APPRAISAL IN RETROSPECT

JAMES H. SCHILT*

		Page
¶ 1.1	Concepts Behind Business Valuation...............	1-2
	[1] Goodwill	1-2
	[2] Fair Market Value	1-3
	[3] Organization and Capitalization of Earnings...	1-3
	[4] Capitalization Rates.........................	1-4
	[5] Formula for Determining Loss of Goodwill ...	1-4
	[6] Value of Intangibles.........................	1-5
¶ 1.2	Evolution of Appraisal Firms.....................	1-5
¶ 1.3	Development of IRS Guides and Manuals	1-7
¶ 1.4	Publication of Recent Standard Texts	1-8
¶ 1.5	Summary of Major Court Decisions	1-9
¶ 1.6	Evolution of Professional Associations............	1-13

Professor James C. Bonbright stated in his classic valuation treatise in 1937 that "the cautious appraiser fights shy of a problem that involves law, economics, accountancy, and commercial appraisal."[1] (The term "commercial appraisal" was frequently used, according to the author, to distinguish going-concern valuation from asset valuation.) Today, however, even the cautious appraiser can move ahead on problems involving these disciplines because of the body of knowledge that has evolved in recent decades on how they relate to business valuation. While today's courses, articles, and books on business valuation and related subjects are excellent and far superior to those of ten or twenty years ago, completing such courses and reading such material remain as starting points rather than final objectives. Before getting into the present text, let us step back and review what has gone before.

The origins of the business enterprise antedate recorded history.

---

* JAMES H. SCHILT, CFA, ASA, is an independent business appraiser in San Francisco, California. The author is a senior member of the American Society of Appraisers, a chartered member of the Institute of Chartered Financial Analysts, and a fellow of the Financial Analysts Federation. In addition to authoring articles for legal and professional journals, he is the founder and editor of Business Valuation Review, the quarterly journal of the Business Valuation Committee of the American Society of Appraisers.

[1] 2 J.C. Bonbright, *The Valuation of Property* 7 (1937 & photo. reprint 1965).

Expansion in individually owned private companies, however, came about only after the demise of medieval feudalism; with the Industrial Revolution, business enterprises grew dramatically in size. This was certainly true in the United States from 1830 to the end of the century, when railroads and banks required large amounts of capital. For example, when the United States Steel Corporation was founded in 1901, it was capitalized at more than $1 billion.

¶ 1.1 Concepts Behind Business Valuation

Business valuation and appraisal historically have revolved around several concepts. These concepts include goodwill, fair market value, and capitalization of earnings and are touched upon in the following pages.

[1] Goodwill

From the beginning, business valuation has revolved around the question of goodwill. One of the early explanations of this intangible comes from John Scott, the first earl of Eldon, who was lord chancellor of England during the first quarter of the nineteenth century. Lord Eldon stated, in an opinion of 1810, that goodwill was "nothing more than the probability that the old customers will resort to the old place."[2]

An often-quoted interpretation of goodwill was written in 1841 by Joseph Story—associate justice of the U.S. Supreme Court and Dane Professor of Law at Harvard University—and published in his *Commentaries on the Law of Partnership*:

> This good-will may be properly enough described to be the advantage or benefit which is acquired by the establishment beyond the mere value of the capital, stock, funds, or property employed therein, in consequences of the general public patronage and encouragement which it receives from constant or habitual customers, on account of its local position, or common celebrity, or reputation for skill and affluence, or punctuality, or from other accidental circumstances, or necessities, or even from ancient partialities or prejudices.[3]

This definition was quoted by the California Supreme Court in 1867[4] and the U.S. Supreme Court in 1893.[5]

---

[2] Cruttwell v. Lye, 17 Ves. 335 (1810).

[3] J. Storey, *Commentaries on the Law of Partnership* § 99 at 170 (6th ed. 1968).

[4] Bell v. Ellis, 33 Cal. 620 (1867).

[5] Metropolitan Nat'l Bank v. St. Louis Post-Dispatch Co., 149 U.S. 436 (1893).

[2] Fair Market Value

Another early building block in appraising, regardless of the type of property, was the concept of fair market value. The Revenue Act of 1918 provided that "when property is exchanged for other property the property received in exchange shall, for the purpose of determining gain or loss, be treated as the equivalent of cash to the amount of its fair market value."[6]

Advisory Tax Board Recommendation (T.B.R.) 57 was issued by the Bureau of Internal Revenue in 1919 to define fair market value. The recommendation stated:

> "Market value" is the price at which a seller willing to sell at a fair price and a buyer willing to buy at a fair price, both having reasonable knowledge of the facts, will trade. It implies the existence of a public of possible buyers at a fair price. The adjective "fair" emphasizes the idea of fairness inherent in this conception of market value, and excludes any possibility of a construction of the words "market value" with reference to a market in which, or to circumstances of sale under which, for any reason a fair price could not be obtained.[7]

[3] Organization and Capitalization of Earnings

The year 1919 also saw the publication of the first edition of Professor Arthur Stone Dewing's monumental work, *The Financial Policy of Corporations*. Dewing, in the various editions of his work, stressed the fact that the going business was more than an aggregate of parts; it had an intangible something that he called "organization." In his description of the organization of a business, "great care has been used to avoid the word 'goodwill' because of the lack of uniformity in usage of this term among accountants, legal writers, court opinions and business men."[8] He also emphasized the capitalization of earnings in determining the value of a business enterprise.

In a 1926 edition of his book, Dewing stated that business appraisals were needed for the purposes of "promotion" (what now is known as the initial public offering), acquisition, merger, and the determination of dissenting shareholder rights. In addition, there was the appraisal of railroads and utility companies by the courts and commissions. "At the best," however, "such valuations are based on arbitrary units comprising the physical structures of the business; at their worst, they bear nothing but a remote historical resemblance to the actual utility business being conducted at the present time by thinking, feeling human beings."[9]

---

[6] Revenue Act of 1918, Pub. L. No. 65-254, § 202(b), 40 Stat. 1057 (1918).
[7] T.B.R. 57, 1919-1 C.B. 40.
[8] A.S. Dewing, *The Financial Policy of Corporations* 285 (5th ed. 1953).
[9] *Id.* at 259 (rev. ed. 1926).

[4] Capitalization Rates

Dewing further stated that "the most searching study of valuation, as a practical business problem, thus far prepared"[10] was Ralph E. Badger's *The Valuation of Industrial Securities*, published in 1925. For this pioneering work, an elaboration of several reports prepared earlier on the valuation of closely held securities for inheritance tax purposes, Badger made a study of the price/earnings multiples or capitalization rates investors were willing to pay for stocks of industrial companies in the period from 1912 to 1921.

The degrees of risk and rates of capitalization found by Badger are shown in Table 1-1.

TABLE 1-1
DEGREES OF RISK AND RATES OF CAPITALIZATION

Class	Degree of Risk	Rate of Capitalization
I	Low risk	12–14.99%
II	Medium risk	15–19.99%
III	High risk	20–24.99%
IV	Very high risk	Over 25%

Source: R. Badger, *The Valuation of Industrial Securities* (1925)

The capitalization rates in Table 1-1 were based upon publicly traded stocks and, of course, represented minority interests only, but they did present a guide in the early days of business appraising. Badger concluded that the results obtained from the use of a capitalization rate with total earnings more nearly conformed to actual values than did the use of book value and capitalization of excess earnings. (In 1928, Badger associated with Harold Torgerson and Harry Guthman to author *Investment Principles and Practices*. By 1963, this book was in its fifth edition and was a text recommended by the Institute of Chartered Financial Analysts for students preparing for the CFA examinations.)

[5] Formula for Determining Loss of Goodwill

The Board of Tax Appeals, in 1920, issued Appeals and Review Memorandum (A.R.M.) 34 for the purpose of providing a formula for determining the amount of goodwill value lost as of March 1, 1913 (the effective date of the first federal income tax law) by breweries, distilleries, and other enterprises put out of business by Prohibition.[11] The suggested formula calls for a reasonable rate of return on the company's tangible assets. It calls any earnings that exceed this amount "excess earnings" and suggests they be capitalized at a rate higher than

---
[10] *Id.* at 264.
[11] A.R.M. 34, 1920-2 C.B. 31.

that allowed for the tangible assets in order to determine the value of intangible assets, or goodwill. Over the years, this formula has received broad acceptance; and it remains widely used today in valuing small, closely held corporate and noncorporate business enterprises.

The memorandum came at a time when there was little or no literature on the subject of valuing closely held securities and no body of rules governing security appraisals. A.R.M. 34, however, codified a formula that had been in common use during the early years of the century: The fair market value of the equity of a corporation is equivalent to its book value plus its goodwill.[12]

[6] Value of Intangibles

In 1927, the doctoral thesis of Y.M. Yang, entitled *Goodwill and Other Intangibles*, was published. The thesis attempted to show that the value of intangibles such as goodwill, trademarks, patents, copyrights, franchises, etc., lies in their ability to produce superior earning power for the specific concern. Yang also make this statement: "It is important to note that the capitalized earning power of an enterprise does not in any definite way indicate the price at which an enterprise might reasonably be sold."[13] What he meant was that selling price is a matter of negotiation between two parties and depends primarily on their horse-trading skills.

¶ 1.2 Evolution of Appraisal Firms

The end of the nineteenth century saw the founding of two of today's major appraisal firms—Coats & Burchard (now Lloyd-Thomas/Coats & Burchard Co.) and The American Appraisal Co. (now American Appraisal Associates, Inc., founded by John L. Moon, a court reporter, and William Young, a building contractor). Both these firms were founded in 1896. During these early years, the principal work for appraisers was insurance related (estimating replacement costs for machinery, equipment, and buildings). The job of estimating hypothetical market prices for closely held companies was done by investment bankers. What is now known as "business valuation" probably got under way in the early part of this century; it was performed by persons trained as real estate appraisers because they were used to capitalizing earnings. It is believed that a business-appraisal section was in operation at the Milwaukee headquarters of The American Appraisal Co. by the 1920s.

Due to poor economic conditions during the 1930s, the appraisal business suffered, employees were dismissed, and fees were lowered. The number of employees at American Appraisal, for example,

---

[12] Badger, Address Before the 1961 Annual Conference of the American Society of Appraisers (June 27, 1961), *reprinted in* Technical Valuation, Oct. 1961, at 13-23.
[13] Y.M. Yang, *Goodwill and Other Intangibles* 143 (1927 & photo. reprint 1978).

dropped from 799 in 1929 to 568 in 1930. Nonetheless, in 1932, Earl P. Marshall, a Los Angeles building inspector who had lost his job, formed Marshall Valuation Service for the purpose of publishing building cost estimates. Four years later, he formed a partnership with Robert W. Stevens, and the name of the company changed to Marshall & Stevens. Stevens had been with General Appraisal Co., a long-established Seattle firm that did lumber-company appraisals; it was acquired by American Appraisal Associates, Inc., in 1969. Both men were civil engineers and experienced building cost estimators. Under the guidance of Marshall, the firm grew to become a large entity in the major valuation fields, including business appraisals in the early 1950s. In 1983, after being owned by two other corporations since 1970, it was purchased by Société Générale de Surveillance Holding S.A. (SGS), a Swiss firm.

SGS had acquired Tait Appraisal Co. eighteen months earlier and merged it into Marshall & Stevens. Stuart C. Tait, a fine-arts appraiser, and Sam Gibson, a machinery and equipment appraiser, had also been with General Appraisal before forming their own firm in the 1930s, to be known as Tait & Gibson Appraisal, later changed to Tait Appraisal.

The 1930s also saw the founding of three business valuation firms, two of which have grown to become important entities in the appraisal industry: Standard Research Consultants, Inc., Management Planning, Inc, and Duff & Phelps. Standard Research was formed in 1933 as the valuation department of Standard & Poor's Corporation. In 1969, it was purchased by American Appraisal Associates, Inc. Management Planning, Inc., was founded in 1939 by Fiduciary Counsel, a New York investment counseling firm, to value privately owned businesses in which their clients had an interest. It subsequently became an independent firm and moved to Princeton, New Jersey. From the early days, the professional staffs of these two firms consisted largely of security analysts, then known as "statisticians," who were well-educated individuals with backgrounds in securities research and investment.

Duff & Phelps Inc. was founded in 1932 through the efforts of William Duff and George Phelps and has become one of the nation's largest investment research and consulting firms providing services in investment management, credit rating, security research (originally known for its expertise in the public utility area), and financial consulting. The company's valuation services, which date back nearly to the founding of the firm, are now provided through a wholly owned subsidiary, Duff & Phelps Financial Consulting Company.

The year 1970 saw the founding of one of the newest entrants to the field of business valuation: the firm of Houlihan, Lokey, Howard & Zukin, Inc. (HLHZ). Now one of the largest and most respected business and security valuation firms, HLHZ has offices in Los Angeles,

Chicago, San Francisco, and New York and maintains a professional staff of over 150 employees whose expertise ranges from accounting to investment banking.

¶ 1.3 Development of IRS Guides and Manuals

The appraisal business was stimulated by the growth in the economy that followed World War II and the estate and gift tax regulations that were part of the Internal Revenue Code of 1954, particularly as they pertained to asset allocation and business valuation.

The Internal Revenue Service (IRS) had maintained a staff of valuation specialists in Washington to pass on valuation of closely held securities and other business interests. With the decentralization of audit activities in 1953, a guide became necessary for audit personnel in the field. This was done by the issuance of a mimeograph in December 1953,[14] most of which was incorporated into Revenue Ruling 54-77[15] and issued in March 1954. The current revision, Revenue Ruling 59-60,[16] was issued in March 1959 with a few material changes from the previous ruling. Since 1959, there have been several amendments issued for clarification.

In early March 1960, the IRS issued the initial text of a training manual for the use of personnel in appellate branch offices throughout the country. This manual has gone through four editions, the most recent in 1985. While it also covers real estate and art objects, most of the text is devoted to business valuation. Since 1978, the manual has been available from Commerce Clearing House, initially as a result of the Freedom of Information Act.

A section in the manual called "Common Errors in Valuation" comes down hard on the use of formulas, such as A.R.M. 34, in place of judgment. Some of the language is worth repeating:

> All that can be said for ARM 34 or a similar method of capitalization using two rates of interest, is that you hope to get a good answer based upon two bad guesses. It is difficult enough to get one reasonably accurate rate of capitalization using normal appraisal methods such as the comparison with market prices for publicly-held stocks. To get two fairly accurate rates, one for tangibles and the other for intangibles, other than by pure guesswork, is impossible.
>
> . . . .
>
> To attempt to segregate value based on earnings as between normal income and that by whatever goodwill or other intangible assets the business may possess, is to aspire to a higher degree of

---
[14] I.R.M. 338 (1953).
[15] 1954-1 C.B. 187.
[16] 1959-1 C.B. 237. Revenue Ruling 59-60 is reprinted in Appendix A at the end of this book.

clairvoyance than has as yet been demonstrated as obtainable by mere man.[17]

Despite these comments, which appeared in the 1967 edition, the IRS issued Revenue Ruling 68-609 in the following year, repeating the formula of A.R.M. 34, along with the caveat that this approach may be used "only if there is no better basis therefor available."[18] (The 1968 ruling was a revision of a similar ruling issued in 1965.)[19]

¶ 1.4 Publication of Recent Standard Texts

In the late 1960s and early 1970s, two books on valuation received wide circulation: *Appraisal Principles and Procedures*, by Henry A. Babcock, and *Valuing a Company* by George McCarthy and Robert Healy.[20] Babcock held a Ph.D. in physics and engineering from Massachusetts Institute of Technology. He felt that his training could be used in appraising, and he became an independent fee appraiser working a great deal with Marshall & Stevens. By the time he wrote his book, when he was in his seventies, he had become a real estate consultant and a university instructor in real estate valuation. While the book was devoted primarily to the valuation of real estate, it did set forth valuation principles for use in all types of appraising and included a section on business valuation and the use of the excess earnings method. McCarthy and Healy were accountants whose book dealt largely with corporations going public, business combinations, tax valuations, and other special situations.

The first "how to" book on business appraisal to receive wide acknowledgment was *Business Valuation Handbook* by Glenn Desmond and Richard Kelley. This book, issued in 1976, was considered a "basic" text, at least for small business valuation, until *Valuing a Business*, by Shannon Pratt, was published in 1980. Pratt followed this book with *Valuing Small Businesses and Professional Practices* five years later. The second edition of *Valuing a Business* was copyrighted in 1989. In 1988, Gordon V. Smith's book, *Corporate Valuation: A Business and Professional Guide* was published. The following year saw the issuance of *Valuation of Intellectual Property and Intangible Assets* by Smith in conjunction with coauthor Russell Parr. A monumental 1989 work on valuing professional practices was in the process of being published by CCH Canadian, Ltd. as this chapter goes to press: *Valuing Professional Practices* by James Horvath.[21]

---

[17] IRS Appellate Conferee Valuation Training Program, Fed. Est. & Gift Tax. Rep. (CCH) No. 49, at 83, 85-86 (Mar. 27, 1978).
[18] Rev. Rul. 68-609, 1968-2 C.B. 327.
[19] Rev. Rul. 65-193, 1965-2 C.B. 370.
[20] H.A. Babcock, *Appraisal Principles and Procedures* (1968 & rev. ed. 1980); G.M. McCarthy & R. Healy, *Valuing a Company: Practices and Procedures* (1971).
[21] G. Desmond & R. Kelley, *Business Valuation Handbook* (1976); S. Pratt, *Valuing a Business: The Analysis and Appraisal of Closely Held Companies* (2d ed. 1989);

¶ 1.5 Summary of Major Court Decisions

The 1970s and 1980s witnessed the growth of many valuation consulting firms in response to a surge in corporate recapitalizations, mergers and acquisitions, employee stock ownership plans, fairness opinions, and stock option planning. It was also a time when major accounting firms began to develop business appraisal departments.

The appraisal of business interests for tax purposes has probably given rise to a larger number of valuations for legal purposes than any other statutory provision. Accordingly, federal tax cases have established precedents for valuation procedures regardless of the reasons for the appraisal. This is in spite of the fact that the courts have frequently split the difference between the contesting parties' valuations.[22] Another area that has resulted in numerous published cases has been the valuation of dissenters' stock under state appraisal statutes.

One of the famous early valuation cases is *Couzens v. Commissioner*,[23] which involved the appraisal of Ford Motor Company common stock under § 202(a) of the Revenue Act of 1918 to establish value, as of March 1, 1913, for ascertaining taxable gain on subsequent sale. The Bureau of Internal Revenue had estimated, in 1919, the value of Ford Motor Company stock for Senator Couzens, a major shareholder.

An accounting staff member of the Bureau reached a value by taking an average book value, average annual earnings capitalized at 10%, and average cash dividends capitalized at 10%. The method was rejected by the Commissioner of Internal Revenue because it did not place enough emphasis on the most recent reported earnings (1912) and the estimated earnings (1913) for a company that was growing at an exceedingly rapid rate. However, it does point out the long-standing use of a weighted average method of valuation. In arriving at a value for the Ford Motor stock, the Board of Tax Appeals (later the Tax Court) said that it was not done by any mathematical formula but by giving consideration to several methods suggested in the course of the trial. The Board also held that value may not be judged by subsequent events, but they may be considered for the purpose of ascertaining "whether such expectations were entertained and whether they were reasonable and intelligent."

The two best-known cases using the weighted average approach are *Bader v. United States*[24] and *Central Trust Company v. United*

S.Pratt, *Valuing Small Businesses and Professional Practices* (1985); G.V. Smith, *Corporate Valuation: A Business and Professional Guide* (1988); G.V. Smith & R. Parr, *Valuation of Intellectual Property and Intangible Assets* (1989).

[22] Englebricht & Davidson, "A Statistical Look at Tax Court Compromise in Estate and Gift Tax Valuation of Closely Held Stock," Taxes 395-400 (June 1977).

[23] 11 B.T.A. 1040 (1928).

[24] 172 F. Supp. 833 (S.D. Ill. 1959).

States.[25] These cases were decided in 1959 and 1962, respectively. In *Bader*, after listening to both parties and without giving a reason, the judge gave earnings a weight of 50%, dividends 25%, and book value 25%. In *Central Trust*, the weights were 50% for earnings, 30% for dividends, and 20% for book value.

The weighted average method became so standard in the state of Delaware that it became known as the "Delaware Block Method." In addition to earnings, dividends, and assets, market price was often used as an important element of value. The method was frequently used for valuation purposes under the state's appraisal statute for dissenting shareholders. Delaware is of particular importance because so many businesses are incorporated in that state.

In 1983, the Delaware Supreme Court held, in *Weinberger v. UOP, Inc.*,[26] another often-cited case, that the weighted average method was clearly outmoded to the extent that it excluded other generally accepted techniques used by the financial community and by the courts. Moreover, the court was in favor of adopting "a more liberal, less rigid and stylized approach to the valuation process."

Referring to advocates' custom of going to extremes in their business valuations in anticipation that the court would split the difference, Judge (later Chief Judge) Tannenwald, in the June 1980 case of *Buffalo Tool and Die Manufacturing Company v. Commissioner*[27] put both sides on notice that he might decide in favor of the party he found more convincing rather than simply make a middle-of-the-road compromise. Judge Tannenwald referred to his previous comments in *Messing v. Commissioner* to the following effect:

> Too often in valuation disputes the parties have convinced themselves of the unalterable correctness of their position. . . . This is the result of overzealous effort, during the course of the ensuing litigation to infuse a talismanic precision into an issue which should finally be recognized as inherently imprecise and capable of resolution only by a Solomon-like pronouncement.[28]

Shortly after *Buffalo Tool and Die*, Judge Tannenwald and other arbiters used similar language in other decisions involving business valuation. In his remarks to various tax groups, Chief Judge Tannenwald has emphasized that he and other Tax Court judges wish to end the custom of tax valuation by compromise.[29]

At one time, many courts held that a projection of earnings was

---

[25] 305 F.2d 393 (Ct. Cl. 1962).
[26] 457 A.D. 701 (Del. 1983).
[27] 74 T.C. 441 (1980).
[28] 48 T.C. 502 (1967).
[29] Bosland, "Tax Valuation by Compromise," 19 Tax L. Rev. 78 (1963); Longenecker, "A Practical Guide to Valuation of Closely Held Stock," Tr. & Est., Jan. 1983, at 20-46.

too speculative to use for valuation purposes. An opinion by Justice Oliver Wendell Holmes, however, in the 1929 case of *Ithaca Trust Company v. United States* is noteworthy: "Like all values, as the word is used in the law, it depends largely on more or less certain prophecies of the future and the value is no less real at the time if later the prophecy turns out false than when it comes true."[30] Nevertheless in 1949, the U.S. Supreme Court, in *Kimball Laundry v. United States*,[31] emphasized the use of excess earnings for goodwill valuation because it considered predicting future earning power too hazardous.

The market prices of comparable listed stocks have long been considered a proper test by the courts in valuing the stock of close corporations. The courts, in two tax-related cases, addressed the fact that at the date of valuation, the stock market was either overvalued or depressed. In the 1928 case of *Parker v. Commissioner*,[32] the Board of Tax Appeals held that if, around the valuation date, the market was so depressed that the representative stock was selling far below its intrinsic value, it was safe to attribute to the stock under appraisal a market value similarly substantially below its intrinsic value. However, in the 1933 case of *Strong v. Roger*,[33] the court recognized a substantial overvaluation and stated that "to ignore the wild and unreasonable prices as obtained in the years 1927, 1928, and 1929 would fail to recognize the conditions which existed at the time and give no effect to the word 'fair' as used by Congress in bearing upon market values."

Again in 1975, the Tax Court, in *Estate of Oakly J. Hall v. Commissioner*, had the opinion that "in time of wide speculation and resulting fluctuations in the stock market we are extremely doubtful that the price on any particular day is truly reflective of what an investor would pay if looking primarily at historical earnings."[34] The court went on to say that the primary emphasis should be on earnings rather than dividend yield and book value, and it would not allow the weighted-average, or formula, approach used in *Bader* and *Central Trust Company*.

The courts and the IRS have been granting larger discounts for lack of marketability and minority interests over the last couple of decades.[35] Part of the reason for increased discounts for closely held corporate stock has to do with observation of discounts on restricted or "letter" stock in relation to the identical freely traded shares and reference to the data on flotation costs published by the Securities and Exchange Commission (SEC). In *Estate of Kirkpatrick v. Commis-*

---

[30] 279 U.S. 151 (1929). *See also* J. Bonbright, *supra* note 1, ch. XII.

[31] 338 U.S. 1 (1949).

[32] 10 B.T.A. 854 (1928).

[33] 14 A.F.T.R. 1207 (1933), *aff'd*, 72 F.2d 455 (3d Cir. 1934), *cert. denied*, 293 U.S. 621 (1934).

[34] T.C. Memo. ¶ 75,141 (1975).

[35] Dant, "Courts Increasing Amount of Discount for a Minority Interest in a Business," Tr. & Est., Dec. 1984, at 22-23.

sioner (1975),[36] for example, the government's witness recommended a 50% discount; and, in *Estate of Little v. Commissioner* (1982),[37] the appraisers for both sides agreed on a 60% discount because of various restrictions and blockage. These compare with discounts of 10% to 20% in the two decades after World War II.[38] (It is interesting to note, however, that as early as 1954 in the tax case of *Whittemore v. Fitzpatrick*,[39] the court allowed a 50% discount for a minority, nonmarketable interest in a closely held stock, albeit a holding company.)

Other noteworthy cases include *Richter v. United States*[40] (1971), where the Court of Claims went into detail regarding the valuation of a closely held corporation. In *Concord Control v. Commissioner* (1982),[41] the Tax Court held that there was no goodwill but that going-concern value did exist; moreover, the court stated that "any assemblage of assets into a functioning, on-going business is capable of giving rise to going-concern value." On remand from the Sixth Circuit Court of Appeals to explain its method of calculating the amount of going-concern value, the Tax Court explained that it used the excess earnings method rather than either the "bargain of the parties" or "residual" method. *Banc One v. Commissioner* (1985)[42] affected purchase price allocation in which the Tax Court called for the residual method to determine goodwill and going-concern value rather than the excess-earnings method, which, the court stated, may be used as a last resort if no better method is available. In *Banc One*, the court commented:

> Determination of the "normal" earnings of a business, the "average return on the tangible assets," and the "appropriate capitalization rate" is a highly subjective task. Indeed, the primary virtue of the residual method is obtaining a more accurate valuation of the acquired intangibles without making speculative assumptions and engaging in unnecessarily complex computations where the total purchase price and the values of the tangible assets are known or ascertainable.[43]

In *Northern Trust Company v. Commissioner* (1986),[44] which involved an estate tax freeze, the court went into detail regarding valuation problems: Discounts were held to be 25% for minority interests and 20% for lack of marketability; gift taxes were to be measured by

---

[36] T.C. Memo. at ¶ 75,141.
[37] T.C. Memo. ¶ 82,026 (1982).
[38] Maher, "Discounts for Lack of Marketability for Closely Held Business Interests," Taxes 562-571 (Sept. 1976).
[39] 127 F. Supp. 710 (D. Conn. 1954).
[40] 439 F.2d 1204 (Ct. Cl. 1971).
[41] T.C. Memo. ¶ 76,301 (1976), *aff'd in part, rev'd & remanded in part*, 615 F.2d 1153 (6th Cir. 1980), *on remand*, 78 T.C. 742 (1982), *acq.*, 1984-1 C.B. 1.
[42] 84 T.C. 476 (1985).
[43] *Id.*
[44] 87 T.C. 349 (1986).

the value of the property passing from the donor; the market comparable approach—using earnings before interest, depreciation, and taxes (EBIDT)—was rejected; debt-free discounted cash flow and the use of beta coefficients were accepted.

Estate of Mark S. Gallo v. Commissioner[45] is noteworthy not only because of the sheer size of the business involved (E. & J. Gallo Winery) but also for the fact the court found that the estate's expert acted reasonably in placing primary emphasis on price/earnings ratios based upon comparative companies' price/earnings ratios and then discounting by 35 percent to reflect the lack of marketability of the shares.

Several important statements were made by the court in *Charles S. Foltz et al. v. U.S. News & World Report et al.*,[46] which involved appraised values of shares in an employee stock ownership plan (ESOP). The sale of *U.S. News & World Report* revealed significant value in its real estate that was not taken into account in the annual appraisals for the ESOP. The plaintiffs, who were retired employees, claimed that the defendant's valuation decisions breached fiduciary duties imposed by the Employment Retirement Income Security Act of 1974. Both the trial court and the appeals court ruled for the defendants. The court of appeals held that the ESOP fiduciaries do not have a duty to maximize its pecuniary benefits to individual plan participants. Moreover, the court supported the proposition that, when valuing minority interest, little weight should be accorded to potential liquidation value of assets when liquidation is not contemplated, nor can this be forced by the minority shareholders. The fact that the employee benefit plan held the majority of the employer's outstanding shares did not mean that its holdings, which constituted minority shares, should have been valued on a control basis. It is interesting to note that the filings in the trial court were reputed to be the largest in any civil case in the history of the U.S. District Court for the District of Columbia.

In 1983, the IRS set forth general principles for determining the value of preferred stock in the recapitalization of a closely held corporation[47]; however, the ruling consisted of no more than basic concepts that had been in use for a number of years.[48]

¶ 1.6 Evolution of Professional Associations

The 1930s marked the founding of many of today's professional appraisal associations. The American Institute of Real Estate Appraisers was formed in 1932 as the appraisal division of the National Association of Real Estate Boards, which subsequently became the National

---
[45] T.C. Memo. ¶ 85,363 (1985).
[46] 865 F.2d 364 (D.C. Cir. 1989).
[47] Rev. Rul. 83-120, 1983, 1 C.B. 170.
[48] *See, e.g.*, Oxford Paper Co. v. United States, 52 F.2d 1008 (Ct. Cl. 1931). The Court of Claims held that similar publicly traded preferred stocks should be considered in addition to underlying asset value.

Association of Realtors. Four years later, the Society of Residential Appraisers was founded. The name was later changed to the more encompassing Society of Real Estate Appraisers.

The American Society of Technical Appraisers (ASTA) was formed in Los Angeles in 1939 by Carl P. Marshall and Robert W. Stevens, founders of Marshall & Stevens, and Stuart C. Tait and Sam Gibson, founders of Tait Appraisal. Most of the original members were fee appraisers who worked primarily with industrial properties. The Technical Valuation Society (TVS) was established in New York in the same year. Many of its early members were employees or consultants in the field of public utility valuation.

In 1952, ASTA and TVS were merged and incorporated as the American Society of Appraisers (ASA), which is, today, a multidiscipline organization with specialists in appraisal administration, appraisal education, machinery and equipment, personal property, public utilities, real property, and technical valuation in addition to business valuation. The first business appraisers in the organization were certified in 1967. Approximately 400 out of a total of about 3,200 tested and certified members are in the business valuation field. The ASA Business Valuation Committee, formed in 1981, is presently composed of 19 members from the United States and Canada. It publishes *Business Valuation Review*, a quarterly journal; sponsors an annual advance business valuation seminar; develops and administers courses and certification examinations in business valuation; and works on valuation theory and standards.

In January 1971, a group of business appraisers in Canada formed an association of professionals interested in the subject of business valuation called The Canadian Association of Business Valuators. In 1985, the name was changed to The Canadian Institute of Chartered Business Valuators. Over 80% of its members are chartered accountants. Business valuations were done for many years in Canada by accounting firms and investment underwriters, but the introduction of a capital gains tax in 1971 gave impetus to the establishment of business appraising as an independent discipline. The institute presently has approximately 300 members who were qualified as a result of a three-year study course and examinations.

The Institute of Business Appraisers, Inc. was founded in Florida in 1978. It now has approximately 1,800 members, many of whom are business opportunity brokers. About 110 of its members are certified as a result of an examination.

In response to concerns about practitioner conduct in the appraisal profession, a self-regulatory organization called the Appraisal Foundation was formed in 1987. The foundation, formed by eight appraisal societies, became the parent entity for the Appraisal Standards Board and the Appraiser Qualifications Board; its object is to promote uniform standards of professional practice and to establish uniform qualifications for appraisers.

The organization's aim is to provide a mechanism for promulgation of consensus standards that can be adopted by states and other government entities and enforced through a state-level licensing and certification procedure. The standards will include criteria for business appraisers as well as for other disciplines.

In 1988, Florida passed a law (State Statute 475) requiring that any person doing business valuation have a real estate broker's license if a sole practitioner or real estate salesperson's license if employed by someone with a broker's license. Only certified public accountants who are licensed in Florida are exempted. The action by the Florida lawmakers brings home the need for uniform licensing and certification.

On August 9, 1989, President George Bush signed into law the Financial Institutions Reform, Recovery and Enforcement Act of 1989 (FIRREA), known as the savings and loan bailout bill, which mandates the certification and licensing of real estate appraisers who are involved in transactions with the federal government. This aspect of FIRREA is a stepping stone toward the licensing of valuation analysts in other disciplines.

2

VALUATION TERMINOLOGY AND METHODOLOGY

JAY E. FISHMAN*

		Page
¶ 2.1	Definitions of Value	2-3
	[1] Fair Market Value	2-3
	[2] Fair Value	2-3
	[3] Investment Value or Intrinsic Value	2-4
	[4] Going-Concern Value	2-4
	[5] Liquidation Value	2-4
	[6] Book Value	2-5
	[7] Enterprise Value	2-5
¶ 2.2	Description of the Particular Asset	2-5
¶ 2.3	Valuation Date	2-6
¶ 2.4	Equity Valuation	2-6
	[1] Understanding the Subject Enterprise	2-7
	[2] Economic- and Industry-Specific Analysis	2-10
¶ 2.5	Financial Statement Analysis and Adjustment	2-11
	[1] Examining the Financial Statements	2-13
	[2] Income Statement	2-13
	[3] Balance Sheet	2-16
	[4] Statement of Changes in Financial Position or Funds Flow Statement	2-17
¶ 2.6	Common-Size Statements	2-17
	[1] Income Statement	2-18
	[2] Balance Sheet	2-18
	[3] Financial Ratios	2-19
	[4] Liquidity	2-20
	[5] Asset Management	2-20
	[6] Accounts Receivable Turnover or Average Collection Period	2-21
	[7] Total Asset Utilization	2-21

---

* JAY E. FISHMAN, ASA, is president of Financial Research, Inc., Ardmore, Pennsylvania. He has been actively engaged in valuing businesses and business interests since 1974 and is a senior member of the American Society of Appraisers, a member of the Business Valuation Committee of the ASA, and a frequent lecturer.

The author wishes to thank Michael J. Bolotsky, ASA, and Bonnie O'Rourke for their invaluable comments on this chapter.

	[8] Debt Management	2-21
	[9] Profitability	2-22
	[10] Adjusting Financial Statements	2-23
	[11] Balance Sheet Adjustments	2-24
	[12] Income Statement Adjustments	2-25
	[13] Mechanics of Adjusting Financial Statements	2-26
¶ 2.7	**Valuation Methodologies**	2-27
¶ 2.8	**Market Comparison Approach**	2-27
	[1] Comparative Company Search	2-27
	[2] Valuation Ratios Derived From Comparatives	2-30
	[3] Sources of Market Information	2-32
¶ 2.9	**Income Approach**	2-34
	[1] Defining the Benefit Stream	2-35
	[2] Time Horizon Used	2-36
	[3] Concept of Risk and Its Application	2-37
	[4] Methods for Determining Cost of Equity	2-38
¶ 2.10	**Cost Approach**	2-42
	[1] Underlying Asset Approach	2-42
	[2] Excess Earnings Approach	2-44
¶ 2.11	**Discounts and Premiums**	2-45
¶ 2.12	**Summary**	2-46

The topics in this chapter cover basic terminology, concepts, and methodologies used in valuing closely held enterprises. Basic terminology in the business valuation profession has evolved from numerous sources, including the courts, the Internal Revenue Service (IRS), the real estate appraisal profession, corporate financial theory, and the accounting profession. Disagreements still exist among professionals concerning even the basics of business appraisal terminology. As recently as 1986, one author thought it necessary to point out that there was no legal difference between the terms "valuation" and "appraisal."[1]

These differences have been quelled to a certain degree with the compilation, by the Business Valuation Committee of the American Society of Appraisers (ASA), of a glossary of business valuation terms, published as *Business Valuation Standard Series #1*. The terminology, concepts, and methodologies in this chapter are consistent with the ASA glossary and the practice of most professionals in the field.

There are a myriad of elements that comprise a business valuation. Most practitioners agree that every business valuation must initially contain three basic elements. Failure to include these elements would result in an unacceptable report. Their inclusion alone without the inclusion of other elements specific to the particular circumstances

---

[1] Reilly, "Standards and Practices for Valuation Services," Practicing CPA, Dec. 1986, at 1.

would not necessarily produce an acceptable report. Every appraisal report must contain (1) a definition of value, (2) a description of the property that is the subject of the appraisal, and (3) the valuation date. Valuation reports written without regard to these factors would not contain the minimum criteria to enable the reader to clearly understand the report. Considerable differences in the expressions of an opinion of value would result without a clear understanding of these elements.

¶ 2.1 Definitions of Value

Value is a term that cannot be used in isolation. The meaning of value can change, depending upon the context within which the term is used. Lack of clarity concerning these concepts often leads to material disagreements in specific valuations. Therefore, the term should never be used unless defined. Practitioners in the business valuation area are aware of a number of definitions of value. The following terms are the most commonly used definitions of value. There is a reasonable degree of agreement as to their meaning.

[1] Fair Market Value

Fair market value is the most commonly used definition of value. *Fair market value* represents the amount at which property would change hands between a willing seller and a willing buyer when neither is acting under compulsion and when both have reasonable knowledge of the relevant facts.[2]

This definition has been used by the IRS, the ASA, and most courts. Fair market value is often used synonymously with the term "market value." Fair market value assumes the sale between a hypothetical willing buyer and willing seller. Accordingly, this concept is a value-in-exchange concept without regard to the specific current owner or specific buyers. This definition of value produces a result that could be achieved if the property were to be sold in an arm's-length transaction.

[2] Fair Value

Fair value, as used in the context of shareholder disputes, is a judicially determined concept of value. It is most often used in the context of a dissenter shareholder's litigation matter. Under the definition of fair value, the appraiser must take into consideration all factors and elements that reasonably might enter into estimating a value, exclusive of any element of value arising from the expectation or accomplish-

---

[2] Rev. Rul. 59-60, 1959-1 C.B. 237, § 2.02. Revenue Ruling 59-60 is reprinted as Appendix A at the end of this book.

ment of the subject corporate transaction. Generally, fair value is determined via consideration of market value, asset value, investment value, and any other relevant valuation considerations. It is essential that the business valuation expert consult the relevant statutes and case law in a particular state when engaged in a valuation for these purposes. (This discussion is not intended to include the usage of the term "fair value" in the context of purchase accounting for financial reporting.)

[3] Investment Value or Intrinsic Value

Investment value and *intrinsic value* are often used interchangeably and are defined as the value to a particular owner or prospective owner. The value produced would reflect the particular knowledge, expectations, and abilities of the owner or synergy of a prospective owner.

[4] Going-Concern Value

The definitions of *going-concern value* favored by the ASA are as follows:

1. The value of an enterprise or an interest therein as a going concern; and
2. Intangible elements of value in a business enterprise resulting from such factors as having a trained work force, an operational plant, and the necessary licensees, systems, and procedures in place.

The first definition of going-concern value is not a true definition of value but an assumption as to the continuity of any given business enterprise. Accordingly, this going-concern concept is a subset of the previously discussed definitions of value. The second definition of going-concern value is most applicable to valuation of intangible assets in business purchases.

[5] Liquidation Value

Liquidation value is usually broken down into two types: orderly liquidation and auction value. The difference between these two concepts of value is the time necessary to dispose of the assets. These definitions reflect the sale of the individual assets of a business enterprise with an allowance for a certain time period to find users who are capable of using these assets. Orderly liquidation usually envisions a six- to nine-month time frame while an auction value considers a much shorter time frame.

The liquidation value of a business enterprise represents the lowest limit of value. It is possible that the fair market value or market value of a business enterprise could be equal to its liquidation value. While the market value of a business enterprise can be lower than the sum of the liquidation value of the enterprise's underlying assets, the market value cannot be lower than the net liquidation value of the enterprise after a consideration of the costs to sell the underlying assets, overhead costs during the sales period, the time to sell the assets, and payment of the business' liabilities and senior equity securities. The book value of a business enterprise could be higher or lower than the liquidation value of a business enterprise.

[6] Book Value

The definitions of *book value* favored by the ASA are as follows:

1. With respect to the assets, the capitalized cost of an asset less accumulated depreciation or amortization as it appears on the books of account of the enterprise; and
2. With respect to a business enterprise, the difference between total assets (net of depreciation, depletion and amortization) and total liabilities of an enterprise as they appear on the balance sheet (it is synonymous with net book value, net worth, or stockholders' equity).

[7] Enterprise Value

Enterprise value is the value of 100% of the owners' equity, on a control basis, of the business enterprise.

¶ 2.2 Description of the Particular Asset

An *appraisal* is an opinion or estimate of the value of an asset. Since financial securities have differing characteristics, it is essential to describe the characteristics of a particular security in the appraisal. The specific characteristics or features of a financial security will have a material effect on its value. In addition, the size of the block, relationships to other blocks, and state of incorporation are other factors that will have a material effect on the value of a particular security.

Knowledge of state corporate laws will enable the practitioner to know the rights of a minority shareholder and the ability of a controlling shareholder to exercise those rights commonly associated with control. *Operational control* is defined as the ability to elect a majority to the Board of Directors. *Absolute control* is defined as the unrestricted ability to exercise all property rights normally associated with ownership, including the right to liquidate the corporation. States differ on the number of shares necessary to effectuate these actions. It is important to know the size of the block in the context of minority, operational control, and absolute control.

Many closely held enterprises also have more than one type of equity. A complete description of the rights of a particular equity holding would be essential in placing the valuation in its appropriate context. The ability of a particular minority issue to represent a *swing block* is also noteworthy. Therefore, it is important to describe the particular block in the context of other blocks of stock.

¶ 2.3 Valuation Date

An appraisal is an opinion or estimate of the value of a specifically defined asset at a given point in time. Value is a dynamic concept that changes because of a multitude of external and internal factors. A business valuation is relevant for a specific point in time. The valuation captures all of the relevant elements at that particular point in time. The practitioner is recreating the market environment in which a willing buyer and willing seller will operate, both knowledgeable of the relevant facts at that time. Factors and events that occurred subsequent to the valuation date that were not discernible or predictable at the valuation date are normally excluded.

¶ 2.4 Equity Valuation

After determining the appropriate definition of value, describing and understanding the asset that is the subject of the valuation, and determining the valuation date, it is necessary to acquire internal and external information about the business enterprise. The rest of this chapter provides a description of the concepts and methodologies used in arriving at an appropriate value of a closely held enterprise that is based on sound valuation and financial theory and that will withstand scrutiny.[3]

It is hard to believe that so many years have passed since the Internal Revenue Service issued Revenue Ruling 59-60. The principal appeal of this revenue ruling is its breadth. The guidelines discussed in Revenue Ruling 59-60 are not formulas or rigid criteria to be used in estimating market value. This revenue ruling contains many of the operational elements seen in the marketplace. Accordingly, the text and spirit of the revenue ruling require the practitioner to consider all those operational elements relevant to any particular valuation assignment.

Revenue Ruling 59-60 discusses eight basic factors that should be considered. These factors are as follows:

---

[3] *Id.* at § 4.

1. The nature of the business and the history of the enterprise from its inception;
2. The economic outlook in general and the condition and outlook of the specific industry in particular;
3. The book value of the stock and the financial condition of the business;
4. The earning capacity of the company;
5. The dividend-paying capacity;
6. The determination of whether the enterprise has goodwill or other intangible value;
7. Sales of the stock and size of the block of stock to be valued; and
8. The market price of stocks of corporations engaged in the same or a similar line of business having their stocks actively traded in a free and open market, either on an exchange or over the counter (OTC).

[1] Understanding the Subject Enterprise

Every appraisal report includes selection of key valuation variables in ultimately coming to an expression of an opinion of value. The selection of those variables is predicated upon a thorough understanding of the business enterprise, its environment, and its financial condition and earning capacity. Therefore, it is essential that the practitioner have a clear understanding of the nature, history, and operations of the business enterprise. Analysis of the history and growth of the business enterprise will provide the practitioner with key insights into the development of the business.

The operating results and financial condition of a business enterprise are recorded in its financial data. Therefore, many practitioners prefer acquisition and cursory analysis of this information prior to a detailed investigation into the history, nature, and operations of a business enterprise. Often, a review of financial data will generate questions concerning specific items recorded in the financial statements or tax returns. Following this cursory review, it is preferable to visit the facilities of an enterprise and obtain additional information from management. For a variety of reasons, this step may not always be possible, and the practitioner should always note the reasons for not being able to visit the facilities in the work notes for the assignment.

An understanding of the history of a business enterprise will be helpful in assessing the current position of a firm. The historical perspective will allow the practitioner a better understanding of the goods or services offered by the firm and the development of its operational characteristics up to the valuation date.

An analysis of the history of an enterprise, including its stock ownership, may lead to transaction information that will be helpful in the valuation process. There may have been previous offers for the subject enterprise from potential buyers. The development of this information in historical perspective represents a good starting point in the analysis of a business enterprise.

In the course of studying the history and nature of the firm, it is usually necessary to classify the firm's activities into one or more groups. One helpful system for classifying establishments by type of activity is the Standard Industrial Classification (SIC) system published by the U.S. Government. This system is helpful in classifying the business activities of the subject enterprise and enables the expert to develop information for comparative purposes within the firm's industry group. The SIC system is described by the Office of Management and Budget (OMB) as follows:

> The Standard Industrial Classification (SIC) is a system for classifying establishments by type of economic activity. Its purposes are: (1) to facilitate the collection, tabulation, presentation and analysis of data relating to establishments, and (2) to promote uniformity and comparability in presentation of statistical data describing the economy. The SIC is used by agencies of the United States Government that collect or publish data by industry. It is widely used by State agencies, trade associations, private businesses and other organizations.[4]

The SIC system was revised by the OMB in 1987. Therefore, care should be used to ensure comparability. A similar system is used by the Securities and Exchange Commission (SEC).[5] The classification of a business enterprise by SIC code or codes will be helpful during the entire appraisal process. Areas that can be enhanced by identification of this code or codes include industry analysis, comparative financial analysis, and the search for comparable publicly traded companies or transactions involving comparable companies.

An understanding of the history and primary economic activity of the business enterprise is a prelude to further analysis. There are many factors that should be considered in analyzing the company business activity. The goal of this inquiry is to understand the operations of the business, its diversity, stability and future. The following is a listing of some of the more important areas of inquiry:

- *Understand the enterprise's management structure.* Included in this area are the job activities of major members of management

---

[4] Office of Management and Budget, Executive Office of the President, *Standard Industrial Classification Manual* 699 (1987).
[5] *See* SEC, *Directory of Companies Required to File Annual Reports With the Securities and Exchange Commission* (Sept. 1987).

and their age, background, and longevity with the industry and firm.
- *Analyze and understand the firm's customer base.* An enterprise that relies on one or two customers for the major portion of its revenue will normally be a comparatively risky enterprise. An analysis of the company's historical customer base and dependency on one or many customers are important in the determination of a reasonable opinion of value.
- *Understand the physical facilities.* In a manufacturing concern, it is important to know the age and condition of the plant. The production capacity of a manufacturing plant in comparison to the current and planned level of production will be important in assessing the future investment needs of a business enterprise. In a service business, the reliance on physical facilities may not be as important as in a manufacturing concern. In a retail establishment, the location will become an important variable affecting its value. A clear understanding of the physical facilities will measurably enhance the valuation.
- *Look for changes in the evolution of the company.* Were there nonrecurring events, including moves, strikes, or natural disasters? Were there major changes in the structure of the firm's activities?
- *Find out the major competitors of the firm.* Management can be a good source of information concerning competition. Also investigate trade associations and industry information. This information may provide useful comparisons between the subject business enterprise and its peer group.
- *Investigate the enterprise's sources of supply.* Determine its level of dependency on one or a few suppliers.

This list was not intended to be exhaustive. Other factors, including regulatory climate, labor availability, and labor relations, backlog, intangible assets, and financial policy, need to be understood. The list of factors to investigate is dynamic and will change with changes in the economic and political climate. For example, increasing environmental awareness has led many governmental agencies to require certifications prior to the exchange of property and these requirements may have a material effect on the value of the property. As society changes, there will undoubtedly be additional areas of inquiry.

The goal of an analysis of the history, nature, and operations of a business enterprise is an understanding of the economic realities that form the basis of its operating results and financial condition. However, business enterprises do not exist in a vacuum. Economic activity is driven by international, national, and local factors. Following an understanding of the history, nature, and operations of a particular business enterprise, it is important to consider that enterprise in the context of these external factors.

[2] Economic- and Industry-Specific Analysis

This area of inquiry is most succinctly addressed in Revenue Ruling 59-60 by the following:

> A sound appraisal of a closely held stock must consider current and prospective economic conditions as of the date of appraisal, both in the national economy and in the industry or industries with which the corporation is allied.[6]

A well-prepared valuation will contain an analysis of the relevant economic and industry research. Clearly, the impact of national and regional trends—both economic and political—need to be assessed. Key influences on overall business activity, including interest rates, securities market trends, gross national production levels, and other general business conditions, and price index changes should be reviewed. Shannon P. Pratt, in his text entitled *Valuing a Business: The Analysis and Appraisal of Closely Held Companies*, has commented that "an understanding of the economic and industry outlook is fundamental to developing reasonable expectations about the subject company's prospects."[7]

General economic analysis should not be restricted to national trends. The regional and local economic factors and local economic environmental factors should also be considered. State, regional, and local agencies may have to be contacted and statistics from those sources should be obtained in areas within which the subject enterprise operates. Demographic data, consumer data, sales data, current and projected levels of employment, and other information is usually available on state, regional, and local levels. Information from all of these sources is combined to enable the practitioner to understand the context within which the subject business operates.

Trade associations, industry groups, and trade journals can be good sources of comparative industry data. Comparative industry data usually are broken down into two types: industry trend information and comparative financial information. Industry trend information will enable the practitioner to understand the growth and development of the industry. The growth or decline of economic activity in a particular industry can be compared to the operating results of the subject enterprise. The market position of a particular business may have significance in its pricing policies and growth prospects.

Comparative financial information will enable the practitioner to compare the operating results and financial condition of the subject

---

[6] Rev. Rul. 59-60, 1959-1 C.B. at 237, § 4.02b.
[7] S.P. Pratt, *Valuing a Business: The Analysis and Appraisal of Closely Held Companies* 174 (2d ed. 1989).

enterprise with its industry peer group. There are numerous sources of general industry information. These include Dun & Bradstreet's *Key Business Ratios*, Robert Morris Associates' *RMA Annual Statement Studies*, Prentice Hall's *The Almanac of Business & Industrial Ratios*, and Financial Research Associates' *Financial Statement Studies of the Small Business*.[8] The most comprehensive set of statistics comes from the Statistics of Income Division of the IRS. These include its *Corporation Source Book*, *Partnership Source Book*, and *Sole Proprietorship Source Book*.[9]

In addition to these sources, there are many industry-specific sources of financial data. These are usually obtained from trade associations or other associations. For example, a number of automobile dealerships participate in minigroups. These groups represent dealerships of similar size that offer the same products. They exchange comparative financial information.

Economic and industry research enables the practitioner to place the subject enterprise within the context of its industry. Where the company fits in its industry and where its industry fits in terms of macroeconomic factors will impact the future operating results of the enterprise.

¶ 2.5 **Financial Statement Analysis and Adjustment**

During the valuation process, it is essential to gather appropriate financial data. The practitioner should determine the availability of specific internal financial information. Financial statements, tax returns, projections, and interim statements are requested routinely. Interim statements are particularly useful if the valuation date falls in the middle of a fiscal year or if there is pronounced seasonality. It is also important to note whether, in the case of financial statements, they are compiled, reviewed, or audited.

The *Statement on Standards for Accounting and Review Services* issued by the Accounting and Review Services Committee of the American Institute of Certified Public Accountants (AICPA) in 1978 defined the requirements for compiled, reviewed, and audited financial statements as follows:

---

[8] Dun & Bradstreet, Inc., *Key Business Ratios* (annual); Robert Morris Associates, *Annual Statement Studies* (annual); L. Troy, *Almanac of Business and Industrial Financial Ratios* (annual); Financial Research Associates, *Financial Studies of the Small Business* (annual).

[9] Statistics Division, Department of the Treasury, "Active Corporations Income Tax Return, July 1985-June 1986," *Source Book; Statistics of Income* (June 1988); Internal Revenue Service, *Source Book; Statistics of Income Sole Proprietorship Returns, 1957* (Nov. 1986); Internal Revenue Service, *Source Book; Statistics of Income Partnership Returns, 1957-1983* (Sept. 1985).

Compilation of financial statements: Presenting in the form of financial statements information that is the representation of management (owners) without undertaking to express any assurance on the statements.

Review of financial statements: Performing inquiry and procedures that provide the accountant with a reasonable basis for expressing limited assurance that there are no material modifications that should be made to the statements in order for them to be in conformity with generally accepted accounting principles or, if applicable, with another comprehensive basis of accounting.

Audited statements contain an auditor's opinion, which, if unqualified, states which financial documents have been audited, and state they present fairly the company's position in conformity with generally accepted accounting principles.[10]

It is also important to determine the subject enterprise's form: regular or "C" corporation, "S" corporation, partnership, or sole proprietorship. If there is more than one entity included, it must be determined whether the statements are combined or consolidated and what type of accounting is used. Related entities, foreign subsidiaries, and joint ventures should be identified.

The data should be examined across the relevant time period for consistency of reporting. A change of accounting firm, accounting methods, or fiscal year during the time under review will have an impact on the analysis. Major changes in the nature of the business should also be ascertained. If, for instance, historical data are reported on a company as a wholesale operation and that wholesale operation has been discontinued, the historical data may not have much relevance to the company's future earnings stream.

As mentioned previously, one of the goals of financial analysis is to identify areas requiring further investigation and possible adjustment. It is usually assumed that the subject company's financial statements are prepared according to generally accepted accounting principles (GAAP) unless the practitioner specifies otherwise in the valuation report.

It should be clear that it is not the responsibility of the valuation expert to audit the subject enterprise's accounting records. It is, however, the responsibility of the valuation expert to analyze the subject enterprise's financial statements and to point out and/or pursue aberrations uncovered during this analysis. It may also be appropriate under certain circumstances and in special cases to enlist the assistance of an accountant to review or verify selected accounts.

---

[10] AICPA, 1 *The Statement on Standards for Accounting and Review Services* 3 (1978).

[1] Examining the Financial Statements

The first step after gathering the relevant financial data is to read the financial statements and tax returns to get an overview of the enterprise's operations and financial performance. It is particularly important to read the notes to the financials, focusing on the particulars of accounting methods used (e.g., inventory method or revenue recognition). The notes should also indicate some off-balance-sheet items, such as unfunded pension liabilities or contingent liabilities.

The federal and state tax returns also yield relevant information, sometimes including the differences between accounting methods employed for tax and book purposes. The Schedule M-1 reconciliation of tax to book on the Form 1120 should be examined to understand differences between the tax and book reported figures.

Generally, a minimum of five full years of historical data should be examined, if available. The purpose of reviewing the historical data is to enable the analyst to estimate the future earnings capacity of the firm and the relevant period should be chosen with that goal in mind. The purpose of the initial review is to identify peculiarities, trends, and areas for further investigation or analysis and items requiring adjustment.

The following sections are devoted to analysis of the income statement and balance sheet, both as presented and in common size form. Select financial ratios are presented and discussed and relevant issues and potential adjustments are discussed within the context of the three valuation approaches. Finally, adjustments are illustrated.

The first step in the analysis is review of the income statement and balance sheet as reported.

[2] Income Statement

The various revenue categories should be examined. Sales growth or decline and the pattern of the revenue over the period should be noted. It is important to ascertain the "quality" of the sales growth by investigating the type of product/service sold and changes during the period under examination and expected future changes that would affect the firm's growth of revenues. Sales in unit (or other measure of real sales volume) as well as nominal growth in dollars should be reviewed (if possible). This should include, of course, investigating such diverse subjects as pricing policies, marketing strategies, and market share (all of which are outside the scope of this chapter).

It is also important to identify at this point the method of revenue recognition. A common accounting basis for revenue recognition is important when comparing entities. For example, the "earnings" reported by a firm on the cash basis of accounting cannot be compared with firms on an accrual basis.

"Other income" categories should be examined to separate *operating* from *nonoperating* income. The latter might include large amounts of interest or dividend income from investments which are unrelated to the company's primary line of business. Gain or loss on disposition of fixed assets is also a common occurrence. The analyst must determine whether or not this type of item should be considered in the valuation of the operating entity.

If any nonoperating income is identified, it must be deducted from the operating income stream of the firm in order to appraise the operating entity.

The next step is to review the expense accounts. This includes cost of goods or services, operating expenses, and other expenses. The components of cost of goods sold should be examined, if possible, noting such areas as inventory accounting methods and trends in purchases.

Trends in individual expense accounts should be examined over time. Any changes in accounts, reclassification, or other differences should be resolved before identifying trends. "Other expense" categories should be examined to separate any additional operating expenses from nonoperating expenses, such as interest expense on long-term financing, or expenses relating to the sale of unneeded assets. Nonoperating expenses related to sales of assets should always be removed when valuing the operating entity. Interest expense on outside financing should be removed if the objective is to value the total invested capital of the entity; however, if the objective is to value the stockholders' equity, the interest expense should remain in the income statement.

The profit from operations, pretax profit, and after-tax profit of the entity should be noted, including the effect of taxes and the general level and trend of profits.

Some specific operating expense accounts typically warrant more specific consideration when appraising a closely held business.

Depreciation may be found as an operating expense and also as part of cost of goods sold in many operations, most notably in manufacturing. The analyst should examine the fixed-asset register or depreciation schedule to determine the various methods of depreciation and the life of the assets being depreciated. It is also necessary to estimate the replacement pattern expected for the future to determine the most likely level of future depreciation. In addition, it is necessary to determine what type of depreciation is being used and is likely to be used in the future. Often, depreciation is added back to net income as a noncash expense in order to estimate the firm's cash flow. It must be remembered that a firm must replace its assets; and although the depreciation expense recorded on the income statement may not be the most appropriate estimate of this replacement cost, some estimate of this expenditure must be built into the analysis if the objective is to determine the true level of ongoing cash flow that the firm could pay out to its equity holders.

Interest expense is related to the debt the firm carries and also to the interest rates it must pay on that debt. It may not be particularly relevant to analyze interest expense as a percent of sales; and given the volatility of interest rates over the past years, the historical level may not predict the company's future burden. It is necessary to assume an expected future level of debt and also to make assumptions about interest rates to estimate future interest expense.

A large *miscellaneous* or *other* account should be examined more closely to determine the specific components. The likelihood that these expenses will be representative of the future expenses must be determined.

The analyst must attempt to identify *nonrecurring* expenses. These may be included as an additional item in an existing account appearing as an increase in that expense account as a percent of sales, or they may be reported in a separate account. Nonrecurring items, such as moving expense or a one-time penalty, should be identified and removed from consideration when determining earnings capacity. According to GAAP, extraordinary items that are both unusual and infrequent should be reported separately and not included in the enterprise's net income. The definition of unusual and infrequent is clearly a matter of judgment; and, for valuation purposes, the analyst should determine whether there are any nonrecurring items embedded in the financial statements.[11]

Finally, the changes in the individual income and expense accounts should be examined in an attempt to explain any fluctuations in the pretax profitability of the firm. The analyst must determine, after reviewing both the financial and operating performance of the entity and looking at the subject firm in comparison with its industry and comparable companies, the most likely future earnings capacity of the firm.

Federal and state income taxes should be examined, including the differences between the statutory rates and the company's effective rate. If there are both permanent differences, such as those generated by payment of officer's life insurance, and timing differences, such as deferred taxes generated by different depreciation methods for tax and book, these should all be understood.

Based on the analyst's expectation for future income, expenses,

---

[11] J.E. Fishman, "Valuation Terminology and Methodology" (working paper 1989).

asset configuration, capital structure, and tax rates, a most likely future after-tax earnings capacity should be determined.

In order to do more than a cursory review of the financials, they must be viewed in perspective. One way to accomplish this is by common-size statement, which will be discussed later in this chapter.

[3] Balance Sheet

The assets on the balance sheet should be examined, noting the categories of assets and again attempting to identify any assets unrelated to the operations of the business. If nonoperating assets are identified, they and any income or expenses associated with them must be adjusted before appraising the operating entity. For example, a building listed on an enterprise's books but not used in operations should be removed from consideration in valuing the operating entity. The cost of the building, together with the accumulated depreciation, should be removed from the balance sheet. In addition, any income, such as rent, expenses, such as depreciation, taxes, utilities, etc., should be identified and removed from the income statement. If the building was financed, the debt and interest expense should also be removed.

The level of assets over time should be noted, keeping in mind that the balance sheet represents a snapshot of a firm's financial position at a single point in time. Any sharp fluctuations should be noted for further exploration. The age of accounts receivable should be determined and the adequacy of reserve for bad debts ascertained, together with the firm's credit policy.

Inventory valuation method(s) used should be noted, and any change in these over the relevant period should also be determined. It is also important to determine the inventory method used before comparing the subject firm with any industry data or comparable companies. If the subject company uses the LIFO method, for example, and the comparable companies report on the FIFO method, the subject company's income stream and asset account must be adjusted before comparisons are made. This information can be obtained from the notes to the financial statements in some cases, or from the firm's accountant. If the inventory account on the balance sheet will require adjustment, this will result in a change in the owner's equity of the firm. In addition, the cost of goods sold will change, resulting in adjustments to income. Tax effects of these adjustments should also be considered.

Fixed-asset accounts must also be closely examined. The type, date of purchase, cost, current book value, operational use, and estimated current market value are all of interest in appraising a business. In certain cases, appraisals of selected fixed assets may be necessary, such as when the analyst suspects the firm's liquidation value may exceed its going-concern value.

It is important to also determine what method(s) of depreciation is used and whether different methods are used for tax and book. This situation may generate positive or negative deferred taxes, depending on the age of the assets. It is also important to ascertain the firm's asset replacement cycle and determine if any departure from the historical cycle is anticipated in the near future.

The practitioner should explore any intangible assets, such as goodwill, patents, and trade names, and may have to determine their value. It is sometimes useful to have intangibles valued separately.

Liabilities should be reviewed, again noting any potential nonoperating entries. Accounts payable and the firm's payment terms from creditors should be noted. The analyst should determine the level and components of long-term debt, note the current and long-term portions, and the acquisition and retirement patterns over the relevant period.

The analyst should note the structure of the firm's equity base, including types and classes of stock as well as their characteristics. If the assignment is to value common equity, the impact of preferred stock and related dividends must be considered.

Again, a common-size statement analysis will facilitate the analysis of the balance sheet.

[4] Statement of Changes in Financial Position or Funds Flow Statement

This statement, if available, should be reviewed, since it is useful in determining how a firm generated funds during the past year and how these funds were used. In addition, this statement can help the analyst pinpoint areas requiring further study and reveal the total depreciation and/or amortization expensed during the period. Other useful information, including the net of new debt acquired and principal repaid, acquisition or retirement of fixed assets, and period-to-period changes in the current asset and liabilities accounts are recorded.

¶ 2.6 Common-Size Statements

After reviewing the financials or tax returns as reported, the subject enterprise's statements should be reduced to common size. The income statement accounts are expressed as a percent of revenues and the balance sheet accounts as a percent of total assets. This allows the analyst to pinpoint changes in the relative composition of the firm's operations removing the effect of absolute size changes. For example, the firm's gross margin could increase in absolute terms but fall as a percent of sales revenue.

[1] Income Statement

Changes in cost of goods sold and gross margin are the first areas that should be examined on the common-size income statement. These levels should be examined over time, and any changes or trends should be further investigated. Changes in product or service mix, production process, costs, or accounting methods could all be potential explanations for changes in margin.

The expense accounts on the income statement are the next area for examination. Large changes in accounts as a percent of sales, volatility, or trends over the relevant period are all indications that further investigation is warranted.

Industry associations often publish operating ratios and common-size statements gathered from their membership. While some bias is to be expected, these can provide a useful benchmark as one comparative measure.

[2] Balance Sheet

The common-size balance sheet expresses the asset, liability, and equity accounts as a percent of total assets. As with the income statement, the balance sheet should be examined over time to identify relative fluctuations that could indicate changes in the company's structure or operations.

Asset accounts should be reviewed and changes in the asset mix noted. For example, an increase in cash as a percent of total assets may indicate excess cash that should be viewed as a nonoperating asset. However, in a firm where management policy is to minimize debt, this build up may be in anticipation of an asset purchase and may be necessary for operations.

Changes in other assets, such as accounts receivable, inventory, and fixed assets as a percent of sales should be noted and trends should be explored further.

Similarly, liabilities should be examined for trends with particular attention to the relative proportion of debt and equity to the company's asset base.

After examining the balance sheet and income statement in both nominal and common-size forms, the next step is to compute and analyze financial ratios.

[3] Financial Ratios

An analysis of financial ratios over time can help the analyst identify areas requiring further investigation. Ratios can assist in pinpointing the company's strengths and weaknesses and can provide a common area for comparisons with similar firms. The ratios must be viewed over time, and they must be viewed in relationship to each other and to the company's industry ratios. The goal of ratio analysis is to identify changes in a firm's operating or financial structure. A marked shift in a ratio should prompt the analyst to investigate why the ratio has changed and whether the change is permanent or temporary and to determine what the impact is on the firm's future earning capacity.

There are many well-known difficulties in utilizing financial ratios, including the problems inherent in comparing companies with different accounting methods. Perhaps the most important problem for valuation purposes is that the ratios, like the company's financial data, examine the historical performance of the firm while valuation requires the projection of expected future results.

Nevertheless, it is helpful, while bearing in mind their various limitations, to examine financial ratios. First, which ratios are not relevant to the subject company should be determined and eliminated from the study. For example, the inventory turnover of a service firm or the times interest earned ratio for a debt-free firm are not likely to be relevant. In addition, it may be useful to recalculate ratios after making selected adjustments to the firm's financial data in order to more accurately assess their position relative to the industry.

The following is a discussion of several commonly used ratios. There are many variations, and any standard financial analysis textbook can be consulted for additional or different ratios. It should also be noted that one of the purposes of ratio analysis is to allow comparison of the subject company to similar firms. To that end, the analyst will often use industry association data or other sources of ratios, including Robert Morris Associates and the IRS source books. It is always essential to read the description of how each source calculates the ratios. For example, a debt/equity ratio, in one source, may include all debt but, in another source, may exclude short-term or non-interest-bearing debt or include only common equity but not preferred equity.

These ratios can be computed on the firm's financial statement as reported. However, it is often necessary to adjust for "structural" differences, such as inventory accounting and nonoperating items, before calculating ratios for the operating entity.

For purposes of this chapter, the ratios will be grouped under four functional classes: liquidity, asset management, debt management, and profitability.

[4] Liquidity

The *current ratio* is the ratio of total current assets to total current liabilities. This is intended to measure the firm's liquidity by examining its ability to "cover" its short-term liabilities, such as accounts payable, with its short-term assets. This assumes that the assets will be converted to cash at their balance sheet amounts or that inventory will be sold at cost and the accounts receivable will be collected in full. This ratio can provide a useful perspective when viewed over time, or in relation to other similar firms. Differences in inventory valuation must be considered when making comparisons to similar firms.

Another more stringent measure of liquidity, is the *quick* or *acid test ratio*. This ratio is calculated by eliminating inventory from current assets and dividing by current liabilities. This is based on the assumption that inventories are the riskiest of the current assets and the least likely to be converted to cash in the near term.

In general, the higher the liquidity ratios, the better; but if the ratios are too high, they could indicate that accounts receivable or inventory levels are too high or that the firm has accumulated excess cash. A review of these accounts on the common-size balance sheet and a comparison of the liquidity ratios with those of similar firms will aid in analyzing these situations.

[5] Asset Management

The *asset management* or *utilization ratios* are intended to assess how effectively the firm is using its assets. Some common measures of asset utilization are:

- Inventory turnover or days of inventory;
- Accounts Receivable turnover or average collection period; and
- Total asset utilization ratio.

Inventory turnover or days of inventory reveals information on the length of time a firm holds its inventory before selling it. Dividing the cost of goods sold by average inventory indicates the number of inventory turns per year. Dividing the number of inventory turns per year into 365 days reveals the average number of days of inventory the company carries.

Caution must be used in interpreting this ratio, especially if the firm experiences seasonality. Quarterly or monthly calculations are helpful but not always feasible. There are many variations in the calculation of this ratio, and it is important to maintain consistency between subject company ratios and the sources of comparison.

In general, if the inventory turnover is slow relative to industry norms, this could indicate obsolete inventory or poor buying practices and could put a strain on the resources of the company. If turnover is much faster than average, this could indicate efficiency in buying or, on the other hand, stock-out situations that could constrain sales volume.

[6] Accounts Receivable Turnover or Average Collection Period

The *accounts receivable turnover ratio* indicates how quickly the firm is collecting its accounts receivable. This ratio, like the inventory turnover ratio, can be expressed in the number of times the accounts receivable turn over in a year or as the average number of days required to collect from customers.

The accounts receivable turnover ratio is calculated by dividing sales by average accounts receivable. This results in the number of times receivables turn over during one year. Dividing this ratio into 365 days reveals the number of days required to collect the average receivable (the average collection period or ACP).

A long ACP could indicate possible uncollectible receivables or poor collection management and possible short-term liquidity problems.

[7] Total Asset Utilization

The *total asset utilization ratio* is a measure of how efficiently assets are generating sales. This ratio is calculated by dividing total assets into sales, and the results indicate that, for every dollar of assets, a certain number of dollars of sales are generated. When viewed over time, the total asset utilization ratio can reveal trends in asset productivity and can indicate, when viewed in relation to similar firms, possible nonproductive or nonoperating assets.

Caution again is urged when interpreting this ratio. The age and hence depreciated book value of fixed assets play a major role in the magnitude of this ratio and should be analyzed carefully.

[8] Debt Management

Debt management ratios or *financial leverage ratios* help measure a firm's financial risk. Two of the most common ratios are the total liabilities/total assets ratio and the debt/equity ratio. In addition, coverage ratios examine the firm's ability to cover interest charges generated by its level of debt. The times interest earned is a commonly used coverage ratio.

Total debt/total assets is calculated by dividing total assets of the firm into its total liabilities. This reveals what percent of its assets is financed by creditors. The proportion of the assets supported by equity holders can be calculated by subtracting the total liabilities/total assets ratio from one.

There is a great variety of *debt/equity* ratios, and the analyst must be especially careful to determine how a ratio is calculated before making comparisons. Generally, these ratios attempt to express how much of the firm is "owned" by creditors and how much by equity holders. Variations of this ratio include dividing total debt by total equity, long-term debt by total equity, long-term debt less deferred taxes by total equity, long-term debt by common equity, and total debt by tangible equity. The higher the debt/equity ratio, in general, the higher the financial risk of the firm. In addition to higher risk, debts also create the potential of higher return to equity holders, and the degree that this potential is realized will determine whether the added risk is justified. Thus, the leverage ratios should be assessed in conjunction with several of the profitability ratios. When valuing closely held entities, it is important to look at the creditors carefully. Frequently, a substantial portion of the "debt" is money loaned to the firm by owners in lieu of contributing additional equity. The analyst must determine whether this should be treated as debt or equity when valuing the firm.

The *times interest earned ratio* is a coverage ratio, measuring the ability of a firm to meet its interest charges. It is calculated by dividing interest expense into earnings before interest and taxes (EBIT). With a higher ratio, it is less likely that a decline in profits will result in inability to pay interest charges. It is important to remember that the firm must repay principal in addition to the interest expense when interpreting this ratio. For this reason, various other coverage ratios, such as total fixed-charges coverage and fixed-charges-to-cash-flow coverage may be useful in the analysis.

[9] Profitability

There are several ratios commonly used to assess a firm's profitability, including:

- Net profit margin;
- Return on assets; and
- Return on equity.

The firm's *net profit margin* is simply its net income divided by sales. (This was addressed in the common-size statement discussion earlier in this chapter.)

Another measure of the firm's profitability is the *return on assets* ratio. This is calculated normally by dividing some measure of debt-free income, such as EBIT or after-operating income, by total assets in order to measure the return to assets without considering how the assets are financed.

The *return on equity* (ROE) is calculated most often by dividing net profit after tax by total common equity. There are, again, several variations; and, if the firm has preferred stock, either the preferred dividends must be deducted from the income before computing the ratio, or the divisor should be adjusted from total common equity to total equity. At times, it is useful to calculate the pretax return on equity; and, in that case, the pretax income is used instead of net income. The return on equity measures the return on the stockholders' investment after a provision for a return to debtholders in the form of interest. This should be viewed in conjunction with the liabilities/assets and the debt/equity ratios for, as mentioned earlier, a high ROE may be the result of *low* owners' equity rather than higher profits.

The variations in a firm's ROE can be analyzed by examining the factors affecting this measure. The du Pont analysis breaks ROE into three components as follows:

$$\text{ROE} = \frac{\text{Sales}}{\text{Assets}} \times \frac{\text{Net Profit}}{\text{Sales}} \times \frac{\text{Assets}}{\text{Equity}}$$

That is, ROE can be viewed as a function of the interaction among asset turnover, net profit margin, and assets/equity. When there is volatility in ROE or when the analyst *identifies* some discrepancy between the subject company and industry ratios, this analysis often proves useful in identifying the sources of the problems. It should be noted that this can be done on a before- or after-tax basis.

[10] Adjusting Financial Statements

Following the preliminary analysis of the enterprise's financial and operating data, the analyst must determine what, if any, adjustments should be made to the reported operating results per the financial statements. A number of these adjustments have been discussed in previous pages. It is important to draw a distinction among types of financial statement adjustments. Some adjustments simply account for the enterprise's assets, liabilities, income, or expenses in an alternative manner. These adjustments are made so that the subject enterprise can be more properly compared to its industry counterparts or similar publicly traded enterprises. Under this category, adjustments may be made for differing inventory accounting methods (LIFO, FIFO, or specific identification) or varying depreciation methods.

A second class of adjustments are made when the subject company has certain attributes, such as nonoperating assets, that are more properly looked at separately from the valuation of the operating business. Examples of nonoperating items include interest or dividend income from investments unrelated to the enterprise's primary line of business.

Other types of adjustments are made so that the historical financial relationships are reasonably reflective or expected future relationships. Specific examples of these types of adjustments include adjustments to remove the effect of nonrecurring events. A nonrecurring item is an item that, under normal circumstances, would not be expected to occur in the future.[12] Examples of nonrecurring items may include gain or loss on disposition of fixed assets, receipt of proceeds from litigation, or extraordinary business interruptions.

It is important that the analyst be cognizant of these various types of adjustments when estimating the enterprise's future earning capacity and also when comparing the subject firm with its industry counterparts or comparables. Several different types of common adjustments are discussed next.

[11] Balance Sheet Adjustments

If the analysis of the firm and its operating statements reveals that the enterprise has nonoperating assets and/or liabilities, these should be removed from the balance sheet. The estimate of the value of the entire firm is produced by valuing the operating entity and adding to it an amount to account for the value of the nonoperating assets, less any associated liabilities. When valuing less than an absolute control position in the firm, the contribution of the nonoperating assets may need to be discounted from the amount that would apply in a valuation of the entire firm.

Another common area of asset adjustment is inventory. If the analyst is comparing the subject company with publicly traded companies, it is advisable to place the subject company on the same inventory accounting basis as the comparative publicly traded companies. For example, it is often necessary to convert the subject enterprise's reported LIFO inventory accounting method to a FIFO basis in order to make meaningful comparisons with other members of its industry group. The LIFO reserve is usually specified in the "Notes to the Financial Statements" or can be obtained from the firm's accountant. The inventory account on the financial statements as reported is adjusted upwards by this amount. Since the increase in the inventory account results in increases in pretax income, income tax expense, and taxes payable, this leads to a corresponding adjustment to the liabilities

---

[12] *IRS Valuation Guide for Income, Estate and Gift Taxes* 83 (IRS Appeals Officer Valuation Training Program No. 44, Oct. 1985).

and owners' equity of the firm. The same treatment should apply to firms using varying depreciation methods.

It is important to remember the interrelationship between the balance sheet and income statement. In the LIFO/FIFO adjustment just discussed, cost of goods sold on the income statement must be adjusted to reflect the change in inventory accounting method.

[12] Income Statement Adjustments

One common adjustment is the removal of nonoperating income. Income generated from nonoperating assets removed from the balance sheet, as already described, should be deducted from the enterprise's income stream as a means of normalizing its future earning capacity. Examples include the income generated from nonoperating investments, including real estate, stocks, bonds, or other investments.

Another common adjustment is the removal of nonrecurring income or expenses. Examples of nonrecurring income include proceeds from the sale of a discontinued operation, the settlement of litigation, or the gain from the sale of fixed assets outside the ordinary course of business.

Likewise, nonoperating losses and nonrecurring losses should also be removed. Examples of nonoperating losses include losses on rental of real estate or capital losses on sale of stocks or bonds. Nonrecurring losses include abnormal bad-debt write-offs, unfavorable settlement of litigation, or loss on the sale of fixed assets outside the ordinary course of business.

In the valuation of many closely held enterprises, the shareholders are also principal employees. In these situations, it may be necessary to make adjustments for salaries beyond reasonable levels of officers' compensation. The guiding principle for these adjustments is the determination of fair compensation for services rendered by a hypothetical replacement employee who possesses the same skills, education, work habits, and job description of the shareholder/employee. The ultimate goal of this adjustment is to determine the amount that would be reasonably paid to the person performing the services. Other factors included in assessing reasonable compensation include the nature of the operation, the customs in the industry, the depth of the management team, the financial performance of the enterprise, and the historical compensation levels of the employee. If there are pension and profit-sharing plans, adjustments consistent with the changes made in base compensation may be necessary. Similarly, if the expert suspects that travel, entertainment, and other related accounts may be excessive, the excess amount may have to be added back to the firm's pretax income.

A reasonable compensation analysis should be part of most valuation assignments. However, the analysis will not necessarily lead to an adjustment of compensation. A consideration of numerous factors, including the size of the block being valued, the premise of value, and the purpose of the assignment will dictate whether the reasonable compensation analysis should result in a reasonable compensation adjustment.

[13] Mechanics of Adjusting Financial Statements

It is possible to specify the adjustments in several ways. The analyst can isolate the adjustment amount and add it (or subtract it) from the appropriate line item on the income statement or balance sheet and thereby arrive at an adjusted financial statement. This is useful if there are substantial structural differences between the enterprise and its industry counterparts or comparative firms. This technique can also be employed if it is desirable to view trends or ratios on an in-depth adjusted basis. In some cases, normalized statements and ratios should be recomputed and analyzed on an adjusted basis.

Another approach is to accumulate all adjustments as additions or reductions of income/expenses, compute the net result of the adjustments, and apply that one figure to the firm's financial statements. Each of these techniques has merits under different circumstances.

In most cases, it is important to recognize the impact of taxes when making adjustments. Adjustments are made to pretax income, and the analyst is calculating an adjusted pretax level of income. The impact of the adjustment for taxes, when relevant, should be considered on both the income statement and, in many cases, the balance sheet as well (e.g., in the adjustment of inventories from LIFO to FIFO). Note, however, that cash or other assets generated by historical accounting practices do not "disappear" when balance sheet adjustments are made. The adjustment to make the accounts representative of other companies or of future trends cannot alter the fact that historical practice has caused the balance sheet to be what it is, and the excess assets that may have been generated by these practices therefore must be accounted for in some manner in the valuation process.

It is important to remember that the purpose of adjusting historical financial statements is to provide a more realistic or appropriate financial picture on the subject enterprise. In addition, adjustments are often made to place the enterprise on a consistent basis to provide meaningful comparison with its industry counterparts or comparative public firms. The application of specific valuation methodology, the size of the block being valued, and the purpose or the premise of value all may dictate the relevance of certain adjustments.

¶ 2.7 Valuation Methodologies

The business valuation discipline recognizes various methodologies to arrive at an estimate of the value of a business enterprise. These methodologies are not mutually exclusive but are interactive. Unfortunately, there is no universally accepted consensus dealing with the nomenclature of these methodologies. Pratt discusses a number of methodologies, including discounted future earnings or cash flow, adjusted net asset value, and capitalization of current, normalized, or historical earnings.[13] Others have discussed similar approaches using the following taxonomy: discounted cash flow approach, value of underlying asset approach, and market comparable approach.[14]

Generally, the business valuation profession recognizes three basic approaches. These are similar to the three classic approaches used in valuing real estate: market data, income, and cost approaches. For purposes of this chapter, these specific business valuation methodologies are called the "market comparison approach," the "income approach," and the "cost approach."

¶ 2.8 Market Comparison Approach

The market comparison approach attempts to estimate the value of a business enterprise or a fractional interest in that enterprise by comparison with exchanges of similar property in the marketplace. It is preferable that the analyst begin this approach by searching for transactions of property as similar as possible to the subject of the appraisal assignment.

[1] Comparative Company Search

The applicability of the market comparison approach hinges on both the comparability of the subject firm to the companies selected as comparatives and the comparability of the size and type of ownership interest to the size and type of ownership interest transfers providing the market evidence. Significant judgment is required in determining companies that may be useful as comparatives. It is highly unlikely that there are two companies alike in all respects or even in all major respects. Revenue Ruling 59-60 directs the expert to consider "the market price of stocks of corporations engaged in the same or similar line of business having their stocks actively traded in a free and open market, either on an exchange or over-the-counter."[15] Similar guidelines would apply when attempting to select comparable purchases of entire businesses to use in valuing controlling interests, except that the

---

[13] S.P. Pratt, *supra* note 7, at 54-55.
[14] R.J. Grabowski, *Closely Held Corporations: Valuation* 3 (1985).
[15] Rev. Rul. 59-60, 1959-1 C.B. at 237, § 4.01.

acquisition price would be substituted for the references to the freely traded market price. Misjudgments as to the degree of comparability can lead to significant distortions in the indicated value of an enterprise or a fractional interest therein.

Objectivity and sound reasoning are required in selecting a relevant group of comparatives. The compilation of a list of factors to be considered in choosing comparative firms could be endless. However, there are some basic considerations that will provide useful guidelines in the selection of comparative publicly traded companies or acquisitions. Some of the more important considerations include the availability of adequate financial and price information; the firm's line of business, location, quality, and depth of management; the size of the comparative firm; trading activity in the stock; and the specific block of stock that is the subject of the appraisal assignment.

The firms selected as comparables should be engaged in the same or similar line of business. It would be inappropriate to compare a large publicly traded company engaged in the construction of chemical plants to a small home builder. One way to identify companies that are similar is to search for comparable companies by their SIC code. The SIC code of the U.S. Department of Commerce is a broad measure for classifying companies. A search by SIC code will allow the expert to narrow the list of potential comparable publicly traded companies or comparable business purchases.

Many databases contain SIC codes by primary and one or more secondary lines of business. The secondary lines of business can be used as further screens and will be important in ensuring that the business activities of the potential comparative companies are as similar as possible to those of the subject enterprise. The databases will usually show what percentage of revenue is generated by each business activity. This tool will enable the analyst to determine the composition of the comparable company's business as compared to the subject enterprise.

It is also important to determine the markets served by the comparable group. If a subject enterprise is serving a region, then, ideally, the comparable group should be serving a similar region. It would be inappropriate to directly compare a multiproduct, international firm to a regional firm. An investigation into the markets served by the subject firm should be followed by a similar investigation of the comparable group.

The quality and depth of management are major issues in the valuation of any business enterprise. The comparative companies and the subject company should be compared regarding their depth of management. If the comparatives are public companies, their filings with the SEC should indicate the number of officers, their age, their years of experience in the industry, and their remuneration. In addition, these filings will indicate their benefit package. The issue of management is not directly related to the selection of a comparable publicly traded company for comparative purposes but rather relates to the advantage or disadvantage these companies have in comparison to the private subject enterprise.

The level of revenues and assets are another set of factors to be considered when selecting comparable companies. Typically, size differences will exist. An investigation should be made as to the nature of these differences. If the revenues of the comparative firms are considerably larger, consideration must be given to the nature of these differences. Is the size difference related to the geographical diversification of the comparative company? Is the comparative company international in scope while the private company is regional? Is the comparative company horizontally integrated or in diverse product areas? Does the relative size of the comparative firm result in a deep management team while the privately held firm is a one-person organization?

These and other factors should be considered when size differences exist. Generally, the larger the revenues of a firm, the less variability in its performance. However, smaller firms may have substantially more attractive growth possibilities since the smaller firm can often more readily capture increased market share than can a larger firm that already holds a significant percentage of a market. Therefore, size and variability must be considered in tandem with growth potential.

An often-overlooked area is the trading volume of a particular publicly traded company. This is particularly true of those publicly traded companies traded OTC. Often, OTC companies do not have sufficient trading volume to generate a market price that is reasonably reflective of their minority share values. Sometimes, there are only one or two trades per week. This is not necessarily indicative of the freely traded market value of these publicly traded shares. In addition, there may be publicly traded companies whose minority shares are speculative and sell for a few cents on the dollar. Again, the market price of these particular publicly traded shares often offer very little insight into value. In order to make meaningful comparisons when seeking an indication of "as if publicly traded" minority value for the subject shares, the publicly traded share price of a comparable company must be traded in a free and active environment.

It is also important to consider the specific block that constitutes the subject of the appraisal. If the subject of the appraisal assignment is a control position in a closely held enterprise, it would be preferable to search and use transactions involving control positions. Conversely, if the assignment is to determine the value of a minority interest in a business enterprise, it would be preferable to locate transactions involving similar minority interests.

While it is certainly possible to determine the minority interest of a closely held enterprise from the acquisition of a control block in a similar enterprise, this would require another level of adjustments to reflect the minority interest that is the subject of the assignment. Similarly, while it would be possible to determine the value of a control position if one relied upon publicly traded minority issues as the basis for comparison, adjustments would need to be made to these minority issues to reflect the control position that is the subject of the assignment. Since the use of similar percentage ownership interest transfers eliminates the need for these additional levels of adjustments, the use of transactions involving similar percentage ownership interests is preferable unless adequate data regarding the transaction and/or the financial position of the comparative are not available.

The preceding has been a brief discussion of some of the important factors that should be considered in selecting publicly traded comparatives or comparative acquisitions. There are numerous other factors, including profitability, growth rate, capital structure, and industry characteristics that should be considered.

[2] Valuation Ratios Derived From Comparatives

Once a relevant group of comparatives is identified, units of comparison are derived from the relationship between the market price of their stock or the acquisition price in a business purchase and operating results. These units of comparison are often referred to as *valuation ratios*. Four typical valuation ratios are as follows:

1. *Price/earnings ratio*—the relationship between the market price of the minority issue or the acquisition price for an entire business and earnings per share;
2. *Price/book ratio*—the relationship between the market price or acquisition price and common shareholders' equity;
3. *Price/dividend ratio*—the relationship between the market price or acquisition price and dividends paid; and
4. *Price/cash flow ratio*—the relationship between the market price or acquisition price and cash flow (often defined as net income available to common shareholders plus noncash charges).

The preceding ratios can be calculated on a per-share basis or on a gross-dollar basis based on total net income, equity, dividends, paid or cash flow. The corresponding gross dollar amount for the market price or the acquisition price would be derived by multiplying the market price or acquisition price per share times the number of shares issued and outstanding.

When utilizing these or any other valuation ratios, it is critical to be consistent concerning the time periods used to calculate these ratios. The consistency also applies to the application of these ratios to the operating results of the subject enterprise. Therefore, it would be inappropriate to take a price/earnings ratio derived from a publicly traded comparative based on its current price to most current year income and apply it to the five-year weighted average, historical earnings of the subject enterprise. When varying capital structure is an issue, the valuation ratios can be calculated on a debt-free basis.

While these valuation ratios provide a representative sample, many other ratios, such as the price/revenues, price/square feet of selling space, or total invested capital/operating income ratios, are used when deemed applicable to particular industries or situations.

During the 1980s, there had been significant activity in the merger and acquisition market. Since acquisition activity normally involves the transfer of control positions, these transactions are especially useful when valuing control positions of closely held enterprises. The criteria concerning the use of a particular transaction or set of transactions, the calculation of the valuation ratios, and the matching of time periods are generally the same as for the selection of publicly traded comparatives and the calculation of their ratios. One significant factor when using mergers or acquisitions as the basis for the market comparison approach is the calculation of the true consideration paid. Since the goal of a business valuation is normally to calculate an amount equal to a fair cash price, the consideration paid in an acquisition must be analyzed to determine if the seller received all cash and, if not, to determine whether the portion of the price not paid in cash is worth more or less than its stated amount.

Factors that would cause the noncash consideration to be worth something other than its stated amount include payment in the form of notes or preferred stock at a coupon rate not equal to a fair market yield or the transfer of unregistered securities to the seller in which various restrictions would prevent the seller from immediately marketing these securities. In those instances, a discount (or, rarely, a premium) may be assigned to the noncash consideration so as to reflect their cash equivalent. It is essential that the analyst understand the terms of each merger or acquisition that is used for comparative purposes in a valuation assignment.

The strength of the market comparison approach lies in the ability to generate units of comparison based on actual market transactions. This strength must be tempered by the degree of comparability the publicly traded comparatives or acquisitions bear to the operating and financial characteristics of the subject enterprise. When comparability exists, the market comparison approach can produce appropriate indications of value.

[3] Sources of Market Information

Much has been written concerning the sources of market information.[16] The search for comparative transactions may include an examination of the subject enterprise, trade associations, and public literature.

An often-overlooked source of comparative information is the enterprise itself. As part of the data-gathering process, it is important to inquire into the history of the ownership position of the business enterprise. Occasionally, this inquiry will reveal a history of transactions involving equity holders of the business enterprise. These transactions should be examined, and documentary information concerning them should be obtained.

Unfortunately, these transactions often do not provide much insight into value. Since the ownership of a private company is usually in the hands of a limited number of shareholders or often one family, most transactions concerning these enterprises are among a limited number of shareholders, often family members.[17] In these instances, great care must be exercised in understanding the circumstances surrounding these transactions. In those cases where the analyst is satisfied that the circumstances surrounding the transaction are representative of normal considerations of typical buyers and sellers, these transactions may provide some insight into value. In addition to providing information regarding transactions in the subject company stock, the company will often have information regarding its major competitors, some of whom may be potential comparatives. The best sources for competitor information is usually the sales, marketing, and research and development departments.

The use of the SIC code as a means of identifying potential comparable publicly traded companies has already been discussed. The starting point in a search for developing similar comparative publicly traded enterprises is a search of the appropriate SIC numbers which apply to the subject enterprise. Data concerning publicly traded companies by SIC group are found in a number of sources, including the SEC's *Directory of Companies Required to File Annual Reports With the Securities and Exchange Commission*.[18] Many databases contain SIC codes by primary and secondary lines of business. These databases

---

[16] For an excellent discussion, see S.P. Pratt, *supra* note 7, at ch. 9.
[17] Rev. Rul. 59-60, 1959-1 C.B. at 237, § 2.03.
[18] See SEC, *supra* note 5.

include Moody's *Manuals* and Standard & Poor's *Register*. In addition, there are a number of computer databases, such as Dialog Information Services, Inc., which allow the searching through numerous databases, including the *Media General, Disclosure*, and Moody's databases.[19]

Merger and acquisition searches are also conducted by relevant SIC code. Various databases exist that will provide information concerning mergers and acquisitions. These include W.T. Grimm's *Mergerstat Review, Mergers & Acquisitions*, and *The Merger Yearbook*.[20] Information gathered from these databases should be considered as a starting point in the analysis. It is advisable to obtain financial information and annual reports to assess the historical performance of the acquired company. Filings with the SEC are also important sources of detailed information concerning the acquired company.

In addition, Houlihan, Lokey, Howard & Zukin, Inc. (HLHZ), a valuation advisory and investment banking firm headquartered in Los Angeles, conducts a quarterly *Control Premium Study* to assess premiums paid for publicly held stock in cash-for-common transactions. An unaffected stock price is selected by HLHZ based on volume and price trends prior to the transaction announcement date. The premium paid over this unaffected price is considered the HLHZ premium. Quarterly median premiums from first-quarter 1986 through first-quarter 1988, for example, have ranged from 31.9% to 60% while twelve-month medium premiums have ranged from 37.5% to 52.3%.

The usual procedure is to identify a broad universe of potential comparable publicly traded enterprises or acquisitions that may be usable in the analysis. After applying an initial set of screening criteria to reduce the broad universe to a more manageable size (often between five and fifteen companies at this stage), detailed information concerning the remaining potential comparatives is obtained and compared to the subject enterprise. These comparisons include many of the criteria mentioned previously as well as salient financial characteristics, including liquidity, efficiency, leverage, and profitability ratios. The list is gradually narrowed to derive the most comparable group. There is no ideal number of final comparatives since the final number is often a function of factors of comparability beyond the control of the analyst, but it is often the case that between four and six comparatives remain after the application of all screening criteria. Units of comparison are

---

[19] Predicast F&S Index (weekly, monthly, supplements, quarterly, and annual cumulations).

[20] W.T. Grimm & Co., *Mergerstat Review* (annual).

then derived from this group and applied to the operating results of the subject enterprise.[21]

¶ 2.9 Income Approach

The *income approach* is based upon the premise that the value of property can be determined by the present worth of future benefits derived from ownership of that property. This is a fundamental principle of valuation. In this context, the term "income" is used in a broad sense encompassing all monetary benefits of ownership excluding compensation for services. As discussed earlier, there are areas of overlap between the market comparison approach and the income approach, and the parameters used in one approach may be derived from the other approach. For example, units of comparison used in the market comparison approach are often measures of income. Similarly, valuation parameters used in the income approach, such as required rates of return, are usually market derived.

There is a certain degree of confusion in appraisal literature regarding the terms "discount rate" and "capitalization rate." When a multiperiod time horizon is used, the rate used to discount benefits to present worth is known as a discount rate, and the factors for each period derived from the discount rate are known as present worth factors or present value factors. The discount rate is synonymous with the required rate of return. When a single period of benefits is converted to an indication of value, the factor is known as a capitalization rate. The capitalization rate normally "impounds" all relevant information necessary to convert the parameter into an indication of value, including but not limited to the required rate of return, less a normalized rate of expected future growth.

Pratt has defined the terms "discount rate" and "capitalization rate" as follows:

> Discount Rate: A rate of return used to convert a series of future income amounts into present value.
>
> Capitalization Rate: A divisor used to convert a defined stream of income to an indicated value.[22]

The reciprocal of the ratio of price to current net income would be a form of capitalization rate applicable to current earnings. Similarly, a dividend yield based on the current indicated dividend would be a form of capitalization rate applicable to current dividends.

---

[21] A.A. Joyce, "Valuation of NonPublic Companies," in *Accountants Handbook* 38.1-38.28 (6th ed. 1981).

[22] S.P. Pratt, *supra* note 7, at 95.

The elements comprising the income approach are interactive. These elements are succinctly characterized by Lester Barenbaum and Thomas F. Monahan when they suggest that the value of any asset is a function of several related factors:

1. The stream of benefits the owner of the assets expects to receive;
2. The timing of the receipt of these benefits; and
3. The risk borne by the owner.[23]

These three elements can be used to describe the principles of the income approach.

[1] Defining the Benefit Stream

Single-period benefits and benefit streams can be determined in various ways. It is essential to understand the nature of the income and to select a discount rate or capitalization rate that is applicable to the income as defined, the type of business being valued, and the size of the appraised ownership interest.[24]

For example, it would be inappropriate to capitalize net income with a rate derived from the debt-free cash flows of comparative companies or to capitalize current net income based on a rate derived from the comparatives' five-year average income. The consistent application of capitalization rates or discount rates derived from like benefit streams will help to avoid inappropriate estimates of value.

A common measure of benefits used by business appraisers is net income. This measure provides the parameter to be capitalized by an earnings/price ratio in the market comparative approach. Because of varying accounting conventions relating to the calculation of net income, various working capital, and capital expenditure requirements and other financial policies, some prefer to use other measures of benefits in addition to net income.[25]

Another commonly used benefit stream is available cash flow, also known as net cash flow. The available cash flow of an entire firm is the proportion of debt-free income that can be distributed once the operational needs of a firm have been met or, in the case of valuation of stockholders' equity, the proportion of income that can be distributed after considering operational needs and the net of debt payments and

---

[23] Barenbaum & Monahan, "Revenue Ruling 59-60: Valuation Theory and Practice Conflict," ASA Valuation, Dec. 1984, at 4.
[24] Pratt, "Understanding Capitalization Rates," ASA Valuation, June 1986, at 12-29.
[25] Rappaport, "Financial Analysis for Mergers and Acquisitions," Mergers & Acquisitions, Winter 1976, at 19-20.

new debt incurred.[26] A similar model is discussed by Pratt and is referred to as net-free cash flow.[27] All of the cash flow models attempt to take into account the working capital needs, capital expenditure needs, and capital structure of the firm in the future. These models are particularly applicable since there is considerable material available on required rates of return applicable to available or net cash flows.

There are a myriad of other means of defining single-period benefits or benefit streams. These include earnings before depreciation, interest, and taxes (EBDIT); EBIT; and earnings before taxes (EBT). All of these measures are after an allowance for reasonable compensation for officers. The EBDIT and EBIT approaches are referred to as debt-free measures, and this type of measurement would determine the value of the total invested capital of a firm. If the purpose of the appraisal is to estimate the equity of an enterprise, the long-term debt, at market, must be subtracted from total invested capital to produce the value of equity.

[2] Time Horizon Used

The present worth of future benefits can be determined on a single-period or multiperiod basis. The choice of using a capitalization rate or discount rate depends on whether a single-period or multiperiod model is used; and, in turn, this is often dependent on the facts and circumstances involving the particular assignment. When a single period is used, the capitalization rate is often a divisor that assumes the benefit stream will continue into perpetuity. In such instances and in those where it is expected that the benefit stream will grow at some normalized rate, the growth rate is subtracted from the discount rate applicable to the multiperiod stream of benefits to derive the capitalization rate applicable to the current period's benefits. An example of a benefit stream model utilizing this single-period approach is the Gordon Dividend Valuation Model.

When the analyst is faced with a situation in which constant growth is not a reasonable option, the benefit stream is estimated over

---

[26] Barenbaum, "Utilizing the Gordon Model: Discounting Net Income vs. Available Cash Flow," J. Bus. Valuation, 1987, at 119-127. The model from the article is as follows:

$$ACF = \frac{Ag - NC(1+g)}{P(1+g)(1+D/E)}$$

where:
- ACF = available cash flow as a percentage of net income
- A = investment in net current assets and gross fixed assets relative to sales
- NC = noncash expenses to sales
- g = expected growth rate in sales
- P = expected profit margin
- D/E = expected debt/equity relationship

[27] S.P. Pratt, *supra* note 7, at 83.

some reasonable time horizon. Generally, a three- to five-year time horizon is used with a terminal value at the end of the relevant time period. However, exceptions exist, and the relevant time horizon is a function of the facts and circumstances of a particular assignment. Under no circumstances can this approach be applied properly unless there is a terminal value. The terminal value can be defined in many ways. One common method is a stabilized level of benefits at the end of the time period capitalized into perpetuity without assuming any growth. Another method applies a capitalization rate in the terminal year that is equal to the discount rate less a perpetual growth rate. Still other approaches involve application of multiples of book value or earnings to the applicable terminal year parameters. In all approaches, to derive a terminal value, the terminal value represents the value of the business or ownership interest as of the terminal year. Therefore, it is always necessary to discount the terminal value to present worth from the terminal year to the appraisal date.

Consistency in matching the appropriate benefit stream to a required rate of return or capitalization rate derived from a consistent time period is also important. For example, the last twelve months' net income of a firm should be converted to value using a current after-tax price/earnings ratio. Using the ratio of projected earnings to price and applying it to historical earnings would produce inconsistent results. When projecting the benefit stream on a multiperiod basis, the appropriate rate used to determine the present value of these flows is the discount rate. As stated earlier, the discount rate or required rate of return should match the benefit stream being discounted.

[3] Concept of Risk and Its Application

The last element in the application of this approach is consideration of the risk borne by the investor. Risk is thought of as the uncertainty regarding the expected rate of return from an investment.[28] The principle that underlies the concept of risk is the financial principle of opportunity costs. The opportunity cost is the return that could be obtained by investing the same amount of money in a similarly uncertain investment elsewhere. This concept is fundamental in the valuation of all assets. For example, the real estate profession discusses these concepts in terms of the "principle of substitution," as follows:

> The principle of substitution presumes that the purchaser will consider the alternatives available and will act rationally or prudently on the basis of the information about those alternatives and a reasonable time is available for the decision. Substitution may assume the form of the purchase of an existing property, with the

---

[28] F.M. Reilly, *Investment Analysis and Portfolio Management* 6-7 (2d ed. 1985).

same utility core, or acquiring an investment which will produce an income stream of the same size with the same risk as that involved in the property in question.[29]

An understanding of the risks associated with a business enterprise begins during the data-gathering phase of any appraisal assignment. A clear understanding of the nature and operations of the business, the way it operates in its environment, and its financial condition and performance are necessary prerequisites to begin to assess the risks associated with the continuation of the expected benefit stream.

In technical terms, risk associated with the firm as a whole is generally broken down into two categories: business risk and financial risk. When partial business interests are being valued, an additional element, liquidity risk, may also be present. Business risk is the uncertainty associated with the operations of the firm and its industry environment. This component of risk is defined as the variability associated with the expected future operating income of a firm. The second component, financial risk, relates to the firm's use of financial leverage in its capital structure. The third component, liquidity risk, can also be incorporated into the total discount rate when applicable, or it can instead be recognized as an explicit discount from the value that would otherwise be derived assuming full liquidity.

When valuing the total invested capital of a firm, only the element of business risk should be considered in the financial analysis while financial risk becomes an input into the choice of discount rate (known in this case as the "weighted cost of capital"). When valuing only stockholders' equity, both the elements of business risk and financial risk are explicitly considered in the financial analysis.

The capital structure of a firm consists of debt and equity. Creditors and equity holders require compensation for their investments; this compensation is termed "cost of debt" for creditors and "cost of equity" for shareholders. Estimating the cost of debt is relatively easy when information within the firm is available concerning its borrowings and the rate at which new borrowings can be made. The cost of equity is more difficult to estimate. The cost of equity is synonymous with the required rate of return for shareholders. There are a number of accepted methods used to estimate the rate required for equity holders in the public market.

[4] Methods for Determining Cost of Equity

There are four commonly used methods for determining the required ROR for equity holders: the Capital Asset Pricing Model

---

[29] *Real Estate Appraisal Terminology* 234 (Byrl N. Boyce rev. ed. 1982).

(CAPM), the buildup method, the arbitrage pricing theory (APT), and the yield-plus-growth method. With the exception of the last approach, which can be applicable to many kinds of benefit streams, depending on how the "yield" is defined, the other three methods are *only* applicable to determining a required rate of return for discounting available cash flow to the equity holder, as defined earlier.

The CAPM is used to determine required rates of return for assets with varying degrees of risk relative to some benchmark average. In this model, risk is broken into two components: systematic and unsystematic risk. Unsystematic risk is risk that can be diversified away when the asset is held as part of a balanced, diversified portfolio. In other words, it is random fluctuations that will tend to be negated by the random fluctuations of other assets in the portfolio. Systematic risk, on the other hand, is equated with nonrandom fluctuations relative to the market as a whole; since the fluctuations are not random, they cannot be diversified away by holding a sufficiently large and diverse portfolio. Since one of the premises underlying the CAPM is that it is used to determine the required rates of return for selecting stocks in a well-diversified portfolio, the model attempts to measure a firm's systematic risk only.

The measure of a firm's systematic risk relative to the market in this model is a factor known as "beta." The beta is a numerical constant for a particular asset, with the beta of the market as a whole set to 1.0. The beta measures the movements of the returns of an individual security as compared to a market proxy. One of the key assumptions in the CAPM is that there is a security that has no nonrandom fluctuations relative to the market—that is, a "zero-beta security." Since the random fluctuations of this security can theoretically be diversified away, the security has no risk of any kind when held in the diversified portfolio. Thus, the fair rate of return on such a security is known as the *risk-free rate*. Although all securities should theoretically have some beta, the yield on a very low beta security, such as U.S. Treasury securities, is usually used as a proxy for the risk-free rate in the model.

By measuring the average difference, over time, between the return on the market as a whole and the risk-free rate, applying the beta to this difference, and then adding the risk-free rate to the resulting product, the CAPM attempts to determine the required return for a particular asset. The difference between the average market return and the risk-free rate is known as the *market risk premium*. The CAPM equation, then, can be succinctly described as the risk-free rate, plus the product of beta and the market risk premium. The higher the beta, the higher the required rate of return. When beta is greater than 1.0, the asset has greater systematic risk and greater required return than the market as a whole; the opposite is the case when beta is less than 1.0. When beta equals zero, the equation reduces to the risk-free rate.

Another method for determining the required rate of return on equity is known as the buildup method. The buildup method is similar to the CAPM (which can be considered a special type of buildup model) in that the basic model requires the return on a riskless security as a base, plus an additional return for the risk of the subject security. The method does not include calculation of a beta or other measure of systematic risk. Usually, a government security is used as a measure for the risk-free portion of the equation while the risk premium starts with some average measure of market risk, such as the "Equity Risk Premium" contained in Ibbotson Associates' *Stocks, Bonds, Bills and Inflation Yearbooks*[30] as a base for the risk premium. Subjective adjustments (up or down) are then made for company-specific factors, both quantitative and qualitative. For a small business, management depth is often one of the key qualitative factors.

As opposed to the CAPM, which assumes a relationship between a single benchmark and the subject security, the APT is a multi-index model. That is, the APT assumes that securities respond, to one degree or another, to the pull of many factors. For each factor, the degree of response of the subject security to that factor is described by a "factor-beta." The factors can be equal to either actual levels of a particular economic variable or equal to the degree of unexpected changes in the level of the variable. Further, the key factors for one security need not be the key factors for a different security. However, if APT is to become usable in practice, it must also be the case that most of the variability in returns from one security to the next are explainable by a limited, manageable number of factors.

The key theory underlying the APT is that the actions of individual investors, when they become aware of riskless arbitrage opportunities (opportunities to generate a guaranteed return with no capital investment), will cause the price of the securities comprising the riskless portfolio to rise or fall until the arbitrage opportunity quickly disappears. It is these actions by investors in an active market that then ensure that each security responds in a predictable and approximately linear manner (described by its factor beta) to changes in the level of the particular factor. These actions also ensure that the rate of return on all riskless investment opportunities is approximately equal, and this rate can then be described as the risk-free rate.

The APT is a much younger method than the other three. The theory has been subjected to limited empirical testing. While it is

---

[30] Ibbotson Associates, *Stocks, Bonds, Bill and Inflation Yearbook: Market Results for 1926-19—* (annual).

hoped that the method will eventually enjoy widespread use, its use in the valuation of closely held firms is currently quite limited.

The final method is known as the yield-plus-growth method. Simply stated, the method assumes that the total return on a security is the sum of the return earned currently plus the future growth expected in the current return. For example, if the goal is to determine a discount rate applicable to a stream of dividends, the starting point would be to determine the sum of the current indicated dividend yield and the expected rate of dividend growth for a sample of public firms in the subject company's industry. The average indicated return would then be adjusted for factors specific to the subject company.

While the yield-plus-growth method has many theoretical and practical weaknesses, it has one advantage over the other three methods. The indicated return produced by the other three methods is applicable only to discounting a projection of available cash flow. The adjustments necessary to make the indicated return from the other methods applicable to discounting any other type of stream involve significant and often speculative assumptions. On the other hand, the yield-plus-growth method is applicable to discounting any kind of stream, depending on how the "yield" is defined.

For example, to discount a stream of earnings, the current earnings yield (current earnings/price ratio) of the public companies would be used as the starting point, to which would be added the estimated growth, to obtain an industry average earnings discount rate. As before, subjective adjustments would then be made for factors specific to the subject company. The process would be similar to determine a rate applicable to discounting a stream of operating cash flow (OCF). The starting point would be the ratio of current OCF to price (the OCF yield) of the public companies, and then the process would flow as before. As long as the current yield is defined analogously to the stream that is discounted, the method can be used for any type of stream.

Each of these models have strengths and weaknesses when applied to closely held firms. The CAPM relies on developing a beta from comparative companies. Again, a particular appraisal assignment may involve a company in which there are no reliable comparatives. The CAPM also measures only the systematic risk of a particular stock and envisions its addition to the well diversified portfolio. This is not always the case in a business valuation and it is a questionable assumption that investors in closely held firms behave in this manner. The buildup method requires judgment as to the extent to which a firm has systematic and unsystematic risk relative to some benchmark. In addition, the premiums derived from the Ibbotson *Yearbooks* are ex ante, and one assumes these premiums will be indicative of the future. This is also a weakness of CAPM when these premiums are used for the equity risk premium in the CAPM equation. One advantage of the buildup method is that it is the only one that does not require comparative companies.

The APT has many of the same strengths and weaknesses as CAPM plus the fact that the theory is not yet widespread in practice and may never be in the valuation of closely held businesses. Theoretically, however, the APT is, in many ways, more well grounded than the CAPM, and the APT also allows for certain real-world imperfections that allow small deviations in the riskless return rate and in the returns of individual securities; in the CAPM, many of these real world imperfections must be assumed away. The yield-plus-growth method is the weakest approach in terms of the theory underlying the method; yet, it is the simplest method to use in many respects and will always be usable unless the comparative companies do not have a positive yield. As with the CAPM and APT, this method requires a group of comparatives.

¶ 2.10 Cost Approach

The *cost approach* in business valuation primarily focuses on the balance sheet of a business enterprise. This approach considers the value of the underlying assets and liabilities of a business enterprise as a means of determining the value of the equity. Therefore, the cost approach is also known as the "underlying asset approach." While most analysts consider the relationship between the market price of minority issues and their shareholders' equity (known as the price/book ratio) as part of the market approach, some consider this relationship to be a form of cost approach. Generally, however, the more common view is that an assessment of the value of underlying assets and liabilities leads to an indication of control value of the business since minority investors lack the power to directly realize the value of the assets. In addition, the cost approach is generally considered to involve identification and valuation of specific groups of underlying assets rather than the application over an overall price/ or value/book ratio.

[1] Underlying Asset Approach

The *underlying asset approach* considers the component parts of a business enterprise. When the primary function of a business enterprise is to hold assets, the cost approach is given considerable weight. For an operating enterprise, the sum of the present worth of the net proceeds from liquidation of its assets less liabilities represents the lowest limit of value for a controlling interest. As mentioned previously, while the market value of a business enterprise can be lower than the sum of the gross liquidation proceeds from sale of the enterprise's underlying assets, the market value cannot be lower than the net liquidation value of the enterprise after consideration of the costs to sell the underlying assets, overhead costs during the sales period, the time to sell the assets, and payment of the business' liabilities and senior equity securities.

The underlying asset approach can be done on either a net liquidation basis or by using the value of the underlying assets in continued use. The former basis is normally applicable when there is a distinct possibility that the business is worth more "dead" than "alive" while the latter basis is normally applicable when there is little possibility of liquidation. When either premise is used, all assets—both tangible and intangible—should be considered. The book value is usually the starting point from which adjustments are made to reflect the various asset values. When real estate appraisals are obtained, it is important to note if the highest and best use contained in the real estate appraisal is consistent with the use contemplated for the business enterprise. If the highest and best use of the real estate is different than the contemplated use, an allowance must be made for this factor.

When analyzing the machinery and equipment and other non-real-estate fixed assets of a business, it is important that the business appraiser acquire information from competent professionals in those fields. When interfacing with those professionals, it is equally important for the business appraiser to understand the terminology and definitions of value used in those disciplines so as to properly apply them in the appropriate context. One term that deserves particular attention is *value in use* for personal property.

The ASA has defined *value in use* for personal property as follows:

> Value in Use is the value of personal property for a specific use or to a specific user, reflecting the extent to which the property contributes to the utility and/or profitability of the enterprise of which it is a part. Included in this value are installation costs, engineering design and layout fees, where applicable.[31]

As stated earlier, value in use is the appropriate starting point for an analysis of a going business enterprise's fixed assets. However, the values reported on this basis must be tested to show that the income stream justifies the values reported. When that situation exists, value in use on an unadjusted basis is appropriate. When the net profits are not sufficient to justify the values reported, a downward adjustment to these values in use must be made.

---

[31] Gadd, "Defining Value-in-Use," ASA Valuation, Feb. 1987, at 5.

Failure to understand these concepts can result in an over or under estimate of value using the underlying asset approach. Ultimately, the underlying asset approach must consider the net profits or cash flow of a business when expressing an opinion of value other than liquidation value. It is important that the income or benefit stream justify the values of the fixed assets in order to properly employ this approach.

Another asset area requiring examination in this approach is the separately identifiable intangible assets. Generally, intangible assets do not explicitly appear on a business enterprise's balance sheet unless they were acquired. Various techniques have been developed that will produce values for clearly identifiable intangible assets. Those methods include the profit advantage approach, relief from royalty approach, and the cost to create approach. (Detailed discussion of these techniques are beyond the scope of this chapter.)

Once the analyst has determined the appropriate separately identifiable asset values, it is also important to look at the liabilities. The liabilities are valued based on economic reality. Favorable financing, favorable loans from shareholders, or other like instruments must be considered and adjusted to their appropriate values.

Finally, in addition to the separately identified intangible assets, additional value may exist in the form of goodwill and other intangibles not separately identified. A commonly used technique for valuing goodwill and other intangible assets not separately identified is known as the excess earnings approach.

[2] Excess Earnings Approach

The excess earnings approach was developed by the U.S. Department of the Treasury in its Appeals and Review Memorandum 34 (A.R.M. 34) in 1920. Its current form is published in Revenue Ruling 68-609.[32] The term "excess earnings" is derived from the capitalization of earnings above and beyond a normal return on tangible assets. In this case, the approach provides an indication of total intangible asset value. Many practitioners also include the separately identifiable intangibles in the assets for which a normal return is deducted from earnings. In this case, the excess earnings then provide an indication of the return attributable only to the intangibles not separately identified. The approach is used primarily to determine the value of goodwill and intangible assets when no better basis exists, and it derives the estimate of value by capitalizing the excess earnings at an appropriate rate.

Because of its longevity and seeming simplicity, courts of competent jurisdiction have cited the excess earnings approach as one method

---

[32] Rev. Rul. 68-609, 1968-2 C.B. 327.

to determine goodwill in certain contexts. The text of the revenue ruling itself clearly indicates that it is the methodology of last resort.

Whatever approach is used to determine goodwill, the value of goodwill is then added to the other net asset values including identified intangibles and a value of the equity on a control basis is then produced. Appropriate discounts would then be necessary if a minority ownership position is being valued.

¶ 2.11 Discounts and Premiums

The interest that is the subject of the appraisal and the methodology employed will dictate consideration of discounts for minority interest, discounts for lack of marketability, or premiums for control. For example, if the subject of the appraisal is a minority interest in a closely held enterprise and the analyst relies on comparisons with minority share prices of publicly traded securities, no minority interest discount is required. The same situation would exist if the data on required rates of return for equity are developed from minority shares of publicly traded securities. In these instances, a discount may be considered for the closely held securities to reflect their illiquidity. This is referred to as a discount for lack of marketability. These discounts are applied to the minority value as if publicly traded to reflect the inability of the minority shareholder to convert his interest into liquid funds as quickly as a shareholder of a publicly traded security. Studies have been conducted that reflect discounts of restricted stock purchases as compared to their publicly traded counterparts. These studies form the basis of one source of information concerning discounts for lack of marketability.[33]

The enterprise value of a firm is usually different than the sum of its aggregate minority issues. When the asset under the appraisal assignment is a control position in a closely held enterprise, an adjustment may be required. The first step in this analysis is a complete understanding of the ownership structure of the firm, the relevant statutes in the state of incorporation and the operating characteristics of the business enterprise.

In most instances where an adjustment for control is appropriate, the adjustment may be made in several interactive ways. An adjustment may be made to the benefit stream to reflect benefits accruing to the control shareholder or that would be available to a prospective owner. It may also be possible to adjust the required rate of return to reflect the additional certainty of a benefit stream to a controlling shareholder. A common method used to arrive at a control position in

---

[33] See S.P. Pratt, *supra* note 7, for an excellent discussion of studies concerning discounts for lack of marketability (ch. 10) and control premiums (ch. 9).

a closely held enterprise is the addition of a premium, when appropriate, to the aggregate minority values produced from the Market Comparative Approach. Many analysts rely upon W.T. Grimm's *Mergerstat Review*[34] as one source of these premiums. (Caution is advised in relying on this source as these premiums sometimes contain synergies.) Another well-respected source is Houlihan, Lokey, Howard & Zukin, Inc.'s *Control Premium Study*.

Conversely, if a value is produced from an acquisition of a controlling interest, no premium is usually required when valuing its closely held counterpart.

An exhaustive discussion of discounts for minority interest, discounts for lack of marketability, and control premium is beyond the scope of this chapter. However, when appropriate, these factors should be considered.

¶ 2.12 Summary

The valuation terminology and methodology explained and analyzed in this chapter are covered in extensive detail in the following chapters in Part 1. In these chapters, practitioners will find market examples, simulated valuation situations, and practical applications on such topics as the concept of fairness versus fair market value, ratio analysis, capitalization and discount rates, and the valuation of fixed-income securities. In addition, a cumulative case study, built around the terminology and methodology from this chapter, is provided. This chapter then serves as the broad reference background for the specific valuation theory analyzed in the following chapters.

---

[34] W.T. Grimm & Co., *supra* note 20; S.P. Pratt, *supra* note 7, at chs. 8-9.

3

FAIRNESS vs. FAIR MARKET VALUE

KENT V. GRAHAM*

		Page
¶ 3.1	Basic Distinction Between Fairness and Fair Market Value	3-2
	[1] When Relevant	3-2
	[a] Mergers and Acquisitions	3-2
	[b] Other Fairness Opinions	3-3
	[2] Parties Involved	3-3
¶ 3.2	**Director Conduct vs. Shareholder Rights**	3-6
	[1] Business Judgment Rule	3-6
	[2] Appraisal Rights	3-7
¶ 3.3	Courts' Concept of Fairness	3-9
	[1] "Entire Fairness"	3-9
	[2] Fair Value	3-11
	[3] Procedural Fairness	3-12
¶ 3.4	**Role of Valuation Expert**	3-13
	[1] Weight Given to Fairness Opinion	3-16
	[a] Independence	3-16
	[b] Sufficient Time	3-16
	[c] Information Available	3-17
	[d] Disclosure to Third Parties	3-19
	[2] Liability of Valuation Experts	3-19
¶ 3.5	**Disclosure Requirements**	3-20
	[1] Federal	3-21
	[2] State	3-23

Fairness, like beauty, is in the eye of the beholder. A transaction may appear fair to a valuation expert because the price represents fair market value. The same transaction, however, may be held to be grossly unfair by a court because of unfair procedures or inadequate disclosure or for a myriad of other reasons.

---

* KENT V. GRAHAM is a partner in the Century City (Los Angeles) office of O'Melveny & Myers. The author specializes in mergers and acquisitions, including going private and leveraged buyout transactions. In addition, he is a member of the board of directors of Plasti-Line, Inc. and has written and lectured on a wide variety of corporate and securities law matters.

¶ 3.1 Basic Distinction Between Fairness and Fair Market Value

At first, the distinction between the terms "fair market value" and "fairness" seems patently obvious. Fair market value is primarily a financial concept. Fairness, on the other hand, is primarily a legal concept that encompasses, yet transcends, the financial aspects of a transaction.

The legal literature and case law are replete with discussion of fairness in a variety of contexts. This chapter focuses on the term as it is likely to arise in connection with the valuation of securities. The purpose of this chapter is not to give a detailed legal treatise on the law in this area; that could, in and of itself, involve volumes. Considerable information from recent important legal decisions is included, however, because valuation experts must understand and appreciate the context within which advice is being given.

[1] When Relevant

A valuation expert's opinion as to the fair market value of an asset may be needed in a variety of situations, including the sale of a business, the buyout of a partner, tax planning, insurance coverage, bank loans, employee stock ownership plans (ESOPs), estate planning, divorce, and death.

Most situations in which the distinction between fairness and fair market value is relevant involve transactions where there are potential conflicts of interest among the parties involved. The expert rendering an opinion involving issues of fairness may find that it is like tiptoeing through a mine field of (1) traditional valuation theory, (2) factors bearing on fairness under the federal securities laws, and (3) evolving standards of valuation theory and practice as set forth in state statutes and legal decisions. This chapter attempts to show a path through this mine field.

[a] Mergers and Acquisitions

By far the most notorious and noteworthy examples of the distinction between fairness and fair market value arise in mergers and acquisitions, particularly "going private" and leveraged buyout transactions. These transactions have led to the development of much of the case law and legal literature on the subject of fairness since, as discussed later, the courts have required such transactions to be fair. The valuation expert will be retained to pass on certain aspects of the fairness.

The terms "going private" and "leveraged buyout" are often—and incorrectly—used interchangeably. A going-private transaction generally occurs when a majority or control stockholder seeks to acquire the remainder of the public shares. This may involve borrowing large sums of money secured by the assets of the company. A leveraged buyout, on the other hand, generally occurs when a third party—often in cooperation with the management of the company—seeks to acquire all the shares of the company in a transaction characterized by the borrowing of large amounts to finance the buyout. Both transactions involve extensive actual and potential conflicts of interests, making valuation opinions extremely important.

Most combinations of publicly traded companies eventually involve a merger of one company with the other pursuant to the corporation statutes of the jurisdictions in which the companies are incorporated. Mergers are used because of the necessity of assuring that the buyer ultimately receives all the shares of the seller. A tender offer, unless followed by a merger, will not result in 100% ownership because there are always stockholders who fail or refuse to tender or who cannot be located. Accordingly, most buyers are faced either with structuring the transaction as a merger at the outset or tendering for shares followed by a second-step "squeeze out" merger to eliminate minority shareholders.

[b] Other Fairness Opinions

Several other situations may require expert opinions as to the fairness of the transaction. For example, under the bankruptcy laws, certain types of arrangements and reorganizations must meet a test of being "fair and equitable" to certain classes of creditors. Expert testimony or opinions may be needed in this context.[1]

In addition, in connection with recapitalization transactions or leveraged buyout transactions involving significant corporate restructuring, issues may arise under the fraudulent conveyance statutes of the states in which the company's assets are located. In this context, the board of directors of the company, the lenders, or both may need advice from an independent expert dealing with the posttransaction ability of the company to pay its debts as they mature, the adequacy of the capital of the posttransaction company, and other related matters. Some of these issues may turn on the question of whether the assets have been transferred or sold for their present fair salable value and whether the posttransaction assets of the company, so valued, exceed the company's liabilities.[2]

[2] Parties Involved

In the typical combination of two unaffiliated companies, the ultimate purpose of a valuation opinion is to help the board of directors of

---

[1] See ch. 10.
[2] *Id.*

the seller satisfy its obligation to exercise sound business judgment in approving the transaction. This business judgment is required of the directors even when no conflicts of interest exist.

Under most state corporation statutes, directors can rely, to a large extent, on opinions expressed by outside experts within the range of their expertise. Under Delaware law,[3] for example:

> A member of the board of directors of any corporation organized under this chapter, or a member of any committee designated by the board of directors shall, in the performance of his duties, be fully protected in relying in good faith upon the books of account or reports made to the corporation by any of its officers, or by an independent certified public accountant, *or by an appraiser selected with reasonable care* by the board of directors or by any such committee, or in relying in good faith upon other records of the corporation.[4]

In some of the recent judicial decisions discussed here, the courts have essentially ignored the valuation work done by experts because of a variety of perceived defects in their selection or work product.

Usually, a number of different parties must consider the fairness of the transaction to them or a constituency they represent. In most transactions of any size or complexity, the following parties generally play a role:

For the company being acquired:

- The board of directors, usually composed both of independent directors and members of management
- The company's investment banker
- The company's regular legal counsel
- A "special" or "independent" committee, composed of the independent directors of the company
- The committee's special legal counsel
- The committee's investment banker or valuation expert

For others:

- Lenders and their legal counsel, sometimes advised by an independent valuation expert

A special committee of the board of directors is generally the key

---

[3] Delaware is the jurisdiction where most of the important judicial decisions with respect to fairness have arisen primarily because it is the jurisdiction in which a high percentage of publicly traded companies are incorporated.

[4] Del. Gen. Corp. L. § 41(e) (emphasis added). *See also* N.Y. Bus. Corp. § 717(2) and Cal. Corp. § 309(b) (1977).

participant attempting to have the transaction meet applicable legal standards. For example:

> Courts will look for objective indicia of compliance with the duty of care. Therefore, where a board establishes a special committee to evaluate a proposed course of conduct, retains independent legal and financial experts, takes its time in addressing the matters before it, and questions its advisors rather than passively receiving information, the board will have taken significant steps toward having made an informed decision. Breaches of the duty of care are usually characterized by either a board's failure to obtain adequate information before acting or by a board's failure to give thorough consideration to a decision. *Although the establishment of a special committee does not satisfy the duty of care standard, the use of a special committee should minimize the risk of breaching the duty of care because the special committee is likely to be a smaller and more objective group that can enhance both the information gathering and deliberative function of the board.*[5]

In addition, in transactions involving ESOPs,[6] the parties involved also include an independent trustee for the ESOP, an independent legal counsel for the trustee, and an independent financial advisor to the trustee. ESOPs are frequently used in leveraged buyouts or going-private transactions to provide part of the funding for the transaction due to the favorable tax benefits available to the company and the lender if the transaction is structured properly.

The primary role of many of these parties is to try to put a transaction that may not, in fact, be at arm's length into a posture as close to arm's length as possible and to ensure that the transaction meets the test of "entire fairness" described later. The duty of fairness generally is owed to public or minority shareholders who, because they are diffused and cannot have a direct voice in the transaction, need the protection of the law.

In general, the standards of fairness that apply to transactions are the same whether the entities involved are public or private, large or small. Because of their visibility in the financial press, large public transactions get the most attention, but the duties owed by the parties are similar regardless of the size or nature of the business enterprise. These duties owed by the parties are discussed in the following pages, with special in-depth coverage of director conduct versus shareholder rights.

---

[5] Simpson, "The Emerging Role of the Special Committee—Ensuing Business Judgment Rule Protection in the Context of Management Leveraged Buyouts and Other Corporate Transactions Involving Conflicts of Interest," 43 Bus. Law. 665, 672 (1988) (emphasis added).

[6] See ch. 8.

¶ 3.2 Director Conduct vs. Shareholder Rights

Directors owe the duties of care and loyalty to the corporations they serve. They must, in general, perform their duties "with such care as an ordinarily prudent person in a like position would use under similar circumstances."[7] They must also, in satisfying the duty of loyalty, avoid conflicts of interest. Although these duties are generally expressed as being owed to the corporation, it is the stockholders, as the owners of the corporation, to whom the duty is really owed and by whom violations of the duty will be asserted.

[1] Business Judgment Rule

The business judgment rule, the touchstone for judging director conduct, is a mechanism developed by the courts to avoid undue second-guessing of director decisions. It may, in certain circumstances not involving any apparent conflict of interest, preclude the court from making inquiry into the fairness aspects of a transaction. It amounts to a presumption that directors are acting properly and are, therefore, not to be second-guessed as long as they act (1) on an informed basis, (2) in good faith, (3) in a manner they reasonably believe to be in the best interests of the stockholders, and (4) without fraud or self-dealing. However, there must be objective evidence of the directors' attempts to be right. The courts make detailed inquiries into how a decision was arrived at, with a great deal of emphasis on the processes involved. Clearly, there is a heightened duty of care in a transaction, such as a leveraged buyout, where management has a significant self-interest.

An expert valuation opinion may be one of the factors taken into account in determining whether the directors possessed sufficient information concerning the transaction and whether they critically examined the information available to them.[8] In *Hanson Trust PLC v. SCM Corporation*,[9] for example, the court was openly critical of the failure to obtain a written fairness opinion from the investment banker and to inquire into what the "range of fair values" was for the assets in question. In *Smith v. Van Gorkom*,[10] the Delaware Supreme Court held that the directors breached their duty of care in approving a merger where they relied primarily on their president's twenty-minute oral analysis; received no written documentation, valuations, or opinions as to the fairness of the transaction; and failed to review any documents concerning the proposed transaction.

---

[7] Rev. Model Bus. Corp. Act § 830(a)(2) (1984).

[8] *See generally* Giuffra, "Investment Bankers' Fairness Opinions in Corporate Control Transactions," 96 Yale L.J. 119 (1986).

[9] 781 F.2d 264 (2d Cir. 1986).

[10] 488 A.2d 858 (Del. 1985).

By contrast, in *Treadway Companies v. Care Corporation*,[11] the court upheld a sale of stock to a friendly party to facilitate a merger where the board had received both a written report detailing the transaction and a written fairness opinion from the company's investment banker.

Blind reliance on outside experts is not enough:

> Nor is SCM's argument that it was entitled to rely on advice of [its legal and investment advisors] dispositive of [a] claim that the SCM directors failed adequately to inform themselves under the duty of care. In general, directors have some oversight obligations to become reasonably familiar with an opinion, report, or other source of advice before becoming entitled to rely on it.[12]

[2] Appraisal Rights

Stockholders who believe that the value of a company is higher than that proposed to be paid are allowed by state merger statutes to dissent from the merger and receive the appraised value of their shares. But because of the cumbersome and time-consuming procedural requirements of appraisal statutes, obtaining an appraised valuation of stock generally is viewed as an unsatisfactory way of seeking to assert a complaint about a transaction.[13] In most jurisdictions, the ability to seek appraisal rights is the *only* remedy that a dissenting stockholder has, with one very important exception.

The exclusivity of appraisal rights can be of great importance in the context of the distinction between fairness and fair market value because in an appraisal proceeding, the only issue is the fair market value of the shares in question, not whether the transaction itself was fair. A key Delaware decision dealing with this issue, *Weinberger v. UOP, Inc.*,[14] radically changed the approach to valuation in appraisal proceedings in Delaware by moving away from the historical "Delaware Block Method" mechanical valuation approach to the following:

> The basic concept of value under the appraisal statute is that the stockholder is entitled to be paid for that which has been taken from him, viz., his proportionate interest in a going concern. By value of the stockholder's proportionate interest in the corporate enterprise is meant the true or intrinsic value of his stock which has been taken by the merger. *In determining what figure represents this true or intrinsic value, the appraiser and the courts must*

---

[11] 638 F.2d 357 (2d Cir. 1980).
[12] Hanson Trust PLC v. SCM Corp., 781 F.2d 264, 275 (2d Cir. 1986).
[13] *See* Note, "*Weinberger* to *Rabkin*: Fine Tuning the Doctrine of Corporate Mergers," 11 Del. J. Corp. L. 839, 843 (1986).
[14] 457 A.2d 701 (Del. 1983).

take into consideration all factors and elements which reasonably might enter into the fixing of value. Thus, market value, asset values, dividends, earning prospects, the nature of the enterprise and any other facts which were known or which could be ascertained as of the date of merger and which throw any light on future prospects of the merged corporation are not only pertinent to an inquiry as to the value of the dissenting stockholders' interest, but must be considered by the agency fixing the value.

This is not only in accord with the realities of present day affairs but it is thoroughly consonant with the purpose and intent of our statutory law.[15]

Besides seeking appraisal rights, a dissenting stockholder engaged in a transaction involving conflicts of interest may allege that the transaction involves nondisclosure, fraud, breach of duty, and so on. In this case, the court is likely to hold that the defendant has the burden of proving that the transaction is fair. (An exception may exist where the transaction has been approved by a majority of the minority stockholders under conditions of full and fair disclosure of all material facts; in this situation, the burden of proof shifts back to the minority to prove that the transaction was unfair.) Accordingly, in most merger transactions involving potential conflicts of interest, court challenges inevitably involve issues beyond the issue of fair market value (i.e., appraisal rights are not the exclusive remedy).

The law in this area is very fluid. In recent years, Delaware courts, in particular, have issued legal decisions that have profoundly changed the law with respect to merger and acquisition activity and related valuation procedures.[16] The Delaware courts are still adjusting to the new valuation techniques described in the previous *Weinberger* quote, and it is not yet clear whether traditional formulations of "fair market value" will, in fact, be coextensive with the valuation standards imposed by the courts. Valuation experts may find themselves pressed to alter their traditional methodology and definitional structures by clients seeking to receive expert advice consistent with the law of the particular jurisdiction involved. For example, simple receipt of an opinion that a transaction is at a price equivalent to fair market value may be relatively useless if, under certain circumstances, the directors are charged with a duty (suggested by the Delaware decision in *Revlon v. MacAndrews and Forbes Holdings, Inc.*[17]) to hold an auction once they have decided to sell the business.

---

[15] *Id.* at 713 (emphasis added).

[16] *See, e.g.*, Note, *supra* note 13, at 839; 1 Balotti & Finkelstein, *Delaware Law of Corporations and Business Organizations* §§ 9.27-9.30 (1986); Graham, "Going Private: Rule 13e-3," in 3 *Securities Law Techniques* ch. 67 (A.A. Sommer, Jr. ed. 1988); Borden, *Going Private* (1986).

[17] 506 A.2d 173 (Dec. 1985). The definitive discussion of the ground rules for a

Revlon arose in the context of a competitive bidding takeover battle for that company. The Delaware Supreme Court held that, while the Revlon board had the right to engage in aggressive defense tactics, once it had decided to negotiate with and sell the company to other bidders, its "role changed from defenders of the corporate bastion to *auctioneers* charged with getting the best price for the stockholders at a sale of the company." It is not unreasonable to interpret this decision as requiring that a board of directors or its committee retain someone to act as financial adviser to give advice on the various strategic alternatives available to the board *prior to* getting to the issue of whether the transaction is fair from a financial point of view. Indeed, the ultimate process of auctioning a company off, assuming a professional and competent job was done, might constitute virtually conclusive evidence of fairness of price and procedure. At a minimum the *Revlon* decision, seems to require that fairness opinions address, either directly or in the procedures followed by the valuation expert, the question of whether the price is as high as it would be if the company were auctioned. In this context the valuation expert and the party to whom the opinion is being given could consider the time and risks associated with auctioning the company compared to losing the transaction at hand.

¶ 3.3 Courts' Concept of Fairness

What, then, does "fairness" mean if it is more than fair market value? What should a valuation expert understand about the distinction between the two? Most recent judicial decisions have focused on the concept of "entire fairness."

[1] Entire Fairness

The broader concept of fairness in transactions involving potential conflicts of interest was brought into focus in the *Singer v. Magnavox Company* decision[18] and in a series of subsequent decisions in Delaware.[19] In *Singer*, the Delaware Supreme Court held that a majority stockholder owed minority stockholders a duty of "entire fairness," encompassing notions of fairness both in the *procedures* followed in the transaction and in the *price* paid. Payment of fair market value, in some cases, is not enough:

> The concept of fairness has two basic aspects: fair dealing and fair price. The former embraces questions of when the transaction

---

corporate auction, as of the publication of this book, is set forth in Mills Acquisition Co. v. MacMillan, [Current Binder] Fed. Sec. L. Rep. (CCH) ¶ 94,401 (Del. 1989).

[18] 380 A.2d 969 (Dec. 1977).

[19] These are discussed in considerable detail in 1 Balotti & Finkelstein, *supra* note 16, §§ 9.28-9.30.

was timed, how it was initiated, structured, negotiated, disclosed to the directors, and how the approvals of the directors and the stockholders were obtained. The latter aspect of fairness relates to the economic and financial considerations of the proposed merger, including all relevant factors: assets, market value, earnings, future prospects, and any other elements that affect the intrinsic or inherent value of a company's stock. [Citations omitted.] However, the test for fairness is not a bifurcated one as between fair dealing and price. All aspects of the issue must be examined as a whole since the question is one of *entire fairness*. However, in a non-fraudulent transaction we recognize that price may be the preponderant consideration outweighing other features of the merger.[20]

Delaware, of course, is not the only jurisdiction that has wrestled with the judicial concept of fairness to minority shareholders. In California, in the seminal case of *Jones v. H.F. Ahmanson & Company*,[21] the court adopted a comprehensive rule of good faith and inherent fairness to the minority in any transaction where control of the corporation is involved. In addition, California provides, by statute, that if one of the parties to a reorganization is controlled by the other, in any action to attack the validity of the transaction, the controlling party shall have the burden of proving that the transaction is just and reasonable to the stockholders of the controlled party.[22]

The interplay between fairness and fair price and the difficulty of separating the two were also highlighted in *Joseph v. Shell Oil Company*.[23] The court ruled that the tender offer price in the transaction was probably below the true value of the shares.

> While I agree with the general rule that a stockholder, if there has been a complete disclosure to him of all germane facts with complete candor, should be left free to make his own decision as to whether to tender or keep his shares, there are exceptions. One such exception is when the maker of a tender offer, *who has a fiduciary duty to the offeree*, structures the offer in such a way as to result in an unfair price being offered and the disclosures are unlikely to call the unwary stockholders' attention to the unfairness.[24]

---

[20] Weinberger v. UOP, Inc., 457 A.2d at 701, 711 (emphasis added). *See also* Moore, "The 'Interested' Director or Officer Transaction," 4 Del. J. Corp. L. 674, 676 (1979); Nathan & Shapiro, "Legal Standard of Fairness of Merger Terms Under Delaware Law," 2 Del. J. Corp. L. 44, 46-47 (1977).

[21] 1 Cal. 3d 93, 460 P.2d 464, 81 Cal. Rptr. 592 (1969).

[22] Cal. Corp. Code § 1312(c) (1977).

[23] 482 A.2d 335 (Del. Ch. 1984).

[24] *Id.* at 341.

[2] Fair Value

Under the *Weinberger* line of cases, the courts have insisted on a concept of "fairness" that includes fair value. Under the best of circumstances, however, valuation and the determination of fair value is an art, not a science. For example, in *Weinberger*, expert testimony gave values ranging from $15 to $32 per share.

There are many different methods of valuation, and no single method can cover every business or every transaction.

> Placing a value on a company of any size or complexity is a major task. . . . Even hired experts cannot reduce this to a pure science. . . .
>
> Another problem in determining what a company is worth is expressed in the question: "Value as of when?" If a present-day assessment leaves out a significant likelihood of future growth and value enhancement for shareholders, it fails to reflect the true value of the company. The board has an obligation to see that shareholders are not short-changed in this way and, in fact, the board may have a responsibility to give greater emphasis to a long-term view than to the short-term one. . . .
>
> A final uncertainty about value is that in the end it may turn out to be neither the seller's nor the buyer's idea of what it should be but, rather, the result of a difficult negotiation process. Despite these and other uncertainties, directors can be held accountable for seeing that every effort is made to get the best price possible.[25]

Even if one were to apply exactly the same techniques and judgments to particular facts, fairness of price does not mean that there is *one* fair price.

> Fairness is a range of prices. The bottom of the range of fairness would be a price which the company could be virtually certain of obtaining in an acquisition if the company sought other offers. Moving up through the range of fairness, the certainty of attracting an offer at any given price diminishes as the prices get higher. The top of the range of fairness would be the highest price that the shareholders could possibly receive in an acquisition under present market conditions.[26]

Also, in some cases, what constitutes fair price depends on the

---

[25] "The Role of Outside Directors in Major Acquisitions for Sales," 1980 Conf. Bd. Res. Bull. 3, 8-9 (1985).

[26] Chazen, "Fairness From a Financial Point of View in the Acquaition of Public Companies: Is Third-Party Sale Value the Appropriate Standard?," 36 Bus. Law. 1439, 1455 (1981).

identity of the buyer. One commentator[27] suggests different measures of financial fairness in three types of transactions: (1) the sale of an entire company to an unaffiliated buyer, (2) the negotiated purchase of a company's publicly held shares by its controlling stockholder, and (3) the acquisition of the publicly held shares where the controlling stockholder unilaterally sets the terms of the transactions. He argues that the economic circumstances of the three kinds of acquisition are so diverse that different standards of financial fairness seem appropriate.

This same commentator makes the following arguments:

> [T]he term fairness has different meanings depending on whether it is applied to an acquisition by a controlling shareholder or a sale to an unaffiliated buyer. In an acquisition by a controlling shareholder a statement that the financial terms are fair has historically meant that the compensation received by the public shareholders was equivalent in value to the shares they are surrendering in the transaction. In a sale to a non-affiliate, on the other hand, fairness is synonymous with reasonableness in relation to other acquisition opportunities.[28]

Of course, in many public transactions—particularly leveraged buyouts—the issue of whether the transaction is being done at a fair price has been largely determined by the marketplace of competitive bidding. During the time between the initial announcement and the closing, the market has ample time and information to enable third parties to make offers counter to management's proposal.

Despite the literature of financial analysis and the abilities of evaluation experts, values are difficult to determine.[29] This has led the courts to consider the nonfinancial, procedural elements of the transaction in assessing fairness.

[3] Procedural Fairness

Partly because of the difficulty of determining the substantive fairness of the price in any transaction, Delaware decisions emphasize *procedural* fairness as a safeguard.[30]

The issue of what constitutes "fair procedures" in a particular transaction is driven by the facts of that transaction. In *Weinberger*, for example, the court held that the failure of the merger proxy statement to disclose the results of a feasibility study prepared by the major-

---

[27] *Id.* at 1439.
[28] *Id.* at 1448.
[29] *See infra* ¶ 3.4.
[30] An interesting discussion in this regard can be found in "Approval of Take-Out Mergers by Minority Shareholders: From Substantive to Procedural Fairness," 93 Yale L.J. 112 (1984).

ity stockholder violated the fiduciary standards of fair dealing applicable to the transaction. The majority stockholder had also imposed very tight time constraints under which the transaction was to be accomplished. Both of these factors were found by the court to be unfair procedural aspects of the transaction. The court noted:

> Since fairness in this context can be equated to conduct by a theoretical, wholly independent, board of directors acting upon the matter before them, it is unfortunate that this course apparently was neither considered nor pursued.[31]

Fairness in the procedures followed may be evidence, in some cases, of the fairness of the price. Such procedural fairness may lead to a presumption that the price is fair, but it is by no means conclusive evidence of fairness. In a decision subsequent to *Weinberger*, a Delaware court commented as follows:

> Of course, if arms-length negotiations took place it would be powerful evidence that the price arrived at was fair. . . . But the failure to arrive at the price by arms-length negotiations does not *ipso facto* indicate an unfair price. It is but one factor to be considered.[32]

Plaintiffs challenging a going-private transaction are in one position if they have to show that the price is *not* fair and in an entirely different position if they can require the defendants to show that it *is* fair. The burden of proof, at least in Delaware, depends upon the use of fair procedures. In general, in a transaction with conflicts of interest, the burden of proving fairness will rest initially on the party with the conflict. If that party can show that fair procedures were followed that in substance, neutralized the conflict, the burden of proving unfairness may shift to the plaintiff.

Some specific procedures relevant to the work of the person providing the fairness opinion are discussed in ¶ 3.4.

¶ 3.4 Role of Valuation Expert

One of the possible indicia of procedural fairness, which also provides support for the determination of price fairness, is the existence of an opinion from an independent expert, such as a valuation consultant or an investment banking firm. Delaware courts have suggested that, while it is not absolutely necessary for the board to have the assistance

---
[31] 457 A.2d at 701, 709 n.7.
[32] Joseph v. Shell Oil Co., 482 A.2d at 335, 343.

of an investment banker in passing on a merger, failure to do so is at the board's own peril.[33]

In general, there is no specific statutory requirement that the opinion of an appraiser, valuation expert, or investment banker be obtained in connection with mergers or similar transactions. An exception is found in Section 1203 of the California Corporations Code, which provides, in substance, that any proposal for a reorganization, sale of assets, or tender offer made to a California corporation or its stockholders by (1) a person or entity directly or indirectly controlling that corporation or (2) an officer, director, or affiliate of the corporation, be accompanied by a written opinion as to the fairness of the consideration to the stockholders of the corporation.

In a typical transaction of the type being discussed, valuation experts would expect to be called upon to give an opinion as to whether the transaction or the consideration to be paid in the transaction is "fair to the [corporation, public stockholders, and so on] from a financial point of view." There does not appear to be any thing in this California statute that would prohibit the use of the qualifier "from a financial point of view"; that would simply make it clear that the experts are not required to considering other procedural aspects of the transaction bearing on fairness. They cannot, however, *ignore* other aspects of the transaction; indeed, they should have a general awareness of the entire transaction. It is conceivable that in the judgment of the experts, some nonfinancial aspects of the transaction may be so unfair that it would be professionally irresponsible for them to render *any* opinion in the transaction, whether or not they conclude that the financial terms are satisfactory.

It is important for a valuation expert to know the context in which the appraisal report will be given. In many appraisals, there is no serious fairness issue. This includes opinions rendered in connection with IRS valuations and for basic planning purposes. In other transactions, there may be fairness issues that the experts should be aware of even if they do not directly affect the opinion being rendered. The nature of a transaction may, for example, affect the expert's perception of the potential of being involved in a lawsuit, which, in turn, would affect the fee charged and the need for indemnification.

The role of fairness opinions is succinctly stated as follows:

> Fairness opinions are most useful when they are the product of thorough research by independent investment bankers and not simply conclusory endorsements of decisions previously made in the corporate boardroom. Their purpose is to provide an objective standard against which directors, shareholders and other inter-

---

[33] *See* Smith v. Van Gorkom, 488 A.2d at 858.

ested parties may measure proposals and opportunities concerning their company. Such opinions also help insulate directors from the charge that they violated their fiduciary duties (particularly with respect to allegations of waste of corporate assets or self dealing) by facilitating their invocation of the business judgment rule.

... The liability of the investment bankers ... generally will turn on the reliability of the fairness opinion, specifically on the nature and depth of the investment banker's investigation of the subject company and on the extent to which weaknesses in the opinion are adequately disclosed to interested parties.[34]

Keep in mind that the valuation expert's area of expertise in the fairness context is limited to the market value of the securities and the prices at which the company could be sold in the merger and acquisition market. It is not a valuation expert's job to determine whether the business judgment rule applies in borderline situations. Valuation experts should apply standards they would normally use in evaluating the financial fairness of transactions without regard to controversies about motive or purpose:

So there are some elements of the valuation process that investment bankers are not competent to do because they represent legal judgments. It seems to me that the appropriate solution to this problem, particularly in the going private area, is for the investment banking firm to receive instructions, preferably from its client but possibly from its own counsel, as to what standards of valuation are to be used.[35]

The scope of the examination that it is reasonable to expect in rendering a fairness opinion is suggested by the following:

The element of fair price, which implies a determination of substantive or economic fairness, requires a detailed financial analysis and embraces considerations that extend beyond a rigid comparison of the proposal with a series of computer-generated financial models. The role of the committee's financial advisor is to assist the committee in determining whether the proposal provides for a fair price—a determination that requires examining the proposal as a whole, including, among other things, (i) the present and future prospects of the corporation, (ii) the existence of other alternatives and the management group's ability to consummate the proposal, (iii) the effect of the proposal on employees, customers, suppliers, creditors, and the communities in which the corpo-

---

[34] Bizily & Weyher, "Selecting a Banker for Fairness Opinions," N.Y.L.J., June 4, 1984, at 2, col. 2.

[35] Feurstein, "Valuation and Fairness Opinions," 32 Bus. Law. 1337, 1338 (1977).

ration operates, and ultimately, (v) the value of the proposal, from a financial point of view, to the public shareholders.

Appropriate factors for the committee and its financial advisor to consider when looking at the present and future prospects of the corporation include historical financial results, present financial condition, cash flow and income projections, the performance history of the corporation's stock, the corporation's ability to fund capital expenditures, the status of research and development and new products, the market and replacement value of assets, and the depth of management. In addition, the committee should ask its financial advisor to compare the corporation, financially and in terms of the performance of its stock, to similar corporations, and to review with management long-term business strategy for the corporation. In examining price, the committee should review alternatives to the proposal and assess the likelihood that the proposal will be consummated. In particular, the committee should focus on whether the management group's financing has been committed or obtained and whether any regulatory or other problems would delay consummating the proposal.[36]

[1] Weight Given to Fairness Opinion

The expert's opinion is not conclusive on the issue of fairness unless it is a negative opinion. It is highly unlikely that a transaction found by the expert to be unfair from a financial point of view would be able to go forward successfully.

If the expert's opinion is positive as to financial fairness, a variety of other factors bear on the question of how much weight, if any, a court will give to that opinion.

[a] Independence

The independence of the valuation expert is of great importance:

> A person who attempts to express a public opinion on the fairness of a transaction such as a merger plan to be acted upon by stockholders have two divergent interests, should be in a position of absolute impartiality.[37]

[b] Sufficient Time

Careful consideration should be given to the nature of the fee arrangements for the valuation opinion. If a material portion of the fee is dependent upon the success of the transaction or any factor other

---

[36] Simpson, *supra* note 5, at 658-687.
[37] Gerstle v. Gamble-Skogmo, Inc., 298 F. Supp. 66, 95 (E.D.N.Y. 1969).

than the mere delivery of the opinion, the independence of the person giving the opinion is likely to be called into question.

If the valuation expert was retained by a majority shareholder or by a person with a conflict of interest, obviously the value and weight given to such opinion by the court will be affected. How dependent will the expert be under these circumstances? If, however, the valuation expert was retained by an independent, fully informed party and was given enough time in which to perform the work, the resulting valuation should be substantial evidence of both procedural and substantive fairness. In *Weinberger*[38] and *Joseph*,[39] time was significantly limited, and the reports were thus essentially ignored by the courts. In *Weinberger*, the Supreme Court of Delaware rejected the validity of a fairness opinion in which "speed was the hallmark," the price was left blank, and the shareholders were given the false impression that the opinion was the product of a "careful study, and it, therefore, was reliable."[40] In *Joseph v. Shell Oil Company*, the opinion was given after "only eight days of scrutiny."[41]

Currently, the standard practice is to give valuation experts as much time as they indicate they need to reach their decisions mostly because of the adverse commentary in many recent Delaware decisions.

[c] Information Available

The amount of information made available to the valuation expert also has had significant bearing on the weight a court gives to the work product. For example, in *Norte & Company v. Huffines*,[42] the court rejected a valuation based on a capitalization of earnings that, on audit, turned out to be overstated. In *Joseph v. Shell Oil Company*, the offerer failed to give the investment banker and stockholders information with respect to oil reserves that the court determined to be highly material. Since the investment banker was, therefore, prevented from doing a proper job, the work product was essentially ignored.

> Here the tender offerer retained [the investment banker] to render an opinion as to the fairness of the price to be offered. Obviously a primary purpose of the fairness opinion of [the investment banker] was to convince the stockholders to whom the tender offer was to be made that the price offered was fair. To believe otherwise is unrealistic. *The maker of the tender offer, however, withheld from [the investment banker] essential facts necessary . . . to arrive at a*

---
[38] 457 A.2d at 701.
[39] 488 A.2d at 858.
[40] 457 A.2d at 712 n. 38.
[41] 482 A.2d at 335.
[42] 304 F. Supp. 1096 (S.D.N.Y. 1986).

fair opinion and accurate opinion as to the value. The essential information withheld was any non-public information about the value of the probable oil reserves. *It would defy reason to find that an oil exploration company such as Shell could be valued without any indepth inquiry into the estimated value of the probable oil reserves.* Indeed, it is possible—although not probable—that the provable reserves may be the single most valuable asset of Shell.

Reasonable men can differ as to opinions as to value. *Indeed, the Court is well aware that expert appraisers usually express different opinions as to value even when they use the same data for arriving at their opinion.* And it is not unusual that an expert appraiser will express a higher value if he has been hired by the plaintiff than if he has been hired by the defendant.

The problem here is not that the valued opinion of [the plaintiff's investment banker] is higher than the value opinion of [the investment banker]—that is expected by sophisticated investors—but rather *that [the investment banker] was not even given the opportunity to examine and evaluate the data relating to the value of the provable reserves. This conduct falls short of the fiduciary duty owed to the stockholders of Shell by the maker of the tender offer.* It shows a failure to make available to the appraiser hired by the offerer the essential information needed by the appraiser if his appraisal was to have any meaning. This would appear to be a breach of fiduciary duty aside from any issue of failure to make full disclosure.[43]

By contrast, in *Beebe v. Pacific Realty Trust*,[44] the court relied almost exclusively, without extensive inquiry, on two fairness opinions in rejecting claims of a class of minority stockholders that the price was inadequate.

Historically, courts have given significant weight to a determination of fairness by an investment banker representing minority interests. There have been occasional exceptions:

> [T]his is a classic case where a dominant minority stockholder was in fact in a controlling position and simply could not deal fairly with the unrepresented majority stockholders no matter how many prestigious outside advisors were brought in to assist in the negotiations.[45]

---

[43] Joseph v. Shell Oil Co., 482 A.2d at 335, 341 (emphasis added).
[44] 578 F. Supp. 1128 (D. Or. 1984).
[45] Kohn v. American Metal Climax, Inc., 322 F. Supp. 1331, 1353-1354 (E.D. Pa. 1971).

[d] Disclosure to Third Parties

An opinion rendered by a valuation expert in a public transaction generally has to be disclosed to outside parties. Disclosure may be required either by applicable law or by the desires of the parties. Accordingly, valuation experts must make certain, to the extent possible, that they have access to all the information needed to accomplish their work and that they are kept informed on a timely basis of developments in the transaction as they occur.

Valuation experts should take these factors into account in several ways. First, they may want to exert contractual control over the manner of dissemination of their work product, the use of it, and any summaries of it. More important, the disclosure aspect will lead experts to want to be certain that their opinion contains an adequate summary of any conflicts of interest they may have, any important assumptions they have made, or any qualifications to the opinion. Failure to do so may result in the expert having assisted in a breach of the duty of "entire candor" required in these transactions by the state court decisions discussed next.[46]

If the valuation expert relies solely on management for information, that factor should be disclosed in the opinion and in any disclosure document (e.g., a proxy statement).

[2] Liability of Valuation Experts

The duty of care owed by a valuation expert in rendering a fairness opinion is not entirely clear. "One argument against imposing liability on investment bankers for negligently prepared fairness opinions is that a workable standard of care cannot be developed."[47]

One commentator has suggested two theories under which the legal responsibility of an investment banker to minority stockholders might be maintained. These are (1) third-party liability for negligent misrepresentation and (2) direct fiduciary duty owed to minority stockholders.[48]

One of the earlier decisions in *Weinberger v. UOP, Inc.* held:

> [A]lthough [the investment banker] has been lumped together with Signal and UOP in plaintiff's allegations of breach of fiduciary duty, plaintiff has offered no authority to indicate that an investment banking firm rendering a fairness opinion as to the

---

[46] *See also* Gerstle v. Gamble-Skogmo, Inc., 478 F.2d 1281 (2d Cir. 1973), on the need to disclose appraisal information.
[47] Giuffra, *supra* note 8, at 137.
[48] *See* Haight, "The Standard of Care Required of an Investment Banker to Minority Shareholders in a Cash-Out Merger: *Weinberger v. UOP, Inc.*," 8 Del. J. Corp. L. 98 (1983).

terms of a merger owes the same fiduciary duty to the minority shareholders as does the majority shareholder who initiated the merger as a direct result of being retained by the management of the controlled subsidiary. Accordingly, judgment will be entered in favor of [the investment banker].[49]

A dissent addressed the issue of the investment banker's liability to minority stockholders, noting the profound impact that an opinion rendered by an investment banker has on stockholders:

> In my view, [the investment banker] had a duty to exercise reasonable care or competence in obtaining or communicating the information as to the value of the UOP shares (that is, in giving its opinion that the proposed merger was "fair and equitable to the stockholders of UOP other than Signal"). If the investment banker were to fail to meet this standard, such failure would make the investment banker liable to the minority stockholders for negligent misrepresentation.[50]

The question of the standard of care owed by the investment banker to the minority in a fairness opinion remains unanswered; the issue was dismissed on reargument in *Weinberger* and the lower court decision just quoted has been withdrawn. One commentator argues that, since the investment banker's opinion is likely to be the single most influential fact considered by minority shareholders in their deliberations over the merger, investment bankers should be held to the same fiduciary standard of care as the majority shareholder. It should be kept in mind, however, that the investment banker in *Weinberger* was hired by the majority and that the rule ought to be different in the case of an investment banker hired by an independent committee.

The terms of a valuation expert's formal engagement should be a significant factor in its liability. Certainly, as between the person who hired the valuation expert and the expert itself, the contractual undertaking should control. It is not uncommon in such contexts for the expert's duty of care to be limited to "gross negligence" or some other similar standard.

¶ 3.5 Disclosure Requirements

Disclosure requirements for the fairness of transaction differ on the federal and state level. These differences can be attributed to the manner in which federal and state law regard their respective fairness statutes. These federal and state disclosure requirements are discussed next.

---

[49] 426 A.2d 1333, 1348 (Del. Ch. 1981).
[50] *Id.* at 1348 n. 38.

[1] Federal

Federal courts generally do not look at the *fairness* of a transaction because the federal securities laws are disclosure statutes, not substantive fairness statutes. Once full and fair disclosure has been made, the inquiry at the federal level is generally at an end.[51]

Some of the disclosure requirements relating to fairness under Rule 13e-3 (the going-private rule of the Securities and Exchange Commission (SEC) are instructive. Among other things, the rule requires the parties involved in the transaction to affirm that they reasonably believe that the transaction is fair to public stockholders.[52] The rule was originally intended by the SEC to be a federal substantive rule governing fairness in going-private transactions. As initially proposed, it would have set forth requirements for the procedures and substantive steps necessary for a transaction not to be found to be unfair under federal securities laws. Due in large part to significant resistance within the legal community and doubts as to the SEC's authority to adopt a substantive regulation, the rule as finally adopted is a "disclosure rule." It sets forth various matters bearing on the issue of fairness that must be disclosed in a going-private disclosure document, but it leaves to the state courts the question of whether the transaction is substantively fair once these disclosure requirements have been satisfied. Nonetheless, the rule has served as a "road map" to guide attorneys to the procedural and substantive issues to be addressed in conflicts-of-interest transactions and is commonly followed by practitioners whether or not the transaction is technically subject to the rule.

A former SEC commissioner, who was a critic of leveraged buyouts in general, stated the following with respect to the purpose of the SEC's going-private rule:

> Rule 13e-3 requires management to express its "reasonable belief" as to whether the transaction is fair to public shareholders. While this requirement may prompt a somewhat better deal than might otherwise be offered, it by no means assures a fair deal. Indeed, given management's conflict of interest, one must question whether its "reasonable belief" as to the fairness of its own offer, or that of its group, provides any meaningful guidance for the seller.... When the commission backed away from the substantive rule of fairness, it sought to achieve the same goal through the detailed disclosure required by Rule 13e-3.[53]

---

[51] Green v. Santa Fe Indus., Inc. 430 U.S. 462 (1977).
[52] 17 C.F.R. § 240.13e-100, item 8(a) (1987).
[53] Speech by SEC Commissioner Bevis Longstreth to the International Bar Association, Toronto, Canada (Oct. 6, 1983), *reprinted in* Longstreth, "Management Buyouts: Are Public Shareholders Getting a Fair Deal?," [1983 Transfer Binder] Fed. Sec. L. Rep. (CCH) ¶ 83,436 (1983).

Transactions subject to Rule 13e-3 generally involve the issuance of a fairness opinion because they are inherently transactions involving conflicts of interest where the parties are seeking support for the pricing from an outside expert. In light of the importance of fairness opinions in such transactions, Rule 13e-3 itself mandates detailed disclosure about any opinion rendered. For example, Item 9 of Schedule 13e-3 requires that the disclosure document "state whether or not the issuer or affiliate has received any report, opinion . . . or appraisal from an outside party which is materially related to the Rule 13e-3 transaction, including, but not limited to, any such report, opinion or appraisal relating to the consideration or the fairness of the consideration to be offered to security holders."

The 1987 decision in *Howing v. Nationwide Corporation* interpreted Rule 13e-3 as requiring "a reasonable detailed analysis of the various financial valuation methods discussed by the Rule and the weights attached thereto. Even if certain valuation methods were not particularly relevant, this should itself have been noted and explained."[54]

The SEC staff interprets Rule 13e-3 quite broadly. A "no action" letter issued by the staff with respect to the disclosures required by Schedule 13e-3 provided as follows:

> The staff has been advised that in a number of going-private transactions, representatives of the investment banking firm have made an oral presentation to the Board of Directors regarding the factors considered by the firm in reaching its fairness determination and has presented only a short-form opinion providing its conclusions as to fairness. In such cases, the oral presentation should be summarized fairly and adequately and any documents, "talking papers," or background materials presented to the Board must be filed as exhibits to the Schedule 13e-3 and provided to shareholders or summarized.[55]

As a result of *Nationwide* and staff interpretations of Rule 13e-3, common practice with respect to disclosures of the methodology and materials prepared in connection with the delivery of fairness opinions in "going-private" transactions has resulted in a significant expansion of such disclosures. Accordingly, a person rendered such an opinion must be particularly sensitive to the ultimate need for expansive disclosure about the work product.

---

[54] 826 F.2d 1470, 1479 (6th Cir. 1987).
[55] Charles L. Ephraim, SEC No-Action Letter (Sept. 10, 1987).

[2] State

At the state court level, recent decisions reflect the fact that full and fair disclosure to minority stockholders is one of the essential components of the entire fairness issue. Disclosure for these purposes means something more than the bare minimum. *Lynch v. Vickers Energy Corporation*, one of the important Delaware cases dealing with disclosure, states that "completeness, not adequacy, is both the norm and the mandate under present circumstances."[56]

In *Smith v. Van Gorkom*, the court held the board of directors liable for approving a cash-out merger because it believed that the minority was not given all the material information concerning the transaction and that the disclosure was not characterized by the requirement of complete candor. The court concluded:

> The director defendants breached their fiduciary duty of candor by their failure to make true and correct disclosure of all information they had, or should have had, material to the transaction submitted for stockholder approval.[57]

Accordingly, one of the very important threads in the tapestry of "entire fairness" is the need for the parties involved in the transaction, including the valuation experts, to assure that the people to whom fairness is owed have received all information about the transaction that a reasonable stockholder would consider important in deciding whether to sell or retain stock.

---

[56] 383 A.2d 278, 281 (Del. 1977).
[57] 488 A.2d at 858, 893.

4

RATIO ANALYSIS FOR EVALUATING FINANCIAL PERFORMANCE

ROBERT SOCOL*

		Page
¶ 4.1	Ratio Analysis and Financial Statements..........	4-2
¶ 4.2	Financial Ratios...............................	4-6
	[1] Liquidity Ratios	4-6
	[a] Current Ratio	4-6
	[b] Quick (or Acid Test) Ratio	4-7
	[c] Cash Ratio..............................	4-10
	[2] Leverage Ratios	4-10
	[a] Total Debt/Total Assets Ratio	4-11
	[b] Total Interest-Bearing Debt/Equity Ratio.	4-12
	[c] Times Interest Earned Ratio	4-12
	[d] Fixed-Charges Coverage Ratio	4-13
	[3] Activity Ratios	4-13
	[a] Inventory Turnover Ratio................	4-13
	[b] Average Collection Period Ratio	4-14
	[c] Fixed-Assets Turnover Ratio	4-16
	[d] Working Capital Turnover Ratio	4-16
	[e] Total Assets Turnover Ratio	4-17
	[4] Profitability Ratios..........................	4-17
	[a] Gross Profit Margin/Sales Ratio..........	4-18
	[b] Profit Margin/Sales Ratio................	4-18
	[c] Return on Total Assets Ratio	4-18
	[d] Return on Net Worth Ratio..............	4-19
	[5] Evaluating the Ratios	4-19
¶ 4.3	Trend Analysis	4-20
¶ 4.4	du Pont System	4-23
¶ 4.5	Financial Leverage	4-23
¶ 4.6	Industry Rates of Return	4-25
¶ 4.7	Comparative Industry Ratios	4-26

* ROBERT SOCOL is a managing director of Houlihan, Lokey, Howard & Zukin, Inc., a valuation advisory and investment banking firm headquartered in Los Angeles, California. He has published several authoritative articles on valuation.

¶ 4.8	Security Analysis	4-27
¶ 4.9	Ratio Analysis Limitations	4-27
¶ 4.10	Summary	4-28

It is becoming increasingly more difficult to compete effectively in today's dynamic business environment. Marketplaces are no longer defined by geographic borders: Companies are now confronted with worldwide competition and the challenge of competing in international marketplaces. Sound financial and business planning are key factors in determining the success of any company. These plans must identify the company's strengths that can be exploited and determine what, if any, corrective measures can be employed to improve its weaknesses. A good plan must establish concrete goals and anticipate surprises.

The planning process plays an integral part in a financial manager's ability to effectively perform his or her job. This job can be divided into a number of functions, including the determination of the company's capital budget, dividend policy, and capital structure. Ultimately, the financial manager is concerned with the cumulative impact of these decisions on the profitability of the firm. Understanding past and present performance is an essential element in developing a viable plan. During this process, a number of critical areas relating to the company's operating performance must be addressed. These include but are not limited to the relative adequacy of the company's liquidity and financial leveraged positions, profitability, asset utilization, and growth prospects.

This chapter focuses on ratio analysis and its application to valuation methods. These discussions will provide useful tools to help the financial manager objectively assess a company's performance.

¶ 4.1 Ratio Analysis and Financial Statements

Financial *ratio analysis* is a convenient method to summarize large quantities of data and to compare companies' performances. Ratios do not always furnish answers but do provide information that allows the proper questions to be asked. Using financial data from the company's balance sheet and income statement, ratios can be easily calculated. Therefore, examination of a company's financial statements is a convenient starting point in performing ratio analysis. The following discussion refers to The Seneca Corporation, a fictitious company, and its financial data contained in Tables 4-1 and 4-2.

The Seneca Corporation was founded sixty years ago by Jim Miller in a small town in Texas. The company initially supplied warehouse space to cotton brokers. Miller's business savvy and relentless determination and energy enabled Seneca to supply a high-quality service at a very competitive price. The company earned an excellent reputation for its high quality of service, which caused sales to increase faster than anticipated; and, seven years after it was founded, Seneca was forced to expand its facility. Nine years later, in an effort to diversify its product line, Seneca acquired a small food processing company in Kankakee, Illinois. Internal growth and several acquisitions transformed the company in its present form as a multinational diversified food processor, with headquarters in Houston, Texas, and facilities located throughout the world.

Miller suffered a heart attack two years ago and is physically unable to devote the long hours necessary to effectively operate the company. Since none of his sons or daughters are interested in running the business, Miller retained an investment banking firm to conduct a thorough investigation of the company and to recommend alternative plans for future operations.

Table 4-1 contains The Seneca Corporation's comparative summary balance sheet for the five years ended December 31, $19X6$. The balance sheet reflects the company's financial position as of a particular point in time.

Seneca's balance sheet indicates that the company has experienced continuous growth in total assets, from $191.390 million as of December 31, $19X2$, to $335.476 million as of December 31, $19X6$. The company's current assets (consisting primarily of accounts receivable and inventories) and fixed assets have followed similar growth patterns. Seneca has expended significant resources in modernizing its facilities in the last two years, as evidenced by the increase in net fixed equipment from $40.059 million as of December 31, $19X4$, to $71.822 million as of December 31, $19X6$. Other assets have remained minimal over the five-year period.

Seneca's total liabilities have consistently increased from $81.662 million as of December 31, $19X2$, to $154.902 million as of December 31, $19X6$. Total current liabilities have generally increased over the period as well. The company's long-term debt and deferred taxes reached period highs of $64.708 million and $13.078 million, respectively, as of December 31, $19X6$. Retained earnings and net stockholders' equity have demonstrated strong growth over the period as a result of the company's profitability and were $182.642 and $180.574 million, respectively, as of December 31, $19X6$. The company's stockholders' equity has been negatively impacted by foreign currency fluctuations, as indicated by the translation adjustments. Seneca's net working capital remained strong over the period, rising from $117.395 million as of December 31, $19X2$, to $180.153 million as of December 31, $19X6$.

The company's income statements for the five-year period ended December 31, $19X6$, are shown in Table 4-2. As contrasted with the

TABLE 4-1
THE SENECA CORPORATION
COMPARATIVE SUMMARY BALANCE SHEET
($000s Omitted)

	As of December 31,				
	19X6	19X5	19X4	19X3	19X2
Assets					
Current assets					
Cash & marketable securities	$ 78,022	$ 80,680	$ 47,428	$ 45,941	$ 28,789
Accounts receivable	88,622	73,959	67,767	65,242	52,623
Inventories	86,686	79,560	92,172	68,406	70,303
Prepaid expenses	3,939	3,579	2,824	2,001	1,588
Total current assets	$257,269	$237,778	$210,191	$181,590	$153,303
Fixed assets					
Land	4,782	4,525	4,311	4,256	4,153
Buildings	45,257	38,106	34,630	33,609	33,384
Equipment	86,293	64,126	54,920	50,603	44,381
Less: Accumulated Depreciation	(64,510)	(58,629)	(53,802)	(52,073)	(48,934)
Net fixed assets	$ 71,822	$ 48,128	$ 40,059	$ 36,395	$ 32,984
Other assets	6,385	5,490	5,083	5,704	5,103
Total assets	$335,476	$291,396	$255,333	$223,689	$191,390
Liabilities and stockholders' equity					
Current liabilities					
Accounts payable	$ 27,754	$ 18,588	$ 18,647	$ 21,186	$ 11,152
Notes payable	6,175	10,621	6,213	1,245	5,372
Current maturities	4,939	4,931	4,986	4,270	3,680
Accrued expenses	35,688	30,122	35,210	22,143	14,169
Income taxes	2,560	2,768	3,610	2,497	1,535
Total current liabilities	$ 77,116	$ 67,030	$ 68,666	$ 51,341	$ 35,908
Long-term debt	64,708	56,185	36,386	41,706	39,779
Deferred taxes	13,078	10,167	8,021	7,842	5,975
Total liabilities	$154,902	$133,382	$113,073	$100,889	$ 81,662
Stockholders' equity					
Common stock	988	988	998	1,007	1,013
Paid-in capital	140	—0—	—0—	—0—	—0—
Retained earnings	182,642	160,574	144,205	123,538	110,112
Less: translation adjustments	(3,196)	(3,548)	(2,943)	(1,745)	(1,397)
Net stockholders' equity	$180,574	$158,014	$142.260	$122,800	$109,728
Total liabilities and stockholder's equity	$335,476	$291,396	$255,333	$223,689	$191,390
Net working capital	$180,153	$170,748	$141,525	$130,249	$117,395

balance sheet, the income statement reflects the results of operations over a period of time.

Seneca's comparative summary income statement reveals a strong growth in revenues from $317.249 million in 19X2 to $589.492 million

TABLE 4-2
THE SENECA CORPORATION
COMPARATIVE SUMMARY INCOME STATEMENT
($000s Omitted)
(Audited)

	Fiscal Year Ended December 31,				
	19X6	19X5	19X4	19X3	19X2
Revenues, net	$589,492	$495,751	$485,572	$392,525	$317,249
Cost of sales (goods sold)	399,163	331,641	328,011	271,321	217,737
Gross profit	$190,329	$164,110	$157,561	$121,204	$ 99,512
Operating expenses					
Distribution	$ 28,529	$ 25,945	$ 22,911	$ 18,709	$ 17,258
Selling	70,376	60,805	53,353	45,354	37,176
General and administrative	38,558	35,608	34,529	27,291	27,135
Total operating expenses	$137,463	$122,358	$110,793	$ 91,354	$ 81,569
Operating income	$ 52,866	$ 41,752	$ 46,768	$ 29,850	$ 17,943
Interest expense	4,838	2,625	1,949	2,377	4,694
Other income (expense)	(325)	22	(94)	263	—0—
Pretax income	$ 47,703	$ 38,149	$ 44,725	$ 27,736	$ 13,249
Income taxes (credit)	21,679	17,127	20,432	12,103	5,730
Net income (loss)	$ 26,024	$ 22,022	$ 24,293	$ 15,633	$ 7,519
Depreciation	$ 10,656	$ 8,112	$ 6,835	$ 5,829	$ 4,623

in 19X6. The magnitude of the increase in revenues is attributable to a strong economic environment since 19X3 combined with a comparatively weak economy in fiscal 19X2. Gross profit demonstrated consistent growth, attaining a period high of $190.329 million in fiscal 19X6. Operating income generally increased over the period and was $52.866 million in fiscal 19X6. With the exception of fiscal 19X5, pretax income and net income experienced continuous growth and were $47.703 million and $26.024 million, respectively, in fiscal 19X6. The decline in profitability in 19X5 is directly attributable to the high level of operating expenses relative to revenues. Capital expenditures and depreciation consistently increased, reflecting the company's commitment to growth and modernization.

In summary, Seneca has experienced increasing profitability over the period while maintaining a strong financial position.

¶ 4.2 Financial Ratios

Ratios typically are classified into four principal categories: liquidity, leverage, activity, and profitability ratios. Each category emphasizes different relationships within the company and allows for a comparative analysis of companies operating in the industry. A comparative financial analysis of Seneca's key ratios with those of six public companies is presented in Table 4-3 on pages 4-8 and 4-9. These public companies operate in similar although not necessarily identical lines of business. More importantly, they are subject to similar inherent economic risks as Seneca.

Comparative public companies are used in the analysis because of the relative ease in obtaining financial data as contrasted to private companies. This type of comparative analysis allows the financial manager to quickly identify Seneca's relative strengths and weaknesses compared to the public companies. A similar type of comparative analysis can be performed utilizing industry statistics. In the following comparative financial analysis, ratios are calculated using December 31, 19$X$6, financial data. The primary reason for using these data is that the industry is seasonal, and interim financial statements could potentially be misleading and distort the ratios. Additionally, all of the public companies have fiscal year-ends of December 31, which coincide with Seneca's, and thereby facilitate the comparative analysis. Seneca's calculations are in thousands of dollars.

[1] Liquidity Ratios

Liquidity ratios measure the ability of a company to meet its short-term financial obligations as they become due. This is the reason bankers and creditors analyze several measures of a company's liquidity before extending credit.

Liquidity ratios can be misleading. Short-term assets and liabilities are subject to rapid change, and, consequently, liquidity ratios can quickly become out of date. Also, companies generally select their fiscal year-end to coincide with a slow business season. This may result in companies reflecting more cash and less short-term debt on their balance sheet than on average or during busier seasons.

Nevertheless, liquidity ratios, by relating cash and other liquid assets to current liabilities, provide a quick indication of a company's liquidity. Three of the most commonly used liquidity ratios are presented here.

[a] Current Ratio

The *current ratio* is computed by dividing current assets by current liabilities. As reflected on Seneca's balance sheet, current assets typically include cash, marketable securities, accounts receivable, inventories, and prepaid expenses. Current liabilities normally consist of accounts payable, notes payable, short-term debt, current maturities portion of long-term debt, other accrued expenses, and accrued income taxes. The current ratio is the most commonly used indication of short-term solvency because it compares the obligations that are anticipated to become due during the next twelve months with the assets that are expected to be converted into cash during that same time period.

Seneca's current ratio is computed here:

$$\text{Current Ratio} = \frac{\text{Current Assets}}{\text{Current Liabilities}} = \frac{\$257,269,000}{\$ 77,116,000} = 3.3$$

$$\text{Public Companies' Median} = 2.3$$

Seneca's ratio of 3.3 is significantly higher than the comparative public companies' median of 2.3. This indicates that Seneca generally has more liquidity to meet its near-term obligations than the public companies. Nevertheless, a comparison using a median may lead to an incorrect conclusion. Differing philosophies in current asset and liability management will result in some well-managed companies being well above the median and others considerably below. However, a ratio that is significantly higher or lower than the median would suggest that the manager needs to perform further analysis to understand the reasons for the variance. The current ratio can be further misleading if a company borrows funds from a bank on a short-term basis and temporarily invests the proceeds in marketable securities. If nothing else on the balance sheet changes, the company's current ratio changes, while its net working capital remains unaffected.

[b] Quick (or Acid Test) Ratio

Inventories are generally the least liquid current asset and, in a forced liquidation, may sell at a price that is substantially below book value. The *quick ratio* (also called the *acid test ratio*) provides a measure of a company's ability to meet current obligations with its liquid assets and is computed by dividing current assets less inventory by current liabilities:

[Text continues on p. 4-10]

TABLE 4-3
THE SENECA CORPORATION
PUBLIC COMPANIES COMPARATIVE FINANCIAL ANALYSIS

	Public Companies							Seneca Fiscal Year-End
	Fiscal Year Ended							
Statistics and Ratios	12/31/X6	12/31/X6	12/31/X6	12/31/X6	12/31/X6	12/31/X6	Range	Median	
Size									
Revenues	$2,997,691	$94,429	$1,433,940	$4,008,699	$689,979	$1,316,175	$94,429–$4,008,699	$1,375,038	$589,492
Total assets	2,208,435	58,949	1,399,176	2,202,299	396,342	877,449	58,949– 2,208,435	1,138,313	335,476
Net worth	840,958	13,594	604,669	1,349,800	179,752	550,639	13,594– 1,349,800	577,654	180,574
Total interest-bearing debt	332,161	26,919	308,944	173,200	55,531	68,134	26,919– 332,161	120,667	75,822
Earnings before interest and taxes	227,994	8,623	184,258	356,700	20,264	232,546	8,623– 356,700	206,126	52,541
Liquidity ratios									
Current ratio	1.8	3.2	2.6	2.0	1.8	2.5	1.8– 3.2	2.3	3.3
Quick ratio	1.0	2.3	0.9	0.9	1.0	1.1	0.9– 2.3	1.0	2.2
Cash ratio	0.6	1.0	0.4	0.5	0.4	0.6	0.4– 1.0	0.6	1.0
Leverage ratios									
Total debt/total assets ratio	0.6	0.7	0.6	0.4	0.6	0.4	0.4– 0.8	0.6	0.5
Total interest-bearing debt/equity ratio	0.4	2.0	0.5	0.1	0.3	0.1	0.1– 2.0	0.4	0.4
Times interest earned ratio	10.4	3.1	4.6	26.5	4.8	21.1	3.1–26.5	7.6	13.1

TABLE 4-3
THE SENECA CORPORATION
PUBLIC COMPANIES COMPARATIVE FINANCIAL ANALYSIS (continued)

| | Public Companies | | | | | | | | Seneca |
| | Fiscal Year Ended | | | | | | | | Fiscal |
Statistics and Ratios	12/31/X6	12/31/X6	12/31/X6	12/31/X6	12/31/X6	12/31/X6	Range	Median	Year-End
Activity ratios									
Inventory turnover ratio	4.5	4.3	2.1	6.6	6.7	4.8	2.1– 6.7	4.7	4.8
Average collection period (in days) ratio	64.6	93.9	50.6	23.1	63.4	40.4	23.1–93.9	57.0	49.7
Fixed-assets turnover ratio	6.9	9.9	5.5	10.3	8.5	8.1	5.5–10.3	8.3	9.8
Working capital turnover ratio	5.1	2.8	3.5	7.3	6.4	5.2	2.8– 7.3	5.2	3.4
Total asset turnover ratio	1.3	1.7	1.1	2.0	1.9	1.5	1.1– 2.0	1.6	1.9
Profitability ratios									
Gross profit margin/sales ratio	29.2%	21.3%	39.5%	24.2%	22.9%	27.6%	21.3–39.5%	25.9%	32.3%
Profit margin/sales ratio	3.2%	3.0%	3.3%	5.0%	1.2%	6.9%	1.2– 6.9%	3.3%	4.4%
Return on total assets ratio	4.2%	5.1%	3.6%	10.0%	2.3%	10.4%	2.3–10.4%	4.7%	8.3%
Return on net worth ratio	10.4%	21.2%	9.1%	14.8%	4.6%	17.4%	4.6–21.2%	12.6%	15.4%

[*Text continues from p. 4-7*]

$$\text{Quick (or Acid Test) Ratio} = \frac{\text{Current Assets} - \text{Inventories}}{\text{Current Liabilities}} = \frac{\$257{,}269 - \$86{,}686}{\$77{,}116} = 2.2$$

$$\text{Public Companies' Median} = 1.0$$

The company's ratio of 2.2 is at the upper end of the public companies' range and well above the median. Seneca's liquid assets can satisfy its current obligations in excess of two times without liquidating inventories.

[c] Cash Ratio

A company's most liquid assets are cash and marketable securities. Consequently, the *cash ratio* reveals the extent to which a company can discharge current obligations with cash and is computed by dividing cash by current liabilities. Financial analysts tend to carefully analyze this ratio, which is computed here:

$$\text{Cash Ratio} = \frac{\text{Cash and Marketable Securities}}{\text{Current Liabilities}} = \frac{\$78{,}022}{\$77{,}116} = 1.0$$

$$\text{Public Companies' Median} = 0.6$$

A ratio exceeding 1.0 implies that the company is able to meet current obligations with its most liquid assets, provided that the marketable securities are reflected on the balance sheet at market value. Conversely, the public companies' median of 0.6 suggests that, collectively, only 60% of their current liabilities could be satisfied with cash and marketable securities. However, this ratio does not reflect the fact that a company may have the ability to borrow funds from a bank to satisfy current obligations. In fact, none of the standard liquidity measures consider a company's "reserve borrowing power," which may play a significant role in the manner in which a company manages its current assets and current liabilities.

[2] Leverage Ratios

Leverage ratios provide information pertaining to (1) the extent to which nonequity is used in a company's capital structure and (2) the company's long-term ability to meet payments to creditors. These ratios are complementary, and most managers examine both sets of ratios as the ratios have a number of significant implications. Creditors examine the amount of owner-supplied capital (or equity) to determine the magnitude of risk associated with making a loan. As the proportion of equity to total financing increases, the amount of risk that is borne by the creditors decreases. If a company is able to raise financing through debt rather than equity, the existing owners will avoid having their ownership interests diluted. Moreover, if borrowed funds earn a rate of return (ROR) that exceeds the cost of borrowing, the owners will realize a higher rate of return on their equity.

Leverage, however, is a double-edged sword. That is, if borrowed funds earn less than the costs of borrowing, the owners' ROR will decrease. Leverage tends to increase a company's risk, and accordingly, a company with a high leverage ratio may exhibit a large volatility in reported earnings. In a recession, a greater risk of loss exists although higher returns are expected when the economy is healthy. Conversely, a company with a low leverage ratio has less risk of loss and lower expected returns. Therefore, decisions concerning the appropriate level of leverage for a company must balance the aspects of increased risks with higher expected returns.

[a] Total Debt/Total Assets Ratio

Accounting treatment of certain balance sheet items can distort leverage ratios. The items to include in the numerator and denominator depend on how liabilities and shareholders' equity are defined. Unfortunately, no general agreement exists in accounting literature or published financial reports on the precise distinction between liabilities and shareholders' equity. The primary issues pertain to the treatment of deferred taxes and preferred stock. When using the total debt/total assets ratio for comparative analysis, consistent treatment of liabilities and equity is required for all companies being analyzed.

The *total debt/total assets ratio* indicates the relative amount of funds provided by all creditors and is calculated by dividing total debt (defined as total liabilities) by total assets. Owners may desire high leverage to either increase returns or prevent dilution. In contrast, creditors prefer to minimize their risk and, therefore, seek moderate ratios.

The total debt/total assets ratio is computed here:

$$\text{Total Debt/Total Assets Ratio} = \frac{\text{Total Debt}}{\text{Total Assets}} = \frac{\$154{,}902}{\$335{,}476} = 0.5$$

$$\text{Public Companies' Median} = 0.6$$

Seneca's ratio of 0.5 is below the comparative public companies' median, which suggests that the company would not find it difficult to borrow additional funds. In fact, the company may not be taking full advantage of its long-term borrowing capacity. This lack of financial leverage could result in foregoing profitable opportunities due of lack of capital and potentially dilute its shareholders' equity ownership interests and reduce the returns on their equity.

[b] Total Interest-Bearing Debt/Equity Ratio

The *total interest-bearing debt/equity ratio* measures the relative amount of funds provided by creditors (lenders) and owners and is computed by dividing the total interest-bearing debt by shareholders' equity:

$$\text{Total Interest-Bearing Debt/Equity Ratio} = \frac{\text{Total Interest-Bearing Debt}}{\text{Shareholders' Equity}} = \frac{\$75{,}822}{\$180{,}574} = 0.4$$

$$\text{Public Companies' Median} = 0.4$$

The company's ratio of 0.4 is identical to the public companies' median of 0.4. This ratio indicates that Seneca uses a similar combination of interest-bearing debt and equity to finance its assets as the public companies.

An alternative method to measure financial leverage is to include the value of leases in the numerator. In industries that rely heavily on lease financing (e.g., the airline industry), it is more appropriate to include the value of lease obligations to debt.

Several valuation issues arise in computing debt/equity ratio. The previous ratios use book (or accounting) values rather than market values. As mentioned previously, the treatment of leases can lead to significantly different conclusions. The leverage ratios just discussed suffer the same limitations as the short-term liquidity ratios because they are derived from the balance sheet and do not focus on the cash flow necessary to service long-term obligations. This shortcoming, in part, has motivated analysts to examine interest coverage ratios.

[c] Times Interest Earned Ratio

The *times interest earned ratio* measures the extent to which interest is covered by earnings before depreciation, interest, and taxes (EBDIT). The numerator uses pretax income since income taxes are computed after interest expense is deducted and do not affect the company's ability to pay current interest charges. The *times interest earned ratio* is computed by dividing EBDIT by interest charges. (This ratio can be modified to exclude depreciation in the numerator. Managers may prefer using EBDIT because depreciation, which is a deductible expense in determining pretax income, is a noncash flow expense and is available to pay interest charges.) A ratio of less than 1.0 indicates that the company is unable to meet its interest obligations, which could lead to legal action by the creditors and ultimately result in bankruptcy.

The times interest earned ratio is computed here:

$$\text{Times Interest Earned Ratio} = \frac{\text{EBDIT}}{\text{Interest Charges}} = \frac{\$63,197}{\$4,838} = 13.1 \text{ Times}$$

$$\text{Public Companies' Median} = 7.6 \text{ Times}$$

Seneca covers its interest charges 13.1 times. The public companies have a median of 7.6. The wide variance from the median implies that the company has an excessive safety margin in its ability to meet its interest charges. This ratio further supports the contention that Seneca is under utilizing debt in its capital structure. Due to the comparatively high coverage ratio, Seneca represents an excellent credit risk and would not have difficulty in borrowing additional funds.

[d] Fixed-Charges Coverage Ratio

Fixed charges are defined as interest plus annual long-term lease obligations. The *fixed-charges coverage ratio* is similar to the times interest earned ratio but is more inclusive because it recognizes that many companies lease rather than purchase assets. As a result, these companies incur long-term lease obligations.

The fixed-charges coverage ratio is preferable to the times interest earned ratio for financial analyses in industries that rely on lease financing. Leases are not a significant financing technique in Seneca's industry and, consequently, the fixed-charges coverage ratio is not included in the analysis here.

[3] Activity Ratios

Activity ratios measure how effectively a company employs its assets. All of the ratios involve comparisons between the level of sales and the investment in certain asset accounts. Activity ratios convey the relationships between sales and various asset accounts, such as inventories, accounts receivable, and fixed and total assets.

[a] Inventory Turnover Ratio

The *inventory turnover ratio* measures the degree of efficiency with which the company utilizes its inventory and is computed by dividing cost of sales (or cost of goods sold) by average inventory. A low ratio implies that the company holds an excessive stock of inventory that is unproductive and represents an investment with a relatively low or negative rate of return. Conversely, a high inventory turnover is regarded as a sign of efficiency and indicates that the company is not holding an excessive amount of obsolete inventory. A high turnover ratio may also imply that the company's inventory is worth at least its book value, which tends to reinforce the applicability of the current ratio. Note also that a high inventory turnover ratio may simply indicate that the company is living hand to mouth.

The inventory turnover ratio is computed here using cost of goods sold rather than cost of sales in the numerator (see explanation in the following paragraphs):

$$\text{Inventory Turnover} = \frac{\text{Cost of Goods Sold}}{\text{Average Inventory}} = \frac{\$399,163}{\$ 83,123} = 4.8 \text{ Times}$$

$$\text{Public Companies' Median} = 4.7 \text{ Times}$$

Seneca's turnover ratio of 4.8 times is similar to the median of 4.7 times for the public companies. This indicates that the company has little excessive or unproductive inventory.

A number of problems arise in computing and analyzing this ratio. One problem is that Dun & Bradstreet and other established providers of financial ratio statistics use sales to inventories to develop the ratio. Since sales are at market prices and inventories are generally carried on the financial statements at cost, it is more appropriate to use cost of goods sold in the numerator. When performing a comparative analysis with statistics compiled by Dun & Bradstreet, however, it is necessary to use sales in the numerator.

The second problem involves the fact that the inventory number reflected on the balance sheet represents the level of inventory at a particular point in time whereas sales occur over the entire year. Therefore, it is preferable to use an average inventory figure in the denominator. This is typically computed by adding the beginning inventory to the ending inventory and dividing by two. An adjustment to this computation is required if it is determined that the company's sales are highly seasonal or if sales experienced a significant upward or downward trend during the year.

[b] Average Collection Period Ratio

The *average collection period* (ACP) measures the length of time that customers take to pay their bills. Alternatively, this represents the average length of time from the making of a sale to the time that the company receives cash. The *average collection period ratio* measures the company's accounts receivable turnover and is computed by dividing annual sales by 360 to determine average daily sales. Average accounts receivable are then divided by the average daily sales to find the ACP for the company or, alternatively, the average number of days that sales are tied up in receivables:

$$\text{Average Collection Period Ratio} = \frac{\text{Average Receivables}}{\text{Sales Per Day}} = \frac{\$81{,}290}{\$1{,}637} = 49.7 \text{ Days}$$

$$\text{Public Companies' Median} = 57.0$$

Seneca's 49.7-day ACP is lower than the industry median and suggests that the company collects its receivables faster than the comparative companies and corrective actions are not needed in its collection department. A low ratio is generally an indication of an efficient collection department although it may be the result of an excessively restrictive credit policy. The ratio also can be analyzed by a comparison of the terms by which the firm sells its goods. For example, Seneca's credit policy allows customers sixty days to pay their bills. The fifty-day collection period indicates that, on average, customers are paying their bills on time.

A rising trend in the ACP over the past several years would be a strong indication that corrective action is required to expedite the collection process. Two issues surface when calculating this ratio. The formula uses total sales since information regarding credit sales is generally unavailable. Because companies have differing percentages of credit sales, the ACP will be understated. It should also be noted that the financial community generally uses 360 rather than 365 days in calculations requiring the number of days in the year.

A nonratio financial schedule that is useful in the analysis of accounts receivable is the *accounts receivable aging schedule,* which identifies the receivables based on the length of time they have been outstanding. Seneca's schedule is provided here:

Age of Accounts (Days)	Percent of Total Value of Accounts Receivable (%)
0–30	40
31–45	30
46–60	16
61+	14
	100

The accounts receivable aging schedule indicates that the company has serious collection problems, with 14% of the accounts receivable overdue. This demonstrates how the average collection period can be misleading. The accounts that are paid promptly reduce the average days and tend to disguise problems.

[c] Fixed-Assets Turnover Ratio

The *fixed-assets turnover ratio* measures the relative efficiency with which the company is utilizing its fixed assets and is computed by dividing sales by average fixed assets:

$$\text{Fixed-Asset Turnover Ratio} = \frac{\text{Sales}}{\text{Average Fixed Assets}} = \frac{\$589,492}{\$59,975} = 9.8 \text{ Times}$$

$$\text{Public Companies' Median} = 8.3 \text{ Times}$$

Seneca's ratio of 9.8 times is above the median of 8.3. A high ratio indicates that the company is utilizing its fixed assets, as a percentage of its capacity, more effectively than other companies in the industry. However, a high ratio may indicate that the company is becoming capacity constrained, and additional capital is required to be invested in fixed assets to facilitate future growth in business. The age of the company's fixed assets and the depreciation method applied to these assets may distort the ratio. A high ratio could be the result of using more aggressive depreciation methods than normal for the industry or old equipment that will need to be replaced shortly.

[d] Working Capital Turnover Ratio

Managers frequently focus on how efficiently working capital is being utilized. This is attributable to the fact that net working capital can be adjusted rapidly to reflect temporary fluctuations in sales. Also, net working capital can generally be measured more accurately than some other assets. The *working capital turnover* ratio is computed by dividing sales by average net working capital:

$$\text{Working Capital Turnover Ratio} = \frac{\text{Sales}}{\text{Average Net Working Capital}} = \frac{\$589,492}{\$175,451} = 3.4 \text{ Times}$$

$$\text{Public Companies' Median} = 5.2 \text{ Times}$$

Seneca's working capital turnover of 3.4 times is below the public companies' median of 5.2 times. The ratio indicates that Seneca has more working capital per dollar of sales, and as a consequence, Seneca appears to have an excessive investment in current assets. A low ratio also suggests that the company may exhibit a better credit risk to suppliers and lenders because it has a high degree of liquidity.

[e] Total Assets Turnover Ratio

The *total assets turnover ratio* measures the turnover of all of the assets of the company and is computed by dividing sales by average total assets:

$$\text{Total Asset Turnover Ratio} = \frac{\text{Sales}}{\text{Average Total Assets}} = \frac{\$589{,}492}{\$313{,}436} = 1.9 \text{ Times}$$

$$\text{Public Companies' Median} = 1.6 \text{ Times}$$

The public companies' median asset turnover ratio of 1.6 times is below Seneca's 1.9 times. A low ratio suggests that the assets of a company are being underutilized and are not generating a sufficient volume of sales to justify their investment. The assets should be disposed of and/or sales must be increased.

Note that the total assets turnover ratio must be examined in conjunction with the profit margin/sales ratio. A company may be confronted with the trade-off of increasing its asset turnover ratio at the expense of decreasing its profit margin/sales ratio.

[4] Profitability Ratios

Financial managers employ another set of ratios to judge how efficiently and profitably companies are using their assets. As will be seen, a great degree of ambiguity is associated with these ratios. For example, how should a lender interpret the fact that a firm has a high profit margin? Perhaps this company operates in a low-volume, high-markup industry. Jewelers operate on considerably higher profit margins than food wholesalers but do not necessarily represent less of a business risk or a more attractive investment risk. What if the company charges higher prices relative to its competition, which may potentially cause it to be noncompetitive? Or perhaps it has lower cost than industry norms, which is a positive sign.

The ratios examined thus far reveal some interesting observations regarding the manner in which companies operate. Profitability is the ultimate result of numerous operating policies and decisions. As such, a *profitability ratio* provides evidence on how effectively the company is managed. Because of the ambiguity associated with profitability ratios, these ratios are best used to identify the important questions rather than to answer them.

[a] Gross Profit Margin/Sales Ratio

The *gross profit margin/sales ratio* measures the gross profit, per dollar of sales, and is computed by dividing gross profit by sales:

$$\text{Gross Profit Margin/Sales Ratio} = \frac{\text{Gross Profit}}{\text{Sales}} = \frac{\$190,329}{\$589,492} = 32.3\%$$

$$\text{Public Companies' Median} = 25.9\%$$

Seneca's higher gross profit margin suggests that its sales price is comparatively higher than industry averages or its cost of sales structure is relatively lower, or both.

[b] Profit Margin/Sales Ratio

The *profit margin/sales ratio* conveys the net income per dollar of sales and is computed by dividing net income by sales:

$$\text{Profit Margin/Sales Ratio} = \frac{\text{Net Income}}{\text{Sales}} = \frac{\$26,024}{\$589,492} = 4.4\%$$

$$\text{Public Companies' Median} = 3.3\%$$

The company's profit margin of 4.4 percent is above the public companies' median of 3.3 percent. This ratio, when analyzed in conjunction with the gross profit margin/sales ratio, reveals that Seneca's cost structure is comparatively higher than the public companies.

[c] Return on Total Assets Ratio

The *return on total assets ratio* measures how efficiently total assets are being utilized by a company—its return on investment (ROI). It is computed by dividing net income by average total assets:

$$\text{Return on Total Assets Ratio} = \frac{\text{Net Income}}{\text{Average Total Assets}} = \frac{\$26,024}{\$313,436} = 8.3\%$$

$$\text{Public Companies' Median} = 5.3\%$$

Seneca has achieved a comparatively high ROI as a result of higher profit margins and more efficient use of its assets.

[d] Return on Net Worth Ratio

The *return on net worth ratio* measures the rate of return on the stockholders' investment and is computed with a numerator of net income available to common shareholders (i.e., net income less preferred dividend payments) and with a denominator of simply the average common shareholders' equity:

$$\text{Return on Net Worth Ratio} = \frac{\text{Net Income Available to Common Shareholders}}{\text{Average Common Shareholders' equity}} = \frac{\$26{,}024}{\$169{,}294} = 15.4\%$$

Public Companies' Median = 13.9%

The company's return on net worth is slightly above the 13.9% median of the public companies. The result is attributable to the combination of Seneca's slightly higher asset turnover and profit margin and similar financial leverage position. A company may experience a high return on assets and a comparatively low return on net worth. (Later in this chapter, the du Pont method of analysis will be applied to the case study and will explain why this phenomenon occurs.)

[5] Evaluating the Ratios

The ratios contained in Table 4-3 provide the company's investment banker, Tim Harrison, with a reasonably good indication of Seneca's relative strengths and weaknesses.

In comparison with the public companies' ratios, Seneca exhibits a stronger liquidity position. The company's quick, current, and cash ratios are substantially above the public companies' medians. Seneca tends to utilize financial leverage to a lesser extent than the public companies. The company has a comparatively low total debt/total asset ratio and a similar total interest-bearing debt/equity ratio. The company's high times interest earned ratio tends to suggest that it is not maximizing its financial leverage capability.

In terms of activity, Seneca generally turns its inventory at a slightly faster rate than the public companies and turns its fixed assets, assets, and accounts receivable at faster rates. However, the company turns its net working capital at a slower rate and generally is more profitable in comparison to the public companies. Its profit margin/sales, return on total assets, and return on net worth ratios are above the public companies' medians.

The foregoing analysis revealed to Harrison several significant weaknesses of the company for which corrective actions must be taken. The activity ratios indicate that the company is not effectively utilizing its working capital. In other words, the company has an excessive investment in current assets and should consider reducing the level of its working capital. Seneca's profitability ratios are above the industry averages, but its profit margin can be improved. The company's gross margins are substantially higher than the industry average, which implies that high operating expenses are depressing profit margins. Further analysis is required to determine the reason for the company's high operating expenses.

Harrison is also concerned about the company's low use of financial leverage. The company has not participated in several profitable opportunities because of its unwillingness to utilize financial leverage. Furthermore, Miller's ownership interest has been diluted from 88% to 51% due to the issuance of new stock to raise capital.

Moreover, the company's capital structure could be modified to increase the return on net worth. Having identified most of the company's apparent problems, Harrison conveyed to Miller the following recommendation: Sell the company in its current configuration at higher multiple of earnings and cash flow than is typically realized in the industry. He provided the following reasoning: the company offers a potential buyer several attractive opportunities, including the following:

- It has the ability to finance part of a transaction through the disposition of Seneca's excessive assets.
- The company's liquidity position allows a purchaser to finance a portion of the purchase price by converting the liquid assets into cash.
- The profitability and asset turnover ratios of the company will be enhanced as a result of the disposition of excess current assets.
- The company's low level of financial leverage allows a substantial portion of the purchase price to be financed through the company's excessive borrowing power.

Alternatively, Harrison suggested that Miller implement these action plans to increase the company's profitability and return on net worth. However, Miller would require a considerable amount of time and dedication to effectuate these changes.

¶ 4.3 Trend Analysis

The preceding ratio analysis is of limited value because it ignores the dimension of time. Although ratio analysis does provide the financial manager with good indications of Seneca's operations at one point in time, the analysis does not address the changing trends that are taking place in the company.

A *trend analysis* allows a manager to determine whether the company has exhibited a change in its relative financial position over a period of time. Trend analysis also allows the individual to compare the company's trends in ratios with those of industry comparative companies or industry norms. If the analysis demonstrates that industry sales have consistently increased over the entire period and industry ratios have remained relatively stable over the period, then any changes in a company's ratios are attributable to internal operations rather than exogenous factor that affect all firms operating within the industry. Tables 4-4 and 4-5 display certain key ratios for the six public companies and ratio over a five-year period.

TABLE 4-4
PUBLIC COMPANIES COMPARATIVE TREND ANALYSIS

Median Statistics	19X6	19X5	19X4	19X3	19X2
Liquidity ratios					
Current ratio	2.3	2.2	2.4	2.9	2.8
Quick ratio	1.0	0.9	1.1	1.4	1.3
Cash ratio	0.6	0.7	0.6	0.8	0.8
Leverage ratios					
Total debt/Total assets ratio	0.6	0.5	0.6	0.7	0.7
Total interest-bearing debt/equity ratio	0.4	0.4	0.5	0.6	0.6
Times interest earned ratio	7.6	9.2	11.1	10.3	6.5
Activity ratios					
Inventory turnover ratio	4.7	5.2	4.0	4.4	4.2
Average collection period (in days) ratio	57.0	59.4	52.0	58.4	56.7
Fixed-assets turnover ratio	8.3	10.2	11.4	9.8	8.7
Working capital turnover ratio	5.2	4.8	5.7	5.4	6.0
Total assets turnover ratio	1.6	1.9	1.9	1.8	1.7
Profitability ratios					
Gross profit margin/sales ratio	25.9%	26.3%	25.4%	23.9%	24.6%
Profit margin/sales ratio	3.3%	4.5%	4.1%	3.9%	3.8%
Return on total assets ratio	5.3%	8.6%	7.8%	7.0%	6.5%
Return on net worth ratio	13.9%	17.2%	19.5%	23.3%	21.7%

The trends indicate that both Seneca's and the median public companies' liquidity ratios have fluctuated within a narrow range during the five-year period. Seneca demonstrated more liquidity than the public companies over the period. Their respective financial leverage ratios, with the exception of times interest earned ratio, followed similar patterns. The median public companies total debt/total assets ratio

TABLE 4-5
THE SENECA CORPORATION
COMPARATIVE TREND ANALYSIS

	Fiscal Year Ended				
Statistics and Ratios	19X6	19X5	19X4	19X3	19X2
Liquidity ratios					
Current ratio	3.3	3.5	3.1	3.5	4.3
Quick ratio	2.2	2.4	1.7	2.2	2.3
Cash ratio	1.0	1.2	0.7	0.9	0.8
Leverage Ratios					
Total debt/total assets ratio	0.5	0.5	0.4	0.5	0.4
Total interest-bearing debt/equity ratio	0.4	0.5	0.3	0.4	0.4
Times interest earned ratio	13.1	19.0	27.5	15.1	4.8
Activity ratios					
Inventory turnover ratio	4.8	3.9	4.1	3.9	4.2
Average collection period (in days) ratio	49.7	51.5	49.3	54.0	N/A
Fixed-assets turnover ratio	9.8	11.2	12.7	11.3	9.4
Working capital turnover ratio	3.4	3.2	3.6	3.2	2.7
Total assets turnover ratio	1.9	1.8	2.0	1.9	1.7
Profitability ratios					
Gross profit margin/sales ratio	32.3%	33.1%	32.0%	30.9%	31.4%
Profit margin/sales ratio	4.4%	4.4%	5.0%	4.0%	2.4%
Return on total assets ratio	8.3%	7.9%	10.0%	7.6%	4.1%
Return on net worth ratio	15.4%	13.9%	17.1%	12.7%	6.9%

has generally been higher than Seneca's whereas their total interest-bearing debt/equity ratios were similar to Seneca's.

Seneca's times interest earned ratio displayed wide fluctuations during the period with recently declining ratios. The public companies' median exhibited milder fluctuations with recently deteriorating ratios. Seneca's ratio was typically higher than the median ratios for the public companies.

In terms of activity, Seneca turned fixed assets and receivables quicker and working capital slower. Inventory turnover and fixed-assets turnover ratios were similar. Seneca realized significantly better gross profit margins. As a result of its higher operating expenses, Seneca realized only slightly higher profit margins. Although Seneca achieved higher returns on total assets, higher debt ratios allowed the public companies to realize higher returns on net worth.

In summary, the public companies' ratios, with a few exceptions, fluctuated mildly over the five years studied. Seneca's current weaknesses—primarily excessive working capital, high operating costs, and insufficient utilization of financial leverage—have been evidenced over the entire five-year period. These weaknesses are a function of poor financial management, which suggests that a management change may be warranted.

¶ 4.4 du Pont System

The *du Pont System* demonstrates how the interaction between activity ratios and profit margin on sales impacts the return on assets or, as commonly referred to, the return on investment (ROI). A modified version of the system is illustrated in Figure 4-1.

FIGURE 4-1 Application of the Du Pont System to the Seneca Corporation

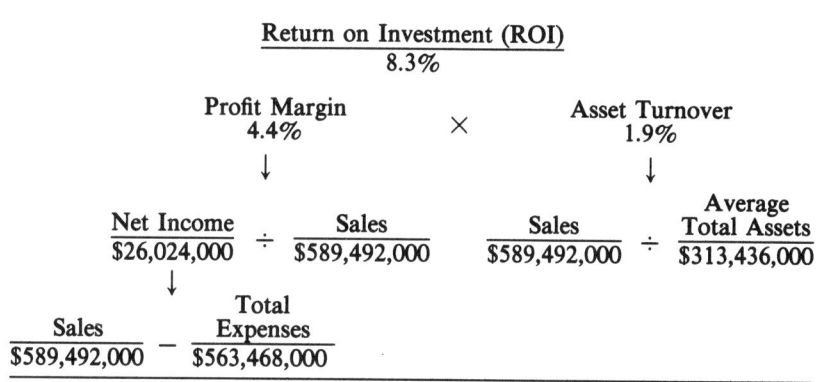

The left side of Figure 4-1 develops the profit margin on sales. Total expenses are subtracted from total sales to arrive at the net income figure. This figure is divided into sales to arrive at the net profit margin on sales figure.

The right side of Figure 4-1 is used to derive the asset turnover number. The company's average total assets are divided into sales to arrive at the company's asset turnover ratio. The resulting ratio is then multiplied by the net profit margin on sales to determine the company's ROI. This is illustrated by the following formula:

$$\frac{\text{Profit}}{\text{Sales}} \times \frac{\text{Sales}}{\text{Average Total Assets}} = \text{ROI}$$

As indicated in Figure 4-1, Seneca's ROI is as follows:

$$4.4\% \times 1.9 = 8.3\%$$

¶ 4.5 Financial Leverage

Financial leverage can be used to increase the return on net worth. How can a company with a return on assets considerably below the industry average realize a return on net worth that is equal to or exceeds the industry average? The company merely uses a larger percentage of debt to finance its investment in assets than the average firm in the industry. Conversely, a company that achieves an average industry ROI but utilizes a comparatively small percentage of debt in its capital structure will realize a return on net worth that is lower than the industry average.

Seneca finances approximately 54% of its assets with equity; the other 46% is financed using debt. The industry mean is approximately 38% equity and 62% debt. Since Seneca's 8.3% ROI was computed after interest charges on debt, the entire 8.3% ROI accrues to the equity holders. Therefore, the financial leverage of a company will have a profound impact on its return on net worth. The formula that quantifies the precise impact of financial leverage on the ROR on net worth is set forth in the following equation:

$$\text{Rate of Return on Net Worth Ratio} = \frac{\text{Return on Assets (ROI)}}{\text{Percent of Assets Financed by Net Worth}} = \frac{<\text{ROI}>}{1.0 - \text{Debt Ratio}}$$

The computation for Seneca is as follows:

$$\text{Rate of Return on Net Worth Ratio} = \frac{8.3\%}{1.0 - 0.46} = \frac{8.3\%}{0.54} = 15.4\%$$

The computation for the industry median is as follows:

$$\text{Rate of Return on Net Worth Ratio} = \frac{5.3\%}{1.0 - 0.62} = \frac{5.3\%}{0.38} = 13.9\%$$

This formula is an easy method for determining the impact of financial leverage on the return on net worth. However, there are limitations to the impact of financial leverage on returns on net worth. The return on net worth increases with leverage, provided the return on assets exceeds the interest rate associated with the debt after giving effect to the tax deductibility of interest payments. The imposition of debt on a company's balance sheet causes its leverage ratios to rise and thereby increases the risk of bankruptcy and endangers the company's stockholders. As a company's leverage ratio exceeds a certain level, creditors will not extend additional loans to the company. Therefore, practical limitations on the magnitude of financial leverage do exist.

However, in today's leveraged buyout environment, transactions are being consummated with minimal amounts of equity capital.

¶ 4.6 Industry Rates of Return

As mentioned previously, rates of return are impacted through the interaction of profit margins and asset turnover ratios. As a consequence, an investor should be indifferent to investing in a firm with a 5% profit margin and a 3 times asset turnover ratio or a firm with a 3% profit margin and 5 times asset turnover ratios. In both cases, the investor is realizing a 15% ROI. However, the risk characteristics of the two firms might be quite different. One company may operate in a highly volatile industry whereas the other may be in a very stable industry with minimal fluctuations in its historical earnings and cash flow levels. An investor requires a higher ROI in a volatile industry than in a stable industry.

The nature of the industry in which a company operates will have a significant impact on its operating ratios. A company with either a substantial investment in fixed-assets or long production periods will experience low asset turnover ratios. A diamond dealer will experience lower asset turnovers than a grocery store. However, the diamond dealer will realize a correspondingly higher profit margin on sales than the grocery store. Managers expect this relationship; that is, a company with a low asset turnover to obtain higher profit margins. If the grocery store realized the same profit margin on sales as the diamond dealer, the grocery store would be significantly more profitable than the diamond dealer. If this were the case, the grocery business would attract a disproportionate amount of investment money, thereby increasing the supply of grocery stores and eroding industry profits and rates of return. The erosion of profits would persist until the rates of return, adjusted for the different industry risk characteristics in both industries, were equal.

In considering the ROR on net worth in different industries, the ability of a company to use leverage must be considered. For example, if companies operating in a certain industry are able to use more financial leverage than companies operating in a different industry, the industry with the ability to obtain more financial leverage will have lower return on assets. The trade-off between higher financial leverage and lower return on assets results in both industries yielding the same risk-adjusted ROR on net worth. Otherwise, more investment money would flow into the industry providing the higher-risk-adjusted rate of return on net worth until an equilibrium ROR on net worth was established between the two industries.

Table 4-6, which contains comparative statistics of a textile manufacturer, a specialty chemical producer, and a wholesale food distribu-

TABLE 4-6
THE SENECA CORPORATION
THE INTERACTION OF TURNOVER, PROFIT MARGIN, AND FINANCIAL LEVERAGE ON RETURNS ON NET WORTH

	Working Capital Turnover Ratio	Profit Margin/ Sales Ratio (%)	ROI (%)	Total Interest-Bearing Debt/ Equity Ratios (%)	Return on Net Worth Ratio (%)
Textile manufacturer	1.6	4.7	7.52	50.0	15.0
Speciality chemical producer	1.2	5.3	6.36	55.0	14.1
Wholesale food distributor	9.2	1.1	10.12	30.0	14.5

tor, illustrates the interaction of turnover ratios, profit margin on sales, and financial leverage. The interaction of profit margins with asset turnover can be observed producing different returns on assets. Also observed are the interactions of financial leverage with various returns on assets and its effect on return on net worth. The food distributor exhibits the highest working capital turnover ratio and lowest profit margin/sales ratio of the three. In contrast, the chemical producer with a high level of fixed assets displays the lowest asset turnover ratio and the highest profit margin/sales ratio of the three, which produce a lower return on assets than the food distributor's. The two ratios for the textile manufacturer fall between the ratios of the chemical producer and the food distributor. The resultant return on assets was between the returns achieved by the other two. All three used financial leverage to enhance the returns on net worth. The chemical producer achieved the greatest benefits on its return on net worth from financial leverage whereas the food distributor received the least value.

¶ 4.7 Comparative Industry Ratios

The analysis of Seneca compared the company with public companies operating in similar lines of business. It was mentioned that industry averages are also appropriate measures to use in comparative ratio analysis. Some of the more commonly used sources are as follows:

- Robert Morris Associates;
- Dun & Bradstreet;
- Federal Trade Commission quarterly reports;
- Bank credit departments;

- Trade associations; and
- Public accountants.

It is not wise to use these ratios blindly. They are most effectively used when how each ratio is computed is understood and how the analysis is performed using comparable data.

¶ 4.8 Security Analysis

Financial ratio analysis is commonly used in security analysis to determine the investment characteristics of different types of securities. The primary focus in security analysis is to determine management's abilities to achieve long-term profitability for a company. As a minority shareholder, an investor has very limited input regarding corporate policy or decisions pertaining to the operating characteristics of the company. Therefore, investors must focus their attention on the relative efficiency with which the existing management team operates the company.

¶ 4.9 Ratio Analysis Limitations

Ratio analysis, as mentioned previously, does have some limitations and is more appropriately used to ascertain what questions need to be asked rather than to answer questions. As an example, a high inventory turnover ratio may indicate that inventories are being effectively managed. It can also mean that the company is experiencing inventory shortages.

Judgment is essential in effectively utilizing ratio analysis. Ratio analysis must not be a perfunctory exercise. The most serious limitation in the application of financial ratios is that they are calculated from accounting data. The data are subject to manipulation because different interpretations of the appropriate application of an accounting principle will yield different accounting data.

In particular, the use of different depreciation and inventory methods; can create lower or higher reported income. In applying ratio analysis, the financial manager must adjust the ratios for these items to make a meaningful comparison. It is essential in any financial ratio analysis to adjust ratios of companies to make accounting treatments comparable. Similar differences in accounting treatment can be found in several areas, including but not limited to research and development costs, pension plan costs, bad-debt reserves, and purchase price accounting involving mergers and acquisitions. Companies' use of different fiscal year-ends can potentially influence the ratios. Furthermore, seasonal factors can cause wide variations in ratios.

Ratios are excellent tools if applied properly. This requires that good judgment be used when applying ratio analysis.

¶ 4.10 Summary

Financial ratio analysis provides a convenient method to summarize large quantities of data and to analyze a company's past and present performance. The ratios develop certain relationships between a company's balance sheet and income statement. The analysis of these ratios provides the financial manager, creditor, or security analyst with insights into the company's relative strengths and weaknesses. As such, it furnishes the essential information that the financial manager needs to effectively plan and anticipate responses to his actions.

5

CAPITALIZATION AND DISCOUNT RATES

RICHARD S. BRAUN*

		Page
¶ 5.1	**Capitalization Rates**	5-2
	[1] Types of Capitalization Rates	5-3
	[a] Price/Earnings Multiple	5-3
	[b] Price/Future Earnings Multiple	5-4
	[c] Price/Cash Flow Multiple	5-4
	[d] Price/Debt-Free Earnings Multiple	5-5
	[e] Price/Debt-Free Cash Flow Multiple	5-6
	[f] Other Debt-Free Capitalization Rates	5-6
	[g] Price/Net Book Value Multiple	5-7
	[h] Other Multiples	5-7
	[2] Computation of Capitalization Rates	5-8
	[a] Numerator Selection	5-8
	[b] Denominator Selection	5-8
	[3] Variation in Capitalization Rates	5-9
	[a] General Economic Conditions	5-9
	[b] Industry-Specific Factors	5-9
	[c] Company-Specific Factors	5-10
¶ 5.2	**Discount Rates**	5-10
	[1] Concept of Present Value	5-11
	[2] Comparison With Capitalization Rates	5-11
	[3] Market Examples	5-12
	[4] Stated Yields vs. Discount Rates	5-13
	[5] Determination of Proper Discount Rate	5-13
	[6] Use of Financial Theory	5-14
	[7] Changing Capital Structures	5-15
¶ 5.3	**Summary**	5-15

* RICHARD S. BRAUN is a managing director of Houlihan, Lokey, Howard, & Zukin, Inc., a valuation advisory and investment banking firm headquartered in Los Angeles, California. He is a senior member of the American Society of Appraisers, and is an active participant on the Business Valuation Committee of the ESOP Association. The author has also appeared as an expert witness and frequent speaker on ESOPs and other valuation matters.

Determining the fair market value of a company is a challenging and complicated task that must take into account a wide variety of factors. The valuation process is dependent on the analyst's choice of inputs. Among the most important inputs in this process are the choices of a *capitalization rate* (the rate used to calculate the present value of a company) and a *discount rate* (a rate important to investors when determining the value of company as a whole).

There is a variety of capitalization rates, of which the most widely known is the price/earnings multiple. This chapter describes and discusses the use of price/earnings and other capitalization rates that are useful to investors and analysts. In addition, the use of discount rates in the analysis of projected earnings and cash flow is addressed later in this chapter.

¶ 5.1 Capitalization Rates

The most widely recognized and utilized investor ratio is the price/earnings multiple. Virtually every newspaper and other publication that carries stock prices also indicates how those prices compare to historical earnings. Such ratios or multiples, of which the well-known price/earnings multiple is but an example, are indicators of investor sentiment that vary greatly between companies and industries, and also change over time. What does it mean when investors are willing to pay, for example, ten times a company's historical earnings in order to purchase its stock, and why is this information important to analysts? The following examples focus on these questions and the answers to them.

> *Example 1.* Assume that two companies, A and B, each made $1 per share during the last year. If investors are willing to pay ten times earnings (or $10 per share) for A but only five times earnings (or $5 per share) for B, they are expressing greater confidence in the future earnings of A.

The higher level of confidence that investors are displaying in the earnings of A may be caused by many factors. However, in general, the level of confidence is determined by investors' perception of both growth and risk. For example, A might be in a growth industry, where earnings are expected to increase in the future, while B may be in an industry that expects little or no growth. Investors would be willing to pay more for A because they expect the company's earnings in the future to be greater than those earned in the past while they expect B to continue to earn about the same or possibly less.

> *Example 2.* Assume that A's earnings are expected to grow

to $2 per share next year while B is expected to continue to earn only $1 per share. With a price of $10 per share, A is selling at five times the anticipated earnings ($10/$2 = 5x). At $5 per share, B is also selling at five times future earnings ($5/$1 = 5x). Thus, A sells at a larger multiple of current or historical earnings than B but not at a greater multiple of anticipated earnings. Investors pay more for A than B because they expect more growth from A.

Risk is also a characteristic that can significantly impact the price investors are willing to pay for securities and, therefore, capitalization rates, as is shown in Example 3.

Example 3. Assume that both A and B earned $1 per share last year. A, however, is in a relatively low-risk industry, where earnings are steady and predictable, while B is in a high-risk industry, where earnings are very cyclical. Investors in A have little risk that future earnings will be substantially less than $1 per share while investors in B are much more likely to suffer an earnings decline. Therefore, investors will pay more for A than B because they have a higher confidence level that A will continue to earn at least $1 per share.

Growth and risk, of course, can take many forms and are dependent on numerous factors, such as leverage, management, competition, barriers to entry, and the quality of goods and services, to mention but a few. The smart investor carefully considers all significant aspects of growth and risk prior to making an investment. Once the price of a security has been established, price/earnings multiples and other capitalization rates can be determined and used as indicators of investor confidence and sentiment toward a particular company, an industry, and even the economy as a whole.

[1] Types of Capitalization Rates

Capitalization rates or multiples can take many forms in addition to the popular price/earnings multiple. It is useful to analyze a variety of capitalization rates that consider cash flow and other things that investors consider important. The more widely accepted capitalization rates or multiples are discussed here.

[a] Price/Earnings Multiple

The price/earnings multiple is the most widely known and utilized capitalization rate. The *price/earnings multiple* uses a numerator that is simply the fair market value of the security (typically stated on a per-share basis) and a denominator that is the historical earnings per share (usually based on the sum of the results for the most recent twelve-month period). *Earnings* typically are defined as net income per share. The price/earnings multiple is illustrated in Example 4.

> *Example 4.* If the fair market value of the stock is $10 per share and the company has earned $1 per share during the most recent twelve months, the price/earnings multiple would usually be expressed as ten times earnings ($10/$1 = 10x).

[b] Price/Future Earnings Multiple

The *price/future earnings multiple* considers the multiple of future or anticipated earnings investors are willing to pay for a company's stock, as shown in Example 5.

> *Example 5.* If the price per share is $10 and the expected earnings of the company for the next twelve months is $2 per share, investors are willing to pay five times future earnings ($10/$2 = 5x). Thus, if investors expect growth in earnings, the price/future earnings multiple will usually be lower than the price/earnings multiple based on historical earnings.

[c] Price/Cash Flow Multiple

The *price/cash flow multiple* is most relevant for companies with large amounts of depreciation and amortization. *Cash flow*, as described here, is the sum of net income plus depreciation and amortization. Since depreciation and amortization reduce net income, they affect price/earnings multiples. It is possible for companies to have very dissimilar price/earnings multiples but much more similar price/cash flow multiples. Thus, reliance solely on price/earnings multiples could give a distorted view of investor sentiment, as shown in Example 6.

> *Example 6.* Assume that both company *A* and company *B* have pretax, predepreciation earnings of $50 per share. However, *A* has depreciation of $30 per share compared to *B*'s depreciation of only $10 per share. Computing the net income and cash flow for the two companies (assuming a 50% tax rate), as shown in Table 5-1, serves to illustrate how reliance solely on the price/earnings multiple could give a distorted valuation of these two companies.

TABLE 5-1
COMPARISON OF NET INCOME AND CASH FLOW FOR DIFFERENT LEVELS OF DEPRECIATION

	Company A	Company B
Pretax, predepreciation earnings	$ 50	$ 50
Less: Depreciation	(30)	(10)
Pretax earnings	$ 20	$ 40
Less: Taxes (50%)	(10)	(20)
Net income	$ 10	$ 20
Plus: Depreciation	30	10
Cash flow	$ 40	$ 30

A value of $100 per share for both companies would result in a higher price/earnings multiple for A ($100/$10 = 10x) than for B ($100/$20 = 5x). However, B would have a higher cash flow multiple ($100/$30 = 3.33x) than A ($100/$40 = 2.5x). While the price/earnings multiples imply that A is more popular than B with investors, the more similar price/cash flow multiples imply just the opposite. The analyst would receive a one-sided and possibly distorted view of investor sentiment if only price/earnings multiples were considered while price/cash flow multiples were ignored.

[d] Price/Debt-Free Earnings Multiple

The *price/debt-free earnings multiple* recognizes that earnings can be materially affected by the existence and magnitude of debt in the company's capital structure. When comparing two companies with greatly different levels of debt, it may be difficult to properly adjust capitalization rates for the difference in risk. By adding back the after-tax effect of interest expense to reported earnings, it is possible to determine the level of earnings a company would have if it had no debt. By dividing price by the debt-free earnings, a capitalization rate for the company on a debt-free basis can be determined, as shown in Example 7.

Example 7. Assume that company A and company B each have pretax, preinterest earnings of $100 per share, but A has interest expense of $50 per share while B is debt free. Their net income and debt-free income (assuming a 50% tax rate) can be computed, as shown in Table 5-2.

TABLE 5-2
COMPARISON OF NET INCOME AND DEBT-FREE INCOME FOR DIFFERENT LEVELS OF INTEREST EXPENSE

	Company A	Company B
Pretax, preinterest earnings	$ 100	$ 100
Less: Interest	(50)	-0-
Pretax earnings	$ 50	$ 100
Less: Taxes (50%)	(25)	(50)
Net income	$ 25	$ 50
Plus: 50% of interest expense	25	-0-
Debt-free earnings	$ 50	$ 50

If A and B are alike in every respect except for the difference in debt, they should have similar debt-free earnings, similar debt-free capitalization rates, and similar value on a debt-free basis. The major difference in their value should be the market value of the debt on A that does not impact the value of B. Thus, if B has equity value of $10 million in aggregate on a debt-free basis and A has $5 million debt, the equity value of A should be approximately $5 million. This is true in theory because an investor could buy A's equity for $5 million, pay off the debt of $5 million for a total investment of $10 million, and be left with an investment that is exactly like that in B, which is also worth $10 million on a debt-free basis. Any other relationship between A and B would imply an inefficient market and an arbitrage opportunity.

[e] Price/Debt-Free Cash Flow Multiple

The *price/debt-free cash flow multiple* is very similar to the price/debt-free earnings multiple, except that operating debt-free cash flow (depreciation and amortization plus debt-free earnings) are used in place of debt-free earnings. Like the debt-free earnings approach, a capitalization of debt-free cash flow makes it easier to compare companies with different capital structures. In addition, because it includes depreciation and amortization, the debt-free cash flow approach tends to smooth the difference between companies with different methods or magnitudes of noncash expenses.

[f] Other Debt-Free Capitalization Rates

In addition to a multiple of debt-free earnings of cash flow, there are other debt-free capitalization rates that may be developed. Two of the most popular are a multiple of earnings before interest and taxes

(EBIT) and a multiple of earnings before depreciation, interest, and taxes (EBDIT). These approaches have the same advantage as the debt-free earnings and cash flow approaches: ease of comparison between companies with substantially different capital structures. In addition, because they are determined pretax, they may minimize distortion caused by differences in tax rates between companies.

[g] Price/Net Book Value Multiple

The *price/net book value multiple* is created by a comparison of fair market value per share to net book value per share. *Net book value* (also known as *stockholders' equity*) is the result of historical costs and expenses added to shareholder investment in the company. Net book value, by itself, is typically not a good proxy for economic or fair market value.

For example, real estate and other assets that tend to appreciate in value are reflected in net book value at their original purchase price plus certain improvements less appropriate depreciation. If real estate was purchased many years ago, it is likely that its fair market value substantially exceeds its net book value. As another example, net book value often includes only tangible assets and excludes any recognition of goodwill and other intangible assets. Goodwill and other intangibles are frequently quite valuable and may have a material impact on fair market value.

[h] Other Multiples

There are a variety of other capitalization rates that may be computed and are useful in some circumstances. For example, it may be appropriate or useful to use a *price/revenues multiple* to capitalize revenues, especially when the company has little or no earnings or cash flow. This approach assumes there is economic value due to the magnitude of the company's market share even if revenues are not currently resulting in a positive bottom line.

In addition to a price/revenues capitalization rate, other multiples may be developed as modifications of other approaches. Price/earnings multiples may be determined on a pretax as well as on an after-tax basis, and cash flow multiples may be determined net of capital expenditures and working capital requirements. While these and other approaches may be useful, they must be viewed carefully in order to determine their value as valid indications of investor confidence and sentiment.

[2] Computation of Capitalization Rates

The computation of capitalization rates involves the selection of an appropriate numerator and an appropriate denominator. This selection process is discussed next.

[a] Numerator Selection

The computation of capitalization rates first requires the determination of the price or fair market value of the company's stock, which is always used as the numerator of the calculation. For publicly traded companies, the price per share is usually determined in the open market and is available from a variety of sources, such as *The Wall Street Journal*. Since a particular capitalization rate is significant only as of a given date, the representative price per share as of the valuation date must be determined. This may require the analyst to retrieve prices months or even years in the past.

The price per share must be viewed cautiously since it may be affected by volatility, premiums, and other factors. The closing price of a publicly traded company as of any given day may be distorted due to volatility in the marketplace that causes stock prices, in general, to rise or fall dramatically. In addition, the price of public companies may contain premiums as a result of potential buyout activity, which tends to inflate the marketable minority interest value of the stock. Therefore, it may be advisable to review stock prices over a reasonable time frame, such as twenty days, in order to determine a price that is more representative of the fair market value of the company than the closing price as of a specific date.

[b] Denominator Selection

Once the value of a company has been determined for the numerator of the capitalization rate computation, the appropriate denominator for the computation must be selected. In a price/earnings multiple computation, the proper denominator is net income over some time frame, typically the latest twelve months, although alternative time frames may be selected where appropriate. A price/cash flow multiple requires operating cash flow (net income plus depreciation and amortization) as the denominator; price/debt-free earnings requires earnings adjusted for interest expense; and so on for the other approaches.

One twist to the selection of the proper denominator may be the need to make adjustments so that the calculation is meaningful. Earnings, for example, should be adjusted for nonrecurring gains and losses if the resulting ratio is to be meaningful. Investors recognize that earnings may be temporarily distorted; and, while prices will vary, they will typically not rise and fall in the same magnitude as such earnings.

[3] Variation in Capitalization Rates

Capitalization rates vary greatly for a wide range of reasons, including the following:

1. General economic conditions;
2. Industry-specific factors; and
3. Company-specific factors.

Anyone who follows the stock market knows that capitalization rates, as a whole, tend to move up or down over time based on investors' perceptions of the general economic outlook. If things are viewed as being good for business as a whole, capitalization rates will begin to rise; as the economic outlook from a macro point of view begins to decline, so, in general, will stock prices and capitalization rates. This is reasonable because few, if any, industries or companies are immune to significant macroeconomic changes. Some may be less exposed to such vagaries and tend to move in smaller increments; others may be counter cyclical; and still others may have greater chances to benefit from an upswing than suffer from a decline. But virtually all investments are affected by general economic conditions to some extent, and so are capitalization rates.

[a] General Economic Conditions

The kinds of general economic conditions that may impact capitalization multiples include the following:

1. Changes in interest rates;
2. Inflation;
3. Recession or depression;
4. A "boom" or economic "bull" market;
5. War or other conflict;
6. Changes in the price or availability of commodities; and
7. Political changes.

[b] Industry-Specific Factors

In addition to general economic conditions, capitalization rates tend to vary by industry. There are certain industries that the market favors with high multiples while others suffer from low multiples. High or low capitalization rates for a particular industry are not static but change over time as investor confidence in that industry changes.

For example, the defense industry is likely to have high multiples during periods of increased defense spending because investors view the industry as having a favorable risk/return trade-off. As defense spending tightens, investors become less enamored with the defense industry, and capitalization rates begin to decline. At the same time, capitalization rates in another industry, such as construction, might begin to rise as the economy shifts its spending from defense to housing.

The types of industry-specific conditions that may impact multiples include the following:

1. Overcapacity or undercapacity;
2. Obsolescence or alternative products;
3. Regulation;
4. Foreign competition;
5. Growth in demand for a particular product or service; and
6. Changes in price or availability of supply.

[c] Company-Specific Factors

There are, in addition, variations in capitalization rates for companies even when they are in the same industry and are subject to the same macroeconomic factors. At the same time that an industry group as a whole is rising or falling in investor's favor, individual companies within that industry may be over- or underperforming in industry as a whole. Those companies performing better than the industry as a whole will typically receive higher capitalization rates and those underperforming the norm will receive lower multiples. Factors that may affect the capitalization rates a particular company receives relative to its industry as a whole include the following:

1. Quality of management;
2. Expected growth in earnings and cash flow;
3. Profitability;
4. Leverage;
5. Liquidity;
6. Market share;
7. Product or service quality; and
8. Geographic location.

¶ 5.2 Discount Rates

A *discount rate* is a form of capitalization rate that is typically applied to projected earnings or cash flow in order to develop an indication of value for the company as a whole. The concept underlying a discount rate is that, while people generally have a propensity to consume rather than save, they may be induced to invest if given a sufficient rate of return. Thus, a small investor is more likely to put $100 in a savings account if he or she expects to get $100 plus interest in return at some future date. The interest is his or her reward for investing rather than consuming.

The interest rate on the investor's savings, plus the ability to get his or her principal back, constitutes the saver's return. An investor who puts money in a savings account at 5% simple interest is said to be getting a 5% rate of return (ROR). The ROR required by an investor on a specific investment is a function of available alternative investments as well as the perceived risk of the investment. The saver, in this example, is unlikely to invest money at a bank across the street at 4% if he or she is already earning 5% unless one bank is riskier than the other. Thus, greater risk increases an investor's required ROR while lesser risk decreases that ROR. The ROR demanded by investors based on the risk of an investment is equal to the required discount rate for that investment.

[1] Concept of Present Value

Present value is the amount an investor would pay today for the right to receive an anticipated stream of payments in the future. A discount rate is typically applied to an investor's projected or anticipated cash payment that indicates the present value of that cash flow. For example, assume an investor expects a cash payment of $110 one year from now from a particular investment. How much is he or she willing to invest today in order to receive the $110 payment? If the investor has a required ROR of 10% to reflect the time value of money and risk associated with receiving this particular cash flow, it would be appropriate to discount the $100 by 10% for one year. Therefore, the investor should be willing to invest the present value of the anticipated cash flow (or $100, in this example) in order to be entitled to $110 one year from now.

In the real world, of course, investments are not as simple and straightforward as in this example. There may be multiple anticipated cash payments that are scheduled over years in various amounts and with different levels of risk associated with each. However, no matter how complex, an investor should never pay more than the present value of anticipated cash flows discounted at their required ROR.

[2] Comparison With Capitalization Rates

Both discount rates and capitalization rates, as already discussed, may be used to quantify the earnings and cash flow of a company, resulting in an indication of value. Thus, both methodologies attempt to quantify the present value of future benefits.

The most obvious difference between the two is that discount rates typically are used to analyze a company's projected earnings or cash flow while capitalization rates usually are applied to historical results. Anticipated growth in earnings or cash flow is captured in projections but missing from historical levels. Discount rates need only reflect the risk associated with achieving the projected results and not include an adjustment for growth since growth is already included in the underlying projections. However, capitalization rates must include an adjustment for growth as well as risk since growth is not included in historical earnings or cash flow. Therefore, it is not appropriate to assume that a company's capitalization rate is the inverse of its discount rate or vice versa. In fact, this would only be true if earnings and cash flow were anticipated to be perpetuities and reflect no elements of growth.

[3] Market Examples

In the public marketplace, the most common examples of discount rates may be seen in the market for bonds and other forms of debt. This is true because such investments typically have a stated yield and a limited life with less upside potential and downside risk than common equity. Since the risk is less and the returns more certain for a debt investment than common equity, it is easier to express the risk of debt in the form of required yield or discount rate.

Examples of debt instrument and discount rates include U.S. Government Treasury securities, corporate bonds, and zero-coupon securities. Treasury securities are considered "risk free" because they are virtually certain not to default on payments of principal and interest. Thus, except for certain tax-enhanced instruments, Treasury securities set a floor on required yields for investors. All other investments are riskier and must yield a greater after-tax ROR.

Even Treasury securities, however, are affected by the term structure of interest rates. Yields on shorter-term Treasuries, such as "T bills," with near-term maturities, typically yield less to an investor than longer-term Treasury bonds whose maturity can stretch up to thirty years. This is because the investor holding a short-term T-bill is less exposed to potential changes in interest rates that may affect the investment's value than the investor holding a longer-term Treasury bond. Corporate bonds vary in risk from relatively riskless blue-chip company debt to relatively high-risk "junk bond" financing. In any case, the ROR is higher on corporate debt than federal government debt because there is more risk. The higher required ROR for corporate and other securities above Treasury securities is known as a *risk premium*. The magnitude of the risk premium varies, depending on the risk of the debt, but it always exists to a certain extent.

Zero-coupon securities do not have a stated yield or fixed interim payments. Instead, they are sold at a discount from *face* or (*stated*) *value*, which is the amount the issuer promises to redeem the securities for at some future date. Thus, the required ROR is implied by the relationship between the price paid for the zero-coupon bond and the face or stated value. For example, suppose a zero-coupon bond is due to mature in one year and will be redeemed by its issuer at $100. If investors are willing to pay approximately $91 for such securities, they are implying a 10% discount on required ROR for the zero-coupon bond.

[4] Stated Yields vs. Discount Rates

With the exception of zero-coupon securities, most debt instruments have a stated yield that typically is expressed as a percentage amount. Stated yields are established by the issuer at the date of issuance and usually remain fixed during the life of the investment. However, due to movements in interest rates in general or changes in the risk of the issuer, the required ROR is likely to change before the instrument's maturity. The value of the security will be affected as investors adjust to changes in required rates of return.

For example, assume a bond is issued with a stated yield of 10%, which is the required ROR on the date of issuance. Over a period of time, the required ROR increases to 20% for a variety of reasons, but the yield remains fixed at 10%. An investor then has a choice between putting his or her money in the original 10% yielding security or buying another security of equal risk with a yield of 20%. Obviously, the investor would choose the higher-yielding security of equal risk unless the price he or she had to pay for the 10% instrument was lowered (in this example, to about half of its original value). Since the required ROR or discount rate is greater than the stated yield, the security is no longer worth face or stated value.

[5] Determination of Proper Discount Rate

The risk-adjusted discount rate for a given investment is not established in a vacuum but must be determined relative to the required ROR on other investments. For example, if risk-free government securities are yielding 5%, discount rates for alternative investments, in general, will be less than if government debt is yielding 10%.

As a first step in determining the appropriate risk-adjusted discount rate for an equity investment, the analyst should consider the required ROR on the company's debt. Since debt by its very nature is less risky than equity, it will command a lower discount rate. If a company is borrowing from a bank at 10%, it is reasonable to assume that the discount rate on the that company's common equity should greater than 10%.

If the company has no debt, it may be appropriate to consider the yields on risk-free government securities and comparable companies' debt. As previously explained, the required ROR on risky investments will always be higher than on risk-free securities. The required ROR on the debt of other companies, especially if comparable to the company being analyzed, is also a good source of information. If the subject company is less risky than the public comparable companies, it is reasonable to assume the required yield on its debt will be lower and vice versa.

When checking the required yields on other companies, it is important to remember the following:

- Debt may vary according to its priority on interest paid, liquidation, and principal repayment.
- Debt may be convertible into common stock or have other associated equity "kickers."
- Debt may be secured or unsecured.
- Debt may have other attributes that impact value and required RORs.

The analyst should consider these and other features when weighing a required yield analysis.

[6] Use of Financial Theory

In addition to the use of market comparables in the selection of appropriate risk-adjusted discount rates, the analyst should consider the use of financial theory. Although there are several methodologies that have received support in their use for the selection of discount rates, probably the most widely accepted and utilized approach is the Capital Asset Pricing Model (CAPM).

A full description of the CAPM, its limitations, and its usefulness, is beyond the scope of this chapter. However, from a conceptual point of view, the CAPM utilizes a variety of inputs to determine a reasonable cost of equity for the firm. In addition, by considering the amount of debt and equity in the capital structure and weighing each according to its percentage, it is possible to develop a weighted average cost of capital (WACC) for the company. The WACC considers the cost of debt weighed by the percentage amount of debt in the company's capital structure as well as the cost of equity and its percentage of total capital.

The cost of equity may be used to discount equity flows, such as earnings or cash flow. In this regard, free cash flow (cash flow minus capital expenditures and changes in working capital) may be the most appropriate equity cash flow to discount since it represents cash available to be paid as dividends to shareholders after the retention of capital necessary to fund the projected operations of the business. The

WACC should be used to discount preinterest cash flow because it considers both the cost and magnitude of equity and debt.

The CAPM, as previously mentioned, does have limitations that make its blind application questionable. In addition to limitations imposed by the model itself, the CAPM has no explicit adjustment to take into account aggressive or volatile projections. Therefore, it is important for the analyst to consider the riskiness of the projections and adjust for a premium where necessary.

[7] Changing Capital Structures

It is not unusual for a company to anticipate changes in its capital structure during the life of the projections. Certainly in a leveraged buyout, the company is burdened with debt when the transaction occurs, but, as debt is repaid, the company will return to a more normal capital structure. As a company's leverage changes, so does its cost of debt and WACC.

If the analyst believes that changes will occur in the company's capital structure, it would not be appropriate to apply the company's current WACC to all future time periods. Instead, it would be reasonable to assume that, as debt is paid, the cost of debt, the cost of equity, and the WACC will all change. Therefore, it is more appropriate to use a "blended" cost of equity or WACC in a present value analysis. Otherwise, the discount rate will be misstated with a resulting increase or decrease in present value.

A blended cost of equity or WACC over a period of time considers how the cost of each component will vary over time, assuming the company's capital structure changes as projected. Each time period has its own anticipated discount rate based on the projected capital structure. It is not appropriate to discount projected cash flows in year 4 by the WACC determined appropriate for year 1 if the capital structure is expected to change. A blended cost of equity or WACC takes into consideration such changes and computes one discount rate that, when applied to the cash flows from every time period, results in a present value equal to the present value determined by discounting each discrete cash flow by its own discount rate and aggregating the present values so calculated.

¶ 5.3 Summary

Capitalization rates and discount rates provide the analyst with tools to help compute the fair market value of a company or its securities. Since the result of most analyses are very sensitive to the selection of inputs, including capitalization or discount rates, the analyst must be careful during the selection process. Rates should not be selected blindly but should consider all relevant facts, including growth, risk, and the availability of alternative investments. The rates selected must be reasonable, supportable, and explainable, and never selected in an arbitrary manner. If rates are selected with diligence and care, the analyst will have a valuable tool for the determination of fair market value.

6

VALUATION CASE STUDY

JOHN G. MAVREDAKIS* AND GLENN GARLICK**

		Page
¶ 6.1	**Purpose**	6-2
¶ 6.2	**General Valuation Considerations**	6-3
¶ 6.3	**Scope of Investigation**	6-4
¶ 6.4	**Corporate Description**	6-5
	[1] Company History	6-5
	[2] Products	6-6
	[3] Customers	6-6
	[4] Marketing	6-7
	[5] Competition	6-7
	[6] Suppliers	6-7
	[7] Personnel	6-7
¶ 6.5	**General Economic Overview and Industry Review**	6-8
	[1] General Economy	6-8
	[2] Industry Review	6-8
¶ 6.6	**Financial Review**	6-9
	[1] Financial Condition and Results of Operations	6-9
	[a] Current Assets	6-14
	[b] Current Liabilities	6-15
	[c] Liquidity	6-15
	[d] Gross Profits	6-16
	[e] Operating Income	6-16
	[f] Profitability	6-17
	[2] Projections	6-17
	[3] Industry Comparison	6-18
¶ 6.7	**Valuation Methodology Overview**	6-20
	[1] Multiple of Earnings and Cash Flow	6-20
	[2] Capitalization of Dividends	6-21
	[3] Market Price to Book Value	6-21
	[4] Discounted Future Debt-Free Cash Flow	6-21
	[5] Adjusted Book Value	6-21

---

* JOHN G. MAVREDAKIS is a managing director of Houlihan, Lokey, Howard & Zukin, Inc., a valuation advisory and investment banking firm headquartered in Los Angeles, California, and is an managing director of its investment banking subsidiary. He has published numerous articles on valuation.

** GLENN GARLICK is a vice president in Houlihan, Lokey, Howard & Zukin, Inc.'s Los Angeles office. He has worked on over 300 valuation engagements.

	[6] Other Indices of Value	6-22
¶ 6.8	**Valuation Analysis**	6-22
	[1] Selection of Comparative Public Companies	6-22
	[2] Comparison of Elcon With Comparative Public Companies	6-23
	[3] Market Comparison Approaches	6-26
	[a] Multiple of Earnings-Price/Earnings Approach	6-26
	[b] Multiple of Cash Flow-Price/Cash Flow Approach	6-29
	[c] Price/EBIT and Price/EBDIT Approaches	6-30
	[d] Capitalization of Dividends and Price/Net Book Value Approaches	6-31
	[4] Discounted Future Cash Flows	6-32
	[5] Adjusted Book Value	6-34
	[6] Other Indices of Value	6-35
¶ 6.9	**Other Valuation Considerations**	6-37
	[1] Premium for Controlling Interest	6-38
	[2] Discount for Minority Interest	6-39
	[3] Discount for Lack of Marketability	6-39
¶ 6.10	**Valuation Summary**	6-40
	[1] Reconciliation of Value Indications	6-41
	[2] Conclusions	6-42

The previous five chapters introduced various concepts related to the valuation of closely held businesses as well as the commonly used methodologies employed. In Chapter 6, a case study illustrating these concepts is presented. For this purpose, a fictitious enterprise, Elcon Company, is used.

¶ 6.1 Purpose

Elcon has operated under the same ownership since it was acquired from a large corporation several years ago. To meet ongoing corporate and personal goals, the owners are contemplating a reorganization. Key elements in the company's strategy include (1) estate planning, (2) the establishment of an employee stock ownership plan (ESOP), and (3) the possible sale of the company. Management has hired a valuation consultant to give opinions of value relative to each of these concerns.

In terms of estate planning, gifts of common stock to children and other family members are being considered in order to pass on future ownership. An opinion of value is required for gift tax purposes.

Elcon is also considering establishing an IRS-qualified ESOP as a motivational tool and a supplementary employee-benefits plan. An ESOP could also provide a market and thus liquidity for privately held stock. The company needs an opinion on the fair market value for potential transactions involving the ESOP. The valuation analysis will consider the value on marketable minority basis because the plan will provide for a "put" option whereby the company or the ESOP trust will purchase shares of stock issued to participants and their beneficiaries.

Management has also been considering the possibility of selling the company. In order to establish a basis for bargaining or to determine the reasonableness of offers, management has asked the valuation consultant to determine the fair market value of a 100% ownership position in the company. A controlling interest can be substantially different from the aggregate value of minority shareholdings in a company.

For all purposes, the valuation date is determined to be the end of the first quarter following the fiscal year-end.

¶ 6.2 General Valuation Considerations

Valuation of closely held securities requires the consideration of all factors that influence the value of the securities. These factors, which are widely recognized by the tax courts, the IRS, and professional investors, are outlined and described in Revenue Ruling 59-60,[1] which has served as a general guideline for the valuation of closely held securities since 1959. The factors set forth in Revenue Ruling 59-60 are:

- The nature of the business and the history of the enterprise from its inception;
- The economic outlook in general and the condition and outlook of the company's specific industry in particular;
- The book value of the stock and the financial condition of the business;
- The earnings capacity of the company;
- The dividend-paying capacity of the company;
- The enterprise's possession or lack of goodwill or other intangible value;
- Sales of the stock and the size of the block to be valued; and
- The market price of stocks of corporations engaged in the same or a similar line of business and currently having their stocks actively traded in a free and open market, either on an exchange or over the counter.

---

[1] 1959-1 C.B. 237. Revenue Ruling 59-60 is reprinted as Appendix A at the end of this book.

¶ 6.3 Scope of Investigation

A valuation analysis that considers all of the previous factors entails extensive data gathering. In the case of Elcon, the investigation included a visit to corporate headquarters and a tour of manufacturing facilities, discussions with management regarding the history and nature of Elcon's business, and a review and discussion with management of all financial data bearing upon recent and proposed operations.

In-depth management interviews provide valuable insight into the strengths and weaknesses of a company as well as the opportunities available to it and the threats it faces. Corporate strategy must be viewed in light of its historical financial results if the reasonableness of management projections is to be properly analyzed.

In the case of Elcon, audited financial statements and tax returns for the five fiscal years ended November 30, 19$X$3, and interim unaudited financial statements for the three months ended February 28, 19$X$4, were provided for review and analysis. It is important to examine financial data up through the date of valuation as well as for a period prior to the date of analysis. A five-year period will provide indications of financial trends and the cyclical nature of a company. Financial statements going back further than five years may be appropriate in some circumstances; but, more often than not, they will not provide any useful data on the current financial condition and earnings capabilities of a company.

Elcon's management provided detailed projections for the next five fiscal years as well as other written materials that would help the analyst understand the history and nature of the company, the financial statements, and the areas of risk. These materials included the following:

- The articles of incorporation;
- Company brochures;
- Management résumés and compensation;
- Copies of contract obligations;
- Stockholders' list;
- Fixed-asset appraisals;
- Customer lists;
- Supplier lists;
- Aged-payables and -receivables lists;
- Inventory lists;
- Equipment lists; and
- Depreciation schedules.

The investigation also included a review of publicly available information on (1) comparable public companies, (2) industry financial ratios and statistics, and (3) general economic and industry outlook.

¶ 6.4 Corporate Description

The valuation of Elcon, like any business, must include a corporate description of the enterprise. This description details Elcon's company history, products, customers, marketing plans, competition, suppliers, and personnel, all of which are analyzed here.

[1] Company History

Elcon began as a division of a large manufacturing company, providing various electronic components for its parent's products. The division eventually began selling electronic connecting products to outside customers—primarily manufacturers of electronic typewriters and other business machines. At the same time that this outside business grew, the division's usefulness as a supplier to its parent dwindled. The parent company was not interested in staying in the electronics-component industry. It therefore sold the division to its managers in a leveraged buyout (LBO) twelve years ago. The division became incorporated and changed its name to Elcon Company.

Shortly after the LBO, Elcon's management directed its marketing and research and development (R&D) efforts toward expansion into the computer and data processing (DP) market. Initially, these efforts were slowed by the need to pay down the borrowed funds used to finance the LBO. Within five years, however, the debt was paid off, and, capitalizing on its strong engineering background, Elcon successfully entered the computer and DP market with innovative connecting products that met the rapidly changing needs of computer manufacturers. A new market opened up for Elcon with the advent of the personal computer. Benefiting from its good reputation, Elcon soon established itself as a major supplier in this burgeoning young industry and enjoyed accelerated growth along with the industry.

More recently, the company has entered into the factory-automation market. This market provides a natural extension of the company's lines of office-based electronic connecting components.

While factory automation has quickly become the fastest-growing segment of the company's business, the computer market remains its largest segment. Despite diversification efforts, the company's reliance on the computer industry has created an area of risk. Accordingly, Elcon experienced its first decline in revenues in fiscal 19X2 when there was a general decline in the computer industry; however, the company continues to diversify into other markets by taking advantage of opportunities that become available.

[2] Products

Elcon develops and manufactures a variety of precision-engineered electronic interconnection products for computer systems and other electronic equipment. Products range from small connector modules for installing semiconductor devices on printed circuit boards to connector cables for connecting systems and peripheral devices. The company's products are designed to provide reliable, cost-efficient interconnection of integrated circuits and are used in electronic computers, DP equipment, business machines, electronic instruments, and industrial electronic controls.

Most of the markets served by Elcon are changing rapidly, resulting in product obsolescence over short periods of time. The company, therefore, puts considerable effort into R&D designed to reduce its exposure to product obsolescence and to maintain state-of-the-art product lines.

Its R&D activities are also directed at developing innovative products that will provide solutions to interconnection problems in both current and new markets. With this market-oriented approach, the company aims to take advantage of opportunities to develop new markets and thus to reduce its dependence on the computer industry. The growing complexity of interconnection needs in current markets should provide opportunities for expansion. Other markets for future growth include telecommunications and consumer electronics.

[3] Customers

The company's customers include hundreds of original equipment manufacturers (OEMs) of computers, peripheral devices, office machines, and industrial automation equipment. In addition, its products are sold to the OEMs' subcontractors and suppliers.

The company is dependent on two large customers for approximately 30% of its business. The largest customer, representing about 20% of the company's business, is a computer and peripheral equipment manufacturer. The other major customer, representing 10% of the business, is in the industrial control market. Elcon does not have long-term contracts with these two companies, and the loss of business from either one would have a significant negative impact on the company. Tremendous effort, therefore, is devoted to maintaining good relations with these customers. Management feels that relations are good at this time, and the primary risk would be in not keeping pace with their technology requirements.

[4] Marketing

The company markets its products nationwide through both its direct sales force and a network of manufacturers' representatives, each of whom is given an exclusive territory and paid on a commission basis. Some product lines are also sold through industrial distributors. The company supports its sales efforts through advertisements in trade magazines, direct mail campaigns, and catalogs by product line. In addition, new product ideas are presented by marketing personnel at trade shows.

[5] Competition

All market segments in which the company does business are highly competitive. There are approximately sixty-five other companies providing electronic connecting components. Some of these competitors are much larger than Elcon in terms of their manufacturing facilities, sales, R&D budgets, and financial resources. It is estimated that Elcon is the eighth largest manufacturer of electronic connectors, with a 3% market share.

Elcon competes primarily on the basis of product quality. Other key customer concerns include product reliability, service, and pricing. Because of the high quality and precision engineering of the company's products, Elcon has been able to sell them at premium prices. However, the industry has become increasingly price sensitive in recent years. With its consistent focus on R&D, Elcon has remained competitive as a low-cost producer known for its high quality.

[6] Suppliers

The raw materials used in Elcon products include brass, copper, aluminum, steel, nickel, gold, silver, and plastics. The company obtains its materials from a number of suppliers. However, there is always the possibility that shortages may cause an increase in the cost of supplies. So far, the company has been able to pass on price increases to its customers.

[7] Personnel

The company currently employs 580 people and expects to employ 625 people by the end of fiscal 19X4. The management team is still headed by the group that purchased the company from its parent corporation. While its operations are not dependent on one key manager, the management team is somewhat lean.

¶ 6.5 General Economic Overview and Industry Review

In order to evaluate the prospects of any business enterprise, it is essential to have a general understanding of the economic environment in which the business functions. This requires an understanding of general national economic conditions as well as conditions in the specific industry in which the company operates.

[1] General Economy

As $19X3$ ended, the economy continued a trend of expansion but at a slower rate than earlier in the year. The gross national product (GNP), after sharply increasing by 9.7% and 7.7% in the second and third quarters, respectively, increased by only 5% in the fourth quarter. Overall, the real GNP (adjusted for inflation) increased approximately 7%. Another positive statistic for $19X3$ was the fact that inflation remained on the low side, with the consumer price index (CPI) increasing only 3.2% during the year.

Other indicators pointing to strength in the overall economy include the following:

- Consumer confidence continues at record high levels.
- Consumer spending has remained strong.
- Retail sales remain at extremely high levels and are expected to remain strong through the spring of $19X4$.
- After-tax profits in $19X3$ rose approximately 13.1% over $19X2$, which powered a strong stock market rally.

Despite the strong economic indicators, however, there are signs of a slower rate of growth in the future. Rising interest rates in the beginning of $19X4$ are expected to slow down the economy, largely in the interest-sensitive areas of housing, automobiles, and durables. Further, employment growth has begun to slow down, and industrial production has increased only modestly.

[2] Industry Review

Elcon designs, manufactures, and markets its products primarily for three end-user markets: computers and peripherals, industrial automation, and business machines. It is, therefore, necessary to review the electronic component industry (with emphasis on electronic connectors).

Electronic components are fundamental to all electronic equipment. Connector products are used to connect wires, cables, printed circuit boards, flat cable, and electronic components to each other and to related equipment. The use of connectors is extremely widespread because electronic and electrical devices must be attached not only to power supplies but to each other.

The electronic components industry rebounded strongly in 19$X$3, following two years of recession. The general economic recovery was largely responsible for the rebound in electronic components. With the present strong demand from major end-user industries and with the rapid pace of technological change, most segments of the electronic components industry, including electronic connectors, are expected to expand at impressive rates in 19$X$4.

Product shipments by the domestic electronic connector industry grew at an inflation-adjusted rate of 10% in 19$X$3, following two years of declining or only slightly increasing shipments. Strong demand from the military and from computer and telecommunications industries fueled the recovery.

Sales of electronic connectors in 19$X$4 and beyond are expected to continue to grow at rates higher than that experienced in 19$X$3. An 11% real growth rate is anticipated for 19$X$4, with a real compound annual growth rate ranging from 13% to 15% anticipated over the next five years. Continued strength in the computer, telecommunications, and defense markets should combine with increasing demand from industrial equipment manufacturers to provide for strong growth.

¶ 6.6 Financial Review

An understanding of the company's operations, the general economy, and the company's industry serve as guides to an understanding of the company's financial statements. Once the company and the economic factors influencing its operations are understood, a complete and thorough financial analysis of the company itself can be undertaken, including an historical review of its operating results and financial condition and an estimate of its near-term profits. Historical trends must be analyzed in order to assess risks, return, and growth.

Information extracted from Elcon's financial statements is shown in Tables 6-1 and 6-2. Financial statistics and ratios have been calculated and are shown in Table 6-3. Finally, financial projections for revenues, earnings, and cash flow are shown in Table 6-4.

[1] Financial Condition and Results of Operations

Table 6-1 shows the company's financial condition as of November 30, 19$X$9, through planned 19$X$4 and as of February 28, 19$X$4. Total assets have grown each year, from $52.687 million as of November 30, 19$X$9 to $63.154 million as of November 30, 19$X$3, and $65.125 million as of February 28, 19$X$4. Much of this growth occurred in 19X0 when the company continued the expansion plans it began in

[*Text continues on p. 6-14*]

TABLE 6-1
ELCON COMPANY
COMPARATIVE SUMMARY BALANCE SHEET
($000s Omitted)

	Planned 19X4	As of 2/28/X4	19X3	19X2	19X1	19X0	19X9
Assets							
Current assets							
Cash and equivalents	$ 8,648	$ 7,636	$ 7,600	$ 6,333	$ 1,833	$ 1,017	$ 611
Accounts receivable	16,263	14,995	13,525	12,068	14,649	13,877	14,099
Inventories	14,476	13,823	12,950	16,438	21,307	20,694	20,205
Other current assets	4,038	4,038	4,613	4,097	2,001	1,704	677
Total current assets	$43,425	$40,492	$38,688	$38,936	$39,790	$37,292	$35,592
Fixed assets							
Land	924	924	924	924	975	1,001	1,001
Building	15,234	15,031	15,031	15,572	15,329	15,141	12,039
Machinery and equipment	27,928	26,395	25,384	23,116	18,421	15,964	13,822
Construction in progress	599	650	650	764	1,723	2,220	1,454
Less: Accumulated depreciation	(22,394)	(21,630)	(20,785)	(18,563)	(16,431)	(14,260)	(12,381)
Net fixed assets	$22,291	$21,370	$21,204	$21,813	$20,017	$20,066	$15,935
Other assets	3,263	3,263	3,262	2,286	1,304	1,000	1,160
Total assets	$68,979	$65,125	$63,154	$63,035	$61,111	$58,358	$52,687

TABLE 6-1
ELCON COMPANY
COMPARATIVE SUMMARY BALANCE SHEET *(continued)*
($000s Omitted)

	Planned 19X4	As of 2/28/X4	19X3	19X2	19X1	19X0	19X9
Liabilities and stockholders' equity							
Current liabilities							
Accounts payable	$ 2,243	$ 2,215	$ 2,206	$ 2,465	$ 2,855	$ 2,522	$ 3,686
Notes payable	225	375	400	1,691	1,478	2,004	-0-
Accrued expenses and other payables	10,769	10,204	10,144	9,937	8,675	8,298	5,529
Income taxes	963	1,112	75	69	677	185	1,185
Total current liabilities	$14,200	$13,906	$12,825	$14,162	$13,685	$13,009	$10,400
Long-term debt	14,538	15,131	14,414	16,196	14,635	14,795	2,021
Total liabilities	$ 338	$ 1,225	$ 1,589	$ 2,034	$ 950	$ 1,786	$12,421
Stockholders' equity							
Common stock	6,173	6,173	6,173	6,173	6,173	6,173	6,173
Retained earnings	49,161	44,664	43,460	41,559	41,096	38,182	34,885
Less: Treasury stock	$ (893)	$ (893)	$ (893)	$ (893)	$ (793)	$ (793)	$ (793)
Net stockholders' equity	54,441	49,994	48,740	46,839	46,476	43,563	40,266
Total liabilities and stockholders' equity	$68,979	$65,125	$63,154	$63,035	$61,111	$58,358	$52,687
Net working capital	$29,225	$26,586	$25,863	$24,774	$26,105	$24,283	$25,192

TABLE 6-2
ELCON COMPANY
COMPARATIVE SUMMARY INCOME STATEMENTS
($000s Omitted)

	Planned 19X4	3 Months Ended 2/28/X4	19X3	19X2	19X1	19X0	19X9
				Fiscal Years Ended November 30,			
Revenue, net	$106,375	$25,131	$87,413	$89,609	$92,231	$87,190	$76,581
Cost of sales (goods sold)	64,499	15,419	55,988	59,376	59,259	57,853	47,184
Gross profits	$41,876	$9,712	$31,425	$30,233	$32,972	$29,337	$29,397
Operating expenses							
Selling & administrative	25,862	641	22,999	24,966	21,761	19,971	15,052
Research and development	5,126	1,240	4,876	4,813	3,875	2,875	3,000
Total operating expenses	$30,988	$7,701	$27,875	$29,779	$25,636	$22,846	$18,052
Operating income	10,888	2,011	3,550	454	7,336	6,491	11,345
Other income (expense)	$1,000	$305	$1,088	$(391)	$214	$575	$748
Pretax income	11,888	2,316	4,638	63	7,550	7,066	12,093
Income taxes (benefit)	$5,563	$1,112	$2,188	$(63)	$3,750	$2,825	$5,672
Net income before extraordinary item	6,325	1,204	2,450	126	3,800	4,241	6,421
Extraordinary item	-0-	-0-	-0-	337	-0-	-0-	-0-
Net income	$6,325	$1,204	$2,450	$463	$3,800	$4,241	$6,421
Depreciation	$3,200	$823	$3,188	$3,047	$2,536	$2,320	$1,405
Dividends	$624	$-0-	$549	$-0-	$886	$944	$948
Research and development % of sales	4.8%	4.8%	5.6%	5.4%	4.2%	3.3%	3.9%

TABLE 6-3
ELCON COMPANY
COMPARATIVE FINANCIAL ANALYSIS
($000 Omitted)

		Fiscal Years Ended November 30,					
Statistics and Ratios	Planned 19X4	19X3	19X2	19X1	19X0	19X9
Size						
Revenues	$106,375	$87,413	$89,609	$92,231	$87,190	$76,581
Total assets	68,979	63,154	63,035	61,111	58,358	52,687
Net worth	54,441	48,740	46,839	46,476	43,563	40,266
Income before taxes	11,888	4,638	63	7,550	7,066	12,093
Net income	6,325	2,450	126	3,800	4,241	6,421
Liquidity ratios						
Quick ratio	2.0	2.0	1.6	1.4	1.3	1.5
Current ratio	3.1	3.0	2.7	3.0	2.9	3.4
Working capital turnover ratio	3.6	3.4	3.6	3.5	3.6	3.0
Leverage ratios						
Total debt/net worth ratio	0.3	0.3	0.3	0.3	0.3	0.3
Total interest-bearing debt/net worth ratio	0.0	0.0	0.1	0.1	0.1	0.1
Profitability ratios						
Gross profit/sales ratio	39.4%	36.0%	33.7%	35.7%	33.6%	38.4%
Pretax income/sales ratio	11.2%	5.3%	0.1%	8.2%	8.1%	15.8%
Pretax income/net worth ratio	22.8%	10.0%	0.1%	16.2%	16.2%	30.0%
Pretax income/total assets ratio	17.2%	7.3%	0.1%	12.4%	12.1%	23.0%
Research and development as % of sales	4.8%	5.6%	5.4%	4.2%	3.3%	3.9%
Activity ratios						
Inventory turnover ratio	4.5	4.3	3.6	2.8	2.8	2.3
Accounts receivable turnover	6.5	6.5	7.4	6.3	6.3	5.4
Total asset turnover	1.5	1.4	1.4	1.5	1.5	1.5
Growth statistics						
Annual revenue growth	21.7%	(2.5%)	(2.8%)	5.8%	13.9%	—
Growth index[*]						
Revenue	1.2	1.1				

[*] Most recent year's revenue divided by revenues four years prior.

[Text continues from p. 6-9]

19X9, with the introduction of new factory automation product lines. As a result, net fixed assets increased from $15.935 million as of November 30, 19X9, to $20.066 million as of November 30, 19X0. Net fixed assets grew more modestly thereafter and even declined slightly in

TABLE 6-4

ELCON COMPANY PROJECTIONS

($000s Omitted)

	19X4	19X5	19X6	19X7	19X8
Revenues, net	$106,375	$125,000	$150,000	$180,000	$205,000
Cost of sales	64,499	737,750	87,000	103,000	115,000
Gross profit	$ 41,876	$ 51,250	$ 63,000	$ 77,000	$ 90,000
Operating expenses					
Selling and administrative	25,862	25,600	29,700	36,500	43,000
Research and development	5,126	6,250	8,500	10,500	12,500
Total operating expenses	$ 30,988	$ 31,850	$ 38,200	$ 47,000	$ 55,500
Operating income	10,888	19,400	24,800	30,000	34,500
Other income (expense)	1,000	1,000	1,000	1,000	1,000
Pretax income	11,888	20,400	25,800	31,000	35,500
Income taxes	5,563	9,800	12,400	14,900	17,100
Net income	$ 6,325	$ 10,600	$ 13,400	$ 16,100	$ 18,400
Plus: Depreciation	3,200	3,300	3,500	3,750	4,000
Less: Capital spending	(4,300)	(6,000)	(6,000)	(4,000)	(4,000)
Plus: Interest (after-tax)	60	15	-0-	-0-	-0-
Net free cash flow	$ 1,935	$ 5,015	$ 7,700	$ 12,300	$ 14,500

19X1 and 19X3 as the company's capital spending was offset by depreciation of capital assets. Capital spending during this period was directed at maintaining state-of-the-art production equipment so as to increase the efficiency and capacity of the company's production process. In 19X0 and 19X1, Elcon disposed of land it had earmarked for a new facility.

[a] Current Assets

Current assets, consisting primarily of accounts receivable and inventories, fluctuated during the period analyzed from a low of $35.592 million as of November 30, 19X9, to a high of $40.492 million as of February 28, 19X4. Accounts receivable generally fluctuated with revenue levels, with the exception of fiscal years 19X9 and 19X2. In 19X9, the company loosened its collection policies with a new customer base (factory automation) while in 19X2, the company toughened its collection policy by demanding cash on delivery from several troubled computer-industry customers. As shown in Table 6-3, average accounts receivable turnover (revenues to accounts receivable), normally at approximately 6.5 times, reached a low of 5.4 times in fiscal 19X9 and a high of 7.4 times in fiscal 19X2. Inventory turnover (cost of sales to inventory) generally increased over the years analyzed, from a low of 2.3 times in fiscal 19X9 to 4.3 in 19X3 and anticipated for fiscal 19X4. This reflects a continued inventory control program that began with an inventory buildup in 19X9 when new factory automation products were introduced and demand was uncertain.

[b] Current Liabilities

Current liabilities, like current assets, have fluctuated somewhat, as shown in Table 6-1, but within a narrow range of approximately $10 million to $14 million since fiscal 19X9. As a result, the company's net working capital level has fluctuated primarily with current assets. Net working capital reached $26.586 million as of February 28, 19X4, as compared to a low of $24.283 million in fiscal 19X0.

[c] Liquidity

As shown in Table 6-3, the company's liquidity position has remained fairly stable since 19X0, as indicated by a current ratio ranging from 2.7 times to 3.1 times and a sales/working capital turnover ratio (revenus/working capital) ranging from 3.4 times to 3.6 times during the period. The company's quick ratio has strengthened each year since 19X0, from 1.3 times to 2.0 times as the company reduced inventory levels and increased cash over the last several years.

Elcon was initially purchased with borrowed funds. Since paying off the acquisition debt, the company's capital needs have primarily been financed with internally generated funds, as indicated in Table 6-3 by the company's low ratios of total debt/net worth total interest-bearing debt/net worth. Long-term debt reached $2.021 million as of November 30, 19X9 as the company borrowed funds to help finance the plant's modernization and expansion. In 19X0, construction in progress (a new production line and new machinery and equipment) was funded primarily with operating cash flow and the use of short-term financing ($2.004 million in notes payable as of November 30) as the company paid down long-term debt. Long-term debt and current notes payable both declined in 19X1 to $0.950 million and $1.478 million, respectively. As of November 30, 19X2, long-term debt increased to a high of $2.034 million, while current notes payable increased to $1.691 million. Since that time, long-term debt has declined each year, to a level of $1.225 million as of February 28, 19X4.

Table 6-2 shows the results of operations for the five fiscal years ended November 30, 19X9, through 19X3, for the three months ended

February 28, 19X4, and for the projected fiscal year ended November 30, 19X4. As indicated in Table 6-2, revenues fluctuated from a low of $76.581 million in fiscal 19X9 to a peak of $92.231 million in fiscal 19X1. Increased revenues from 19X9 to 19X1 reflected the success of new factory automation product lines introduced in 19X8. Sales of these factory automation connector products continued to grow through the valuation date; however, the sales volume and prices of computer-related connectors began to decline in 19X1 due to the general recession and a resulting decline in shipments by the company's customer base in the computer industry. As a result, the company's revenue declined in fiscal 19X2 to $89.609 million and declined still further in fiscal 19X3, to $87.413 million. Volume began to pick up late in fiscal 19X3, and sales have been strong in early fiscal 19X4. Annualized first-quarter sales indicate revenues in excess of $100 million while management projects fiscal 19X4 sales of $106.375 million. This increase reflects an expected price recovery as well as sales generated from recently introduced products.

[d] Gross Profits

Gross profits and gross profit margins have fluctuated with sales. As shown in Table 6-3, the company's gross profit/sales ratio was 38.4% in fiscal 19X9, but declined to 33.6% in fiscal 19X0, owing to the high cost of materials and the high labor costs related to implementing new machinery and equipment. As a result, gross profits declined slightly despite increased revenues. In fiscal 19X1, the margin improved with improved purchasing and more efficient production. Gross profits increased accordingly, to a high of $32.972 million, as shown in Table 6-2. As sales dropped in 19X2, the margins also dropped with reduced prices, resulting in a decline in gross profits to $30.233 million. Despite declining revenues in 19X3, gross profits increased to $31.425 million, reflecting improved production efficiency and a cost reduction program that included a reduction in the labor force. During 19X4, continued cost controls and continued improvement of the company's state-of-the-art production facilities will result in continued improvement in the gross profit margin. As a result, gross profits are anticipated to reach $41.876 million in fiscal 19X4.

[e] Operating Income

Operating income has fluctuated, as shown in Table 6-2, from a high of $11.345 million in fiscal 19X9 to a low of $0.454 million in fiscal 19X2. Operating income reached $3.550 million in fiscal 19X3 and is anticipated to reach $10.888 million in fiscal 19X4. Operating expenses grew each year through fiscal 19X2, reflecting the company's increased selling efforts, expansion of distribution channels, and continued emphasis on R&D. With revenues declining in fiscal 19X2, the company chose to cut its dividend and use borrowed funds rather than risking future growth by enhancing profitability via cost reductions. However, with continued declines in revenues in fiscal 19X3, it became apparent that the company's overhead was excessive, and so it embarked on a cost-reduction program. With its costs reduced, profitability is expected to improve in fiscal 19X4, with operating income reaching $10.888 million.

[f] Profitability

The company's fluctuating profitability is shown in Table 6-3. Income before taxes to sales, net worth, and total assets all peaked in fiscal 19X9 and declined to lows in fiscal 19X2. The profitability ratios all improved in fiscal 19X3 and are projected to improve still further in fiscal 19X4 although they are not expected to reach the levels recorded in fiscal 19X9. It should be noted that R&D expenses continued to rise as a percent of sales from a low of 3.3% in 19X0 to 5.6% in fiscal 19X3.

In summary, Elcon has exhibited steadily increasing assets, with fluctuating revenue levels and profitability. The company's financial condition has been strengthening since 19X2, with liquidity, leverage, profitability, and activity ratios all improving. Continued asset growth and continued high research and development expenses, despite declining revenues in 19X2 and 19X3, are an indication of management's commitment to long-term growth even at the expense of short-term profitability. As a result, Elcon has remained a low-cost producer in the industry while retaining high quality in its production. Further, Elcon's strong financial condition has allowed the company to finance its growth primarily with internally generated funds with the flexibility to use debt for capital needs during downturns.

[2] Projections

Historical operating performance serves as a meaningful guideline for determining the future earnings capacity of the enterprise. Financial projections are, however, an important part of any valuation analysis, regardless of previous performance because a prospective buyer of the securities will participate only in the company's future earnings and cash flow.

As discussed previously, Elcon's management expects revenues to reach $106.375 million in fiscal 19X4 with operating income of $10.888 million (see Table 6-2). The recent turnaround in the industry, combined with Elcon's introduction of new products for the telecommunications and consumer-electronics industry, should result in increased revenues. With R&D budgeted to increase as a percent of sales over the next five years, the increased investment in new products and enhancements to current product lines are projected to contribute to an annual revenue growth rate of nearly 20% through 19$X$7.

In addition, during fiscal 19$X$4, management is directing significant resources to put in place a management infrastructure and distribution channel to handle future incremental increases in sales. As a result, selling and administrative expenses will increase substantially in 19$X$4 but only marginally in 19$X$5. In future years, selling general and administrative expenses are anticipated to grow with increasing revenues.

Capital expenditure needs are anticipated to increase to $6 million per year to increase capacity in the near term. It is expected that capital spending will decline to current levels of approximately $4 million in 19$X$7 and beyond. Working capital needs will also grow with revenues; however, it is anticipated that working capital turnover will increase as well. Finally, interest-bearing debt is expected to be paid off by 19$X$5.

In summary, Elcon is benefiting from (1) a strong turnaround in demand for its products and (2) the success of its new product introductions. It therefore anticipates strong growth in 19$X$4, which will continue into the near term. Based on the outlook in the industry in general and the company's financial results, these projections do not appear to be unreasonable. Further, management's long-term planning during difficult times bode well for the future.

[3] Industry Comparison

A more thorough understanding of the financial characteristics of a company can come from comparing it to industry composite statistics. From this analysis, conclusions as to strengths and weaknesses relative to industry norms as well as a more thorough assessment of risk can be made.

In Table 6-5, key financial ratios and statistics for Elcon are compared with those of companies within the same general industry classification of "manufacturers—electronic components and accessories."[2]

From this table, it can be seen that Elcon is slightly larger in terms of revenues and slightly smaller in terms of assets than the composite RMA companies. Elcon has stronger quick ratios and similar current ratios and sales/working capital turnover ratios. Elcon's low ratios of liabilities to net worth indicate a strong leverage position for Elcon. Elcon's profitability ratios are similar, and its inventory turnover, accounts receivable turnover, and asset turnover are stronger.

Based on these statistics, Elcon appears to have a stronger finan-

---

[2] Robert Morris Associates, *Annual Statement Studies* (1983 & 1984).

TABLE 6-5
ELCON COMPANY
PUBLIC COMPANIES' COMPARATIVE FINANCIAL ANALYSIS

Statistics and Ratios	Elcon	Elcon	RMA*	Elcon	RMA*	Subject Comparability
	Projected 11/30/X4	11/30/X3	19X5–19X4	11/30/X2	19X2–19X3	
			Fiscal Year Ended			
Size ($ millions)						
Revenue (RMA mean)	$106,375	$87,413	$80,390	$89,609	$84,701	Slightly larger
Total assets (RMA mean)	$ 68,979	$63,154	$69,569	$63,035	$73,186	Slightly smaller
Liquidity ratio						
Quick ratio	2.0	2.0	1.3	1.6	1.4	Stronger
Current ratio	3.1	3.0	2.8	2.7	2.7	Similar
Working capital turnover ratio	3.6	3.4	3.1	3.6	3.2	Similar
Financial leverage ratios						
Total debt/net worth ratio	0.3	0.3	0.7	0.3	0.6	Stronger
Profitability ratios						
Gross profit/sales ratio	39.4%	36.0%	36.4%	33.7%	30.7%	Similar
Income before taxes to						
Sales ratio	11.2%	5.3%	9.1%	0.1%	7.3%	Similar
Net worth ratio	22.8%	10.0%	16.7%	0.1%	16.2%	Similar
Total assets ratio	17.2%	7.3%	9.0%	0.1%	9.9%	Similar
Activity ratios						
Inventory turnover ratio	4.5	4.3	2.6	3.6	3.3	Stronger
Accounts receivable turnover ratio	6.5	6.5	5.0	7.4	5.8	Stronger
Asset turnover ratio	1.5	1.4	1.1	1.5	1.2	Stronger

* Robert Morris Associates, *Annual Statement Studies* (1983 & 1984); asset size: $50 million–$100 million; industry classification: "manufacturers—electronic components and accessories"; SIC #3671 (72, 74, 76, 77); 1983—26 companies reporting; 1984—25 companies reporting.

cial condition than do the composite industry comparative companies. An investment in Elcon, therefore, appears to be less risky than an investment in any of the composite companies. In other words, an investor would place a higher value relative to return on Elcon.

¶ 6.7 Valuation Methodology Overview

With Elcon's operational background and financial results understood, the analysis can proceed to a determination of the value of the company. Several approaches to valuation should be considered and applied before a conclusion is drawn. The various limitations of each approach should also be considered so that the appropriate conclusion can be determined from the various indications of value yielded by the methodologies.

[1] Multiple of Earnings and Cash Flow

The value of closely held stock of an operating enterprise is usually expressed as a multiple of its earnings capacity. This approach, often referred to as "multiple of earnings," has application in a variety of business valuation problems and is based on the theory that the subject investment will yield a return sufficient to recover its initial cost and to justly compensate the investor for the inherent risks of ownership.

The multiple rate used is generally derived from the prices paid for stock of public companies with similar investment attributes. Consideration is, therefore, given to the informed investor and what he is willing to pay for the stock of public companies with similar investment attributes, adjusted for the specific circumstances of the subject company.

Another form of the multiple of earnings approach is the multiple of operating cash flow method. This approach is used primarily in instances where the operating assets of the business, and the resulting depreciation expenses, are large relative to total assets, total revenues, and net income. This approach tends to compensate for differences in the depreciation practices of companies, which could result in differing net income figures when the operating cash flow for each is more comparable.

Still another form of the multiple of earnings approach is the comparison of market price to earnings before interest and taxes (EBIT) or earnings before depreciation, interest, and taxes (EBDIT). The use of earnings or cash flow on a debt-free basis may be useful when comparing companies with substantially different levels of financial leverage. This approach reduces distortions in price/earnings or price/cash flow ratios that might be present due to the use of various degrees of debt in the company's capital structure. Further, the use of EBIT and EBDIT reduce distortions related to various tax structures.

[2] Capitalization of Dividends

Dividends paid (or dividend-paying capacity) is another factor to be considered in arriving at an opinion as to the fair market value of a company. In considering dividends, the most commonly accepted basis for comparison is what is known as the "yield rate," which is a percentage established by dividing the dividends paid by the value placed on the stock. The relationship between the dividends and the prices paid for the stock of comparable public companies serves as a guideline in establishing an appropriate yield rate to apply to the dividend-paying capacity of the subject company. This approach is sometimes referred to as the capitalization of dividends method.

[3] Market Price to Book Value

Still another approach, used when a business has a substantial investment in its tangible assets or when its tangible assets are highly liquid and its operating earnings are providing a reasonable return on investment, is to analyze market price to net book value. This approach should be carefully analyzed both from the standpoint of whether the net book value is reasonably close to the asset value and from the standpoint of the market price/net book value ratios of comparable public companies.

[4] Discounted Future Debt-Free Cash Flow

The discounted future debt-free cash flow approach is another method for determining the value of a business enterprise. The procedure is one of estimating the present worth of the estimated future debt-free cash flow to be generated from the business and theoretically available (though not necessarily paid) to the stockholders as dividends and debt holders as principal and interest. Provision is also made for the value of the enterprise at the termination of the forecast period. The resulting debt-free cash flow and terminal value, discounted at an appropriate risk rate, yields an indication of value for the total invested capital (including debt and equity) of the enterprise.

[5] Adjusted Book Value

An alternative approach can be developed by expressing the value as a function of the underlying assets. This technique, referred to as the asset approach, generally is applicable to businesses with substantial capital investments in tangible assets or for which the operating earnings are relatively insignificant as an indicator of investment value.

Obvious examples of such businesses include real estate or natural resource holding companies and mutual funds. In theory, the value of all tangible assets, less outstanding liabilities, provides an indication of the fair market value of ownership equity.

[6] Other Indices of Value

Use of recent acquisitions of similar companies is probably one of the best indicators of value, especially if there is information available pertaining to the basis of the sales price. Multiples of earnings, cash flow, and net book value are analyzed in conjunction with a risk assessment to arrive at indications of value for a controlling interest in a company. Unfortunately, it is usually difficult to find information regarding the sale of similar closely held companies.

Finally, indications of value can be derived from a study of prior sales of the company's stock or consideration of bona fide offers for the purchase of the company by outside interests. In considering actual prior sales made, it must be determined if the stock was traded in an arm's-length transaction and whether any restrictions were made in the transaction. Further, isolated sales or shares traded in thin or erratic markets are often found to trade at prices that vary with fair market value. Sales of this nature should be carefully analyzed before being considered as indicators of value. Where there are frequent, significant sales of the stock between third parties, this approach can be given the most weight.

¶ 6.8 Valuation Analysis

The valuation of Elcon would not be complete without the comparison of its financial performance with other comparable companies. The selection of those companies and a description of the market comparison approaches available to the analyst are discussed next.

[1] Selection of Comparative Public Companies

Several of the previously discussed valuation methodologies rely on the prices of publicly traded stocks in comparison with various benchmarks, such as earnings, cash flow, net book value, and dividends. The indicated ratios, or multiples, for the public companies serve as a guide in selecting appropriate multiples for the subject company. Therefore, it is advantageous to obtain a representative list of publicly traded companies that are similar to the company being valued in those respects carrying the greatest weight with the investing public. Companies may be considered to be similar from an investment standpoint even when they are engaged in a rather broad variety of operations. The selected public companies should offer financial and economic similarity in the areas of major importance to the investing public and offer a similar degree of investment risk and growth potential.

The search for such companies includes reviewing various published and on-line research information sources containing pertinent financial and operating information on actively traded public companies. Sources of information include *Moody's Industrial Manual, Standard & Poor's Corporate Records, Value Line Investment Survey,* and various on-line databases, such as Dow Jones News Retrieval, Dialog-Information Services, and Compustat. In establishing the parameters to be used in selecting comparative companies for Elcon, four basic criteria have to be met:

1. The company must be engaged in developing and manufacturing electronic components, primarily electronic connectors for computers, data processing equipment, business machines, and other electronic devices;
2. The common stock must be outstanding in the hands of the public;
3. The trading market of the company must be relatively active in order to obtain true investor sentiment; and
4. The company must make its financial information public.

After reviewing the companies in the same general industry as Elcon, six were selected for comparison based on their products, customers, and operating characteristics: (1) Alpha, (2) Beta, (3) Gamma, (4) Delta, (5) Sigma, and (6) Theta.

[2] Comparison of Elcon With Comparative Public Companies

An analysis of the size, financial condition, and operating performance of Elcon with the comparative public companies is shown in Table 6-6. It was found that Elcon exhibits the following characteristics when compared with these companies:

1. **Size.** Elcon is generally smaller in terms of revenues, total assets, and net worth.
2. **Liquidity.** Elcon has somewhat higher quick and current ratios and is similar in terms of its working capital turnover.
3. **Leverage.** Elcon is somewhat stronger in terms of leverage.
4. **Profitability.** Elcon is slightly weaker in terms of profitability.
5. **Activity.** Elcon turns inventories, accounts receivable, and assets faster.
6. **Growth.** Elcon is similar in terms of growth.

In addition, more industry-specific data were examined. It was found that Elcon's R&D costs as a percentage of its revenues were

[Text continues on p. 6-26]

TABLE 6-6
ELCON COMPANY
PUBLIC COMPANIES' COMPARATIVE FINANCIAL ANALYSIS

Statistics and Ratios	Alpha	Beta	Gamma	Delta	Sigma	Theta	Range	Elcon	Elcon	Subject Comparability
	12/31/X4	10/31/X4	12/31/X4	12/31/X4	12/31/X4	12/31/X4		11/30/X4	11/30/X3	
			Fiscal Year Ended							
Size (millions)										
Revenues	$759.7	$201.7	$1,670.5	$603.4	$64.9	$1,057.0	$64.9 – 1,670.5	$106.4	$87.4	Smaller
Total assets	$660.5	$172.0	$1,594.2	$462.3	$46.9	$804.8	$46.9 – 1,594.2	$69.0	$63.2	Smaller
Net worth	$333.5	$95.0	$877.5	$322.2	$40.3	$478.7	$40.3 – 877.5	$54.4	$48.7	Smaller
Liquidity ratios										
Quick ratio	1.1	1.7	1.7	1.4	3.2	1.3	1.1 – 3.2	2.0	2.0	Higher
Current ratio	2.2	2.9	2.5	3.2	5.6	2.2	2.2 – 5.6	3.1	3.0	Higher
Working capital turnover ratio	3.3	10.5	3.3	2.5	2.3	5.2	2.3 – 10.5	3.6	3.4	Similar
Leverage ratios										
Total debt/net worth ratio	1.0	0.8	0.8	0.4	0.2	0.7	0.2 – 1.0	0.3	0.3	Lower
Total interest-bearing debt/net worth ratio	0.5	0.3	0.5	0.2	0.0	0.1	0.0 – 0.5	0.0	0.0	Lower

TABLE 6-6
ELCON COMPANY
PUBLIC COMPANIES' COMPARATIVE FINANCIAL ANALYSIS (continued)

Statistics and Ratios	Alpha	Beta	Gamma	Delta	Sigma	Theta	Range	Elcon	Elcon	Subject Comparability
	12/31/X4	10/31/X4	12/31/X4	12/31/X4	12/31/X4	12/31/X4		11/30/X4	11/30/X3	
			Fiscal Year Ended							
Profitability ratios										
Gross profit margin/sales ratio	21.7%	36.8%	37.0%	42.5%	56.2%	29.6%	12.7 – 56.2%	39.4%	36.0%	Similar
Income before taxes/sales ratio	3.5%	6.7%	7.9%	13.5%	17.1%	16.0%	3.5 – 17.1%	11.2%	5.3%	Similar
Net worth ratio	7.9%	14.2%	15.0%	25.2%	27.5%	35.4%	7.9 – 35.4%	22.8%	10.0%	Similar
Total assets ratio	4.0%	7.8%	8.2%	17.6%	23.7%	21.1%	4.0 – 23.7%	17.2%	7.3%	Similar
Activity ratios										
Inventory turnover ratio	3.0	2.6	3.9	1.8	1.9	4.9	1.8 – 4.9	4.5	4.3	Faster
Average accounts receivable turnover ratio	5.1	4.2	4.5	5.1	9.3	7.0	4.2 – 9.3	6.5	6.5	Faster
Asset turnover ratio	1.2	1.2	1.0	1.3	1.4	1.3	1.0 – 1.4	1.5	1.4	Faster
Growth statistics										
Annual revenue growth	(3.3%)	(9.4%)	(8.3%)	(2.0%)	10.0%	11.2%	(9.4) – 11.2%	21.7%	(2.5%)	Similar
Growth index*	1.2	1.0	0.9	1.5	1.7	1.5	0.9 – 1.7	1.2	1.1	Similar

*Most recent year's revenue divided by revenues years prior.

[*Text continues from p. 6-23*]

slightly below the mean of the industry. This implies less research and development effort and less product development. On the other hand, it was found that Elcon had been more stable in its research and development efforts, keeping them at high levels in declining years while others had cut back. Elcon thus appeared to have historically put more effort into its product development. Other factors compared included the depth of management, the customer base, and growth expectation in markets served. This analysis indicated that Elcon was relatively thin in management, with little backup for key management responsibilities. Further, Elcon appeared to be more dependent upon fewer customers, leaving it more exposed to losses of key customers. On the other hand, Elcon was serving higher growth markets.

[3] Market Comparison Approaches

By using public sources of statistical and financial data, the analyst was able to develop price/earnings ratios for each of the comparable public companies.

[a] Multiple of Earnings-Price/Earnings Approach

In its simplest form, this ratio is computed by dividing the price paid for the stock as of the appraisal date or an average trading price over a reasonable time period just prior to the valuation date by the net earnings for the latest fiscal year preceding the valuation date. The result is known as the current price/earnings ratio. The use of this approach can be expanded to include latest twelve months' earnings, average earnings, or other refinements dictated by the particular circumstances in computing price/earnings ratios.

In the Elcon case, the average prices of the public companies over the twenty trading days just prior to the valuation date were divided by their five-year average earnings to determine their price/earnings ratios. The industry's cyclicity made a five-year/average earnings level more indicative of representative earnings than would earnings in any one year.

The price/earnings ratios determined for the selected comparative public companies are shown along with other multiples in Table 6-7.

The selection of an appropriate price/earnings ratio requires an in-depth analysis of the subject company in comparison with the comparable public companies. In summary, based on the previously discussed comparison, Elcon appears to generally reflect a slightly stronger financial condition than the comparative public companies based on its stronger liquidity, leverage, activity ratios, and similar profitability ratios. Furthermore, Elcon is anticipating strong growth

TABLE 6-7
CAPITALIZATION RATIOS OF COMPARATIVE PUBLIC COMPANIES

	Ratios			
	Price/Earnings	Price/Cash-Flow	Price/EBIT	Price/EBDIT
Alpha	15.6	11.5	12.0	9.3
Beta	18.9	15.0	15.0	12.2
Gamma	13.5	8.6	10.6	8.2
Delta	16.0	10.1	13.1	9.2
Sigma	11.2	7.6	8.7	7.2
Theta	12.6	8.6	9.6	8.1
Range	11.2–18.9	7.6–15.0	8.7–15.0	7.2–12.2
Median	14.6	9.4	11.3	8.7
	Price/Net Book Value Ratio	% Dividend Yield		
Alpha	1.3	0.6%		
Beta	1.4	0.5%		
Gamma	1.0	1.6%		
Delta	1.2	1.0%		
Sigma	1.4	1.2%		
Theta	1.0	0.8%		
Range	1.0–1.4	0.5–1.6%		
Median	1.2	0.9%		

in the future, with weak markets turning around and new products being introduced. While this is also true for the comparables, Elcon is expected to benefit more because of the markets it serves relative to the markets served by the comparables. The fastest-growing markets are the computer and industrial automation markets, where Elcon has a strong reputation for quality and service. While the public companies also serve these markets, they are more dependent upon other, slower-growing markets, such as consumer, telecommunications, and others. Further, despite recent declines in sales and cash flow, Elcon has maintained its assets through capital investments and its level of research and development activity, which was not the case for all of the public comparables. Still further, an analysis of Elcon's depreciation expenses relative to the depreciation expenses of the comparables indicates that

Elcon has a higher degree of noncash expenses compared to net income. This "high quality" of earnings should be considered in the analysis.

On the other hand, Elcon is generally smaller than the comparative public companies and is highly dependent on two key customers. The customer base of the public companies is larger and more diverse, implying a higher degree of risk for Elcon relative to the public companies. Also, Elcon is managed by a relatively thin management team. In general, the public companies exhibit more management depth, again implying a greater degree of risk for an investment in Elcon relative to the public companies.

Accordingly, Elcon appears to represent a slightly greater investment risk but with a higher quality of earnings. Based on these and other considerations, a price/earnings multiple slightly above the median or 15.0 times representative earnings appears reasonable for Elcon as of the valuation date.

An essential ingredient of the multiple of earnings–price/earnings approach is the appropriate level of earnings to multiply. The earnings level to capitalize should be the expected earnings level of the subject company as of the valuation date and is determined primarily by an analysis of past, present, and projected earnings of the company. In other words, the representative earnings level of a company that has shown rapid and dramatic growth or decline in revenues and profits over several years might be the company's current and projected earnings. However, the representative earnings level of a company that has experienced fluctuating profitability over the last few years might be arrived at through an averaging or weighted average. In any event, the analyst will need to look closely at the individual circumstances of the company being appraised in order to determine the earnings level to multiply.

In the case of Elcon, the company as well as its competitors have experienced fluctuating revenues and earnings over the last five years. The company anticipates increasing revenues and profits in the future, but this growth will depend on a stabilization in its industry and the success of new product lines. Therefore, a representative level of earnings to multiply was selected based on a five-year average of actual $19X0$ through projected $19X4$ results.

Earnings were adjusted for nonrecurring and extraordinary items, including a $101,000 loss in $19X1$ and a $436,000 loss in $19X2$ on disposal of assets. During $19X1$ and $19X2$, Elcon disposed of land that it had set aside for a new facility that never materialized. The losses did not occur in the normal course of doing business and will not recur.

A representative level of earnings of $3.5 million was selected as shown in Table 6-8.

TABLE 6-8
COMPUTATION OF EARNINGS LEVEL TO CAPITALIZE

Fiscal Year	Net Income		Plus: Nonrecurring Expenses		Adjusted Net Income
Planned 19X4	$6,325,000	+	$ -0-	=	$6,325,000
19X3	2,450,000	+	-0-	=	2,450,000
19X2	126,000	+	349,000*	=	475,000
19X1	3,800,000	+	81,000*	=	3,881,000
19X0	4,241,000	+	-0-	=	4,241,00
5-year average = $3.500 million (rounded)					

*Assumes 20% marginal tax rate on land sales.

In summary, the multiple of earnings–price/earnings approach involves developing a representative expected earnings level and multiplying the earnings level by a reasonable multiple, which takes into account a risk-adjusted return required by an investor based on the risk factors associated with the company being valued. Applying the selected price/earnings ratio of 15.0 to the representative earnings level of $3.5 million yields an indication of value as follows:

Price/Earnings Ratio		Representative Earnings		Indicated Value
15.0	×	$3,500,000	=	$52,500,000

[b] Multiple of Cash Flow-Price/Cash Flow Approach

Through a similar analysis, indications of value are developed by using other market comparison approaches. In the case of the multiple of cash flow or price/cash flow method, operating cash flow (net income) plus depreciation, is used in place of earnings, and multiples are based on price/cash flow ratios of the comparative public companies.

The price/cash flow ratios for the comparative public companies are presented in Table 6-7 and indicate a range of ratios from 7.6 times to 15.0 times cash flow, with a median of 9.4. Based on the same analysis for the selection of a price/earnings ratio, a price/cash flow ratio was selected for Elcon. However, it should be noted that the selected price/earnings ratio considered the company's quality of earnings due to high noncash expenses, which is not a consideration when selecting a price/cash flow multiple. A price/cash flow ratio, therefore, slightly below the median, or 9.0 times, appears reasonable for Elcon as of the valuation date.

A representative level of cash flow to multiply is determined by adding the five-year average of depreciation of $2.85 million (rounded) to the previously determined representative earnings level as follows:

Representative earnings	$3,500,000
Plus: 5-year average depreciation	2,850,000
Representative cash flow	$6,350,000

Applying the selected price/cash flow ratio of 9.0 times to the representative cash flow level of $6.35 million yields the following indication of value:

Price/Cash Flow Ratio		Representative Cash Flow		Indicated Value
9.0	×	$6,350,000	=	$57,150,000

[c] Price/EBIT and Price/EBDIT Approaches

Price/EBIT and price/EBDIT multiples were also computed for the public companies by dividing the mean stock price, adjusted for a premium for control, plus the value of interest-bearing debt by the five-year average EBIT and EBDIT levels, respectively. The public companies' equity values were adjusted to reflect the control premium because total invested capital value (debt plus equity value) is expressed on an enterprise or controlling interest basis. The computed ratios are also presented in Table 6-7 and indicated a price/EBIT range of 8.7 to 15.0 times EBIT with a median of 11.3 times, and a price/EBDIT range of 7.2 to 12.2 times EBDIT, with a median of 8.7 times. Based on all the evidence analyzed, a price/EBIT ratio of 11.5 times and a price/EBDIT ratio of 8.5 times appear reasonable for Elcon.

Applying the selected multiples to the five-year average adjusted EBIT level of $6.4 million and the five-year average EBDIT level of $9.25 million yields indications of value of total invested capital. Therefore, the value of debt capital must be subtracted from the indicated value of total invested capital to determine the indicated value of the company's equity. Further, because the multiples computed for the public comparatives were computed with a premium for control, the indicated values will be on a controlling interest level of value. Value indications using the price/EBIT and price/EBDIT approaches were determined, as shown in Table 6-9.

TABLE 6-9
INDICATIONS OF VALUE USING THE
PRICE/EBIT AND PRICE/EBDIT RATIOS

	Price/EBIT	Price/EBDIT
Representative EBIT or EBDIT	$ 6,400,000	$ 9,250,000
Capitalization rates	11.5	8.5
Total invested capital	$73,600,000	$78,625,000
Less: Debt	(1,225,000)	(1,225,000)
Enterprise value of equity	$72,375,000	$77,400,000

[d] Capitalization of Dividends and Price/Net Book Value Approaches

The capitalization of dividends and price/net book value methods follow similar principles. In the capitalization of dividends method, dividends paid by the public companies are compared to their prices to determine dividend yield rates. In the case of Elcon, dividend yield rates were determined by dividing five-year average dividends by current stock prices in order to account for cyclicity in the industry. These ratios, shown in Table 6-7, range from 0.5% to 1.6% for the selected comparative public companies, with a median of 0.9%.

Based on all the evidence analyzed, a dividend yield rate of 1.0% appears reasonable for Elcon. Applying this yield rate to Elcon's five-year average dividend of $600,000 yields an indication of value as follows:

Five-Year Average Dividend	Dividend Yield	Indicated Value
$600,000	÷ 0.01	= $60,000,000

Price/net book value ratios for the comparative public companies are also shown in Table 6-7. Once again, an appropriate multiple to be applied to Elcon's net book value is selected based on a comparison with the similar publicly traded companies. Price/net book value ratios for the public companies ranged from 1.0 to 1.4, with a median of 1.2. Based on all the evidence analyzed, a price/net book value ratio of 1.1 appears reasonable as of the valuation date, to apply to the company's reported net book value of $49.944 million. Applying this approach yields an indication of value as follows:

Net Book Value as of 2/28/X4		Price/Net Book Value Ratio		Indicated Value
$49,944,000	×	1.1	=	$54,938,000

[4] Discounted Future Cash Flows

Future debt-free cash flows, theoretically available to stockholders as dividends and debt holders as interest and principal, consist of estimated operating debt-free cash flow (debt-free net income plus depreciation) less capital expenditures and increases in working capital requirements. The sum of all discounted net debt-free cash flows, including the liquidation or terminal value, yields an indication of value for total invested capital in the company. Another form of discounted cash flow is to determine net free cash flow available only to equity holders, in which case provisions would have to be made for interest and principal payments on debt.

Projections were discussed previously, and projected earnings and cash flow are shown in Table 6-4. Discount rates used to calculate the present values of future net cash flows are based on the overall risks inherent in realizing the net cash flow stream. The appropriate discount rate for debt-free cash flows is the weighted average cost of capital (WACC). The WACC is determined by weighting the return demanded by equity holders (cost of equity, or K_e) and the return demanded by debt holders (interest rate) using the following formula:

$$\text{WACC} = \frac{E}{E+D}(K_e) + \frac{D}{E+D}(i)(1-t)$$

where

E = value of equity
D = value of debt
K_e = cost of equity
i = interest rate on debt
t = tax rate

The Capital Asset Pricing Model (CAPM), which states that the return on any risky asset must be greater than the risk-free rate, is often used to calculate K_e. The formula used to calculate the company's cost of equity (K_e) is:

$$K_e = R_f + [(R_m - R_f) \times (B_l)]$$

where

R_f = risk-free rate of return
R_m = return on market portfolio
B_l = leveraged beta

The betas of the public companies are listed in Table 6-10. Betas are influenced by the capital structure or leverage of a company; therefore, it is best to determine a beta for all companies on a debt-free basis (unleveraged beta). An appropriate unleveraged beta is selected for the subject company and adjusted for the subject company's capital structure to determine a leveraged beta.

TABLE 6-10

LEVERAGED AND UNLEVERAGED BETAS OF PUBLIC COMPARABLES

	Leveraged beta	Unleveraged beta
Alpha	1.3	1.0
Beta	1.2	1.1
Gamma	1.4	1.1
Delta	0.9	0.8
Sigma	1.2	1.2
Theta	1.1	1.1
Median	1.2	1.1

Based on an analysis of the betas for the public companies, an unleveraged beta for Elcon of 1.1 appears reasonable and, because Elcon has so little debt, a leveraged beta of 1.1 is also appropriate for Elcon. Assuming the excess return on a market portfolio ($R_m - R_f$) of 8% and a risk-free rate of 9%, the CAPM yields a K_e for Elcon of approximately 18%, as follows:

$$K_e = 9\% + (8\% \times 1.1) = 17.8\%$$

Because Elcon has so little debt, K_e approximates WACC; therefore, 18% was used to calculate the present value of net-free cash flows.

To account for the enterprise or residual value at the end of 19X8, cash flows beyond 19X8 must be capitalized. The Gordon Growth

Model capitalizes future cash flows into perpetuity, assuming a steady growth rate. The formula used in the Gordon Growth Model is as follows:

$$\text{Terminal value} = \frac{CF_{TY} \times (1 + G)}{(K_e - G)}$$

where

CF_{TY} = cash flow in terminal year
G = growth rate assumption
K_c = cost of capital

An alternative method of determining terminal value is to multiply earnings and cash flow using a selected price/earnings and/or price/cash-flow ratio. However, these ratios reflect current market conditions and growth expectations that can be significantly different five years down the road.

Applying the Gordon Growth Model to Elcon's cash flow in 19X8 and assuming a 5% annual growth into perpetuity yields a terminal value of $117.115 million as follows:

$$\text{Terminal value in } 19X8 = \frac{(\$14,500,000 \times 1.05)}{(0.18 - 0.05)} = \underline{\$117,115,000}$$

The present value of future cash flows plus the present value of the company's terminal value in 19X8 are summarized in Table 6-11.

Based on the discounted net debt-free cash flow method, the indicated value for the company is $75,122,000.

[5] Adjusted Book Value

The adjusted book value approach expresses the value of the company as a function of its underlying tangible assets. The approach is simply a restatement of the company's balance sheet, substituting the fair market value of its assets and liabilities for its book value. Elcon's land, buildings, machinery, and equipment have been appraised assuming an arm's-length transaction. All other assets have been assumed to have a fair market value equal to book value because of their high liquidity. The value of all liabilities is assumed to be book value.

A summary of Elcon's adjusted balance sheet based on appraised values for its fixed assets is shown in Table 6-12.

The indicated value assumes an ongoing business enterprise and does not include liquidation costs or taxes on sales of assets that would

TABLE 6-11
PRESENT VALUE OF FUTURE CASH FLOWS AND
PRESENT VALUE OF COMPANY'S TERMINAL VALUE

Year	Projected Cash Flow	Present Value at 18% †
19X4*	$ 1,559,000	$ 1,374,000
19X5	5,015,000	3,744,000
19X6	7,700,000	4,872,000
19X7	12,300,000	6,596,000
19X8	14,500,000	6,589,000
Terminal value	117,115,000	53,222,000
Indicated value of total invested capital		$76,397,000
Less: Debt		(1,275,000)
Equity value		$75,122,000

*Final 9 months.
†Present value calculations are determined based on the assumption of receiving cash flows at year end.

occur if the business were to be liquidated. In addition, intangible assets and goodwill are not included or considered in the previous analysis.

[6] Other Indices of Value

Other indications can be drawn from recent acquisitions of similar companies, recent prior sales of the subject company's stock, and bona fide offers to purchase the company. Elcon has not had any bona fide offers to purchase the company but has had several inquiries from interested parties. Inquiries to purchase have always been politely refused, with discussions going no further than the initial inquiry. Transactions involving common stock included a recent purchase of stock from one of the original founders when he retired. The transaction was at book value, with little analysis involved.

In terms of recent acquisitions in the industry, a competitor that was formerly publicly traded was purchased for $100 million. Because this company was publicly traded, an analysis similar to a comparison of the publicly traded companies can be performed that will give an indication of value on a controlling interest basis (see the following

TABLE 6-12
ELCON COMPANY
SUMMARY OF ADJUSTED BALANCE SHEET

(As of 2/28/X4)
($000s omitted)

	Net Book Value	Estimated Fair Market Value
Current assets	$40,492	$40,492
Fixed assets	42,980	25,500
Less: Accumulated depreciation	(21,610)	-0-
Net fixed assets	$21,370	$25,500
Other assets	3,263	3,263
Total assets	$65,125	$69,255
Less: Total liabilities	15,181	15,181
Net value indication	$49,944	$54,074

table). Based on publicly available information, the following market multiples were calculated for the company purchased:

Price/earnings multiple (5-year average)	20.3
Price/cash-flow multiple (5-year average)	12.2
Price/net book value multiple	1.5
Dividend yield	-0-

In addition, a comparative analysis indicates that Elcon is smaller with a slightly stronger financial condition in terms of leverage, liquidity, profitability, and activity. Elcon has exhibited stronger growth and serves similar markets, but again Elcon has more dependence on a few customers and less management depth. Balancing all these factors, it appears that Elcon exhibits a similar investment risk. Applying the transaction multiples of Elcon's competitors yield indications of value on a controlling-interest basis for Elcon as follows:

Capitalization of earnings	$ 3,500,000	× 20.3 =	$71,050,000
Capitalization of cash flow	$ 6,350,000	× 12.2 =	$77,470,000
Price/net book value	$49,944,000	× 1.5 =	$74,916,000

¶ 6.9 Other Valuation Considerations

As noted earlier, the valuation analysis for Elcon is to be used for three different purposes: (1) estate planning, (2) establishing an ESOP, and (3) selling the company. For each of these purposes, a separate and distinct value may be determined dependent on the circumstances.

The size of the block itself is a relevant factor to be considered in valuation. If a specific block allows the purchaser to control a corporation, a higher value (relative to a minority position) is justified. Thus, transactions for a controlling interest in Elcon command a higher price than transactions involving minority interest. Examples of minority interests are the shares to be gifted and shares that will be distributed to ESOP participants.

Just as a controlling interest is worth more on a per-share basis than a minority interest, a marketable minority interest is worth more than a nonmarketable minority interest. This is a distinction that can be drawn between ESOP minority shares that have a put option and shares to be gifted that do not have access to a market for its stock (currently). Thus, there are three relative levels of fair market value, as shown in Figure 6-1.

In Figure 6-1, the three levels of value are for (1) a controlling interest, (2) a marketable minority interest, and (3) a nonmarketable minority interest. Notice the distinction between the discount for minority interest and the discount for lack of marketability; these two discounts are often erroneously considered by some to be synonymous rather than viewed as distinct considerations. When both of these discounts are applied, they are sequential. Further, it should be noted that, whereas a premium for control would be applied to bring a marketable minority-value indication to an enterprise level of value, a minority-interest discount represents the mathematical inverse and would be applied to an enterprise value indication in determining a level of value on a marketable minority-interest basis. The relative levels of value are discussed in more detail next.

FIGURE 6-1 Three Levels of Fair Market Value

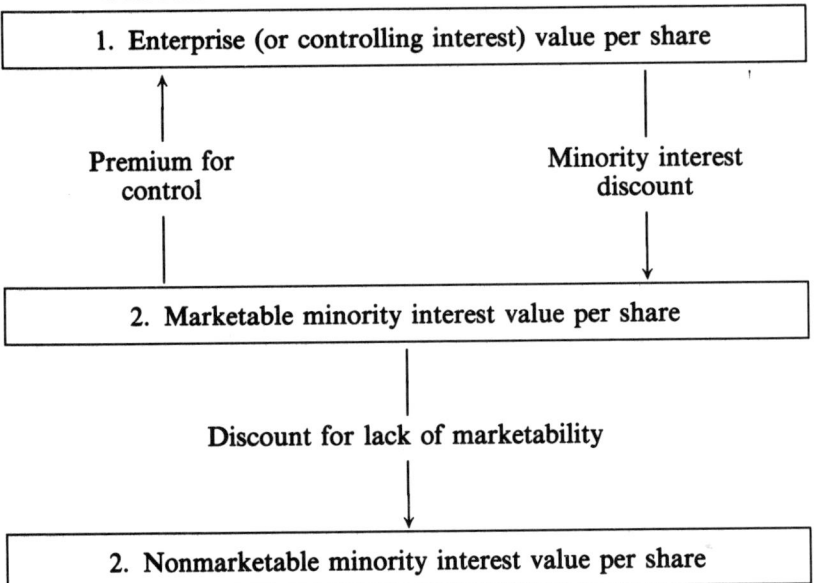

[1] Premium for Controlling Interest

Controlling (or majority) blocks of stock generally have the power to effect changes in the overall corporate structure and to influence corporate policies. Minority shareholders, of course, do not have this ability. Consequently, a controlling interest is considered to be worth more per share than a minority interest.

A measure of the difference in value between a controlling interest in a corporation and a minority interest can be found in public tender offerings where the tender offer, if successful, will give the acquirer a control position. The market price of the stock prior to the tender offer is related to the higher tender-offer price, resulting in the premium paid for the control position. A study by Houlihan, Lokey, Howard & Zukin, Inc. on recent tender-offer premiums indicates a median control premium of approximately 40%.[3] In the case of Elcon, a particularly good measure of a premium for control is the control premium paid for the competitor that was recently purchased. Based on preannouncement stock prices and the tender-offer price, a control premium of 36% was paid. For Elcon, a 35% premium for control is considered reasonable.

---

[3] Houlihan, Lokey, Howard & Zukin, Inc. Research Department, *HLHZ Control Premium Study* (1988).

[2] Discount for Minority Interest

In many valuation situations, the block of stock to be appraised represents minority ownership interests in the company. Minority blocks of stock, by themselves, generally do not have the power to effect change in the bylaws of a corporation, effect any significant corporate change, sellout, recapitalization or other conversion of assets, determine dividend policies and employee shareholder salaries, or effect any other significant change in corporate policy. A minority stockholder without a ready market for his stock would also find it difficult to dispose of his stock and realize a capital gain.

The fair market value of a marketable minority interest is the price at which the securities trade in a free and active market. In essence, the prices quoted in the *Wall Street Journal* for public companies whose shares trade on any of the various exchanges or in the over-the-counter market represent the per-share value of marketable minority interests. It therefore follows that a discount is inapplicable in instances where the value of the subject company minority position is predicated upon indices derived from prices of securities of publicly traded companies.

On the other hand, where indications of value are predicated upon control or complete ownership, a discount must be applied to provide indications of value for a minority or less-than-controlling interest. In short, discounts for the subject minority interest are appropriate for some methodologies but inappropriate for others.

The appropriate discount to apply to control indications of value for Elcon would be the mathematical inverse of the 35% control premium, or a discount of 26%.

[3] Discount for Lack of Marketability

Relative to the value applicable to a marketable minority interest, it is accepted valuation practice to discount the value of minority interests that are not traded in a free and active market. Minority interests in closely held companies lack the inherent liquidity of traded securities, and thus some discount is justified. While the magnitude of the discount depends upon the particular facts and circumstances, it will generally fall in the range of 10% to 50% of the value otherwise determined.

An analysis of historical court cases can provide an indication of the magnitude of discounts allowed by the courts in cases involving valuation of fractional interests. While in many cases analysts have tended to determine marketability discounts by using rules of thumb and an ultimate reliance on "professional judgment," recent cases suggest that these methods may not be acceptable. Empirical evidence measuring the differences in value between a marketable and nonmarketable security can often be found in private placement transactions involving publicly traded securities restricted under Rule 144 of the Securities and Exchange Act of 1934. Because of the marketability restrictions imposed under Rule 144, public data on discounts for lack of marketability in transactions involving restricted securities can provide information on appropriate discounts for other nonmarketable securities. Revenue Ruling 77-287,[4] issued by the Internal Revenue Service and based on the SEC Institutional Investor Study performed in 1971, provides guidance in determining discounts for lack of marketability.

For gifting purposes, where the stock has no ready market, a discount for lack of marketability would be appropriate. Based on an analysis of transactions of publicly traded securities restricted under Rule 144, a discount of 35% was considered appropriate for Elcon stock.

In the case of the closely held company that adopts an ESOP, employer securities and other assets may be accumulated in the ESOP for the benefit of the employees and for later distribution to the plan participants upon termination of employment, retirement, etc. When the ESOP is designed to offer the participants a "put" option to redeem their stock at fair market value after distribution, the plan will effectively create liquidity for the ESOP securities. Assuming prudent administration and planning, the ESOP or the company plays the counterpart of an organized securities exchange by providing liquidity for the employer securities. However, the existence of a put option is not enough to disregard the discount for lack of marketability. The analyst must carefully analyze future repurchase liabilities and the company's ability to honor such options. Thus, where put options exist, such as in ESOPs, and where liquidity exists to satisfy the option demands, it is inappropriate to discount for lack of marketability.

In the case of Elcon, an IRS-qualified ESOP would have such a put option and provide a market for ESOP shares. Further, contributions will be made to satisfy liquidity needs of satisfying the puts. Therefore, no discount for lack of marketability is considered appropriate for ESOP purposes.

¶ 6.10 Valuation Summary

All valuation methodologies can yield widely ranging indications of value. These indications of value must be adjusted and compared, as is discussed next, before a final valuation can be reached.

---

[4] 1977-2 C.B. 391.

[1] Reconciliation of Value Indications

The valuation methodologies outlined above yielded widely ranging indications of value, from as low as $52.550 million to a high of $77.400 million. Before trying to arrive at a conclusion, the indications of value must be adjusted and compared in terms of the relative level of fair market value they represent. Valuation methodologies using comparative public companies develop indications of value on an aggregate minority-interest basis. In order to provide an indication for a controlling interest in the company, these approaches should be adjusted to reflect a premium for control. Using a control premium of 35%, selected because it is based on an analysis of public tender offers and giving consideration to Elcon's specific circumstances, the market approaches provide indications of value on a marketable minority-interest basis and controlling-interest basis as shown in Table 6-13.

TABLE 6-13
INDICATIONS OF VALUE BASED ON MINORITY INTEREST
AND CONTROLLING INTEREST

	Aggregate Marketable Minority Interest	Control Premium	Controlling Interest
Capitalization of earnings	$52,500,000	1.35	$70,875,000
Capitalization of cash flow	$58,500,000	1.35	$78,925,000
Capitalization of dividends	$60,000,000	1.35	$81,000,000
Capitalization of price to net book value	$54,993,000	1.35	$74,240,000

Conversely, all other approaches discussed provide indications of value for the enterprise as a whole on a controlling interest basis. In order to bring enterprise value indications to marketable minority-interest levels of value, a minority-interest discount representing the mathematical inverse of the control premium should be applied to the indicated values. The appropriate discount, based on a 35% control premium, is 26%. Applying this discount to the various indications of value on a controlling interest basis yields indications of value as shown in Table 6-14.

Conclusions can now be drawn for both minority- and controlling

TABLE 6-14
INDICATIONS OF VALUE BASED ON MINORITY-INTEREST DISCOUNT AND CONTROLLING INTEREST

	Controlling Interest		26% Discount for Interest		Aggregate Marketable Minority Interest
Price/EBIT	$72,375,000	−	$18,818,000	=	$53,557,000
Price/EBDIT	$77,400,000	−	$20,124,000	=	$57,276,000
Discounted future debt-free cash flow	$75,492,000	−	$19,628,000	=	$55,864,000
Adjusted book value	$54,074,000	−	$14,059,000	=	$40,015,000
Competitor acquisition	$74,479,000	−	$19,365,000	=	$55,114,000

interest levels of value. There is no acceptable mathematical model available to use in weighting the conclusion of various approaches. The weights assigned to various conclusions are dependent on the judgment of the analyst.

In the case of Elcon, some of the indications are more pertinent than others. The market approaches appear to provide particularly relevant indications because of the high degree of similarity of the comparatives to Elcon. The discounted future cash flow analysis provides strong support for conclusions within the range indicated by the market approaches. The adjusted book value approach does not provide a good indication of value for ongoing profit-oriented business (because investors are more concerned with assets from a functional standpoint with respect to their adequacy to generate future benefits) than they are with individual asset values.

[2] Conclusions

As discussed previously, the valuation analysis for each of the three purposes will yield different conclusions due to the level of value to be considered. For gifting purposes, the fair market value is to be determined on a nonmarketable minority-interest basis; therefore, a 35% discount will be applied to the value otherwise determined on a marketable minority-interest basis. Because of the put option, the value determined for ESOP purposes will be on a marketable minority-interest basis based on a review of the marketable minority value indications. Based on the analysis outlined above, an aggregate fair market value conclusion for ESOP purposes of $55 million appears reasonable as of the valuation date. Applying the 35% discount for lack of marketability yields an aggregate value on a nonmarketable minority interest of $35.750 million for gift tax purposes as follows:

Aggregate marketable minority interest	$55,000,000
Less: 35% discount for lack of marketability	(19,250,000)
Aggregate nonmarketable minority interest	$35,750,000

The determination of the fair market value of the enterprise for the potential sale of the company is based on the analysis and indications of value on a controlling-interest basis. Based on a control premium of approximately 35%, and considering the value indications mentioned previously on a controlling-interest basis, a value of $75 million appears reasonable for Elcon as of the valuation date.

7

VALUATION OF FIXED-INCOME SECURITIES: BONDS AND PREFERRED STOCK

Marko A. Budgyk*

		Page
¶ 7.1	Bonds vs. Preferred Stock	7-2
¶ 7.2	Basic Valuation Principles	7-2
¶ 7.3	Issue-Specific Risk	7-3
	[1] Duration	7-3
	[2] Dividend and Interest Protection	7-5
	[3] Asset Protection	7-6
	[4] Corporate Protection	7-7
	[a] Callability	7-7
	[b] Exchangeability	7-7
¶ 7.4	Company-Specific Risk	7-8
	[1] Nature of Capital Structure	7-8
	[2] Variability of Operations	7-9
¶ 7.5	Measuring and Quantifying Risk	7-9
	[1] Measures of Risk	7-9
	[2] Issue-Specific Risk	7-10
	[a] Duration	7-10
	[b] Position in Capital Structure	7-11
	[c] Collateralization	7-12
	[3] Callability	7-13
	[4] Company-Specific Risk	7-14
¶ 7.6	Summary	7-16

    The valuation of fixed-income securities differs from the valuation of common stock and yet shows certain similarities as well. The similarity occurs in that the value of *any* security can be broken down into the same basic components: a future income stream and the expected risk and growth of that income stream. The main difference arises in that bonds and preferred stock have predetermined, or contractually

---

* MARKO A. BUDGYK is a senior vice president of Houlihan, Lokey, Howard & Zukin, Inc., a valuation advisory and investment banking firm headquartered in Los Angeles, California. He is also the chief investment officer of the firm's investment management subsidiary, which specializes in high-yield bonds.

fixed, income streams as opposed to the uncertain, or contingent income stream of common stock. In addition, valuation of bonds and preferred stock must emphasize risk considerations because fixed-income securities do not generally participate in the growth of a firm.

¶ 7.1 Bonds vs. Preferred Stock

As fixed-income securities, bonds and preferred stock should be valued according to the same general valuation principles. However, it is important to take into account the somewhat subtle differences between them.

The first and most basic difference lies in their relative position in a company's capital structure. Bonds always have a senior claim to a firm's cash flows and assets. Preferred dividends cannot be paid until all interest obligations to bondholders have been satisfied. In a liquidation, no proceeds can be made available to preferred shareholders until all bondholders' claims have been paid. Different bonds issued by the same firm may have their own seniority structures, but no preferred shareholder is entitled to any returns until *every* bond obligation has been met. In conjunction with the explicit seniority of bonds in the firm's capital structure comes another right not accorded preferred shareholders: *the right to force bankruptcy.* Missed interest payments constitute a default; missed dividends merely accumulate as arrearages that must be paid before any dividends can be declared on common stock.

The other key difference between bonds and preferred stock lies in their different tax treatment. To the issuer, bond interest is tax deductible while preferred dividends must be paid out of net income. To the holder, preferred dividends are 80% tax excluded if the holder is a corporation.

¶ 7.2 Basic Valuation Principles

The process required to value fixed-income securities is simpler than the process required to value common stock. The cash flows attributable to fixed-income securities are both specific and predetermined. These cash flows consist of interim payments in the form of either interest or dividends and/or a series of terminal payments or redemptions. Bonds always have a maturity, the date of the last payment made to the holder; preferreds may pay dividends into perpetuity or may have a maturity.

Since the cash flows to fixed-income securities are known, valuation can be reduced to an assessment of risk, which is a measurement of uncertainty. The quantification of risk is expressed as a required yield that, when used to discount the contracted cash flows, will generate a fair market value.

The appropriate quantification of risk attributable to a specific security requires consideration of two distinct but somewhat interrelated sources. The first component, issue-specific risk, is the risk inherent in the actual security itself, as delineated in its complex set of rights, privileges, and limitations. Second is the risk associated with the overall credit quality of the issuing firm. This is referred to as company-specific risk.

¶ 7.3 Issue-Specific Risk

Issue-specific risk is, itself, comprised of a multitude of factors. These factors can be generally categorized as (1) duration, (2) dividend and interest protection, (3) asset protection, and (4) corporate protection.

[1] Duration

A key factor in determining the required yield of a fixed-income security is its duration (or holding period). A longer duration is typically associated with a higher required yield. Evidence of the relationship between yield and duration can be derived from the government bond market. It is almost always the case that required yields on ten-year bonds will exceed those on five-year bonds, which, in turn, will exceed those on one-year bills. (There have been brief periods when the reverse has been true. However, these periods are generally considered to be anomalies.)

Investors require lower yields on shorter-term obligations because a shift in interest rates will have less impact on fair market value of a short-term obligation than it will on the fair market value of a long-term obligation. To illustrate, consider the difference between a one-week obligation and a thirty-year bond. Even a dramatic change in interest rates will leave a one-week obligation virtually unaffected because the principal is scheduled to be paid to the holder in one week. In contrast, almost any movement in interest rates will have an impact on a thirty-year obligation because of the effect of compounding the required yield on cash flows into the distant future. In sum, it is the security's susceptibility or sensitivity to interest-rate changes that results in the direct relationship between required yield and duration.

To illustrate the relationship between duration and interest-rate sensitivity numerically, consider Table 7-1, which depicts the present value of $100 to be received at various points in the future. If interest rates (and the appropriate discount rates) rise from 10% to 20%, the change in value of a one-week obligation is minimal, less than 1%. By

TABLE 7-1
RELATIONSHIP BETWEEN DURATION AND INTEREST-RATE SENSITIVITY

Present Value of $100 to Be Received at Different Times in the Future

Time Until Payment of $100	10%	20%	Change in Value Resulting From Increase in Discount Rate
1 week	$99.82	$99.65	− 0.2%
1 year	90.91	83.33	− 8.3%
5 years	62.09	40.19	−35.3%
10 years	38.55	16.15	−58.1%
30 years	5.73	0.42	−92.7%

contrast, the change in value on a payment thirty years hence is staggering—92.7%!

The security's effective duration is a function of the actual schedule of interim and terminal payments, taking into account their sizes and timing. For example, a bond with one payment in twenty years and no interim payments has, by definition, a duration of twenty years. Interim interest payments as well as early redemptions through a sinking fund provision have the effect of reducing duration by shifting the timing of various cash flows into earlier years.

The impact of various payment structures can be seen in Table 7-2. Four alternatives are presented for comparison. In each case, the security's maturity is twenty years. D represents a zero-coupon bond, which is a promise of one payment at the security's maturity date with no interim interest. A zero-coupon bond, therefore, by definition, has a duration equal to its time to maturity and is, in this example, exactly twenty years. A and B are the most commonly found in the public market and consist of a combination of interim interest payments and retirements. A, without a sinking fund, is retired in one payment in twenty years; B, with a sinking fund, is retired in a series of payments prior to and including a final retirement payment in twenty years. The existence of a sinking fund entails the earlier payment of certain cash flows and, therefore, reduces B's effective duration relative to A.

Another variation that affects duration is the existence of an adjustable yield feature, as depicted by C. Adjustables typically link the security's yield to the level of interest rates prevailing in the government bond sector or to the prime rate. Yields are reset periodically from as frequently as every seven weeks with money market preferreds to annually. The readjustment of rates protects the holder from the

FIGURE 7-1

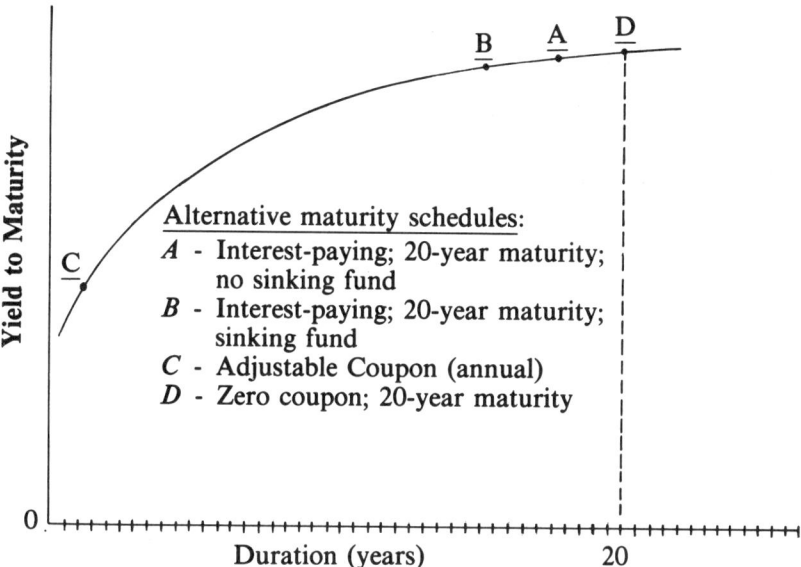

FIGURE 7-1 Impact of Alternative Maturity Schedules on Required Return

Alternative maturity schedules:
A - Interest-paying; 20-year maturity; no sinking fund
B - Interest-paying; 20-year maturity; sinking fund
C - Adjustable Coupon (annual)
D - Zero coupon; 20-year maturity

interest rate sensitivity associated with longer-term obligations. Therefore, the duration of an adjustable will approximate the time interval between coupon adjustments.

[2] Dividend and Interest Protection

As discussed previously, bonds are accorded an interest preference versus all classes of equity, and preferred equity has a dividend preference versus common equity. Missed bond interest payments typically constitute a default while missed preferred dividends do not. The feature that protects preferred shareholders is the cumulative dividends provision, which prevents the payment of any proceeds to common shareholders until all unpaid preferred dividends have been paid. Arrearages may or may not bear any interest, however; and their value can be watered down over time.

Noncumulative dividend preferreds are very rare in the public marketplace, but they are common among closely held concerns. The impact of this feature varies widely, depending upon the other rights and privileges of the preferred stock. In many instances, a noncumulative preferred may be virtually worthless, especially if the security has no mandatory redemption or other mechanism ensuring the payment of some form of return to shareholders. In other instances, a cumulative provision may be unnecessary, such as when the preferred class possesses effective voting control and, thus, can compel the declaration and payment of dividends.

An important variation on the preferences accorded bonds and preferred stock occurs when a fixed-income security is a zero coupon. Zeros consist of one payment—a redemption at the maturity date—and are valued at a discount to the redemption amount based on required yield and time to maturity. As no payments are made in the interim, a zero-coupon bond may effectively surrender its interest priority because junior securities may still receive cash payments. If the issuing firm were to be rendered insolvent prior to the zero coupon's maturity, the bond would maintain its preference in liquidation while having, to a certain extent, forgone the interim payments.

[3] Asset Protection

The hierarchy of a company's capital structure dictates the order in which proceeds from a liquidation of assets will be made available to different classes of security holders. Bondholders are always entitled to full restoration of their investments before any proceeds are made available to preferred or common shareholders. If any assets remain after satisfaction of the bondholders' claims, they must be dedicated toward the preferred shareholders' complete restitution before any payment can be made to common shareholders.

Practically speaking, in the event of a bankruptcy and subsequent liquidation, it is likely that bondholders will receive far less than their full entitlement and that equity holders will receive no return whatever. Thus the impact of asset preference is far more valuable to bondholders but may offer only a very limited measure of protection against loss.

An important variation in the value of asset preference occurs when a bond is collateralized, or secured. Common examples found in the marketplace are mortgages and equipment trusts. The benefits of securitization vary widely, depending on the assets used as collateral. The best assets for the purposes of securing a bond are those that are easily salable and have multitude of valuable applications to a wide variety of potential purchasers, assets such as airplanes or automobiles. Far less desirable are assets like factories or plants because their value depends greatly on their ability to generate profits. If a factory is unable to produce sufficient cash flow to meet bond interest obligations, its fair market value suffers and thus provides very little additional protection as collateral.

[4] Corporate Protection

While the holders of fixed-income securities often have a myriad of protective rights and privileges, certain features protect the corporate issuers. Two of these key provisions are callability and exchangeability.

[a] Callability

The purpose of a call provision is to give the issuing corporation financial flexibility if interest rates decline substantially following the issuance of the security. Once the security is called and redeemed, the issuer can then reissue new securities at lower rates and reduce interest or dividend "costs."

The vast majority of publicly traded fixed-income securities are callable by the issuing firm at prespecified prices and times. Typically, a newly issued security is not callable prior to a moratorium period, which averages five years. At the end of the moratorium, issuers can purchase the security from the holder at prices that vary from par to a slight premium (up to 10%) above par. It is also most often the case that the call premium declines toward par over a several-year period following the expiration of the moratorium.

The impact of a call provision is analogous to that of any call option. The (negative) value is related to the time until callable, the call price, and the security price. The volatility of the security is a function of its interest-rate sensitivity, which is, in turn, related to its duration. Other important considerations are (1) the issuing firm's financial ability to redeem the security and (2) the transaction costs if a reissuance is planned at lower yields.

[b] Exchangeability

The second provision that benefits the corporate issuer emerged fairly recently but is currently being used with great frequency. This feature, exchangeability, is also used as a mechanism to provide the issuer with enhanced financial flexibility and has been used on preferred stock issues.

An exchangeable preferred is one in which the issuer has the option of exchanging a preferred issue into a bond (typically subordinated) with very similar, if not identical, coupon and maturity. The advantage to the issuer is the ability to transform after-tax dividends into pretax interest. The timing of the exchange, from the corporation's perspective, should coincide with the firm's ability to take advantage of the tax deductibility of the interest expense.

As discussed previously, preferred dividends and bond interest get somewhat different tax treatments and therefore attract different holders. Preferreds, for example, are largely held by corporations that can benefit from the tax exclusion. The exchange of a preferred into a bond, therefore, will leave the holder no better off and quite possibly worse off on an after-tax return basis. Thus the granting of this privilege to an issuer must entail a diminution of value from the holder's point of view, and an exchangeable preferred must have a fair market value less than a nonexchangeable preferred if all other features are identical.

¶ 7.4 Company-Specific Risk

The other major source of risk as applicable to the valuation of fixed-income securities is the overall credit quality of the issuing firm (or the company-specific risk). This component of risk reflects the likelihood that the issuing firm can generate the cash flow needed to meet the mandatory dividend, interest, and redemption requirements. Company-specific risk as it pertains to fixed-income securities is, in turn, a function of the interplay of two distinct factors: (1) the nature of the firm's capital structure and (2) the variability of the company's operations.

[1] Nature of Capital Structure

The securities that make up a firm's capital structure (i.e., bonds, preferred, common) form the priority basis by which the cash flows produced by the firm's operations are allocated to investors. As discussed previously, no security can receive any cash returns until all senior securities' obligations have been satisfied. Thus, from the perspective of a bondholder, the greater the level of cash flows available to lower-priority equity holders, the greater the protection against any decline in operation performance. Similarly, the greater the level of cash flows available to common stockholders, the greater the protection enjoyed by preferred shareholders against an unexpected decline.

Another way of expressing the protection accorded fixed-income securities is to examine the aggregate values of each layer of financing. A firm comprising 90% debt and 10% equity has a very small cushion protecting its bondholders while a firm with 10% debt and 90% equity affords its bondholders a very comfortable safety margin. By the same logic, the preferred shareholder's absolute protection can be viewed as the common equity layer.

As important as the aggregate value of the common equity, from a preferred shareholder's standpoint, is the size of the firm's debt obligations. The greater the aggregate amount of debt relative to common equity, the smaller the relative protection enjoyed by preferred shareholders and the greater the vulnerability of preferred dividends to a decline in operations.

[2] Variability of Operations

If a firm's operations were so predictable that future cash flows could be forecast with complete certainty, there would be no need for cushion in the capital structure. Such a firm could consist of 100% debt and the debt would be riskless because the payments would be known and assured.

There is, of course, no such thing as a completely riskless operation. However, the spectrum of operating risk is quite wide, stretching from the very low risk in utilities to the extremely high risk in mining companies. A firm's operating risk is affected by factors such as its size, diversification, cost structure (variable versus fixed), and the nature of the industry in which it operates.

Since bondholders and preferred shareholders do not participate directly in a firm's growth, they are not rewarded by "positive surprises," such as unexpected improvements in operating results. Fixed-income securities are, however, affected by "negative surprises," such as declines in profitability. Therefore, from a bondholder's or preferred shareholder's perspective, certainty and stability are always preferable to uncertainty and variability in a firm's operations.

The variability of a firm's operations also has a direct impact on the degree of protection supplied a given capital structure. The greater the variability of operations, the greater the equity cushion needed to provide a given level of safety to bondholders and the greater the common-equity cushion needed to provide a given level of safety to preferred shareholders.

Since the risk involved in highly variable operations can be offset by a less risky capital structure, and vice versa, the combination of the two factors ultimately determines the degree of company-specific risk affecting a fixed-income security.

¶ 7.5 Measuring and Quantifying Risk

The valuation of fixed-income securities must take into account the measuring and quantifying of risk. There are several measurements of risk, including issue-specific and the callability feature, and company-specific risk, all of which are discussed next.

[1] Measures of Risk

In one sense, valuating fixed-income securities is simpler than valuating common stock. While there are many ways to value common stock, there is only one appropriate approach to the valuation of fixed-income securities—the discounted cash flow approach. Naturally, alternative methods are necessary when there is no likely stream of payments to discount—such as when the issuing company is in default or bankrupt.

Since cash flows are generally contractually fixed, valuation should focus on the appropriate risk-adjusted discount rate. The discount rate that equates the interim interest or dividends plus subsequent redemptions into a present value is referred to as the security's yield to maturity. *Current yield*, another commonly used measure, is defined as the annual interest or dividend payment divided by the value of the security. Current yield is a component of yield to maturity but ignores the impact of the capital gain (or loss) portion of total return. When the redemption price of a security exceeds its present value, yield to maturity is greater than current yield, and vice versa.

Yield to maturity is usually a far more relevant measure of risk than is current yield because it reflects total return. However, many preferred issues do not have a maturity or specified redemption and, therefore, do not have a yield to maturity. Current yield then becomes the appropriate indicator of risk and return.

Another important exception to consider occurs when bonds or preferred shares contain a call option or an early redemption option. This feature permits the issuer to redeem or call an issue earlier than the scheduled maturity date. In many cases, the call option may entail the payment of a slight premium to the holders of the security. The possibility of early redemption creates an alternative set of cash flows to discount. The associated risk measurement (or yield to call) assumes that the issue will be redeemed at the first possible call date. Yield to call typically becomes the relevant measure of risk when the likelihood of call is great—that is, when the issuing firm can reduce its interest expense by refinancing at lower rates.

[2] Issue-Specific Risk

Measuring issue-specific risk is usually the more difficult aspect of the valuation of a fixed-income security. The magnitude of impact upon yield varies widely and often depends upon a myriad of factors that are inherently difficult to measure with any degree of precision. As with any type of valuation, it is best to look for public market analogs in trying to assess how a particular feature either increases or decreases required yields.

[a] Duration

As discussed previously, the duration of a fixed-income security varies directly with its required yield—in general, the longer the duration, the greater the yield needed to compensate for increased interest-rate sensitivity. Fortunately, the government bond market and, to a lesser extent, the corporate bond market provide means of measuring the relationship between duration and yield. The government bond market is a better indicator because all issues are presumed to have the same degree of default risk (e.g., none), and yield differences can, therefore, be attributed solely to duration. The corporate bond market contains issues of various risks and features, and it may therefore be difficult, if not impossible, to separate the duration component of yield.

In general, the government bond yield corresponding to the duration of the issue being considered is an excellent starting point from which to calculate a required yield to maturity for a corporate bond. By definition, the corporate bond must have a yield in excess of the government issue, which has no default risk. The analysis should then focus on the yield premium required to compensate the holder of the corporate bond for the incremental risk assumed in holding a risky security.

The valuation of a preferred, however, is a bit more tricky because there exists no government preferred market, and the corporate preferred market is very small compared to the corporate bond market. Ideally, one would begin with the highest quality preferreds of various durations as a proxy for a risk-free preferred yield curve, with the analysis being focused on the additional yield needed to offset the risk of the subject company's preferred.

[b] Position in Capital Structure

The less senior the fixed-income security vis-à-vis other securities in a firm's capital structure, the greater the required yield. The magnitude of the increment in required yield needed to offset an inferior position, however, is again difficult to determine and based on a multitude of considerations. An issuer may have any combination of senior debt or subordinated debt that, in turn, may be secured or unsecured. Subordinated debt requires a higher yield than senior debt, and junior subordinated debt requires a higher yield than either subordinated or senior subordinated debt.

In the public marketplace, the exact yield spreads among all these instruments varies, taking into account the amount of claims at each layer of the company's capital structure. Another important consideration may be the extent to which certain assets of the issuer have been pledged as collateral.

Using the public marketplace as a guide, yield spreads vary widely between senior and subordinated issues of the same issuer. In some cases, especially among better overall credits, spreads may be 50 basis points or less while, in other cases, they may exceed 300 basis points.

According to ongoing research at Houlihan, Lokey, Howard & Zukin, Inc. (HLHZ), the yield spreads between senior and subordinated issues *average* 100 to 150 basis points when all other factors are constant. While this average is valuable as a starting point from which to form a frame of reference, it should be stressed that the individual circumstances of the issuer may lead to substantially different conclusions.

While it may seem intuitive that junior securities are entitled to higher yields than are senior securities, an important exception exists when comparing company preferred stock to bonds. Although preferred stock is junior to subordinated debt in a company's capital structure, the yield on preferred is not always nor should it always be greater than the yield on a company's debt security. The difference arises from the different tax treatments accorded preferred dividends and bond interest. Preferred dividends are 80% tax excluded to corporate holders, while debt interest is fully taxable (except, of course, to tax exempt entities). This advantageous tax treatment tends to lower the required pretax yield and offset the increase in required yield attributable to preferred stock's junior position in the capital structure.

Research at HLHZ has indicated that preferred yields are typically lower than debt yields of the same issuers of relatively strong credit standing. Among very good credits, the benefit of the tax preference outweighs the impact of capital structure because the probability of default is extremely low. However the converse is true for relatively weak credits because the priority of debt overwhelms the tax advantage of preferred stock dividends. Thus valuation of preferred stock requires much more than simply adding a risk premium to debt yields.

[c] Collateralization

In many instances, bonds may be secured by pledging collateral in case of default. Commonly found secured bonds include equipment trust certificates and mortgages. The impact upon risk of this attribute varies widely and is often difficult to quantify. The corporate bond market, however, can provide clues as to the impact of different types of collateral upon yield.

It is important to realize that the existence of collateral sets up an either-or situation: Either the company generates sufficient cash flow to service the debt, or the asset will be used to satisfy the obligation. The risk of the security should reflect the likelihood that both cash flow *and* asset value will be inadequate to satisfy debt obligation. If asset value varies inversely with cash-flow capability, then debt will be riskless because one or the other will satisfy the obligation. At the other extreme is the case where the underlying asset's value is directly correlated with the firm's earning capacity. In this instance, the collateral will not mitigate the risk of the debt because its value will diminish as its capacity to satisfy obligations diminishes.

Practically speaking, asset values tend to be closely, but not perfectly, related to cash-flow generation. Some assets, such as airplanes or other conveyances, are liquid, have a multitude of potential users, and thus have values somewhat independent of the earnings capability of the company operating them. Other assets, like plants and machinery, are highly illiquid, have a very limited number of potential users, and hence have values closely related to their cash-flow-generating capability.

Another important factor to consider in assessing the impact of collateral on a risk is the proportion of pledged versus nonpledged assets. In general, the greater the proportion of assets that have been pledged as collateral, the higher the yield that will be required on an unsecured debt.

While the impact of collateralization is difficult to quantify, some guidelines can be gleaned from the corporate bond market. In examining issues of secured and unsecured debt from the same issuer, yield spreads may range from 0 to 1,000 basis points or more. Commonly found secured debt issues such as mortgages, especially on utilities plants, have yields virtually identical to unsecured issues. At the other extreme are airline-equipment trust certificates, which often have yields 500 to 1,000 basis points lower than unsecured bonds of similar duration.

[3] Callability

The impact of callability on a bond or preferred stock price is more easily quantifiable than is its impact on some of the issue-specific features discussed previously. In general, call options detract value from a security because they are an option of the issuer designed to facilitate refinancing.

In the absence of a callability feature, a drop in interest rates will be accompanied by a drop in required returns on bonds and preferred stocks. This can only be accomplished by an increase in bond and preferred prices sufficient to reduce the security's yield to maturity. If a bond or preferred *does* contain a call option, the required increase in price may exceed the price of the call. If it does, the issuer has a financial incentive to redeem the security and explore refinancing at the new, lower rates.

If the required yield to maturity on a bond or preferred suggests a price in excess of the current call value, it is generally appropriate to assume that the issue will be redeemed. In this event, the cash flows prior to call plus the call price should be discounted at the risk-adjusted required yield (or yield to call) to arrive at a value for the security. The impact of the call, therefore, will be simply the difference in value if all cash flows to maturity are made minus the value implied by an early redemption.

[4] Company-Specific Risk

Arriving at an appropriate risk-adjusted discount rate for a preferred stock or bond is a process similar to the process used in selecting a market multiple for the valuation of common stock. In general, as with common stock, the ideal method of quantifying risk is to find publicly traded analogies to the company and security in question. Unfortunately, finding publicly traded "twins" is difficult.

Since the required yield of a fixed-income security is directly related to risk, the key valuation consideration is the *measurement* of risk. In general, risk can be measured in the same manner as it is measured in the valuation of common stock. The ratios used to measure size, liquidity, profitability, and leverage are equally valuable in determining the risk interest in a fixed-income security. Growth is not directly of importance to bonds or preferred—it may, in fact, be negative if it is accompanied by a high degree of uncertainty.

Determining required yield then becomes a process of calculating a series of risk measures for the subject company and comparing these measures to similarly calculated measures for a group of publicly traded companies whose bond or preferred yields are known. The subject company's appropriate bond yield can be estimated by determining its risk relative to the group of comparables and then setting a required return commensurate with the relative risk.

In selecting the comparable issues for comparison purposes, it is important to consider issues which, to the extent possible, have similar rights and privileges. A key feature to take into account is duration, either in the selection process itself or by calculating each security's yield premium above government bonds of comparable duration.

A *convertible bond* (or preferred) gives the holder the right to exchange the security for common shares of the issuer. Typically, the convertibility feature specifies a fixed number of common shares into which the bond or preferred can be converted. Therefore, if the price of the common shares increases, the value of the convertible will also increase.

Having elements of common stock appreciation as well as a priority fixed-income stream, a convertible security represents a hybrid of debt and equity. The value of a convertible can be broken into debt and equity components.

The *equity component* can also be referred to as the security's "convertible value" and is defined as the value of common stock that it is convertible into today. It is computed as the common share price multiplied by the number of shares into which the security is convertible. A convertible must be worth at least its convertible value because of the holder's right to convert and to realize this value immediately.

Convertibles are nearly always worth a premium above their convertible value. The premium arises because of the debt component of value, which can be referred to as "excess" dividends or interest. The term "excess" refers to the fact that in general, a convertible pays its holder a current return that exceeds the dividends that could be realized by conversion into common stock.

In essence, a convertible can be thought of as a package of common stock plus a series of dividends or interest payments greater than those paid on the common stock. The value of a convertible, therefore, is the sum of its convertible value plus the present value of excess dividends or interest.

Since a convertible's equity portion is known with certainty (assuming the value of the common stock is known), the key to valuating a convertible is determining the debt or excess-interest value. The factors that have an impact on the debt portion are (1) the size of the excess-payment stream, (2) the expected length of the stream, and (3) the riskiness of the payments.

The size of the excess dividends or interest is a function of three variables: (1) the payments on the convertible, (2) the dividends on the common, and (3) the expected growth in dividends on the common. Dividends or interest on the convertible are fixed throughout the life of the security—dividends on common are usually expected to grow over time. Thus the excess payments stream is typically expected to diminish and, in some cases, shrink to zero or even become negative. As long as the holder of a convertible can command greater current return through the preferred or bond, there is no economic incentive to convert voluntarily. If the dividends on the common grow sufficiently, the common may return a higher payment and encourage conversion.

The length of the excess payment stream will also be a function of the expected growth in common dividends and factors that have an impact on the size of the stream. An additional and important consideration is the existence of a call on the security. All publicly traded convertible securities are callable, usually under similar terms to the calls on nonconvertible securities. A call has an impact on the value of a convertible by shortening the expected length of the excess-payment stream. Once a convertible is called, the holder may either elect to convert or receive the call price. Practically speaking, firms call their convertible securities only when the holder has an incentive to convert. Issuers have an incentive to force conversion as soon as possible under any scenario in order to avoid, as much as possible, the payment of excess dividends or interest that, by their existence, detract value from common shareholders. Thus when a security's convertible value exceeds its call price, the issuing firm will generally respond by calling the security.

The third important factor in determining the debt portion of the value is the riskiness of the excess payments themselves. The appropriate discount rate for arriving at a present value should be the same one that would be used on nonconvertible debt and should be determined using the methodology and approaches applicable to a nonconvertible security.

In actually computing the excess payment value of a convertible security, it is usually impossible to know all the factors with perfect certainty. Common dividends are set at irregular intervals, being susceptible to increases or decreases over time. The timing of when a call is permitted is always known, but it cannot be precisely anticipated as to when the convertible value will increase to a sufficient level to *warrant* a call. These parameters can be estimated only by using the best data available, and the valuation will still involve some subjectivity.

¶ 7.6 Summary

The basic valuation principles for fixed-income securities are based, first, on an understanding of the differences and similarities of bonds and preferred stock. Once these are established, risk factors—issue-specific risk, company-specific risk, and risk measurement and quantification—must then be considered.

Risk is an important factor because fixed-income securities typically do not participate in the firm's growth. Valuation thus must take into account the subtle difference among general valuation principles between bonds and preferred stock, such as their corporate structure and their tax treatment. Measuring and quantifying risk by taking into account industry-specific risk (e.g., risk duration, capital structure position, collaterization, and callability) as well as company-specific risk, is the final step in the process of valuing fixed-income securities.

II

VALUATION FOR SPECIFIC PURPOSES

II
VALUATION FOR SPECIFIC PURPOSES

Part II Introduction II-3

ESOP Valuations... 8-1

Valuation Litigation 9-1

Valuation of Common Equity Securities When Asset Liquidation Is an Alternative 10-1

Valuation in Marital Dissolutions 11-1

Valuation of Start-ups, Initial Public Offerings, and Private Placements 12-1

Solvency Analysis in Leveraged Transactions 13-1

PART II INTRODUCTION

Financial Valuation: Businesses and Business Interests devotes its entire Part II to "Valuation for Specific Purposes." Part II includes six chapters, which provide realistic applications of the practice of valuation in specific market situations.

Chapter 8 on "ESOP Valuations" by Richard S. Braun considers the special aspects of both leveraged and nonleveraged ESOPs and their impact on value. Leveraged ESOPs in particular involve economic benefits to the sponsoring company as well as to other participants to the transaction; the valuation expert thus must be aware of both the regulatory and legal considerations for all parties. The chapter's focus is on equity allocation approaches. A natural transition is then made to the valuation topic of adequate consideration, including fair market value, premiums and marketability, and independence. The chapter closes with an analysis of the methods that the valuation expert can use to judge whether the transaction is fair to both the ESOP and other parties from a financial point of view. Special features of the chapter include four market examples, several tables, and an appendix on the Department of Labor regulations on adequate consideration.

Chapter 9 on "Valuation Litigation" by Charles F.G. Kuyk, Robert F. Howard, and Peter B. Frank analyzes the specific litigation issues in valuation. The chapter covers much legal ground, from statutory law to regulatory and administrative law to case law and finally to the rules of civil procedure and evidence. The valuation expert is taken through the litigation process, with succinct guidelines for the expert witness to follow. The expert witness is then introduced to the most common valuation case types, all of which are analyzed and supported by case history. The chapter closes with situations involving recovery of damages. Special features of the chapter include two appendixes, one of the Federal Rules of Evidence Article VII on opinions and expert testimony and another on a sample litigation retainer agreement.

Chapter 10 on "Valuation of Common Equity Securities When Asset Liquidation Is an Alternative" by Michael J. Bolotsky analyzes the specific mechanics of liquidation analysis from three perspectives: a determination of "combined highest and best use," a determination of gross liquidation proceeds, and the reduction of gross proceeds to net liquidation value. Examples of liquidation analysis—including liquidation of an entire entity and liquidation of a portion of the entity—are then applied. The chapter then moves on to the valuation expert's choice of a discount rate and evaluates both a low-risk and a high-risk scenario. The chapter closes with an analysis of contingent liquidation considerations, such as liquidation value of assets versus liquidation value of stock, intangible asset value, the value of minority interests, to name a few. Special features of the chapter include two tables, many formulas, expert calculations, and an appendix on the details of the liquidation value computations from the chapter tables.

Chapter 11 on "Valuation in Marital Dissolutions" by Jan C. Gabrielson takes a case law approach to the meaning of value—market value, investment value, and compulsion value—in the specific context of marital disolutions. Judicial attitudes towards the valuation methods and formulas used are analyzed, with a discussion focusing on how most methods are approved on appeal. Other factors that the valuation expert must take into account in marital dissolutions—buy-sell agreements, potential tax liabilities, tactical problems and concealed income, to name a few—are discussed and supported by case law. The chapter closes with discussions of the components of value (e.g., "hard assets," accounts receivable, goodwill, and loans to shareholders), the effect of separation on earnings and the apportionment of premarital and marital property, problems encountered while the marital dissolution is pending (especially where one or both spouses work in the business), and dealing with professional practices.

Chapter 12 on "Valuation of Start-ups, Initial Public Offerings, and Private Placements" by Roger C. Davisson focuses on the specific valuation of enterprises with limited operating histories. The chapter opens with a concise analysis of the similarities among start-ups, initial public offerings (IPOs), and private placements, including the common element of financing, the return on investment (ROI), and the ROI analysis. Then, the chapter makes equally concise distinctions among the three types of enterprises. The valuation of start-ups includes the analysis and application of such key determinants as required ROI, valuing what exists, and the expected upside. The valutaion of IPOs concentrates on valuation in theory and valuation in practice, including the use of comparables, projections, practical examples, the limitations of the price/earnings multiple, and after-market considerations. The valuation of private placements includes an analysis of such key considerations as required ROI, expenditures to date, the expected upside, the need for additional capital, and risk. The chapter closes with a realistic tracking of "performance versus promise" in these enterprises. Special features of the chapter include many market calculations and seven tables.

Chapter 13 on "Solvency Analysis in Leveraged Transactions" by Jeffrey R. Greene and Lori M. Price provides the legal theory in the specific case of fraudulent conveyances. The chapter takes into account recent court decisions on these conveyances. The valuation expert is then introduced to the components of a solvency analysis, starting with due diligence and moving on to the balance sheet test, cash flow test, and reasonable capital test. The chapter closes with the application of solvency analysis—including the three solvency tests just mentioned—to a case study of the leveraged buyout of a fictitious company, Bornwell Industries, Inc. Special features of the chapter include many market examples and calculations, four illustrative graphs, and ten tables.

8

ESOP VALUATIONS

RICHARD S. BRAUN*

		Page
¶ 8.1	What Is an ESOP?	8-2
¶ 8.2	Proposed Adequate Consideration Regulations	8-3
¶ 8.3	Types of ESOPs	8-3
	[1] Nonleveraged ESOPs	8-3
	[a] Stock Contributions	8-4
	[b] Cash Contributions	8-5
	[2] Leveraged ESOPs	8-6
	[a] Stock Purchases	8-6
	[b] Dilution Impact	8-7
	[c] Decline in Value	8-7
¶ 8.4	Quantification of ESOP Benefits	8-8
¶ 8.5	Multi-Investor Equity Allocation Issues	8-9
	[1] Equity Allocation Approaches	8-10
¶ 8.6	Adequate Consideration	8-11
	[1] Fair Market Value	8-11
	[2] Premiums and Marketability	8-12
	[3] Independence	8-13
¶ 8.7	Effective Date of Appraisal	8-14
¶ 8.8	Report Format and Content	8-14
¶ 8.9	Fairness	8-15
¶ 8.10	Conclusion	8-15
Appendix 8-1 DOL Proposed Regulation Relating to the Definition of Adequate Consideration		8-15

The valuation of stock for employee stock ownership plan (ESOP) purposes must consider many of the same factors which are discussed elsewhere in this book. The purpose of this chapter is to describe and discuss the special and sometimes unique aspects of ESOPs and their impact on value. In addition, there are regulatory and legal aspects

---

* RICHARD S. BRAUN is a managing director of Houlihan Lokey Howard & Zukin, Inc., a valuation advisory and investment banking firm headquartered in Los Angeles, California. He holds an M.B.A. from Harvard University, is a senior member of the American Society of Appraisers, and is currently chairman of the Business Valuation Committee of the ESOP Association. The author also has appeared as an expert witness and is a frequent speaker on ESOPs and on other valuation matters.

that the appraiser must consider when valuing shares for transactions involving ESOPs.

¶ 8.1 What Is an ESOP?

An *ESOP* is an employee benefit plan whose primary investment goal is to purchase and own the equity of the sponsoring company. In order to encourage the use of ESOPs, the federal government has instituted tax benefits for the sponsoring company, lenders, and owners who participate in ESOP transactions. As this chapter went to press, Congress was considering a number of proposals that may reduce or modify the economic benefits of an ESOP. Under existing law, however, the more significant benefits include the following:

1. *Contributions of stock or cash by the sponsoring company are deductible from pretax income, similar to other qualified employee benefit plans.* However, since an ESOP must invest primarily in employer securities, the contribution does not leave the company to fund a diversified portfolio of investments. Instead, the contribution reduces taxes but is retained by the company, thus enhancing the cash flow and value of the employer. From an economic point of view, this sheltering of cash flow from taxes is typically the most significant tax benefit available to an ESOP-sponsoring company.
2. *Fifty percent of the interest income received by qualified lenders on loans to an ESOP is excluded from the taxable income of the lender.* This results in a greater after-tax rate of return to the lender that encourages lenders to make such loans. In addition, lenders are usually willing to share some of this economic benefit with the borrower, resulting in a reduced rate of interest on an ESOP loan compared to conventional methods of financing.
3. *Dividends paid on ESOP-held securities may be deducted from pretax income if they are paid out to plan participants or are used to amortize ESOP debt incurred to buy such securities.* The ability to pay debt with ESOP dividends is especially significant because it may be used in lieu of or in addition to contributions, which are limited to 25 percent of covered payroll for the payment of principal. This feature may be used to shelter additional cash flow from taxes, may pay off ESOP indebtedness more quickly, and may have additional beneficial economic impacts on an ESOP transaction.
4. *If 30 percent of the equity in a nonpublicly traded company is sold to an ESOP, capital gains taxes may be postponed virtually indefinitely if the proceeds are reinvested on a timely basis in other qualified domestic securities.* This has proven to be a powerful economic incentive to the owners of closely held com-

panies who desire to diversify their portfolio of investments but do not want to incur taxes.

There are other economic benefits that participants in an ESOP transaction may receive, but these are the most significant and give an ESOP transaction a unique character with valuation implications.

¶ 8.2 Proposed Adequate Consideration Regulations

During May 1988, the Department of Labor (DOL) issued its long-anticipated proposed regulations on adequate consideration in ESOP transactions. In their final form, the DOL's adequate consideration regulations will have a significant influence over the use of leveraged ESOP transactions. A number of practitioners and organizations have suggested modifications or clarifications of the DOL's *proposed* regulations, and the precise content of the *final* regulations is not known as of the book's publication date.

It is likely, however, that many issues raised in the proposed regulations will be contained in the final regulations. Therefore, the proposed regulations in their entirety are included as Appendix 8-1 at the end of this chapter. In addition, many of the more significant aspects of the proposed regulations, such as independence, premiums, effective date of appraisal, and the definition of adequate consideration itself will be covered in this chapter.

¶ 8.3 Types of ESOPs

Fundamentally, there are two basic forms of ESOPs: leveraged and nonleveraged. While there are many similarities between these forms of ESOP, there are also significant differences from both a legal and an economic point of view. Economically, these differences may involve both the value of the sponsoring company in the aggregate as well as value on a per-share basis.

[1] Nonleveraged ESOPs

A nonleveraged ESOP is an ESOP that does not borrow money to purchase the shares it acquires. Since ESOPs typically do not have significant cash or other nonemployer assets, this limits the dollar amount of stock a nonleveraged ESOP can typically acquire at any given point to the maximum amount the employer can contribute to the ESOP on a tax-sheltered basis.

Over a period of time, however, a nonleveraged ESOP may acquire a significant amount of employer securities. Each year, the company decides how much it wishes to contribute to the ESOP in either stock or cash, and the ESOP acquires a given number of shares based upon the fair market value of such shares at the time of contribution or purchase. For example, if a company contributes $1 million of stock to its ESOP when the value per share is $10, the ESOP must receive 100,000 shares. For the same contribution when the value is $20 per share, the ESOP is entitled to receive only 50,000 shares. Thus, the number of shares a nonleveraged ESOP will receive over time is unknown and is a function of both the size of future contributions and the value of shares on the date of contribution.

[a] Stock Contributions

A stock contribution to a nonleveraged ESOP may be in the form of virtually any employer equity security, including preferred, convertible preferred, or common. Since the employer is able to deduct the value of the stock contribution from pretax income, a tax shelter is created that enhances both cash flow and aggragate equity value. Offsetting this increase in aggregate value is dilution caused by newly issued shares now owned by the ESOP, as shown in Example 1.

Example 1. Assume a company with $1 million in pretax income and a 40% tax bracket makes a $1 million, nonrecurring contribution to an ESOP. The company's after-tax cash flow is increased by $400,000, as shown here:

	ESOP	No ESOP
Pretax income	$1,000,000	$1,000,000
Less: ESOP contribution	1,000,000	-0-
Adjusted pretax	$ -0-	$1,000,000
Less: Taxes	-0-	400,000
Net income	$ -0-	$ 600,000
Plus: ESOP contribution	1,000,000	-0-
Cash flow	$1,000,000	$ 600,000

Therefore, if the company was worth $10 million without the ESOP stock contribution, it would be worth $10.4 million because of the stock contribution and the associated $400,000 tax shelter. However, while the value of the company in aggregate has increased by $400,000, the value per share may have declined as a result of dilution caused by the new ESOP shares. In order for the company to qualify for a $1 million tax deduction, the ESOP must receive $1 million in stock. If the ESOP has $1 million in stock and if the entire company is worth $10.4 million, the non-ESOP shareholders aggregate value must have declined from $10 million pre-ESOP to $9.4 million post-ESOP.

Since the number of non-ESOP shares outstanding remains the same but the aggregate value of such shares has declined, the value per share must likewise have fallen. Presuming 1 million non-ESOP shares outstanding, the value per share has declined from $10 per share to $9.40 per share, as follows:

	Pre-ESOP	Post-ESOP
Aggregate value	$10,000,000	$10,400,000
Less: ESOP value	-0-	1,000,000
Non-ESOP value	$10,000,000	$ 9,400,000
Number non-ESOP shares	÷ 1,000,000	÷ 1,000,000
Value per share	$10.00	$ 9.40

For the ESOP to receive $1 million of stock at $9.40 per share, the ESOP must receive 106,383 shares. In many cases, the impact of contributions to a nonleveraged ESOP on aggregate equity value may be harder to calculate than in the simplified Example 1, which assumed a one-time, nonrecurring contribution of $1 million. While contributions to nonleveraged ESOPs are typically discretionary, they may be recurring in nature.

For example, a company's ESOP contribution may take the place of contributions to more conventional pension or profit sharing plans. If ESOP contributions were terminated, it may be reasonable to assume that conventional plan contributions would have to be substituted in order to attract and retain a qualified work force. In such a case, it is probably appropriate to adjust representative earnings and cash-flow levels only to the extent that an ESOP contribution is in excess of normalized conventional plan contributions. This would reduce the impact of dilution on non-ESOP shareholders. As in a valuation engagement, all facts and circumstances must be considered before such adjustments are made.

[b] Cash Contributions

A cash contribution to a nonleveraged ESOP may also have an impact on value. Typically, cash is contributed to an ESOP either to fund the repurchase of shares from terminating plan participants or to give the ESOP the ability to buy shares from existing shareholders.

If the contribution is used to fund the put rights of terminating plan participants, the result is a cash outflow from the company without any reduction in the number of shares outstanding. The impact of such contributions on value depends both on what their size is and whether they are expected to continue into the future. If they are expected to be ongoing, they should be viewed as any other cash expense with an appropriate reduction in value.

The other primary reason to make cash contributions to a nonleveraged ESOP is to purchase shares from existing shareholders. Such contributions reduce cash flow available to the company but do not have an offsetting antidilutionary impact. Again, the key issues regarding impact on value include whether such contributions are expected to be recurring, whether they replace more conventional plan contributions, and what the magnitude of such contributions is.

[2] Leveraged ESOPs

A leveraged ESOP differs from a nonleveraged ESOP in several substantial respects. Unlike a nonleveraged ESOP, which acquires its shares over a period of time, a *leveraged ESOP* buys a block of stock at one time with debt and pays for the shares over a period of time.

In order to encourage the use of leveraged ESOPs, the federal government has endowed them with significant tax advantages not found in nonleveraged ESOPs. For example, the employer can make a tax deductible contribution of up to 25% of payroll to the ESOP for principal payments on the ESOP loan plus an unlimited deduction for interest payments. In addition, dividends paid on ESOP stock acquired with the debt may be used to amortize the debt in addition to or in lieu of contributions. Qualified lenders may exclude 50% of interest income on ESOP loans from taxable income typically resulting in a below market rate of interest on the ESOP loan. Finally, if a block of at least 30% of a nonpublic company's equity is sold to an ESOP, the sellers are able to postpone the payment of capital gains taxes and are thus encouraged to sell to an ESOP. The purchase of such a large block of stock can rarely be accomplished without the use of leverage.

[a] Stock Purchases

A leveraged ESOP may purchase either convertible preferred stock or the most senior class common stock. The convertible preferred stock must be convertible any time into the most senior class of common stock. The conversion premium, which is measured by the difference between the price paid for the convertible preferred and the value of the common into which it is convertible, must not be unreasonable. To take an extreme example, a convertible preferred purchased for $100 that was convertible into one share of common worth $1 per share would be viewed as having an unreasonable conversion premium.

In its simplest form, an ESOP borrows money from a bank or other qualified lender and uses the proceeds to purchase shares from the company or existing shareholders. Over time, the company makes contributions and dividend payments to the ESOP that are used to repay the loan.

Lenders are often reluctant to loan directly to an ESOP because the note is nonrecourse to plan participants, is secured only by the stock purchased with the loan, and is dependent upon contributions or dividends for repayment. Therefore, in a structure known as a *mirror loan*, lenders typically loan directly to the company, which, in turn, reloans to the ESOP on substantially the same terms. A *mirror loan* allows the lender to become a senior-secured lender to the company and still to preserve the special rights of lending directly to an ESOP, such as the ability to exclude 50% of interest income from taxable income. Contributions and dividends flow from the company to the ESOP, which are then used to repay the loan between the company and the ESOP. The company takes such payments and uses them to amortize the loan between the company and the lender. The contributions and dividends create a tax-sheltered cash flow, which allows both principal and interest to be paid in pretax dollars.

[b] Dilution Impact

Offsetting this increase in aggregate value is dilution caused by newly issued shares owned by the ESOP. The present value of tax and other cash-flow benefits to the company provided by the ESOP may not equal the value of stock given to an ESOP. If employees are willing to give wage or other benefit concessions in exchange for an ESOP, the dilutive impact may be minimal. However, in most cases, the issuance of newly issued shares to a leveraged ESOP typically will result in an increase in aggregate value and a decrease in value per share.

A more widely used application of leveraged ESOPs is the purchase of shares from existing shareholders. If an ESOP and other investors purchase all outstanding shares, the potential negative impact on per-share value is of concern only to the new owners of the company. Existing shareholders, who receive fair market value in exchange for their shares, do not care how the purchase is financed or what the possible impact on posttransaction value may be. Indeed, to the extent they are willing or able to take advantage of a tax-deferred rollover of the proceeds, they may be better off economically to sell to the ESOP rather than to another investor.

[c] Decline in Value

The use of a leveraged ESOP may result in a decline in per-share values, as shown in Example 2.

Example 2. Assume that a company whose equity is worth $100 million borrows $50 million and reloans it to an ESOP, which then purchases 50% of existing shareholders stock. Since the company in effect gave away $50 million, its value must have declined by about $50 million. However, the number of outstanding shares has not declined but is now simply owned 50% ESOP and 50% non-ESOP. If value declined in the aggregate but shares outstanding remain the same, value per share must also have declined.

Why would existing shareholders sell to an ESOP if the value per share of their remaining stock declines? First, existing shareholders may need cash or want to diversify their investments. It may be substantially easier to sell stock in a nonpublic company to an ESOP than find a motivated, third-party investor willing to make a similar investment. Second, to the extent such shareholders are willing to reinvest the proceeds in qualified securities, they can postpone the payment of capital gains taxes and may be better off on an after-tax basis. Third, the decline in value caused by the ESOP is somewhat offset by the present value of tax and other economic benefits created either directly or indirectly by the use of a leveraged ESOP.

¶ 8.4 Quantification of ESOP Benefits

As previously discussed, the use of a leveraged ESOP brings economic benefits to the sponsoring company as well as to other participants to the transaction. Benefits to the company may include the following:

1. *The ability to repay ESOP debt in pretax dollars.* Contributions and dividends paid to the ESOP are deductible from taxable income. The ESOP uses them to repay its debt to the company, which, in turn, uses them to repay the bank in the mirror loan structure, described earlier. Thus, principal payments as well as interest are repaid by pretax dollars, creating a tax shelter with value.
2. *Reduced interest expense on ESOP loan.* Because qualified lenders are able to exclude 50% of interest income and ESOP loan from taxable income, their after-tax rate of return is improved. Typically, lenders are willing to share some of this economic benefit with the company in the form of below-market interest rates.
3. *Wage or benefit concessions.* In many leveraged ESOP transactions, future ESOP contributions are not simply layered on existing wages and benefits but are conditional on the reduction or even elimination of compensation. Like any reduced expense, compensation concessions increase cash flow and thus value.

These and other possible economic benefits to the company are typically not indefinite in nature and may exist only during the life of the ESOP loan. They may be projected with reasonable accuracy and then discounted to a present value and added to the value of the company not considering such benefits. The sum of the value of the company without the ESOP plus the present value of the ESOP-related benefits would equal the value of the company's equity posttransaction, as shown in Example 3.

Example 3. Assume that a company worth $100 million pretransaction borrows $70 million and reloans it to an ESOP payable over seven years to buy existing shares. In addition, assume the company has a 40% tax rate and a reduction in interest expense from a market-driven 12% to a ESOP influenced 10% per year. The company will save $4 million per year in taxes as a result of the ability to repay debt in pretax dollars plus 2% per year in the form of reduced interest expense. Assuming that the risk associated with enjoying these savings was reasonably expressed by a discount rate of 15%, the present value of the ESOP-related benefits would equal approximately $20.4 million, as shown here:

Year	Tax Savings ($Millions)	Interest Savings ($Millions)	Total Savings ($Millions)	Present Value at 15 Percent ($Millions)
1	$ 4.0	$1.4	$ 5.4	$ 4.7
2	4.0	1.2	5.2	3.9
3	4.0	1.0	5.0	3.3
4	4.0	0.8	4.8	2.7
5	4.0	0.6	4.6	2.3
6	4.0	0.4	4.4	1.9
7	4.0	0.2	4.2	1.6
Total	$28.0	$5.6	$33.6	$20.4

In our simplified Example 3, the company's pretransaction value of $100 million would have declined to $50.4 million posttransaction as follows:

Pretransaction value	$100.0 million
Less: Debt	70.0 million
	$ 30.0 million
Plus: ESOP-related benefits	20.4 million
Posttransaction value	$ 50.4 million

¶ 8.5 Multi-Investor Equity Allocation Issues

As described previously, the use of an ESOP may result in a decline in value per share if the ESOP-related economic benefits are worth less than the stock that the ESOP receives. Thus, an increase in aggregate equity value may be more than offset by dilution and the impact of additional debt. This problem becomes particularly acute in leveraged ESOP transactions that include non-ESOP investors.

Most leveraged buyouts done by an ESOP include non-ESOP investors. A leveraged ESOP does not bring hard dollars in the form of cash to the deal but brings instead soft dollars in the form of ESOP-related benefits. Most lenders are unwilling to loan an ESOP enough to affect a 100% buyout without the inclusion of investors who are willing to provide a cash cushion in the form of equity or subordinated debt. In addition, lenders are anxious to ensure that the company will have competent, experienced, motivated management posttransaction. This is frequently accomplished by including incentive stock as part of an overall compensation package to key members of management outside of the ESOP.

> *Example 4.* Using Example 3, assume a leveraged ESOP and other investors decide to purchase a $100 million company and finance the transaction with $70 million in ESOP debt and $30 million in investor cash. Initially, it might seem reasonable to allocate posttransaction equity value 70% to the ESOP and 30% to the cash investors. However, as previously described, the use of the ESOP provides just $20.4 million in economic benefits while the ESOP debt imposes a $70 million burden on the company. Therefore, posttransaction equity value declines from $100 million to $50.4 million.

If the cash investors receive 30% of the company posttransaction, they will have paid $30 million for an investment, which is immediately worth only $15.1 million as follows:

Posttransaction value	$50.4 million
Cash investor's equity allocation	× 30%
Cash investor's equity value	$15.1 million

This is not an investment that any reasonable or prudent investor would make.

[1] Equity Allocation Approaches

Suppose, in Example 4, that the cash investor is not a third party but simply another employee plan with cash that wishes to buy the company in conjunction with the ESOP. Surely, no fiduciary would make an investment on behalf of the plan with cash that would see its value decline immediately from $30 million to $15.1 million. It would seem ironic if a plan could purchase a company with all cash or all debt but could not do so with a combination of cash and debt.

There have been numerous approaches taken on the issue of equity allocation in multi-investor, leveraged ESOP transactions. Perhaps the best approach is to consider the cash flows both ESOP and non-ESOP investors will enjoy, adjusted for risk and timing, and allocate equity on that basis. For example, the ESOP receives a disproportionate amount of interim cash flows, which it uses to amortize its debt. In order to not penalize other investors, it would seem reasonable to give the non-ESOP investors a somewhat larger allocation of terminal or equity value. This may be accomplished in a variety of ways, including the issuance of different classes of stock to ESOP and non-ESOP shareholders.

Although it has been critical of some equity allocation approaches used in various transactions over the years, the DOL has not issued formal regulations or proposed guidelines in this area. In the resulting gray area of equity allocation, the ESOP's financial adviser must consider the deal the ESOP is getting on a relative basis to other investors as well as on an absolute basis. Experience in dealing with equity allocation issues and sensitivity to potential regulatory concerns are vital to structuring a transaction that is both economically rational and fair to the ESOP from a financial point of view.

¶ 8.6 Adequate Consideration

From the viewpoint of both the DOL and the Internal Revenue Service (IRS), an ESOP may not pay more than adequate consideration for the shares it receives. ESOP transactions that fall under the DOL's authority are prohibited from paying greater than adequate consideration. The IRS's concern is that a company is not allowed to take a tax deduction for an ESOP contribution unless the ESOP has received securities worth a similar amount.

[1] Fair Market Value

In the DOL's proposed adequate consideration regulations, which are attached as Appendix 8-1 at the end of this chapter, it is specified that a determination of adequate consideration must include a determination of fair market value. Fair market value is a term that has been defined in various court cases and regulations, perhaps most notably in Revenue Ruling 59-60.[1] In essence, *fair market value* is the amount that would be paid by a willing buyer to a willing seller in an arm's-length negotiated transaction, presuming they were both knowledgea-

---

[1] 1959-1 C.B. 237. Revenue Ruling 59-60 is reprinted as Appendix A at the end of this book.

ble about all relevant facts and neither was under compulsion to conduct the transaction. This concept precludes the use of formula approaches because they cannot, by their very nature, consider all relevant facts.

[2] Premiums and Marketability

In addition to factors that affect the fair market value of the underlying company, there may be additional factors that affect the particular class or block of stock purchased by the ESOP. One factor that has a significant impact on value is the relative level of value associated with the stock held by the ESOP. Essentially, most transactions in the stock of publicly traded companies are done on a marketable minority interest basis. The blocks are small minority blocks that have a great deal of liquidity because they can be easily bought and sold but have little influence and no control over company matters.

When large blocks of stock are purchased in the public market, a premium typically is paid by the buyer to acquire the shares. These premiums, sometimes called *control premiums* or *enterprise-level value*, are paid for a variety of reasons. The buyer may be willing to pay a premium if he or she can acquire significant influence or control over company matters. Through sales of assets, changes in management, cutting of costs, changes in capital structure, or other actions, the buyer may be able to increase value. The buyer, therefore, maybe willing to pay a premium to attain control. On the other hand, the seller will demand a premium whether the buyer receives control or exercises his or her prerogatives in that regard. Stock, after all, is a commodity whose value rises as demand for it increases, which is precisely what happens when a large block of stock is purchased.

Premiums range widely from transaction to transaction. Studies of transactions involving 100% change of ownership or an acquisition of control, however, indicate that the median control premiums have ranged from 40-50%. While the median control premium cannot be used blindly for every ESOP transaction, it does indicate how much value can be influenced if a premium is justified.

The proposed adequate consideration regulations state that an ESOP should pay a "control" premium only to the extent that a third party would also pay such a premium for the acquired block of stock. In addition, the ESOP must receive voting control and control in fact. This language raises some interesting questions that the proposed regulation does not answer:

- Is every premium above marketable minority interest value a "control" premium, or might some premium be justified even if the ESOP does not attain control?

- If the ESOP is justified in paying a "control" premium only when attaining control and if other parties to the same transaction do not get control, does that justify the ESOP paying a higher price than other investors?

These and many other potentially interesting questions await further clarification in the form of regulations or court cases.

Another factor that may have a significant impact on value is marketability. As previously mentioned, publicly traded securities are generally very marketable and easy to buy or sell. The shares of nonpublic companies, by their very nature, do not have this form of liquidity. From a theoretical point of view, marketable securities should be more valuable than nonmarketable securities because investors have a preference for liquidity and the ability to turn an asset like stock into cash when desired. Studies on restricted stock have shown this to be true, with discounts of 30% or more from marketable minority interest value justified based on the extent and duration of such restrictions.

Most ESOPs are designed with put rights, which allow terminating plan participants to receive the fair market value of their stock in the form of cash or notes when they leave the company. In the absence of such put rights or in cases where they may not be honored due to a lack of liquidity on the part of the company or the plan, a discount for reduced marketability may be appropriate. The appraiser must consider both the put right and the capacity to honor such puts in determining how much of a discount, if any, to take on the stock held by an ESOP.

[3] Independence

The proposed adequate consideration regulations require that an ESOP have either an independent fiduciary or an independent financial adviser prior to entering into a transaction. Once again, the proposed regulations are not clear regarding who is independent and who is not. For example, if an organization provides services to the company that are unrelated to the transaction, is it independent for purposes of acting as the ESOP's financial adviser? At this point, these and other such questions remain unanswered.

One area where there is general agreement regarding independence is the issue of contingent payments. Most practitioners agree that a fee contingent on the closing of the proposed transaction could arguably encourage the financial adviser to approve a potentially unfair transaction in order to collect his fee. It is much more desirable from both an appearance as well as from a practical point of view for the financial adviser to have a fixed fee that is paid whether the transaction is consummated or not. Similarly, a fee that is not fixed but is based on a percentage of the transaction amount could also put the ESOP's interests in conflict with its financial adviser and should be avoided.

As a final note on the issue of independence, the financial adviser should be careful to ensure that he or she is hired by and reports to the ESOP committee or trustee who will make the final investment decision on behalf of the ESOP. The company may be responsible for the payment of fees or indemnification of the financial adviser without potential conflict. But to maintain independence, it should be clear that the financial adviser works only for the fiduciary on behalf of the ESOP.

¶ 8.7 Effective Date of Appraisal

The value of a company's stock changes over time based on a variety of micro- and macroeconomic factors. These changes may be relatively small and immaterial, or they may be large and significant. In any case, it is not possible to come to a reasonable conclusion of value unless an analysis is conducted as of a given date.

One important feature of ESOP transactions is the requirement that they be conducted at no more than fair market value. An appraisal conducted weeks or even days prior to an actual transaction may no longer be relevant for ESOP purposes if values have declined. Therefore, the DOL's proposed regulations specify that the effective date of appraisal for ESOP transactions is the actual date of the transaction. This requires the ESOP's financial adviser to conduct a full analysis prior to the transaction and update it as of the actual transaction date, using the most recent information regarding the company and the environment in which it operates.

¶ 8.8 Report Format and Content

The DOL's proposed adequate consideration regulations make it clear that the financial adviser's analysis and conclusions must be documented in an extensive narrative report that clearly describes assumptions, valuation approaches, restrictions, and conclusions. Without listing all the factors suggested for inclusion in the report, it is obvious that the DOL feels that a relatively stand-alone document describing in detail the financial adviser's process and conclusions is important. Such a report helps to document the depth and breadth of investigation and analysis that was conducted and provides the basis for reasonable and supportable conclusions of value. In addition, it ensures that the fiduciary has received sufficient information on which to base the final investment decision and has not relied blindly on the financial adviser's conclusions.

¶ 8.9 Fairness

Frequently, the financial adviser to an ESOP transaction is required to issue an opinion that the proposed transaction is fair to the ESOP from a financial point of view. This type of opinion goes beyond the determination of fair market value; it merely provides a threshold for fairness. Fairness from a financial point of view must also consider relative fairness to the ESOP compared to other parties to the transaction. Arguably, an ESOP could pay no more than fair market value for its stock yet receive a deal which was unfair compared to other investors. Financial fairness may also consider the terms of the financing and the ultimate equity allocation in a multi-investor, leveraged ESOP transaction.

¶ 8.10 Conclusion

The valuation of stock for ESOP transaction purposes must consider all of the factors required in any stock valuation. There are, however, certain unique aspects of ESOP transactions that have a significant impact on both aggregate and per share value. Issues such as ESOP-related tax benefits, dilution, security design, and equity allocation make ESOP transactions difficult and complicated to analyze and value. This chapter has attempted to shed light on some of these issues and the legal framework in which they must operate.

Appendix 8-1 DOL Proposed Regulation Relating to the Definition of Adequate Consideration*

DEPARTMENT OF LABOR

Pension and Welfare Benefits Administration

29 CFR Part 2510

Proposed Regulation Relating to the Definition of Adequate Consideration

AGENCY: Pension and Welfare Benefits Administration, Department of Labor.

ACTION: Notice of proposed rulemaking.

SUMMARY: This document contains a notice of a proposed regulation under the Employee Retirement Income Security Act of 1974 (the Act or ERISA) and the Federal Employees' Retirement System Act of 1986 (FERSA). The proposal clarifies the definition of the term "ade-

---

* 53 Fed. Reg. 17632 (1988).

quate consideration" provided in section 3(18)(B) of the Act and section 8477(a)(2)(B) of FERSA for assets other than securities for which there is a generally recognized market. Section 3(18)(B) and section 8477(a)(2)(B) provide that the term "adequate consideration" for such assets means the fair market value of the asset as determined in good faith by the trustee or named fiduciary (or, in the case of FERSA, a fiduciary) pursuant to the terms of the plan and in accordance with regulations promulgated by the Secretary of Labor. Because valuation questions of this nature arise in a variety of contexts, the Department is proposing this regulation in order to provide the certainty necessary for plan fiduciaries to fulfill their statutory duties. If adopted, the regulation would affect plans investing in assets other than securities for which there is a generally recognized market.

DATES: Written comments on the proposed regulation must be received by July 18, 1988. If adopted, the regulation will be effective for transactions taking place after the date 30 days following publication of the regulation in final form.

ADDRESS: Written comments on the proposed regulation (preferably three copies) should be submitted to: Office of Regulations and Interpretations, Pension and Welfare Benefits Administration, Room N-5671, U.S. Department of Labor, 200 Constitution Avenue NW., Washington, DC 20216. Attention: Adequate Consideration Proposal. All written comments will be available for public inspection at the Public Disclosure Room, Pension and Welfare Benefits Administration, U.S Department of Labor, Room N-5507, 200 Constitution Avenue NW., Washington, DC.

FOR FURTHER INFORMATION CONTACT: Daniel J. Maguire, Esq., Plan Benefits Security Division, Office of the Solicitor, U.S. Department of Labor, Washington, DC 20210, (202) 523-9596 (not a toll-free number) or Mark A. Greenstein, Office of Regulations and Interpretations, Pension and Welfare Benefits Administration, (202) 523-7901 (not a toll-free number).

SUPPLEMENTARY INFORMATION:

A. Background

Notice is hereby given of a proposed regulation under section 3(18)(B) of the Act and section 8477(a)(2)(B) of FERSA. Section 3(18) of the Act provides the definition for the term "adequate consideration," and states:

The term "adequate consideration" when used in part 4 of subtitle B means (A) in the case of a security for which there is a generally recognized market, either (i) the price of the security prevailing on a national securities exchange which is registered under section 6 of the Securities Exchange Act of 1934, or (ii) if the security is not traded on such a national securities exchange, a price not less favorable to the plan than the offering price for the security as established by the current bid and asked prices quoted by persons independent of the issuer and of any party in interest; and (B) in the case of an asset other than a security for which there is a generally recognized market, the fair market value of the asset as determined in good faith by the trustee or named fiduciary pursuant to the terms of the plan and in accordance with regulations promulgated by the Secretary.

The term "adequate consideration" appears four times in part 4 of subtitle B of Title I of the Act, and each time represents a central requirement for a statutory exemption from the prohibited transaction restrictions of the Act. Under section 408(b)(5), a plan may purchase insurance contracts from certain parties in interest if, among other conditions, the plan pays no more than adequate consideration. Section 408(b)(7) provides that the prohibited transaction provisions of section 406 shall not apply to the exercise of a privilege to convert securities, to the extent provided in regulations of the Secretary of Labor, only if the plan receives no less than adequate consideration pursuant to such conversion. Section 408(e) of the Act provides that the prohibitions in sections 406 and 407(a) of the Act shall not apply to the acquisition or sale by a plan of qualifying employer securities, or the acquisition, sale or lease by a plan of qualifying employer real property if, among other conditions, the acquisition, sale or lease is for adequate consideration. Section 414(c)(5) of the Act states that sections 406 and 407(a) of the Act shall not apply to the sale, exchange, or other disposition of property which is owned by a plan on June 30, 1974, and all times thereafter, to a party in interest, if such plan is required to dispose of the property in order to comply with the provisions of section 407(a) (relating to the prohibition against holding excess employer securities and employer real property), and if the plan receives not less than adequate consideration.

Public utilization of these statutory exemptions requires a determination of "adequate consideration" in accordance with the definition contained in section 3(18) of the Act. Guidance is especially important in this area because many of the transactions covered by these statutory exemptions involve plan dealings with the plan sponsor. A fiduciary's determination of the adequacy of consideration paid under such circumstances represents a major safeguard for plans against the potential for abuse inherent in such transactions.

The Federal Employees' Retirement System Act of 1986 (FERSA) established the Federal Retirement Thrift Investment Board whose members act as fiduciaries with regard to the assets of the Thrift Savings Fund. In general, FERSA contains fiduciary obligation and prohibited transaction provisions similar to ERISA. However, unlike ERISA, FERSA prohibits party in interest transactions similar to those described in section 406(a) of ERISA only in those circumstances where adequate consideration is not exchanged between the Fund and the party in interest. Specifically, section 8477(c)(1) of FERSA provides that, except in exchange for adequate consideration, a fiduciary shall not permit the Thrift Savings Fund to engage in: transfers of its assets to, acquisition of property from or sales of property to, or transfers or exchanges of services with any person the fiduciary knows or should know to be a party in interest. Section 8477(a)(2) provides the FERSA definition for the term "adequate consideration" which is virtually identical to that contained in section 3(18) of ERISA. Thus, the proposal would apply to both section 3(18) of ERISA and section 8477(a)(2) of FERSA.

When the asset being valued is a security for which there is a generally recognized market, the plan fiduciary must determine "adequate consideration" by reference to the provisions of section 3(18)(A) of the Act (or with regard to FERSA, section 8477(a)(2)(A)). Section 3(18)(A) and section 8477(a)(2)(A) provide detailed reference points for the valuation of securities within its coverage, and in effect provides that adequate consideration for such securities is the prevailing market price. It is not the Department's intention to analyze the requirements of section 3(18)(A) or section 8477(a)(2)(A) in this proposal. Fiduciaries must, however, determine whether a security is subject to the specific provisions of section 3(18)(A) (or section 8477(a)(2)(A) of FERSA) or the more general requirements of section 3(18)(B) (or section 8477(a)(2)(B)) as interpreted in this proposal. The question of whether a security is one for which there is a generally recognized market requires a factual determination in light of the character of the security and the nature and extent of market activity with regard to the security. Generally, the Department will examine whether a security is being actively traded so as to provide the benchmarks Congress intended. Isolated trading activity, or trades between related parties, generally will not be sufficient to show the existence of a generally recognized market for the purposes of section 3(18)(A) or section 8477(a)(2)(A).

In the case of all assets other than securities for which there is a generally recognized market, fiduciaries must determine adequate consideration pursuant to section 3(18)(B) of the Act (or, in the case of FERSA, section 8477(a)(2)(B)). Because it is designed to deal with all but a narrow class of assets, section 3(18)(B) and section 8477(a)(2)(B) are by their nature more general than section 3(18)(A) or section 8477(a)(2)(A). Although the Department has indicated that it will not issue advisory opinions stating whether certain stated consideration is "adequate consideration" for the purposes of section 3(18), ERISA Procedure 76-1, § 5.02(a) (41 FR 36281, 36282, August 27, 1976), the Department recognizes that plan fiduciaries have a need for guidance in valuing assets, and that standards to guide fiduciaries in this area may be particularly elusive with respect to assets other than securities for which there is a generally recognized market. *See*, for example, *Donovan v. Cunningham*, 716 F.2d 1455 (5th Cir. 1983) (court encourages the Department to adopt regulations under section 3(18)(B)). The Department has therefore determined to propose a regulation only under section 3(18)(B) and section 8477(a)(2)(B). This proposal is described more fully below.

It should be noted that it is not the Department's intention by this proposed regulation to relieve fiduciaries of the responsibility for making the required determinations of "adequate consideration" where applicable under the Act or FERSA. Nothing in the proposal should be construed as justifying a fiduciary's failure to take into account all relevant facts and circumstances in determining adequate consideration. Rather, the proposal is designed to provide a framework within which fiduciaries can fulfill their statutory duties. Further, fiduciaries should be aware that, even where a determination of adequate consideration comports with the requirements of section 3(18)(B) (or section 8477(a)(2)(B) of FERSA) and any regulation adopted thereunder, the investment of plan assets made pursuant to such determination will still be subject to the fiduciary requirements of Part 4 of Subtitle B of Title I of the Act, including the provisions of sections 403 and 404 of the Act, or the fiduciary responsibility provisions of FERSA.

B. Description of the Proposal

Proposed regulation 29 CFR 2510.3-18(b) is divided into four major parts. Proposed § 2510.3-18(b)(1) states the general rule and delineates the scope of the regulation. Proposed § 2510.3-18(b)(2) addresses the concept of fair market value as it relates to a determination of "adequate consideration" under section 3(18)(B) of the Act. Proposed § 2510.3-18(b)(3) deals with the requirement in section 3(18)(B) that valuing fiduciary act in good faith, and specifically discusses the use of an independent appraisal in connection with the determination of good faith. Proposed § 2510.3-18(b)(4) sets forth the content requirements for written valuations used as the basis for a determination of fair market value, with a special rule for the valuation of securities other than securities for which there is a generally recognized market. Each subsection is discussed in detail below.

1. General Rule and Scope.

Proposed § 2510.3-18(b)(1)(i) essentially follows the language of section 3(18)(B) of the Act and section 8477(a)(2)(B) of FERSA and states that, in the case of a plan asset other than a security for which there is a generally recognized market, the term "adequate consideration" means the fair market value of the asset as determined in good faith by the trustee or named fiduciary (or, in the case of FERSA, a fiduciary) pursuant to the terms of the plan and in accordance with regulations promulgated by the Secretary of Labor. Proposed § 2510.3-18(b)(1)(ii) delineates the scope of this regulation by establishing two criteria, both of which must be met for a valid determination of adequate consideration. First, the value assigned to an asset must reflect its fair market value as determined pursuant to proposed § 2510.3-18(b)(2). Second, the value assigned to an asset must be the product of a determination made by the fiduciary in good faith as defined in proposed § 2510.3-18(b)(3). The Department will consider that a fiduciary has determined adequate consideration in accordance with section 3(18)(B) of the Act or section 8477(a)(2)(B) of FERSA only if both of these requirements are satisfied.

The Department has proposed this two part test for several reasons. First, Congress incorporated the concept of fair market value into the definition of adequate consideration. As explained more fully below, fair market value is an often used concept having an established meaning in the field of asset valuation. By reference to this term, it would appear that Congress did not intend to allow parties to a transaction to set an arbitrary value for the assets involved. Therefore, a valuation determination which fails to reflect the market forces embodied in the concept of fair market value would also fail to meet the requirements of section 3(18)(B) of the Act or section 8477(a)(2)(B) of FERSA.

Second, it would appear that Congress intended to allow a fiduciary a limited degree of latitude so long as that fiduciary acted in good faith. However, a fiduciary would clearly fail to fulfill the fiduciary duties delineated in Part 4 of Subtitle B of Title I of the Act if that fiduciary acted solely on the basis of naive or uninformed good intentions. *See Donovan v. Cunningham, supra*, 716 F.2d at 1467 ("[A] pure heart and an empty head are not enough.") The Department has therefore proposed standards for a determination of a fiduciary's good faith which must be satisfied in order to meet the requirements of section 3(18)(B) or section 8477(a)(2)(B) of FERSA.

Third, even if a fiduciary were to meet the good faith standards contained in this proposed regulation, there may be circumstances in which good faith alone fails to insure an equitable result. For example, errors in calculation or honest failure to consider certain information could produce valuation figures outside of the range of acceptable valuations of a given asset. Because the determination of adequate consideration is a central requirement of the statutory exemptions discussed above, the Department believes it must assure that such exemptions are made available only for those transactions possessing all the external safeguards envisioned by Congress. To achieve this end, the Department's proposed regulation links the fair market value and good faith requirements to assure that the resulting valuation reflects market considerations and is the product of a valuation process conducted in good faith.

2. Fair Market Value

The first part of the Department's proposed two part test under section 3(18)(B) and section 8477(a)(2)(B) requires that a determination of adequate consideration reflect the asset's fair market value. The term "fair market value" is defined in proposed § 2510.3-18(b)(2)(i) as the price at which an asset would change hands between a willing buyer and a willing seller when the former is not under any compulsion to buy and the latter is not under any compulsion to sell, and both parties are able, as well as willing, to trade and are well-informed about the asset and the market for that asset. This proposed definition essentially reflects the well-established meaning of this term in the area of asset valuation. *See,* for example, 26 CFR 20.2031-1 (estate tax regulations); Rev. Rul. 59-60, 1959-1 Cum. Bull. 237; *United States v. Cartwright,* 411 U.S. 546, 551 (1973); *Estate of Bright v. United States,* 658 F.2d 999, 1005 (5th Cir. 1981). It should specifically be noted that comparable valuations reflecting transactions resulting from other than free and equal negotiations (e.g., a distress sale) will fail to establish fair market value. *See Hooker Industries, Inc. v. Commissioner,* 3 EBC 1849, 1854-55 (T.C. June 24, 1982). Similarly, the extent to which the Department will view a valuation as reflecting fair market value will be affected by an assessment of the level of expertise demonstrated by the parties making the valuation. *See Donovan v. Cunningham, supra,* 716 F.2d at 146 (failure to apply sound business principles of evaluation, for whatever reason, may result in a valuation that does not reflect fair market value).[1]

---

[1] Whether in any particular transaction a plan fiduciary is in fact well-informed about the asset in question and the market for that asset, including any specific circumstances which may affect the value of the asset, will be determined on a facts and circumstances basis. If, however, the fiduciary negotiating on behalf of the plan has or

The Department is aware that the fair market value of an asset will ordinarily be identified by a range of valuations rather than a specific, set figure. It is not the Department's intention that only one valuation figure will be acceptable as the fair market value of a specified asset. Rather, this proposal would require that the valuation assigned to an asset must reflect a figure within an acceptable range of valuations for that asset.

In addition to this general formulation of the definition of fair market value, the Department is proposing two specific requirements for the determination of fair market value for the purposes of section 3(18)(B) and section 8477(a)(2)(B). First, proposed § 2510.3-18(b)(2)(ii) requires that fair market value must be determined as of the date of the transaction involving the asset. This requirement is designed to prevent situations such as arose in *Donovan v. Cunningham, supra.* In that case, the plan fiduciaries relied on a 1975 appraisal to set the value of employer securities purchased by an ESOP during 1976 and thereafter, and failed to take into account significant changes in the company's business condition in the interim. The court found that this reliance was unwarranted, and therefore the fiduciaries' valuation failed to reflect adequate consideration under section 3(18)(B). *Id.* at 1468-69.

Second, proposed § 2510.3-18(b)(2)(iii) states that the determination of fair market value must be reflected in written documentation of valuation[2] meeting the content requirements set forth in § 2510.3-18(b)(4). (The valuation content requirements are discussed below.) The Department has proposed this requirement in light of the role the adequate consideration requirement plays in a number of statutory exemptions from the prohibited transaction provisions of the Act. In determining whether a statutory exemption applies to a particular transaction, the burden of proof is upon the party seeking to make use of the statutory exemption to show that all the requirements of the

---

should have specific knowledge concerning either the particular asset or the market for that asset, it is the view of the Department that the fiduciary must take into account that specific knowledge in negotiating the price of the asset in order to meet the fair market value standard of this regulation. For example, a sale of plan-owned real estate at a negotiated price consistent with valuations of comparable property will not be a sale for adequate consideration if the negotiating fiduciary does not take into account any special knowledge which he has or should have about the asset or its market, .*eg.*, that the property's value should reflect a premium due to a certain developer's specific land development plans.

[2] It should be noted that the written valuation required by this section of the proposal need not be a written report of an independent appraiser. Rather, it should be documentation sufficient to allow the Department to determine whether the content requirements of § 2510.3-18(b)(4) have been satisfied. The use of an independent appraiser may be relevant to a determination of good faith, as discussed with regard to proposed § 2510.3-18(b)(3), *infra,* but it is not required to satisfy the fair market value criterion in § 2510.3-18(b)(2)(i).

provision are met. *Donovan v. Cunningham, supra*, 716 F.2d at 1467 n.27. In the Department's view, written documentation relating to the valuation is necessary for a determination of how, and on what basis, an asset was valued, and therefore whether that valuation reflected an asset's fair market value. In addition, the Department believes that it would be contrary to prudent business practices for a fiduciary to act in the absence of such written documentation of fair market value.

3. Good Faith

The second part of the Department's proposed two-part test under section 3(18)(B) and section 8477(a)(2)(B) requires that an assessment of adequate consideration be the product of a determination made in good faith by the plan trustee or named fiduciary (or under FERSA, a fiduciary). Proposed § 2510.3-18(b)(3)(i) states that as a general matter this good faith requirement establishes an objective standard of conduct, rather than mandating an inquiry into the intent or state of mind of the plan trustee or named fiduciary. In this regard, the proposal is consistent with the opinion in *Donovan v. Cunningham, supra*, where the court stated that the good faith requirement in section 3(18)(B):

> is not a search for subjective good faith * * * The statutory reference to good faith in Section 3(18) must be read in light of the overriding duties of Section 404.

716 F.2d at 1467. The inquiry into good faith under the proposal therefore focuses on the fiduciary's conduct in determining fair market value. An examination of all relevant facts and circumstances is necessary for a determination of whether a fiduciary has met this objective good faith standard.

Proposed § 2510.3-18(b)(3)(ii) focuses on two factors which must be present in order for the Department to be satisfied that the fiduciary has acted in good faith. First, this section would require a fiduciary to apply sound business principles of evaluation and to conduct a prudent investigation of the circumstances prevailing at the time of the valuation. This requirement reflects the *Cunningham* court's emphasis on the use of prudent business practices in valuing plan assets.

Second, this section states that either the fiduciary making the valuation must itself be independent of all the parties to the transaction (other than the plan), or the fiduciary must rely on the report of an appraiser who is independent of all the parties to the transaction (other than the plan). (The criteria for determining independence are discussed below.) As noted above, under ERISA, the determination of adequate consideration is a central safeguard in many statutory exemptions applicable to plan transactions with the plan sponsor. The close relationship between the plan and the plan sponsor in such situations raises a significant potential for conflicts of interest as the fiduciary values assets which are the subject of transactions between the plan and the plan sponsor. In light of this possibility, the Department believes that good faith may only be demonstrated when the valuation is made by persons independent of the parties to the transaction (other than the plan), *i.e.*, a valuation made by an independent fiduciary or by a fiduciary acting pursuant to the report of an independent appraiser.

The Department emphasizes that the two requirements of proposed § 2510.3-18(b)(3)(ii) are designed to work in concert. For example, a plan fiduciary charged with valuation may be independent of all the parties to a transaction and may, in light of the requirement of proposed § 2510.3-18(b)(3)(ii)(B), decide to undertake the valuation process itself. However, if the independent fiduciary has neither the experience, facilities nor expertise to make the type of valuation under consideration, the decision by that fiduciary to make the valuation would fail to meet the prudent investigation and sound business principles requirement of proposed § 2510.3-18(b)(3)(ii)(A).

Proposed § 2510.3-18(b)(3)(iii) defines the circumstances under which a fiduciary or an appraiser will be deemed to be independent for the purposes of subparagraph (3)(ii)(B), above. The proposal notes that the fiduciary or the appraiser must in fact be independent of all parties participating in the transaction other than the plan. The proposal also notes that a determination of independence must be made in light of all relevant facts and circumstances, and then delineates certain circumstances under which this independence will be lacking. These circumstances reflect the definitions of the terms "affiliate" and "control" in Departmental regulation 29 CFR 2510.3-21(e) (defining the circumstances under which an investment adviser is a fiduciary). It should be noted that, under these proposed provisions, an appraiser will be considered independent of all parties to a transaction (other than the plan) only if a plan fiduciary has chosen the appraiser and has the right to terminate that appointment, and the plan is thereby established as the appraiser's client.[3] Absent such circumstances, the appraiser may be unable to be completely neutral in the exercise of his function.[4]

---

[3] The independence of an appraiser will not be affected solely because the plan sponsor pays the appraiser's fee.

[4] With regard to this independence requirement the Department notes that new section 401(a)(28) of the Code (added by section 1175(a) of the Tax Reform Act of 1986) requires that, in the case of an employee stock ownership plan, employer securities which are not readily tradable on established securities markets must be valued by an independent appraiser. New section 401(a)(28)(C) states that the term "independent appraiser" means an appraiser meeting requirements similar to the requirements of regulations under section 170(a)(1) of the Code (relating to IRS verification of the value assigned for deduction purposes to assets donated to charitable

4. Valuation Content—General

Proposed § 2510.3-18(b)(4)(i) sets the content requirements for the written documentation of valuation required for a determination of fair market value under proposed § 2510.3-18(b)(2)(iii). The proposal follows to a large extent the requirements of Rev. Proc. 66-49, 1966-2 C.B. 1257, which sets forth the format required by the IRS for the valuation of donated property. The Department believes that this format is a familiar one, and will therefore facilitate compliance. Several additions to the IRS requirements merit brief explanation.

First, proposed paragraph (b)(4)(i)(E) requires a statement of the purpose for which the valuation was made. A valuation undertaken, for example, for a yearly financial report may prove an inadequate basis for any sale of the asset in question. This requirement is intended to facilitate review of the valuation in the correct context.

Second, proposed paragraph (b)(4)(i)(F) requires a statement as to the relative weight accorded to relevant valuation methodologies. The Department's experience in this area indicates that there are a number of different methodologies used within the appraisal industry. By varying the treatment given and emphasis accorded relevant information, these methodologies directly affect the result of the appraiser's analysis. It is the Department's understanding that appraisers will often use different methodologies to cross-check their results. A statement of the method or methods used would allow for a more accurate assessment of the validity of the valuation.

Finally, proposed subparagraph (b)(4)(i)(G) requires a statement of the valuation's effective date. This reflects the requirement in proposed § 2510.3-18(b)(ii) that fair market value must be determined as of the date of the transaction in question.

5. Valuation Content—Special Rule

Proposed § 2510.3-18(b)(4)(ii) establishes additional content requirements for written documentation of valuation when the asset being appraised is a security other than a security for which there is a generally recognized market. In other words, the requirements of the proposed special rule supplement, rather than supplant, the requirements of paragraph (b)(4)(i). The proposed special rule establishes a nonexclusive list of factors to be considered when the asset being valued is a security not covered by section 3(18)(A) of the Act or section 8477(a)(2)(A) of FERSA. Such securities pose special valuation

---

organizations). The Department notes that the requirements of proposed regulation § 2510.3-18(b)(3)(iii) are not the same as the requirements of the regulations issued by the IRS under section 170(a)(1) of the Code. The IRS has not yet promulgated rules under Code section 401(a)(28).

problems because they are not traded or are so thinly traded that it is difficult to assess the effect on such securities of the market forces usually considered in determining fair market value. The Internal Revenue Service has had occasion to address the valuation problems posed by one type of such securities—securities issued by closely held corporations. Rev. Rul. 59-60, 1959-1 Cum. Bull. 237, lists a variety of factors to be considered when valuing securities of closely held corporations for tax purposes.[5] The Department's experience indicates that Rev. Rul. 59-60 is familiar to plan fiduciaries, plan sponsors and the corporate community in general. The Department has, therefore, modeled this proposed special rule after Rev. Rul. 59-60 with certain additions and changes discussed below. It should be emphasized, however, that this is a non-exclusive list of factors to be considered. Certain of the factors listed may not be relevant to every valuation inquiry, although the fiduciary will bear the burden of demonstrating such irrelevance. Similarly, reliance on this list will not relieve fiduciaries from the duty to consider all relevant facts and circumstances when valuing such securities. The purpose of the proposed list is to guide fiduciaries in the course of their inquiry.

Several of the factors listed in proposed § 2510.3-18(b)(4)(ii) merit special comment and explanation. Proposed subparagraph (G) states that the fair market value of securities other than those for which there is a generally recognized market may be established by reference to the market price of similar securities of corporations engaged in the same or a similar line of business whose securities are actively traded in a free and open market, either on an exchange or over the counter. The Department intends that the degree of comparability must be assessed in order to approximate as closely as possible the market forces at work with regard to the corporation issuing the securities in question.

Proposed subparagraph (H) requires an assessment of the effect of the securities' marketability or lack thereof. Rev. Rul. 59-60 does not explicitly require such an assessment, but the Department believes that the marketability of these types of securities will directly affect their price. In this regard, the Department is aware that, especially in situations involving employee stock ownership plans (ESOPs),[6] the

---

[5] Rev. Rul. 59-60 was modified by Rev. Rul. 65-193 (1965-2 C.B. 370) regarding the valuation of tangible and intangible corporate assets. The provisions of Rev. Rul. 59-60, as modified, were extended to the valuation of corporate securities for income and other tax purposes by Rev. Rul. 68-609 (1968-2 C.B. 327). In addition, Rev. Rul. 77-287 (1977-2 C.B. 319), amplified Rev. Rul. 59-60 by indicating the ways in which the factors listed in Rev. Rul. 59-60 should be applied when valuing restricted securities.

[6] The definition of the term "adequate consideration" under ERISA is of particular importance to the establishment and maintenance of ESOPs because, pursuant to section 408(e) of the Act, an ESOP may acquire employer securities from a party in interest only under certain conditions, including that the plan pay no more than adequate consideration for the securities.

employer securities held by the ESOP will provide a "put" option whereby individual participants may upon retirement sell their shares back to the employer.[7] It has been argued that some kinds of "put" options may diminish the need to discount the value of the securities due to lack of marketability. The Department believes that the existence of the "put" option should be considered for valuation purposes only to the extent it is enforceable and the employer has and may reasonably be expected to continue to have, adequate resources to meet its obligations. Thus, the Department proposes to require that the plan fiduciary assess whether these "put" rights are actually enforceable, and whether the employer will be able to pay for the securities when and if the "put" is exercised.

Finally, proposed subparagraph (I) deals with the role of control premiums in valuing securities other than those for which there is a generally recognized market. The Department proposes that a plan purchasing control may pay a control premium, and a plan selling control should receive a control premium. Specifically, the Department proposes that a plan may pay such a premium only to the extent a third party would pay a control premium. In this regard, the Department's position is that the payment of a control premium is unwarranted unless the plan obtains both voting control and control in fact. The Department will therefore carefully scrutinize situations to ascertain whether the transaction involving payment of such a premium actually results in the passing of control to the plan. For example, it may be difficult to determine that a plan paying a control premium has received control in fact where it is reasonable to assume at the time of acquisition that distribution of shares to plan participants will cause the plan's control of the company to be dissipated within a short period of time subsequent to acquisition.[8] In the Department's view, however, a plan would not fail to receive control merely because individuals who were previously officers, directors or shareholders of the corporation continue as plan fiduciaries or corporate officials after the plan has acquired the securities. Nonetheless, the retention of management and the utilization of corporate officials as plan fiduciaries, when viewed in conjunction with other facts, may indicate that actual control has not passed to the plan within the meaning of paragraph

---

[7] Regulation 29 CFR 2550.408b-(j) requires such a put option in order for a loan from a party in interest to the ESOP to qualify for the statutory exemption in section 408(b)(3) of ERISA from the prohibited transactions provisions of ERISA.

[8] However, the Department notes that the mere pass-through of voting rights to participants would not in itself affect a determination that a plan has received control in fact, notwithstanding the existence of participant voting rights, if the plan fiduciaries having control over plan assets ordinarily may resell the shares to a third party and command a control premium, without the need to secure the approval of the plan participants.

(b)(4)(ii)(I) of the proposed regulation. Similarly, if the plan purchases employer securities in small increments pursuant to an understanding with the employer that the employer will eventually sell a controlling portion of shares to the plan, a control premium would be warranted only to the extent that the understanding with the employer was actually a binding agreement obligating the employer to pass control within a reasonable time. *See Donovan v. Cunningham, supra*, 716 F.2d at 1472-74 (mere intention to transfer control not sufficient).

6. Service Arrangements Subject to FERSA

Section 8477(c)(1)C) of FERSA permits the exchange of services between the Thrift Savings Fund and a party in interest only in exchange for adequate consideration. In this context, the proposal defines the term "adequate consideration as "reasonable compensation", as that term is described in sections 408(b)(2) and 408(c)(2) of ERISA and the regulations promulgated thereunder. By so doing, the proposal would establish a consistent standard of exemptive relief for both ERISA and FERSA with regard to what otherwise would be prohibited service arrangements.

Regulatory Flexibility Act

The Department has determined that this regulation would not have a significant economic effect on small plans. In conducting the analysis required under the Regulatory Flexibility Act, it was estimated that approximately 6,250 small plans may be affected by the regulation. The total additional cost to these plans, over and above the costs already being incurred under established valuation practices, are estimated not to exceed $875,000 per year, or $140 per plan for small plans choosing to engage in otherwise prohibited transactions that are exempted under the statute conditioned on a finding of adequate consideration.

Executive Order 12291

The Department has determined that the proposed regulatory action would not constitute a "major rule" as that term is used in Executive Order 12291 because the action would not result in: an annual effect on the economy of $100 million; a major increase in costs of prices for consumers, individual industries, government agencies, or geographical regions; or significant adverse effects on competition, employment, investment, productivity, innovation, or on the ability of United States based enterprises to compete with foreign based enterprises in domestic or export markets.

Paperwork Reduction Act

This proposed regulation contains several paperwork requirements. The regulation has been forwarded for approval to the Office of Management and Budget under the provisions of the Paperwork Reduction Act of 1980 (Pub. L. 96-511). A control number has not yet been assigned.

Statutory Authority

This regulation is proposed under section 3(18) and 505 of the Act (29 U.S.C. 1003(18) and 1135); Secretary of Labor's Order No. 1-87; and sections 8477(a)(2)(B) and 8477(f) of FERSA.

List of Subjects in 29 CFR Part 2510

Employee benefit plans, Employee Retirement Income Security Act, Pensions, Pension and Welfare Benefit Administration.

Proposed Regulation

For the reasons set out in the preamble, the Department proposes to amend Part 2510 of Chapter XXV of Title 29 of the Code of Federal Regulations as follows:

PART 2510—[AMENDED]

1. The authority for Part 2510 is revised to read as follows:

   Authority: Sec. 3(2), 111(c), 505, Pub. L. 93-406, 88 Stat. 852, 894, (29 U.S.C. 1002(2), 1031, 1135); Secretary of Labor's Order No. 27-74, 1-86, 1-87, and Labor Management Services Administration Order No. 2-6.
   Section 2510.3-18 is also issued under sec. 3(18) of the Act (29 U.S.C. 1003(18)) and secs. 8477(a)(2)(B) and (f) of FERSA (5 U.S.C. 8477)
   Section 2510.3-101 is also issued under sec. 102 of Reorganization Plan No. 4 of 1978 (43 FR 47713, October 17, 1978), effective december 31, 1978 (44 FR 1065, January 3, 1978); 3 CFR 1978 Comp. 332, and sec. 11018(d) of Pub. L. 99-272, 100 Stat. 82.
   Section 2510.3-102 is also issued under sec. 102 of Reorganization Plan No. 4 of 1978 (43 FR 47713, October 17, 1978), effective December 31, 1978 (44 FR 1065, January 3, 1978), and 3 CFR 1978 Comp. 332.

2. Section 2510.3-18 is added to read as follows:

§ 2510.3-18 Adequate Consideration

(a) [Reserved]

(b)(1)(i) *General.* (A) Section 3(18)(B) of the Employee Retirement Income Security Act of 1974 (the Act) provides that, in the case of a plan asset other than a security for which there is a generally recognized market, the term "adequate consideration" when used in Part 4 of Subtitle B of Title I of the Act means the fair market value of the asset as determined in good faith by the trustee or named fiduciary pursuant to the terms of the plan and in accordance with regulations promulgated by the Secretary of Labor.

(B) Section 8477(a)(2)(B) of the Federal Employees' Retirement System Act of 1986 (FERSA) provides that, in the case of an asset other than a security for which there is a generally recognized market, the term "adequate consideration" means the fair market value of the asset as determined in good faith by a fiduciary or fiduciaries in accordance with regulations prescribed by the Secretary of Labor.

(ii) *Scope.* The requirements of section 3(18)(B) of the Act and section 8477(a)(2)(B) of FERSA will not be met unless the value assigned to a plan asset both reflects the asset's fair market value as defined in paragraph (b)(2) of this section and results from a determination made by the plan trustee or named fiduciary (or, in the case of FERSA, a fiduciary) in good faith as described in paragraph (b)(3) of this section. Paragraph (b)(5) of this section contains a special rule for service contracts subject to FERSA.

(2) *Fair Market Value.* (i) Except as otherwise specified in this section, the term "fair market value" as used in section 3(18)(B) of the Act and section 8477(a)(2)(B) of FERSA means the price at which an asset would change hands between a willing buyer and a willing seller when the former is not under any compulsion to buy and the latter is not under any compulsion to sell, and both parties are able, as well as willing, to trade and are well informed about the asset and the market for such asset.

(ii) The fair market value of an asset for the purposes of section 3(18)(B) of the Act and section 8477(a)(2)(B) of FERSA must be determined as of the date of the transaction involving that asset.

(iii) The fair market value of an asset for the purposes of section 3(18)(B) of the Act and section 8477(a)(2)(B) of FERSA must be reflected in written documentation of valuation meeting the requirements set forth in paragraph (b)(4), of this section.

(3) *Good Faith*—(i) *General Rule.* The requirement in section 3(18)(B) of the Act and section 8477(a)(2)(B) of FERSA that the fiduciary must determine fair market value in good faith establishes an objective, rather than a subjective, standard of conduct. Subject to the

conditions in paragraphs (b)(3)(ii) and (iii) of this section, an assessment of whether the fiduciary has acted in good faith will be made in light of all relevant facts and circumstances.

(ii) In considering all relevant facts and circumstances, the Department will not view a fiduciary as having acted in good faith unless

(A) The fiduciary has arrived at a determination of fair market value by way of a prudent investigation of circumstances prevailing at the time of the valuation, and the application of sound business principles of evaluation; and

(B) The fiduciary making the valuation either,

(1) Is independent of all parties to the transaction (other than the plan), or

(2) Relies on the report of an appraiser who is independent of all parties to the transaction (other than the plan).

(iii) In order to satisfy the independence requirement of paragraph (b)(3)(ii)(B), of this section, a person must in fact be independent of all parties (other than the plan) participating in the transaction. For the purposes of this section, an assessment of independence will be made in light of all relevant facts and circumstances. However, a person will not be considered to be independent of all parties to the transaction if that person—

(1) is directly or indirectly, through one or more intermediaries, controlling, controlled by, or under common control with any of the parties to the transaction (other than the plan);

(2) Is an officer, director, partner, employee, employer or relative (as defined in section 3(15) of the Act, and including siblings) of any such parties (other than the plan);

(3) Is a corporation or partnership of which any such party (other than the plan) is an officer, director or partner.

For the purposes of this subparagraph, the term "control," in connection with a person other than an individual, means the power to exercise a controlling influence over the management or policies of that person.

(4) *Valuation Content.* (i) In order to comply with the requirement in paragraph (b)(2)(iii), of this section, that the determination of fair market value be reflected in written documentation of valuation, such written documentation must contain, at a minimum, the following information:

(A) A summary of the qualifications to evaluate assets of the type being valued of the person or persons making the valuation;

(B) A statement of the asset's value, a statement of the methods used in determining that value, and the reasons for the valuation in light of those methods;

(C) A full description of the asset being valued;

(D) The factors taken into account in making the valuation, including any restrictions, understandings, agreements or obligations limiting the use or disposition of the property;

(E) The purpose for which the valuation was made;

(F) The relevance or significance accorded to the valuation methodologies taken into account;

(G) The effective date of the valuation; and

(H) In cases where a valuation report has been prepared, the signature of the person making the valuation and the date the report was signed.

(ii) *Special Rule*. When the asset being valued is a security other than a security covered by section 3(18)(A) or the Act or section 8477(a)(2)(A) of FERSA, the written valuation required by paragraph (b)(2)(iii) of this section, must contain the information required in paragraph (b)(4)(i) of this section, and must include, in addition to an assessment of all other relevant factors, an assessment of the factors listed below:

(A) The nature of the business and the history of the enterprise from its inception;

(B) The economic outlook in general, and the condition and outlook of the specific industry in particular;

(C) The book value of the securities and the financial condition of the business;

(D) The earning capacity of the company;

(E) The dividend-paying capacity of the company;

(F) Whether or not the enterprise has goodwill or other intangible value;

(G) The market price of securities of corporations engaged in the same or a similar line of business, which are actively traded in a free and open market, either on an exchange or over-the-counter;

(H) The marketability, or lack thereof, of the securities. Where the plan is the purchaser of securities that are subject to "put" rights and such rights are taken into account in reducing the discount for lack of marketability, such assessment shall include consideration of the extent to which such rights are enforceable, as well as the company's ability to meet its obligations with respect to the "put" rights (taking into account the company's financial strength and liquidity);

(I) Whether or not the seller would be able to obtain a control premium from an unrelated third party with regard to the block of securities being valued, provided that in cases where a control premium is taken into account:

(1) Actual control (both in form and in substance) is passed to the purchaser with the sale, or will be passed to the purchaser within a reasonable time pursuant to a binding agreement in effect at the time of the sale, and

(2) It is reasonable to assume that the purchaser's control will not be dissipated within a short period of time subsequent to acquisition.

(5) *Service Arrangements Subject to FERSA.* For purposes of determinations pursuant to section 8477(c)(1)(C) of FERSA (relating to the provision of services) the term "adequate consideration" under section 8477(a)(2)(B) of FERSA means "reasonable compensation" as defined in sections 408(b)(2) and 408(c)(2) of the Act and §§ 2550.408b-2(d) and 2550.408c-2 of this chapter.

(6) *Effective Date.* This section will be effective for transactions taking place after the date 30 days following publication of the final regulation in the **Federal Register.**

Signed in Washington, DC, this 11th day of May 1988.

David M. Walker,

Assistant Secretary, Pension and Welfare Benefits Administration, U.S. Department of Labor.

[FR Doc. 88-10934 Filed 5-16-88; 8:45 am]

9

VALUATION LITIGATION

CHARLES F.G. KUYK, ROBERT F. HOWARD, AND
PETER B. FRANK*

		Page
¶ 9.1	The Litigation Setting	9-4
	[1] Common Valuation Litigation	9-5
	[2] Uniqueness of the Legal Context	9-6
	[a] Statutory Law	9-6
	[b] Regulatory and Administrative Law	9-7
	[c] Case Law	9-7
	[d] Rules of Civil Procedure and Evidence	9-8
	[3] The Judicial Process	9-11
	[a] The Complaint	9-11
	[b] The Answer	9-12
	[c] Discovery	9-12
	[d] Motions, Stipulations, and Requests for Admission	9-15
	[e] Pretrial Hearings	9-16
	[f] Trial	9-17
	[g] Judge and Jury	9-18
	[h] The Verdict	9-19
¶ 9.2	Guidelines for the Expert Witness	9-19
	[1] Attributes of the Valuation Expert Witness	9-19
	[a] Personal Attributes	9-20
	[b] Professional Attributes	9-21
	[2] The Litigation Engagement	9-22
	[a] Expert Witness or Consultant	9-22
	[b] The Exercise of Professional Judgment	9-24
	[c] Conflicts of Interest	9-24
	[d] Inconsistencies With Prior Case Testimony	9-25
	[e] Engagement Acceptance Considerations	9-26
	[f] Testimony Evidence Submitted	9-27

* CHARLES F.G. KUYK, CPA, is a partner with Price Waterhouse in its San Francisco, California, office. ROBERT F. HOWARD is a managing director, Houlihan Lokey, Howard & Zukin, Inc., a business valuation and investment banking advisory firm headquartered in Los Angeles, California. PETER B. FRANK, CPA, is a partner with Price Waterhouse in Los Angeles, California, and is its chairman of litigation services.

	[g]	Reliance Upon Company Financial Statements	9-28
	[h]	What to Expect From the Opposition	9-28
	[i]	What to Expect in the Deposition	9-30
	[3] The Valuation Report and Expert Testimony		9-31
	[a]	Standards of Report Content	9-31
	[b]	Preparation for Testimony	9-32
	[c]	Conduct in Depositions	9-33
	[d]	Conduct in Trial	9-33
¶ 9.3	**Valuation Litigation by Case Type**		**¶ 9-35**
	[1] Dissenting Shareholder Statutes		9-35
	[a]	Appraisal Rights	9-35
	[b]	Standard of Value	9-37
	[c]	Entire Fairness	9-39
	[d]	Burden of Proof	9-39
	[e]	Valuation Approaches	9-40
	[f]	Other Factors	9-42
	[g]	The Level of Value	9-42
	[h]	Summary	9-45
	[2] Corporate or Partnership Dissolution Statutes		9-46
	[a]	Forms of Liquidation	9-46
	[b]	Voluntary vs. Involuntary Dissolution	9-49
	[c]	Partnership Dissolution vs. Corporate Dissolution	9-50
	[d]	The Valuation Date	9-52
	[e]	Summary	9-52
	[3] Business Valuations Under Federal Statutes		9-52
¶ 9.4	**Recovery of Damages**		**9-54**
	[1] Corporate Damages		9-54
	[a]	Origins of Litigation	9-54
	[b]	Valuation vs. Damage Determination	9-55
	[c]	Legal Theory of Damages	9-57
	[d]	Elements of Recovery	9-58
	[2] Human Capital Valuation		9-62
	[a]	Elements of Damage	9-62
	[b]	Medical and Funeral Expenses	9-63
	[c]	Personal Injury Lost Earnings	9-64
	[d]	Wrongful Death/Lost Earnings	9-65
	[e]	Assessing the Impact of Inflation	9-72
	[f]	Discounting Future Earnings	9-73
Appendix 9-1	Federal Rules of Evidence—Article VII. Opinions and Expert Testimony		9-76
Appendix 9-2	Sample Litigation Retainer Agreement		9-78

Litigation has become an ever-present fact of life in the business community. Indeed, the experienced appraiser who has *not* been called upon to give an opinion on the value of a closely held company in a legal proceeding is rare. Yet, unless an appraiser has either learned the "dos and don'ts" of expert testimony the hard way—in the courtroom, with perhaps less than satisfactory results—he or she will find little published guidance on the subject that is readily usable by the practitioner. The purpose of this chapter is to alleviate, to some degree, this condition.

Despite the professional hazards associated with testifying as an expert witness (and they are many), this dimension of the valuation expert's professional practice can be both challenging and rewarding. Each time this analyst renders a value opinion in court, he or she does no less than place his or her professional reputation on the line. Few practitioners would disagree that the time spent sitting opposite an attorney (often accompanied by the opposing valuation expert witness) who is carefully reviewing your report with the sole intent of finding flaws is one of an analyst's most memorable moments! However, for the trained and experienced professional who has properly prepared for the occasion, testifying in a deposition or in the courtroom can be an intellectually invigorating and professionally satisfying experience.

Valuation litigation can and perhaps should be viewed as one important stage in the business valuation process. While it is customary to view the written valuation report as the culmination of most valuation engagements, if the report is submitted as evidence in a legal proceeding, the appraiser's work has, in many respects, just begun. That is why the astute valuation expert learns, before accepting a valuation assignment, whether or not the appraisal report will be reviewed in litigation proceedings. It is equally vital when expert witness testimony is anticipated that the analyst carefully estimate and communicate to the client the significant level of effort required to prepare for testimony. Unless the client is willing to compensate the appraiser for testimony preparation above and beyond time spent producing the report, the valuation analyst should consider declining the assignment.

The experienced valuation analyst is also alert to the circumstance of a client with a preconceived value (amount) such that any significant deviation from this amount by the appraising expert witness is "unsatisfactory." At such times, the analyst must be vigilant in satisfying his or her professional obligations of independence and objectivity before accepting such an assignment or rendering an opinion. Failure to do so would constitute a potential breach of professional ethics. In any event, developing testimony around a preestablished value is almost certainly doomed since the opposing attorney will be sure to explore any biases or inconsistencies in the valuation report.

While litigation is not without its risk, the rewards are commensurately numerous. Aside from the personal satisfaction of having persuasively communicated a well-supported opinion, the valuation expert can take great pride in knowing that he or she has provided a valuable service not only to the attorney-client but to the litigants and judge and jury as well. It is important to remember that no one appreciates an easily read, well-supported valuation report and lucid courtroom testimony more than the judge and jury who are faced with the responsibility of determining the "right" value.

Serving as an expert witness also provides a boost to an appraiser's professional qualifications. It forces the mastery of acceptable valuation techniques as well as a clear understanding of why other techniques are unacceptable or inappropriate for a particular case. It encourages high standards of research, analysis, and documentation since it is virtually certain the other side will do its utmost to uncover weaknesses. The litigation setting also fosters consistency in valuation methodology from one appraisal to the next since reports issued in previous cases are often studied by the opposing attorneys and experts to uncover differences relative to the current testimony.

Unlike many other valuation engagements, where the means of expressing a company's value is through a written report, litigation allows the appraiser to communicate his or her findings verbally. And most importantly, testifying as an expert witness is an excellent way to gain recognition in the business community as an authority on the subject—which, in turn, is unquestionably one of the best ways to expand a professional practice.

While no single chapter can explore the full range of situations likely to be faced by the appraiser in a litigation setting, hopefully this chapter will at least acquaint the practicing business appraiser with the unique characteristics of this valuation phase. At a minimum, the chapter is sufficiently broad to serve as a guide for further research. This, after all, is often what is most needed by the skilled valuation analyst facing a unique valuation setting. Finally, the chapter is intended as a bench mark for reviewing prior to accepting a valuation engagement that is likely to lead to litigation and as an aid in preparing for valuation testimony.

¶ 9.1 The Litigation Setting

The foundation of expert witness testimony is thorough preparation. The valuation analyst must research past and current valuation cases as well as become conversant with all aspects of the selected legal concept—statutory law, regulatory and administrative law, case law, and, most importantly, the Rules of Civil Procedure and Evidence. The preparation needed for all these aspects of the litigation setting are discussed next.

[1] Common Valuation Litigation

Disputes over the value of a company arise for a variety of reasons. Those most often requiring the opinion of a professional valuation expert, however, generally fall into one or more of the following categories:

- Dissenting shareholder actions;
- Corporate or partnership dissolutions;
- Divorces; and
- Recovery of damages in litigation through such actions as breach of contract, antitrust violation, tortious actions, insurance claims, and personal injury or wrongful death.

Each of these case types, with the exception of divorce (which is the subject of Chapter 11), is discussed in some detail later in this chapter.

The fundamental objective in valuing a company under one of these scenarios is no different from any other valuation setting. Unique to the litigation environment, however, is the fact that the interested parties are, by definition, in considerable disagreement over the monetary value of the company. The valuation analyst is thus entering a relatively hostile environment and one in which the rules may be established by a third party, such as a judge or arbiter. The experienced analyst recognizes the unique conditions of litigation and takes extra care in preparing his or her valuation report, knowing full well that the opposition will take issue with many, if not all, of the report's assumptions and methods.

It is vital that the valuation analyst be familiar with the fundamental legal and economic issues of a particular case. If so prepared, the analyst can provide valuation testimony both relevant to the appraised company and consistent with applicable statutory case law. Failure to deal with the applicable legal issues or precedents early in the case can prove disastrous to the expert witness later when, for example, his or her well-recognized valuation methodology proves to have been wholly disallowed in one of the jurisdiction's prior court rulings. Accordingly, the analyst should work closely with his or her client attorney to learn what appraisal methods have been successfully used—or rejected—within a given jurisdiction.

[2] Uniqueness of the Legal Context

While the basic principles and procedures for valuing a company for a legal proceeding are no different from those for other valuation engagements, the practitioner should be aware of two important distinctions. First, the care and preparation that the analyst must take in such cases may be far greater than those required for other valuation contexts. In fact, the primary ingredient of success for a valuation witness is simply hard work, particularly when preparing for testimony. In no other valuation setting will the analyst's work—not to mention his or her own professional qualifications—be more diligently scrutinized than in the litigation setting.

A second major distinction of a litigation environment is the influence exerted by the body of statutes, regulations, case law, and rules of evidence and civil procedure. These conventions may not only influence the methodology used in appraising a company but will also govern if and how the expert witness testifies to his or her findings and opinions as well. The makeup, authority, and implementation of these rules are, of course, subjects covered in a school of law. Nevertheless, some aspects have been summarized here to highlight their effect upon the valuation process.

[a] Statutory Law

Statutes are, fundamentally, the laws established by federal, state, or local legislative bodies (governments). While there are numerous categories of statutes, the broadest classifications are probably those of *general statutes*—laws that apply to the general population—and *private or personal statues*—laws that pertain to individuals or groups of individuals. Similarly, there are public statutes governing the social and commercial behavior of citizens within the entire country, state, or community.

Statutes will often determine both the valuation issues to be addressed in the particular case and the ways (valuation methods) in which the court will arrive at an appraised value. This is particularly true in cases such as dissenting shareholder actions where each state has its own laws governing when and how shareholders are to be compensated for events such as corporate "squeeze-outs."

Different statutes also govern different legal issues. For example, federal statutes regulate estate and gift tax matters and damage cases in federal courts, such as those arising from federal antitrust or patent infringement matters. State statutes govern many other proceedings, such as divorce, dissenting shareholder actions, personal injury and condemnations, and business litigation under state law.

Statutes vary from state to state and from federal to state jurisdictions. Statutes, of course, also change periodically. The careful valuation analyst should learn—often from the client attorney—which statutes are relevant to the case at hand and should become familiar with the major issues surrounding these statutes.

[b] Regulatory and Administrative Law

Regulations and administrative rulings essentially are supplements to statutes designed to provide clarification and guidance on statute implementation. Some regulations and rulings have the same force as statutes; others, such as the Internal Revenue Service (IRS) revenue rulings, are expressions of opinion or are interpretive in nature. Again, it is the responsibility of the valuation analyst to become familiar with any regulations and rulings pertinent to a particular case.

[c] Case Law

Case law is the law that governs a particular issue based upon decisions made by courts in earlier similar cases. Case law arises from the outcome of prior cases. It provides a means for courts to use precedents to guide their decisions in later cases. The obvious, although not always valid, justification for using this form of law is that decisions reached after careful deliberation on similar issues in the past should be equally sound in later cases. The dilemma of this supposition when the value of a company is at stake is the difficulty involved in finding cases with identical issues and circumstances.

Since case law is often the primary reason for ruling on a given issue, it is essential that the appraiser be familiar with the case law bearing on a particular valuation dispute. As with statutes, case law varies from jurisdiction to jurisdiction and is also subject to change. While courts first look to prior rulings within their own jurisdictions for guidance, it is not uncommon for courts to base decisions on other states' rulings, particularly those states with a greater volume of commercial enterprise and litigation (e.g., California, New York, Illinois, Delaware, and Texas).

Identifying applicable case law on valuation issues is not an uncomplicated task. After all, the process of researching case precedents that may relate to a particular matter is clearly within the domain of attorneys. But, while many valuation experts rely exclusively upon the client attorney to provide the relevant case law, it is common today to find appraisers with extensive research capabilities in the form of valuation law libraries, electronic legal and economic research capabilities (e.g, LEXIS or COMPUSTAT), and work product files organized by individual valuation issue. The proper use of such facilities allows the expert to thoroughly and efficiently prepare for a particular valuation assignment. Of course, legal research by the expert can be viewed only as a supplement—and not as a replacement—for research and case strategy implemented by the client attorney.

Despite the huge body of case law in the United States, new economic and business transactions continue to occur at a rapid pace, often resulting in litigation for which little, if any, case law exists. This places increased responsibility on the valuation expert to maintain an up-to-date awareness of economic and valuation trends and to use sound professional judgment when valuing a company within the litigation setting.

[d] Rules of Civil Procedure and Evidence

Valuation analysts exposed to valuation in a legal setting for the first time are often surprised by the profusion of legal rules and customs guiding the process of collecting and disclosing evidence. While understanding and applying these rules is the responsibility of the attorneys, basic knowledge of the rules should be part of the analyst's litigation arsenal.

The *Federal Rules of Civil Procedure*, as the title implies, govern the procedures that attorneys must follow in pleading their cases (civil cases) before the district courts of the United States.[1] The rules direct, for example, the ways in which complaints and answers are prepared, delivered, and amended; how depositions are conducted and used in court proceedings; how documents are requested and admitted as evidence; and how various motions are filed with the court.

The actual categories of civil procedure rules are as follows:

- Scope of Rules—One Form of Action;
- Commencement of Action, Service of Process, Pleadings, Motions, and Orders;
- Pleadings and Motions;
- Parties;
- Deposition and Discovery;
- Trials;
- Judgment;
- Provisional and Final Remedies and Special Proceedings;
- Appeals;
- District Courts and Clerks; and
- General Provisions.

---

[1] *Federal Civil Judicial Procedures and Rules* (1987).

Of particular relevance are the rules governing the discovery of witnesses. Considerable literature exists on the subject of expert witness discovery, so it will not be examined in detail here. However, the relevant sections governing expert witness discovery are within Rule 26, "General Provisions Governing Discovery," and are as follows:

- *Scope of Discovery*;
- *Trial Preparation: Materials* (this section governs work products and essentially creates an attorney work product privilege for "consultants" (i.e., not expert witnesses) working with attorneys to protect "conclusions, opinions, or legal theories"); and
- *Trial Preparation* (this section governs the process of gaining information from individuals identified as expert witnesses).

The basic purpose of the attorney work product rule is to preserve the attoneys' rights to prepare for trial with enough privacy to let them examine both the favorable and unfavorable aspects of the case without divulging their findings to the opposition.

As might be expected, there has been considerable debate over the interpretation of these rules, particularly those dealing with what work products are protected, who is available for discovery, and to what extent an expert witness is required to testify. The valuation analyst should determine, with the client attorney, what is "protected work product" and what are "facts and opinions" that will be subject to discovery. Also, it is important that the analyst recognize his or her role as either a consultant (and subject to the protection afforded by Rule 26(b)(3)) or an expert witness (and subject to discovery under Rule 26(b)(4)). In many instances, an individual may be initially retained as a consultant to work with the attorney in developing valuation, economic, or accounting theories and then subsequently "evolve" into an expert witness to render opinion testimony (at which point, it is likely that all previous consulting work may become discoverable). The valuation analyst engaged to work on a litigation should thus be sensitive to the distinction between "consultant" and "expert witness" and ensure that his or her role is clearly defined.

If there is even a possibility that the valuation analyst will be asked to serve as an expert witness, it is best to assume that full discovery will take place. The analyst should thus guard against retaining extraneous and outdated work products that do not contribute to the testimony but that might provide a fertile field for inquiry at a deposition or at trial.

In addition to the Federal Rules of Civil Procedure, each federal court has its local rules covering such things as timetables and deadlines. Each of the states also has its own rules of evidence and procedure. No attempt is made here to identify these, but the appraiser should discuss the rules with his or her client-attorney when starting an assignment.

The *Federal Rules of Evidence* govern the admissibility of evidence at trials. As stated in the rules, the purpose of rules of evidence is "construed to secure fairness in administration, elimination of unjustifiable expense and delay and promotion of growth and development of the law of evidence to the end that truth may be ascertained and proceedings justly determined.[2]

The articles of the Federal Rules of Evidence, within which the individual rules are stated, are as follows:

- Article   I.   General Provisions
- Article   II.   Judicial Notice
- Article III.   Presumptions in Civil Actions and Proceedings
- Article IV.   Relevancy and its Limits
- Article   V.   Privileges
- Article VI.   Witnesses
- Article VII.   Opinions and Expert Testimony
- Article VIII. Hearsay
- Article IX.   Authentication and Identification
- Article   X.   Contents of Writings, Recordings, and Photographs
- Article XI.   Miscellaneous Rules

From this list of articles, it is clear that Article VII, "Opinions and Expert Testimony," is of most interest to the valuation analyst. The individual rules within this article include the following:

- Rule 701.   Opinion Testimony by Lay Witness;
- Rule 702.   Testimony by Experts;
- Rule 703.   Bases of Opinion Testimony by Experts;
- Rule 704.   Opinion on Ultimate Issue;
- Rule 705.   Disclosure of Facts or Data Underlying Expert Opinion; and
- Rule 706.   Court Appointed Experts.

While the valuation expert witness is certainly not expected to possess an in-depth understanding of these rules, a basic awareness of their purpose and application can contribute significantly to the expert's efficient rendering of useful testimony. The rules of evidence contained in Article VII are reproduced at the end of this chapter as Appendix 9-1.

---

[2] Fed. R. Civ. Proc. 102, "Purpose and Construction."

[3] The Judicial Process

The judicial process (guided by the previously mentioned Federal Rules of Civil Procedure and Federal Rules of Evidence) governs the way in which each party submits its arguments and evidence to the court and the way in which each side examines and refutes the arguments and evidence presented by the opposing litigants. If the valuation analyst is familiar with these rules, he or she can concentrate on rendering truly "expert" testimony rather than devoting attention to less critical procedural concerns.

Unlike courtroom scenes depicted on television, which often include dramatic testimony completely unexpected by opposing counsel, federal and state civil proceedings guard against such "surprise" testimony. Each side is given ample opportunity to explore the other side's testimony and evidence before presenting its case to the judge and jury. This includes the investigation of each party's position relative to statutory case law, the facts to be relied on, and, in the case of expert valuation testimony, the opportunity to examine the methodologies, the facts relied upon, and the opinions of opposing expert witnesses.

The following paragraphs provide only a brief outline of the stages of the judicial process that the appraiser can expect to see in valuation litigation. Readers interested in greater detail are encouraged to study the Federal Rules of Civil Procedure, the Federal Rules of Evidence, and state rules or to make inquiries of an attorney.

[a] The Complaint

The judicial process begins when one party, the plaintiff, files a complaint alleging that some action by the defendant violated a legal right of the plaintiff and thereby caused injury to the plaintiff. The *complaint*, drafted by the plaintiff's attorneys with assistance from the plaintiff, is the legal document that initiates the legal proceeding. It sets forth statutory or other legal precedents involved, the actions by the defendant which led to the violation of law, and, in general terms, the resulting damages suffered by the plaintiff as a result of the defendant's allegedly illegal acts. The complaint is filed with the applicable court, and copies are served by the court clerk upon the defendant under cover of a summons.

In some cases, business valuation experts are retained to assist in the drafting of the complaint's damage assertions. Retention of experts at this stage can prevent the future embarrassment of pleaded damages widely divergent from amounts calculated by the expert witness.

[b] The Answer

As the name implies, the *answer* is the defendant's response to the plaintiff's allegations voiced in the complaint. Filed with the court issuing the summons and complaint, the answer responds to each claim asserted and either admits or denies the claims (*averments*). In response to the claim, the defendant may elect to file a motion (a *demurrer*) to strike the complaint because there are defects in the claim, such as lack of jurisdiction or failure to state a claim upon which relief can be granted. The answer may also include so-called affirmative defenses, which set forth reasons why the claim is without legal merit even if the plaintiff's contentions are valid. Examples of affirmative defenses include contributory negligence, fraud, and statute of limitations.

The complaint and answer, referred to as *pleadings*, provide the basic foundation—both legal and factual—of the case. The valuation analyst employed to render expert witness testimony should carefully review the complaint and answer (including all amendments) as the first step in understanding the issues of a particular case. These documents will also provide considerable insight into the statutory and case law being relied upon by either side, thereby allowing the appraiser to initiate research into the relevant appraisal issues.

[c] Discovery

The Federal Rules of Civil Procedure govern the procedures by which the attorneys for each litigant "discover" all that they can about the opposition's theories and arguments. Thus, *discovery* (or *pretrial discovery*) is the legal name given to the fact-finding process. When expert witnesses are involved, questions regarding the scope of testimony, methodologies used, facts relied upon, and the opinion as to a company's value are among the central targets of discovery. Many attorneys consider the main objective of expert discovery to be preparation for cross-examination rather than just fact-finding.

In discovery, two fundamental types of information are sought: (1) documentation, such as financial statements, memoranda, correspondence, or operating statistics, relevant to the issues and (2) the testimony of witnesses, including expert witnesses. The primary instruments used to obtain this information are depositions, interrogatories, and requests for production of documents.

Depositions are taken by attorneys of witnesses to gather information prior to the trial about the issues and to understand the nature (or identify weaknesses) of each potential witness's testimony. Depositions also help attorneys gauge the strength of both their own and the opposition's arguments as a basis for conducting settlement negotiations. It is important to note that, like testimony at trial, a deposition is testimony under oath and may be presented at trial. The questions and answers are recorded verbatim by a court reporter and, after corrections are made, are provided to both sides in written form.

The following areas generally are covered in depositions of an expert witness:

- The expert's credentials, both academic and professional, including any publications, speeches, and classes taught;
- The expert's prior litigation experience and testimony (this often includes detailed inquiry into prior cases in which the expert testified, the objective of which is to uncover contradictory testimony);
- The specific nature of the work performed (or to be performed) by the expert, including the identification and work scope of staff who assisted in the valuation;
- The fee and billing arrangements among the expert witness, the attorneys, and the litigant;
- The expert witness' opinion on the relevant issues together with a description of all materials relied upon to form such an opinion;
- A detailed review of all assumptions made and calculations performed by the expert in arriving at his or her opinion; and
- A detailed review of all documents upon which the expert relied or which the expert produced.

As might be expected, plaintiff attorneys will attempt to elicit answers from the defense's witnesses that will support the plaintiff's allegations. In contrast, defense attorneys will seek to discover weaknesses in the plaintiff witness's testimony. The client attorney, present throughout the deposition, will attentively monitor the proceeding. If the inquiries are improper in form or enter into areas either beyond the expert's scope or upon potentially privileged areas, the attorney may object to the question or, in a more extreme instance, may move to preclude further examination into certain areas.[3]

While the valuation expert witness should attempt to be as prepared as possible prior to being deposed by opposition counsel, trial schedules occasionally prevent this. In such instances, the expert witness can only respond honestly that his research has not been completed as of the deposition date and that it will be finished by time of trial. This is certainly a better response than to incorrectly guess at an answer in the deposition and then have to give a different answer to the same question at trial. As described in the rules of civil procedure,

---

[3] See Daniels, "Protecting Your Expert During Discovery," 71 A.B.A.J. 50 (1985).

"any deposition may be used by any party for the purpose of contradicting or impeaching the testimony of deponent as a witness or for any other purpose permitted by the Federal Rules of Evidence."[4] Since credibility is one of an expert witness's most valued attributes, the expert must carefully guard against any testimonial infractions which might tarnish his credibility. If work is incomplete, however, there may be undesirable ramifications, such as a trial delay, a second deposition, or even preclusion of the expert as a witness. It is thus critical to work closely with the client attorney on timetables and deadlines.

Valuation analysts, whether retained as consultants or expert witnesses, often play a role during the deposition of the opposing witness. While individuals other than the attorney conducting the deposition are prohibited from asking questions of the witness, the analyst can suggest questions to the attorney by passing notes or by discussing lines of inquiry during breaks. Since the analyst is familiar with the concepts and terminology used by the opposing expert witness, he or she is in an excellent position to recommend that certain weak areas in the testimony be more fully explored.

Finally, depositions should be viewed positively as a means of "testing" the expert witness's arguments as well as his or her capabilities as an expert witness. In many cases, a strong performance by an appraiser in a deposition can encourage the opposition to consider settlement in a different light.

Interrogatories are sets of written questions prepared by each side and submitted to the opposing side for their response. In general terms, written interrogatories are intended to obtain any information (excluding that which is privileged) that is relevant to the subject matter in the pending action. Like depositions, interrogatories are completed well before the trial so that each side has an opportunity to learn as much as it can about the facts.

A litigant, through an interrogatory, is entitled to learn a considerable amount of information concerning the testimony of the opposition's expert witness. For example, the Federal Rules of Civil Procedure state that the following may be requested:

- The identity of expert witnesses;
- The subject matter upon which the expert witness is expected to testify;
- The substance of the facts and opinions to which the expert witness is expected to testify; and
- A summary of the grounds for each opinion.

---

[4] Fed. R. Civ. Proc. 32(a)(1).

While interrogatories are prepared by the attorneys, it is not uncommon for the lawyers to seek assistance from the valuation expert when drafting questions focused upon the financial or economic aspects of the case. The expert witness can contribute significantly to this process since specificity in drafting interrogatories often yields more valuable information than less precise inquiries.

Conversely, when responding to interrogatories about the nature of expert testimony, the expert witness can assist his or her attorney in drafting the answer. The attorney will generally respond to an interrogatory as succinctly as possible. On one hand, divulging too much information may provide fuel for the ensuing cross-examination whereas a response that is too brief could be grounds for further expert witness discovery. It is ultimately up to the attorney to strike the appropriate balance.

Requests for production of documents are the procedures whereby attorneys obtain relevant existing materials (e.g., accounting and operational data, correspondence, memoranda, and financial forecasts) from the opposition. Valuation expert witnesses can provide assistance in the drafting of these requests. Unless the relevant documentation is obtained during discovery, it will be more difficult, if not impossible, to secure later on.

The focus of inquiry by analysts invited to assist in the drafting of a document production request should be on any financial, operational, or administrative document likely to have been produced by the appraised company that would be of value in performing the valuation. As with interrogatories, requests for production that explicitly identify—by actual name, if possible—the documents required will often yield far better results than requests for "generic" accounting or financial materials.

The discovery process coupled with the complaint and answer thus comprise the measures used by attorneys to elicit information from opposing litigants and witnesses. For the expert witness, the deposition marks the end of a substantial effort to analyze facts, assess alternative approaches, and formulate opinions. As witnesses can be precluded from adding new testimony at trial, it is imperative that the expert witness be able to clearly convey the essence of the testimony at the deposition. Major shifts in testimony between the time of deposition and trial can serve to undermine an expert witness's credibility.

[d] Motions, Stipulations, and Requests for Admission

Other procedures which frequently occur during litigation warrant mention. The first is that of a motion. A *motion* is an application to the court by one of the litigant's attorneys for a court order. Within the context of valuation litigation, the most common motions are motions to reject all or portions of the claim due to various inadequacies in the claim; motions to challenge the use of certain data as evidence; motions seeking to bar individuals as witnesses or specific testimony or exhibits; and, finally, motions for directed verdicts or motions for judgment seeking a decision and judgment from the court.

A *stipulation* is an agreement among the litigants concerning the issues to be considered in the trial. The primary purpose of stipulations is to make the litigation process more efficient by eliminating all issues other than those on which the parties disagree. Stipulations govern not only issues of fact but also address applications of statutory and case law and rules of evidence and procedure. To the expert witness, stipulations concerning admissions of fact are of primary concern. Stipulations are generally recorded in writing with each litigant's attorney signing to acknowledge agreement.

As a simple example, in business valuation litigation, the attorneys might wish to stipulate that the measure of value for the closely held company owned by litigants in a divorce proceeding be fair market value. In this case, the valuation expert witness should be consulted by the attorney prior to agreeing to the stipulation to ensure that fair market value is a fair and appropriate basis of value and that fair market value—as contrasted from some other definition of value—was properly defined in the stipulation. Stipulations may also be entered as to the reliability of certain financial documents or as to the accuracy of a table of data.

A *request for admission*, like a stipulation, is a means whereby the litigating parties can agree on certain facts. A *request for admission* is essentially a request for a statement from the opposition that a certain fact is true. If the parties can agree to such facts, it is unnecessary to "muddy the litigation waters" with uncontested issues. Again, the expert valuation witness can play a role by identifying to the attorney those factual elements less likely to be contested.

[e] Pretrial Hearings

A *pretrial hearing* (or conference) is a meeting between the litigants' attorneys and the trial or pretrial judge to (1) clearly define those issues on which there is agreement and those for which there is dispute, (2) resolve issues relating to discovery, (3) agree upon a schedule for discovery motions and trial, and (4) assess the potential for settlement. Like stipulations, pretrial hearings seek to streamline the litigation process by focusing attention on critical issues. Based upon the pretrial conference and the attorney's written agreement on factual and legal issues in dispute (submitted prior to the conference), the judge will prepare a *pretrial order* setting forth these agreements. This order is filed with the court and becomes the controlling document of the legal action.

Because this hearing strongly influences the issues to be addressed and the evidence to be considered, the valuation expert witness can again play an important role by counseling his or her client attorney as to the key valuation issues involved.

[f] Trial

The trial addresses three basic facets of a case, in separate phases[5]:

1. *Liability*—whether the defendant has violated a statute or a right of the plaintiff which is actionable in a court of law;
2. *Proximate cause*—whether the action of the defendant was the immediate cause of injury to the plaintiff; and
3. *Damage*—what is a determination of the loss sustained by the plaintiff because of the wrongful actions of the defendant.

In most instances, the involvement of the business appraiser is restricted to the damages element of the case. If liability or proximate cause is not established, the expert witness testifying as to damages may never be examined at trial. In some cases, such as business interruption, product or lender liability, or breach of contract, the expert witness may be asked to testify as to proximate cause. For example, in a product liability lawsuit, the expert retained by the defendant may rebut the assertion of proximate cause by illustrating the many internal and external factors (e.g., regulatory changes or general economic downturns) other than the product's defects that led to the plaintiff company's demise.

As the plaintiff usually has the burden of proving the allegations, counsel for the plaintiff presents its case first. This process includes the introduction of evidence in the form of documentation and testimony by witnesses. Witnesses for the plaintiff are first directly examined by plaintiff counsel and then cross-examined by the opposing counsel. Redirect examination of the witness allows clarification of points raised during cross-examination. Following the presentation of plaintiff's arguments and evidence, the defense is allowed to introduce its own evidence and testimony to rebut the plaintiff's case.

Having taken the depositions of each side's expert witness, the attorneys are largely aware of the substance of each expert witness' testimony. Because of this, the plaintiff expert witness, who is first to testify, has an advantage. That is, in anticipation of the opposing expert's testimony, the plaintiff expert witness can, in his or her direct examination, be the first to raise and effectively defuse the arguments

---

[5] Dykeman, *Forensic Accounting, The Accountant as Expert Witness* 8 (1982).

expected later by the opposition's expert witness. The risk of this tactic is that the plaintiff is presenting elements of the defense's case that in fact, the defense might not have been planning to introduce.

The defense expert witness, on the other hand, has the advantage of being first to hear the opposition's expert testimony. This affords the defense counsel and expert witness the opportunity to refine the direct examination as well as to prepare for cross-examination. Regardless of the analyst's role as plaintiff or defense expert witness, however, the need for close cooperation between attorney and expert witness is obviously an important factor in the case.

[g] Judge and Jury

In most civil cases where the value of a company is to be determined, it is a *jury*, comprised of anywhere from six to twelve individuals of varying educational and professional backgrounds, that decides in favor of plaintiff or defendant. Because valuation litigation can involve relatively complex concepts within the disciplines of valuation theory, accounting, economics and financial analysis, it is important that the expert witness testify with the utmost clarity. Effective and persuasive communication is as much a requirement of the successful expert witness as is sheer intelligence and experience. Furthermore, the expert witness who can develop easy-to-understand and compelling demonstrative evidence—charts, graphs, and illustrations—will have an edge over mundane testimony that fails to keep the jury's interest.

As an expert witness, it is important to remember that it is within the jury's discretion to consider—or not consider—the testimony of the expert. As finders of fact, jurors bear the responsibility of listening to witnesses, analyzing the evidence presented, weighing the credibility of witnesses, and rendering a verdict. If that means disregarding the testimony of an expert witness, then the jury is not restricted from doing so. This fact underscores the need for the expert witness to not only provide logical and well-supported testimony but also to present the evidence in a manner that makes it easy for the jury to understand and believe. Furthermore, without becoming an advocate of the *client*, the expert witness should certainly be an advocate of his or her own theories, judgments, opinions, and work products.

The *judge* has duties that are sufficiently broad and of such magnitude as to place an adequate description of those responsibilities beyond the scope of this chapter. Suffice to say that, during the trial, the judge is responsible for, at a minimum, the following:

- Deciding upon the litigated issues of law;
- Instructing the jury on how to resolve the facts at issue and how to apply the relevant law;

- Governing the actual conduct of courtroom proceedings; and
- Making effective and efficient use of judicial resources.

The requirement for lucid testimony by the expert witness is equally applicable to the judge because he or she, like the jury, is expected to understand the facts and testimony of expert witnesses so that a just verdict can be rendered. Judges are extremely busy individuals who listen to the testimony of hundreds of witnesses. The expert who clearly conveys his or her message will be greatly appreciated by most judges. Thus, the valuation analyst, as an expert witness, is responsible to two bodies—the judge and jury—for the rendering of logical, easily understood testimony.

[h] The Verdict

In its simplest sense, the *verdict* is the decision of the jury (or judge if he or she hears the case without a jury) reported to and accepted by the court. The most common form of verdict is the general verdict in which the jury finds in favor of one party or the other. If the plaintiff receives a favorable verdict, the jury also establishes the amount of damages to be awarded. A *special verdict* involves a separate ruling on each issue placed by the court before the jury. Once the verdict has been returned, the losing party has a number of options, ranging from motions to the court to set aside the verdict to the granting of a new trial. If these attempts fail, the losing party can pursue the appeals process.

¶ 9.2 Guidelines for the Expert Witness

There is little in the way of published guidelines about the attributes of a successful valuation expert witness. This section seeks to provide such guidance with the recognition that these recommendations should be tailored to the individual appraiser. Ultimately, the best way to learn is by doing—but since mistakes on the stand can be enormously damaging, the skilled expert will pay heed to a few basic rules.

[1] Attributes of the Valuation Expert Witness

Expert witnesses come in all sizes, races, genders, and backgrounds. There is no one stereotype that identifies the good expert witness. There are, however, certain characteristics that may indicate how well a person will perform either in a deposition or on the witness stand. Make no mistake: Giving oral testimony *is* a kind of performance since the appraiser must clearly communicate the results of his or her analysis and persuade the audience (i.e., the judge and jury) that the appraiser's analysis and opinion are the just and proper ones.

[a] Personal Attributes

While it is difficult to list the personal attributes that all valuation experts should possess, there are a number of characteristics that generally are desirable in an expert witness. Some of these attributes are necessarily the same found in competent appraisers in nonlitigation settings and include intelligence, sound judgment, objectivity, and resourcefulness. There are other desirable attributes, however, that are particularly important for the expert witness.

☐ *Maintaining a sense of self.* The first rule expert witnesses should follow when on the witness stand is to be themselves. Of course, the experts should behave in a professional and self-confident manner but also should *not* try to be someone they are not, much as an actor would assume a role in a play. The expert should maintain a sense of self since it is *his or her* opinion that is offered to the court. Furthermore, assuming a different or more formal air can be harmful since the jury may see through it and it may lead to erratic behavior under cross-examination. Remember: The expert's credibility is on trial at all times.

☐ *Communication skills.* The "product" of an expert witness is expressed orally so it is essential that the expert be an effective and convincing communicator. A weak presentation can undermine even the best valuation report so the expert should be prepared to give concise, easy-to-understand testimony. This includes the ability to use graphic or visual support in appropriate places to reinforce testimony. Strong communication skills can be particularly important when testifying on valuations in which little empirical data is available to support the conclusion. The test of success then becomes whether the expert can verbally support the rationale for his or her conclusions.

☐ *Demeanor.* The ability to stay calm, especially during cross-examination, can be of great benefit to the expert witness. A calm demeanor conveys competence and self-confidence. Attorneys cross-examining an excitable or combative witness may get the witness confused about his or her own analysis or may paint the witness as biased in favor of the client. Recognize that one of the objectives of the examining attorney is precisely to unsettle the witness such that doubt is cast upon his or her testimony. Preparation and confidence in the quality of the work will serve to deter this attack.

☐ *Handling stress.* The ability to think clearly under pressure is an attribute the valuation expert must possess. It is expected that any witness will feel the tension of being on the witness stand. Anxiety exists even during direct examinations. Such tension can be magnified many times during cross-examination when the attorney may be perceived as "winning" by asking questions which the witness has difficulty in answering. This is normal. A good expert witness is one who can think clearly under cross-examination and respond assertively to questions. This will reinforce the court's opinion of him or her as a competent professional.

☐ *Open-minded.* The effective expert witness is able to see both sides of an issue and is willing to concede a point if justified. The expert witness also recognizes his or her own limitations. The ability to acknowledge not knowing the answer to a question is important since to do otherwise would raise doubts in the jurors minds as to the integrity of the witness. Some witnesses have personality characteristics that will not allow them to concede even the smallest point to the other side. Such a trait can be damaging. In an area as subjective as business valuations, it is important to remember that there is often no *one* right answer but, rather, a range of reasonable answers.

☐ *Patience.* The skilled expert witness is patient when listening and responding to questions posed by both plaintiff and defendant attorneys. Impulsive answers can serve as traps which the opposing attorney will later spring on the unwary witness. Deposition questions can trap the unwary since the testimony is simply reduced to writing and then resurrected at trial. The valuation expert should always carefully consider each question before answering.

☐ *Professional attitude.* Maintaining a professional attitude allows the expert witness to accept criticism during cross-examination without taking it personally. The expert witness who can remain emotionally detached from the proceeding, especially during cross-examination, stands a far better chance of preserving his objectivity and persuading the court.

[b] Professional Attributes

One of the best professional qualifications a valuation expert witness could bring to the witness stand would be as a market maker—someone who is actively involved as an agent for the purchase and sale of the type and size of business in question and who has recently completed a number of such transactions. However, this type of qualification is relatively rare so most valuation expert witnesses tend to fall into the category of theoretical appraisers. That is, they are experienced in the art of performing business valuations assuming a hypothetical transaction.

Because valuation courses have only recently been added to the curriculum of a few universities, the primary academic grounding for appraisers has been in accounting, finance, economics, or business management. Coupled with this background, actual experience in securities financial analysis and business valuations is likely the single most important qualification the valuation expert witness can offer. It is this experience that provides the foundation upon which the valuation opinion is based.

In addition to academic background and valuation experience, the attainment of recognized professional designations is also important. For valuation expert witnesses, the most common professional certifications include Senior Member of the American Society of Appraisers (ASA), with business valuation designations, Chartered Financial Analyst (CFA), and Certified Public Accountant (CPA). Each of these designations is achieved through a combination of experience and written examinations. The ASA credential is the most relevant to business valuations, followed by the CFA and CPA designations. However, since currently there are relatively few business valuation ASAs, it has become commonplace for CFAs and CPAs to provide business valuation services. Finally, postgraduate degrees such as M.B.A.s and Ph.D.s with concentrations in finance are also credentials that can establish the witness as an expert.

While there is no substitute for experience in the valuation field, it is important to underscore the fact that a valuation expert does not have to be an industry expert. Rather, the expert must be an expert in the *process of valuing businesses.*

[2] The Litigation Engagement

For the appraiser facing a litigation engagement, there are a number of factors to consider. Some are simply good engagement management practices while a number are unique to the litigation environment.

[a] Expert Witness or Consultant

The objectives and scope of work for a valuation litigation engagement will vary dramatically depending upon the valuation analyst's role. If the analyst is retained as an expert witness, then his or her objective is to render an expert opinion at trial. If retained as a consultant to the attorney, the analyst's objective is to provide business valuation advice. He or she "consults" with the attorney throughout the case on matters of valuation theory and practice and may assist the attorney in gathering data and cross-examining adverse experts.

A fundamental difference between the two roles concerns the "discoverability" of the valuation analyst's work. As mentioned earlier, a general (although not absolute) rule is that the appraiser as consultant is protected by the attorney work product privilege. This means that the other side is restricted from obtaining the analyst's work papers except under "exceptional circumstances."[6] This privilege affords the consultant considerable flexibility in pursuing alternative valuation solutions without having to reveal the results of his or her calculations to the opposition. The role of the consultant is thus aligned with that of the advocate where the client's best advantage is utmost in mind.

In contrast to the consultant's role is the expert witness's role. The expert witness is retained to render an independent, unbiased opinion. Accordingly, work product of the appraiser as an expert witness is generally subject to subpoena and review by the opposition. These documents are "discoverable." Because of this, valuation analysts retained as expert witnesses need to consider a number of precautions:

- Engagement letters between the valuation analyst and his or her client attorney are discoverable documents. If they describe the approach the analyst intends to follow and the nature of the information he or she intends to rely upon, any departure from these plans will provide fertile ground for inquiry by the opposing attorneys.
- Similarly, work defined in the engagement letter that is simply not completed may also invite the attention of opposing counsel who may draw the inference that, because the appraiser did not comply with his or her own plan, any testimony offered would be based on incomplete work. The analyst retained as an expert witness should thus weigh the benefits of an engagement letter against these risks. If the appraiser requires the protection such a letter provides or if the attorney or the client requests one, an engagement letter should be brief and, regarding the scope of work, should be stated in broad terms.
- Work plans that may or may not accompany an engagement letter should also be developed and retained with the understanding that they will be discoverable. These also should be general in nature to afford the expert flexibility in completing the engagement.
- Determine early in the engagement if a written report is required. In many cases, the lawyers do not want a written report and instead prefer to rely upon the expert witness's verbal testimony.
- The analyst should carefully control the content of his or her work papers. Indeed, work papers should be kept to a minimum. Extraneous materials showing the results of alternative calculations or notes taken during meetings should be eliminated on a contemporaneous basis. Once a subpoena has been received for the production of expert witness work papers, no eliminations can be made.

---

[6] Fed. R. Civ. Proc. 26(b)(4)(B).

[b] The Exercise of Professional Judgment

Business valuation is, by its very nature, a process requiring considerable professional judgment and insight gained from experience. Variables such as earnings capitalization rates or discount factors for present value calculations are determined both quantitatively and qualitatively. The value ascribed to a closely held company is the best estimate of value based upon accepted valuation methods and upon the sound judgment of the valuation analyst.

The problem with this element of judgment is its inherently human nature. Although the expert witness may be an individual of impeccable professional qualification and unblemished character, he or she is still human and subject to human frailties. The frailty sought most earnestly by opposing attorneys is unquestionably that of bias. After working closely, sometimes over an extended period, with the client attorney and perhaps the attorney's client, the possibility for bias exists.

To counter the appearance or fact of bias, a number of guidelines can be followed:

- Recognize the potential for bias in favor of your attorney's client and ensure that calculation variables requiring judgment are thoroughly screened for the actual presence or even appearance of bias. Conservatism and objectivity are the standards by which an expert witness should judge his or her testimony. A good test of bias is to try to place yourself in the shoes of the opposing expert as he or she reviews your assumptions and calculations. Will he or she concur with your approach? If not, why not? Assess both sides of a given variable, and carefully weigh the support for each before coming to any conclusions.
- Reduce, to the greatest extent possible, the use of calculation variables rather than subjective judgment. For example, if appropriate, a weighted average of past years' earnings as a proxy for future earnings would probably be easier to defend than a purely arbitrary estimate of future earnings based on your "judgment" or assessment of earning potential.
- When adjusting variables based upon judgment, obtain sufficient and pertinent supporting documentation such that refuting the calculation on the grounds of bias will be difficult. The greater the amount and higher the quality of external data, the easier it will be to defend your judgment.

[c] Conflicts of Interest

Checking for potential conflicts of interest should be a standard procedure prior to accepting a litigation engagement. There are essentially two ways in which a conflict can occur. One is when the valuation analyst is in some way affiliated with the appraised company or its owners such that there is either an actual lack of independence from the company or, equally important, such that there is the appearance of a lack of independence. Since the valuation analyst is offering, above all, an objective, unbiased opinion of the value of a company, the slightest hint of such a conflict—whether real or perceived—should be discussed with the attorney before accepting the engagement.

The second dimension of potential conflict arises if an analyst is involved in a litigation engagement and a current client or, in some cases, a past or future client is the adverse party. At stake here is not so much the analyst's independence from the appraised company but rather the analyst's professional obligations to his or her other clients. In some instances, the litigant-client is a large corporation with frequent legal actions pending (such as with large banks), and they are only an ancillary litigant in the case. It is possible to render an opinion of value against that litigant. However, accepting such an engagement should be done only after considering all ethical and legal ramifications and after discussing the matter fully with all involved parties.

[d] Inconsistencies With Prior Case Testimony

For valuation analysts who have testified often, in a variety of litigations, and for both plaintiffs and defendants, it becomes increasingly important to consider the consistency of testimony. With expert testimony being part of the public court record, it is relatively easy for opposing attorneys to research past testimony to perhaps uncover contrary opinions of the expert. In fact, during a deposition, it is common for an attorney to ask an expert witness for transcripts of all prior testimony which the witness has retained. While the circumstances from one appraised company to the next are always different, an expert witness's testimony can be severely undermined if the opposition can show that he or she testified to an opposite conclusion in an earlier case.

An example would be the use of a particular formula employing the cost of equity and debt for determining a capitalization rate (as in the capital asset pricing model). If this formula was used in one case but an entirely different formula was used in another case involving, for example, a company in the same industry, the expert witness should plan on explaining at length in his or her deposition why different methods were used for the two cases.

For the analyst who plans to testify frequently in business valuation litigation, the best defense against such a dilemma is to do the following:

- Ensure that the methodologies employed in valuing companies in the early litigations are based on accepted valuation methods,

on careful financial and economic research of both the company and the industry, and on thorough documentation of the reasons supporting judgmental variables.
- Maintain an awareness of past testimonies to ensure against inconsistencies. When circumstances dictate that different methodologies or factors be used, the expert witness should at least be aware that they vary from prior testimony. This will allow preparation for the cross-examination seeking to invalidate current testimony due to inconsistencies with past testimony. This should not be construed to mean, however, that all testimony transcripts be retained. As mentioned earlier, they will be requested and may provide grist for expert witness impeachment.
- Maintain an up-to-date awareness of changes in the discipline of valuation to maintain currency as well as to support departures from past testimony, when warranted.

[e] Engagement Acceptance Considerations

There are a number of factors that the appraiser should bear in mind when considering a litigation engagement opportunity. These factors are taken into account in the "Sample Litigation Retainer Agreement" in Appendix 9-2 at the end of this chapter.

- The appraiser should determine whether or not he or she is qualified to do the work. While this may seem so obvious as to not warrant mentioning, it is essential that the appraiser be satisfied that his or her training and experience are closely related to the issues at hand. Client attorneys will, of course, be the first to judge the qualification of a prospective expert, but it is not uncommon for attorneys to expand the scope of testimony of an expert, in some cases beyond the "comfort zone" of the appraiser. To illustrate, in the case of *Joseph E. Seagram & Sons, Inc. v. Hawaiian Oke & Liquors, Ltd.*,[7] the plaintiff's witness, an accountant, had only limited experience in business valuation. His testimony on valuation issues was thus not admitted. Similarly, in *California Steel and Tube v. Kaiser Steel Corporation*,[8] the testimony of qualified economist was rejected since his testimony was directed at determining whether or not the company priced below marginal cost—an issue upon which an accountant would be better qualified to respond. It is thus incumbent upon the appraiser to be candid with his or her client attorney if the nature of the work exceeds the appraiser's qualifications.

---

[7] 416 F.2d 71 (9th Cir. 1969).
[8] California Steel & Tube v. Kaiser Steel Corp., 469 F. Supp. 265 (C.D. Cal. 1979).

- The reputation of the law firm and the law firm's client should be evaluated.
- The attorney and the attorney's client (the party) should determine whether they will give full freedom to the appraiser with regard to obtaining required client information, interpreting facts, and forming conclusions of value.
- Billing arrangements should always be on a reimbursable basis and should in no way be dependent upon the outcome of the case. Even when working with attorneys who are on a contingent fee arrangement, the expert witness's fees should be paid in accordance with standard billable rates. (In typical contingent fee agreements, the client agrees to pay costs and expert witness fees currently.) Most attorneys are well aware of the requirement for such billing arrangements since Disciplinary Rule 7-109(c) of the American Bar Association's Model Code of Professional Responsibility proscribes "payment to a witness contingent upon the content of his testimony or the outcome of the case."
- The timetable within which the valuation services are to be performed should be clearly understood. If insufficient time has been allowed by the attorneys to perform a proper appraisal, the work should be declined. Similarly, if current work loads are such that accepting a litigation engagement, with its often stressful and time-sensitive demands, will overload an appraiser's existing staff, the engagement should perhaps not be undertaken. As many valuation analysts will attest, the litigation engagement that consumes *only* the originally planned level of effort is indeed a rare engagement!

[f] Testimony Evidence Submitted

Expert witness testimony requires a firm foundation in both fact and methodology to be accepted by the court. This requires the expert witness to clearly document and organize the documents and studies that support his or her testimony.

The expert witness should rely to the greatest extent possible upon facts which he or she (or the staff) has obtained first-hand. As a general rule, reliance upon other individuals for important facts (hearsay evidence) is never as reliable or persuasive as facts gained by direct observation. For this reason, the Federal Rules of Evidence contain a rule (Rule 802) concerning hearsay evidence essentially excluding evidence submitted by witnesses that is judged to be based on hearsay.

However, the Federal Rules of Evidence also grant considerable latitude to the witness designated as an expert witness as to hearsay evidence. The expert witness may rely upon research, academic literature, discussions with other experts in the field, or almost any other source needed to render an opinion. All such materials, although derived second-hand, are allowable as the basis for an opinion formed by the expert witness. So long as there is suitable "indicia of trustworthiness" or "reasonable basis of reliability," experts are permitted wide latitude as to the materials on which they may base their testimony.[9] This becomes particularly important when relying upon information provided by industry experts with whom the valuation analyst consulted when performing industry research.

[g] Reliance Upon Company Financial Statements

All valuations of closely held companies rely to a great extent upon financial statements—balance sheets, income statements, statements of changes in financial position and cash flow, and accompanying footnotes. Whether these statements are audited, reviewed, or compiled by outside auditors, they comprise one of the most important sources of information for the appraiser.

Another important exception to the hearsay rule (Rule 803(6)) relates to financial statements and the business records (e.g., source documents, journals, and ledgers) that underlie the statements. In essence, the expert witness may rely upon such statements without having to "audit" these records if they are normal business records prepared in the ordinary course of the business. However, while this exception may provide some level of protection, it is important to note that the opposition may present evidence that the statements are in error and thus cast doubt upon the expert witness's testimony.

The expert witness should, therefore, recognize the risks of relying upon financial statements (particularly those which are unaudited) and, if the risks seem excessive, take additional measures to value the company. Such measures may include performing an appraisal with no reliance upon the financial statements (in the case of smaller enterprises) or requesting that a financial audit be performed. While an audit by a reputable certified public accounting (CPA) firm does not provide ironclad protection from the risks of inaccurate or fraudulent financial reporting, it does provide a level of assurance that is generally recognized to be adequate for purposes of business valuation. Nevertheless, the valuation expert should still be alert to obvious errors in the financial statements.

[h] What to Expect From the Opposition

One of the best ways for valuation experts to prepare both their reports and themselves for testimony is to anticipate what the opposing

---

[9] Brett, "Expanded Use of Expert Witnesses Pose New Problems for Counsel," Nat'l L.J., Dec. 31, 1979, at 22; *see also* Fraier v. Continental Oil Co., 566 F.2d 378 (5th Cir. 1978). *See also* Fed. R. Evid. 803, "Hearsay Exceptions."

attorneys and expert witness will do with their testimony. One practice often followed in a number of business valuation firms is to have a colleague or team of reviewers independently critique the valuation report to uncover any weaknesses prior to its submission as evidence. If any of the in-house reviewers have previous personal experience in lengthy depositions, the appraiser can be sure of their careful attention to detail!

It is also helpful to understand what the other side is likely to do with the appraiser's report. Here are a number of activities often followed when examining the opposition's valuation report for the first time:

- Perform a general walk-through of the document, being alert to any obvious irregularities or inconsistencies. Such inconsistencies would include pages or tables out of order, an illogical report format, or the omission of major report sections.
- Perform a second, more detailed examination highlighting such items as all grammatical errors, misspelled words, typographical errors, and incorrect references.
- Analyze all financial schedules to uncover simple mathematical errors or to find inconsistencies among schedules. For example, ensure that the income statement, balance sheet, and statement of shareholder equity agree with each other and agree from year to year. Assess the downstream impact of such errors on the appraised value.
- Review the footnotes to financial statements to identify accounting practices for which the analysis failed to make adjustments. For example, a company using last-in, first-out (LIFO) inventory valuation may present inventory and cost of sales amounts on a basis inconsistent with some definitions of economic value.
- The majority of financial schedules prepared today are developed using electronic spreadsheet software, such as Lotus 1-2-3, Symphony, or Framework. Despite the enhanced appearance of such spreadsheets, they can be fraught with errors. Two common errors to bear in mind when reviewing such spreadsheets are logic errors (e.g., incorrect totals due to erroneous formulas) and rounding errors. Look for errors—particularly logic errors—when reviewing spreadsheets. Conversely, when developing such spreadsheets, take precautions to avoid such errors. The use of "spreadsheet audit" software can make this job easier.
- Review any "boiler plate" in the report to identify any references or citations that are irrelevant to the case at hand. These may indicate that the expert simply added the boiler plate without actually researching the references or relying upon them in conducting the appraisal. Such references might also support a contrary valuation conclusion.

- Carefully test the theories, methodologies, and assumptions used in the valuation. Are they applicable to the particular circumstances of the appraised company and its industry? Have the proper valuation methods been used? Have the valuation methods used been properly computed? Are the assumptions supported by fact, or are they conjecture?
- Test the comparable sales/price data to ensure true comparability. Vouch the authenticity of the quoted data (e.g., sales figures, price/earnings ratios, financial performance ratios, etc.).
- Perform alternative computations using the basic framework of the report but without the previously mentioned errors (if any) and under different assumptions. Perform sensitivity analyses on the computation variables to understand which variables have the greatest leverage upon the result.
- Locate other appraisals by the same expert witness, and compare methods and results to the current appraisal report. Focus particularly upon cases where the expert witness was working with the other side (e.g., if he or she is currently working with the plaintiff, find cases where the expert witness represented the defendant).
- After reviewing the approaches and variables used, conduct research to identify authoritative literature which refutes the approaches or variables. Rule 803(18) of the Federal Rules of Evidence makes "learned treatises" admissible as evidence which can be used to impeach an expert. Even if an expert is not used to validate the treatise, the attorneys can present it such that the "court can even take judicial notice of its prominence and reliability."[10]

[i] What to Expect in the Deposition

As mentioned earlier, the primary objectives of the deposition are to learn about the nature of the witness's testimony, to examine the qualifications and characteristics of the witness, and to gather information that will help in the trial cross-examination process. To accomplish these objectives, an attorney generally will cover the following areas when deposing an expert witness:

- Personal and professional background;
- The identification and, if available, authentication of prior statements of the expert that may provide grounds for impeachment, including publications, speeches and public statements (e.g., testimony before governmental bodies), prior expert testimony, reports or opinions in other consulting assignments, and statements made as an expert in another context;

---

[10] McElhaney, "Expert Witnesses and the Federal Rules," 2 Litigation 34 at 39 (1975).

- A description of his or her engagement by the adverse party, including the nature and basis of the compensation paid;
- A description of the scope of work that he or she has undertaken, including an identification of all documents and other materials the expert witness has reviewed;
- Identification of all the facts and opinions about which he or she will testify and the basis for each opinion;
- Identification of all assumptions, facts, and data upon which he or she is relying;
- Identification of any and all rules, principles, standards, and authorities within the witness's area of expertise upon which he or she is relying;
- A reconstruction of the steps followed by the expert witness in making any calculations, financial models, or exhibits; and
- The demand for production of work papers identified during the deposition and not previously produced (to be followed up with a formal document request, if necessary).[11]

[3] The Valuation Report and Expert Testimony

The valuation analyst will be expected to prepare a valuation report and to provide expert testimony based on that report. The following guidelines will help make that process more effective.

[a] Standards of Report Content

There is no standard report used for expert testimony related to a business valuation. The form of report can range from a standard full-length narrative business valuation report to no report at all. Something in between is generally the norm. The decision as to the form of report to be used is determined by the expert witness in conjunction with the client attorney. The important factors influencing this decision include the form of report with which the expert witness feels most comfortable, the form of opinion that will best communicate the expert witness's opinion to the court, and the form the client attorney may need to highlight certain aspects of the valuation. However, in some jurisdictions, a full written report is required by the court.

A report form frequently used is one with little narrative accompanying the valuation computations. This is done typically in outline or bullet-point form to highlight various aspects of the business and the industry. The expert witness must then verbally expand upon these items. This form of report presents graphs, charts, calculations, and exhibits supporting the valuation opinion. The expert witness then explains how the qualitative and quantitative aspects affect the valua-

---

[11] See R.D. Kennedy, *California Expert Witness Guide* § 7.8 (1989) (a publication of California Continuing Education of the Bar) for a more detailed description of the expert witness disposition process.

tion opinion. This form of report is highly dependent upon the expert witness's ability to clearly and persuasively communicate the analysis. It may also lead to the omission of important factors affecting the opinion of value. This approach does, however, allow the witness the opportunity to simplify a complicated process such that the court can understand the analysis and conclusions.

The primary advantage of the full narrative report is that the court will have a readily available and complete record of which factors were considered and how they were weighted in the valuation. A second advantage is that a thick narrative report may be impressive to the court as tangible evidence of the efforts put forth by the valuation expert in developing his or her opinion. On the other hand, a full narrative report may be too complex and cumbersome for the court, especially for a nontechnical jury. The full report may also prove difficult for the expert to testify from in a concise manner. Furthermore, the more narrative appearing in the report, the more exposure the expert witness has to the opposing attorney's cross-examination. For example, opposing counsel might take a sentence out of context or exaggerate its meaning to cast doubt upon the reasonableness of the entire report. The advantage, therefore, to testifying from a brief valuation report is that it limits the scope of cross-examination by the opposing attorney.

However, a brief report is disadvantaged in that the court must depend entirely upon the verbal testimony of the expert witness. If the trial is lengthy, the impact and substance of the expert's testimony may be muted as time passes. Furthermore, if the opposing expert is equally well-qualified and provides a report, there may be a tendency to refer more to the opponent's report as tangible evidence of the effort put forth in developing a conclusion.

Thus, the form of report used by the valuation expert witness will vary depending upon the unique circumstances of each case. Regardless of the approach taken, the expert witness who can provide understandable and convincing evidence will have a decided advantage over the witness providing vague or unsubstantiated testimony.

[b] Preparation for Testimony

The first step in preparing for testimony, once the report has been developed, is to prepare for direct examination. First, the expert witness should be thoroughly familiar with the analysis, the data relied upon, and the steps taken in arriving at his or her opinion. This is particularly important if major segments of the analysis were delegated to more junior staff. Next, the expert witness should work on communicating his or her analysis and the opinion in a manner conducive to the court's easy understanding of the testimony. During this process, the expert witness should meet with the client attorney so that they can both become familiar with the nature and content of the testimony. This may include rehearsals of the direct examination. However, memorizing lines should be avoided since it can make the testimony appear too "coached" and since it can lead to embarrassing confusion if the attorney fails to ask the preplanned questions. Thorough preparation by both witness and attorney should ensure a smooth direct examination.

The expert witness should also spend considerable time preparing for cross-examination. This requires a comprehensive understanding of the case and the valuation to allow an objective assessment of any weaknesses in the analysis. After his or her deposition and the review of the opposing expert witness's report, the effective expert witness can generally anticipate the areas that opposing counsel will attack during cross-examination. It is also helpful to have the client attorney provide input regarding areas vulnerable to attack. These steps, coupled with careful preparation, should lead to few unexpected questions at trial.

[c] Conduct in Depositions

While the substance of testimony should be the same during deposition and trial testimony (assuming no new information was discovered after the disposition), the manner in which the testimony is delivered is different. Depositions are used for fact-finding and preparation for cross-examination by opposing counsel. The expert must understand this and avoid the temptation to impress opposing counsel with his or her knowledge and experience. The expert's role in a deposition is simply to answer the questions posed—nothing more, nothing less. The deposition can provide opposing counsel with ammunition to later attack the expert witness in trial and/or obtain information helpful to the opposing counsel's own case. Therefore, the expert witness should respond in a direct and brief manner. In situations where a yes or no answer is called for, the answer should be limited to yes or no. If the opposing attorney wants a more thorough explanation, it is his or her responsibility to ask the appropriate questions. It is often tempting for expert witnesses to display their wealth of knowledge. A deposition is not the place to do it.

Depositions can also identify to the expert witness likely areas in which he or she will be cross-examined at trial. This allows the expert witness to focus on certain areas more thoroughly such that the cross-examination yields little ground.

[d] Conduct in Trial

The proper place for valuation experts to demonstrate their depth of knowledge is during the testimony at trial. In the courtroom during direct examination, expert witnesses have considerable flexibility in advancing their arguments. Such testimony can be likened to the classroom lecture of a college professor. Often, the expert witness and the client attorney have prepared a series of questions that allow the expert to provide a full explanation of his or her analysis and opinion.

Direct testimony is relatively straightforward for well-prepared expert witnesses. It is in cross-examination, however, that their skill, preparation, and professional judgment is tested. It is also in cross-examination that expert witnesses can be most convincing since lucid responses rebutting the opposing attorney's attack are often given greater weight by the jury than well-rehearsed direct testimony. In those cases where the expert has been deposed and has had an opportunity to review the opposing side's valuation report, there should be few surprises. In fact, effective expert witnesses can frequently turn part of the cross-examination into their own forum in which to advance their arguments and display their knowledge. In situations where expert witnesses feel that they have more to add in an answer than a simple yes or no, they can often get the court's permission to explain their answers in greater detail. If done properly, this can discourage the opposing attorney from further cross-examination on certain issues.

Finally, there are a few basic rules of conduct that should generally be followed by a valuation expert witness during court testimony:

1. *Professional appearance.* A professional appearance and attitude should always be maintained. Trying to entertain the court in the form of jokes or anecdotes should be avoided. This is not to suggest the expert witness should appear humorless or insensitive. Rather, it is appropriate to be demonstrative within one's own character.
2. *Address the court.* Whenever possible, the expert witness should directly address the judge and/or jury when answering questions or providing explanations. After all, these are the decision makers in the case.
3. *Avoid speculation.* Speculation is generally harmful. This is true both in deposition and courtroom testimony. Often, the most effective answer is "I don't know." As mentioned earlier, courts are well aware that no single individual has all the answers. Attempts to finesse a question with speculation can be dangerous.

As with most things, a valuation analyst becomes a better expert witness with experience. One of the biggest difficulties frequently encountered by analysts wishing to become expert witnesses is simply getting the opportunity to testify. This requires nothing less than convincing the attorney that you are a qualified witness. In addition, the analyst who wishes to become an effective expert witness can gain valuable insight by observing the testimony of experienced valuation expert witnesses and by participating in trial advocacy programs sponsored by law schools and legal associations throughout the country.

¶ 9.3 Valuation Litigation by Case Type

The following discussion identifies valuation litigation by case type. The valuation analyst also is familiar with the typical and unique scenarios characterizing each type of case.

[1] Dissenting Shareholder Statutes

In most engagements, the analyst's task is to determine the fair market value of either a company or a block of securities. However, in the context of valuations under dissenting shareholder statutes in most states and Canada, the "fair market value" of the company or block of securities may not be acceptable to the courts. Further, questions arise regarding which valuation methodologies are acceptable. Most importantly, however, the courts are not in agreement as to what level of value (i.e., nonmarketable minority, marketable minority, controlling interest, or a premium above controlling interest) is a fair and acceptable remedy for the dissenting shareholder. This section will provide the appraiser with an understanding of some of the legal and valuation issues unique to dissenting shareholder jurisprudence.

[a] Appraisal Rights

At common law, any significant change in the financial structure or business of a company required an affirmative vote of all shareholders.[12] As the laws were relaxed to allow such action upon the vote of a super majority and later a vote of a simple majority of shareholders, the courts recognized that, by allowing a simple majority of shareholders to materially alter the state of the company over the objections of the minority shareholders, a great injustice to the dissenting shareholders could result. Consequently, a statutory remedy was developed for those shareholders objecting to altering the status of the corporation.

---

[12] See Chicago Corp. v. Munds, 172 A 452 (Del. 1934). *See also* Eisenberg v. Central Zone Property Corp., 306 N.Y. 58, 63, 115 N.E.2d 652, 655 (1953), which stated:

> At common law neither the majority stockholders nor the directors could bring about a sale or cause a transfer of any portion of the property, essential for the transaction of its customary business, of a solvent, prosperous corporation, which was justifying the reason for its corporate existences against the will of the minority however small.

See also Skinner v. Smith, 134 N.Y. 240, 31 N.E. 911 (1982); Butler v. New Keystone Copper Co., 10 Del. Ch. 371, 93 A. 380 (1915); Beardstown Pearl Button Co. v. Oswald, 130 Ill. App. 290 (1906); 1 R.F. Balotti & J.A. Finkelstein, *The Delaware Law of Corporations and Business Organization* § 9.26 at 481-482 (1985).

The statutory remedy is the right to appraisal. This right, as defined in *Tri-Continental Corporation v. Battye*, is as follows:

> The basic concept of value under the appraisal statute is that the stockholder is entitled to be paid for that which has been taken from him, viz., his proportionate interest in the corporate enterprise is the true or intrinsic value of his stock which has been taken by the merger.[13]

Although the situations which give rise to valuation rights depend on the statutes of the various jurisdictions, most state statutes are fairly similar.[14] The following, taken from Section 302A.471 of the Minnesota Business Corporation Act, illustrates the type of corporate changes that typically give rise to a dissenting shareholder's right to valuation:

(a) An amendment of the articles that materially and adversely affect the rights of the dissenting shareholder in that it:
 (1) Alters or abolishes a preferential right of the shares;
 (2) Creates, alters, or abolishes a right in respect of the redemption of the shares, including a provision respecting a sinking fund for the redemption or repurchase of the shares;
 (3) Alters or abolishes a preemptive right of the holder of the shares to acquire shares, securities other than shares, or rights to purchase shares or securities other than shares;
 (4) Excludes or limits the right of a shareholder to vote on a matter, or to cumulate votes, except as the right may be limited by dilution through the issuance of securities with similar voting rights;
(b) A sale, lease, transfer or other disposition of all or substantially all of the property and assets of the corporation not made in the usual or regular course of its business, but not including a disposition in dissolution described in section 302A.725, subdivision 2, or a disposition pursuant to an order of a court, or a disposition for cash on terms requiring that all or substantially all of the net proceeds of disposition be distributed to the shareholders in accordance with their respective interests within one year after the date of disposition;
(c) A plan of merger to which the corporation is a party, except as provided in subdivision 3;
(d) A plan of exchange pursuant to which the shares of the corporation are to be acquired; or

---

[13] Tri-Continental Corp. v. Battye, 31 Del. Ch. 523, 74 A.2d 71 (1950).

[14] F.H. O'Neal, *Oppression of Minority Shareholders*, ch. 5, § 5:28, at 168-173 (1977). *See also* Note, "Valuation of Dissenters' Stock Under Appraisal Statutes," 79 Harv. L. Rev. 1453 (1966).

(e) Any other corporate action taken pursuant to a shareholder vote with respect to which the articles, the bylaws, or a resolution approved by the board directs that dissenting shareholders may obtain payment for their shares.

It should be noted that, in Delaware, where approximately one half of all U.S. corporations are incorporated, the right to appraisal is basically limited to certain mergers and consolidations.[15]

[b] Standard of Value

In the evolution of dissenting jurisprudence, the primary concern of the courts has been the fair treatment of the dissenting minority shareholder. Consequently, in Canada and various state statutes and in their respective judicial decisions, the concept of fairness is described in terms of "fair value," "real value," "actual value," "fair cash value," "true value," "intrinsic value," and "full market value." In general, these terms are treated synonymously by the various jurisdictions and, for the purposes of this chapter, will be referred to collectively as "fair value." Although there is no precise legal definition of the term fair value, current jurisprudence suggests that fair value is *not* fair market value. In essence, "fair value" appears to be a legal concept separate and distinct from "fair market value," which is an appraisal concept.

In order to better understand the subtle distinctions between fair value and fair market value, a review of the definition of fair market value is in order. The IRS's Revenue Ruling 59-60[16] defines fair market value as "the price at which the property would change hands between a willing buyer and a willing seller when the former is not under any compulsion to buy and the latter is not under any compulsion to sell, both parties having reasonable knowledge of relevant facts." Further, the word "fair" in fair *market* value modifies the word market, perhaps implying an open and active market. On the other hand, the word "fair" in fair value modifies the word value, perhaps suggesting a just and equitable value. In situations involving dissenters' rights, a fair market value may imply a different value than fair value. James C. Bonbright described the difference as follows:

> Overlooking entirely the questions whether the market prices are "fair" in the sense that they reflect the bids and offers of intelligent investors, the fatal objection to market value is that it reflects the influence of the very sale or merger against which the dissenter is

---

[15] 1 F.R. Balotti & J.A. Finkelstein, *supra* note 12. *See also* 8 Del. Ann. Code § 262(a).

[16] 1959-1 C.B. 237. Revenue Ruling 59-60 is reproduced as Appendix A at the end of this book.

seeking a remedy. The market does not wait until the corporate action has taken place before it discounts the event.[17]

In Ohio, where the state statutes use the term "fair cash value," the court in *Roessler v. Security Savings and Loan Company* stated:

> Nowhere in the statutes is the term "fair cash value" defined. However, many states have statutes similar to the one in question and, where such statutes have come before the courts, the term "fair cash value" and similar terms have been so construed as to allow dissenting shareholders the intrinsic value of their shares. We believe that to be the correct interpretation of this phrase. Intrinsic value is the true interest, and essential value; it is not synonymous with *market value*.[18]

Other important state court decisions supporting the notion that fair value is not fair market value include *Santee Oil Company, Inc. v. Cox* where the court said:

> Offers for merger and consolidation are likely to be made to a corporation, and accepted by it, when the market price of its stock is depressed in relation to certain other valuation criteria. The majority may be willing to force out minority shareholders at a low value, since those remaining will be left with a bigger share of the corporate potential. Therefore, limiting the dissenter to the market price of his shares may enrich the majority at his expense.[19]

In *Robbins v. Beatty*, the court stated:

> The authorities substantially agree in rejecting the argument that such terms as value or actual, true, fair or real value of minority stock mean market values.[20]

Finally, in *Atlantic States Construction, Inc. v. Beavers*, the court stated that "we believe that confusion will best be avoided by refraining from the use of the 'willing seller/willing buyer' test to define 'fair value'...."[21]

---

[17] 2 J.C.Bonbright, *The Valuation of Property* 828 (1965).
[18] 72 N.E.2d 259 (Ohio 1947) (emphasis added).
[19] 265 S.C. 270, 217 S.E.2d 789 (1975).
[20] 67 N.W.2d 12 (Iowa 1954).
[21] 169 Ga. App. 584, 314 S.E.2d 245 (1984).

[c] Entire Fairness

Based upon the court opinions just discussed, it appears that in most cases the professional business appraiser should use the fair value standard as opposed to fair market value. Although the business appraiser may be conditioned to thinking of fair value from a strictly financial point of view, in Delaware, it is clear that fair value encompasses the concept of "entire fairness."[22]

The concept of entire fairness was first brought to the forefront in *Singer v. Magnavox Company*,[23] where fairness encompassed procedural fairness as well as financial fairness. In *Weinberger v. UOP, Inc.*, the court concurred with the notion of entire fairness as brought out in *Singer*, stating:

> The concept of fairness has two basic aspects: fair dealing and fair price. The former embraces questions of when the transaction was timed, how it was initiated, structured, negotiated, disclosed to the directors, and how the approvals of the directors and the stockholders were obtained. The latter aspect of fairness relates to the economic and financial considerations of the proposed merger including all relevant factors: assets, market value, earnings, future prospects, and any other elements that affect the intrinsic or inherent value of a company's stock. . . . However, the test for fairness is not a bifurcated one as between fair dealing and price. All aspects of the issue must be examined as a whole since the question is one of *entire fairness*.[24]

Since the issue of fair dealing and fair price "must be examined as a whole," the professional business appraiser should make him or herself aware of all facts and circumstances surrounding the transaction in determining fair value. Notwithstanding the concept of entire fairness in a dissenting shareholder case, the court recognized the primary importance of the fair price component, stating that "in a nonfraudulent transaction, we recognize that price may be the preponderant consideration outweighing other features of the mergers. . . ."[25] However, this should not be interpreted to mean that a premium over market price assures entire fairness.[26]

[d] Burden of Proof

Weinberger also shed light on which parties in a dissenting shareholder action shoulder the burden of proof and under what circum-

---

[22] Weinberger v. UOP, Inc., 457 A.2d 711 (Del. 1983).
[23] 380 A.2d 969 (Del. 1977).
[24] 457 A.2d at 711 (citations deleted and emphasis added).
[25] *Id.*
[26] See Smith v. Van Gorkom, 488 A.2d 858 (Del. 1985).

stances.[27] In general, the burden of proof rests on the majority shareholder "to demonstrate intrinsic fairness by a preponderance of the evidence."[28] However, it rests upon "the plaintiff attacking the merger to demonstrate some basis for invoking the fairness obligation."[29] The court in *Weinberger* went on to state that, where a transaction has been "approved by an informed vote of the majority shareholders, the burden entirely shifts to the plaintiff to show that the transaction was unfair to the minority."[30] Notwithstanding this fact, the concept of "shareholder approval does not shift the burden of proof if explanatory material submitted to shareholders was misleading."[31]

[e] Valuation Approaches

Over the years, the courts in many states and Canada have recognized the imperfect nature of a valuation process. In an English case from the House of Lords, *Gold Coast Selection Trust, Ltd. v. Humphrey*,[32] the court stated: "Valuation is an art, not an exact science. Mathematical certainty is not demanded, nor indeed is it possible." Nonetheless, prior to *Weinberger*, significant Delaware case law, as well as in most other states and Canada, suggested "elements of value" common to all valuations of businesses that must be considered. The Maine Supreme Judicial Court in *Libby, McNeill & Libby* said:

> The case indicates that there is no definite rule for determining "fair value," but that proper results in each case will depend upon the particular circumstances of the corporation involved. Among other jurisdictions with valuation statutes similar to our own, we do find, however, a consensus that the component elements to be relied upon in determining "fair value" are *stock market price, investment value, and net assets value.*
>
> While it is generally agreed that the process of stock appraisal involves consideration of all three of those elements of value, the weight to be given to the three factors depends upon the circumstances of each individual case. The courts have consistently declined to lay down hard and fast rules. All three components of "fair value" may not influence the result in every valuation proceeding, yet all three should be considered.[33]

In Delaware, prior to *Weinberger*, the courts had required the use of these three approaches: market value, earnings (investment) value,

---
[27] 457 A.2d at 701, 703.
[28] 1 F.R. Balotti & J.A. Finkelstein, *supra* note 12, at 492.
[29] 457 A.2d at 703.
[30] *Id.*
[31] *See* David J. Greene & Co. v. Dunhill Int'l, 249 A.2d 427 (Del. Ch. 1969).
[32] 1948 A.C. 459, 19482 All E.R. 379.
[33] 406 A.2d 54, 59-60 (Me. 1979) (emphasis added).

and asset value. In general, the three approaches would be used to develop three different indications of value. The three value indications would then be weighted according to the particular facts and circumstances of the case in arriving at a weighted average value conclusion. The use of these three approaches became known as the "Delaware Block Method."[34]

In determining a weight to assign a given valuation approach, the appraiser could choose not to assign a weight to an approach that was considered inappropriate. In *Endicott Johnson Corp. v. Bade*, the court expressed this concept as follows:

> While, in order to provide the elasticity deemed necessary to reach a just result, all three factors are to be considered, the weight to be accorded to each varies with the facts and circumstances in a particular case.... [A]ll three elements do not have to influence the result in every valuation proceeding. It suffices if they are all considered. Compelling the consideration of all of them, including those which may turn out to be unreliable in a particular case, has the salutary effect of assuring more complete justification by the appraiser of the conclusion he reaches. It also provides a more concrete basis for court review.[35]

Weinberger greatly liberalized the valuation process in Delaware by allowing the consideration of valuation approaches other than the market, earnings, and asset approaches by stating:

> Accordingly, the standard "Delaware Block" or weighted average method of valuation, formerly applied in appraisal and other stock valuation cases, shall no longer exclusively control such proceedings. We believe that a more liberal approach must include proof of value by any techniques or methods which are generally considered acceptable in the financial community and otherwise admissible in court....[36]

Consequently, in Delaware at least, the business appraiser is given wide latitude in selecting and weighing the valuation approaches most suitable to the case given its own particular set of relevant facts and circumstances. Nevertheless, because of the tradition of the courts, the business appraiser in a dissenting shareholder case should at a minimum consider the three Delaware Block approaches and should be

---

[34] "Fair Value and Minority Shareholder Appraisal Rights," Address by R. Ward, Jr. at the American Society of Appraisers/Canadian Institute of Chartered Business Valuators' 1986 Joint Business Valuation Conference (Oct. 23-24, 1986).

[35] 376 N.Y.S.2d 103 (N.Y. 1975).

[36] 457 A.2d at 712-713.

prepared with sound arguments as to why any of the three did not effect the value conclusion if such is the case.

[f] Other Factors

☐ *Postmerger effects.* In Delaware, Section 262(h) of the General Corporation Law suggests an appraisal standard that excludes any effect on value as a result of the proposed merger as follows:

> The Court shall appraise the shares, determining their fair value exclusive of any element of value arising from the accomplishment or expectation of the merger, together with a fair rate of interest, if any, to be paid upon the amount determined to be the fair value.

However, in *Weinberger*, the court took exception to the narrow interpretation of Section 262(h), suggesting that nonspeculative merger effects on value can be considered, stating:

> [E]lements of future value, including the nature of the enterprise, which are known or susceptible of proof as of the date of the merger and not the product of speculation, may be considered.[37]

In Canada, relevant jurisprudence seems to suggest that the exclusion of postmerger benefits could be unfair to the minority shareholder. In the Canadian case of *Ripley International, Ltd.*, the court was faced with the situation where the company, after the squeeze-out, would have significant tax savings. The court ruled as follows:

> If [the small shareholders] are not to be eliminated, against their wishes . . . the price to be paid for their shareholdings would not be fair and reasonable . . . unless it reflected a pro rata participation in the tax savings. In other words, their shareholdings should be valued as if they would have been able to remain as shareholders in the newly constituted private corporation.[38]

[g] The Level of Value

The first determination that a valuation analyst must make when receiving a new valuation assignment is the appropriate level of value (i.e., control, minority, or nonmarketable minority) in light of the relevant facts and circumstances surrounding the case. In a dissenting shareholders action, the securities always represent a minority interest in the subject company. Notwithstanding the fact that the subject securities represent a minority interest, the courts, although far from

---

[37] *Id.* at 713.
[38] 1 B.L.R. 269 (Ont. H.C. 1977).

conclusive, appear to prefer a pro rata controlling interest value for the minority shares.[39]

☐ *The case for control.* Canadian jurisprudence is generally consistent when dealing with the issue of valuing a minority interest as a pro rata of the enterprise value of a company in dissenting shareholder cases. In the Canadian case of *Diligenti v. RWMD Operations Kelowna, Ltd.*, et al. the court eloquently reasoned as follows:

> [I]n my view, under the law applicable we are dealing here not with market value but with fair price or fair value. This is not an arid distinction, but a real one which recognizes and gives effect to the particular situation where there has been oppressive or unfair conduct which justifies an order that the shares of the minority be purchased by the majority or by the company. Again it is true that the first step in valuation is to determine the value of the business as a going concern which is determined, so far as is possible to do so, on the basis of estimated market value. But when it comes to determining the price to be paid for the shares in these circumstances, the test is not market value of those shares—where a minority discount would apply—but what price is fair in the circumstances.[40]

In *Woodward et al. v. Quigley*,[41] the court rejected the use of a minority discount, saying:

> In considering the value for tax purposes it is proper and necessary to discount the value because it is a minority interest. The statutory protection afforded the minority interest in cases of the kind here involved distinguishes this case from the tax cases . . . the statute is designed to protect the minority from the very considerations which result in a discounted value in tax cases.

More recently, the Delaware Court of Chancery declared:

> The amount of the holdings of a particular dissenting stockholder is not relevant, except insofar as they represent that shareholder's proportionate interest in the corporation's overall "fair value." That a particular dissenting stockholder's ownership represents only a minority stock interest is, therefore, legally immaterial in determining the corporation "fair value. . . ." The "minority" and

---

[39] Johnson, "Dissenting Shareholder Valuations: A Study of Cases and References," Bus. Val. Rev., Mar. 1988, at 9-17.
[40] 4 B.C.L.R. 134 (B.S.C. 1977).
[41] 133 N.W.2d 38 (Iowa 1965).

a "nonmarketable" discounts advocated are improper under Delaware law.[42]

☐ *The case for minority.* Notwithstanding the previously cited decisions by Delaware, Iowa, and Canadian courts that concluded that minority interest discounts were inappropriate, some American courts suggest that, because the subject securities in a dissenting shareholder context represent a minority interest, they should be valued as a minority interest.

In *Atlantic States Construction, Inc. v. Beavers*, the court reasoned as follows:

> If in a given case the minority nature of the interest diminishes the worth of the stock itself, there is nothing we can find in the statutory appraisal scheme that would prevent the trial court from considering the "minority interest" factor into account when he purchased the stock. Failure to account for that factor in the appraisal process would unfairly compensate the shareholder for "value" not properly attributable to his shares of stock.[43]

The court went on to further say that "the focus of the valuation process is on the value of the stock held by dissenting shareholders, not on the value of some specified percentage of the corporate worth."

Further, on February 25, 1985, the New York State Supreme Court, in *Fleischer v. Gift Pax, Inc.*, specifically addressed the issue of a control premium, saying:

> The record clearly indicates that such premiums are paid only when 100 percent of the stock or controlling interest in the stock of a corporation is acquired. In the case at bar, Gift Pax is acquiring only one-third of its common stock. Therefore, no premium should be added.[44]

☐ *The case for nonmarketable minority interest.* In the same case, *Fleischer v. Gift Pax, Inc.*, the court also addressed the issue of marketability, ruling as follows:

> In determining the "fair value" of the shares of a closely held corporation, discounts for lack of marketability of such shares are appropriate and do not provide a windfall to the majority share-

---

[42] Cavalier Oil Corp. v. William J. Harnett, Civ. Action Nos. 7959, 7960, 7967, 7968 (Del. Ch., Feb. 22, 1988).
[43] 169 Ga. App. at 584, 314 S.E.2d at 249.
[44] 486 N.Y.S.2d 272 (Sup. Ct. App. Div. 1985).

holders merely because the shares to be purchased by the majority pursuant to their election under Business Corporation Law Section 1118 constitutes a minority interest in the corporation.[45]

☐ *The case for a premium above control.* Only in Canada have the courts allowed a premium above control for the forcible taking of minority shares allowable under statute. In the celebrated Canadian case, *Domglas, Inc. v. Jarislowsky, Fraser and Company*, Mr. Justice Greenberg allowed a 20 percent premium above the pro rata controlling interest value and reasoned as follows:

> In cases of the "squeeze-out" of the dissenting shareholders, which is equivalent to an expropriation, "fair value" goes beyond the concept of "intrinsic value" in that the former must include a premium for forcible taking, and is not subject to a minority discount. In this Court's opinion, in a "squeeze-out" situation, as exists in the case at Bar, the absence of a discount in valuing a minority holding, and the increment or premium for forcible taking, are the essence of the distinction between "fair market value" and "fair value."
>
> . . . .
>
> The payment by the Petitioner of a "fair value," even if more than the "intrinsic value" of the shares, is the price that must be paid by it for the privilege of effecting the amalgamation over the protest of the dissenting shareholders who in effect are being ousted from the corporation.[46]

[h] Summary

When by vote of a simple majority of the shareholders the structure and business of a company could be altered in a material way, a body of law was developed to protect dissenting shareholders. The primary protection afforded the dissenting shareholder is the right of appraisal. In general, depending upon the jurisdiction, the right of appraisal allows for the purchase of the dissenting shareholders interest at "fair value." In most states and Canada, fair value, although not defined by statute, is not fair market value.

Further, the concept of fair value is broader than a purely financial concept. It encompasses both the fairness of the price as well as the fairness of the procedures. Consequently, the appraiser cannot simply focus on the financial aspects of the case alone.

---

[45] *Id.*
[46] C.S. 925, 13 B.L.R. 135 (1980), *aff'd*, C.S. 377, 22 B.L.R. 121; 138 D.L.R.3d 521 (Que. C.A. 1982).

In the landmark case *Weinberger v. UOP, Inc.*, the court went beyond the narrow use of the so-called Delaware Block valuation approaches to allow for "any techniques, or methods which are generally considered acceptable to the financial community and otherwise admissible in court. . . ."[47] This case should not be interpreted to mean that the approaches utilized under the Delaware Block Method can be ignored but rather that all relevant valuation approaches should be addressed. Sound reasoning may justify the rejection of an accepted approach.

Furthermore, the courts in Canada and Delaware, if not elsewhere, have recognized that the dissenting shareholder should not only receive the pro rata fair value of his or her shares as of the day prior to the vote of shareholders on the merger but should also include any nonspeculative benefits that accrue to the postmerger company.

Court decisions regarding the appropriate level of value (nonmarketable minority, minority, or control) for a dissenting shareholder's interest appear contradictory. Nevertheless, there exists a significant body of jurisprudence that suggests that the proper value for a dissenting shareholder's interest is at the control level. In Canada, the court has even deemed a premium above control to be appropriate in order to compensate the dissenting shareholder for being forced out. Regardless, the question of what level of value to use is a legal question and when involved in a dissenting shareholder action the appraiser should rely on the advice of counsel.

[2] Corporate or Partnership Dissolution Statutes

Corporate and partnership dissolutions can take place for a variety of reasons. They can be voluntary or involuntary and can be forced on a company or partnership by minority interest holders, majority interest holders, state regulatory bodies, or the business entity's creditors. For the appraiser involved in this type of litigation, it is important to understand the distinctions between different forms of liquidation and voluntary and involuntary dissolutions. It is also important to distinguish between corporate and partnership dissolutions.

[a] Forms of Liquidation

In most state statutes the terms dissolution and liquidation appear to be used interchangeably. Nevertheless, one author indicates a subtle distinction between liquidation and dissolution. He defines liquidations as "the process of paying off or making provisions for the corporate debts, and disposition of all corporation's assets, either by sale

---

[47] 457 A.2d 712-713.

(with distribution of the proceeds to the shareholders) or by direct distribution in kind to the shareholders."[48]

This same author defines dissolution as "the formal termination of corporate existence, the expiration or revocation of the franchise granted to the corporation by a state."[49] Thus, collectively, a dissolution and a liquidation of a corporation or partnership could be defined simply as the termination of the business entity's existence through the sale and distribution of its assets.

☐ *Tangible asset liquidation.* The most common form of corporate dissolution arises in the area of bankruptcy proceedings. (Discussions of the Federal Bankruptcy Codes and practices are beyond the scope of this chapter.) Accordingly, when the layperson considers liquidation, he or she contemplates the sale of the *tangible* assets in a manner that generally *precludes* any value for *goodwill*. The proceeds of the sale of the tangible assets are then used to satisfy the claims of the creditors. Any proceeds beyond that needed to satisfy the claims of the creditors are then distributed to the shareholders and the underlying business ceases to exist.

In situations outside of bankruptcy, however, a company or partnership in dissolution may be solvent. When the earnings of a solvent corporation or partnership are insufficient to indicate a value greater than what would be realized in a liquidation of the tangible assets of the same entity, then the valuation of the tangible assets of the entity may be appropriate. The Iowa court in *Woodward v. Quigley* stated:

> [Utilizing net tangible asset value] offers protection to the minority stockholders in a corporation with a poor earnings record. In such instance the value as a going concern might be less than the dissolution value of the assets. It would not be fair to limit the minority interests to a value influenced by poor earnings, when the minority might prefer to liquidate and convert the assets into cash, and at the same time place the majority in a position where it would later liquidate and receive the entire benefit of the greater liquidation value.[50]

☐ *Going-concern liquidation.* In situations outside of bankruptcy, it is not unusual for a corporation or partnership in a dissolution, where the corporation or partnership entity ceases to exist, to have the

---
[48] *Closely Held Corporations*, pt. V (1971).
[49] *Id.*
[50] 257 Iowa 1077, 1083, 133 N.W.2d 38, 41, *modified*, 257 Iowa 1104, 136 N.W.2d 280 (1965).

underlying business continue. For example, under the Uniform Partnership Act (UPA), which governs the dissolution of partnership in most states (in the absence of a partnership agreement to the contrary), a partnership ceases to exist upon the death of a partner. When a partner dies, it is very likely that the underlying business could continue, perhaps even without interruption, if there are one or more surviving partners to operate it as a going concern. In that case, the proceeds from the sale of the tangible assets of the partnership could be less than if the business were sold as a going concern. For example, Section 2000 of the California Corporation Code recognizes the necessity of valuing a company in a dissolution proceeding as a going concern, when appropriate, stating:

> [The "purchasing parties"] may avoid the dissolution of the corporation . . . by purchasing for cash the shares owned by the plaintiffs or by the shareholders so initiating the proceeding . . . at their fair value. The fair value shall be determined as of the valuation date but taking into account, if any, the sale of the entire business as a going concern in liquidation.

Regardless of a state's dissolution statute's language pertaining to valuing the business entity as a going concern and thus accounting for the goodwill in the entity, the courts have generally recognized the necessity of liquidating a business entity on a going concern basis, if possible, as a matter of equity and as the fiduciary duty of the board of directors. In *Godley v. Crandall & Godley Company*, a case where the board of directors did not liquidate the company on a going concern basis, the court stated:

> It was the duty of the directors if they decided to discontinue the business to make an honest attempt to realize on the goodwill. . . . The directors did not discharge their fiduciary duties simply by realizing on and honestly accounting for the tangible assets.[51]

The utilization of the highest value indicated by a going-concern liquidation or a tangible asset liquidation appears to be justified as a matter of equity. In support of this view, the court in *Page v. Page* stated:

> A partner may not dissolve a partnership to gain the benefits of the business for himself, unless he fully compensates his co-partner for his share of the business opportunity.[52]

---

[51] 212 N.Y. 121, 105 N.E. 818 (1914).
[52] 55 Cal. 2d 192, 196-197, 10 Cal. Rptr. 643, 646, 359 P.2d 41, 44 (1961).

Accordingly, it is important for the appraiser to consider both the tangible asset liquidation value as well as the going-concern liquidation value and utilize the higher value of the two approaches as the fair value of the subject company or partnership.

[b] Voluntary vs. Involuntary Dissolution

At common law, significant changes in the structure of a corporation required a unanimous vote of all shareholders. As corporations in the nineteenth century grew in size, the number of shareholders required to financially support such large corporations grew accordingly. However, as the pace of technological change accelerated, a single shareholder could stop economically necessary corporation actions to the detriment of the majority shareholders. Consequently, statutes arose allowing significant corporate changes to occur upon the vote of the majority of shareholders[53] (and, under some state statutes, 50 percent of the shareholders).[54] As a result, the majority under most state statutes can also force the liquidation of the corporation in a voluntary dissolution.[55]

Depending on the terms of the individual partnership, a typical partnership agreement allows for a majority of the partners to liquidate the partnership. This, too, is considered a voluntary dissolution. (For a discussion of the remedies available to shareholders or partners dissenting from the vote of the majority for a dissolution of the business entity, see the previous section on "Dissenting Shareholder Statutes.")

In order to protect minority shareholders from actions of the majority that do not trigger remedies under dissenting shareholder statutes, many states adopted statutes that allowed a significant number of the minority shareholders of a corporation to seek a dissolution of the company. A dissolution brought by an action of the minority is termed an involuntary dissolution. A significant minority typically can force an involuntary dissolution under certain circumstances, including the following[56]:

- Internal dissension between two or more factions of shareholders that causes the directors or management of the corporation to become unable to conduct the affairs of the company without impairing company assets;
- Liquidation necessary for the protection of the rights and interest of minority shareholders; or

---

[53] See *supra* note 12.
[54] Cal. Corp. Code, ch. 19, § 1900, "Voluntary Dissolution."
[55] F.H. O'Neal, *supra* note 14, ch. 5, § 5:21, at 120-121.
[56] *Example*: Cal. Corp. Code, ch. 18, § 1800, "Involuntary Dissolution."

- Other reasons, including fraud, mismanagement, or abuse of authority by controlling shareholders.

Many states have adopted statutes that specifically address this topic, while similar legal rights for minority shareholders have evolved in other states through case law. The California Corporations Code, one such statute, contains the provision that majority shareholders facing such a suit can avoid dissolution by repurchasing the shares of the dissenting minority at their "fair value."[57] (The concept of "fair value" is discussed at length in the previous section, "Dissenting Shareholder Statutes: Standard of Value.")

[c] Partnership Dissolution vs. Corporate Dissolution

☐ *Partnership dissolution.* The most important valuation issue that can arise in a partnership dissolution is to correctly identify the assets of the entity at the relevant date. The UPA (in the absence of a partnership agreement to the contrary) states that, upon dissolution, the business of the partnership ceases, and the surviving partners have a reasonable period of time to wind up the affairs of the partnership, including settlement of outstanding debts and completion of unfinished business. The surviving partner is generally entitled to additional compensation for winding up the affairs of the partnership.[58] After the business is completed, each partner is entitled to his or her pro rata share of the net assets of the dissolved partnership. This process is called an "accounting."[59]

There are two important items to note. First, as discussed earlier, while it is the pro rata share of net assets that is to be valued, this does not necessarily mean that "liquidation" asset values are appropriate. A determination of the amount of goodwill, if any, that belongs to the partnership (and is, hence, an asset to be included in net assets) is required.[60] However, often the goodwill of a personal service firm, like a law or medical partnership, is viewed as personal in nature. Since this goodwill belongs to the partners individually and not to the partnership, it is not included in the determination of the net assets of the partnership.[61]

Second, unfinished business is not necessarily valued at the date of dissolution but may be valued at the actual amount ultimately realized

---

[57] Cal. Corp. Code., ch. 20, § 2000, "General Provisions Relating to Dissolution."
[58] *Example*: Cal. Corp. Code § 15683, "Winding Up of Partnership—Compensation to Limited Partners."
[59] Uniform Partnership Act §§ 15040, 15043.
[60] *See* Lebold v. Inland Steel Co., 136 F.2d 876 (7th Cir.), *cert. denied*, 320 U.S. 787 (1943).
[61] *See cf.* Carr v. Carr—O'Brien Co., 386 Pa. 196, 125 A.2d 607 (1956).

at some date in the future. As an example, consider a construction partnership that is half way through a long-term project when one partner dies. The deceased partner's estate has an interest in the uncompleted project (its pro rata share of the partnership's interest). In this case, determining the value of the project would depend primarily on the profits ultimately realized (net of additional compensation allowed to the surviving partner for completing the project).

The task of valuing an interest in a dissolved partnership boils down to the identification of the bundle of all the assets and liabilities belonging to the partnership and the determination of their value. The assets may include work in progress, favorable leases, physical assets or working capital, contracts, customer lists and other intangibles, and goodwill or going-concern value. Liabilities may include debt (valued using market rates), the expenditures required to complete unfinished business (including special compensation, if any), and other economic obligations of the partnership. Contingent assets or liabilities may be valued at the amounts ultimately realized. Otherwise, a probabilistic determination of their value may be necessary.

In the case of partnerships, it is very easy to think in terms of the death of a partner causing the dissolution of a partnership. There are, however, many other events which may force a dissolution. One is the absence of a partner. Under the UPA, if a partner leaves the partnership (rather than dying) and the partnership is liquidated, the "surviving" partner who must wind up the affairs of the partnership receives no special compensation from the departed parties assets.[62] However, if a partner is deceased, the partner winding up the affairs receives a distribution from the deceased partner's interest as compensation for his or her work in winding up the affairs of the partnership. Consequently, as unfair as it may seem, a "surviving" partner would be better off if his or her partner died rather than left the firm. This simply demonstrates the importance of having a thorough partnership agreement that addresses all relevant issues rather than relying on the UPA, which can have a seemingly inequitable impact upon application.

☐ *Corporate dissolution.* State statutes that allow for involuntary dissolution can generally be divided into two types. One type of statute allows for the majority to elect to buy out the minority shareholder; and, thus, the minority shareholder is compelled to sell at a price that is determined by the court.[63] The other type of statute provides the court with the authority to take one of several different actions. To the extent the court chooses, it can even force the minority shareholder

---

[62] Uniform Partnership Act § 15018(f).
[63] For a further discussion of the two types of dissolution statutes, *see* F.H. O'Neal, *supra* note 14, ch. 7, § 7:21, at 157-159.

seeking dissolution to purchase the shares from the majority.[64] Consequently, a minority seeking to end his or her relationship with the corporation may find him- or herself as the sole shareholder of the corporation.

[d] The Valuation Date

As in other types of statutes, state dissolution statutes also dictate the date of valuation. An example of this is Section 2000 of the California Corporation Code. Section 2000 indicates different valuation dates depending upon which form, voluntary or involuntary, the dissolution takes. In a voluntary dissolution "initiated by the vote of shareholders representing only 50% of the voting power," the valuation date is the date upon which the dissolution proceeding was initiated. In an involuntary dissolution, the valuation date is "the date upon which the action was commenced." Notwithstanding these circumstances, the court may "for good cause shown, designate some other date as the valuation date."

[e] Summary

Dissolutions of corporations and partnerships are provided for in federal and state statutes and sometimes, in the case of partnerships, in the partnership agreement itself. In most voluntary dissolutions (requiring an affirmative vote of the majority), a dissenting shareholder would most likely seek legal remedies under dissenting shareholder statutes or federal fraud statutes and not state dissolution statutes.

In involuntary dissolutions where state statutes allow, the majority may avoid dissolution by purchasing the minority's interest (or, in some cases, by the minority's purchasing the majority's interest) at its "fair value." As is the case under dissenting shareholder statutes, fair value appears to be a legal concept and not one defined by appraisers. Consequently, an appraiser should consult counsel when performing an appraisal under state dissolution statutes.

Finally, state dissolution statutes or individual partnership agreements dictate the date of the appraisal. Unique to partnerships, upon the death of a partner, the value of unfinished business may be valued at the actual amount realized in the future rather than the date of dissolution. In addition, compensation must be allotted to the surviving partner for the winding up of the affairs of the partnership.

[3] Business Valuations Under Federal Statutes

Although state statutes provide protection to minority shareholders in cases of fraud and misrepresentation, federal statutes provide a

---
[64] *Id.*

more favorable forum than state dissenting shareholder and dissolution statutes. The federal statute most often used in cases of fraud is Rule 10(b)-5, which "prohibits fraud in connection with the purchase or sale of any security." In order to prove fraud, the plaintiff must show that there was a "misrepresentation of a material fact made with scienter on which the plaintiff relies suffering damage as a consequence."[65]

Unlike dissenting shareholder statutes and, to a certain extent, dissolution statutes, the offended party in a Rule 10(b)-5 action has the choice to select rescission or recovery of out-of-pocket damages. This unique characteristic of Rule 10(b)-5 is extremely important to the appraiser because two valuations on two separate dates are required for the plaintiff to make an informed decision to seek recision or recovery of damages.

For example, consider the following set of facts. An investor, because of a material misrepresentation of fact, purchases securities for $2 million that have a true fair value of $1 million as of the date of the transaction. Upon discovery of the fraudulent misrepresentation, the investor sues the seller under Rule 10(b)-5. If the investor seeks rescission, the investor would exchange the securities for his or her original $2 million. However, if, subsequent to the transaction date, the subject company received an unanticipated windfall such that the securities as of the trial date had a fair value of $4 million, then, in that case, the investor could choose to hold on to the securities but seek damages of $1 million for paying $2 million on the transaction date when the fair value was only $1 million. Although the longer the time between the transaction date and the trial date, the more valuable the rescission versus recovery of damages decision is, courts may revoke the plaintiff's right to choose if his or her decision to seek rescission or recovery of damages is not made in a timely manner.[66]

From a valuation perspective, the primary difference between state statutes and Rule 10(b)-5 concerns the choice of recovery of damages or rescission. There does not appear to be any significant difference in either valuation methodologies or fair value definitions between state statutes and Rule 10(b)-5.

In summary, business valuations under Rule 10(b)-5 provide relief to investors in fraudulent transactions. Of considerable importance to the appraiser is the need to value the business on two different dates (i.e., the date of transaction and the date of trial). In situations involving publicly traded companies where, because of fraud, the publicly traded price did not reflect the true value of the subject securities the court may utilize a third valuation date (i.e., the date the fraud was

---

[65] *Id.*, ch. 8, § 8:10, at 28.
[66] *See also* John Hopkins Univ. v. Hutton, 325 F. Supp. 250, 262 (D. Md. 1971).

publicly discovered). The different valuation dates are necessary for the plaintiff to make the decision to seek rescission or recovery of damages that may result in a recovery greater than the original loss. The ability to choose either rescission or recovery of damages is the primary difference between Rule 10(b)-5 and state statutes from a business valuation perspective.

¶ 9.4 Recovery of Damages

The quantification of damages to the injured party is the topic of the following discussion. Both corporate damages and human capital valuation are analyzed in this context.

[1] Corporate Damages

Many of the techniques employed in valuing businesses are readily and appropriately applied to one of civil litigation's most basic objectives: the quantification of damages suffered by the injured party. Since the intent of civil litigation is to restore the harmed party (the plaintiff) to a financial condition that it would have enjoyed without the illegal act, the focus of the court is to ascertain how much damage has been sustained. This, in turn, often requires a comparison of two states of plaintiff financial condition: (1) where it was after the illegal act (a *known* condition) and (2) where it would have been but for the illegal act (a *hypothetical* condition). It is with respect to the latter condition that expert witnesses are most often expected to testify.

The following discussion on the recovery of damages presumes that the issues of liability in a particular case have already been decided. That is, if the court had found the defendant innocent, there would be no need for determining damages. Since the primary role of valuation specialists arises during the damage phase of a case, the analysis is restricted to damage issues. Of course, it is common for attorneys to consider both liability and damage issues simultaneously, depending upon the merits and financial risks of a particular case. Further, it is important to note that the Federal Rules of Evidence—in particular Rule 704—permit an expert witness to express an opinion on an "ultimate issue" to be decided upon by the judge and jury.[67]

[a] Origins of Litigation

While damage determination and recovery is a fundamental component of civil litigation, cases requiring business valuation expertise for determining damages generally fall into the following categories:

- Breach of contract;

---

[67] Fed. R. Evid. 704.

- Antitrust violations;
- Tortious actions;
- Lost business opportunities; and
- Insurance claims.

In addition, legal actions such as patent or trademark infringement, where the financial viability of a company is based upon ownership of a patent or trademark, may also require business valuation expertise. Similarly, in product liability proceedings, the worth of a company (or some portion thereof) can be the measure of damages if the company owned a measurable amount of its value to the product at issue. For example, if a company purchases a computer system and relies heavily upon it for its basic operations, the failure of that system could severely hamper the operations of the company. One basis of damages might be the diminution in the enterprise value of the company.

[b] Valuation vs. Damage Determination

While business valuation methods are appropriately used in determining the extent of damages, there are a number of fundamental differences concerning the objectives of valuations in the typical nonlitigation setting and the objectives of damage quantification in court. These differences center around (1) the entity to be valued, (2) the elements of value to be recognized, and (3) the approaches used in quantifying the value (or value lost). Since the latter two differences are closely related, they are examined together next.

□ *Entity to be valued.* In a standard business valuation, where the purpose is the expression of an opinion regarding the company's fair market value, the entity valued is the entire company (often called *enterprise value*). Even if the appraisal is to measure the value of a minority interest, the starting point of the valuation is a measure of the value of the business as a whole.

While measuring the value of an entire company is frequently required in damage determinations, it is also often the case that the *entity* to be valued is a subset of the company such as a division or department. In some cases, such as in patent infringements, the object of valuation can be limited to a single product or product line. Similarly, in a breach-of-construction contract or insurance casualty claim, the entity to be valued might be an office building or a manufacturing facility.

In some instances of valuation litigation, the entity to be valued is one that, in fact, never existed at all except in the minds of its owners.

A good example of this is in a breach-of-contract matter where two parties agree to form a new corporation based either on new technology or on the special expertise and financial resources of the parties. This often occurs in situations where management takes over a company through a leveraged buyout.

If the agreement is breached by one of the parties, one measure of damages would be the value of the business that would have resulted but for the breach. Here, the credibility of the new venture's business plan and the strength of its financial backing and proposed management become critical elements in convincing the jury that the valuation of the prospective company is sound. In addition, comparisons to other similar companies can be made to support the reasonableness of the damage claim, particularly with regard to a rate of return that could have been expected from the new venture.[68]

Unlike most business valuations in which information gained after the valuation date ("hindsight" information) is restricted, in such breach-of-contract matters, where the basis of damages is that of the business plan and/or financial projections, most of the information relied upon is prospective in nature. Naturally, damages in such cases are won and lost on the merits of the assumptions and underlying documentation of the business plan and/or other financial projections.

☐ *Elements of value and valuation methodology.* The difference in valuation objectives are most telling when the elements of value and the ways for determining that value are examined.

In nonlitigation valuation, the appraiser considers two fundamental aspects of business value: (1) the current value of the existing assets and (2) the present value of the future assets (generally expressed through future earnings). Of course, the valuation method used tends to place greater emphasis upon either the current value (as with asset-based valuation methods) or future value (as with earnings capitalization or discounted future earnings methods). Market-based valuation methods theoretically recognize both dimensions since they are based upon the market's assessment of both current and future value.

In litigation, however, the element of value that is most often measured is that of lost profits. That is, what is the value (i.e., amount) of profits foregone by the plaintiff as a result of the defendant's illegal

---

[68] Berge v. International Harvester Co., 142 Cal. App. 3d 152, 162, 190 Cal. Rptr. 815 (1983). *See also* "Evaluating and Proving Damages in Business Litigation," Program Material Presented at the California Continuing Education of the Bar Conference (1987).

acts.[69] Here, the focus of quantification is upon the incremental profits lost by the plaintiff rather than upon the business as a whole. Of course, in litigation involving illegal acts that bring about the demise of an entire company, for example, in certain antitrust violations, the focus is upon the company as a whole.

Lost profit measurements generally require two basic ingredients: profits that actually occurred after (in the presence of) the illegal acts and profits that would have occurred but for the acts. The latter profits are often identified as *"but for" profits*. The difference between the two profit amounts is the measure of damages.

Lost profits are generally computed based on one of two basic methods. In the first method, an incremental profit margin concept is used whereby the profit that each unit of lost sales would have contributed to the plaintiff's income is determined and then is multiplied by the volume of lost sales. In the second method, the plaintiff's overall profits, both before and after the illegal act, are computed, the difference between the two being the extent of damages suffered.

Damage measurements also span a finite period of time, starting generally from the date of infraction to either the date of restraining order (to halt the illegal acts, as in restraint of trade activities) or the current period. In cases where damages are expected to occur in the future, a finite number of future years is used, in much the same way a financial forecast or a budget is developed.

While the objectives of lost profit measurement are quite simple, the quantification of lost profits is another matter entirely. The root of this difficulty, common to most valuations, is that of prediction. In lost profit computations, the expert witness is faced with predicting what the plaintiff's profits would have been without the alleged illegal acts. This estimation is, in turn, the product of two other predictions: plaintiff revenues and plaintiff costs without the illegal acts. As discussed later, these predictions are based upon numerous assumptions, each requiring clear and logical justification by the expert witness.

[c] Legal Theory of Damages

To understand damages and damage computations, it is important to see how they fit within the litigation process. In order to be awarded damages, the plaintiff must prove that (1) the defendant violated a legal

---

[69] Substantial case law provides guidance on the proper measure of damages. In addition, many state statutes also contain definitions of damages. For example, Cal. Civ. Code § 3300 (West 1987) defines measurement of damages in breaches of contract to be "the amount which will compensate the party aggrieved for all the detriment proximately caused thereby, or which, in the ordinary course of things, would be likely to result therefrom."

right of the plaintiff and (2) the violation caused harm to the plaintiff.[70] The third and final element involves determining the amount of damages.

As an example, within the context of antitrust violations, to prove the *fact* of damages, the plaintiff must establish two things: (1) the defendant committed acts that violated the antitrust laws, and (2) the violation was the cause of a loss to the plaintiff.[71]

In some cases, when damages can be proven to have been sustained, this is considered sufficient evidence that the violation caused harm to the plaintiff, thereby satisfying condition (2).[72]

It is also important to note that the standards of proof concerning, on one hand, the *fact* of damage and, on the other, the *amount* of damages are quite different. While the *fact* of damage must be established with "reasonable certainty," the basic standard for determining the *amount* of damages is more flexible in that the plaintiff must "only establish the extent of damages as a matter of just and reasonable inference based on evidence in the record, but cannot resort to mere speculation or guess."[73] In other words, the plaintiff's burden is to present the best evidence possible under the circumstances to permit a reasonably accurate estimate. Damages need not be quantified with absolute mathematical certainty.[74]

The justification for this comparatively relaxed standard regarding the amount of damages is to recognize the difficulty in reconstructing what might have occurred absent the defendant's violations.[75] Indeed, the difficulty arises precisely because of the acts of defendant. Thus, the burden of dealing with uncertainty in quantifying damages is shifted to the defendant. What this means to the financial expert witness is that, as long as reasonable assumptions are used and the best information available is relied upon, the expert has considerable latitude in developing lost profits calculations.

[d] Elements of Recovery

Within the context of antitrust violations, the plaintiff is permitted recovery of the reasonably foreseeable but for losses to its business.

---

[70] M.J. Wagner & P.B. Frank, *Litigation Services Technical Consulting Practice Aid* 4 (1986) (a publication of the AICPA).

[71] Story Parchment Co. v. Paterson Parchment Paper Co., 282 U.S. 555, 562-563 (1931).

[72] Bigelow v. RKO Radio Pictures, Inc., 327 U.S. 251, 264 (1946).

[73] Eastman Kodak Co. v. Southern Photo Materials Co., 272 U.S. 359, 379 (1927); Hacker Pipe & Supply Co. v. Chapman Value Mfg. Co., 17 Colo. App. 2d 265 (1936).

[74] Berge v. International Harvester Co., 142 Cal. App. 3d at 152, 190 Cal. Rptr. at 815.

[75] *See also* Contemporary Mission, Inc. v. Famous Music Corp., 557 F.2d 918 (2d Cir. 1977).

These losses generally fall into three categories: increased costs, lost profits, and loss of going-concern value.[76]

☐ *Increased costs.* When a plaintiff has been forced to buy goods at conspiratorially high prices as a result of, for example, price fixing, the plaintiff has been injured in part to the extent of those higher prices. The basis for a portion of the damage determination is thus the difference between what the plaintiff did pay and what he or she would have paid in a free market.[77]

☐ *Lost profits.* Lost profits generally are when a plaintiff is deprived of revenue (and thus income) that could have been earned in a free market but for the unlawful business practices of competitors. Common examples of such unlawful activity include below-cost pricing or tying arrangements between competitors. Included in lost profits are both past and future profits.[78] In addition, net profits, rather than gross profits, are the measure of recovery.[79] The mechanics of computing the lost profits from lost sales involve the use of cost/volume/profit relationships experienced without the violation applied to the incremental lost sales. This assumes, of course, that the relevant range of production has not materially changed. If it would have changed in the but-for model, an adjustment for increased fixed-cost absorption should be included.

As an aside, the use of microcomputers and spreadsheet software has become virtually a standard tool in the development of but-for lost profit models. Assuming the logic within a spreadsheet is sound, such models allow the user to change assumptions and quickly see the impact on total lost profits. In addition, microcomputer models provide the basis of developing graphic demonstrative evidence (e.g., graphs, charts, and schedules) that can be extremely useful in supporting expert testimony.

Lost profits are generally calculated using any of three basic methods[80]:

1. *The "before and after" method.* The *before-and-after method* compares the plaintiff's profit performance prior to and after the violation. The basic assumption in this computation is that, but for the violation, the plaintiff would have continued to

---

[76] J. Bodner, Jr., *Developments in the Proof of Fact of Damage, Causation and the Amount of Damage* 15-16 (1986).
[77] Ohio Valley Elec. Corp. v. General Elec. Co., 244 F. Supp. 911 (S.D.N.Y. 1965).
[78] Fontana Aviation, Inc. v. Beech Aircraft Corp., 432 F.2d 1080 (7th Cir. 1970).
[79] Kuffed v. Seaside Oil Co., 11 Cal. App. 3d 367, 90 Cal. Rptr. 217 (1970).
[80] J. Bodner, Jr., *supra* note 75, at 17; *see also* 3 C.L. Knapp, *Commercial Damages: A Guide to Remedies in Business Litigation*, ch. 54 (1986).

earn profits in much the same way he had before the violation. Comparing before-and-after profits yields the amount of damages. A necessary ingredient in such computations is sufficient reliable financial data, both before and after the violation, to support the comparison. A classic example of the application of the before-and-after method to compute lost profits was the *Continental Baking Company v. Old Homestead Bread Company* case.[81] In this case, one of the plaintiffs derived its lost profits by demonstrating the amount of profits that would have been gained but for the violation. The method involved showing the extent of (1) projected lost sales and (2) the incremental profit margin related to each lost sale. On the other hand, another plaintiff used actual sales during the complaint period multiplied by the alleged higher price that would have been attained as the basis for lost profits.

2. *The "yardstick" method.* The *yardstick method* is based upon a comparison of the plaintiff's sales and profits during the violation period to another similar company or companies' sales and profits which were not affected by the violation. This method is not unlike the market-based valuation of a closely held company whereby price/earnings multiples of similar, publicly traded companies are used to derive a fair market value for the appraised company. The method is based on the assumption that the injured company would have enjoyed sales and profits similar to the comparable companies but for the anticompetitive practices of the defendant(s). As with the valuation of a closely held business, one of the more difficult burdens faced by the plaintiff employing this method is that of identifying truly comparable businesses as a basis for demonstrating lost profits. In some case, the most comparable business is, in fact, the defendant company, which would be an inappropriate comparison since it might have the effect of awarding the plaintiff company illegally gained profits.[82] The yardstick method is often suited to cases in which the plaintiff company has not been in business long enough to establish a "before" track record needed in the before-and-after method previously discussed.

3. *The market-share method.* As the name implies, the *market-share method* involves estimating the extent of lost market share suffered by the plaintiff as a result of the anticompetitive practices of the defendant(s). Once this lost share is determined, the plaintiff then translates the loss into lost sales (or units of sales) and multiplies the loss by an appropriate profit margin. It shares the concept of pre- and postviolation time periods with the before-and-after method by examining the plaintiff's market share both with (after) and without (before)

---

[81] Continental Baking Co. v. Old Homestead Bread Co., 476 F.2d 97 (10th Cir. 1973).
[82] Farmington Dowel Prods. Co. v. Forster Mfg. Co., 421 F.2d 61 (1st Cir. 1970).

the violation. Under this method, the plaintiff must provide evidence of (1) the economic profile of the relevant industries, (2) the plaintiff's share of that market prior to the violation, (3) the profit margins experienced prior to the violation, and (4) a reasonable basis for using at least previolation margins for the postviolation period.

☐ *Loss of "going concern" value.* In instances where an illegal act, such as an antitrust violation, has caused the total demise of the plaintiff company, the basis for determining damages is logically the value of the entire company. Value in such cases has often been defined to be *"going-concern value"* or "the price a willing buyer would have paid and a willing seller would have accepted for the business if the anti-competitive practices had not diminished or destroyed his business."[83] In such cases, valuation methods applicable to any other valuation setting with similar objective should be applied.

It is interesting to note that the previously mentioned categories of damages are not necessarily mutually exclusive. That is, under the proper circumstances, a plaintiff may recover *both* lost profits and loss of going-concern damages so long as they are not directed at the same period.[84] For example, in the *Farmington Dowel Products Company v. Forster Manufacturing Company* case,[85] the plaintiff recovered lost profits from the date of the violation to the date it had gone out of business. In turn, it recovered loss of going-concern value as of the date it went out of business. This same approach can be applied in cases where only a portion of a plaintiff's business has been damaged by the defendant. The company would be valued in its damaged state and then would be compared to a valuation estimated for the company, had it been undamaged. The difference or loss in value could be ascribed the defendant's violation.

It is important to note that the standards of valuation methodology used in the going-concern damage computation should be no different from any other appraisal environment. As evidenced in this case, for example, the plaintiff's expert witness attempted, unsuccessfully, to establish going-concern value based on capitalizing expected profits, assuming a steady increment of profit on sales, without examining changes in the relevant marketplace, future costs of labor, and other external factors.[86]

---

[83] Albrecht v. Herald Co., 452 F.2d 124 (8th Cir. 1971).
[84] C.L. Knapp, *supra* note 80, at 54-25.
[85] 421 F.2d at 61.
[86] C.L. Knapp, *supra* note 80, at 54-77.

[2] Human Capital Valuation

Negligently inflicted personal injury or wrongful death is often the subject of considerable expert witness debate due to the many variables influencing the determination of these damages. While generally the domain of economists, expert witnesses for such actions have been drawn from the ranks of CPAs, investment bankers, valuation specialists, and financial analysts. It is appropriate that valuation professionals be relied upon in personal injury and wrongful death cases because of the similarities between valuing a business and valuing the pecuniary loss of a human life.

The range of issues and the diversity of opinion issued by the courts in these matters preclude an in-depth analysis here of each variable affecting the damage calculation. Nevertheless, an introduction to these issues and a discussion of prevalent views and methodologies serve as a foundation for further research. In large part, valuation methodology is influenced by case decisions and federal and state statutes. For the prospective expert witness, this discussion underscores the need for careful research concerning the computation of damages and for close coordination with client attorneys.

[a] Elements of Damage

The elements of compensable damage in wrongful death cases vary from one jurisdiction to another but generally include the following:

- Medical expenses;
- Funeral expenses;
- Lost earnings;
- Pecuniary value of personal services rendered by the decedent in behalf of the decedent's immediate family; and
- Pecuniary value of the decedent's "society" contributions (i.e., love, affection, care, attention, companionship, comfort, and protection).

Extensive debate has been waged in the courts on the issue of recovering pecuniary and nonpecuniary consortium (society) losses; and, as might be expected, different courts have established different precedents. For example, some states have permitted recovery for temporary loss of consortium in persona injury cases while at the same time denying recovery in wrongful death cases.[87] However, the quantification of such consortium losses is typically an arbitrary lump-sum

---

[87] *See* Liff et al. v. Schildkrout, 49 N.Y.2d 622 (1980); Millington v. Southeastern Elevator Co., 22 N.Y.2d 498 (1968).

amount set by the court. As this element of damages is generally outside the scope of the financial expert witness's testimony, it has been excluded from consideration here.

While the quantification of medical and funeral expenses is frequently a direct process, establishing a logical and defensible damage amount for the other elements is often a greater challenge. This situation arises from the "single recovery" or "lump sum" rule that provides for the award of all past, present, and future losses stemming from the injury or death at the single time when judgment is rendered. This required lump-sum computation compels the expert witness—and the judge and jury—to project future losses. The expert witness tries to reduce the level of ambiguity in such projections, thereby contributing to fair and reasonable damage awards.

Controversy in wrongful death or personal injury cases often centers around issues of lost earnings. To satisfy the objective of "making whole" the injured party (or heirs of the decedent), the court must decide upon an appropriate level of earnings that presumably would have been earned but for the injury/death. The following is cited from the case of *Allen v. Toledo*:

> The measure of damages [in a wrongful death action] is the value of the benefits the heirs could reasonably expect to receive from the deceased if [he or] she had lived.[88]

In essence, the future earnings stream foregone by the injured party or the survivors is the measure of damages (for this element of recovery).

[b] Medical and Funeral Expenses

The plaintiff generally enters evidence of the actual cost of medical expenses (and/or funeral expenses) incurred through a medical expert witness. Often, the plaintiff will submit a claim for anticipated future medical expenses. Such future costs usually are determined by the medical experts, with the financial expert's role, if any, being limited to vouching for (or disputing) the mathematical accuracy of such projections.

The difficulty inherent in accurately predicting the cost of future medical payments resulting from personal injuries, particularly in times of inflation and increasing medical costs, has influenced the use of periodic payment settlements as an alternative to lump-sum awards. Such settlements provide defendants a future income stream, in some cases as long as the plaintiff's remaining life, to cover the plaintiff's

---

[88] 109 Cal. App. 3d 415 (1980).

future medical expenses. Payment comes directly from the defendant or from the earnings of a lump-sum deposit made or annuity purchased by the defendant.

Settlements of this nature often work to the benefit of both plaintiff and defendant since the plaintiff is assured a steady flow of income to offset expenses and the defendant is not burdened with a sometimes crippling lump-sum payment. Also, the plaintiff is freed from managing the often large lump-sum payment to ensure its continuing earnings power needed to offset future expenses.[89]

[c] Personal Injury Lost Earnings

Computing lost earnings damages for personal injury and wrongful deaths are similar; the ensuing paragraphs will thus treat them as essentially identical. However, there are a number of characteristics of personal injury cases that are not shared by wrongful death actions. These differences relate to (1) the duration of impairment and (2) the extent of impairment (i.e., the injury may result in the injured party's ability to earn some wage, albeit smaller than his or her preinjury earnings).

☐ *Duration of impairment.* Responsibility for estimating the duration of impairment generally rests with the medical expert witness. Once determined, this period becomes the term over which the financial expert will compute lost earnings.

Where injury results in incapacitation, the period used to estimate lost earnings is from (1) the injury date to trial date and (2) the judgment date to the plaintiff's expected date of retirement (for preretirement earnings) added to (3) the time between the expected retirement date and an actuarially determined date of death for post-retirement earnings. Often, due to the effects of discounting to present value the distant years' earnings, no distinction is made between the estimated retirement date earnings and the subsequent postretirement date earnings. Rather, lost earnings are simply computed assuming a preretirement earnings level from date of judgment to a normal life expectancy. However, adjustments to this term must logically be made to accom-

---

[89] For a detailed discussion of periodic payments, see N.J. Itzkoff, *Dealing With Damages* (1983); Elligett, "The Periodic Payment of Judgements," 46 Ins. Counsel J. 130 (1979); Krause, "Structural Settlement for Tort Victims," 66 A.B.A.J. 1527 (1980); Note, "Variable Periodic Payments of Damages: An Alternative to Lump Sum Awards," 64 Iowa L. Rev. 138, 142 (1978); Hindert & Hindert, "New Rules for an Old Game: An Evaluation of the Uniform Law Commissioner's Model Periodic Payment of Judgements Act," 15 Int'l Soc'y Barristers Q. 359 (1982); Henderson, "Periodic Payments of Bodily Injury Awards," 66 A.B.A.J. 734 (1980).

modate such factors as absences from the work force and the probability of premature death.

☐ *Extent of impairment.* Unlike wrongful death cases where alternative gainful employment is of course irrelevant, an important factor in personal injury cases is the extent to which the injured party can obtain gainful employment during the recovery period or, in the case of permanent disability, for the remainder of his or her life. The financial expert witness is seldom responsible for opining upon the plaintiff's vocational and earnings potential but rather relies upon the testimony of another expert (e.g., a vocational counselor, a doctor, or a psychologist).

The vocational expert identifies the type of employment and appropriate potential earnings levels for which the injured party is capable. Absent this testimony and assuming the injured party has not yet reentered the work force, the financial expert witness can determine an appropriate wage by using, at one extreme, the minimum wage and, as a preferable measure, the average wage levels published by the Department of Labor (Bureau of Labor Statistics (BLS)) segregated by major job category. The closer the relationship between the nature of actual work that now will be performed by the injured party and the occupational category from the BLS data, the more reliable the estimate.

[d] Wrongful Death/Lost Earnings

To the trained economist, accountant, or financial analyst, computing a decedent's future lost earnings in a wrongful death action is fairly rudimentary. However, a number of variables complicate the process and cause abundant debate among experts and attorneys alike. As expected, the variables cited here center around the uncertainty inherent in prediction. While the variables listed are not all the factors affecting the computations, they provide a good checklist for the expert witness when analyzing lost earnings.

☐ *Variables affecting the calculation of lost future earnings.* The following represent the key variables a financial expert witness should consider when conducting lost earnings computations, which are examined in greater detail throughout this section:

- The work life expectancy of the decedent (prior to wrongful death) and the probability of survival to that age;

- The extent and timing of separations from the work force that would have occurred throughout the decedent's remaining work life;
- Expected wage increases attributable to merit, bonuses, or promotions;
- The effects of inflation on projected lost earnings;
- The use of pre- or posttax earnings levels, including fringe benefits, in the projection of lost future wages;
- The selection of an appropriate discount rate for computing the present value of future lost earnings;
- The extent to which future lost earnings should be reduced to recognize outlays that the decedent would have spent on his own behalf (i.e., money not contributed to the support of his or her family); and
- In the case of the wrongful death of persons with no work history, the determination of a probable profession or line of work and resultant earnings that would have been attained by the deceased.

☐ *Projecting lost earnings—the economic profile of the decedent.* The projection of the lost earnings of a decedent should first consider the "economic profile" of the decedent. As with the valuation of businesses or tangible assets, it is important to recognize the fundamental characteristics and uses of the property (here, the individual) in order to perform a relevant appraisal. Generally, individuals who are victims of wrongful death fall into one of five economic categories[90]:

1. Employees;
2. Professionals (e.g., doctors, lawyers, accountants, or appraisers);
3. Business people (e.g., executives or proprietors);
4. Juveniles; and
5. Homemakers.

Of course, a decedent may fall into more than one category—for example, the working mother (an employee or professional) who also performs the traditional duties of the housewife or the employee who also owns and operates a side business.

The decedent's category will influence the earnings projection methodology, the factors considered, and, to a large extent, the relative accuracy of the projection. Thus, the expert witness must recognize early in the valuation engagement into which category the decedent falls so that the valuation can yield accurate results and be conducted in an efficient manner.

---

[90] S.M. Speiser, *Recovery for Wrongful Death Economic Handbook* 49 (1970).

Earnings base. The projection of foregone future earnings often starts with examining the individual's past earnings history. For decedents whose past and presumably future earnings had remained static or moved in stable increments, the starting point for prospective future earnings will be some embodiment of past earnings. When establishing a representative earnings base for the projection, a weighted average of the decedent's recent (generally the past five years) earnings experience may be appropriate. Weighting the latest years places increased value upon more recent history under the presumption that those years will more accurately predict future earnings. However, for individuals with relatively static earnings, weighting is unnecessary since it results in roughly the same amount as the nonweighted average.

The best source for earnings data is generally the decedent's income tax or payroll records. Included in earnings should be all stock options, bonuses, and fringe benefits. Where there is little past history—as in the case of the wrongful death of juveniles—the expert must develop an earnings base considering age, sex, race, education, training, work experience, and family background.

An alternative method for projecting earnings would employ data from the BLS, relative to the decedent's age, sex, geographic location, and present or likely occupation. Similarly, for individuals employed in the civil service or academia, fixed salary scales can be used, including estimates for in-grade durations and promotions to higher grades.

Work-life expectancy. The next step determines the decedent's work-life expectancy—the term over which the earnings will be projected. In the simplest scenario, this period dates from the decedent's death to his or her compulsory retirement. If no compulsory retirement age exists—as is the case with many professionals—then the expert witness might again rely upon BLS data (i.e., Tables of Working Lives for Men and Women).

It is important for the valuation expert to note the decedent's *life* expectancy in contrast to his or her *work-life* expectancy. If the decedent's life expectancy (using actuarially sound projections based upon the individual's age, sex, health, race, and occupation) is less than his or her work-life expectancy, this *life* expectancy would be the date used for projecting future earnings (from employment) rather than his or her *work-life* expectancy. The most appropriate way to factor in life expectancies is to adjust each year's earnings by the probability of mortality by that date. Actuarial tables and methods make this calculation relatively straightforward.

For decedents with spouses, it is also important to recognize the life expectancy of the spouse.[91] For example, if the decedent's life

---

[91] *Id.* at 57.

expectancy exceeded work-life expectancy, it is reasonable to expect retirement benefits in the form of profit and/or pension distributions as well as social security benefits. If, as is normally the case with spouses of male decedents, the spouse would have outlived the decedent and would have been entitled to those retirement benefits; these foregone benefits become part of the lost earnings calculation.

Additional adjustments to lost earnings. Once the valuation analyst has examined these factors, the baseline earnings projection is simply the sum of the adjusted annual earnings (historical earnings) remaining until the expiration of work life. The next step involves modifying this projection for the following factors, as appropriate:

- The amount the decedent would have expended for his or her own maintenance (personal consumption);
- Wage increases based on past wage increases or wage increases which would arise from increases in productivity or from likely promotions;
- Wage increases from cost-of-living (inflation) adjustments (COLAs);
- The probability of early death; and
- The likelihood of absences from the work force (i.e., unemployment).

Adjustment for personal consumption expenditures. Lost future earnings must be reduced by expenditures the decedent would have made on his or her own behalf, thereby reducing earnings which would contribute to family support. Heirs cannot logically claim the portion of the decedent's earnings dispensed for his or her own support as an element of lost earnings since the heirs would not have benefited from such amounts, had the decedent lived.

While this adjustment seems reasonable, the difficulty (as always) lies in determining an appropriate amount. The factor that most influences this adjustment is often the decedent's family size. There are essentially two relevant categories of decedents: those who were single individuals and those who were married and supported a spouse and/or family.

The best indication of what the single individual did not spend on him- or herself probably is his or her annual savings rate. If there is no evidence that the decedent had regularly set aside money from his or her earnings, it would be difficult to justify significant lost earnings for the benefit of the relatives (other than any residual estate). For example, in one case involving the death of a number of single individuals, the court reduced the lost earnings projection by a factor of 94%.[92]

---

[92] Butler v. United States, 726 F.2d 1057 (5th Cir. 1984).

This adjustment was upheld based on the defendant's expert testimony, uncontroverted, that 97% of the decedent's earnings went to personal expenditures.

For decedents with families, the primary determinant of the personal expenditure adjustment is based upon the number of family members supported by the decedent. BLS statistics support the fact that, the greater the number of family members, the greater the contribution to the family. In wrongful death matters, this results in a smaller reduction for the decedent's personal expenditures. In such cases, expert witnesses generally rely either on BLS data or, if the BLS data do not fairly represent the circumstances of the particular decedent, on historical data compiled by the expert witness that more accurately reflects the decedent's family contributions.

Adjustment based on past earnings growth rate. A number of expert witnesses adjust future earnings for likely merit increases based upon the incidence of past similar increases. Rather than attempting to segregate merit increases from base earnings, such computations simply look at the decedent's historical trend in earnings growth and assume that similar growth would have continued. Various methods can be used to make this projection, ranging from the use of simple extensions of the past earnings trend (using a ruler and pencil) to the use of regression analysis techniques.

Regardless of method used, this approach assumes that trends experienced in the past will continue into the future. Such an approach depends, to varying degrees, upon the employment circumstances of the individual decedent. However, the vagaries of the modern-day economy and the impact on employment trends of, for example, rapidly changing technology, make projections based solely on past trends increasingly difficult to justify. This is particularly true in instances where the deceased is relatively young, thus requiring the expert witness to make long-term earnings projections. Also, the analysis must take into account that past salary increases have been, in part, adjustments for inflation. To the extent the rate of inflation in the past is different from future inflation, the use of the historical trend will be in error.

Adjustments for productivity and inflation. In determining damages for personal injury or wrongful death, perhaps no single factor has generated as much debate as that of how damages are to be adjusted for the effects of productivity and/or inflation. It is difficult to address this adjustment factor without simultaneously discussing the discount factor used in the present value calculation. The close relationship among productivity, inflation rates, and the present value discount factor arises since courts often use these factors to increase or decrease the lost earnings calculation. As discussed later, adjustments to earnings projections for inflation or productivity can be neutralized by the discount factor used in the present value operation.

Because of the considerable body of written material on the subject (court decisions, law review articles and texts), the following is only an overview of the major issues and a summary of approaches used successfully in different courts. Under the Federal Tort Claims Act, questions concerning the measure of damages are governed by the law of the state having jurisdiction over a particular matter. This has resulted in a variety of decisions throughout the country as to the admissibility and measurement of productivity and inflation on lost earnings. Thus, the expert engaged to compute lost earnings should familiarize him- or herself with the precedents established in the applicable state as well as in previous federal causes of action.

Decedents with a record of employment logically would expect salary increases throughout their careers as compensation for merit or productivity improvement. Similarly, a deceased employee would likely have received salary increases to compensate for the rising cost of living. Despite the reasonableness of these statements, the application of these two factors to lost earnings computations has proven to be a formidable task.

Perhaps the court decision that had, until recently, provided the principal guidance on these issues was *Johnson v. Penrod Drilling Company*, which stated:

> The influence on future damages of possible inflation or deflation is too speculative a matter for judicial determination." Therefore, triers of fact "should not be instructed to take into account future inflationary or deflationary trends in computing future lost earnings, nor should the jury be advised to consider such alternative descriptions of inflationary and deflationary trends as the purchasing power of the dollar or the consumer price index.[93]

In addition to prohibiting the admission of evidence concerning the impact of inflation, the *Johnson* case had the extended, although unintended, effect of prohibiting evidence concerning raises due to merit or productivity, which are increases theoretically unaffected by inflation. This was due primarily to the difficulty in isolating the inflation component from future wage increases. As noted in the court's opinion in *Culver v. Slater Boat Company*, the "practical effect of Penrod is often to throw the baby of future merit increases out with the inflationary washtub waters."[94]

---

[93] 510 F.2d 234 (5th Cir. 1975).
[94] 688 F.2d 280 (5th Cir. 1982).

However, subsequent cases recognized that inflation and productivity were indeed separate factors to be addressed and that productivity increases could be considered by the jury.[95] Thus, based upon these and other cases, the expert witness should determine if a particular decedent would probably have received future merit-based pay raises (above and beyond COLAs) and include these in the projection of lost future earnings.

The acceptance and application by the courts of evidence concerning the changing purchasing power of the dollar (inflation) have proven still more difficult than that of the productivity issue. When courts have considered inflation's impact on lost earnings, they have been concerned with three fundamental attributes of its admission as evidence[96]:

1. Its accuracy, efficiency, and predictability;
2. The accuracy of estimates as to future rates of inflation;
3. The efficiency with which it can be presented to and considered by the court; and
4. The measure of predictability as to its occurrences as estimated.

Thus, the central issues become how the issue of inflation can be efficiently submitted to the jury and how an accurate and predictable inflation factor can be applied to the damages.[97] The expert witness, as might be expected, plays an important role in contributing to each of these objectives.

As described by the Court of Appeals for Second Circuit in *Doca v. Marina Mercante Nicaraquense, S.A.*, the jury should consider the issue of inflation in any one of three ways[98]:

1. By allowing expert opinion;
2. By requiring the factfinder (judge and jury) to apply its own knowledge; and
3. By permitting the factfinder to apply its own knowledge together with expert testimony.

As consideration by the jury of expert witness testimony generally leads to a more informed jury, it is expected that courts will continue to follow option (3).

---

[95] *See* Hamilton v. Canal Barge Co., 395 F. Supp. 978 (E.D. La. 1975); Feldman v. Allegheny Airlines, Inc., 524 F.2d 384 (2d Cir. 1975).

[96] Hurney, Jr., "Tort Damages: The Adjustment of Awards for Lost Future Earning Capacity to Compensate for Inflation and Increased Productivity: *Kuczkowski v. Bolubasz* [491 Pa. 561 (1981)]," 7 U. Dayton L. Rev. 139 (Fall 1981).

[97] Doca v. Marina Mercante Nicaraquense, S.A., 634 F.2d 30 (2d Cir. 1980).

[98] *Id.*

[e] Assessing the Impact of Inflation

A review of court rulings shows that three fundamental approaches to calculating the inflation effect have most often been used[99]:

1. The traditional approach;
2. The middle-ground approach; and
3. The evidentiary approach.

The *traditional approach* is essentially embodied in *Johnson* where the influence or future damages of possible inflation was considered too speculative a matter for judicial determination. In essence, the inflation factor is ignored. While this method at first seems logically unsound, it nevertheless easily accommodated the objectives of eliminating speculation and providing efficiency. Therefore, for considerable time, it served as the guiding decision. It should be noted that, in addition to disallowing consideration of inflation, this method nevertheless required the discounting of future earnings to present value, thereby, in many critic's minds, undercompensating plaintiffs.

The *middle-ground* approach, in going a step further, allowed the fact finder to consider the effects of inflation and increased productivity on lost future earnings but prohibited the introduction of expert witness testimony on either subject.[100] In essence, this approach allowed inflation to be considered by the judge and jury using only their own pooled knowledge and experience as a guide. Again, while this method seems unsound, it too met the tests of efficiency and, to a lesser extent, accuracy, since at least the combined knowledge of the judge and jury concerning inflation was applied. As noted in a number of court opinions, it also avoided the introduction of expert witness testimony that might serve to "confuse the jurors and divert their attention from the central issues."[101]

Finally, the *evidentiary approach*, manifested in several variants, provides the fact finder with expert testimony on the impact of inflation. This approach, while perhaps neglecting the goal of efficiency through the introduction of often complex testimony, nevertheless significantly enhanced the court's opportunity to fulfill the objectives of accuracy and predictability. The trend for many courts has been in the direction of allowing such expert testimony on future inflation and its likely effects on a decedent's future wages.

---

[99] Hurney, *supra* note 96, at 140.

[100] *Id.* at 141; see also Johnson v. Serra, 521 F.2d 1289 (8th Cir. 1973); Riba v. Jasper Blackburn Co., 516 F.2d 840 (8th Cir. 1975).

[101] Johnson v. Penrod Drilling Co., 510 F.2d at 234.

Adjustment for future income taxes. Following the axiom that "in life there are only two certainties: death and taxes," another necessary adjustment to future lost earnings is that of future federal income taxes of the decedent. Since income taxes claim a substantial and regular portion of an individual's earnings, it is only logical to expect that future earnings would likewise be reduced by income taxes.

Despite this reasoning, courts have not always permitted consideration of the effects of future income taxes on lost earnings calculations. In fact, it is more likely that exclusion of this offset to future earnings has occurred more often than it has been included. One California case, *Canavin v. Pacific Southwest Airlines*,[102] provides considerable guidance on why future income taxes should or should not be included in the lost earnings computation. It, along with several other cases,[103] should be reviewed by the appraiser faced with this issue.

[f] Discounting Future Earnings

The final step in the computation of lost earnings is the discounting to present value of the stream of future net earnings. Discounting is required as plaintiffs are compensated through lump-sum awards *today* for losses they will suffer in the *future*. The gross damage amount is discounted (reduced) to give effect to the time value of money attributable to the award's ability to earn interest income over time. The most important step in this process is, of course, selecting the proper discount rate. It should be noted that this discounting process for lost earnings computations is analogous to the commonly used discounted future earnings method of business valuation.

In 1916, the U.S. Supreme Court mandated that awards for future damages be discounted to present value to avoid overcompensating plaintiffs.[104] The fundamental problem today revolves not around whether or not to discount but rather around how to discount and what factors (e.g., inflation) to consider in the discounting process.

In simple terms, the question of how to discount a stream of future earnings to present value involves the following issues:

- Should the projected future earnings be adjusted to recognize future inflation (as distinguished from increases due to productivity increases)?
- Should the present value discount factor be adjusted for inflation?

---

[102] 141 Cal. App. 3d 577 (1983).

[103] Norfolk & Western R.R. Co. v. Leipelt, 444 U.S. 490 (1980); Rodriguez v. McDonnell Douglas Corp., 87 Cal. App. 3d 620 (1978); Plourd v. Southern Pac. Transp. Co., 513 P.2d 1140 (Or. 1973); Scalise v. Central R.R. Co. of N.J., 323 A.2d 525 (N.J. Super. 1974); Raines v. New York Cent. R.R. Co., 283 N.E.2d 230 (Ill. 1972).

[104] Chesapeake & Ohio R.R. v. Kelley, 241 U.S. 485 (1916).

- What is an appropriate discount factor for the present value calculation?

There have been a number of mathematical approaches used to reconcile the two factors of inflation and interest ("real" earning power of money invested) in selecting a discount rate. As described fully in a *Wisconsin Law Review* comment:

> At one extreme, courts will create a conclusive presumption that the rate used to discount to present value and the future inflation rate totally offset each other. They do this by making no changes in the award. They neither discount to present value nor account for future inflation. At the other extreme, courts discount at normal rates and make no inflation adjustment. In the middle, some courts take account of future inflation by reducing the discount rate.[105]

For the practitioner faced with understanding and, in turn, applying these alternative methods, the following summarizes the major approaches that have been used in the courts.

☐ *Total offset method*

- *Description*: The discount rate for the present value computation is presumed to equal the future inflation rate. One "offsets" the other. Thus, no discount (present value) calculation is required.
- *Case precedent: Beaulieu v. Elliott.*[106]
- *Advantages:* (1) It avoids speculation as to future inflation and real interest rates; (2) it is simple to apply and understand; (3) it requires no expert testimony.
- *Disadvantages:* It includes the erroneous assumption that the rate of inflation used in projecting earnings and the discount rate are equal.

☐ *Variable adjusted discount rate*

- *Description:* This considers expert testimony for appropriate rates for both discounting and inflation. "Variable" refers to the relationship between inflation rates and interest rates and assumes long-term parallel movement in the rates with a difference equal to the real rate of interest.

---

[105] Winer, "Adjusting Damage Awards for Future Inflation," 3 Wis. L. Rev. 397 (1982).
[106] 434 P.2d 665 (Alaska 1967).

- *Mathematical application:* (1) Inflate earnings projections to recognize future inflation, and then discount to present value using a nominal (i.e., including inflation) discount rate, or (2) do not inflate the earnings projection and discount to present value using a *real* (i.e., net of inflation) discount factor.
- *Legal precedents:* For (1), *District of Columbia v. Barriteau*[107] and *Kaczkowski v. Bolubasz*[108]; and for (2), *Feldman v. Allegheny Airlines, Inc.*[109]
- *Advantages:* It offers increased accuracy due to the separate consideration of each factor and the admission of expert testimony.
- *Disadvantages:* (1) It is less efficient due to admission of expert testimony on complex subject matter; (2) it includes the potential for confusing jurors; and (3) long-term parallelism in rates must be assumed and the real rate of interest must be identified.

☐ *Fixed adjusted discount rate*

- *Description:* This assumes that a fixed relationship exists between the inflation rate and the interest rate such that a fixed discount rate can be used in all present value calculations. Note that this is essentially the same as option (2) under the above variable adjusted rate.

  Note: Nominal risk-free interest rates are generally recognized to contain two elements: a factor of inflation and a factor for "real" interest. Since the real rate, many economists maintain, has been historically constant at approximately 2-3%, this method allows for inflation to be disregarded in the calculation by using only the net real rate of interest in the present value discounting process. Using this rate negates the need to inflate the earnings projection.
- *Legal precedent: Doca v. Marina Mercante Nicaraquense, S.A.*[110]
- *Advantages:* (1) It is simple to apply; (2) it is efficient (no expert testimony required); and (3) it is relatively accurate.
- *Disadvantages:* It may be erroneous to the extent that inflation and the real rate of interest are not positively correlated.

These three methods represent the major approaches to addressing the issue of *how* (as opposed to *if*) to account for the rate of inflation in present value calculations. From an economic perspective, it is difficult to dispute the fact that both factors should be addressed in a lost earnings calculation.

---

[107] 399 A.2d 563 (D.C. Ct. App. 1979).
[108] 491 Pa. 561 (1981).
[109] 382 F. Supp. 1271 (D. Conn. 1974).
[110] 634 F.2d at 30.

Similarly, considerable economic research supports the view that a strongly correlated relationship exists between interest rates and inflation rates. Accordingly, the use of either the fixed or variable adjusted discounting methods in computing future lost earnings in personal injury or wrongful death litigation is supported.

Appendix 9-1 Federal Rules of Evidence—Article VII. Opinions and Expert Testimony

Rule 701.

OPINION TESTIMONY BY LAY WITNESS

If the witness is not testifying as an expert, his testimony in the form of opinions or inferences is limited to those opinions or inferences which are (a) rationally based on the perception of the witness and (b) helpful to a clear understanding of his testimony or the determination of a fact in issue.

Rule 702.

TESTIMONY BY EXPERTS

If scientific, technical, or other specialized knowledge will assist the trier of fact to understand the evidence or to determine a fact in issue, a witness qualified as an expert by knowledge, skill, experience, training, or education, may testify thereto in the form of an opinion or otherwise.

Rule 703.

BASES OF OPINION TESTIMONY BY EXPERTS

The facts or data in the particular case upon which an expert bases an opinion or inference may be those perceived by or made known to the expert at or before the hearing. If of a type reasonably relied upon by experts in the particular field in forming opinions or inferences upon the subject, the facts or data need not be admissible in evidence.

Rule 704.

OPINION ON ULTIMATE ISSUE

(a) Except as provided in subdivision (b), testimony in the form of an opinion or inference otherwise admissible is not objectionable because it embraces an ultimate issue to be decided by the trier of fact.

(b) No expert witness testifying with respect to the mental state or condition of a defendant in a criminal case may state an opinion or inference as to whether the defendant did or did not have the mental state or condition constituting an element of the crime charged or of a defense thereto. Such ultimate issues are matters for the trier of fact alone.

Rule 705.

DISCLOSURE OF FACTS OR DATA UNDERLYING EXPERT OPINION

The expert may testify in terms of opinion or inference and giving his reasons therefor without prior disclosure of the underlying facts or data, unless the judge requires otherwise. The expert may in any event be required to disclose the underlying facts or data on cross-examination.

Rule 706.

COURT APPOINTED EXPERTS

(a) Appointment. The court may on its own motion or on the motion of any party enter an order to show cause why expert witnesses should not be appointed, and may request the parties to submit nominations. The court may appoint any expert witnesses agreed upon by the parties, and may appoint witnesses of its own selection. An expert witness shall not be appointed by the court unless he consents to act. A witness so appointed shall be informed of the witness's duties by the court in writing, a copy of which shall be filed with the clerk, or at a conference in which the parties shall have opportunity to participate. A witness so appointed shall advise the parties of his findings, if any; his deposition may be taken by any party; and the witness may be called to testify by the court or any party. The witness shall be subject to cross-examination by each party, including a party calling him as a witness.

(b) Compensation. Expert witnesses so appointed are entitled to reasonable compensation in whatever sum the court may allow. The compensation thus fixed is payable from funds which may be provided by law in criminal cases and civil actions and proceedings involving just compensation under the Fifth Amendment. In other civil actions and proceedings the compensation shall be paid by the parties in such proportion and at such time as the court directs, and thereafter charged in like manner as other costs.

(c) **Disclosure of appointment.** In the exercise of its discretion, the court may authorize disclosure to the jury of the fact that the court appointed the expert witness.

(d) **Parties' experts of own selection.** Nothing in this rule limits the parties in calling expert witnesses of their own selection.

Appendix 9-2 Sample Litigation Retainer Agreement

The following shall constitute a retainer agreement ("Agreement hereinafter) between the law firm of _____ ("Law Firm" hereinafter) and the *XYZ* Valuation Company ("*XYZ*" hereinafter), under which *XYZ* shall provide such consulting services as Law Firm may reasonably require pertaining to the appraisal of the *ABC* Company ("Company" hereinafter), and related areas, relative to the pending litigation. *XYZ*'s analyses and conclusions may be documented in a narrative report ("Report" hereinafter) or such other document as may be mutually agreed upon. It is further understood and accepted by *XYZ* that *XYZ* may be required to furnish judicial testimony, and otherwise advise Law Firm in judicial procedures concerning the substance of said analyses.

Law Firm agrees that the conclusions expressed by *XYZ* in any form shall be based on methods and techniques that *XYZ* considers appropriate under the circumstances. Law Firm further agrees to make available to *XYZ* on a timely basis, and in a format satisfactory to *XYZ*, such information as *XYZ* may reasonably require. Any reports, data, worksheets or other documents prepared by us in connection with this engagement will be submitted solely to Law Firm and will not be furnished to any other person or party without *XYZ*'s prior written consent.

Law Firm agrees to pay *XYZ* a fee based on an hourly rate of $_____ to $_____ for professional staff time, plus out-of-pocket expenses that may be incurred by *XYZ* on Law Firm's behalf, payable as follows: (a) upon the signing of this Agreement, $_____; and (b) the remainder promptly (within 30 days) upon submission of monthly billings. Out-of-pocket expenses shall include, but not be limited to, all travel expenses, research data, duplicating charges, computer charges, and long-distance telephone calls incurred by *XYZ* on Law Firm's behalf.

If either party to the Agreement brings an action based on this Agreement, the prevailing party shall be entitled to reasonable expenses therefor, including, but not limited to attorney's fees and court costs. This Agreement shall be governed by the laws of the state of _____, and both parties hereby agree that exclusive jurisdiction to enforce any of the terms of this Agreement shall reside in the courts of the state of _____.

This Agreement shall become effective upon the last party hereto affixing his signature below, and shall include all work done by XYZ prior to, and subsequent to, such signing.

XYZ VALUATION COMPANY

_____ _____, 19__

By _____
   Name
   Title

LAW FIRM
Address
csz

_____ _____, 19__

By _____
   Name
   Title

10

VALUATION OF COMMON EQUITY SECURITIES WHEN ASSET LIQUIDATION IS AN ALTERNATIVE

MICHAEL J. BOLOTSKY[*]

		Page
¶ 10.1	The Mechanics of Liquidation Analysis..........	10-3
	[1] Determination of "Combined Highest and Best Use"......................................	10-3
	[a] Liquidation vs. Continued Operation	10-4
	[b] The Role of Intangible Assets	10-5
	[2] Determination of Gross Liquidation Proceeds	10-5
	[3] Reduction of Gross Proceeds to Net Liquidation Value.........................	10-5
	[a] Reduction for Costs and Taxes and Comparison to Going-Concern Value	10-5
	[b] Reduction to Present Worth and Comparison to Going-Concern Value	10-6
	[4] Summary.....................................	10-7
¶ 10.2	Examples of Liquidation Analysis	10-10
	[1] Liquidation of the Entire Entity	10-10
	[2] Liquidation of a Portion of the Entity........	10-11
¶ 10.3	Choice of Discount Rate	10-12
	[1] Comparison to the Discount Rate for an Operating Company.........................	10-14
	[2] Factors to Consider	10-15
	[3] Quantification of the Factors	10-16
	[4] Selection of a Discount Rate	10-18
	[a] Low-Risk Scenario	10-18

---

[*] MICHAEL J. BOLOTSKY, ASA, is an independent business consultant headquartered in Plainsboro, New Jersey, and was formerly a senior consultant with American Appraisal Associates, Inc., in its Princeton, New Jersey, office. The author has been engaged in valuing businesses and business interests since 1978, is a member of the ASA Business Valuation Committee and chairman of its Exam Development Committee. In addition, he has served as the coeditor of *Federal Tax Valuation Digest* (1985 Cumulative Edition) and is a frequent instructor for business valuation and financial valuation courses and seminars.

	[b] High-Risk Scenario	10-19
	[5] Relative Risk in Liquidation vs. Continued Operation	10-20
¶ 10.4	**Additional Considerations**	10-21
	[1] Liquidation Value of Assets vs. Liquidation Value of Stock	10-21
	[2] Liquidation Value of Assets as the "Floor" of Value of the Stock	10-21
	[3] Intangible Asset Value	10-22
	[4] Factoring in Both Liquidation and Continued Operation	10-23
	[5] The Value of Minority Interests	10-23
	[a] When and How to Factor in Liquidation	10-24
	[b] Applicability of a Minority-Interest Discount	10-25
	[c] Fairness Considerations	10-26
	[d] Discount for Lack of Marketability	10-26
	[6] Shareholder-Level Taxes and the Value of Common Stock	10-27
¶ 10.5	**Summary**	10-30
Appendix 10-1 Detail of Table 10-1 Liquidation Value Computations		10-30

The valuation of businesses or business interests in situations where underlying asset liquidation is an alternative incorporates both the concepts applicable to the more common "going-concern assumption" securities valuations and the concepts applicable to underlying tangible and intangible asset valuations. Accordingly, these valuations typically place both business valuators and asset appraisers into unfamiliar and uncomfortable territory. More often than not, the course of action followed is to assume the exclusion of the liquidation alternative when doing the valuation. However, while a properly worded qualifying caveat will protect the valuator, it may not provide the client with the needed information; and, in a testimony situation, a successful attack on the qualifying caveat may render the entire valuation moot. This chapter will demonstrate the benefits that may be gained from analyzing the impact of asset liquidation on securities values.

Misconceptions regarding the correct application of a liquidation approach abound in the popular concept of the "liquidation valuation" of a business. The following statements shed some light on what a liquidation valuation is *not*:

- The liquidation value of a business is the net of the liquidation value of its underlying assets and liabilities.

- The value of an unrestricted 100% control interest cannot fall below the sum of the liquidation value of its net assets.
- In a business liquidation, the value of the business's intangible assets falls to zero.
- The value of a business is determined by the higher of its value in liquidation or its value as a going concern. The two indications of value are never averaged.
- Liquidation value is never an issue in the valuation of a minority interest.
- Taxes at the shareholder level are irrelevant in determining the value of common stock.

There have been many variations on these statements in valuation literature or valuation reports. Most valuation practitioners have used verbiage similar to at least one of these statements in reports or writings. Yet each of these statements has one attribute in common: Either in the general case or in specific instances, they are all false. In providing a framework for common stock valuations when the liquidation alternative will affect the final determination of value, each of the issues raised by the previous statements will be discussed.

¶ 10.1 The Mechanics of Liquidation Analysis

Business liquidation valuations most commonly apply in the case of an unrestricted 100% control interest. These situations present the simplest entry into the conceptual framework, and examples drawn from actual valuations of this type will, therefore, be used before the discussion proceeds to the less common applications of liquidation concepts.

[1] Determination of "Combined Highest and Best Use"

Valuation of an unrestricted 100% control interest involves a consideration of all means of realizing the value of the shares followed by the selection of the "*combined* highest and best use" of the business assets that will result in the realization of the maximum value of the shares. Note the use of the term *combined* highest and best use; the qualifier "combined" is important. While each particular asset may, in isolation, have a determinable highest and best use, putting the asset in question to its highest and best use will often preclude the realization of highest value from other assets of the business. For example, a 3-acre parcel of land on a corner property zoned "commercial/light industrial" may have a shutdown service station and undeveloped woodland on it. While the highest and best use of the existing structure may have been determined to be a real estate agency or small retail store, an analysis of the land and building together may show that higher net proceeds can be realized from leveling the structure and woodland and selling the entire 3 acres for commercial development. Under this scenario, the service station contributes *negatively* to the total proceeds (zero ongoing value less the cost of demolition), but the *combined* proceeds are higher than they would be if the value of the structure alone were maximized. Thus, what the analysis must determine is the optimum mix of uses for all the business assets combined such that the maximum value is obtained for the assets as a whole, whether or not the value of individual assets is maximized.

[a] Liquidation vs. Continued Operation

The initial step in the process is to place the business into one of three categories:

1. Liquidation in any form is clearly not the highest-value alternative.
2. Some form of liquidation clearly is the highest-value alternative.
3. Additional investigation is required before the determination can be made.

Sometimes a business is clearly worth more "dead" than alive. An example would be a small, marginally unprofitable, capital-intensive business with a strong current asset position, no debt, and a single key employee who intends to retire from an active role in the business in the near future. Conversely, it is often clear without valuing the underlying assets that the going-concern alternative provides the greater value. An example would be a highly profitable labor-intensive service business whose assets are primarily both intangible in nature and not salable separate from the business as a whole. These two scenarios correspond to the previous categories 1 and 2.

In many situations, however, the "dead or alive" choice is not nearly as clear-cut. In these cases, the next step is to determine a reasonable range of value for the shares of the business under the going-concern alternative. Then, the combined highest value in alternate use of the business assets and liabilities, both *tangible* and *intangible*, must be determined.

In determining the combined highest value in alternate use, it is important that the asset appraisers be given clear instructions regarding the desired premise of value. It is usually best to request the value of the assets under conditions of both orderly liquidation and forced liquidation. Each valuation analyst must be instructed to operate with the identical definition of value for these terms because the assumptions of time required for sale and the definition of duress in forced liquidation will often vary from analyst to analyst in the absence of a standard definition.

[b] The Role of Intangible Assets

Regarding intangible assets, the intangibles must be identified and analyzed to determine which ones, if any, have value separate from the going business. These assets must then be valued under a premise of business liquidation. Normally, these assets will have value only under an orderly liquidation premise although the premise of "combined highest and best use" may, in rare occasions, dictate that all the assets of the business be valued under a forced liquidation premise, even though this may render the intangibles valueless. The intangibles should be valued by an appraiser experienced in the separate identification and valuation of items of intangible property. A simple "excess earnings" goodwill valuation will not be sufficient in this context. If the business appraiser is experienced in intangible asset valuations under liquidation scenarios, then these assets may be valued by him or her.

[2] Determination of Gross Liquididation Proceeds

In addition to the fixed assets and other noncurrent assets on the balance sheet, the current assets excluding receivables should be valued at the gross proceeds actually realizable in a liquidation and to this should be added the expected collections of receivables. These amounts will often be far less than the stated book value, particularly for work in process inventories and certain classes of receivables.

Included, for valuation purposes, as one of the liabilities applicable to the common stock should be the liquidation preference of all equity securities senior to the shares in question (e.g., various classes of preferred stock). These amounts must be deducted as if they were a nonequity liability.

[3] Reduction of Gross Proceeds to Net Liquidation Value

Once the gross liquidation proceeds of all assets and liabilities have been identified, the next steps involve a reduction of the gross proceeds by various types of liquidation costs and time value considerations, with a comparison to the reasonable range of value as a going concern at each step in the process.

[a] Reduction for Costs and Taxes and Comparison to Going-Concern Value

Specifically, if the amount of the gross liquidation proceeds of all assets less liabilities under both the orderly and forced liquidation premises is less than the bottom of the reasonable range established under the going-concern assumption, the process need go no further. In this case, the going-concern assumption clearly represents the combined highest and best use of the business assets. If the gross liquidation proceeds are not less than the range of value as a going concern, the next step is to deduct the direct costs of liquidating the assets, and then again test versus the going-concern range. If this amount still exceeds the bottom of the going-concern range, the corporate tax consequences of liquidating (e.g., depreciation recapture tax, corporate capital gains taxes subsequent to the repeal of the *General Utilities* doctrine, investment tax credit (ITC) payback) should be deducted, and the amount derived should again be compared to the bottom of the going-concern range.

If liquidation still appears viable, the expected indirect expenses of liquidation and interim operating loss (gain) prior to liquidation should be deducted. These items must include shutdown costs, such as personnel expenses, triggered by the liquidation. These expenses should be tax effected at ordinary rates to the extent of recapture income and other ordinary gain upon sale. Subsequent to the repeal of the *General Utilities* doctrine, additional expenses to the extent of corporate capital gains should be tax effected at the applicable capital gain rate. (For the near term, it appears that this rate will be the same as the ordinary income tax rate.) However, any indirect and interim operating expense in excess of gain realized prior to and during liquidation should *not* be tax effected if the resulting tax loss will not carry over following the liquidation of the corporate shell and the tax benefit will thus never be realized.

[b] Reduction to Present Worth and Comparison to Going-Concern Value

If the proceeds from liquidation to this point in the analysis still exceed the minimum range of value as a going concern, the final step is to discount to present worth at an appropriate rate each of the inflows and outflows previously described from the time when they are actually expected to be paid or received. The present worth thus derived is then compared once more to the range of value as a going concern.

If the present worth is in *excess* of the *maximum* of the going-concern range of value, then the present worth, otherwise known as the *liquidation value* of the common stock, clearly represents the best use of the business assets and, therefore, equals the value of the stock. If the present worth is *less than* the *minimum* of the going-concern range of value, then some going-concern indication of value within this range clearly represents the best use of the business assets and liquidation is not an economically viable alternative. Finally, if the liquidation value lies somewhere within the reasonable range of value on a going-concern assumption, it is quite reasonable to consider both means of realizing value from the business because the reasonable range of value as a going concern indicates a market of potential owners, some of whom would favor liquidation and some of whom would favor continued operation. In this instance, the value in liquidation and the value as a going concern can justifiably be correlated rather than one being chosen over the other.

[4] Summary

It should be noted that the preceding analysis assumes a sale or collection of all the business assets pursuant to Section 337 of the Internal Revenue Code and a liquidation of the corporate entity pursuant to Section 336. Under the Tax Reform Act of 1986 (TRA '86), capital gain would be taxed at the corporate level; and the analysis, therefore, should include both the tax on ordinary income items, such as Sections 1245, 1250, and 291 gain or LIFO reserve recapture; tax credit recaptures such as Section 47 ITC payback; and other applicable ordinary income items as well as the additional tax on corporate capital gain, if any, in excess of the ordinary amounts. Tax law prior to these changes enabled the corporation to pay only tax on ordinary income items in a Section 336/337 situation.

In summary, liquidation value of a 100% control interest in common stock is calculated as follows:

	Liquidation Value of All Tangible and Intangible Assets
Less:	Direct liquidation cost (e.g., commissions)
Less:	Taxes on income from asset dispositions
Less:	Payback of tax credits
Less:	Indirect liquidation costs and interim operating loss (gain), tax-effected at appropriate rates to the extent of gain from asset dispositions
Less:	Liquidation value of all liabilities
Less:	Liquidation preference of all equity securities senior to the shares in question
Compute:	Present worth of all inflows and outflows previously described, discounted at an appropriate rate.

The present worth thus derived is equal to the indicated value of the common stock under a liquidation premise. As described earlier, the final step is to compare the value thus derived to the value under a going-concern premise.

[*Text continues on p. 10-10.*]

TABLE 10-1
ABC AND XYZ COMPANY COMBINED FAIR MARKET VALUE BALANCE SHEET
(AS OF _____, 19___)

	Value as Per Books, ABC $	Value as Per Books, XYZ $	Combined Value as Per Books $	Combined Fair Market Value $	Explanation of Difference Between Combined Book Value and Fair Market Value
Assets					
Cash	$ 11,506	$859	$ 12,365	$ 12,365	
Trade notes and accounts receivable	515,235	-0-	515,235	722,728	As of 8/31/X2, receivables due XYZ totaled $207,493. These did not appear on the books since XYZ filed on the cash basis.
Less: Reserve for uncollectible amounts	(85,000)	-0-	(85,000)	(750,826)	Fair market value of ABC reserve is $48,000. Additionally, $202,826 of XYZ receivables are deemed uncollectible.
Net trade notes and accounts receivable	$430,235	$-0-	$430,235	$ 471,902	
Inventories					
Paper	N.A.*	-0-	N.A.*	144,000	$144,000 is based on written opinion of owner.
Ink	N.A.*	-0-	N.A.*	17,000	$17,000 is based on physical count of ink supplies.
Other	N.A.*	-0-	N.A.*	N.A.*	
Total inventories	$ 29,285	$-0-	$ 29,285	$ 161,000	
Less: expenses related to resale	-0-	-0-	-0-	40,250	There is a 15% reduction for restocking and transportation and a 10% reduction for unusable amounts acquired in bulk. The total reduction is 25%.
Net inventories	$ 29,285	$-0-	$ 29,285	$ 120,750	
Other current assets	17,165	-0-	17,165	17,165	
Gross plant, property, and equipment	792,154	-0-	792,154	-0-	
Less: accumulated depreciation	(508,771)	-0-	(508,771)	-0-	
Net plant, property, and equipment	$283,383	$-0-	$283,383	$ 662,000	This is explained in Appendix 10-1.
Security deposit on lease for premises	-0-	-0-	-0-	8,000	Held in XYZ name, but not appearing as a prepaid asset on the company's books.
Favorable lease agreement	-0-	-0-	-0-	112,000	As explained in Appendix 10-1.
Other assets	250	-0-	250	250	
Total Assets	$771,824	$859	$772,683	$1,404,432	
Liabilities					
Accounts payable	$374,277	$-0-	$374,177	$ 374,177	
Mortgages, notes, bonds payable in less than one year	45,771	-0-	45,771	45,771	
* N.A. — not applicable					

TABLE 10-1
ABC AND XYZ COMPANY COMBINED FAIR MARKET VALUE BALANCE SHEET
(AS OF _____, 19__) (continued)

	Value as Per Books, ABC $	Value as Per Books, XYZ $	Combined Value as Per Books $	Combined Fair Market Value $	Explanation of Difference Between Combined Book Value and Fair Market Value
Other current liabilities	35,113	-0-	35,113	127,113	XYZ had liabilities to _____ and _____ to pay withholding amounts. Fair market value of these liabilities is $92,000, as per Appendix 10-1. This amount was not on the XYZ books because the company was on the cash basis.
Loans from stockholders	83,986	-0-	83,986	-0-	This is a loan bearing no interest and with no fixed repayment schedule. If the assets of the business were sold, no amount would be realized by the sole shareholder from this corporate liability. Instead, the personal asset and corporate liability would eliminate one another.
Mortgages, notes, bonds payable in one year or more	20,492	-0-	20,492	20,492	
Estimated business broker expense	-0-	-0-	-0-	78,275	This is 10% of proceeds from sale of inventories and plant, property and equipment.
Estimated other closeout costs	-0-	-0-	-0-	24,000	This consists of estimated two weeks severance pay and legal fees.
Ordinary income tax payable from gain on sale of assets, collection of receivables, and payment of expenses	-0-	-0-	-0-	156,818	704,475 = Amount realized from sale of inventories and plant, property, and equipment, after business broker expense (312,668) = Net book value of inventories and PP&E 391,807 = Ordinary income from recapture of depreciation and write up of inventories (92,000) = Expense recognized on payment of withholding and unemployment taxes 41,667 = Gain recognized from collection of receivables ($471,902 - $430,235) (24,000) = Other closeout costs 317,474 = Net ordinary income 156,818 = State and local income taxes, federal taxes at graduated rates on first $100,000, and federal taxes at 46% thereafter
Investment tax credit recapture	-0-	-0-	-0-	46,000	This is explained in Appendix 10-1.
Capital gains tax payable	-0-	$-0-	-0-	-0-	All gain is subject to ordinary income taxes.
Total liabilities	$559,539		$559,539	$ 872,646	
Net worth	$212,285	$859	$213,144	$ 531,786	Total assets minus total liabilities.
			Rounded to	$ 532,000	

* N.A. — not applicable

[*Text continues from p. 10-7.*]

¶ 10.2 Examples of Liquidation Analysis

The following two examples are drawn from actual valuations. Both examples deal with the 100% control situation previously described. In each case, ignoring the liquidation alternative would have had a drastic effect on the value concluded, to the detriment of the client. Conversely, however, following the normal practice in liquidation situations of simply adding the liquidation value of each asset and subtracting liabilities would have untenably overstated the liquidation value of the stock. Note in each case the very significant difference between the liquidation value of the stock and the sum of the liquidation value of the underlying assets due to the inclusion of liquidation costs and taxes and a consideration of present worth. Note also that, just as assets not on the balance sheet are identified and valued, so also are non-balance-sheet liabilities. An estimate of the liquidation claim of all contingent liabilities and similar items must be included in the analysis.

[1] Liquidation of the Entire Entity

The first example is that of a small, incorporated trade printing company. The company had an affiliated cash-basis sole proprietorship. In combination, the two entities had less than $250,000 book value of net worth and showed little or no profit in most years. Only tax statements were available. An examination by an independent certified public accountant (CPA) retained by the client did not disclose any reason to believe that the business owner was generating unreported profits or removing cash from the business in any other manner. The owner was not paid an excessive salary. The client was the spouse of the owner, and the valuation was required in connection with a marital dissolution. The corporation is the *ABC* Company, and the sole proprietorship is the *XYZ* Company. The assets of each business could not be distinguished by location or by nature and the companies accordingly were treated as one for liquidation valuation purposes.

Table 10-1 on pages 10-8 and 10-9 shows the determination of liquidation value of the common stock. Appendix 10-1 at the end of the chapter shows the justification for using liquidation value as the proper representation of the fair market value of the stock rather than value under a going-concern assumption and also provides additional detail regarding the computations. Note that, while the book net worth of the companies was $213,144 and the sum of the liquidation value of the assets and liabilities was $901,897, the liquidation value of the stock after a consideration of liquidation costs, time value, and taxes was $532,000, two and one-half times the book value but 42% less than the simple sum of the asset and liability values in liquidation.

A capitalization of earnings and book value approach would have demonstrated a nominal value for the stock of $100,000 or less. In the absence of any liquidation analysis, the valuator would have been hard-pressed to refute this conclusion. In the end, a value of about $450,000 was agreed to out of court. This represents at least a 350% increase over the amount that might have been concluded in the absence of a liquidation value analysis.

[2] Liquidation of a Portion of the Entity

The second example involves a proposed purchase of four affiliated manufacturing companies followed by a reorganization of the companies into a single corporate entity. The total sales of the four entities could be handled by the manufacturing capacity of the two largest entities. The two largest entities were profitable, while the two smallest entities were not currently profitable and were not expected to become profitable in the foreseeable future. The assignment was to both value each entity under the correct premise of value as determined by the valuator and to counsel the client regarding the optimum restructuring of the entities.

The analysis indicated that the maximum value would be obtained by continuing to operate the two larger entities. The two smaller entities should be liquidated by having the larger entities "cherry-pick" the best machine units and usable inventories and reinstall them at the larger entities' facilities, with the less desirable machine units sold at auction or to a dealer. After emptying the plant, disposing of all unwanted inventories, and collecting receivables to the extent possible, the land and building could then be sold vacant for its highest and best use. As with the earlier example, appropriate taxes and costs were considered as well as present worth. To the extent that the sale of assets might take more than twelve months and to the extent of certain asset sales to affiliated corporations, additional tax considerations may have to be factored into the analysis. These additional considerations are not included in the simplified example shown in Table 10-2. The table shows the determination of the value of the common shares for one of the two smaller entities for which asset liquidation was the preferred alternative.

Although the presentation is somewhat different from that in Table 10-1, the concepts applied are identical. Note again that, while the unadjusted book value of stockholders' equity is $1.767 million and the sum of the liquidation value of all assets and liabilities is $3.828 million, the liquidation value of the common stock is $1.721 million, representing 97.4% of the book value but only 45% of the sum of the

TABLE 10-2

Page 1
HEAVY MANUFACTURING COMPANY
ORDERLY LIQUIDATION
(NET ASSET VALUE)

	($000)	
Stockholders' equity per financial statements		$1,767
Accounts receivable adjustment		(24)
Inventory adjustment		(67)
Appraised value of property, plant, and equipment*		
Property, plant, and improvements	$1,670	
Machinery and equipment	1,826	
Total	$3,496	
Less: net cost	1,344	
Appraised value over net cost		$2,152
Net asset value		$3,828
Net asset value per share		$ 656

*Orderly liquidation value

liquidation value of the net assets, due to the costs, tax ramifications, and present worth considerations. Note also that this valuation was done prior to the repeal of the *General Utilities* doctrine, so no corporate capital gains taxes are reflected in the computations.

Had all four entities been maintained as going concerns, the ongoing combined net cash flow generated by the businesses would have been significantly lower than it would have been if the two smaller businesses were liquidated, and the combined value of the businesses would also have been significantly lower.

¶ 10.3 Choice of Discount Rate

In both of the previous examples, the present worth of net proceeds to the common shareholder before the shareholders' personal taxes is considered to be the value of the common stock. Thus, the methodology is nothing more than a variation of a standard discounted cash flow (DCF) technique. The only difference from a more common DCF projection is that the flows have a limited and (usually) short duration under the liquidation premise. Yet, it is frequently written that, in order to induce a buyer to purchase a business for liquidation purposes, the liquidation value of the business must be reduced to pro-

TABLE 10-2

Page 2

HEAVY MANUFACTURING COMPANY
ORDERLY LIQUIDATION
(COMMON STOCK VALUE)

	Present Worth of Net Proceeds ($000)	Reduction of Net Asset Value ($000)
Machinery and equipment	$1,826	
Less: 20% selling costs and uncertainty	(365)	
Total	$1,461	
Discounted at 20% for 9 months	×0.8722	
	$1,274	$ (552)
Real estate	1,670	
Less: 10% selling cost	(167)	
	$1,503	
Discounted at 20% for 3.5 years	×0.5283	
	$ 794	(876)
Estimated taxes, maintenance, insurance for 3.5 years discounted at 20%		(64)
Severance and medical		(22)
Management expense 22,000 per month for 12 months discounted at 20%		(128)
3,000 per month for next 30 months discounted at 20%		(31)
ITC recapture		(85)
Depreciation recapture		(349)
Total reduction of equity value		$ (2,107)
Plus: orderly liquidation net asset value (Table 10-2, Page 1)		3,828
Valuation in liquidation: Total		$ 1,721
Per share (rounded)		$ 290

vide the purchaser a profit on the transaction. In light of the conceptual framework previously discussed, it can be seen that such a reduction of liquidation value would result in a double-counting of the profit aspect.

In doing a standard DCF analysis on a going concern, the process of discounting to present worth the projected net cash flow builds into the value an allowance for a return sufficient to compensate the purchaser for the risks incurred. The present worth thus derived is not further reduced to provide the purchaser an additional profit incentive. Similar logic applies for the specialized form of DCF known as *liquidation valuation*, in which the discounting of the proceeds to present worth at an *appropriate* rate builds in the investor's return requirements. Clearly, if the liquidation could be accomplished instantaneously, if the amount of the liquidation proceeds were perfectly knowable, and if the administrative labor of the investor were compensated as payment for services rendered, then there would be *no* justification for building in a return since the investment would have associated with it neither uncertainty nor opportunity holding costs.

As the time required to effect a liquidation increases from zero and as the amount of the net proceeds is subject to greater uncertainty, an implicit profit is built in through a higher discount rate that is subject to increased "negative compounding" to present worth as the holding period increases. Accordingly, if the appropriate discount rate is selected, there is no justification for an additional reduction of the time-zero present worth any more than there would be justification for doing this in a going-concern assumption DCF valuation.

[1] Comparison to the Discount Rate for an Operating Company

The question of determining an appropriate required rate of return (ROR) for the liquidation valuation analysis is more complicated than first appearances might indicate. Initially, it might appear that the business' normal cost of equity, K_e would be the proper discount rate to use. However, K_e is the proper rate to discount an *operating* projection, given the *possibility* of business failure and the attendant bankruptcy costs. In the asset liquidation scenario, what is dealt with instead is a nonoperating projection of net cash flow under the conditional probability that a form of business failure (asset liquidation) *will* occur.

Given this scenario, it might be assumed that the correct thought process in deriving the rate would be to modify the rigorous Modigliani-Miller formulation (positing a linear relationship between leverage and K_e) to account for potential bankruptcy costs, thereby deriving an upwards curvilinear relationship, with the typical liquidating firm being near the upper end of the curve. However, this reasoning leads to a form of "double penalty" since the projection of net cash receipts to be discounted in a liquidation analysis *explicitly* factors in many of the costs of bankruptcy while the bankruptcy-cost-adjusted discount rate is intended for application to an operating projection and is intended to factor in a consideration of the possible bankruptcy costs *not* explicitly factored into the projection. Thus, when applied to a projection of net liquidation receipts, this procedure will cause the bankruptcy costs to be factored in twice and will result in an understated conclusion of value.

Clearly, the assumptions underlying the theory of discount rate selection for operating firms make that theory applicable to the liquidation scenario only with significant modifications. The issues surrounding the choice of a discount rate for a liquidating firm based on market evidence from operating firms are complex. The best starting point is to discuss the factors that affect the relative required returns *among* liquidating firms, and once these relationships are understood, then the differences between required returns for liquidating firms and operating firms can be discussed.

[2] Factors to Consider

In assessing the factors that make the required return higher for one liquidating firm than for another, it is clear that the input of business risk, so important to an assessment of overall risk for an operating firm, is a relatively unimportant distinguishing factor in the liquidation scenario. While the business may operate for a short period, it will be in a "wind-down mode," and the relative uncertainty of future prospects for one industry versus another is not particularly relevant. On the other hand, the relative uncertainty of future liabilities from *past* decisions in one industry versus another is *very* important, as will be shown later.

In addition, the element of financial risk, the other primary element that distinguishes risk in operating firms, is explicitly recognized in the projection of net cash receipts for the liquidating firm since the projection includes the payoff of the debt as an absolutely certain liability and a consequent cash outflow. Accordingly, it would be incorrect to explicitly recognize the degree of leverage in the discount rate as well (although it will indirectly enter into one of the factors discussed later). Finally, the element of stock liquidity risk is again not a factor (in the 100% control scenario) when the premise of value is the sale of underlying assets and liquidation of the business. (The issue of stock liquidity risk for ownership interests unable to force liquidation will be addressed later in the chapter.)

The previous discussion appears to indicate that there are no distinguishing risk characteristics among liquidating firms. This is, of course, not the case. In reality, three factors determine the relative required return. Initially, these factors will be qualitatively described; then they will be fitted into an adapted pricing model; and finally examples of how these factors impact the return of two very different liquidating firms at opposite ends of the spectrum will be described. The three factors are:

1. Degree of predictability, in an *absolute* sense, of projected cash flows, quantified as the variance of the cash flows (this is a step towards determining the following factor);
2. *Relative* predictability of projected cash flows, quantified as the coefficient of variation of the cash flows; and

3. The effect of unpredictable contingencies—in other words, potential liabilities of a nature that they are not subject to even a "best guess" of their mean and variance.

Note that the first two factors consider total variability rather than only the systematic covariance of the projected cash flows versus some bench mark. In other words, there is no factor that would be analogous to "beta" in the Capital Asset Pricing Model (CAPM). It is illogical to speak of the "beta" of a firm that is not a going business. While the net receipts from asset liquidation likely have some systematic relationship to the stock market as a whole, that relationship is a part of the total variability and it need not and should not be separately calculated. Therefore, if one term in the model is a function of the coefficient of variation, then the term for incremental systematic covariation should be zero.

[3] Quantification of the Factors

These factors can be adapted into the following model:

S^2 = variance of projected net cash receipts

S = standard deviation of projected net cash receipts

$\bar{X}$ = mean of projected net cash receipts

$\dfrac{S}{\bar{X}}$ = coefficient of variation of projected net cash receipts; this is a function of the activity of the market for the underlying assets of the firm and the degree of available information on prices received in liquidation for these assets (both of which contribute to the determination of S), and the magnitude above zero of the best expectation of net cash receipts ($\bar{X}$) (as discussed earlier, it is in this respect that financial risk enters into the equation: The higher the leverage, everything else being equal, the lower is $\bar{X}$, and, therefore, the higher the coefficient of variation)

$F_1\left(\dfrac{S}{\bar{X}}\right)$ = an increasing function that relates the magnitude of the coefficient of variation to some incremental required return in excess of the risk-free rate

Unit UC = the historical experience of firms in the subject company's industry regarding unpredictable contingencies subsequent to a base year, related to events prior to the base year, stated as a percent of some logical parameter in the base year (e.g., as a percent of sales volume, number of employees, or asset base).

$(UC)_{i,0}$ = the estimate of future unpredictable contingencies for the liquidating firm at time zero, given *absolute certainty* that the firm would mirror the average historical industry experience; computed as (Unit UC) × (Parameter$_{i,0}$).

$\dfrac{(UC)_{i,0}}{\bar{X}_i}$ = the (UC) as a percentage of the mean of projected net cash flow

$F_2\left(\dfrac{(UC)_{i,0}}{\bar{X}_i}\right)$ = an increasing function that relates the magnitude of the unpredictable contingencies as a percentage of projected net cash flow under complete certainty to some incremental return in excess of the risk-free rate; since the unpredictable contingencies are so variable that they are not subject to even a meaningful mean estimate to be factored into the projection of cash flow, the effect of this term is to factor in an excess return in lieu of explicitly building the negative amount of the contingency into the projection

R_f = the risk-free rate.

R_m = the return on the market index of stocks

$\beta_{L,i}$ = the beta of the subject firm in liquidation, defined herein to be *incremental* systematic variation not captured in the S term and assumed to be equal to zero

$K_{L,i}$ = the required return for the subject firm, conditional on the asset liquidation having a 100% probability of occurence.

Given this terminology:

$$K_{L,i} = R_f + \beta_{L,i}(R_m - R_f) + \left[F_1\left(\frac{S}{\bar{X}}\right)_i\right] + \left[F_2\left(\frac{UC}{\bar{X}}\right)_i\right]$$

$$K_{L,i} = R_f + (0.0)(R_m - R_f) + \left[F_1\left(\frac{S}{\bar{X}}\right)_i\right] + \left[F_2\left(\frac{UC}{\bar{X}}\right)_i\right]$$

$$K_{L,i} = R_f + \left[F_1\left(\frac{S}{\bar{X}}\right)_i\right] + \left[F_2\left(\frac{UC}{\bar{X}}\right)_i\right]$$

[4] Selection of a Discount Rate

The previous equation cannot be used to derive a specific required return since the two functions F_1 and F_2 have not been specified. However, the basic application of the equation can be demonstrated through an analysis of 100% control interests in two very different companies, both analyzed in the liquidation scenario.

[a] Low-Risk Scenario

The first company is an unleveraged investment company holding only a diversified portfolio of readily marketable securities with no history as an operating company at any time in its past and only two employees, one the sole owner. This company has the following characteristics:

- It has market value of holdings, $50 million.
- Its time to liquidate is five days (the same as normal time required to receive cash for sale of stock).
- Variability of expected receipts is a function only of systematic risk since the nature of the underlying assets (a diversified portfolio of marketable securities) is such that sale of the assets will not be accompanied by unsystematic risk; this will be diversified away. Also, company is unleveraged. Therefore, the $F_1\left(\frac{S}{\bar{X}}\right)_i$ term will collapse to $\beta(R_m - R_f)$ where the beta is applicable to a diversified unleveraged portfolio of securities and is therefore equal to 1.0.
- The possibility of unpredictable contingencies is very low since the business was never an operating company and since only one of the two employees has an incentive to sue or otherwise bring any potential lien against the business. For discussion purposes, say that the $F_2\left(\frac{UC}{\bar{X}}\right)_i$ factor is 1.0 percent.

- R_f equals 7.0%, and $(R_m - R_f)$ equals 6.0% for discussion purposes.

Therefore:

$$K_{L,i} = R_f + F_1\left(\frac{S}{\overline{X}}\right)_i + F_2\left(\frac{UC}{\overline{X}}\right)_i$$

$$K_{L,i} = R_f + \beta(R_m - R_f) + F_2\left(\frac{UC}{\overline{X}}\right)_i$$

$$K_{L,i} = 0.07 + (1.0)(0.06) + 0.01$$

$$K_{L,i} = 0.14 \text{ annual}$$

or:

$$K_{L,i} = 0.0025, \text{ compound rate for 5 business days.}$$

[b] High-Risk Scenario

The second company is a very specialized chemical processor, with the following characteristics:

- Liquidation value of current assets is equal to operating liabilities (including predictable liabilities created by the liquidation).
- It has an extremely uncertain market for the specialized plant, property, and equipment. The best estimate of receipts is $50 million but with a standard deviation of $25 million.
- Its time required to liquidate is one year.
- Its outside debt is $40 million.
- Based on average industry data, unexpected contingencies over a seven-year future span might average $1 million per year for every $100 million of current sales. Current sales prior to liquidation were $75 million.
- As before, R_f equals 0.07.

Based on the foregoing, the unlevered $\frac{S}{\overline{X}}$ is 0.5 calculated as (25 ÷ 50). However, the leveraged $\frac{S}{X}$ is 2.5, calculated as (25 ÷ (50−40)). In addition, the unlevered $\frac{UC}{\overline{X}}$ is 0.015 per year, calculated as ((1.0 ÷ 100) × 75) ÷ 50) or 0.105 over a seven-year span.

However, the leveraged $\frac{UC}{X}$ is 0.075, calculated as

$$\left(\frac{(1.0 \div 100.0) \times ((1.0 \div 100) \times 75 \div (50 - 40))}{50.0 - 40.0}\right) \text{ or } 0.375 \text{ over a}$$

seven-year span. Clearly, the leveraged process plant requires a significantly higher required return than the unleveraged investment company. For discussion purposes, assume that $F_1(2.5)$ equals 0.25 and $F_2(0.375)$ equals 0.13. Therefore:

$$K_{L,i} = R_f + \left[F_1\left(\frac{S}{X}\right)_i\right] + \left[F_2\left(\frac{UC}{X}\right)_i\right]$$

$$K_{L,i} = 0.07 + 0.25 + 0.13$$

$$K_{L,i} = 0.45 \text{ (annualized)}$$

In the preceding example, the investment company's required return in liquidation of a 100% control interest is 14% annual while that of the process plant is only 45% annualized back.

[5] Relative Risk in Liquidation vs. Continued Operation

Clearly, there are factors that distinguish among liquidating firms in terms of the appropriate discount rate, based on the nature of the holdings, the coefficient of variation of the predictable inflows and outflows, and industry experience regarding the unpredictable outflows. However, since the pricing model derived for this scenario looks considerably different from the CAPM equation, the relative risk of an average liquidating firm versus that of an average operating firm cannot readily be determined. Evidence based on experience indicates that while the appropriate required return for an average liquidating firm should be considerably higher than that for an average operating firm, the appropriate required return for the least risky types of liquidating firms can be well within the range of typical operating firms. Qualitative arguments to support this position are as follows:

- Covariance (systematic risk) only is the major determinant of relative required return when the investment can become an ongoing part of a balanced and diversified portfolio. For a liquidating firm, however, total variance of cash flow, including both systematic *and* unsystematic factors, becomes the major determinant of relative required return.
- Unknown and unknowable potential liabilities triggered by the liquidation are a factor in liquidating firms but not in operating firms.
- The receipt of net cash flow is an ongoing process in the operating firm but is a "one-shot deal" in the liquidating firm. Thus,

extraordinary efforts might correct in the future the negative impact of a single, unexpected poor year in the operating firm. In the liquidating firm, if net cash receipts end up lower than expected, the investor doesn't get a second chance.
- Partially balancing these considerations is the fact that business risk and financial risk do not impact the liquidating firm as strongly as the operating firm.

On balance, the appropriate discount rate for the average liquidating firm is usually considerably higher than that for the average operating firm. However, as was demonstrated earlier in the example of the unleveraged investment firm, when there is an active, low-variability market for the assets of the firm, a lack of leverage, and little likelihood of unexpected contingencies, the appropriate required return for the liquidating firm can be lower than that of risky operating firms and potentially lower than that of the average market portfolio as a whole (R_m).

¶ 10.4 Additional Considerations

To this point, a basic framework has been established for the development of a net cash flow projection and discount rate applicable to the valuation of a 100% unrestricted control interest under the liquidation scenario. In light of this framework, each of the statements made earlier on page 10-20 can be assessed in the succeeding discussion.

[1] Liquidation Value of Assets vs. Liquidation Value of Stock

"The liquidation value of a business is the net of the liquidation value of its underlying assets and liabilities."

Clearly, this statement leads to a considerable overvaluation of the business in liquidation since it does not consider direct costs, indirect costs, taxes triggered, tax credit paybacks, and present worth.

[2] Liquidation Value of Assets as the "Floor" of Value of the Stock

"The value of an unrestricted 100% control interest cannot fall below the sum of the liquidation value of its net assets."

As a corollary of the first statement, this commonly held misconception also proves to be incorrect due to a lack of consideration of costs, taxes, and present value.

[3] Intangible Asset Value

"In a business liquidation, the value of the business' intangible assets falls to zero."

Recall the first example with *ABC* Company and *XYZ* Company. Among the assets valued was an intangible asset (a favorable lease). This asset could be included in the liquidation proceeds, albeit in a reduced amount, as detailed in Appendix 10-1 at the end of this chapter, because it was an intangible asset whose value could be realized separately from the business as a whole. Among many other classification criteria, intangible assets can be divided into those that are separately salable from the business as a whole and those that are not. Intangible assets in the former category may contribute value in liquidation while those in the latter category will always be valueless in liquidation. Among the assets in the former category are favorable leases (leasehold interests), licensor's rights under license agreements, certain licensee's rights under license agreements, codified proprietary know-how, patents, trademarks, favorable financing relating to assumable debt obligations, and mailing lists. Among the intangibles in the latter category are the assembled work force, uncodified proprietary know-how, and goodwill.

In a liquidation scenario, the initial step is to identify all intangible assets and to segregate each of them into one of these two categories. Then, for those that are separately salable from the business as a whole, each type of intangible must be assessed to determine whether, in the particular scenario in question, the asset will realize any net proceeds in liquidation. An example is shown in Table 10-1 and Appendix 10-1, where the full value of the favorable lease is reduced due to certain factors related to the liquidation.

It is important to note that certain intangible assets may have an associated tax cost at the corporate level under Section 111 of the Internal Revenue Code. This tax cost is similar to tax upon depreciation recapture, and it can be triggered in many circumstances, including sale or disposition in a business liquidation. Generally, assets "included" under Section 111 are those that relate to expenses previously deducted for tax purposes for which an event, subsequent to the year that the deduction was taken, provides an indication that the conceptual basis for the deduction is no longer valid. The associated tax cost is equal to the marginal federal tax rate multiplied by the lesser of the historical expense or the fair market value of the asset to which the expense relates. These tax costs must be figured into the liquidation value analysis.

Separately salable intangible assets generally considered not vulnerable to such treatment include assets related to expenses deducted under Section 174 of the Internal Revenue Code (e.g., many patents, drawings, and some computer software), assets whose existence relates to a change in market conditions rather than to previous expenditures by the business (e.g., favorable leases and favorable licensee's rights), and any assets that do not relate to prior expenses deducted for tax purposes. Subsequent to the repeal of the *General Utilities* doctrine under TRA '86, any gain not subject to Section 111 treatment would be treated as capital gain, and currently, the capital gains tax rate is the same as the marginal ordinary rate.

[4] Factoring in Both Liquidation and Continued Operation

"The value of a business is determined by the higher of its value in liquidation or its value as a going concern. The two indications of value are never averaged."

As discussed earlier, this statement is generally true when the reasonable range of liquidation value and when the reasonable range of value as a going concern have no areas of overlap. In that case, the higher premise of value is the correct one. However, when there is overlap in the reasonable range of value determined under each assumption, a situation results where some rational owners might prefer liquidation and some might prefer continued operation. In that case, it would be flying in the face of the market if either of the two alternatives were totally ignored. A consideration and correlation of the value derived under each of the two assumptions is both warranted and recommended in this case.

[5] The Value of Minority Interests

"Liquidation value is never an issue in the valuation of a minority interest."

A more correct rewording of this statement might be: "Liquidation value is far less often an issue in the valuation of a minority interest than in the valuation of a 100% control interest." In assessing whether liquidation value applies in the minority interest situation, a case-by-case approach should be used. The first step is to determine the purpose of the valuation and the correct premise of value applicable to that purpose. One example of when liquidation value might influence minority stock value can be drawn from the public marketplace. Stock prices in the aftermath of failed tender offers may, in some cases, indirectly reflect a consideration of potential liquidation value. If a stock's price does not drop to its original level subsequent to the failed offer, it can be the case that the market is factoring in the possibility of a future buyout. In so doing, the market must factor in the likely price as well as the probability of an offer. One of the components of the likely offer price for many companies is the optimum breakup value of the business in the hands of the controlling interest, which will include a consideration of liquidation value for some of the business units. Although the connection is indirect, it nonetheless is a factor to be considered.

[a] When and How to Factor in Liquidation

Moving to a situation more relevant to the valuation of the closely-held firm, return to the second example. (See Table 10-2.) Keep the general fact pattern the same, except that, instead of four affiliated but separate corporations, there are now four wholly owned subsidiaries of a single parent corporation, and there are a number of minority ownership positions in the parent as well as an 80% control position.

First, assume that the controlling shareholder has already retained a consultant to help him or her determine how to reorganize the business operations and, in particular, what to do with the two unprofitable operations. The unprofitable operations have been unprofitable on average for the past five years, for the past three years, and for the last year, and they are expected to remain unprofitable. There is excess capacity spread over the four operations, but operations would be at 85-90% of capacity if the two larger, profitable operations did all of the manufacturing. Independently, the minority investors have hired a valuator to determine the fair market value of a typical minority interest in the parent.

Should the liquidation value of the two unprofitable subsidiaries be considered in the determination of minority interest value? Clearly, the answer is "yes," albeit reduced by some probability factor p for likelihood and timing of occurrence, given the $1 - p$ possibility that the controlling interest may not choose the rational, value-maximizing liquidation options. When considering the $1 - p$ alternative of continuing the unprofitable operations, then, to the extent of expected future losses, should the valuator factor the losses (and the drain on net cash) from these operations into the total parent income to be capitalized (and cash flow to be discounted)? Again, the answer is "yes." The middle-ground position is often taken wherein liquidation proceeds are not figured in but the losses from continued operation of unprofitable units are also ignored and removed from total parent earnings. Except under special circumstances, this position is not supportable. Either the business is run with continued losses and an associated probability factor, $1 - p$, or it is shut down and liquidated for its net proceeds, with an associated probability factor, p_1. The middle ground does not exist.

As a second example, alter the previous fact pattern slightly such that the controlling interest has not yet retained a consultant to study the optimal business reorganization but it is obvious that some action should be taken shortly by any rational owner. It is uncertain whether this controlling owner is rational and whether he or she would consider selling out to someone else who is rational. All other facts remain the same. Should the liquidation alternative be considered on the unprofitable subsidiaries in the minority interest valuation of the parent? Absolutely, albeit with a lower probability factor, p_1, to account for the fact that the controlling interest has not yet taken the concrete step of retaining the consultant. Should the subsidiary losses (and negative net cash flow) be factored into the parent earnings (and cash flow) under the continued operation alternative? Again, the answer is "yes," albeit with a higher probability factor, $1 - p_1$.

The two hypothetical examples just discussed, derived from the actual valuation situation discussed earlier, represent one of many instances where liquidation value can be a relevant factor in the determination of minority interest value. It can be particularly relevant in the case of reserve-rich natural resource companies. As the reader has probably noted, however, the issues of the magnitude of a minority-interest discount and discount for lack of marketability as they apply to liquidation situations have not yet been discussed.

[b] Applicability of a Minority-Interest Discount

In the previous examples, should the expected liquidation proceeds to the shareholders be subject to a minority discount if the purpose is minority interest value? The answer is "no." The liquidation proceeds themselves represent imminently received cash flow in return for sale of assets, the same cash flow per share for the controlling interest as for the minority. When the impact of the liquidation proceeds to the parent is reduced by a probability factor p, consideration is already being factored in that, even though liquidation may be the rational alternative, the minority cannot cause it to occur. Accordingly, subjecting the parent shares to an additional minority discount under the liquidation alternative would represent a double penalty. Of course, under the continued operation alternative with probability of $1 - p$ the shares should be valued in the normal fashion as a minority interest including a minority interest discount, if appropriate.

The logic of this position can be seen by taking it to the extreme, given that the probability of the liquidation alternative, p, is 100% (i.e., it has been announced that a liquidation will occur and it is scheduled to begin immediately). Under this scenario, it can be seen that it is illogical to subject the present worth of the liquidation proceeds to the minority to any discount below the amount received by the majority. Such a discount would imply that cash to be paid out, most likely in a year or less, should be worth less per share to one fractional interest than to another. Clearly, under this reasoning, no one would want to buy in at the control price if he or she could purchase a minority block at the lower price.

[c] Fairness Considerations

What about the situation where the liquidation alternative yields a *lower* indicated value than the value of a *control* block in continued operation but a *higher* indicated value than the value of a minority interest block in continued operation? If the subject company actually does have a single control block large enough to force liquidation as well as at least one small minority block, this becomes one of the most interesting of all valuation problems and one that must be approached strictly on a case-by-case basis. Clearly, the controlling interest has no personal economic incentive to liquidate but has, at the same time, a responsibility to run the company in the best interest of the minority investors as well. Yet, the minority investors would be better off if the business *were* liquidated. There is no single correct answer, but relevant considerations include the degree of fiduciary responsibility the control block has to the minority under applicable state law; the degree of minority shareholder rights and type of recourse under the state law; and the degree of affiliation, if any, between the control block and the minority shares.

[d] Discount for Lack of Marketability

What about the discount for lack of marketability (DLOM) applicable to a closely held minority interest when liquidation is an alternative? The answer becomes clearer if the DLOM is viewed a little differently than usual, as a by-product of another process rather than as a process in and of itself. If lack of liquidity is viewed as a factor that, through its restriction of freedom of choice, causes greater investment uncertainty for closely held shares relative to publicly and actively traded shares, then the lack of liquidity would result in a higher required return on the part of the investor. The amount known as a "discount for lack of marketability" can then be viewed as the result of discounting expected cash flows in a closely held firm at a higher rate than one would apply to otherwise identical public shares.

A necessary corollary of this viewpoint, then, would be the statement that, *ceteris paribus*, the magnitude of the DLOM is directly related to the average duration of the investment's cash flows. At one extreme, cash flows immediately received could not be subject to any DLOM. Conversely, given a very large duration, the compounding effect of the increase in the discount rate would produce an exceedingly high DLOM.

Returning, then, to the previous example, the parent stock's freely traded value was assessed based on the value derived from the p alternative and the $1 - p$ alternative. For the p alternative, liquidation of two of the subsidiaries, the parent cash flows have components from continued operations on the two larger subsidiaries and from near-term liquidation proceeds on the two smaller subsidiaries. On balance, the duration of cash flows in the p alternative will be lower than in the $1 - p$ alternative where all four subsidiaries would continue operations and where there would be no large lump-sum near-term cash flow from liquidating two of the subsidiaries. If there is a DLOM applicable to the $1 - p$ alternative of, say, 35%, then the DLOM applicable to the p alternative will be somewhat less, and the weighted average DLOM for the stock, considering both alternatives, will be less than 35% but greater than for the p alternative.

The same logic will apply as one of the relevant factors in assessing the DLOM in any liquidation alternative applicable to a minority interest. At the extreme, where liquidation of the entire corporate entity is both planned and imminent, little or no DLOM will apply to shares in a private company relative to shares in a hypothetical identical but public company. On the other hand, when liquidation might be a low probability alternative, the DLOM will approach the normal amount applicable to the subject company in continued operation.

[6] Shareholder-Level Taxes and the Value of Common Stock

"Taxes at the shareholder level are irrelevant in determining the value of common stock."

The example to be discussed will apply specifically to a 100% control interest where liquidation is the preferred alternative. With some minor modification, the concepts to be discussed will apply to other specific applications of the general statement.

Again, the starting point is to assess the environment and the premise of value inherent in the assignment. When the assignment is to determine "fair market value" for estate or gift tax purposes, the hypothetical (and representative) willing buyer and seller must be assumed. In this case, individual tax considerations cannot be factored in (at least not explicitly). However, when the assignment is more of a consulting nature, for example determining the maximum that a buyer should offer or the minimum a seller should sell for, or determining the relative merits of adopting a particular ownership form, then all relevant factors must be considered and individual tax ramifications can become very pertinent. Investors ultimately compare the cash that leaves their pocket to make an investment today with the cash expected to return to their pocket in the future, after all outflows, including the outflow represented by personal taxes due the government. In fact, it is impossible to correctly evaluate the investor's compound rate of return for certain investments, such as limited partnership tax shelters, without a consideration of after-personal-tax cash flows. While simplifying assumptions have been developed that allow us to value common stock without a consideration of the typical investor's personal tax status, it is nonetheless true that the investor will, if he or she is behaving rationally, make an investment decision between common stock and a limited partnership tax shelter by comparing the relative risk and after-personal-tax ROR on a tax shelter not to the relative risk and pre-personal-tax rate of return on a common stock but rather to the stock's relative risk and after-personal-tax return.

In determining the price of common stock in a liquidation situation, personal taxes become relevant in the analysis although in a significantly different manner than for a limited partnership tax shelter. Indeed, the personal tax consequences can make or break a market, as the ensuing examples shows.

Assume the following fact pattern:

Liquidation is clearly desirable in comparison to continued operation	
Net proceeds at corporate level upon liquidation (after corporate taxes and all costs but before present value considerations)	$115.00
Time of receipt of net proceeds to corporation from asset sale	12 months
Time of dissolution of corporation and distribution of $115 to sole shareholder	12 months
Sole shareholder's adjusted stock basis	$150.00
Sole shareholder's applicable tax rate (28% bracket at an income level above the 33% personal exemption elimination bracket)	28%
There are no state or local personal income taxes	
Pre-personal-tax required return (annual)	15%
After-personal-tax required return (annual)	12%

The current stockholder will receive $115 in 12 months, show a loss of $35, and receive a credit of $9.80 in taxes. The transaction is worth $111.43 to him or her [($115 + $9.80) = $124.80, discounted for one year at 12%] while the indication of value for the common stock itself under this approach is $100 ($115 discounted for one year at 15%).

Now, assume there is a potential purchaser for the shares—an individual rather than a corporation. The purchaser would also intend to liquidate the corporation; he or she would receive the same proceeds in the same time span and would have the same required return. The purchaser feels absolutely confident of being able to claim long-term capital gains treatment on the stock at the date of liquidation, and his or her applicable personal tax rate is also 28%, at a level of income above the 33% bracket.

At what minimum price would the current owner be willing to sell the shares, and at what maximum price would the purchaser be willing to buy? The seller will want to receive at least $111.43 after personal taxes immediately to be neutral versus the alternative of holding and liquidating. He or she can accomplish this by selling the stock immediately for a minimum of $96.43 ($96.43 plus tax credit of $15.00 on capital loss equals $111.43, the present worth of not selling and liquidating). The buyer, on the other hand, will be willing to offer as much as $98.57 for the shares. (The $98.57 will generate a tax on future liquidation of $4.60. Subtracting $4.60 from the $115 corporate liquidation proceeds yields an amount of $110.40, which, when discounted to present worth at 12% for one year, equals the $98.57 price paid.) Thus, a market can be made, for a share price anywhere between $96.43 and $98.57.

Now, assume the same situation except that the seller's adjusted stock basis is $25, not $150. If the seller holds and liquidates, he or she will now receive $115 in twelve months and owe a capital gain tax of $25.20; and the transaction would be worth only $80.18 to him or her [($115 − $25.20) = $89.80, discounted for one year at 12%]. The indication of value for the common stock under the liquidation approach would still be $100.

The seller would now be willing to sell the stock immediately for a minimum of $101.64 ($101.64 less capital gains tax of $21.46 equals $80.18, the present worth of not selling and liquidating). The buyer, however, will again be willing to offer a maximum of only $98.57 for the shares. (The $98.57 will generate a tax at ordinary rates on future liquidation of $4.60. Subtracting $4.60 from the $115 corporate liquidation proceeds yields $110.40, which, when discounted to present worth at 12% for one year, equals the $98.57 price paid.) Note that *no market can now be made*. The buyer's maximum offer is $98.57, and the seller's minimum price is $101.64. The seller's only alternative is to hold and liquidate, realizing an after-personal-tax present worth of $80.18. Paradoxically, the value concluded for the stock itself, $100, is *higher* than the price range in the earlier scenario ($96.43 to $98.57) within which a market could be made; yet, the seller would have received greater value and would have been considerably better off under the earlier scenario. The apparent paradox between "value of the transaction" and "price of the stock" is resolved when personal taxes are considered.

¶ 10.5 Summary

This chapter did not specifically treat the subject of the breakup value of business units. This can be an entirely different situation than the asset liquidation scenario since the business units typically represent viable freestanding entities. Valuation considerations and tax considerations, for example, may be considerably different. However, the general conceptual framework of a consideration of gross proceeds, less costs, less taxes, less (plus) interim losses (gains), all discounted to present worth, will still apply whether the liquidation is by asset or by business unit.

Finally, the two examples discussed earlier in this chapter are from actual valuations that predate TRA '86 and therefore ignore the effect of the various changes in tax rates and the repeal of the *General Utilities* doctrine. Following the general conceptual framework outlined earlier, however, as modified by the inclusion of additional strata of taxes or different rates where applicable, the analysis of liquidation value after the 1986 tax law changes would not be a substantially more difficult undertaking than was the case prior to TRA '86.

Appendix 10-1 Detail of Table 10-1 Liquidation Value Computations

The following material is abstracted from the narrative valuation report accompanying the calculations included in Table 10-1.

An investigation of the highest and best use of the companies' assets considered the following:

- Current reported earnings of the business;
- Potential current and future earnings capacity of the business;
- Potential dividend paying capacity of the business;
- Current reported book value of the business;
- The multiples of earnings and book value paid for both minority and controlling shares in similar businesses;
- The existence of assets and liabilities not currently on the balance sheet of either of the companies and the effect on the companies of realizing the value of the assets and liabilities; and
- The amount realizable from a liquidation of the companies' assets and liabilities, including a consideration of all expenses and tax ramifications from liquidation.

The investigation indicated that the highest and best use of the business assets would be to sell the inventories and plant, property, and equipment through a broker or a dealer acting as broker to a buyer or several buyers who would use these assets at alternate locations, leaving *ABC* Company to collect on the remaining assets and to pay off all liabilities. The highest and best use equates roughly to an orderly sale of the inventories and plant, property, and equipment, and an orderly realization of the remaining assets and liabilities of the companies.

Under this premise, a prospective buyer would not choose to purchase any other assets of the business besides the inventories and plant, property, and equipment because of tax related matters to be discussed later in this report and because of *XYZ* Company's significant problem receivables. A prospective purchaser also would not choose to assume any of the companies' liabilities since these would more easily be left for *ABC* and *XYZ* to pay off from the proceeds of the sale.

The amount that could be realized from a sale of the plant, property, and equipment would be equal to the fair market value in continued use of the plant, property, and equipment, less the freight and installation required to set the assets up elsewhere. This amount equates roughly to the "value from a dealer" of the assets.

Similarly, for the inventories, the purchaser would be willing to pay fair market value in continued use, less transportation and restocking costs. For both the inventories and plant, property, and equipment, the proceeds to the seller would be reduced by the fee of a business broker or an equipment dealer acting as broker who would be required to effect an orderly and timely sale of these assets. Given market conditions at the date of appraisal, certain of the assets could be sold immediately, but a waiting period of from six to twelve months would be required to dispose of much of the machinery at the "from a dealer" value.

The value to the companies of the lease agreement is related to the amount at which the space could be sublet to a sublessee after the machinery has been sold and the space has been vacated compared to the lower amount that the lessee would have to pay to the landlord. The value also considers the outflow associated with the payment of rent by the lessee for the period during which the assets are being sold and the subrental income from existing sublessees at the appraisal date.

Based on the conceptual framework just described, Table 10-1 details the computation of the combined fair market value of the companies as indicated by the highest and best use study. Further explanation of the computation of the fair market value of each account classification is shown here:

☐ *Cash.* This is self-explanatory.
☐ *Accounts receivable.* An investigation of the *ABC* reserve for uncollectible amounts indicated that the original reserve of $85,000 was higher than the fair market value of the reserve, and the reserve should be restated at $48,000, or a reduction of $37,000 ($85,000 − $48,000). In addition, $4,667 of the *XYZ*

receivables were considered collectible. Adding these adjustments to the $430,235 book value of the receivables, a fair market value of $471,902 is indicated ($430,235 + $37,000 + $4,667).

- ☐ *Inventories.* The amount of the paper inventory, $144,000, is based on an estimate submitted in a signed document dated _____, by _____, the sole shareholder and active manager of *ABC*. The $17,000 of ink was based on a physical count of the ink supplies. Both amounts are reduced by 15% for transportation and restocking and by 10% to account for any unusable inventories. As stated earlier, it is impossible to separate the *ABC* and *XYZ* inventories.

- ☐ *Other current assets.* Market value is assmed to be equal to book value.

- ☐ *Plant, property, and equipment.* The total of $662,000 is based on the following: *Machinery*—the value of *$654,175* is based on estimated proceeds from sale of $727,000 with a waiting period averaging nine months. The proceeds from sale were then discounted to the present worth of $654,175; *general plant equipment*—the value of *$2,325* is equal to 25% of fair market value in continued use; *office furniture, fixtures, and equipment*—the value of $5,500 is equal to 25% of fair market value in continued use; *leasehold improvements*—these are not included in the valuation.

- ☐ *Security deposit.* *XYZ* paid $8,000 as security, refundable at termination of lease.

- ☐ *Favorable Lease Agreement.* The lessee is paying $1.90 per square foot until _____, 19__, and $2.03 per square foot thereafter. The lease expires on _____, 19__. The lessee is currently subletting to two entities. Rental income from the sublessees is $20,760 annually, or $1,730 per month. Machinery will be sold in six to twelve months, say nine months. During this period lessee will pay rent as follows:

Date 1—Date 2
$\overline{27,000 \text{ sq. ft.} \times \$1.90 \div 12 = \$4,275.00/\text{month}}$

Date 2—Date 3
$\overline{27,000 \text{ sq. ft.} \times \$2.03 \div 12 = \$4,567.50/\text{month}}$

The lessee will receive rental income of $1,730 per month. Therefore, net rental expense will be as follows:

Date 1—Date 2
$\overline{\$1,730.00 - \$4,275.00 = (\$2,545.00)}$

Date 2—Date 3
$\overline{\$1,730.00 - \$4,567.50 = (\$2,837.50)}$

The present worth of these monthly cash outflows, at 1.5% monthly in advance, is ($23,498).

After the machinery is sold, the lessee would be free to sublease the entire premises. Although the market rate is between $5 and $6, considering the remaining lease term and other negative factors, the space could immediately be sublet, after the removal of the machinery, at $4.25 per square foot, and this is similarly the amount upon which the lessor would base an offer to buy the lease from the lessee. Whether the lease is sold back to the lessor or the lessee chooses to sublet, the value of realizing the favorable lease nine months from the appraisal date would be as follows:

Market rent − contract rent (monthly)—
($4.25 − $2.03) × ($27,000) ÷ (12) = $4,995

Present worth factor in advance at 1.5% monthly to end of lease term—30.916

Total present worth to date 3—
30.916 × $4,995 = $154,425

Present worth factor at 1.5% monthly from date 3 to date 1—0.8746

Therefore, the present worth of the favorable lease beyond date 3, discounted back to date 1, is $135,060 (0.8746 × $154,425). Finally, the net value of the favorable lease is the present worth of the favorable lease beyond date 3, less the present worth of the net rental expense from date 1 to date 3, or *$112,000* ($135,060 − $23,498 = $111,562, rounded to $112,000).

☐ *Other assets.* Market value is assumed to be equal to book value.

☐ *Accounts payable.* Market value is assumed to be equal to book value.

☐ *Current portion of debt.* Market value is assumed to be equal to book value.

☐ *Other current liabilities.* Included here is the book value of $35,113, plus $92,000 related to the failure to pay withholding and unemployment taxes, plus accrued penalties and interest. The amount of $92,000 represents amounts paid subsequent to Date 1, less interest accrued between Date 1 and the date of payment, less an amount representing potential overcharges of penalties and interest by _____ and _____, for which the Companies' accountant has stated he has put in a claim for $25,000. The amount of the overcharge has been included at the midpoint of the minimum refund (-0-) and the amount of the claim ($25,000) (i.e., at an amount of $12,500 for purposes of the computation).

- ☐ *Loans from stockholders.* As indicated on Table 10-1, this is a liability that would be negated by the personal loan receivable of the sole shareholder in the event of a sale of the business.
- ☐ *Long-term portion of debt.* Market value is assumed to be equal to book value.
- ☐ *Estimated business broker expense.* This is based on a standard fee for selling the inventories and plant, property, and equipment of 10% of the proceeds ($120,750 + $662,000) × 0.1 = $78,275).
- ☐ *Estimated other closeout costs.* These are as explained on Table 10-1.
- ☐ *Ordinary income tax payable.* As explained on Table 10-1, this relates to federal and state taxes on all ordinary income realized from sale of the inventories and plant, property, and equipment, collection of the other assets, and payment of liabilities. The sale of the plant, property, and equipment triggers ordinary income from recapture of depreciation. Since the *XYZ* inventory was previously expensed in the cash basis accounting, a similar recapture of expense would be recognized when the inventory is sold. Both gains would be reduced by the business broker fee required to sell the assets. A gain would be recognized on collection of receivables in excess of book value. The total gain would be reduced by the recognition of expense related to the withholding and unemployment tax payments and by the expense related to closeout costs.
- ☐ *Investment tax credit recapture.* This is based on a recapture of 100% of ITC on post-1980 recovery property, 100% of ITC on Section 1245 property less than 3 years old, $66^2/_3$% of ITC on Section 1245 property between 3 and 5 years old, and $33^1/_3$% of ITC on Section 1245 property between 5 and 7 years old.
- ☐ *Capital gains tax payable.* As indicated on Table 10-1, the entire gain from sale and collection of the assets and payment of liabilities would be considered subject to taxes at ordinary rates, since the sales proceeds do not exceed the original cost of the assets.

11

VALUATION IN MARITAL DISSOLUTIONS

JAN C. GABRIELSON*

		Page
¶ 11.1	Valuing Businesses for Purposes of Marital Dissolution.....................................	11-3
¶ 11.2	The Meaning of Value in the Context of Marital Dissolution.....................................	11-4
	[1] Market Value..............................	11-4
	[2] Investment Value	11-5
	[3] Compulsion Value	11-5
¶ 11.3	Formulas..	11-5
	[1] Uses of Formulas	11-6
	[2] Derivation of Formulas	11-6
	[a] Tax Rulings and Cases..................	11-6
	[b] "Creative" Appraisal Methods	11-7
	[c] Problems With Formulas	11-7
¶ 11.4	Judicial Attitude Toward Valuation Methods	11-8
	[1] Most Methods Approved on Appeal	11-8
	[2] Mandated Methods	11-8
	[3] Forbidden Methods	11-8
	[a] Price/Earnings Ratio	11-9
	[b] Stock-for-Stock Transactions as Comparable Prices......................	11-9
	[4] Splitting the Difference.....................	11-9
	[5] Reservation of Jurisdiction Over Contingencies	11-10
¶ 11.5	Other Factors in Valuation	11-10
	[1] Buy-Sell Agreements	11-10
	[a] Binding Values	11-11
	[b] Influential Tax Cases	11-11
	[c] Specific Provisions for Marital Dissolutions............................	11-11
	[d] Legal Issue or Valuation Issue?..........	11-12
	[2] Potential Tax Liabilities	11-12

---

* JAN C. GABRIELSON, Esq., is a shareholder in the firm of Walzer & Gabrielson in Los Angeles, California. The author is a certified family law specialist and a fellow of the American Academy of Matrimonial Lawyers. In addition, he has written and lectured extensively on all aspects of family law.

¶ 11.6	Tactical Problems	11-13
	[1] Concealed Income	11-13
	[2] Assertions of Confidentiality	11-14
	[a] Trade Secrets; Patient and Client Records	11-14
	[b] Privacy of Business Associates	11-14
¶ 11.7	**Components of Value**	11-14
	[1] "Hard" Assets	11-15
	[2] Accounts Receivable	11-15
	[a] Reduction for Taxes	11-15
	[b] Receivables and Alimony: The Double Dip	11-15
	[c] Vanishing Separate Accounts Receivable	11-16
	[3] Goodwill	11-16
	[a] Goodwill as Property in a Marital Dissolution	11-16
	[b] Problems of Valuing Goodwill	11-16
	[c] Discount for Relocating	11-17
	[4] Loans to Shareholders	11-17
	[a] Loan Accounts	11-17
	[b] Handling the Balance at Separation	11-17
	[c] Handling Additions After Separation	11-18
¶ 11.8	**Effect of Separation**	11-18
	[1] Earnings Become Nonmarital Property	11-18
	[2] Effect of Postseparation Work	11-18
	[3] Restrictions on Earnings History	11-19
	[a] Postseparation Earnings	11-19
	[b] How the Valuation Is Affected	11-19
	[c] Applicability of Rule to Spouse's Earnings	11-20
	[d] Comparing Preseparation Earnings With a Comparable Period	11-20
	[4] Definition of Separation	11-20
¶ 11.9	**Apportionment of Premarital Property and Marital Property**	11-20
	[1] Fair Return on Separate Capital Method	11-21
	[2] Reasonable Compensation Method	11-21
	[3] Court Discretion to Determine Method	11-21
¶ 11.10	**Date of Valuation**	11-22
	[1] Statutory and Decisional Provisions	11-22
	[2] Distinction From Restrictions on Earnings History	11-23
¶ 11.11	**Management and Control Problems That Affect Valuation While Marital Dissolution Is Pending**	11-23
	[1] One Spouse Working in the Business	11-23
	[2] Both Spouses Working in the Business	11-24
¶ 11.12	**Professional Practices**	11-24

[1] Professional Practices as Assets 11-24
[2] Absence of a Market 11-24
[3] Income Usually Produced by Current Work .. 11-25
[4] Small Share in a Big Firm 11-25
[5] Valuation of License and Education 11-25
¶ 11.13 Distribution of Business Interests Between the
Spouses 11-26
[1] Corporate Stock 11-26
[2] Both Spouses in the Same Business 11-26

¶ 11.1 Valuing Businesses for Purposes of Marital Dissolution

If valuing businesses for business purposes is an art, not a science, then valuing businesses for the purposes of divorce borders on the occult.

Marriages often come apart with all the grace of a splitting atom, and the spouses' anger toward each other can have a long enough half life to taint every issue in the case. Business valuation experts find themselves drawn into the fray when the warring spouses hire them as proponents of their preconceived ideas of what the family business must be worth.

In the marketplace, the buyer wants a low value, and the seller wants a high one. In divorce, the spouse who operates the business and wants to keep it becomes an unwilling buyer while the other spouse plays the reluctant seller, asking an outrageously high price. In this climate, business valuation experts find their desire to be fair and objective thwarted by their client's desire to obtain a high or low value.

Not only is the process encumbered with the emotional baggage of a shattered relationship and not only are the parties locked into dealing only with each other for the business, but a whole new set of bizarre rules also confronts the appraiser—rules that vary from state to state and often clash with rational economic analysis. Valuation experts find themselves labeled "husbands' " or "wives' " appraisers, depending on whom their work helped the most in their last few cases. They try, often in vain, to shed such labels.

This chapter is not a comprehensive treatise on valuing business interests in marital dissolutions. It is simply an overview of some of the problems to be encountered in the area and how those problems have been approached by the courts. Although a California bias may appear from time to time, the legal and economic principles are transferable from state to state.

Mention should be made here of the concept of marital or community property since that concept pervades the discussion in this chapter. Different states use different terms, but the basic idea is the same.

Community property states (generally on the Pacific Coast, in the Southwest, and in Louisiana) use the words "community" and "separate" property. Noncommunity property states usually speak of "marital" and "nonmarital" property.

Separate or *nonmarital property* is usually property that is owned by one spouse before marriage or that is received by one spouse during marriage by gift or inheritance. *Community* or *marital property* is generally property that results from the efforts of either spouse during marriage. States differ as to whether the passive earnings of separate property are separate or community.

Upon divorce, community or marital property is divided between the spouses. California is in the minority in requiring equal division. Most states have some form of equitable division in which the judge can divide property unequally, applying rules that vary from state to state. Separate or nonmarital property is not divided.

Although the national trend is to change the term "divorce" to "marital dissolution" to take away some of the negative emotional charge of the former term, most people still call a divorce a divorce. In this chapter, the terms are used interchangeably.

¶ 11.2 The Meaning of "Value" in the Context of Marital Dissolution

For most people, the value of something is what they could sell it for; that is called *market value*. In divorce, some assets that do not have a market are valued anyway and distributed to the husband or wife. In states that have equal or equitable distribution of marital property, every asset that is not divided equally in kind—an equal portion to each spouse—must be valued, whether or not it can ever be sold. The need to establish a value where there is no reliable market value leads to such concepts as investment value and compulsion value.

[1] Market Value

Assets that are readily bought and sold, such as real estate, jewelry, cars, and publicly traded stock, present no particular valuation problem in marital dissolutions. Determining market value is more difficult in the case of closely held business interests. Many business owners object to being awarded the family business at what they considered a high value over protests that the business could not be sold for anything close to that value.

That lament falls on deaf ears in divorce court. Case after case holds that the absence of a market for a business interest does not mean it cannot be valued and the value allocated to one of the spouses in a divorce.[1] The other spouse is then awarded other assets of comparable value to balance the division. The spouse who gets the business may be even more distressed if the balancing assets given to his or her spouse are readily marketable.

While market value is not the last word in divorce valuation, it is certainly relevant and persuasive. For example, a discount in the value of shares may be appropriate where a business is not marketable.[2] If a business is of a kind that is readily bought and sold, market value is still the best indicator of value. If the parties do not like the value that results from analyzing the market or if there is no market at all, other concepts of value are available.

[2] Investment Value

In response to the argument by one of the parties to a divorce that the court should use market value in valuing the family business, courts have held that using market value was not required and that investment value would satisfy the requirements of the law in dividing marital property. A pivotal case in point is *Marriage of Hewitson*.[3]

Investment value, according to the case of *Marriage of Hewitson*, is simply value as determined by a method other than an analysis of the market, for example: capitalization of earnings, capitalization of dividends, book value, or net asset value.

[3] Compulsion Value

Compulsion value is not itself a valuation method; rather, it is a recognition of the unique circumstances surrounding the valuation and distribution of business interests in divorce. Data for finding the market value of an interest come from transactions on the open market between a willing buyer and a willing seller, neither being under any compulsion to buy or sell. But when an interest is not readily marketable, the spouse who expects to keep the business becomes an unwilling buyer and the other spouse an unwilling seller. The concept of compulsion value also recognizes the problems inherent in forcing one spouse to accept intangible assets at a judicially contrived value and pay for them with tangible assets, as in the case of *Marriage of Lopez*.[4]

¶ 11.3 Formulas

Formulas for valuing businesses under specific conditions are discussed elsewhere in this book so the material will not be repeated here.

---

[1] *See, e.g.*, Marriage of Foster, 31 Cal. App. 3d 577, 117 Cal. Rptr. 49 (1974).
[2] Arneson v. Arneson, 120 Wis. 2d 236, 355 N.W.2d 16 (Wis. App. 1984).
[3] 142 Cal. App. 3d 874, 191 Cal. Rptr. 392 (1983).
[4] 38 Cal. App. 3d 93, 110, 113 Cal. Rptr. 58 (1974).

Instead, the focus here is on the reasons for using formulas in marital dissolutions and on some of the problems that arise from their use.

[1] Uses of Formulas

In many cases, business assets cannot be valued for divorce purposes by using market data because some business interests simply cannot be sold. The business may be too personal to its owner or may involve risks that few investors other than its founder are willing to take. Some kinds of businesses, such as law practices, have legal constraints against selling them. Yet, it is elementary law that business interests must be valued and included in the distribution of marital assets on divorce.

The courts, then, are obliged to find values where market values are nonexistent or are unrepresentative of the value of a particular business. They turn to business valuation experts to offer expert testimony as to value. These experts, in turn, are expected to come up with an opinion of value. When market data fails them, they turn to formulas.

[2] Derivation of Formulas

Formulas derived from the marketplace pose no particular problem in business valuation. For example, accounting practices are actually sold for one year's gross earnings. But for businesses that have no real market, the validity of valuation formulas is also subject to question. These formulas have two primary sources: the methods used by taxing authorities and the imagination of forensic experts.

[a] Tax Rulings and Cases

The Internal Revenue Service (IRS) faces the same problem that a divorce court does when it must find a value for business interests in order to determine the amount of estate or gift tax upon transfer of the interest. Even business interests that have no market must be valued. For that reason, the IRS has issued a number of rulings stating how business interests are to be valued for tax purposes. Three of these rulings have probably been the most influential in valuation for marital dissolutions. Appeals and Review Memorandum 34 (A.R.M. 34), promulgated in the 1920s, set out a formula that, in effect, calls for capitalizing the profit of the business.[5]

Revenue Ruling 59-60, while not prescribing any particular formula, reviews at length how appraisers should approach the valua-

---

[5] 1920-2 C.B. 31.

tion of business interests and lists factors that they should consider.[6] Several courts have approved the use of Revenue Ruling 59-60 for valuing businesses in marital dissolutions.[7]

A.R.M. 34 was superseded in 1968 by Revenue Ruling 68-609,[8] which described the process of valuing businesses using a formula that capitalizes earnings.

[b] "Creative" Appraisal Methods

Since the courts are not limited to market value and rely heavily on appraisers in valuing divorce assets, appraisers are often willing to use "creative" appraisal methods. Sometimes, such creativity is commendable, but it can result in a severe miscarriage of justice.

For example, a highly respected forensic accountant and business appraiser in Los Angeles arbitrarily uses three months' gross receipts to value the goodwill of a professional practice. He adjusts that figure for the profitability of the practice as determined by the ratio of its gross receipts to its net income. One reason he does not like the excess earnings method is because many times it yields no goodwill. There is not valuable goodwill in every practice, and any method that always finds some is subject to question.

Three months' gross receipts seems to be a popular basis for valuing a professional practice. In two California cases, *Marriage of Foster*[9] and *Marriage of Barnert*,[10] the trial courts used that formula to value medical practices. In *Foster*, three months' gross receipts were used to value the goodwill only while in *Barnert* the same formula was used to value the entire practice, including tangible assets. The California Court of Appeal affirmed both, approving the trial court's exercise of discretion. Some lawyers cite those cases as prescribing the method used even though the appellate court would likely have approved almost any method that the trial court found appropriate.

[c] Problems With Formulas

Valuation formulas that are not based on actual market data tend to be arbitrary. Where the business is not transferable, a business has no value except to its owner. Formulas cannot evaluate what the owner honestly believes the business is worth to him or her and so do not take it into account. Finally, most formulas applied to highly per-

---

[6] 1959-1 C.B. 237. Revenue Ruling 59-60 is reproduced as Appendix A at the end of this book.
[7] *See* Lavene v. Lavene, 162 N.J. Super. 187, 392 A.2d 621 (Ch. Div. 1978); Marriage of Hewitson, 142 Cal. App. 3d at 874, 191 Cal. Rptr. at 392.
[8] 1968 2 C.B. 327.
[9] 42 Cal. App. 3d 577, 117 Cal. Rptr. 49 (1974).
[10] 85 Cal. App. 3d 413, 149 Cal. Rptr. 616 (1978).

sonal service businesses do not give adequate weight to the amount of personal labor that the owner of the business must continue to provide in order to realize any benefit from the business.

¶ 11.4 Judicial Attitude Toward Valuation Methods

With few exceptions courts leave valuation methodology to forensic appraisers. Rarely do they prescribe a specific valuation method. The following discussion focuses on both mandated (such as they exist) and forbidden methods of valuation, with splitting the difference in the face of conflicting valuations as well as on an analysis of reserving jurisprudence over contingencies.

[1] Most Methods Approved on Appeal

Expert witnesses in divorce valuation cases are allowed to testify to a wide variety of conclusions arrived at by many different methods.[11] Once the trial court selects from among the evidence and settles on a value, it is almost impossible to convince an overworked appellate court that a different method should have been used. As a result, there are as many methods and variations on those methods as there are valuation experts. Similarly, the same case can be decided with a completely different result by different judges.

The message for lawyers should be clear: Select your expert witnesses and your judges carefully. In most cases, the battle will be fought on the facts presented, not on the law.

[2] Mandated Methods

Occasionally, it does happen that an appellate court will reverse, holding that the trial court should have valued a business in a specific manner. For example, in *Marriage of Fortier*, the trial court valued a medical practice using the formula advocated by a forensic accountant.[12] A partner of the doctor, however, had bought into the practice about a year and a half before the divorce, and the trial court was reversed for not using that buy-in price as the value of Dr. Fortier's interest.

[3] Forbidden Methods

While it is usually true that appellate courts tend not to overturn valuation methods accepted by the trial court, there are some exceptions.

---

[11] *See, e.g.*, Arneson v. Arneson, 120 Wis. 2d at 236, 355 N.W.2d at 16.
[12] 34 Cal. App. 3d 384, 109 Cal. Rptr. 915 (1973).

[a] Price/Earnings Ratio

Two California cases have disapproved the exclusive use of price-earnings ratios derived from sales of publicly traded stock to determine the value of closely held stock: *Marriage of Lotz*[13] and *Marriage of Hewitson*.[14] The reason for this rule is the inherent difference between closely held and publicly traded corporations. A Wisconsin court in *Dean v. Dean*[15] allowed the use of such comparisons, provided the difference is taken into account. The court noted that stock in a close corporation lacks marketability and investors will pay more for a listed stock than an unlisted one having identical factors of earnings, dividend payments, and book value. The cost of going public is another, although less important, factor.

However, even in California, as in the case of *Marriage of Hewitson*, if an appraiser can convince the court of its necessity and relative reliability, the court might allow the use of the price-earnings ratio as a cross-check on the other approaches used to determine the value of closely held shares.[16]

[b] Stock-for-Stock Transactions as Comparable Prices

When one corporation is acquired by another, cash is rarely paid for the acquired company. It is usually bought in exchange for stock in the acquiring company. In such a case, the acquiring company will pay a premium because the actual cost is less to the acquiring company. For this reason, it was held in *Marriage of Hewitson*[17] to be improper to use prices of stock that were derived from corporate acquisitions of comparable companies.

[4] Splitting the Difference

When the courts are presented with conflicting valuation evidence, the temptation to split the difference between the two values is overwhelming. In *Marriage of Webb*, the husband owned a one-man detective agency.[18] He testified that it had no goodwill value. His wife's valuation expert testified that its goodwill had a value of $31,000. The court found a value of $16,000 and was affirmed on appeal. However, in *Marriage of Hargrave*,[19] the California Court of Appeal held that finding an arbitrary value between two values testified to by expert wit-

---
[13] 120 Cal. App. 3d 379, 174 Cal. Rptr. 618 (1981).
[14] 142 Cal. App. 3d at 874, 191 Cal. Rptr. at 392.
[15] Dean v. Dean, 87 Wis. 2d 854, 275 N.W.2d 902 (1979).
[16] *Id*
[17] *Id.*
[18] 94 Cal. App. 3d 335, 156 Cal. Rptr. 334 (1979).
[19] 163 Cal. App. 3d 346, 209 Cal. Rptr. 764 (1985).

nesses was not proper unless the court gave its reasons for finding that value.

[5] Reservation of Jurisdiction Over Contingencies

To appraise a business requires a valuation expert to make judgments about the future course of the business. Except when appraising liquidation value, the assumption must be made that the business will be able to continue operation. Other contingencies, such as the probable future income, the loyalty of customers, and the availability of raw materials, are routinely considered by appraisers and figured in the valuation.

In a valuation done for the purpose of finding a purchase price for the business, the buyer considers the risks inherent in the business. Those risks influence the price he or she is willing to pay. Absent fraud, the buyer takes the business and lives with its future ups and downs. In a marital dissolution, on the other hand, the value is not always fixed when the case is settled or the judgment signed. Most courts have the right to reserve jurisdiction over some marital assets to value and divide them at an appropriate time in the future.[20]

When the occurrence of a contingency is critical to the operation of a business, it may be appropriate for the divorce court to exercise its power to defer its decision and reserve jurisdiction over valuation and distribution of the business until the contingency has occurred or can no longer occur. Thus, in *Marriage of Munguia*,[21] one of the marital assets was a tavern. Crucial to its continued operation was the renewal of its lease, which was about to expire. At the time of the divorce, no one knew whether the lease would be renewed. The trial court valued the tavern anyway and was reversed by the court of appeal, which held that it was error not to have reserved jurisdiction over the valuation and distribution of the tavern until it was known whether the lease would be renewed.

¶ 11.5 Other Factors in Valuation

Among the other factors to consider in business valuations for purposes of divorce are buy-sell agreements that protect the assets and continuity of the business in question, and potential tax liabilities that may result from the valuation. Both factors are discussed next.

[1] Buy-Sell Agreements

Many businesses that are owned by more than one person are subject to formal agreements between partners or shareholders. These

---

[20] *See, e.g.*, Cal. Civ. Code § 4800(a) (Deering 1989).
[21] 146 Cal. App. 3d 853, 195 Cal. Rptr. 199 (1983).

buy-sell agreements usually set a value or provide a method of determining a value for the business in the event one of the principals dies, withdraws from the business, or is forced out. Since the purpose of such buy-sell agreements is to protect the assets and continuity of the business, the values tend to be conservative and to reflect what the principals would be willing to pay for a particular interest in the business. (Values on death may be higher since the buyout is usually funded by life insurance.) Business owners are usually proponents of using the value prescribed by the agreement as the value for divorce purposes since the buy-sell value is usually lower than what the spouse's valuation expert calculates by using a formula.

[a] Binding Values

Although some cases approve the use of business values found in buy-sell agreements,[22] most recent decisions hold that while they may be persuasive evidence of value, they are not binding on the divorce court. In *Marriage of Slater*,[23] for example, the trial court used the value in the buy-sell agreement of a medical group to value the interest of one of the members for his divorce. The trial court considered itself bound by the agreement, but the appellate court reversed, pointing out that the doctor's wife was not a direct party to the agreement and that it was not written for purposes of divorce.

Likewise, New Jersey has not held buy-sell valuations to be binding in divorce litigation. But where the agreement provides a means to value an owner's interest and the formalities provided in the agreement have been observed, as in the case of *Stern v. Stern*,[24] then the value provided in the agreement is the presumptive value for purposes of divorce.

[b] Influential in Tax Cases

In *Estate of Seltzer*,[25] a shareholder of a corporation died and her shares were sold to the corporation at the value specified in the shareholders' buy-sell agreement. When the IRS assessed estate tax on a higher (fair market) valuation, the tax court held that the lower value in the buy-sell was controlling.

[c] Specific Provisions for Marital Dissolutions

Most buy-sell agreements provide for a value on death, expulsion, or withdrawal from the business. Although the spouses often sign

---
[22] *See, e.g.*, Marriage of Rosan, 24 Cal. App. 3d 885, 101 Cal. Rptr. 295 (1972); Marriage of Aufmuth, 89 Cal. App. 3d 446, 152 Cal. Rptr. 668 (1979).
[23] 100 Cal. App. 3d 241, 160 Cal. Rptr. 686 (1979).
[24] 66 N.J. 340, 331 A.2d 157 (1975).
[25] T.C. Memo. 1985-519.

them, few agreements attempt to set a value on divorce probably because most happily married couples find advance planning for divorce distasteful. In most states, married persons have the right to make agreements with each other regarding their property, subject to requirements of full disclosure and the absence of undue influence. If people overcome their aversion to such agreements, the agreements can be binding on the court in a divorce.

[d] Legal Issue or Valuation Issue?

Some valuation analysts refuse to consider values set out in buy-sell agreements when they appraise businesses—perhaps from fear that their services will not be necessary. Their rationale is that the buy-sell value was not necessarily arrived at by sound valuation principles. Where there is a market price for the business, using the buy-sell value may not be appropriate. In the common situation, however, where the business interest has no market, a value agreed on in good faith by the principals of the business is usually at least as accurate as a value found by an arbitrary formula.

Perhaps those valuation experts are right, and perhaps their conclusions should not be tainted by a value agreed to by the owners of the business. The independent work of these experts can serve as a cross-check on the reliability of the buy-sell value. In those jurisdictions where the buy-sell value is not binding, its proponent usually has the burden of proving to the court that its value is reasonable, so the valuation expert's work will not be wasted.

When relying on a buy-sell agreement for valuation, offering evidence of the business purposes of the agreement is a "must." Not only are courts impressed by such things, but it is also important to emphasize in a positive way that the agreement was not contrived by the partners to cheat their spouses.

[2] Potential Tax Liabilities

When a business is sold, taxes may have to be paid on the transaction. The spouse who expects to be awarded the business wants to argue that those future taxes should reduce the value of the business that will be charged to him or her in the divorce. Because of the near impossibility of computing what those taxes will amount to in some future year, many states, such as California in *Marriage of Fonstein*,[26] hold that the tax consequences must be immediate and specific before they can be used by the court to reduce the value charged to the recipient of the business. Otherwise, the court must speculate on the year the sale will take place, the value of the business in that year, the tax

---

[26] 17 Cal. 3d 738, 131 Cal. Rptr. 873 (1976).

rates in that year, the other income the business owner will have, and the availability of tax shelters.

Similarly, the New Jersey case of *Stern v. Stern*[27] held that the value of the husband's law practice should not be reduced by the income tax he would have to pay on his accounts receivable when they would be collected.

On the other hand, where the court is convinced at the time of the divorce that immediate and specific tax consequences will affect the value of the business, some cases hold that the taxes must be subtracted from the value.[28]

Some states allow expert testimony on the tax consequences of proposed divisions of marital property.[29] In those states, it is wise to offer such evidence in an appropriate case since most lawyers and judges are not equipped to do accurate tax calculations.

¶ 11.6 Tactical Problems

There are several tactical problems to be resolved in valuations in marital dissolutions. Among the most common problems that valuation analysts must address are concealed income and assertions of confidentiality.

[1] Concealed Income

Many small business owners do not keep records of all of their cash receipts and do not report all of their income on their tax returns. In divorce proceedings, unreported income artificially lowers the value of the business since the income of a business is a critical factor in most valuation methods. When a business owner has unreported income, his or her spouse often knows about it or suspects it and urges his or her lawyer to prove it to the court.

Dealing with unreported income is difficult at best. Most of the time, it is impossible to prove. Even when diligent accounting and detective work show its existence, it may still be impossible to reduce it to numbers that are exact enough to enable the court to take it into account. Furthermore, the spouse of the tax evader has usually filed joint tax returns for the years in which income was not reported. If he or she is successful in proving unreported income, both spouses are exposed to back taxes as well as civil and criminal penalties.

Finally, the attitude of many judges toward concealed income makes it almost not worth pursuing. The evidence may be largely

---

[27] 66 N.J. at 340, 331 A.2d at 257.
[28] *See, e.g.*, Marriage of Clark, 80 Cal. App. 3d 417, 145 Cal. Rptr. 602 (1978); Marriage of Epstein, 24 Cal. 3d 76, 154 Cal. Rptr. 413 (1979).
[29] *See* Marriage of Fonstein, 17 Cal. 3d at 738, 131 Cal. Rptr. at 873.

speculation and therefore inadmissible. Even if the evidence is admissible and probative, some judges will refuse to hear it because it will hurt both spouses. Others insist on calling in the tax authorities.

[2] Assertions of Confidentiality

For an appraiser to do a thorough study of a business, records must be reviewed. Secret processes may be important assets of the business that the appraiser must evaluate. The atmosphere of suspicion in marital dissolutions and other litigation adds to the reluctance of the business owners to give any information to the other side's appraiser, especially where trade secrets, patents, and client records as well as the privacy of business associates are concerned.

[a] Trade Secrets; Patient and Client Records

Most states allow some degree of protection to trade secrets when a party tries to get them by judicial discovery procedures. Similarly, when professional practices are valued, doctors and lawyers are reluctant to impair their clients' right to confidentiality when the spouse's valuation expert asks to look at the client and patient lists and, worse yet, their files and charts. Most courts will limit the amount of material to be made available to the opposing valuation expert in such situations. Clients and patients are often assigned a code so that information on them that is relevant to the valuation can be given to the appraiser without violating their confidence.

[b] Privacy of Business Associates

Some states do not allow unlimited discovery of financial information when a business owner is going through a divorce. The theory behind such restrictions is that, while the divorcing spouse's own finances are relevant and discoverable, the privacy of his or her business associates should not be invaded. To do a thorough valuation, however, it is often necessary to know how much money the business pays to other people in the business. Such privacy restrictions, as in the case of *Marriage of Rifkind*,[30] make the valuation analysts's job more difficult.

¶ 11.7 Components of Value

The components of value in a business valuation for marital dissolution purposes run the gamut from "hard assets" and loans to shareholders, which are usually easily appraised, to accounts receivable goodwill, which may be more difficult to appraise.

---

[30] 123 Cal. App. 3d 1045, 177 Cal. Rptr. 82 (1981).

[1] "Hard" Assets

Equipment, furniture, real estate and other tangible property of businesses pose no particular problem in marital dissolutions. They can be valued at market by appraisers of those assets and their value added to the value of the other components of the business.

[2] Accounts Receivable

The accounts receivable of a business are an asset of that business.[31] A discount for noncollectibility is appropriate in marital dissolutions as in other appraisals. But when the business is valued because of a divorce, there are some special problems of which to be aware.

[a] Reduction for Taxes

The business owner will argue that the value of his or her accounts receivable must be reduced for the income taxes he will have to pay when he collects them. Since most receivables must be collected within a few months if they are ever to be collected, the business owner argues that the taxes are necessarily immediate and specific.[32]

The valuation expert for the other spouse will argue, on the other hand, that a small corporation may pay little or no tax and that, since the receivables went to pay operating expenses, they were offset by deductions and therefore not taxed.

[b] Receivables and Alimony: The Double Dip

The spouse who is awarded the business in a divorce usually gets all of the assets of the business, including its accounts receivable. He or she is charged with those accounts receivable so that the other spouse gets other property of the same value to balance the distribution. Then, the spouse with the business finds he or she has to use some of those receivables as they are collected to pay alimony. The argument has been made that it is not fair to charge that spouse twice for the same receivables.

The argument, although compelling, was not successful in *Marriage of Marx*.[33] There, the court held that the accounts receivable as of the date of separation were community property and properly chargeable to the husband who got them. Support, on the other hand, is payable from postseparation earnings which in California are separate property. The receivables from which support is paid are, therefore, separate property and are not the same receivables as those that

---

[31] Stern v. Stern, 66 N.J. at 340, 331 A.2d at 257.
[32] *See* ¶ 11.5[2] for a discussion on when future taxes can reduce the value of an asset.
[33] 97 Cal. App. 3d 552, 159 Cal. Rptr. 215 (1979).

were allocated to the husband in the property division. Therefore, the business owner is not charged twice for the same asset, at least not in theory.

[c] Vanishing Separate Accounts Receivable

It often happens that one spouse owns a business that has accounts receivable on the date of marriage. When there is a divorce, it appears logical to find the marital portion of the receivables by subtracting the total on the date of marriage from the total on the date of separation (or date of trial, depending on local law).

But the court in *Marriage of House*[34] had a different approach. The receivables at the date of marriage no longer existed, having been collected and spent long before separation. To the extent they had been spent for community purposes, the court presumed that a gift to the marital community was intended. The receivables that accumulated during marriage, on the other hand, were community property and chargeable to the business owner when the business was awarded to him.

[3] Goodwill

The most difficult asset to value in a divorce is goodwill, especially for small, personal businesses and professional practices.

[a] Goodwill as Property in a Marital Dissolution

There is little question in most jurisdictions that the goodwill of a business is property and must be valued and distributed in marital dissolutions.[35] Similarly, it will almost always be awarded and charged to the spouse who has been the operator of the business.[36]

[b] Problems of Valuing Goodwill

Where the business is such that it can be sold and most of the customers are likely to patronize the new owner, a reasonable estimate of the value of the goodwill can be made. Some businesses have a rule of thumb, using the gross receipts for some period of time as the amount of the goodwill (or of the whole business). For others, the valuation expert can compute the profits of the business and multiply them by a factor that represents the period of time in which a buyer would expect to recapture his investment and then begin making a profit. Or the buyer can divide the profits by a capitalization rate that represents the return a buyer would expect to get on his investment.

---

[34] 50 Cal. App. 3d 578, 123 Cal. Rptr. 451 (1975).
[35] *See, e.g.,* Golden v. Golden, 270 Cal. App. 2d 401, 75 Cal. Rptr. 735 (1969).
[36] *See, e.g.,* Marriage of Smith, 79 Cal. App. 3d 725, 145 Cal. Rptr. 205 (1978).

When the business is not transferable, a theoretical analysis of its appeal to a prospective buyer is far less reliable. It is in those cases that valuation experts sometimes arbitrarily select a formula to value the business or its goodwill.

[c] Discount for Relocating

Since a large part of goodwill is the expectation that customers will return to the old location, the goodwill of a business may suffer if the divorce requires a business owner to relocate. The loss of future public patronage, as in the case of *Marriage of Asbury*,[37] should be considered in the value of the goodwill.

[4] Loans to Shareholders

Loans to shareholders must be taken into account both at and after separation in a business valuation for marital dissolution purposes. Situations involving these loans are discussed next.

[a] Loan Accounts

Many owners of small, closely held corporations do not pay themselves a regular salary. Rather, they draw the equivalent of a salary, and the corporation carries the disbursements on the books as "loan to officer." Later, often in a new calendar year, a salary is declared and used to pay the outstanding loans. The device is used to defer income into subsequent taxable years. Loan accounts are also used, when for convenience, the officer has the corporation pay his personal expenses. As common as the practice is, loan accounts continue to confuse lawyers and judges and cause serious accounting errors in the division of property.

[b] Handling the Balance at Separation

A loan receivable from an officer at the date of separation is an asset of the corporation and increases the value that will be charged to the spouse awarded the business.[38] However, the business owner must be sure to explain to the valuation experts and to the court that for the loan to have value to the corporation, it must be repayable. Since it was borrowed before separation in lieu of salary, it will have been used in most cases for marital purposes and therefore be a marital debt. The logical person to repay the loan is the spouse who is awarded the business. That spouse must then be given credit in the property division for the obligation to repay the loan. The net result is that the receiva-

---

[37] 144 Cal. App. 3d 918, 193 Cal. Rptr. 562 (1983).
[38] Marriage of Lotz, 120 Cal. App. 3d at 379, 174 Cal. Rptr. at 618.

ble and the debt neutralize each other, provided both are assigned to the same spouse.

[c] Handling Additions After Separation

It can be hazardous to allow a loan account to increase after separation. In states where assets are valued at the date of trial, the increase in the loan account will increase the value of the corporation. Since the loans were made after separation, however, they are separate debts and do not result in a credit to the payor in the division of the marital property. In states where postseparation earnings are nonmarital property, the business owner may find that he or she effectively got no salary for all the work done between separation and trial. In some states, any increase in the value of a corporation attributable to work after separation is the nonmarital property of the spouse doing the work. The value of the corporation at the time of trial must, therefore, be apportioned between marital and nonmarital property, as in the California case of *Marriage of Imperato*.[39] However, even in states where apportionment is required, the danger is real that the judge will not understand how to handle the problem.

¶ 11.8 Effect of Separation

The date of separation is significant in a business valuation for divorce purposes because it can change the fruits of work from marital to nonmarital property. Postseparation work and whether it can be used for valuation are factors that the valuation expert must take into account.

[1] Earnings Become Nonmarital Property

In most states, the fruits of work done by either spouse before separation are marital or community property that must be divided at dissolution. In many states, however, earnings become nonmarital or separate property upon separation and are not divided with the other spouse.[40] This rule complicates business valuations for purposes of divorce.

[2] Effect of Postseparation Work

If the spouse has a small business that is marital property and its value increases between separation and trial, he or she will argue that the increase in value is nonmarital property and not divisible in divorce. The argument was accepted in *Marriage of Imperato*,[41] which

---

[39] 45 Cal. App. 3d 432, 119 Cal. Rptr. 590 (1975).
[40] *See, e.g.*, Cal. Civ. Code § 5118 (Deering 1989).
[41] 45 Cal. App. 3d at 432., 119 Cal. Rptr. at 590.

also gave some guidance as to how to determine whether the increase in value is marital or nonmarital. One method allocates a fair return on the value of the business at the date of separation to marital property and the balance of the increase in value is the separate property of the spouse who did the work. The other method would determine the reasonable value of the services of the spouse to the business after separation less any draws or salaries actually taken in the same period. This additional sum is allocated to separate property and the balance of the increase in value is marital property.

[3] Restrictions on Earnings History

Some states impose limitations on the time period during which the earnings of a business may be considered in valuing a business. These restrictions raise other issues and cause confusion, as is discussed next.

[a] Postseparation Earnings

In *Marriage of King*,[42] the husband had a one-man consulting business. His wife's appraiser based his opinion of the value of the business in part on the earnings of the business for a period after separation. The trial court used his value and was reversed on appeal. Since the postseparation earnings of the husband were his separate property, they could not be used in valuing the business.

[b] How the Valuation Is Affected

In cases where postseparation earnings are higher, it is to the advantage of the business operator that they not be used since he will likely be awarded the business at a lower value. It is a common misconception that *King* requires businesses to be valued as of the date of separation. In most cases, all valuation factors other than earnings will be evaluated as of the date of trial.

If the earnings of the business decline after separation, there is an argument that would allow the court to consider the decline in earnings. When the value increases solely because of higher postseparation earnings, the increase in value is separate property. If there is a change, however, in value of the marital portion of the business, it should be as admissible as any other factor affecting the value of the marital property.

---

[42] 150 Cal. App. 3d 304, 197 Cal. Rptr. 716 (1983).

[c] Applicability of Rule to the Spouse's Earnings

Where the earnings of a business increase after separation, courts may choose to exclude only those earnings attributable to the spouse. Since the increase in value of the entire business because of the higher earnings produced by the other participants is passive, the spouse's share in that part of the increased value is still arguably marital property.

[d] Comparing Preseparation Earnings With a Comparable Period

Since the goodwill of a business is often determined by comparing its earnings to some standard of average earnings, it is only logical to compare those earnings with statistically average earnings for the same dates. If an increase in earnings between separation and trial is because of inflation, using comparable earnings from the time of separation will not necessarily result in a lower value. But if the business has grown substantially between separation and trial, the business owner may benefit from the rule against using postseparation earnings in business appraisals for divorce.

[4] Definition of Separation

Although separation changes the fruits of work from marital to nonmarital property, what constitutes the date of separation is not always clear. In California, for example, the earnings and accumulations of the parties "while living separate and apart" are separate property.[43] The language of the statute seems to describe physical separation. In *Marriage of Baragry*,[44] however, the husband and wife lived apart for four years and were held not to be separated. The property that had been accumulated while they were living in separate residences was held to be community. The *Baragry* case set out the test for separation as "a complete and final break in the marital relationship."[45]

¶ 11.9. Apportionment of Premarital Property and Marital Property

Where a spouse owns separate property before marriage and the value of that separate property increases substantially during marriage, a portion of the increase in value may be due to the skill and efforts of the spouse who has managed that property. The fruits of that skill and effort are considered a community or marital asset; and, to the extent

---

[43] *See, e.g.*, Cal. Civ. Code § 5118 (Deering 1989).
[44] 73 Cal. App. 3d 444, 140 Cal. Rptr. 779 (1977).
[45] *Id.* at 448, 140 Cal. Rptr. at 779.

that it has increased the value of the separate property asset, the marital estate is entitled to some portion of the increase. Where the asset is a business, there are two basic formulas for allocating the increase in value.

[1] Fair Return on Separate Capital Method

The *fair return on separate capital method* allocates a fair return on the spouse's separate property capital at the time of the marriage. Any increase in the value of the asset that exceeds the separate capital plus a fair return on separate capital is assumed to have resulted from the efforts of the spouse during marriage and is therefore allocated to community. The community's portion of the increase in value, as in the case of *Pereira v. Pereira*,[46] is the amount by which the actual increase in value exceeds the return that the initial capital investment could have been expected to earn without any personal management by the spouse.

[2] Reasonable Compensation Method

The *reasonable compensation* method requires the court to find a reasonable value for the services performed by the spouse in connection with managing his or her separate property business by considering what it would have cost to hire a third party to perform the services performed by the spouse. This reasonable compensation cost (which may exceed the actual compensation paid to that spouse over the years) is allocated to the community. The balance of the increase in value of the assets is the spouse's separate property.[47] This method is usually preferred by the spouse claiming the separate interest because, in many states, the living expenses of both parties are deducted from the reasonable compensation before it is allocated to marital property.

[3] Court Discretion to Determine Method

The courts have discretion to determine which of the two previous formulas to use. However, since the return on separate capital method often favors marital property, the case law in some states indicates that the courts should apply the return on separate capital method whenever that the skill and efforts of the spouse were the major factors in producing the increase. When natural increases in the value of the capital and capital assets would have resulted with little or no effort by the spouse, the reasonable compensation method may be appropriate.

---

[46] 156 Cal. 1, 103 P. 488 (1909).
[47] *See* Van Camp v. Van Camp, 53 Cal. App. 17, 199 P. 885 (1921).

¶ 11.10 Date of Valuation

Business valuation experts and those working with them must know as of what date the business must be valued under local law. Depending on the state and the circumstances of the individual case, the valuation date may be before separation, the day of separation, some date between separation and trial, or the time of trial. Where the judgment entered at trial is vacated or reversed, a valuation date after trial may be appropriate.

[1] Statutory and Decisional Provisions

California requires that assets and liabilities of the marital community be valued at a date as close as practicable to the date of trial.[48] But a party can give notice to the other of the intention to seek a different valuation date. If the court is satisfied that good cause exists, one or more assets can be valued at a date other than trial. Failure to comply with discovery has been held to be good cause, as in the case of *Marriage of Stallcup*.[49] But the mere passage of time between separation and trial has been held insufficient cause, as in the case of *Marriage of Priddis*.[50] The same is true of the failure to pay support voluntarily during separation, as in the case of *Marriage of Koppleman*.[51]

The rules, however, vary from state to state. Ohio, for example, allows its courts to use any date which is reasonable under the facts of the individual case in order to make an equitable award, as in the case of *Berish v. Berish*.[52] In the Montana case of *Marriage of Popp*,[53] the trial court was reversed for valuing crops in February instead of at harvest time. Even though Montana had no fixed rule for the date of valuation, valuing them in February effectively eliminated a marital asset.

New Jersey uses for a valuation date the same date as of which the marital assets are determined (i.e., the date of filing the complaint). But the court can make adjustments for changes in value by alimony or by its manner of distributing the property.[54]

---

[48] Cal. Civ. Code § 4800(a) (Deering 1989).
[49] 97 Cal. App. 3d 294, 159 Cal. Rptr. 679 (1979).
[50] 132 Cal. App. 3d 349, 183 Cal. Rptr. 37 (1982).
[51] 19 Cal. App. 3d 627, 205 Cal. Rptr. 629 (1984).
[52] 69 Ohio 2d 318, 432 N.E.2d 183 (1982).
[53] 671 P.2d 24 (Mont. 1983).
[54] Borodinsky v. Borodinsky, 162 N.J. Super. 437, 447 (App. Div. 1978).

[2] Distinction From Restrictions on Earnings History

In some states, the law forbids the use of earnings after separation as a basis of valuing a business.[55] Some lawyers and valuation experts are confused by this restriction and think it means that businesses must be valued as of the date of separation. In states where assets are valued as of the trial date, all other factors, such as the age of key persons, the economic climate, interest rates, the intensity of competition, and the availability of essential raw materials, are evaluated as of the trial date. Use of a restricted earnings history does not change the overall valuation date.

¶ 11.11 Management and Control Problems That Affect Valuation While Marital Dissolution Is Pending

The period while a marital dissolution is pending presents some special factors for the valuation expert to consider. Among them are disputes over control of working in the business.

[1] One Spouse Working in the Business

Where one spouse has had the primary responsibility of operating a business and has the knowledge and skill to do it, it makes sense for the court not to disturb his or her management when a divorce is started. Even in states where husbands and wives have equal rights to manage and control marital property, there are often specific provisions that a spouse who has been operating a business has the sole or primary right of management over that business.[56]

Even when the other spouse expresses fear that the business may be mismanaged because of the divorce, courts are reluctant to interfere. Courts are simply not equipped to supervise the management of a business. Absent some serious defalcation which would justify the appointment of a receiver, the managing spouse has few restrictions on his or her management powers while the litigation is pending.

However, if some deliberate inappropriate activity on the part of the managing spouse can be proved, the court might take those facts into consideration at trial. In *Marriage of Barnert*,[57] the court found that a physician had deliberately attempted to depress his income as a result of the divorce. An adjustment was made in the value of the medical practice to take into account the doctor's intentionally lowered income.

---

[55] *See, e.g.*, Marriage of King, 150 Cal. App. 3d at 304, 197 Cal. Rptr. at 716.
[56] *See, e.g.*, Cal. Civ. Code § 5125(d) (Deering 1989).
[57] 85 Cal. App. 3d 413, 1499 Cal. Rptr. 616 (1978).

[2] Both Spouses Working in the Business

When both spouses have operated the same business during the marriage, the start of divorce proceedings may precipitate a fight for control of the business. The outcome of that battle may affect the value of the business.

In *Marriage of Rives*,[58] each spouse operated one of two closely-related businesses. When the divorce was started, the wife asked the court to exclude the husband from the business and allow her to operate it. Eventually, the husband agreed to the order. Then, the wife, through neglect, destroyed the business that the husband had managed until the divorce. After the court awarded it to him at a value that was now absurdly high, the court of appeal reversed.

¶ 11.12 Professional Practices

Despite their personal and often nontransferable nature, professional practices are issues that must be addressed where they exist in the marital estate. They are businesses and must be valued but present a whole different set of problems, which are discussed below.

[1] Professional Practices as Assets

A professional practice owned by one of the spouses is an asset and must be valued and distributed in divorce proceedings, as in the case of *Marriage of Lopez*.[59] If that practice has goodwill, as in the case of *Dugan v. Dugan*,[60] the goodwill is also a marital asset to be dealt with. In most cases (e.g., *Marriage of Smith*[61]), the practice can only be awarded to the spouse with the license to practice. Since the other spouse does not risk receiving the practice in the property distribution, that spouse argues for the maximum possible goodwill value.

[2] Absence of a Market

Although professional practices are sometimes bought and sold, their personal nature makes valuing them on the basis of market transactions difficult. For example, some kinds of accounting practices are considered transferrable and can be valued at market while law practices are often encumbered with ethical and legal restraints against sale.[62]

---

[58] 130 Cal. App. 3d 138, 181 Cal. Rptr. 572 (1982).
[59] 38 Cal. App. 3d at 93, 113 Cal. Rptr. at 58.
[60] 92 N.J. 423, 457 A.2d 1 (1983).
[61] 79 Cal. App. 3d at 725, 145 Cal. Rptr. at 205.
[62] *See, e.g.*, Geffen v. Moss, 53 Cal. App. 3d 215, 125 Cal. Rptr. 687 (1975).

[3] Income Usually Produced by Current Work

The income from professional practices is rarely passive, and it must be generated by the current work of the professional. For this reason, professionals usually consider the placing of a goodwill value on their practice to be unfair. If the practice produces no income other than an average salary directly from current work, there is a strong argument that the goodwill of the practice has no real economic value.[63]

[4] Small Share in a Big Firm

Professionals who are partners or shareholders in big firms have a serious valuation problem. Most big firms have agreements that give the partners no interest in particular assets of the firm and provide for very limited benefits upon withdrawal from the firm. In such a firm, there is no conceivable scenario under which the partner could ever take possession of any of the assets. The only benefit of partnership is the right to a share of the income. But the income is usually based on the professional's current output, which should not be a marital asset after separation.

Many valuation experts find a total value for the entire firm, including intangibles, such as accounts receivable and goodwill. These experts then apply to that total value the percentage interest the divorcing partner has in the firm's income in order to find the value of his interest. This method, which often yields huge artificial values, has several inherent problems. It assumes that there is some basis of value for an asset that is not transferable. It assumes that the interest has some inherent value to the professional who must usually continue to work hard to realize any value from it. It also assumes the liquidation of the firm since that is the only conceivable situation in which any firm assets would be distributed to the partner. In reality, when a law firm dissolves, receivables become almost worthless, and the debts to be paid usually exceed whatever revenue there is from the sale of used equipment and furnishings.

Whether the goodwill to be valued is a share of the firm's goodwill or the personal goodwill of the professional is a subject of debate, as it was in the case of *Marriage of Fenton*.[64]

[5] Valuation of License and Education

The suggestion that the professional education and license of a professional should be treated as marital property to be valued and charged to him or her has received recent acceptance in a few states,

---

[63] *See, e.g.*, Dugan v. Dugan, 92 N.J. at 423, 457 A.2d at 1.
[64] 134 Cal. App. 3d 451, 184 Cal. Rptr. 597 (1982).

such as Michigan and New York.[65] Some states do not deal with the professional education and license as a marital asset if a practice has been established and is supporting the couple. In that situation, the education and license are deemed merged into the value of the practice itself.

In California, attempts to establish such property rights were headed off by legislative action.[66]

¶ 11.13 Distribution of Business Interests Between the Spouses

Sometimes it is clear from the beginning of the divorce process which spouse will be awarded the business. But when the parties do not agree which spouse will get the business, the valuation battle takes on a whole different character.

[1] Corporate Stock

The manner in which the stock of closely held corporations is distributed varies with the situation and with the state. It can be appraised and awarded to one spouse, usually the one who operates the business. It can also be divided in kind: in half, or in some other portion to each spouse. Distribution of one half to each spouse avoids valuation problems and shares future risks, contingencies, and taxes equally.[67] But hostility between the spouses may make it impractical for them to be co-owners. In at least one case—*Marriage of Behrens*[68]—ownership of stock in a corporation operated by her former husband was forced on a wife against her vehement protest. The court was satisfied that her rights as a minority shareholder were adequately protected under corporation law.

Another court in *Borodinsky v. Borodinsky*[69] has held that, before divorcing spouses should be forced to be in business together, the court should consider their former relationship and decide whether they are capable of working together.

[2] Both Spouses in the Same Business

When both spouses work in the management of the same business, the fight for control and eventual ownership of the business can be the central issue in their divorce. If one spouse has most of the knowledge, skill, or contacts necessary to run the business, most courts will maximize the benefit to the marital estate by awarding the business to that

---

[65] *See, e.g.*, Woodworth v. Woodworth, 337 N.W.2d 332 (Mich. App. 1983); O'Brien v. O'Brien, 106 A.D.2d 223, 485 N.Y.S.2d 548 (2d Dep't 1985).
[66] *See* Cal. Civ. Code § 4800.3 (Deering 1989).
[67] *See* Marriage of Brigden, 80 Cal. App. 380, 145 Cal. Rptr. 716 (1978).
[68] 137 Cal. App. 3d 562, 187 Cal. Rptr. 200 (1982).
[69] 162 N.J. Super. at 437, 447.

spouse.[70] Where both are equally qualified, the award of the business to one or the other may be completely arbitrary.

Where one spouse is awarded the joint business and charged with its value in the distribution of marital property, what prevents the other spouse from opening up next door and hustling the old customers? Courts may not have the power to impose a covenant not to compete on the spouse who is not awarded the business because it is a restriction on that spouse's right to earn a living. Yet, the potential for an unfair award is real.[71]

---

[70] Marriage of Smith, 79 Cal. App. 3d at 725, 145 Cal. Rptr. at 205.
[71] *See, e.g.*, Marriage of Shelton, 118 Cal. App. 3d 811, 173 Cal. Rptr. 629 (1981).

12

VALUATION OF START-UPS, INITIAL PUBLIC OFFERINGS, AND PRIVATE PLACEMENTS

ROGER C. DAVISSON*

		Page
¶ 12.1	Start-ups, IPOs, and Private Placements: General Similarities	12-2
	[1] Common Element of Financing	12-2
	[2] Driving Force of the ROI	12-3
	[3] Key Differences	12-3
	[4] Comparables	12-3
	[5] ROI Analysis	12-4
	[a] Dilution	12-5
	[b] Premoney vs. Postmoney Valuations	12-6
¶ 12.2	Valuing Start-Ups	12-6
	[1] Key Determinants	12-6
	[a] Required ROI	12-6
	[b] Valuing What Exists	12-7
	[c] Expected Upside	12-7
	[d] Additional Capital Requirements	12-8
	[e] Risks	12-8
	[2] Rules of Thumb	12-8
¶ 12.3	Valuing IPOs	12-9
	[1] Valuation Theory	12-10
	[a] Mathematical Basis	12-10
	[b] Application to IPOs	12-11
	[2] Valuation in Practice	12-12
	[a] Use of Comparables	12-12
	[b] Projections	12-13
	[c] Finding Comparables	12-16
	[d] Practical Example	12-16
	[e] Limitations of Price/Earnings Multiples	12-25
	[f] After-Market Considerations	12-25

* ROGER C. DAVISSON is a general partner at Brentwood Associates, a venture capital investment firm headquartered in Los Angeles, California. The author has also served as a director of several corporations and as chairman of the Business School Trust at the Stanford Graduate School of Business.

¶ 12.4	**Valuing Private Placements**	12-25
	[1] Key Considerations	12-26
	[a] Required ROI	12-26
	[b] Expenditures to Date	12-26
	[c] Expected Upside	12-27
	[d] Need for Additional Capital	12-27
	[e] Remaining Risk	12-27
	[2] Rules of Thumb	12-28
	[a] Performance vs. Promise	12-29
	[3] Calculation Case Study	12-29
¶ 12.5	**Summary**	12-31

The focus of this chapter is the valuation of enterprises with limited operating histories. A *start-up* may be at the stage of an idea for a new business while an *initial public offering (IPO)* generally occurs when a firm has achieved revenues and (usually) earnings sufficient to indicate at least some stability and staying power. A *private placement*, as the term is used here, refers to a company somewhere in between the start-up and IPO stages.

Changing financial market conditions may turn one year's IPO candidate into a private placement; conversely, in extraordinarily bullish public market environments, even start-ups have been done as IPOs. In general, however, a new business goes through three financing stages in the start-up, private placement, IPO sequence and typically increases in valuation at each stage.

Of course, not all businesses are founded with the objective of becoming large publicly owned companies. This chapter concentrates on those that do—and are, therefore, likely to be financed by professional and generally institutional investors.

¶ 12.1 Start-ups, IPOs, and Private Placements: General Similarities

The valuation expert begins the appraisal of start-ups, IPOs, and private placements by considering their similarities. Those similarities are discussed in the following discussion.

[1] Common Element of Financing

Regardless of which stage applies to an enterprise, the valuation task is virtually always associated with a financing event—the raising of new equity capital to fund the firm's next stage of growth. This capital is typically provided by growth-oriented investors seeking capital appreciation.

Different types of investors typically are active in the three different types of investing. Start-ups are generally financed by venture capitalists (i.e., professionally managed funds whose full-time activity is the investment of relatively large pools of capital in a portfolio of primarily early stage enterprises) and by speculative (i.e., high-risk-accepting) private investors.

IPOs are, by definition, sold to "the public," which encompasses both institutions and individuals. Unlike start-up and private placement financings, the buyer of an IPO issue has no say in the valuation; he or she must "take it or leave it" based upon the analysis of the attractiveness of the valuation that the company and its investment banker have determined to be appropriate.

Private placements, which technically include start-ups, involve investments by a variety of institutions, ranging from venture capitalists to pension and trust funds, insurance companies, and other "mezzanine" investors—so called because they invest in situations between the "ground floor" start-up and the higher-priced, generally lower-risk IPO.

[2] Driving Force of the ROI

Although each class of investor has a different risk profile, all have essentially one overriding criterion in determining what investments to make—and at what price to make them: return on investment (ROI). In essence, *ROI* refers to the stream of income (whether dividends or interest) that the investor will receive as long as the investment is held plus the value received upon selling the security. (For high-growth companies, dividends are generally small or nonexistent, so the ending value is key.) Of course, there is uncertainty associated with any investment, and early-stage companies are generally riskier than more established ones, so the expected ROI must be evaluated in the context of the risk involved.

[3] Key Differences

The three classes of investment appeal to different types of investors because they offer different ROI and risk profiles. Start-ups present the least information to the prospective investor because they have no operating history; they have the most "blue sky" prospects—both in terms of risk and upside potential. IPOs generally offer some successful operating history and credibility. Private placements span the spectrum in between, from just post-start-up to "prepublic" (i.e., the last financing before an IPO, to the degree that event is predictable).

[4] Comparables

Although much analysis is applied to the valuation of early-stage companies, the process is far from scientific. Wide swings in the valuations of publicly held companies are a well-known phenomenon; these swings are generally only partially explicable by conventional means of value analysis. Heavily influenced by public stock and bond markets, private securities' valuations depend strongly upon prevailing "investor psychology." Hence, there is a need to know how similar companies in the same or similar industries are being valued when analyzing the value of an early-stage enterprise. These so-called comparables provide a measure of current market psychology, which fluctuates with the health and growth prospects of the particular industry involved, as well as the overall health of the economy and business conditions in general.

Comparables are used heavily in the valuation of IPOs partly because data are most readily available for this class of early-stage financing. Public companies' Securities and Exchange Commission (SEC) filings, including the registration statements done in connection with IPOs, are fruitful sources of data on the performance and prospects of similar or related businesses. The public market valuations of these companies are readily available on a daily basis, providing a dynamic measure of the buyers' and sellers' collective judgments of the value of the companies' securities.

[5] ROI Analysis

As used by equity investors, an ROI is a compound rate of growth. In the simplest case of an investment made at time zero and sold after n years, the ROI of the investment is just the annual rate of growth that yields the sales price. The general mathematical formulation is:

$$\text{ROI} = (\text{Sales Price/Investment})^{1/n} - 1$$

where

$n =$ the number of years the investment is held

For example, to compute the ROI (before taxes) of a stock investment at $10 per share held for four years and sold for $40 per share, the formula would work like this:

$$\begin{aligned}
\text{ROI} &= (\text{Sales Price/Investment})^{1/n} - 1 \\
&= (40/10)^{1/4} - 1 \\
&= 4^{1/4} - 1 \\
&= 1.41 - 1 \\
&= 0.41 \\
&= 41\%
\end{aligned}$$

Table 12-1 gives the ROI's implied by various multiples of the original investment realized upon sale (40/10, or 4 times, in the previous example) as a function of the number of years the investment is held.

TABLE 12-1

ROIs IMPLIED BY VARIOUS MULTIPLES OF ORIGINAL INVESTMENT

Years Held	\multicolumn{9}{c}{Multiple of Cost}								
	1x	1.5x	2x	3x	5x	7x	10x	15x	20x
1	0%	50%	100%	200%	400%	500%	900%	1400%	1900%
2	-0-	22	41	73	124	165	216	287	347
3	-0-	14	26	44	71	91	115	147	171
4	-0-	11	19	32	50	63	78	97	111
5	-0-	8	15	25	38	48	58	72	82
6	-0-	7	12	20	31	38	47	57	65
8	-0-	5	9	15	22	28	33	40	45
10	-0-	4	7	12	17	21	26	31	35

[a] Dilution

The term *dilution* refers to the reduction in percentage ownership that occurs when a company issues additional stock in a financing, acquisition, or other transaction. Investors in start-ups and IPOs expect future dilution in most cases because most early-stage companies raise equity in "rounds," giving up appropriate amounts of equity in each. This reduces the amount at risk in the very early stages of the business and allows the firm to raise capital at higher prices if progress is made. Hence, early-round investors must expect their investment to be diluted and compute their ROI estimates accordingly.

Example 1. An investor who purchases 10% of the equity of a start-up company for $100,000 expects that the company will be worth $5 million in five years and that it will have to sell an additional 25% ownership share to finance itself over that period. The investor would then own 75% (100% − the 25% sold to later investors) of 10%, or 7.5%, of an entity worth $5 million; this partial ownership would be worth $375,000, or 3.75 times the investment. Since $3.75^{1/5} - 1 = 0.30$, the expected ROI is 30%.

If the potential dilution was not taken into account, the investor would mistakenly compute the ownership value as 10% of $5 million, or $500,000, a 5 multiple; the apparent ROI would then be $5^{1/5} - 1 = 0.38$, or 38%. On the other hand, if the company fares less well than it expects and is forced to sell 50% of its equity for capital, the initial investor's return would be reduced to 50% × 10% × $5 million, or $250,000, and the ROI would only be

$2.5^{1/5} - 1 = 0.20$, or 20%. Clearly dilution can affect ROI dramatically.

[b] Premoney vs. Postmoney Valuations

Since early-stage valuations nearly always involve providing capital to the company as opposed to purchasing equity from selling shareholders, the distinction between "premoney" and "postmoney" valuations becomes relevant. A *premoney valuation* refers to the value placed upon the enterprise before the addition of the capital provided by the financing while a *postmoney valuation* is the value after the capital is added. The postmoney valuation, then, is simply the premoney valuation plus the amount of new capital added to the equity of the firm. When doing ROI calculations, it is the postmoney valuation that must be used as the starting valuation because it is that base from which the firm's value must grow to provide a return to the investor.

¶ 12.2 Valuing Start-ups

There are several key rules of thumb the valuation expert can use to value start-ups, as discussed next.

[1] Key Determinants

Fundamentally, the value of an enterprise at the point of start-up is determined by these factors:

- The ROI that the investor seeks;
- The value of what exists already;
- The expected upside;
- The anticipated requirement for additional capital; and
- The risks.

The first item (the desired ROI) is closely correlated with the last item (the risks inherent in the start-up). The more risk that an investor must undertake, the higher the reward he or she will seek. Hence, if the expected upside is not in proportion to the risks involved, the enterprise will be financeable only if an investor motivated by considerations beyond the ROI can be found. A good example would be a family member financing a relative's start-up; the desire to help a relative may be more important than achieving an appropriate ROI (i.e., an ROI that would be achievable in a comparable investment without the family tie).

[a] Required ROI

As Table 12.1 illustrates, ROIs above 30% quickly lead to significant multiples of the original investment. In most cases, investors in start-up situations think in terms of a multiple of their investment when they analyze upside because it is generally accepted that start-ups are the riskiest kind of companies in which to invest and therefore should offer ROI rewards of 40% to 50% or more. More specifically, a venture capital investor will usually not consider a start-up that does not offer a believable opportunity to achieve 10 times to 20 times the initial investment in a five-to-seven-year period. This translates to a *40% to 82% ROI range* before taking into account the effects of dilution. The lower end of this range would be considered marginal unless there were a real chance to significantly exceed the upper end.

[b] Valuing What Exists

Although the term "start-up" connotes a firm with no history, there must be some elements with value in place for the company to be financeable. The entrepreneur or his or her family and friends may have invested capital in a so-called seed phase to develop a business plan. Some professional funds also currently make such seed investments.

Of greater importance than this seed capital are the unique contributions that the start-up managerial and technical teams bring. These may include proprietary technology in the form of inventions, patents, prototypes, special technical skills, and know-how. Sometimes, a new business concept or a franchise that precludes competition may be a key element of value. The key aspect is proprietariness—a protectable advantage over competition that will last at least long enough to allow the new firm to become established.

The skill and the experience of management are other key parts of the value of what exists in a start-up. A management team that has done it before can command significant value in the capital-raising process because most investors recognize the importance of experience and a proven track record. Even an inexperienced management team, if it has a backable idea and technological base, can expect to receive some value for its entrepreneurial contribution in conceiving a start-up.

[c] Expected Upside

To compute an expected ROI, the prospective investor needs to estimate the expected future value of the contemplated investment. The management of the start-up usually provides financial projections and justifies them on the basis of these factors:

- The significance of the proprietary edge the firm is expected to enjoy;
- The size of the market the firm will address; and
- The quality of the management team, which suggests how well it will execute its strategy.

Each prospective investor must decide how achievable the firm's projections are and must either accept those provided or adjust them to a level believed appropriate. Armed with projections that are comfortable, the investor must then estimate an expected future value for the firm based on price-earnings or other valuation techniques.[1] The potential attractiveness of the firm as an acquisition by a larger company is also an important element in estimating upside.

[d] Additional Capital Requirements

The need for additional capital significantly affects the ROI of an investment. Hence, the prospective investor must estimate this need and factor it into the ROI calculation.

[e] Risks

Investors participate in risky ventures because they hope to achieve high ROIs. Among the key risks usually inherent in start-up enterprises are:

- Unanticipated capital requirement;
- Time delays in developing, manufacturing, or selling the firm's product or service due to unanticipated difficulties; and
- Management execution failures.

Even if all the challenges have been accurately anticipated, the management team invariably has some weaknesses that affect execution of the strategy. Delays and cost increases may occur in (1) product development, (2) marketing (generating and closing prospects), and (3) manufacturing.

[2] Rules of Thumb

The intangibility and subjective nature of the value determinants just cited make the use of broad guidelines and rules of thumb commonplace in valuing start-ups. The ROI—or, rather, multiple of investment—ranges mentioned previously are one of these, but they still require an estimate of future value to derive a financing value.

---

[1] See ¶ 12.3 on IPO valuation.

In practice, most start-up valuations of venture-capital-backed companies fall in the $1 million to $5 million premoney valuation range. An alternative way of expressing this is that entrepreneurs generally retain 20% to 50% of a start-up after venture capitalists have invested from $1 million to $5 million. Future dilution will reduce the entrepreneurs' and the original investors' ownership, especially in capital-intensive companies. Generally, early-stage investors provide only enough capital to prove the business concept, which typically includes developing the product and perhaps testing it in a friendly user's environment. Capital to develop manufacturing and marketing capabilities is usually raised in later rounds.

There are start-up situations where these valuation ranges may not apply as follows:

- Some situations are extraordinarily capital intensive. If very large amounts of capital equipment are required by an enterprise and the equipment cannot be financed other than with equity, the start-up valuation must be lower to account for the dilution that the capital equipment will cause.
- Modest enterprises oriented toward penetrating small market niches or toward developing personal service or boutique retail businesses often command much lower premoney valuations.
- Occasionally, a widely known and respected business executive, with a proven track record at developing successful new business(es), commands a significantly higher valuation than most start-ups. (Examples of $10 million premoney valuations are not unheard of.) The combination of reduced risk and possibly higher expected upside that a proven entrepreneur brings to a start-up are clearly of great value.

¶ 12.3 Valuing IPOs

When a company is judged ready to "go public," a great deal is known about it that was only guessed at when it was at the start-up phase. Hence, substantial analysis can be applied to valuing the IPO.

The theoretical methods applicable to securities valuation[2] suggest that, if four variables are known, mathematical techniques can be used to derive the underlying security's value (assumed herein to be a common stock). The four variables are:

1. The current earnings per share;
2. The future earnings per share (or the growth rate(s) in earnings per share) over the next twenty years or so;

---

[2] See ch. 10 on valuation of common equity securities.

3. The current and future dividend payouts (how much of the earnings will be paid in the form of dividends); and
4. The potential investors' "discount rate" (the return, or ROI, that investors require to accept the risk inherent in investing in the company in question).

Of course, all of these are never known, although they can be estimated or forecast. The following discussion shows how these variables form the theoretical underpinning of securities' valuations in the IPO context.

[1] Valuation Theory

While a detailed discussion of the theoretical methods of valuing a financial asset is beyond the scope of this chapter, a brief summary of the fundamental principles is included.

[a] Mathematical Basis

The theoretical value of a financial asset is the *discounted present value of the expected future cash flow(s)* that the asset will provide to its owner; assuming (as is in this discussion) the asset is an equity security (generally common or preferred stock), the cash flows will come from dividends and the ultimate sale or liquidation of the security. Both are uncertain (i.e., subject to the risk of variability in amount and timing).

The *discount rate* reflects the risk of achieving the dividends and ultimate sales price: The higher the risk is perceived to be, the higher the discount rate the prospective investor wants to apply to the cash flows. The formula for the present value of a series of cash flows is as follows.

$$P_o = \sum_{t=1}^{n} \frac{D_t}{(1+d)^t} + \frac{P_n}{(1+d)^n}$$

where

P_o = present value of security
n = number of years security will be held
D_t = dividend in year t
d = discount rate
P_n = value received when security is liquidated in year n

Note that a security that pays an annual dividend of 10% of its purchase price and is eventually sold for exactly its purchase price has the same present value as a security with no dividend that is sold for a price equal to its purchase price times $(1.10)^n$ where n is the number of years the security is held. In other words, the present value formula is indifferent between an annually paid return and a compounded growth that pays off only when the security is sold. This is the essential reason why investors participate in early-stage corporate financings: They seek long-term gains, which may have favorable tax treatment, depending upon current tax policy, instead of annual income. Nevertheless, most finance theorists agree that the value of stock without dividends is predicated on the ultimate expectation of future dividends. So-called growth companies that pay no dividends are considered attractive because the investor believes their growth allows them to reinvest capital in their own business and make at least as high a rate of return as the investor could if the earnings were received in the form of dividends.

[b] Application to IPOs

Given the current earnings per share, future earnings per share, dividend payouts, and discount rates (three of which can only be estimated), the present value formula just presented allows the determination of the price/earnings ratio that a security should enjoy. In the case of an IPO, this ratio gives the theoretical price at which the offering should occur.

Example 2. Assume that Acme Company has earnings of $1 million and 1 million shares of stock outstanding; its earnings per share are, therefore, $1. Assume further that Investors believe earnings can grown at 10% per year and that it will pay out 50% of its earnings in the form of dividends. The prospective investor believes Acme to be fairly risky and applies a 15% discount rate to the cash flow stream. Assuming it is held indefinitely (i.e., not sold), the theoretical P_o of Acme's stock is computed as follows:

$$P_o = \sum_{t=1}^{\infty} \frac{(0.5)(1.10)^t}{1.15^t}$$

Mathematically, this equation can be simplified as follows:

$$P_o = (0.5)\left[\frac{(1.10/1.15)}{(1-(1.10/1.15))}\right]$$
$$= (0.5)\frac{(0.9565)}{0.0435}$$
$$= 11$$
$$= \$11 \text{ per share}$$

The investor should be willing to pay this amount, which implies a price/earnings ratio of 11.

Note that if the investor (or investment bank with which the company may be negotiating its IPO value) argues that the risk is higher—say, a 20% discount rate—the previous computation yields a value of only $5.50, so that price/earnings ratio is halved to 5.5. On the other hand, a lower discount—say, 12.5%—yields a present value of $22, or a price/earnings ratio of 22. As the discount rate (the required return, which is proportional to perceived risk) drops to close to the expected growth rate, the implied price/earnings ratio grows very rapidly.

What happens with a stock with no dividends, as is the case with most IPOs? The value is predicated upon the expectation of *future* dividends; the investors implicitly assume that the firm will compensate for the lack of early payout by eventually paying substantial dividends from the enhanced earnings stream, which its high growth and early retention of earnings will develop.

Theoretical price/earnings ratios for various combinations of growth rates, dividend payouts, and discount risk rates can be analytically calculated. Table 12-2 illustrates the results of such calculations for a variety of classes of business. Company types in the lower half of the table, especially types P through U, are high-growth, low-dividend cases, which could apply to many IPO situations.

[2] Valuation in Practice

The theoretical price/earnings table is useful as an indicator of appropriate price/earnings ratios for a potential IPO, but it cannot give a certain answer because no one can know the right growth, payout, and discount rates to apply. In practice, these are never known with certainty and are often subject to much guesswork.

Probably the most useful way of coping with these uncertainties is the careful analysis of both the fundamental performance and market price behavior of comparable companies.

[a] Use of Comparables

The experience of other companies in a firm's industry suggests what kind of earnings growth can be achieved in that industry, and the price/earnings ratios of similar companies suggest what potential investors' discount rates and expectations are. Price/earnings ratios rise and fall with overall stock market conditions and, to a lesser extent, with changes in an industry's general health and each specific company's performance. Hence, the price/earnings ratios of comparable firms are vital parameters in IPO valuation analysis.

Other key ratios are also considered, especially when the company going public has little or no earnings record upon which to base a price/earnings multiple. The other ratios most commonly analyzed are (1) the price/sales ratio and (2) the price/book value ratio. Generally, these data are tabulated and compared over various time periods, including the current year, the following year (projected), the last three years (usually averaged), and the last five years (usually averaged).

Many other operating and financial data are scrutinized and compared to those of similar firms to validate comparability of valuations or suggest appropriate adjustments. The following are the most often used financial data:

- Revenue history and average compound annual growth rate;
- Pretax and after-tax net income and average compound annual growth rates;
- Pretax and after-tax net profit margins (as percentages of sales);
- Return on average common equity;
- Return on average total assets;
- "Cash flow"—funds from operations and average compound annual growth rate;
- Capital expenditures;
- Research and development budget and the proportion externally financed; and
- Capitalization including short-term debt, long-term debt, and debt/equity ratio.

The IPO will usually change the capitalization of the company dramatically, and the so-called pro-forma, or post-IPO, capital structure is critical. It is a key determinant of the stability and financial staying power of the firm, and the elimination of debt that the IPO may make possible can materially change the income statement of the firm.

[b] Projections

The SEC does not allow the presentation of financial projections in the prospectuses of companies making public offerings of their securities. Most underwriters are wary of implying projections because of potential liability to disappointed investors if the projections are not achieved. However, analysts of public securities are paid to develop projections, and they will do so basing their estimates on the firm's prior results and the information on markets, customers, and prospects presented in the company's registration statement and during its "road

[Text continues on p. 12-16.]

TABLE 12-2
THEORETICAL PRICE/EARNINGS RATIOS AS A FUNCTION OF EARNINGS GROWTH, DIVIDEND PAYOUTS, AND DISCOUNT RATES

Company Type	Annual Growth and Dividend Payout[a]	Time Segments - Years				Discount Rate						
		1-5	6-10	11-20	20+	0.06	0.08	0.09	0.10	0.11	0.12	0.13	0.15
A	g	-0-	-0-	-0-	-0-	16.67	12.50	11.11	10.00	9.09	8.33	7.69	6.67
	$1-b$	1.00	1.00	1.00	1.00								
B	g	0.03	0.03	0.03	0.03	20.60	12.36	10.30	8.83	7.72	6.87	6.18	5.15
	$1-b$	0.60	0.60	0.60	0.60								
C	g	0.04	0.04	0.04	0.04	31.20	15.60	12.48	10.40	8.91	7.80	6.93	5.67
	$1-b$	0.60	0.60	0.60	0.60								
D	g	0.05	0.05	0.05	0.05	52.50	17.50	13.12	10.50	5.75	7.50	6.56	5.25
	$1-b$	0.50	0.50	0.50	0.50								
E	g	0.06	0.06	0.06	0.06	∞	26.50	17.67	13.25	10.60	8.83	7.57	5.89
	$1-b$	0.50	0.50	0.50	0.50								
F	g	0.06	0.06	0.06	0.06	∞	21.20	14.13	10.60	8.48	7.07	6.06	4.71
	$1-b$	0.40	0.40	0.40	0.40								
G	g	0.06	0.06	0.06	0.04	∞	17.35	13.19	10.50	8.65	7.31	6.30	4.90
	$1-b$	0.06	0.06	0.06	0.04								
H	g	0.50	0.50	0.50	0.60	41.20	19.00	14.70	11.89	9.93	8.49	7.39	5.85
	$1-b$	0.07	0.06	0.05	0.04								
I	g	0.50	0.50	0.50	0.60	39.91	18.66	14.52	11.81	9.90	8.50	7.43	5.91
	$1-b$	0.08	0.07	0.05	0.04								
J	g	0.50	0.50	0.50	0.60	43.59	20.27	15.73	12.76	10.68	9.15	7.98	6.32
	$1-b$	0.10	0.08	0.06	0.04								
K	g	0.40	0.45	0.50	0.60	52.94	23.72	18.08	14.42	11.88	10.02	8.61	6.64
	$1-b$	0.12	0.10	0.07	0.04								
L	g	0.35	0.40	0.45	0.60	66.85	28.80	21.57	16.91	13.70	11.39	9.65	7.26
	$1-b$	0.15	0.12	0.08	0.04								
M	g	0.30	0.40	0.50	0.60	90.92	38.70	28.77	22.37	17.97	14.79	12.42	9.15
	$1-b$	0.15	0.15	0.10	0.04								
N	g	0.20	0.20	0.40	0.60	116.44	46.29	33.27	25.04	19.47	15.53	12.64	8.80
	$1-b$	0.20	0.20	0.40	0.60								

TABLE 12-2
THEORETICAL PRICE/EARNINGS RATIOS AS A FUNCTION OF EARNINGS GROWTH, DIVIDEND PAYOUTS, AND DISCOUNT RATES *(continued)*

Company Type	Annual Growth and Dividend Payout[a]	Time Segments - Years				Discount Rate						
		1-5	6-10	11-20	20+	0.06	0.08	0.09	0.10	0.11	0.12	0.13	0.15
O	g	0.15	0.15	0.12	0.10	∞	∞	∞	∞	95.37	44.51	27.84	14.91
	1-b	0.30	0.30	0.40	0.60								
P	g	0.20	0.15	0.10	0.04	126.29	43.45	28.91	20.07	14.35	10.50	7.81	4.50
	1-b	-0-	-0-	-0-	0.60								
Q	g	0.20	0.15	0.10	0.04	139.01	53.20	37.48	27.63	21.03	16.41	13.06	8.67
	1-b	-0-	0.20	0.30	0.60								
R	g	0.25	0.15	0.10	0.04	170.49	65.25	45.97	33.88	25.79	20.13	16.02	10.63
	1-b	-0-	0.20	0.30	0.60								
S	g	0.30	0.20	0.30	0.04	252.21	94.43	65.68	47.73	35.79	27.47	21.48	13.71
	1-b	-0-	-0-	0.10	0.60								
T	g	0.40	0.20	0.30	0.04	365.32	136.78	95.13	69.14	51.84	39.79	31.12	19.87
	1-b	-0-	-0-	0.30	0.60								
U	g	0.50	0.30	0.15	0.04	1185.64	438.02	302.55	218.32	162.50	123.82	96.11	60.44
	1-b	-0-	-0-	0.30	0.60								

[a] g is the annual growth rate in earnings; 1 - b is the payout ratio, dividends/earnings.

Source: Based J.G. McDonald, *The Solvay Group* (1976), a Standord University Graduate School of Business case that was provided by Brentwood Associates (1986).

[*Text continued from p. 12-13.*]
show" tour when it makes presentations to prospective investors. Thus, although IPOs lack the company-prepared projections that start-up and private placement financings routinely provide, there usually are informal projections available to interested investors.

As the financial asset pricing theory previously outlined indicates, the price/earnings ratio that a company will enjoy (or regret) is heavily dependent upon the earnings growth rate that the investment community thinks it will achieve. Therefore, the projected earnings of the firm are key in pricing its IPO. Moreover, if the company is going public prior to achieving significant (or any) earnings, projections are necessary if any kind of price/earnings analysis is to be done. In most cases of an IPO prior to profitability, however, more emphasis will be placed upon price/sales ratios or on more intangible indicators of potential future value (e.g., status and potential market impact of technology).

[c] Finding Comparables

What makes a company "comparable"? Similar markets, products, technologies, growth curves, and financial results, especially key operating ratios, are the primary criteria. Sometimes, it is difficult to find closely comparable firms; this may suggest valuable uniqueness in the subject firm's product/market niche. Some usefully comparable firms can invariably be found, sometimes by invoking analogies between unrelated industries with similar characteristics.

[d] Practical Example

Once appropriate comparable publicly held firms have been identified (along with their key dissimilarities), detailed "spreadsheets" comparing the IPO company with the comparables are prepared, usually by the investment banker(s) involved (or seeking to be involved) in taking the company public. Tables 12-3 through 12-7 illustrate the kinds of comparisons generally made; they are taken from documents actually prepared by prospective underwriters of a company in the educational supply industry, A-1 Educational Supply Corporation (a fictitious name). As is often the case, no directly comparable firm existed; therefore, a number of firms in related businesses (including textbook publishing, day-care services, and test-scoring systems) were used.

Table 12-3 provides basic stock market information along with summaries of earnings per share, price/earnings multiples, book values, and dividend rates, along with brief descriptions of each firm (to help qualify it as a comparable, and allow readers to form their own judgment about just how comparable it is).

[*Text continues on p. 12-22.*]

TABLE 12-3
A-1 EDUCATIONAL SUPPLY CORPORATION
CURRENT MARKET DATA OF SELECTED EDUCATIONAL SUPPLY/SERVICE COMPANIES

	Addison-Wesley Publishing Company, Inc.	Grolier, Inc.	Kinder-Care Learning Centers, Inc.	Macmillan, Inc.
Current price (7/9/X6)	$40.50	$9.125	$14.375	$47.125
52-week price range	$31.25-$42.00	$4.625-$11.75	$12.00-$17.25	$27.00-$53.375
Shares outstanding (000)	2,563.9	12,746.8	33,545.5	22,292.8
Market value (000)	$103,838.0	$116,314.6	$482,216.6	$1,050,548.2
Earnings per share				
Current[a]	$1.99	$0.48	$0.88	$2.00
Projected[b]				
19X6	$2.77	$0.79	$0.76	$2.25
19X7	$3.15	$0.73	$0.96	$2.65
Price/earnings multiples				
Current	20.4x	19.0x	16.3x	23.6x
Projected				
19X6	14.6x	11.6x	18.9x	20.9x
19X7	12.9x	12.5x	15.0x	17.8x
Book value per share:	$19.69	$4.57	$6.58	$10.95
price/book	2.1	2.0	2.2	4.3
Current indicated annual dividend	$0.80	-0-	$0.06	$0.60
Current dividend yield	2.0%	-0-	0.4%	1.3%
Symbol	ADSHB	GLR	KNDR	MLL
Exchange traded on	OTC	NY	OTC	NY
Description of company	Publisher of educational materials for the elementary through college markets; also publishes training material for business and government, reference books, and software for the professional market and books for the retail trade	World's largest publisher of encyclopedias and reference sets; publisher and distributor of children's books, educational materials, and reference and educational software	Nation's largest professional operator of day-care centers; day care services provided for children between the ages of 2-6 years through over 1,000 centers	Publisher of textbooks for the elementary, secondary, college, and professional markets; also publishes home learning and reference materials, educational software, and books for the retail trade; operates technical/vocational schools

[a]Based on fully diluted EPS from continuing operations (excluding nonrecurring charges) as of 3/31/X6, except for Kinder-Care which is as of 3/14/X6
[b]Based on each company's fiscal year (Institutional Brokers Estimating Service (IBES) (1986))

Source: Brentwood Associates (1986)

¶ 12.3[2][d]   FINANCIAL VALUATION   12-18

TABLE 12-4
A-1 EDUCATIONAL SUPPLY CORPORATION SUMMARY COMPARATIVE OPERATING DATA OF SELECTED EDUCATIONAL SUPPLY/SERVICE COMPANIES
($ Millions Except Per-Share Amounts)

	Addison-Wesley Publishing Company, Inc.	Grolier, Inc.	Kinder-Care Learning Centers, Inc.	Macmillan, Inc.
Fiscal year ended	11/30/X5	12/31/X5	8/30/X5	12/31/X5
Latest 12 months ended	3/31/X6	3/31/X6	3/14/X6	3/31/X6
Net sales				
Latest 12 months	$141.8	$308.4	$215.7	$709.5
19X5	139.4	296.1	192.2	676.9
19X4	123.8	286.0	156.3	529.7
19X3	114.3	286.2	128.1	430.5
19X2	102.2	333.2	116.5	384.3
19X1	91.5	344.8	87.0	404.5
Compound growth	11.1%	(3.7%)	21.9%	13.7%
Operating income and margins				
Latest 12 months	$12.2 8.6%	$40.7 13.2	$28.2 13.1%	$87.1 12.3%
19X5	14.8 10.6	40.7 13.8	24.1 12.5	88.8 13.1
19X4	14.5 11.7	34.2 12.0	19.6 12.5	63.7 12.0
19X3	14.5 12.7	32.2 11.3	15.2 11.9	44.5 10.3
19X2	12.9 12.6	36.6 11.0	14.2 12.2	35.6 9.3
19X1	10.7 11.7	34.3 10.0	10.7 12.3	33.5 8.3
Compound growth	8.4%	4.4%	22.5%	27.6%
Pretax income and margins				
Latest 12 months	$9.2 6.5%	$13.5 4.4%	$26.1 12.1%	$82.3 11.6%
19X5	11.7 8.4	13.2 4.5	21.8 11.3	82.6 12.2
19X4	10.6 8.6	9.6 3.4	18.7 12.0	60.4 11.4
19X3	11.5 10.1	15.5 5.4	13.4 10.5	46.4 10.8
19X2	9.6 9.4	7.9 2.4	8.3 7.1	41.4 10.8
19X1	8.3 9.1	17.6 5.1	5.4 6.2	30.1 7.4
Compound growth	9.0	(6.9%)	41.7%	28.7%
Net income and margins				
Latest 12 months	$5.1 3.6%	$6.1 2.0%	$29.5 13.7%	$44.7 6.3%
19X5	6.7 4.8	5.9 2.0	23.7 12.3	44.7 6.6
19X4	5.9 4.8	4.8 1.7	17.1 10.9	33.1 6.2
19X3	5.6 4.9	11.5 4.0	11.2 8.7	25.1 5.8
19X2	4.6 4.5	4.4 1.3	6.7 5.8	21.8 5.7

12-19 START-UPS, IPOs, PRIVATE PLACEMENTS ¶ 12.3[2][d]

TABLE 12-4
A-1 EDUCATIONAL SUPPLY CORPORATION SUMMARY COMPARATIVE OPERATING DATA OF SELECTED EDUCATIONAL SUPPLY/SERVICE COMPANIES *(continued)*
($ Millions Except Per-Share Amounts)

	Addison-Wesley Publishing Company, Inc.		Grolier, Inc.		Kinder-Care Learning Centers, Inc.		Macmillan, Inc.	
19X1	3.6	3.9	14.3	4.1	4.3	4.9	14.2	3.5
Compound growth	16.8%		(19.9%)		53.2%		33.2%	
Earnings per share								
Latest 12 months	$1.99		$0.48		$0.88		$2.00	
19X5	2.63		0.45		0.81		2.01	
19X4	2.37		0.36		0.64		1.55	
19X3	2.25		1.02		0.46		1.19	
19X2	1.84		0.37		0.33		0.93	
19X1	1.46		1.31		0.22		0.52	
Compound growth	15.9%		(23.4%)		38.5%		40.2%	
Return on average common equity; return on average total assets								
Latest 12 months	10.3%	5.2%	11.7%	2.1%	17.6%	5.4%	19.5%	9.0%
19X5	12.2	16.4	11.3	2.1	15.7	5.2	21.3	8.8
19X4	11.8	6.0	10.5	2.0	18.5	4.9	20.0	8.3
19X3	12.4	6.0	N.M.	4.9	18.0	4.9	16.3	7.6
19X2	11.1	5.6	N.M.	1.7	18.5	5.0	12.8	7.0
19X1	9.2	4.9	N.M.	5.0	16.1	4.2	7.3	3.7
Average	11.2%	5.7%	11.2%	3.0%	17.4%	4.9%	16.2%	7.4%
Funds from operations; capital expenditures								
Latest 12 months	$19.3	$1.9	$19.2	$2.6	$36.7	$101.7	$84.3	$15.4
19X5	20.5	2.1	18.4	2.5	28.0	121.7	80.3	13.1
19X4	22.7	1.3	13.5	9.5	22.7	77.0	58.0	18.9
19X3	15.8	0.6	17.4	2.2	16.9	30.7	39.6	16.4
19X2	14.8	2.1	8.3	1.7	12.1	9.4	29.8	6.0
19X1	11.7	0.9	14.9	1.9	9.3	6.5	28.5	5.1
Compound growth	15.1%	23.6%	5.4%	7.1%	31.7%	108.0%	29.6%	26.6%

Source: Brentwood Associates (1986)

TABLE 12-5
HISTORICAL MARKET DATA OF SELECTED EDUCATIONAL SUPPLY/SERVICE COMPANIES

	Addison-Wesley Publishing Company, Inc.			Grolier, Inc.			Kinder-Care Learning Centers, Inc.			Macmillan, Inc.		
Price per share												
19X6	$33.500	—	$42.000	$6.250	—	$11.750	$12.000	—	$17.250	$34.4000	—	$53.375
19X5	28.000	—	36.500	3.000	—	6.750	9.875	—	16.000	21.625	—	38.125
19X4	21.250	—	32.750	2.750	—	5.000	7.375	—	12.250	12.750	—	23.375
19X3	16.000	—	29.000	2.375	—	8.375	4.125	—	13.500	11.250	—	18.875
19X2	8.750	—	16.000	1.625	—	3.000	3.125	—	4.625	5.625	—	11.625
19X1	10.125	—	14.625	1.250	—	3.125	3.875	—	5.250	5.750	—	8.500
Earnings per share; price/earnings range												
Latest 12 months	$ 1.99	16.8x	— 21.1x	$ 0.48	13.0x	— 24.5x	$ 0.88	13.6x	— 19.6x	$ 2.00	17.0x	— 26.7x
19X5	2.63	10.6	— 13.9	0.45	6.7	— 15.0	0.81	12.2	— 19.8	2.01	10.8	— 19.0
19X4	2.37	9.0	— 13.8	0.36	7.6	— 13.9	0.64	11.5	— 19.1	1.55	8.2	— 15.1
19X3	2.25	7.1	— 12.9	1.02	2.3	— 8.2	0.46	9.0	— 29.3	1.19	9.4	— 15.9
19X2	1.84	4.8	— 8.7	0.37	4.4	— 8.1	0.33	9.5	— 14.0	0.93	6.0	— 12.5
19X1	1.46	6.9	— 10.0	1.31	1.0	— 2.4	0.22	17.6	— 23.9	0.52	11.1	— 16.3
Book value per share; price/book range												
Latest 12 months	$19.69	1.7x	— 2.1x	$ 4.57	1.4x	— 2.6x	$ 6.58	1.8x	— 2.6x	$10.95	3.1x	— 4.9x
19X5	22.66	1.2	— 1.6	4.59	0.7	— 1.5	6.05	1.6	— 2.6	11.06	2.0	— 3.4
19X4	21.01	1.0	— 1.6	3.94	0.7	— 1.3	3.67	2.0	— 3.3	8.93	1.4	— 2.6
19X3	19.13	0.8	— 1.5	4.02	0.6	— 2.1	3.23	1.3	— 4.2	8.11	1.4	— 2.3
19X2	18.10	0.5	— 0.9		N.M.		1.87	1.7	— 2.5	7.45	0.8	— 1.6
19X1	16.30	0.6	— 0.9		N.M.		1.71	2.3	— 3.1	7.04	0.8	— 1.2

TABLE 12-5
HISTORICAL MARKET DATA OF SELECTED
EDUCATIONAL SUPPLY/SERVICE COMPANIES (continued)

	Addison-Wesley Publishing Company, Inc.			Grolier, Inc.	Kinder-Care Learning Centers, Inc.			Macmillan, Inc.		
Dividends paid; yield range										
19X5	$ 0.75	2.7% —	2.1%	$0.00	$ 0.06	0.6% —	0.4%	$ 0.54	2.5% —	1.4%
19X4	0.65	3.1 —	2.0	0.00	0.06	0.8 —	0.5	0.45	3.5 —	1.9
19X3	0.55	3.4 —	1.9	0.00	0.05	1.2 —	0.4	0.38	3.4 —	2.0
19X2	0.50	5.7 —	3.1	0.00	0.04	1.3 —	0.9	0.29	5.2 —	2.5
19X1	0.50	4.9 —	3.4	0.00	0.04	1.0 —	0.8	0.24	4.2 —	2.8
Dividend payout ratio										
19X5		28.5%		-0-		7.4%			26.9%	
19X4		27.4		-0-		9.4			29.0	
19X3		24.4		-0-		11.4			31.9	
19X2		27.2		-0-		12.1			31.2	
19X1		34.3				18.2			46.2	

Source: Brentwood Associates (1986)

[Text continued from p. 12-16.]

Table 12-4 provides much more detail about operating performance of the comparable companies. Profit margins are viewed as a good measure of the strength of a firm's proprietary position and of its ability to sustain earnings growth. The compound growth rate of those earnings is an important indicator of the appropriate price/earnings ratio for the firm's stock. (In fact, a widely used rule of thumb holds that this ratio should be at most roughly equal to the average long-term earnings growth rate.)

Table 12-5 is important because it provides perspective on the stock market performance of firms in A-1's industry. Given the importance of comparables in pricing an IPO, the parties involved want to be sure that current market conditions are reasonably representative of relatively long-term trends rather than recent aberrations.

Armed with this data, the firm and its underwriter may then proceed to develop the analysis in Table 12-6. In practice, a number of these analyses would be prepared, reflecting different net income and growth rate assumptions (shown in the upper right hand corner of the table). Note the following in Table 12-6:

- The data are grouped into "children's market" and "other related" companies; the former group is judged more comparable than the latter, so it is averaged separately; and
- A-1's "implied valuation" is computed in two ways for each comparable: (a) using the comparable's price/earnings ratio and (2) using the comparable's "growth-adjusted" price/earnings ratio.

The latter is determined by computing what percentage the comparable's conventional price/earnings ratio is of its estimated earnings growth rate and then applying that percentage to A-1's expected growth rate. This demonstrates the importance attached to earnings growth as a determinant of the price/earnings ratio and therefore a fundamental indicator of value.

Table 12-7 shows the computations done to determine what comparable companies might be expected to yield to investors. The internal rate of return (IRR) is essentially the ROI that an investor in each comparable firm would achieve if the firm's earnings grew as shown in the Expected Earnings Growth Rate column and the stock was sold after five years (the holding period) at the Exit Price/Earnings Ratio shown in the last three columns. These ROIs are then compared to those expected from A-1's stock, with various assumptions regarding A-1's IPO price and subsequent growth rates, to determine whether A-1 would constitute an attractive stock in relation to others in its industry.

[Text continues on p. 12-25.]

**TABLE 12-6
A-1 EDUCATIONAL SUPPLY CORPORATION
Valuation Based on Price/Earnings Ratios and Growth Adjusted Price/Earnings Ratios of Selected Comparables**

	Total Shares Outstanding (Millions)	Market Value ($Millions)	Fiscal 19X6 Earnings Per Share[a,b]	Current Price[c]	Price/Earnings Ratio	Implied Valuation for A-1[d] ($Millions)	Fiscal 19X6 net income $2.8 million Growth rate 28%		Implied Price Earnings Ratio for A-1[e]	Implied Valuation for A-1[d] ($Millions)
							Estimated Growth Rate	Price/Earnings Ratio as a Percentage of Growth Rate		
Childrens' Market										
Kinder Care Centers (KNDR)	44.727	$637.4	$0.83	$14.25	17.2X	$48.1	25%	69%	13.7 X	$38.5
Oshkosh B'gosh (GOSHA)	5.469	315.8	2.55	57.75	22.6	63.4	28%	113%	22.6	63.4
Scholastic, Inc. (SCHL)	2.067	53.7	1.43	26.00	18.2	50.9	15%	121%	24.2	67.9
Western Publishing (WPGI)	20.000	382.5	1.25	19.13	15.3	42.8	28%	77%	15.3	42.8
				Average	18.3X	$51.3	28%		19.0 X	$53.1
Other related companies										
Harcourt Brace Jovanovich (HBJ)	34.173	$1,144.8	$1.92	$33.50	17.4X	$48.9	15%	116%	23.3 X	$65.1
Hasbro (HAS)	24.082	1258.3	4.00	52.25	13.1	36.6	22%	59%	11.9	33.3
Hunt Manufacturing (HUN)	7.060	193.3	1.42	27.38	19.3	54.0	15%	129%	25.7	72.0
Jostens (JOS)	21.400	706.2	2.03	33.00	16.3	45.5	12%	135%	27.1	75.9
Scan-Trow (SCNN)	3.357	65.5	0.94	19.50	20.7	58.1	25%	83%	16.6	46.5
				Average	17.4X	$48.6	18%		20.9 X	$58.5

[a] Institutional Brokers Estimating Service (IBES) and Morgan Stanley & Co. estimates
[b] All earnings per share are normalized for A-1 Educational Supply's December fiscal year-end
[c] Closing price on 7/14/19X6
[d] Based on projected fiscal 19X6 fully taxed income of $2.8 million (taxed at 46%)
[e] Based on an expected growth rate for A-1 Educational Supply of 20%

Source: Brentwood Associates (1986)

TABLE 12-7
A-1 EDUCATIONAL SUPPLY CORPORATION
Expected Internal Rates of Return for Investors for Selected Comparables

Holding period	5.0 years		Price/earnings ratios	15X 20X 25X	Expected IRR Based on Exit Price/Earnings		
Company	Per-Share Price July 14, 19X6	Fiscal 19X6 Earnings Per Share	Expected Earnings Growth Rate		15X	20X	25X
Kinder Care (KNDR)	$14.25	$0.83	25%		3.5%	9.6%	14.6%
Oshkosh B'gosh (GOSHA)	57.75	2.55	20		5.9	12.2	17.3
Scholastic (SCHL)	26.00	1.43	15		18.4	25.4	31.1
Western Publishing (EPGI)	19.13	1.25	20		17.9	24.9	30.6
Harcourt Brace Jovanovich (HBJ)	33.50	1.92	15		12.2	18.9	24.3
Hasbro (HAS)	52.25	2.00	22		14.2	21.0	26.5
Hunt Manufacturing (HUN)	27.38	1.42	15		10.7	17.2	22.6
Jostens (JOS)	33.00	2.03	12		14.5	21.3	26.9
Scan-Tron (SCNN)	19.50	0.94	25		16.4	23.3	28.9
			Average		12.6%	19.3%	24.8%

Source: Brentwood Associates (1986)

[*Text continued from p. 12-22.*]

[e] Limitations of Price/Earnings Multiples

Although price/earnings ratios are the most frequently used measures in determining how to value IPOs, they are not without shortcomings. As even a casual follower of the public stock markets knows, price/earnings ratio levels are subject to fairly wide fluctuations, often with very imperfect correlations with the current performance of the economy. Auction markets (like the stock exchanges) are subject to the "pendulum effect": When prices get out of equilibrium (i.e., either too high or too low in relation to underlying fundamentals), they eventually will correct and generally overshoot the appropriate midpoint. Of course, these swings provide buying or selling opportunities; without them, strong markets receptive to IPOs of young companies might occur rarely, if at all.

How should the company going public make allowances for the volatility of price/earnings ratios? They should be viewed as reasonableness tests, and their changes over a five- or ten-year period should be analyzed to provide some perspective. Finally, a very useful exercise for a company about to go public is to calculate what earnings growth it must accomplish to justify the price of its stock. Unless management has fairly strong confidence that it can accomplish that growth, it should seriously consider whether it is overreaching in its IPO valuation.

[f] After-Market Considerations

Most underwriters agree that an IPO is not truly successful unless the stock "behaves well" in the public market that it has entered. In practice, this means that the price of the stock should not drop below the offering price. Pressure exists, therefore, for management to deliver consistently growing earnings per share on a quarterly basis (subject, of course, to any seasonality known to exist in the industry). If earnings stability is fragile, a higher discount rate is applicable to the firm's stock and a lower price/earnings ratio is likely appropriate. The bottom line is that the maximum IPO price is not necessarily the best price when viewed over the long term. A bit more dilution in the IPO may buy much investor patience and goodwill in the after-market.

¶ 12.4 Valuing Private Placements

Private placement, as used herein, refers to the sale of equity securities of a firm (typically in its early stages of growth) to private investors. These investors are generally professionally managed funds, such as venture capitalists, pension and trust funds, insurance companies, and the like.

Private placements represent a middle case between start-ups and IPOs. To the degree a firm has made progress in completing its management team, developing and beginning to produce its products or services, and selling them to actual customers, the risks inherent at its start-up phase will have been reduced. If profitability has been achieved, the company may be ready for a public offering. (However, generalizing about the conditions that make a firm suitable for an IPO is difficult because stock market conditions change regularly and sometimes rapidly.) The investor seeking to value a private placement can use some of the tools of both the start-up investor and the IPO underwriter.

[1] Key Considerations

The valuation expert must take into account a number of key considerations when valuing private placements. Among them are the required ROI, the expenditures to date, the expected "upside" (the potential size and profitability of the business), the need for additional capital, and the remaining risk. Each of these factors is discussed next.

[a] Required ROI

As in the other cases, the required ROI of a private placement is central to its valuation. Generally, the further along a company is in executing its business plan, the less risk remains and the lower the ROI the prospective investor should require. *Reducing risk reduces required ROI.* However, institutional private placement investors are generally seeking compound annual ROIs in the 35% to 50% range. For a company nearly qualified for an IPO, the lower end of the range would apply (occasionally an ROI in the 25% to 35% range might be acceptable to an institution if little remaining risk were perceived). Conversely, a firm with significant remaining product, market, or management risks would need to demonstrate the chance to provide the investor well above a 50% ROI.

[b] Expenditures to Date

Certainly, the amount of money already invested in a firm is an important indicator of value; unless assets have been wasted, or significant negative changes have occurred in the firm's industry, the amount invested already in the company should represent a "floor" of value for the firm.

As already mentioned, progress in executing the firm's business plan (product development, marketing arrangements, sales results) serves to reduce risk and consequently increases value. As in start-ups, time delays are the enemy of the ROI, so the closer the firm is to achieving profitable operations, the more it is worth.

[c] Expected Upside

In determining what value to place on an investment, the private placement investor must estimate the potential size and profitability of the business. The company almost always provides detailed financial projections, and the investor must analyze these and accept or adjust them (either up or down, but generally the latter) based upon a view of these factors:

- The proprietariness and significance of the products or services the firm is developing;
- The size of market addressable by the firm and its expected market penetration ("share"); and
- The quality of the management team and its ability to achieve its expectations (the prospective investor bases this judgment upon the managers' prior experience and their execution to date of the firm's business plan).

Having estimated the future performance of the firm, the interested investor must estimate what value this performance will yield to the shareholder. Usually this involves two steps:

1. Estimating the price/earnings ratio the firm should enjoy if it goes public; and
2. Examining examples of acquisitions of similar companies to determine values achieved if this route to liquidity is taken.

[d] Need for Additional Capital

The effect of dilution on ROI has been discussed previously. The private placement investor must take into account the firm's plans for later equity offerings in analyzing the potential ROI.

[e] Remaining Risk

There are three primary categories of risk usually associated with private placement candidates. These categories are as follows:

1. *Unanticipated* capital requirements;
2. Time delays; and
3. Execution risks, including (a) product development (i.e., technological hurdles and the need to develop extensions and enhancements to the product), (b) marketing (i.e., developing

sales at the rate and within the marketing budget proposed), and (c) operations and the management of growth.

Of course, these risks are heavily interrelated. The prudent private placement investor will develop as detailed an understanding of them as possible before determining the price to pay for the company's securities.

[2] Rules of Thumb

There is a widely used method for at least generating a starting point in determining value, which then can be analyzed using the foregoing criteria. It helps estimate an appropriate "markup" over the *postmoney valuation* of the prior round of financing, which may have been the start-up or an earlier private placement.

If progress has been made against the company's prior business plan, management and prior investors will expect the current private placement to be at a value above—perhaps *significantly* above if substantial risk reduction has occurred—the prior round's postmoney value. How much above can vary greatly depending upon the times.

In "normal" times, institutional investors, including venture capitalists, are accustomed to seeing price increases (markups) on the order of 30% to 50% from round to round of financing for a development-stage company.

In times of strong bull markets with heavy IPO activity, markups of two to three times are sometimes seen. But when markets are weak (and private placement markets can be weaker or stronger than IPO or public markets in general, but they are correlated), very small or even no markups may occur. Even in healthy market periods, if too many firms have been founded to pursue the same market (as occasionally occurs in the venture-capital financed arena), markups will be small or nonexistent.

If progress against the business plan has been poor, resulting in the need for unanticipated capital, management changes, or similar upheavals, writedowns (from the prior postmoney level) may be required to complete a financing. The term "restart" has been coined to apply to situations where a firm has to drop its private placement valuation to essentially that of a start-up, even though it may have spent several years and millions of dollars of prior equity attempting (unsuccessfully) to achieve its business plan. Such restarts are only done when investors (often including both prior and new participants) can be convinced that the fundamental appeal of the company (usually based upon proprietary technology) justifies another try at success. New management—and often major changes in strategy—are often involved.

[a] "Performance vs. Promise"

The closer a company is to being a "real business," with revenues and, perhaps, earnings, the less relevant the prior financing round valuation becomes. Performance is almost always a more reliable measurement of potential success than the expectations upon which start-ups are founded. Sometimes, this leads to the curious result that a *higher* valuation may be obtained at an earlier stage of financing, simply because the severity—or even the existence—of some of the risks facing the business may not be fully perceived at the early stage. Progress, especially when it involves market feedback, may temper upside expectations. This phenomenon is captured in the epigram, "The sizzle is often more appealing than the steak."

[3] Calculation Case Study

Assume that Beta Corporation is seeking to raise $2 million of equity capital in a private placement. Its financial status is as follows:

Current revenues	$-0- (but shipments about to begin)
Investment to date	$1.5 million at start-up
Ownership percentage for investors	40%
Projected earnings in fifth year (from present)	$3.7 million
Projected future equity capital requirements	$2.5 million in year 3
Estimated price/earnings ratio of company in year 5	15 to 25

With this information, the following computations may be done:
Postmoney valuation of prior round (start-up):

$$\frac{\$1,500,000}{0.40} = \$3,750,000$$

Possible premoney valuations of this round:

30% markup: 1.3 × $3,750,000 = $4,875,000
50% markup: 1.5 × $3,750,000 = $5,625,000
2 times markup: 2 × $3,750,000 = $7,500,000

Potential dilution from anticipated $2 million financing in three years:

If this round is done at the $5.6 million premoney level (a 50% markup), it will result in a $5.6 million + $2 million, or $7.6 million postmoney valuation. Assuming another 50% markup in three years, the premoney valuation will be 1.5 × $7.6 million, or $11.4 million. The firm will, therefore, have to sell 18% [$2.5 million/($11.4 million + $2.5 million)] of its equity to raise the $2.5 million, resulting in a 100% − 18% = 82% dilution factor for this round's investors. Since this round's price (much less the next round's) is not yet known, the future dilution is approximated by 80%.

Range of possible company valuations in year 5:

Price/Earnings Ratio	Earnings	Company Value	80% of Company Value
15	$3,700,000	$55,500,000	$44,400,000
20	$3,700,000	$74,000,000	$59,200,000
25	$3,700,000	$92,500,000	$74,000,000

Now it is possible to calculate the potential ROIs that would result from the various possible premoney valuations just listed. Since no interim cash flows are involved (it is assumed that no dividends will be paid by Beta), the ROI of this potential five-year investment is found by determining the fifth root of the ratio of the realized value (the last column in the previous table) to the postmoney valuation of the present investment ($2 million plus the assumed premoney valuation).

Premoney Valuation	Postmoney Valuation	Price/Earnings Ratio	Realized Value (from "80%" column)	ROI
$4,875,000	$6,875,000	15	$44,400,000	45.2%*
$4,875,000	$6,875,000	20	$59,200,000	53.8%
$4,875,000	$6,875,000	25	$74,000,000	60.8%
$5,625,000	$7,625,000	15	$44,400,000	42.2%
$5,625,000	$7,625,000	20	$59,200,000	50.7%
$5,625,000	$7,625,000	25	$74,400,000	57.5%
$7,500,000	$9,500,000	15	$44,400,000	36.1%
$7,500,000	$9,500,000	20	$59,200,000	44.2%
$7,500,000	$9,500,000	25	$74,000,000	50.8%

* Example of calculation: $(44,400,000/6,875,000)^{(1/5)} - 1 = 0.452$, or a 45.2% ROI

This table shows that an assumed price/earnings ratio of 20 yields ROIs in the 44% to 54% range *if the company achieves its projections*. The prospective investor will invariably consider cases where the projections are not attained, at least in the time projected. If six years (rather than the five projected) are required to achieve the $3.7 million earnings level, then the 44% to 54% range (at a price/earnings ratio of 20) would be reduced to *36% to 43%*—a substantial change. Typically, an investor would prepare several tables like the previous ones, using various earnings levels and time horizons. Different methods of estimating the firm's ending value may also be used. (The investor can consider IPO valuation criteria like those in the prior section of this chapter, assuming Beta is a potential IPO candidate.) If the analyst is able to assign probabilities to the varying scenarios under consideration, the expected values and probability distributions describing the expected return can be computed.[3]

If the investor(s) can be convinced that Beta could command a price/earnings ratio of 20 in five years and that it has a very good chance of making its $3.7 million earnings projection in that time and that a 50% ROI adequately compensates the investor(s) for the risks involved, it appears that the $5.625 million pre-money valuation (a 50% markup from the prior round) is appropriate, since it gives a generally acceptable 42.2% to 57.5% ROI range, given a 15 to 25 price/earnings ratio range.

In practice, of course, the actual determination of valuation will depend upon a negotiation process. The number of investors interested in participating will be an important factor because competition to invest tends to support a higher price. Prudent companies will avoid an "auction" approach, however, because the private placement investor will become a long-term partner, perhaps called upon to make later, unplanned equity infusions. Treating the investor fairly, which includes providing a defensible, appropriately rewarding valuation in the financing, is important in making the relationship healthy. A strong, supportive investor group is generally considered to be more important than avoiding marginal additional dilution that may occur due to a valuation below the maximum potentially attainable.

¶ 12.5 Summary

The valuations of start-ups, IPOs, and private placements are all based to a material extent upon uncertain, future events, that is, upon *expectations*.

During good economic times (which are usually reflected in good equity markets), both fundamental expectations and the way they are translated into valuations (e.g., price/earnings ratios and discount rates) tend in the direction of higher valuations. Fundamentals and valuation "multiples" are psychologically correlated, and this is true in both good times and bad.

Ultimately, the law of supply and demand prevails. The valuation of a security is what someone will pay for it. A strong public market affects all the classes of investment considered in this chapter. It raises the expectations of earlier-stage investors, who can pay a higher price

---

[3] See "The Pricing of a Venture Capital Investment" in *Pratt's Guide to Venture Capital Sources* (S.E. Pratt & J.K. Morris, 10th ed. 1986).

and maintain their desired ROI if the higher price/earnings ratios of a bull market remain long enough to allow an investment to benefit (from an IPO or acquisition by a public company).

Start-ups, being furthest from the public market stage, are least affected by public market conditions while later-stage private placements are strongly affected. IPOs themselves, of course, rise in value when the market is strong; investment bankers, who vie with one another for the right to take quality firms public, compete partially on the price level that they attempt to justify to a potential client. Comparables enjoying high multiples make this justification (and delivery on the promise) easier.

In addition, strong financial markets usually stimulate additional money to enter the arena of earlier-stage investing because the apparently higher ROIs available there become more and more attractive (relative to high-priced public securities). New entrepreneurs may also be stimulated to emerge, so the supply of investment opportunities often tends to rise along with the supply of investable funds. This helps to explain the general long-term stability of start-up valuations.

A weak public market environment reduces the visibility of an "exit" for private placement investors, making those investments seem less attractive. Long bear markets can substantially reduce the level of private placement activity (the mid-1970s are a good example) because both entrepreneurs and investors become discouraged about their prospects.

Overall, then, the valuations of early-stage companies from start-up through IPO are driven by two factors:

1. Their fundamental product (or service), its market, and the strengths of the management team (these and their associated risks are evaluated by the investor community, which translates them into expectations for future corporate performance); and
2. The health of the securities marketplace, i.e., the public stock market (this affects IPO valuations the most and start-ups the least).

Most experienced observers of the financial markets for early-stage enterprises believe that there is a prevailing tendency to overvalue in good times and undervalue in bad. The challenge to the investor in these enterprises is to maintain a long-term perspective and participate in investments with valuations that can lead to acceptable returns in "normal" times. Returns will fluctuate but should average out acceptably if this perspective is maintained.

13

SOLVENCY ANALYSIS IN LEVERAGED TRANSACTIONS

JEFFREY R. GREENE AND LORI M. PRICE*

		Page
¶ 13.1	The Legal Framework of Fraudulent Conveyances	13-2
	[1] Recent Court Decisions	13-5
	[2] Accountants' Solvency Letters	13-5
¶ 13.2	Components of a Solvency Analysis	13-6
	[1] Due Diligence	13-7
	[2] Balance Sheet Test	13-8
	[a] Valuing a Company's Assets	13-8
	[b] Valuing Interest-Bearing Debt	13-8
	[c] Valuing Contingent Liabilities	13-9
	[3] Cash Flow Test	13-10
	[4] Reasonable Capital Test	13-10
¶ 13.3	Solvency Case Study	13-10
	[1] Overview of the Company	13-11
	[2] Balance Sheet Test	13-11
	[a] Historical Financial Summary	13-11
	[b] Normalized Earnings and Cash Flow	13-12
	[c] Market Multiple Selection	13-12
	[d] Discounted Cash Flow Approach	13-18
	[e] Asset Valuation Summary	13-19
	[f] Valuing Liabilities: Guarantee of Subsidiary's Debt	13-20
	[g] Valuing Liabilities: Convertible Subordinated Debt	13-21
	[h] Summary	13-21
	[3] Cash Flow Test	13-21
	[4] Reasonable Capital Test	13-24
	[a] Revenue Growth and Margin Sensitivity	13-24

---

* JEFFREY R. GREENE is a managing director in the New York office of Houlihan, Lokey, Howard & Zukin, Inc., a valuation advisory and investment banking firm headquartered in Los Angeles, California. The author manages the firm's national solvency opinion practice and has written many articles on such topics as fraudulent conveyance issues and employee stock ownership plans (ESOPs). LORI M. PRICE is a vice president in the Los Angeles office of Houlihan, Lokey, Howard & Zukin, Inc. and is responsible for coordinating the firm's product development effort for solvency-related analysis on the West Coast.

	[b] Volatility of Asset Prices...............	13-25
	[c] Maturity Structure of Fixed and Contingent Obligations	13-25
¶ 13.4	Summary	13-25

One of the most important applications of valuation analysis of late has been in the area of solvency or capital adequacy. Once a minor checklist item supplied by a company's accountants, solvency opinions are now a central feature of most leveraged buyouts (LBOs) and recapitalizations. Lenders and directors as well as attorneys and financial advisers look to the solvency expert to provide an independent assessment of the company's posttransaction financial viability.

Solvency concerns originate in federal and state law dealing with fraudulent transfers and with corporate distributions to shareholders. Anyone examining proxies or prospectuses for today's LBOs and recapitalizations will find several pages devoted to relevant statutes and cases.

This chapter explores the following topics to facilitate an understanding of the concepts and techniques applied in the rendering of solvency opinions:

1. The legal framework;
2. The components of a solvency analysis; and
3. An LBO case study.

The following discussion will be best understood by readers with a basic mastery of the valuation fundamentals covered in chapter 2.

¶ 13.1 The Legal Framework of Fraudulent Conveyance

The valuation expert should understand the critical aspects of fraudulent conveyance law embodied in the U.S. Bankruptcy Code (the Code) and the following state statutes: the Uniform Fraudulent Transfer Act (UFTA) and the Uniform Fraudulent Conveyance Act (UFCA). Fraudulent conveyance laws are designed to prevent shareholders, secured creditors, and others from benefiting at the expense of unsecured creditors.[1]

When a company goes bankrupt because of an improperly structured LBO, courts can, under certain circumstances, unwind the prior transaction. The results can be the following:

---

[1] For valuation experts, lawyers, accountants, and other practitioners who want more information on fraudulent conveyance law, see Kirby, McGuinness & Kandel, "Fraudulent Conveyance Concerns in Leveraged Buyout Lending," 43 Bus. Law. 27 (1987); Cook, Marañoti & Miller, "Fraudulent Transfers," in J.J. Cunningham & C.D. Lobell, *Financing Leveraged Buyouts and Acquisitions* 195 (1989).

- Lenders could lose their security interests in the bankrupt company's assets.
- Selling shareholders may have to disgorge their sale proceeds.
- Directors and company advisers could be subjected to costly litigation.

The laws focus on both *intentional* fraud and *constructive* fraud. *Intentional fraud* occurs when conveyances, or transfers, are made with actual intent to hinder, delay, or defraud present or future creditors. In cases of intentional fraud, use of the federal Racketeer Influenced and Corrupt Organizations (RICO) Act may expose the lender to treble damages, attorney's fees, and even criminal liability.

Constructive fraud provisions present a greater risk to prudent lenders and directors. For *constructive fraud* to occur, the bankruptcy trustee or unsecured creditors do not need to prove actual intent to defraud; rather, the determination of constructive fraud rests on an objective inquiry into the value of the transfers and the posttransaction capital adequacy of the debtor. The elements of constructive fraud are addressed in the following pages.

As shown in Figure 13-1, an LBO typically involves a number of transfers, any one of which can be jeopardized by application of the fraudulent conveyance laws. For example, assume the following:

1. Lender takes a security interest in debtor company's assets.
2. Loan proceeds are paid to selling shareholders.
3. Company issues debentures to selling shareholders as noncash portion of selling price.
4. Subsidiary (OPCO) guarantees debt of its corporate parent.

FIGURE 13-1 LBO Transfers That May Be Jeopardized

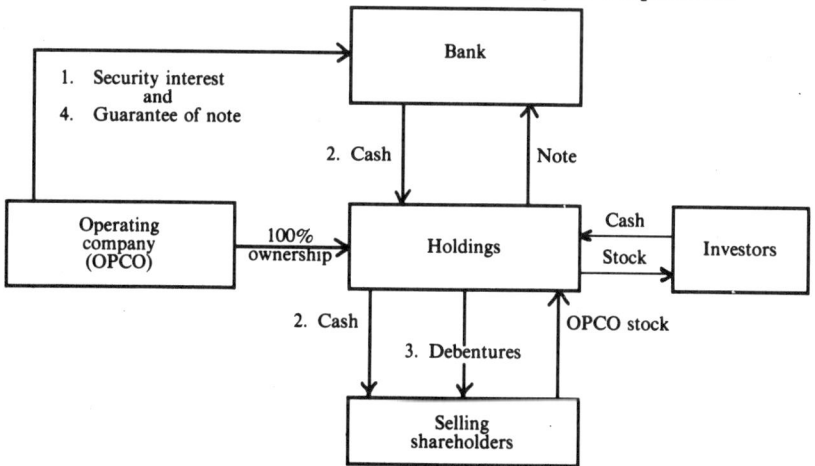

The most likely first step on the road to a fraudulent conveyance judgment under the constructive fraud provisions is for the subject company, posttransaction, to file a bankruptcy petition. The trustee or secured creditors must show that the transfer made in connection with the LBO was for less than "reasonably equivalent value." As a practical matter, "value" is defined in economic, not accounting, terms and may depend on the circumstances of the case.

If the transfer was not made for reasonably equivalent value (which is the case with most LBOs since the loan proceeds typically do not stay with the debtor), the trustee or unsecured creditors then look to the financial condition of the company at the time of the transfer in determining whether a fraudulent transfer has occurred (*constructive fraud*). Section 548 of the Code sets up three tests of financial condition, which specify conditions that the court must determine about the debtor. Those conditions are:

- [The debtor] was insolvent on the date that such transfer was made or such obligation was incurred or became insolvent as a result of such transfer or obligation. . . .
- [The debtor] intended to incur, or believed that [he] would incur, debts that would be beyond his ability to pay as such debt matured. . . .
- [The debtor] was engaged in business or was about to engage in business or a transaction, for which any property remaining with the debtor was unreasonably small capital. . . .

If any *one* of these conditions existed when the transfer was made *and* there was no reasonably equivalent value given, the transfer would be considered fraudulent under the Code. The trustee or unsecured creditor can then seek to have the transfer set aside.

A lender whose security interest is set aside in this manner loses its priority claim on the bankrupt company's assets. The lender must then share the liquidation proceeds with unsecured creditors and likely recover a much smaller dollar amount from the company. In addition, former shareholders who sold out for cash in an LBO face the risk of having to return their proceeds if the company's payment to them is deemed a fraudulent transfer. Directors may also be sued for breaching their fiduciary duty to creditors.

Under the Code, a transaction may be attacked as a fraudulent conveyance if it occurred within one year of the date of the filing of the bankruptcy petition. However, Section 544(b) of the Code incorporates state fraudulent conveyance laws. This enables a trustee to attack a transaction for significantly longer periods after the date of the transfer (e.g., California and Texas, four years; New York, six years).

[1] Recent Court Decisions

Even though fraudulent conveyance law has existed in some form since the 1600s, it has only recently received prominent attention because of growing numbers of LBOs and several key court findings. The case of *United States v. Tabor Court Realty Corporation* (the *Gleneagles Appeal*)[2] is the most referenced decision in a small but growing body of fraudulent conveyance cases. In reviewing a failed LBO company, the *Gleneagles* court actually voided lenders' security interests under the Pennsylvania UFCA. The court found evidence of *intentional* fraud in addition to constructive fraud in the case, so application to well-meaning LBO participants is somewhat unclear. Nevertheless, the *Gleneagles* decision stands as a primary factor behind current concerns over fraudulent conveyance liability in leveraged transactions.

The 1985 decision in *Credit Managers Association of Southern California v. Federal Company*,[3] resulted in security interests being upheld as a result of prudent analysis of the LBO company's projections performed by one of the deal participants.

One of the newest phenomena in fraudulent conveyance exposure has appeared in the form of the preemptive legal attack. When the $4.2 billion Safeway Stores LBO was proposed in July 1986, a major union filed suit alleging the transaction would involve a fraudulent conveyance with respect to the employees as unsecured creditors. The union claimed the LBO would render Safeway insolvent or severely undercapitalized, thereby jeopardizing the company's ability to meet accrued wages, vacation pay, pension contributions, and other unsecured claims. As part of a settlement in June 1987, Safeway agreed to pay up to $35 million in severance benefits for employees terminated as part of the company's restructuring.

[2] Accountants' Solvency Letters

The rising number of large, complex LBOs in the mid-1980s combined with growing concern over fraudulent conveyance liability led to demands by lenders and directors for independent solvency analyses. This need was met largely by the major accounting firms who routinely issued "solvency letters" for their clients' leveraged transactions. The letter was based on limited procedures and gave only negative assurance or cold comfort: "[W]e are not aware of anything that would

---

[2] 803 F.2d 1288 (3d Cir. 1986). In *Tabor Court Realty*, the Court of Appeals for the Third Circuit affirmed the three related district court opinions of United States v. Gleneagles Inv. Co., 565 F. Supp. 556 (M.D. Pa. 1983), 571 F. Supp. 935 (M.D. Pa. 1983); 584 F. Supp. 671 (M.D. Pa. 1984). The *Tabor Court Realty* case thus became known as the *Gleneagles Appeal* case.

[3] 629 F. Supp. 175 (C.D. Cal. 1985).

cause the company to be unable to pay its debts as they come due...."
One alarming limitation placed on the accountant's work was the prohibition on opinions covering projections longer than one year. Since the statute of limitations for fraudulent conveyance attacks extends beyond one year in most states, these opinions gave extremely cold comfort.

In February 1988, the American Institute of Certified Public Accountants (AICPA) issued a formal policy statement barring its members from providing solvency opinions.[4] The AICPA's main concerns appeared to be the following:

- The solvency letter might be interpreted as giving legal advice; and
- A solvency analysis requires procedures that may change over time as the case law evolves (this does not lend itself to well-defined criteria for assessing solvency).

The exit of accounting firms from solvency analysis as the LBO market grew meant lenders and directors had to turn to a few professional valuation firms for independent opinions. Unhampered by the AICPA's rules and procedures, the valuation firm could apply rigorous corporate finance techniques to determine solvency in leveraged transactions.

¶ 13.2 Components of a Solvency Analysis

Since a fraudulent transfer investigation can be triggered by anything from late-trade creditor payments to a bankruptcy filing, an obvious goal in any transaction is to minimize the potential for financial distress by properly pricing and structuring the transaction. To protect themselves in an LBO, participants must make sure the post-LBO company will not fail the constructive fraud tests.

The financial questions of solvency posed by the Code can be summarized into a three-part analysis at the time of the LBO:

- *Balance sheet test.* Does the value of the company's assets exceed its liabilities?
- *Cash flow test.* Is there a reasonable expectation that the company will be able to pay its debts as they come due?
- *Reasonable capital test.* Is the "equity cushion" determined in the balance sheet test large enough? Is the "safety margin" in the projections adequate?

---

[4] AICPA, *Responding to Requests for Reports on Matters Relating to Solvency: An Interpretation of Statement on Standards for Attestation Engagements* (Feb. 1988). (This interpretation rescinds Report on Solvency, AU Section 9504.23-35.)

[1] Due Diligence

A complete solvency analysis must begin with collecting information about the company's historical performance, its industry, and its prospects for the future.

This information comes from two kinds of sources: (1) documents prepared by the company and its advisers and (2) interviews with key managers and deal participants. Basic solvency due diligence is similar to that for any valuation analysis, but it emphasizes the following key areas:

- *Recession behavior.* How sensitive are the company's revenues to general economic downturns?
- *Cost structure.* Given a revenue decline, how will earnings and free cash flow be affected?
- *Financial flexibility.* If the company experiences an unexpected operating cash shortfall, can it sell assets, temporarily cut capital expenditures, or otherwise cope without jeopardizing future performance?

Figure 13-2 outlines the key components of a thorough due diligence analysis.

FIGURE 13-2 Due Diligence for Solvency Analysis

☐ *Investigation topics*
- Historical performance
- Projections
- Industry trends
- Product/market strategies
- Operating cost structure
- Capital spending program
- Contingent liabilities
- Financial contingency plans

☐ *Field investigations*
- Interview corporate and division management
- Visit major facilities

☐ *Interview advisers and other professionals*
- Lenders and investment bankers
- Accountants
- Attorneys
- Industry experts

☐ *Document review*
- SEC filings
- Projections
- Operating and strategic plans
- Financing and loan documents
- Disclosure schedules
- Market studies
- Industry information

[2] Balance Sheet Test

The balance sheet test requires an economic valuation of the company as a going concern and a consideration of liabilities, including contingent liabilities. The critical valuation steps are as follows:

1. Review the industry environment.
2. Assess the company's strategic and operating plans.
3. Analyze the company's historical financial performance.
4. Determine normalized earnings and cash flow levels.
5. Select comparable public companies.
6. Compare the company's risk profile and growth prospects with the selected comparable companies.
7. Choose appropriate capitalization ratios for market multiple approaches and discount rates for discounted future cash flow approach.
8. Evaluate liabilities, including contingent items.

[a] Valuing a Company's Assets

The valuation of a company's assets is generally completed on a debt-free basis (without regard to capital structure). Some of the public company approaches commonly used to develop indications of value include the following ratios: price/earnings before income and taxes (price/EBIT), price/earnings before depreciation, interest, and taxes (price/EBDIT), price/debt-free earnings (price/DFE), and price/debt-free cash flow (price/DFCF) (as well as price/revenues in certain industries). Analysis of comparable transactions will help determine an appropriate control premium to use in the public company approaches and will provide a useful guide in selecting multiples.

The discounted cash flow approach (completed on a debt-free basis) must exclude all interest and principal payments, preferred dividends, transaction fees or disbursements, amortization of transaction-related items and anything else that represents a payment to investors or payment associated with the consummation of the transaction. Financial projections should be discounted using the weighted average cost of capital (WACC) as a discount rate. WACC should be developed based on the optimal capital structure for the particular industry. The posttransaction capital structure or the industry average capital structure are often used as surrogates for the theoretical ideal structure.

[b] Valuing Interest-Bearing Debt

The value of posttransaction interest bearing debt (including existing debt to be maintained posttransaction, if any) should be computed on a face value basis for the balance sheet test unless the company or the company's legal counsel advises that market value be used.

(Face value typically approximates market value for new transaction debt that is priced at a fair rate.) If the market value of debt is less than the face value, the posttransaction equity cushion will be understated by the difference between market value and face value. The market value of subordinated debt can be determined by analyzing analog companies that are publicly traded and that have similar equity size (on an absolute and on a relative basis), volatility of underlying assets, and financial leverage. Once an appropriate market yield has been determined, projected interest and principal payments can be discounted back to present value to determine the market value of the debt.

[c] Valuing Contingent Liabilities

Contingent liabilities can be either on- or off-balance sheet but are usually either disclosed in the financial statement footnotes or not formally disclosed at all. Regardless of disclosure, a solvency analysis must investigate and consider contingent items such as those listed in Figure 13-3, among others. While commonly known approaches exist for valuing liabilities such as interest-bearing debt, advanced financial theory may need to be applied to such contingent claims as debt guarantees and convertible bonds. Other items, such as potential liability for a Superfund site cleanup may need to be determined through an interdisciplinary effort of engineers, attorneys, and financial analysts.

FIGURE 13-3 Contingent Liability Examples

- *Convertible securities*
- *Letters of credit*
- *Debt guarantees*
- *Take-or-pay contracts*
- *Throughput agreements*
- *Taxes due*
  - Planned and unplanned asset sales
  - Unremitted foreign earnings
  - Future IRS audit exposure
- *Government contract audit exposure*
- *Litigation*
- *Superfund (CERCLA) liabilities*
- *Pension plan funding*
- *Employment contracts*
- *Postretirement health benefits*

The solvency case study later in this chapter considers two examples of contingent items: a third-party debt guarantee and a convertible bond.

[3] Cash Flow Test

The cash flow test can be broken down into a three-step analysis of the company's projections:

1. Examine the consistency of the projections with historical performance, current product/market strategies, and the current operating cost structure.
2. Evaluate proposed changes by new owners, including corporate overhead reductions, organizational changes, and planned asset sales.
3. Test the sensitivity of the projections to changes in key variables, such as revenue growth, operating margins, capital expenditures, and interest rate fluctuations.

In testing cash flows, reasonable downside scenarios must be developed to determine the "safety margin" available to deal with unexpected downturns in a Company's ability to generate operating cash flow.

[4] Reasonable Capital Test

The reasonable capital test follows directly from the balance sheet and cash flow tests. The determination as to whether the net assets remaining with the company constitute unreasonably small capital involves an analysis of various factors, including the following:

- The degree of sensitivity to revenue growth and margin assumptions demonstrated in the cash flow test;
- The historical and expected volatility of asset values;
- The maturity structure of the company's fixed obligations;
- The magnitude, timing, and nature of contingent liabilities;
- The prevalent capital structures within the industry; and
- The amount of flexibility allowed by the financial covenants in the credit agreements.

These issues are dealt with in detail in the following case study.

¶ 13.3 Solvency Case Study

The solvency analysis is applied in this case study to the LBO of Bornwell Industries, Inc. (BII). BII management has proposed a $410 million LBO to be effective on January 1, 19X9. The following are sources and uses of cash required to consummate the transaction:

Sources of cash	$ Millions
Excess company cash	$ 40[a]
Secured bank debt at 10.5%	165
Senior unsecured notes at 12.0%	75
Convertible subordinated debt at 9.0%	100
New equity	30
Total sources	$410
Uses of cash	
Refinance existing debt	$100
Purchase common stock	290
Transaction costs	20
Total uses	$410

[a] Includes $25 million proceeds from sale of subsidiary

[1] Overview of the Company

BII manufactures and distributes corrugated cardboard and plastic boxes to a variety of industries nationwide. Its customers include pharmaceutical companies, automobile aftermarket wholesalers and electronics manufacturers. BII has just completed a four-year program to expand its production capacity and its distribution resources. As a result, sales and operating earnings have grown appreciably over the past four years, as summarized here:

	19X8
Revenues	$ 608MM
Net income	$ 21MM
Return on sales (ROS)	3.5%
Return on equity (ROE)	16.2%
Total assets	$ 414MM
Net worth	$ 131MM
4-year sales growth	25%/year
4-year operating income growth	37%/year

[2] Balance Sheet Test

Solvency analysis based on the balance sheet test must take into account the factors described in the following pages.

[a] Historical Financial Summary

Detailed statistics on BII's historical financial performance are shown in Tables 13-1 through 13-3. BII's expansion is the dominant theme evident in the financial statements; revenues, assets and profits have grown rapidly since 19X4. The company has reached a new plateau in performance as opposed to a cyclical peak. While sales and asset growth will likely slow in the future, profitability is expected to increase as market development expenses decline relative to sales.

[b] Normalized Earnings and Cash Flow

Since the latest fiscal year operating results appear to be most representative of the company's sustainable levels (because of BII's consistent improvement in operating performance), the 19X8 figures will be used as representative in the market multiple approaches. The resulting computations are shown as follows:

		$ Million
EBIT		$55
Less:	Interest	(20)
	Taxes (40%)	(14)
Net income		$21
Plus:	Interest (after-tax)	10
	Depreciation	29
DFCF		$60

[c] Market Multiple Selection

A comparison of BII with similar publicly traded companies is summarized in Table 13-4. This analysis compares BII to the selected comparables on the basis of risk and growth characteristics to determine the overall investment risk of BII relative to that of the selected public companies. Ultimately, the public companies' multiples will be used as a guide in selecting appropriate multiples for BII since public company multiples reflect investors' expectations of risk/reward requirements and growth expectations. Based on the relative comparison of risk and growth, consideration of quantitative factors deemed to be relevant for comparison purposes, and the public company multiples displayed in Table 13-5, the selected multiples for BII are as follows:

Approach	Selected Multiple
Price/DFE	14.5x
Price/DFCF	8.0x
Price/EBIT	8.0x

Application of price/DFE, price/DFCF, and price/EBIT approaches involves the multiplication of the selected multiples with the selected representative DFE, DFCF and EBIT levels. The resulting conclusions represent indications of value for the total invested capital (TIC) or debt plus equity of the firm.

[Text continues on p. 13-18.]

TABLE 13-1

BORNWELL INDUSTRIES, INC.
COMPARATIVE SUMMARY BALANCE SHEET
($ Millions)

	Fiscal Year Ended December 31,				
Assets	19X8	19X7	19X6	19X5	19X4
Current assets					
Cash and equivalents	28	25	20	14	19
Accounts receivable	56	63	54	34	20
Inventories	71	76	63	58	55
Prepaid expenses	5	5	2	15	12
Total current assets	160	169	139	121	106
Fixed assets					
Land and improvements	29	20	16	11	10
Machinery and equipment	189	165	146	129	117
Building and improvements	118	107	68	53	45
Automotive equipment	27	20	16	12	12
Furniture and fixtures	19	18	13	10	3
Less: Accumulated depreciation	(144)	(121)	(97)	(78)	(61)
Net fixed assets	238	209	162	139	126
Other assets	16	5	2	-0-	2
Total assets	414	383	303	260	234
Liabilities and stockholders' equity					
Current liabilities					
Accounts payable	70	82	65	54	53
Notes payable	31	32	7	21	4
Current portfolio long-term debt	23	17	17	14	12
Accrued expenses	14	19	14	10	6
Total current liabilities	138	150	103	99	75
Long-term debt	105	95	88	75	80
Deferred income taxes	40	28	19	11	5
Total liabilities	283	273	210	185	160
Stockholders' equity					
Common stock	7	7	7	7	7
Paid-in capital	2	2	2	2	2
Retained earnings	122	101	84	66	65
Net stockholders' equity	131	110	93	75	74
Total liabilities and stockholders' equity	414	383	303	260	234

TABLE 13-2

BORNWELL INDUSTRIES, INC.
COMPARATIVE SUMMARY INCOME STATEMENT
($ Millions)

	Fiscal Year Ended December 31,				
	19X8	19X7	19X6	19X5	19X4
Revenues, net	608	547	373	260	246
Cost of sales (goods sold)	432	398	260	198	188
Gross profit	176	149	113	62	58
Operating expenses					
Selling and administrative	104	93	65	38	35
Delivery	17	14	11	8	7
Total operating expenses	121	107	76	46	42
Operating income	55	42	37	16	16
Other income (expense)					
Interest expense	(21)	(17)	(15)	(21)	(11)
Other—net	(1)	1	5	1	3
	(20)	(16)	(10)	(20)	(8)
Income (loss) before taxes	35	26	27	(4)	8
Income taxes (credit)	14	8	9	(5)	2
Net income	21	18	18	1	6
Depreciation	29	24	20	18	12

TABLE 13-3

BORNWELL INDUSTRIES, INC.
COMPARATIVE FINANCIAL ANALYSIS
($ Millions)

Statistics and Ratios	Fiscal Year Ended December 31,				
	19X8	19X7	19X6	19X5	19X4
Size					
Revenues	$608	$547	$373	$260	$426
Total assets	414	383	303	260	234
Net worth	131	110	93	75	74
EBIT	54	43	42	17	19
Net income	21	18	18	1	6
Working capital	22	19	36	22	31
Liquidity ratios					
Quick ratio	0.6	0.6	0.7	0.6	0.7
Current ratio	1.2	1.1	1.3	1.2	1.4
Net working capital turnover ratio	28.0	27.8	10.4	11.8	7.9
Leverage ratios					
Total non-interest-bearing debt/equity ratio	0.9	1.2	1.1	1.0	0.9
Total interest-bearing debt/equity ratio	1.2	1.3	1.2	1.5	1.3
Activity ratios					
Inventory turnover ratio	6.0	5.3	4.1	3.4	3.4
Accounts receivable turnover ratio	10.9	8.7	7.0	7.6	12.5
Fixed-assets turnover ratio	1.5	1.4	1.2	1.0	1.1
Profitability ratios					
Gross profit margin/sales ratio	29.0%	27.3%	30.1%	24.0%	23.4%
EBIT					
Sales	8.9%	7.9%	11.3%	6.3%	7.2%
Net worth	41.5%	39.0%	45.3%	21.7%	23.9%
Total assets	13.1%	11.2%	13.9%	6.3%	7.6%
Growth statistics					
Annual revenue growth	11.3%	46.6%	43.6%	5.6%	−5.7%
Growth index[a]					
Revenue	2.5	2.1	-0-	-0-	-0-

[a] Most recent years' revenue divided by revenues four years' prior.

TABLE 13-4
BORNWELL INDUSTRIES, INC.
PUBLIC COMPANIES COMPARATIVE FINANCIAL ANALYSIS
($ Millions)
Public Companies

Statistics and Ratios	Alpha Corp.	Gamma Corp.	Iota Corp.	Lambda Corp.	Rho Corp.	Tau Corp.	Range	BII
	12/31/X8	12/30/X8	12/31/X8	10/31/X8	12/31/X8	12/31/X8		12/31/X8 (Pro Forma)
Fiscal Year Ended								
Revenues	$57.0	$350.2	$678.1	$483.0	$1,244.4	$1,766.3	$57-$1,766	$608
Total assets	$17.9	$330.9	$342.4	$480.6	$1,006.7	$1,759.4	$18-$1,759	$439
Net worth	$11.0	$197.2	$114.2	$207.6	$303.6	$936.3	$11- $936	($105)
EBIT	$2.8	$38.5	$62.3	$45.5	$114.6	$243.9	$3- $244	$55
Net income	$1.6	$22.1	$24.5	$20.0	$33.7	$117.7	$2- $118	$14
Working capital	$3.2	$46.2	$46.3	$20.8	$158.9	$318.9	$3- $319	$61
Liquidity Ratios								
Quick ratio	0.8	1.3	0.9	0.7	1.0	1.6	0.7-1.6	0.9
Current ratio	1.6	2.6	1.6	1.3	2.0	2.4	1.3-2.6	1.6
Net working capital turnover ratio	17.8	7.6	14.6	23.2	7.8	5.5	5.5-23.2	10.0
Leverage Ratios								
Total non-interest-bearing debt/equity ratio	0.4	0.2	0.3	0.2	0.2	0.2	0.2- 0.4	0.3
Activity Ratios								
Inventory turnover ratio	11.1	6.9	9.8	9.4	6.1	7.4	6.1-11.1	6.0
Accounts receivable turnover ratio	13.3	11.3	11.3	8.5	10.0	11.5	8.5-13.3	10.9
Fixed-asset turnover	3.2	1.1	2.0	1.0	1.2	1.0	1.0- 3.2	1.5

TABLE 13-4
BORNWELL INDUSTRIES, INC.
PUBLIC COMPANIES COMPARATIVE FINANCIAL ANALYSIS (continued)
($ Millions)

	Public Companies							
	Fiscal Year Ended							
Statistics and Ratios	Alpha Corp. 12/31/X8	Gamma Corp. 12/30/X8	Iota Corp. 12/31/X8	Lambda Corp. 10/31/X8	Rho Corp. 12/31/X8	Tau Corp. 12/31/X8	Range	BII 12/31/X8 (Pro Forma)
Profitability ratios								
Gross profit margin/sales ratio	22.5%	25.2%	16.3%	21.1%	25.7%	26.4%	16.3%-26.4%	29.0%
EBIT/sales	4.9%	11.0%	9.2%	9.4%	9.2%	13.8%	4.9%-13.8%	8.9%
EBIT/total assets	15.6%	11.6%	18.2%	9.5%	11.4%	13.9%	9.5%-18.2%	13.1%
Growth statistics								
Annual revenue growth	26.1%	27.9%	13.1%	29.4%	89.8%	18.3%	13.1%-29.4%	11.3%
Growth index[a]								
Revenues	1.2	1.4	1.8	1.3	3.3	1.3	1.2-3.3	2.5

[a] Most recent year's revenues divided by revenues four year's prior.

[*Text continued from p. 13-12.*]

TABLE 13-5

BORNWELL INDUSTRIES, INC.
CAPITALIZATION RATES OF COMPARATIVE COMPANIES

	Mean Price[a]/DFE
Alpha Corp.	14.9
Gamma Corp.	16.0
Iota Corp.	11.9
Lambda Corp.	19.6
Rho Corp.	17.0
Tau Corp.	13.6
Range	11.9-19.6
Median	15.5

	Mean Price[a]/DFCF
Alpha Corp.	8.0
Gamma Corp.	8.1
Iota Corp.	8.1
Lambda Corp.	10.8
Rho Corp.	8.4
Tau Corp.	7.8
Range	7.8-10.8
Median	8.1

	Mean Price[a]/EBIT
Alpha Corp.	8.5
Gamma Corp.	10.2
Iota Corp.	6.3
Lambda Corp.	12.7
Rho Corp.	9.4
Tau Corp.	8.0
Range	6.3-12.7
Median	9.0

[a] Price includes both debt and equity (TIC)

[d] Discounted Cash Flow Approach

Table 13-6 develops projected net debt-free cash flows for BII, which is discounted to a net present value using a WACC of 14 percent. (See the computation in Table 13-7.) The terminal value calculated assumes 4% growth in free cash flow after 19X4. Like the market multiples approach, the resulting conclusion represents an indication of value for the total invested capital or debt plus equity of the firm.

TABLE 13-6

BORNWELL INDUSTRIES, INC.
PROJECTED NET DEBT-FREE CASH FLOW
($ Millions)

	19X9	19X0	19X1	19X2	19X3	19X4
Net income	$14	$23	$35	$49	$58	$68
Plus: Depreciation	36	48	55	52	55	55
Interest expense (after-tax)	21	20	19	18	16	15
Less: Working capital investment	8	(4)	(5)	(6)	(6)	(7)
Capital expenditures	(52)	(50)	(50)	(54)	(57)	(65)
Net debt-free cash flow	$27	$37	$54	$59	$66	$66
Terminal value						$661
WACC	14.0%					
Present value of TIC	$523					

TABLE 13-7

BORNWELL INDUSTRIES, INC.
COST OF CAPITAL

Cost of capital = (% debt) × (Cost of debt) × (1 − Tax rate)
+
(% equity) × (Cost of equity)

Cost of equity = Risk-free rate + Market premium × Beta
Market premium = Market return − Risk-free rate
Beta = Company-specific risk parameter

where

Tax rate = 50%
Cost of debt = 14%
% debt = 75%
Risk-free rate = 7%
Market premium = 8%
Beta (leveraged) = 3.5
Cost of equity = 35%
Cost of capital = 14%

[e] Asset Valuation Summary

Based on the four indications of value and giving equal weight to each, a value for BII's operations of $475 million is reached.

Approach		Value Indication
Price/DFE		
14.5 × $31,000,000	=	$450,000,000
Price/DFCF		
8.0 × $60,000,000	=	$480,000,000
Price/EBIT		
8.0 × $55,000,000	=	$440,000,000
Discounted cash flow	=	$523,000,000
Concluded value of operations	=	$475,000,000

The next step in the solvency analysis will be to evaluate liabilities.

[f] Valuing Liabilities: Guarantee of Subsidiary's Debt

The market value of interest-bearing debt and value of contingent claims, if any, must be subtracted from total invested capital to arrive at an indication of value for the company's total equity. Prior to effecting the LBO, BII plans to spin off a subsidiary and guarantee the subsidiary's $75 million zero-coupon note. What value should be used for the guarantee in the balance sheet test? There are at least two methods for valuing this type of contingent liability.

A simplified option pricing approach would treat the guarantee as though BII had written a put option on the subsidiary's assets. The key variables in valuing an option are:

Subsidiary's asset value	$60 million
Face value of note (exercise price)	75 million
Time to exercise	5 years
Risk-free rate	7%
Volatility	0.25

Making the appropriate computations and adjustments yields a market value of approximately $10 million.

The second approach is somewhat easier to explain and involves determining the market yield that the subsidiary would have received if it had issued the note without the BII guarantee. The credit quality analysis of the subsidiary on a stand-alone basis indicates a market yield of 16 percent. The proceeds on the notes would have been $33 million as compared to actual proceeds of $43 million with the guarantee. This implies a $10 million value for the guarantee, in agreement with the option pricing approach.

[g] Valuing Liabilities: Convertible Subordinated Debt

BII's new issue of $100 million in convertible debt poses an interesting solvency valuation issue. Because of the convertibility feature the security carries a below-market coupon of 11%, as compared to a market rate determined through analysis to be 16% for a comparable straight debt issue without a convertibility feature. Computing a present value for the straight debt component of the security at 16% results in a market value of $75 million. There is currently some disagreement in the legal community over which figure should be used for the value of the liability in the balance sheet test. In this example, the more conservative approach will be taken, and the face value of $100 million will be used.

[h] Summary

As shown here, the equity cushion for the BII deal is $65 million or approximately 14% of total asset value:

Value of aggregate assets	$475,000,000
Value of liabilities	
Existing debt to be maintained	($ 60,000,000)
Secured bank debt	($165,000,000)
Senior notes	($ 75,000,000)
Convertible subordinated debt	($100,000,000)
Guarantee of subsidiary's debt	($ 10,000,000)
Value of equity capital	$ 65,000,000

[3] Cash Flow Test

The purpose of the cash flow test is to determine whether the company can reasonably be expected to meet its anticipated fixed (stated and identified contingent) obligations as they mature and come due. As a first step, the reasonableness of the company's base case projections must be determined. The projections shown in Table 13-8 demonstrate the effects of transaction debt and key financial covenants imposed by the lenders. Table 13-9 displays a comparison of certain of BII's forecast assumptions relative to its historical performance. BII expects revenue growth to slow while profitability increases relative to the 19X4 to 19X8 period. This is consistent with the company's evolution from an expansion strategy to one that focuses on rationalizing both manufacturing and marketing expenses.

TABLE 13-8

BORNWELL INDUSTRIES, INC.
PROJECTED CASH FLOW STATEMENT
($ Millions)

	19X9	19X0	19X1	19X2	19X3	19X4
Revenues	$687	$776	$862	$957	$1,043	$1,105
Gross profit	203	233	267	306	334	365
Net income	14	23	35	49	58	68
Depreciation	36	48	55	52	55	55
Working capital	8	(4)	(5)	(6)	(6)	(7)
Capital expenditures	(52)	(50)	(50)	(54)	(57)	(65)
Net cash flow from operations	$6	$17	$35	$41	$50	$51
Principal repayment						
Existing debt	-0-	(5)	(5)	(5)	(5)	(5)
Bank debt	-0-	(10)	(20)	(25)	(30)	(30)
Senior notes	-0-	-0-	-0-	-0-	-0-	(10)
Subordinated debt	-0-	-0-	-0-	-0-	-0-	-0-
Cash excess (shortfall)	$6	$2	$10	$11	$15	$6
Ending cash balance	$19	$21	$32	$42	$57	$63
EBIT coverage						
Actual	1.67	2.14	2.83	3.68	4.54	5.54
Covenant	1.40	1.60	2.10	2.70	3.20	3.80
Debt service coverage						
Actual	2.54	2.42	2.58	2.80	3.01	2.94
Covenant	2.00	2.10	2.20	2.30	2.40	2.40

TABLE 13-9

BORNWELL INDUSTRIES, INC.
REVENUE AND PROFITABILITY ASSUMPTIONS

	Historical (19X4-19X8)	19X9	19X0	19X1	19X2	19X3	19X4
Revenue growth							
Range	(5.7%)-46.6%	13.0%	13.0%	11.0%	11.0%	9.0%	6.0%
Average	18.5%						
Gross profit margin							
Range	23.4%-29.0%	29.5%	30.0%	31.0%	32.0%	32.0%	33.0%
Average	26.8%						
Operating expenses/revenues							
Range	17.1%-20.4%	19.5%	19.0%	18.5%	18.2%	18.0%	18.5%
Average	19.0%						

The next step involves sensitivity testing of key assumptions underlying the projections. Table 13-10 provides a sensitivity test for BII's projected gross profit margin (GPM). In this example, the GPM reaches the break-even level when the company's cash balance turns negative, which occurs for a five-year average GPM 2 percentage points lower than the base case. The cash balance is adjusted for funds available under revolving credit facilities.

TABLE 13-10

SENSITIVITY TO GROSS PROFIT MARGIN
ANNUAL FREE CASH FLOW
($ Millions)

Gross Profit Margin	19X9	19X0	19X1	19X2	19X3	19X4	19X4 Cumulative Cash
Base	$6	$ 2	$10	$11	$15	$ 6	$63
−1.0%	4	(2)	6	6	9	(1)	36
−1.5%	3	(4)	4	3	6	(4)	22
−2.0%	3	(6)	1	1	4	(7)	8
−2.5%	2	(8)	(1)	(2)	1	(10)	(6)
−3.0%	1	(10)	(3)	(5)	(2)	(14)	(20)
−3.5%	0	(12)	(5)	(7)	(5)	(17)	(33)

Additional sensitivity tests require analysis of reasonable downside scenarios that combine lower inputs for key variables to facilitate the determination of whether a reasonable degree of comfort exists that the company would be able to pay its debts even in the presence of reasonably foreseeable adverse conditions. A two-variable test is conceptually represented in Figure 13-4. The maximum revolver curve represents the break-even line where the company's cash availability is exhausted. The interest coverage covenant line graphs the break-even points for this financial covenant. Figure 13-4 also depicts the only two years in recent history when the company's performance fell below the projected five-year averages. This supports a conclusion that BII should reasonably be expected to be able to pay its debts as they come due.

FIGURE 13-4 Combined Sensitivity Analysis

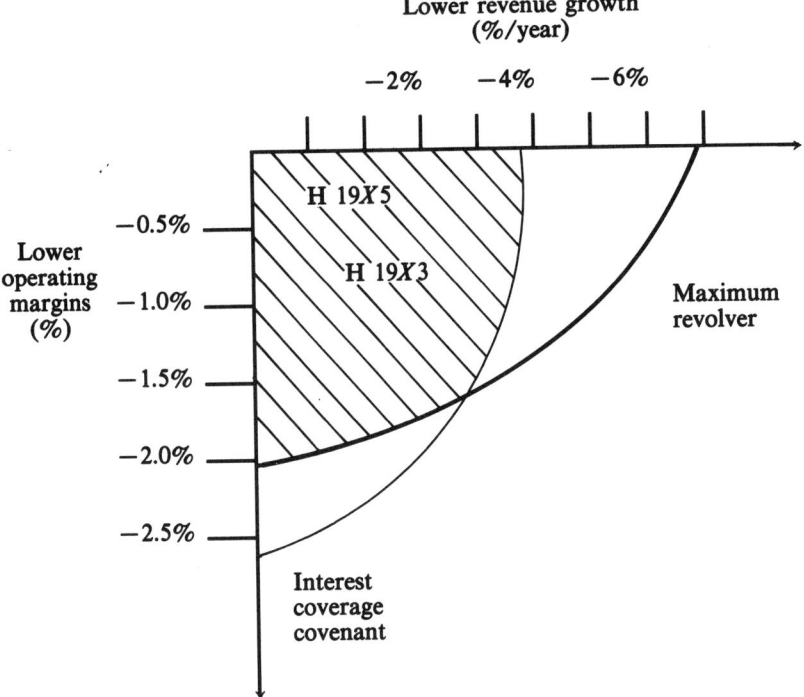

These sensitivity tests have been performed without any counterbalancing adjustments, such as reducing or delaying capital expenditures in the lower revenue growth scenarios. Capital expenditures related to maintenance items typically cannot be delayed, but growth-oriented investments might be postponed to provide an extra cash flow cushion.

[4] Reasonable Capital Test

The reasonable capital test focuses on a subjective analysis of the results obtained in the balance sheet and cash flow tests—both the equity cushion derived in the balance sheet test and the safety margin found in the cash flow test must be examined. The assessment of capital adequacy incorporates consideration of several factors, including those in the following discussion.

[a] Revenue Growth and Margin Sensitivity

Based on the combined sensitivity analysis (see Figure 13-4), BII should have a sufficient cushion to survive temporary shortfalls in revenue and earnings performance.

[b] Volatility of Asset Prices

The equity value can also be thought of as the amount available to cushion against a fall in the overall value of the company. In BII's case, the company's aggregate asset value can fall by $65 million without falling below the current value of liabilities.

[c] Maturity Structure of Fixed and Contingent Obligation

The repayment schedule and covenants shown in Table 13-8 appear to give BII enough operational flexibility both to meet its debt obligations as they come due and to avoid a technical default on the financial covenants during the debt paydown period. In the unlikely event that the outstanding contingent item (the subsidiary debt guarantee) becomes a real liability in $19X3$ BII should be able to fund the $75 million note through its operating cash flow and/or its available debt capacity. The base case cash balance is projected at $58 million, and $105 million of debt is expected to have been repaid.

¶ 13.4 Summary

From a financial point of view, the LBO proposed for BII has been structured prudently. The analysis of the base case projections indicates the company should be able to weather any reasonably foreseeable downturn in operating cash flow while remaining current on its debt. Based on the solvency analysis outlined in this case study, a complete, unqualified opinion on the financial aspects of solvency could be issued.

III
VALUATION BY INDUSTRY

III

VALUATION BY INDUSTRY

Differentiating Valuation Approaches by Industry Group 14-1

Manufacturing 15-1

Service Industries 16-1

Financial Institutions 17-1

Insurance Companies and Agencies 18-1

Natural Resources 19-1

Professional Practices 20-1

Canadian Financial Valuation 21-1

PART III INTRODUCTION

Financial Valuation: Business and Business Interests devotes its entire Part III to descriptions and analyses of "Valuation by Industry." Part III includes eight chapters whose comprehensive topics range from valuation approaches by industry groups to specific studies of manufacturing, service industries, financial institutions, insurance companies and agencies, natural resources, professional practices, and, finally, Canadian financial valuation.

Chapter 14 on "Differentiating Valuation Approaches by Industry Group" by Shannon P. Pratt focuses on choosing valuation approaches and techniques. The chapter analyzes the business situations where valuation approaches may or may not be readily adaptable from one business to the next. After a brief explanation of the use of Standard

Industrial Classification (SIC) codes, the discussion devotes itself to identifying the twelve industry characteristics and market factors that affect the selection of a valuation approach. The chapter closes with a definitive analysis of the availability and nature of comparative transaction data as well as industry valuation formulas.

Chapter 15 on "Manufacturing" by Wallace F. Forbes dissects the complicated task of valuing the wide variety of businesses that are involved in manufacturing. This diversity within the manufacturing industry is explained in the opening pages of the chapter, which then proceeds to the types of analytical techniques that must be part of any valuation of a manufacturing business: company qualitative analysis, company financial analysis, and industry analysis. The chapter, which includes eight practical tables, concludes with an explanation and an application of the accepted valuation approaches.

Chapter 16 on "Service Companies" by Donald P. Jacobs and Charles H. Stryker focuses on the wide range of service companies, including those services listed in the SIC manual, from hotels and other lodgings to personal, business, health, legal, educational, and social services as well as to entertainment, recreation, and art education services, to name a few. This industry study analyzes the valuation of the intangible assets that characterize the service industry, such as its work force, customer contracts, software and databases, customer base, employment and other contracts, and trade names. The chapter, which includes eight hands-on tables, closes with a study of the special financial considerations and valuation approaches that characterize service industries.

Chapter 17 on "Financial Institutions" by Jack W. Berka is a pivotal chapter on the valuation of the financial institutions industry, taking into account this industry's unique role as an instrument of public policy and its regulation by a number of overlapping agencies. After a detailed overview of the financial institutions industry, with special focus on the changes taking place during the 1980s, the chapter moves on to savings and loan analysis and commerical bank analysis, supported by eleven practical tables. The chapter closes with a discussion of other valuation considerations, particularly accounting and management issues.

Chapter 18 on "Insurance Companies and Insurance Agencies" by Russell R. Miller and Mark S. Lefenfeld is divided into two areas of focus: The first part of the chapter is devoted to an analysis of the valuation of insurance companies, and the second part is devoted to an analysis of the valuation of insurance agencies, with both parts supported by ten tables. The study of insurance companies starts with the business reasons for valuation, including the economic dynamics of mergers and acquisitions, long-term planning, initial public offerings, employee stock ownership plans, and demutualization. This analysis moves on to the steps in the valuation process, the evaluation of management practices, and an analysis of the business. The first part of the chapter concludes with a financial report review and a study of the generally accepted valuation methods for insurance companies. The study of insurance agencies opens by dispelling the myths pervading this type of valuation and then moves on to an analysis of the valuation methods and factors in the valuation of insurance agencies. The chapter concludes with a brief summary and comparison of the valuation of insurance companies and insurance agencies.

Chapter 19 on "Natural Resources" by Alex W. Howard focuses on the predominant company in the natural resources industry—the exploration and production company. The techniques to value oil and gas, coal, and timber companies are explored in depth, with special consideration paid to ownership forms, partnerships, operational data, and taxation, accounting, and valuation methods. The chapter closes with an analysis of other extractive industries, including all types of mining.

Chapter 20 on "Professional Practices" by Ralph Arnold and Shannon P. Pratt presents the valuation of a professional practice as a two-step process: the sale of the practice or an interest in the practice and the distribution of the assets in a divorce. The valuation of these practices' balance sheets is analyzed in depth. The chapter devotes many pages to the topic of goodwill—the practice of goodwill and professional goodwill, and the elements of goodwill in purchase, sales, and divorce valuations. The chapter closes with a practical approach to valuing the professional practice, including the following accepted valuation methods: the excess earnings method, the capitalization of earnings method, and the multiples of revenues method.

Chapter 21 on "Canadian Financial Valuation" by Richard M. Wise parlays the similarities and differences between U.S. and Canadian valuation practices into an in-depth focus on Canadian valuation methodology. This comprehensive chapter opens with an exposition of the relevant statutes governing Canadian valuation and then moves on to an analysis of commerical transactions. This discussion covers mergers and acquisitions, corporate reorganizations, going private or going public, partnership/shareholder buy-sell agreements, employee stock option plans, allocation of purchases, related-party transactions, financial solvency analyses, and government privatization. The chapter then moves on to the litigation that supports valuation methods in Canada and a description of the Canadian valuation profession. The chapter, which is supported by four tables, closes with an explanation of Canadian valuation terms and a study of applicable case law and regulatory pronouncements and practices, including those from leading judicial decisions, from Revenue Canada, Taxation, from the Ontario Securities Commission, and the British Columbia Securities Commission.

14
DIFFERENTIATING VALUATION APPROACHES BY INDUSTRY GROUP

SHANNON P. PRATT*

		Page
¶ 14.1	Valuation Approach Concerns	14-2
¶ 14.2	The SIC Code System	14-3
	[1] Classifications	14-3
	[2] Usefulness	14-4
	[3] Limitations	14-4
	[a] Method of Classification	14-4
	[b] Obsolescence	14-5
	[c] Trend Away From Homogeneity	14-5
¶ 14.3	Industry Characteristics That Affect Valuation Approaches	14-5
	[1] Capital Intensity	14-5
	[2] Nature of Assets	14-5
	[a] Financial Assets	14-5
	[b] Inventory	14-6
	[c] Real Estate	14-6
	[d] Furniture, Fixtures, Machinery, and Equipment	14-7
	[e] Natural Resources	14-8
	[3] Extent of Off Balance Sheet Factors	14-8
	[4] Regulatory Environment	14-9
	[5] Ease of Entry	14-9
	[6] Degree of Product or Service Differentiation Among Competitors	14-10
	[7] Degree of Industry Homogeneity	14-10
	[8] Business Continuity Characteristics	14-11
	[9] Owner-Manager Personal Involvement	14-11

---

* SHANNON P. PRATT, CFA, FASA, DBA, is president of Willamette Management Associates, Inc. in Portland, Oregon. The author has also written two books on business valuation: *Valuing a Business: The Analysis and Appraisal of Closely Held Companies* (2d ed. 1989), and *Valuing Small Businesses and Professional Practices* (1986).

	[10]	Manner in Which Benefits Are Realized by Owners	14-12
	[11]	Specialized Accounting Practices	14-13
	[12]	Size of Business Unit	14-13
¶ 14.4	**Market Factors That Affect Valuation Approaches**		14-15
	[1]	Supply and Demand Conditions	14-15
	[2]	Typical Terms of Sale and Types of Consideration Paid	14-15
		[a] Notes or Contracts Receivable	14-15
		[b] Stock	14-16
		[c] Convertible Securities	14-16
		[d] Earnout Provisions	14-16
	[3]	Channels Through Which Industry Units Are Sold	14-16
¶ 14.5	**Availability and Nature of Comparative Transaction Data**		14-17
	[1]	Public Market Trading Data	14-17
	[2]	Merger, Acquisition, and Divestiture Data	14-18
	[3]	Small Private Company Sales Data	14-18
¶ 14.6	**Industry Rule-of-Thumb Valuation Formulas**		14-18

The value of a business depends upon the cash payments and other benefits it generates for its owners. These payments and benefits can come from one or from a combination of three sources:

1. Ongoing business activity (operations and investments);
2. Liquidation of assets; and
3. Sale of all or a partial interest in the entity or a pledge of interest as collateral for borrowing.

How these benefits are generated by the company and how they can be measured and translated into values perceived by owners varies greatly from one industry to the next.

Businesses that appear to be in dissimilar industries may share characteristics that make the valuation approaches and expertise derived from one fairly readily adaptable to the other. On the other hand, the characteristics of some industries are so unique that it is essential that the valuation of a company in that industry be done by a firm with specific experience in valuing similar entities.

¶ 14.1 Valuation Approach Concerns

Some concerns that must be addressed in choosing valuation approaches and techniques include the following:

- To what extent is the value of the business dependent upon its tangible-asset values, and to what extent is it dependent upon its earning power?
- What degree of attention should be focused on the various indications of earning power: gross revenues, any of several definitions of *cash flow*, operating income, and net income? (Note, of course, that the choice of what indication of earning power is to be capitalized also becomes an essential consideration when it comes to defining and developing appropriate capitalization rates.)
- To what extent should earning power approaches focus on historical data, and to what extent should they focus on projected data?
- To what extent is it possible or appropriate to derive capitalization rates and other market parameters from specific transactions in comparative companies versus more generalized (and thus less precisely comparable) market data?
- What is the type and extent of adjustments that the analyst would expect to have to make for valuation purposes?

To a great extent, answers to these questions are dependent upon the characteristics of the industry in which the subject entity operates.

This chapter introduces the basic topic of industry classifications and characteristics and how they influence the choice of appropriate valuation approaches and techniques.

¶ 14.2 The SIC Code System

The Standard Industrial Classification (SIC) code system was developed by the United States government for the purpose of gathering, analyzing, and publishing financial and other data by industry group. Every corporation and partnership that files a tax return is identified by a primary SIC code.

[1] Classifications

SIC codes are based on a four-digit system; all industry groups fall into one of 11 broad classifications as follows.

A. Agriculture, forestry, and fishing (01— through 09—)
B. Mining (10— through 14—)
C. Construction (15— through 17—)
D. Manufacturing (20— through 39—)
E. Transportation, communications, electric, gas, and sanitary services (40— through 49—)
F. Wholesale trade (50— through 51—)
G. Retail trade (52— through 59—)

H. Finance, insurance, and real estate (60— through 67—)
I. Services (70— through 89—)
J. Public administration (91— through 97—)
K. Nonclassificable establishments (99—)

A list and definition of all industry groups is published in the *Standard Industrial Classification Manual*.[1]

[2] Usefulness

In addition to being a generally understood and widely used numerical system of classifying companies by industry group, the SIC system has the advantage of being the only game in town. Databases that use the system for the classification or indexing of companies by industry include *Acquisition/Divestiture Weekly Report*, *Directory of Companies Required to File Reports with the Securities and Exchange Commission*, *Mergerstat Review*, Moody's manuals, *Annual Statement Studies*, *Predicasts F&S Index of United States*, Standard & Poor's *Corporate Records*, and Willamette Management Associates' Business Sale Data Base. As a consequence, the SIC system can be very useful as a tool in the process of locating comparative company transactions and other data for input into the valuation process.

[3] Limitations

While SIC codes are useful, the valuation analyst cannot use them mechanically without understanding their limitations. The most important limitations arise from the method of classification, the obsolescence of the codes in light of technical innovation, and the trend away from homogeneity.

[a] Method of Classification

The distinctions used in classifying companies by SIC group are not necessarily the distinctions relevant in choosing valuation approaches and techniques. For example, manufacturer's representatives are classified under wholesale trade and grouped by the type of products they distribute. From a valuation viewpoint, manufacturer's representatives are much more like service businesses than merchant wholesalers that operate physical distribution centers and take title to and possession of large inventories.

---

[1] U.S. Office of Management and Budget, *Standard Industrial Classification Manual* (1987).

[b] Obsolescence

Technological progress and other innovations have resulted in the formation of many industries not in existence when the SIC system was developed. The result has been to squeeze many companies in emerging industries into categories that are not particularly good fits.

[c] Trend Away From Homogeneity

While it used to be true that there were many companies within each of many industries that were essentially similar to each other, that has become less true in more recent years. Companies are tending to become more diversified and unique, making generalizations based on a single SIC code less relevant.

¶ 14.3 Industry Characteristics That Affect Valuation Approaches

Many industries have one or more inherent characteristics that have a bearing on determination of the most relevant valuation approaches. The analyst must understand the industry characteristics of the company being valued and the implications of these characteristics for choosing valuation approaches. Failure to do so will result in square company valuation criteria being applied to round and amoeba-shaped companies, necessarily resulting in an invalid estimation of value.[2]

[1] Capital Intensity

As one might expect, asset-related approaches tend to play a greater role in valuations of companies in industries where a considerable amount of capital is required; earnings-related approaches usually dominate the valuation process in industries requiring little capital.

[2] Nature of Assets

The nature of the assets used in a business has considerable bearing when it comes to choosing or emphasizing a valuation approach. Broadly speaking, the more liquid the assets, the more directly they will be considered in the valuation process.

[a] Financial Assets

Much emphasis is generally placed on balance sheet items in valuations of companies in industries with large amounts of financial assets such as stocks, bonds, notes, contracts, or financial leases. Such companies include the following:

---

[2] *See* S.P. Pratt, "Economic and Industry Data," in *Valuing a Business: The Analysis and Appraisal of Closely Held Companies*, ch. 7 (2d ed. 1989).

- Banks and savings and loans;
- Insurance underwriters;
- Mortgage bankers; and
- Investment holding companies.

If a particular company in any of these categories has unusually large financial assets, it may be necessary to modify the valuation approaches used for that industry in order to reflect the full value of the assets.

[b] Inventory

When inventory represents a major part of total assets—as it does in retailing and wholesale merchandising, for example—inventory value must be a major factor in the valuation of the total entity. The value of inventory can also be an important factor in some manufacturing and extraction companies.

[c] Real Estate

The appropriate valuation approaches when real estate is involved depend, to a considerable degree, on whether the real estate is usable only for the purpose for which it is currently being used or is adaptable to other uses. The greater the extent to which the real estate can be expected to remain in its current use, the greater the emphasis on income-related approaches; the greater the likelihood that the real estate will be sold or converted to some other use, the greater the attention accorded to the market value of the real estate as such.

The degree of flexibility with respect to potential uses of real estate depend upon either the nature of the property itself or upon zoning or contractual restrictions. Aluminum plants and electric-power-generating facilities are examples of special-purpose properties where income approaches, as opposed to asset approaches, would be expected to dominate the valuation process. A farm subject to permanent agricultural zoning or a dedicated golf course are also examples of properties where the focus would be expected to be on income rather than asset valuation.

If a company owns real estate in an industry where real estate is more commonly leased (e.g., retailing, the restaurant business, many types of manufacturing, and most service businesses) it is common to impute a market rate of rent to the expenses, value the business without the real estate, and then add an appropriate amount for the real estate owned.

Where improved real estate is a major asset factor—as it is in hotel chains and shopping centers, for example—cash flow rather than net income will be used as an indicator of earning power. This is because the depreciation charges on improved real estate generally do not represent a genuine diminution in economic value, provided that adequate maintenance and replacements are allowed for in the cash-flow stream.

[d] Furniture, Fixtures, Machinery, and Equipment

The nature and extent of non-real estate fixed assets will have a bearing on whether the income approaches focus on cash flow, net income, or some variation of one of these variables. The key is the extent to which the depreciation charged on the income statement represents a genuine decrement to value. In a typical restaurant, the useful life of the equipment may be about twice the depreciable life used for tax purposes. In a construction company in Alaska, the useful life of the equipment may not exceed the depreciable life used for taxes. One of the most common errors made in business valuations, especially valuations of smaller businesses, is to focus the income approach on earnings before depreciation without adequately reflecting the cash outflow needed for replacements.

Most machinery and equipment cannot be liquidated for anywhere near its book value, much less its cost. Therefore, companies in industries heavily dependent upon machinery and equipment normally should not be valued with a heavy emphasis on asset-value approaches even when they can be considered capital-intensive, but income approaches should be designed carefully to reflect the true economic life of the equipment.

Users of appraisals should also be wary of the "depreciated replacement cost" approach to the valuation of an industrial plant. This approach starts by estimating what it would cost to build a new plant with equivalent productive capacity. The estimated replacement cost is then adjusted to reflect whatever decrement to that value may be inherent in the existing plant as a result of functional and economic obsolescence (in an oversimplified definition, the excess production costs inherent because of outmoded facilities and factors exogenous to the plant itself, such as excessive power costs in the particular locale). Finally, an estimate is made of the remaining useful life of the existing facility as a percentage of the estimated total useful life of the hypothesized replacement facility. This requires more estimations, often with less basis in fact, than discounted future earnings or cash-flow approaches! When you are all through, what does it mean? Investors would not buy the plant at the value indicated by that approach if the plant could not generate enough earnings to justify that value, so it does not indicate a minimum value. On the other hand, investors could not go out and buy the hypothetical depreciated replacement facility as an alternative to the subject facility, so neither does the approach indicate a maximum value.

[e] Natural Resources

For companies that own a finite amount of natural-resource assets—such as mining, oil and gas, and timber companies—an asset-valuation approach usually is included as part of the total valuation process. Obviously, the extent of reliance on historical operating results in an income approach for a natural resource company depends on the extent to which adequate supplies of the resource remain as well as on the concurrence or lack of it between the historical economic factors that affect the resource and the current and prospective factors that affect the resource.

[3] Extent of Off Balance Sheet Factors

Some industries have many off balance sheet factors that need to be incorporated into the valuation approaches; other industries have few. They are called "off balance sheet" items because they do not appear as line items on the balance sheet although, in general, they may be susceptible to estimation and inclusion as reserve accounts or by footnote reference as a contingency. Some typical off balance sheet factors are the following:

- Unfunded or overfunded past service costs;
- Requirements to comply with environmental regulations or the Occupational Safety and Health Act (OSHA);
- Employment or "noncompete" agreements; and
- Other contractual agreements.

It is hard to generalize about which off balance sheet factors are most prevalent in which industries. Suffice it to say that the nature of the industry should trigger a person's thinking about the possibilities of various off balance sheet factors.

It is also hard to generalize about how the many different off balance sheet factors should be reflected in valuation approaches. In some cases, it is appropriate to reflect off balance sheet factors by making specific adjustments to asset values or to an income stream to be capitalized. In other cases, the factors may merely represent risks that can best be reflected through an appropriately risk-adjusted capitalization or discount rate.

[4] Regulatory Environment

The regulatory environment is one broad category to be considered when selecting and implementing a valuation approach. The analyst must consider the impact that the current and prospective regulatory environment in the industry will have on important variables such as the pricing of a company's products or services, its cost structure, its operating policies, its competition, its expansion opportunities, its taxes, and many other items that will have a bearing on its value.

The past decade has ushered in a sweeping set of changes in the regulatory environment. These changes have had a profound effect on the way in which the value of a company is determined. One obvious impact of regulatory change on valuation approaches is the lessening of reliance on a company's historical record in arriving at an earnings base to capitalize in industries heavily affected by regulatory change, such as banking, other financial services, most forms of transportation, and telecommunications.

Furthermore, state laws, regulations, and court decisions may dictate different valuation approaches in different states or local areas for companies in the same industry. Limitations to entry tend to move the valuation focus away from asset-value approaches and toward income-related approaches. Examples of industries where such regulations vary greatly from one locale to another include taxi services, garbage collection and disposal services, and package and on-premise alcoholic beverage outlets, including nightclubs and restaurants. Valuations of professional practices for divorces are an example of court decisions mandating different valuation approaches in different states for entities in the same industry.

[5] Ease of Entry

The greater the ease of entry to a particular industry, the more the valuation approaches emphasize asset values. The harder it is to establish a comparable unit de novo, the more the valuation approaches focus on earning power, which may result in a substantial amount of intangible value. For example, individual hardware stores, auto-parts stores, and hobby shops tend to sell very close to their tangible-asset values because opening comparable new stores is a readily available alternative in most cases.

Impediments to entry originate from different sources in different industries. Such sources include government regulation (discussed in the previous section), the time needed to create productive operations (e.g., tree farming, paper production), the time needed to build up a clientele (e.g., most types of professional practices, consumer products marketed through brand-name recognition), the limited availability of qualified personnel or other resources, or the technological complexity of the products or services offered.

[6] Degree of Product or Service Differentiation Among Competitors

Many industries are considered "commodity industries" because their products cannot be differentiated from those of their competitors in the marketplace. Examples of these industries are sawmills; plywood mills; and many farming, seed, and food processing operations. The selling prices of commodities produced by companies in these industries are subject to market forces outside the control of the company, and earnings of such companies thus tend to be highly cyclical. The valuation analyst must focus heavily on the cost structure compared with competitors when trying to assess the earning power of such companies because the revenues per unit or production will be set by market forces. When using a valuation approach based on historical earnings, the historical time period analyzed should be long enough to reflect cyclical influences. Comparative companies from which market parameters are to be derived must be chosen carefully on the basis of how they are affected by the same cyclical influences. It is normally appropriate to accord more than the average amount of attention to economic factors affecting the industry in an attempt to evaluate the extent to which recent cyclical history may be repeated versus the extent to which economic and industry factors have changed so that future expectations must be based on a new scenario.

The more an industry is characterized by differentiated products and services, the more the valuation approaches can properly focus on factors within the company as opposed to factors outside the company's control and the more likely it is that the company may have created some intangible value for itself as a result of its ability to control its own destiny. Examples of companies with differentiated products and services would be those that have succeeded in taking full advantage of patents, copyrights, brand names, trademarks, and firm name recognition.

[7] Degree of Industry Homogeneity

The more that companies within an industry are like one another, the more the valuation approaches can make good use of comparable company data.

The more that the future earnings prospects for the subject company relative to its most recent earnings resemble its peer companies' prospects relative to their recent earnings, the more valid the approach of using comparable companies' price/earnings ratios as an indicator of value for the subject company. Similarly, the more alike the subject company and its peers in various respects (cost structure, capital structure, growth prospects, nature of assets, and so on), the more valid it is to use comparable companies to derive various parameters indicative of market value, such as price/cash flow ratios, price/sales ratios, price/ book value ratios, and price/adjusted book value ratios.

As noted earlier, industries are tending to become less homogeneous over time. However, many, if not most, industries have enough company characteristics in common to make approaches using comparative company analysis useful, providing that it is done carefully, with the proper adjustments. Examples of industries in which there are many companies with enough in common to make comparative company analysis useful are individual grocery stores and chains, restaurant chains, cable television companies, securities brokers, travel agencies, insurance agencies, and electric and natural gas distribution companies, to name a few.

[8] Business Continuity Characteristics

Generally speaking, the more a buyer feels that he can rely on the continuity of a business, the more willing he is to determine the price he will pay on the basis of the business's earning power rather than its asset values.

Businesses in industries that generate orders almost exclusively on the basis of competitive contract bidding—such as construction subcontractors and ship-repair facilities—tend to be valued with a heavy emphasis on asset values rather than earning power because there is little or no assurance of business continuity. On the other hand, businesses in industries that tend to have predictably persistent customers, such as newspapers and property and casualty insurance agencies, tend to be valued heavily on their ability to generate revenues and earnings, usually resulting in significant intangible value.

[9] Owner-Manager Personal Involvement

The extent to which a particular business is dependent upon the personal services of its owner or manager will have a major bearing on the valuation approach used.

The more dependent a business is on its people rather than its physical attributes (such as its assets or location), the more intangible value it may have, value resulting from the ability of its people to generate revenues and earnings. However, it may be very important in the valuation process to try to identify the extent to which the implied intangible value really is an integral part of the entity being valued, as opposed to personal goodwill, which may be removed at the pleasure of one or more individuals. For example, the value of a property and casualty insurance agency, engineering practice, CPA practice, or almost any kind of personal services business or practice may be substantial with the existence of an employment contract or "noncompete" agreement with one or more key individuals but negligible without such contractual arrangements. In other words, the more dependent an entity is on its key people, the more the choice of valuation approach depends on the existence of provisions for continuity of these people or, at least, protection from competition from them.

[10] Manner in Which Benefits Are Realized by Owners

The value of a business depends upon the value of the benefits that can be realized by its owners. The more quantifiable, in dollar terms, those benefits are, the more business valuation approaches can focus on the ability of the business to generate earnings, cash flow, and dividend-paying capacity.

There are two general categories of reasons why benefits are less easily quantifiable in some industries than in others.

1. *Bookkeeping and disbursements policies.* In many industries (travel publications, for example), it is common for benefits to owners to be so buried in indirect compensation and expenses that they defy an analyst's ability to sort them out. In others (primarily cash businesses, such as taverns, nightclubs, and many types of concessions), the books often fail to reflect all revenues and expenses fully and accurately.
2. *Benefits nonquantifiable in dollars.* There are certain industries in which a dollar return on investment may not be the primary, or at least the only, motivation for investment. Owners perceive benefits other than dollar returns from operations such as sports franchises, horse racing stables, and other businesses that provide their owners a forum for expression and audiences with notable people and attendance at notable events.

To the extent that there are problems in assessing the nature and necessity of some expense items, valuation approaches may focus on gross revenues rather than actual cash flow or earnings as an indication of potential earning power. The approaches may then impute earnings or may simply focus on multiples of revenues found in the prices at which comparable companies have sold. If gross revenues are not reliably ascertainable, earning-power approaches may focus on some physical measure of volume—such as kegs of beer sold or number of customers coming through the gate—again developing imputed earning power or relying on market observations of the relationship between price and physical volume at which comparable entities have been sold.

Similarly, in industries where non-dollar-denominated benefits are perceived by owners, valuation approaches may focus on multiples of gross revenue or dollars per unit of physical volume, such as dollars per subscriber.

[11] Specialized Accounting Practices

Some industries have specialized accounting practices either because of the nature of the business or, more commonly, because of regulatory requirements. These include:

- Banks and savings and loans;
- Insurance underwriters (both life and property and casualty);
- Automobile and equipment dealerships;
- Utilities (electric, gas, telephone);
- Railroads;
- Airlines;
- Forest products companies with federal timber-cutting contracts;
- Natural resource companies;
- Contractors;
- Securities brokers and underwriters; and
- Shopping centers.

In industries where specialized accounting practices exist, it is essential to have the valuation performed by a firm familiar with these practices so that the schedules or statements containing items accorded specialized accounting treatment can be properly interpreted, adjusted, and evaluated for valuation purposes.

Generally speaking, industries using cash-basis accounting require adjustments to an accrual basis for valuation purposes. In some industries, the purpose of the valuation will dictate how the specialized accounting data is to be used and what approaches should be taken. For example, regulatory authorities have widely adopted discounted cash-flow techniques, with certain definitions of "cash flow," for valuation of railroads and utilities for ad valorem taxes, while other approaches might receive more emphasis for mergers and acquisitions.

[12] Size of Business Unit

While in theory, valuing large and small businesses is essentially the same, in practice, the approaches used tend to be considerably different. Smaller business units tend to be found particularly among the following industry groups:

- Specialty retailers;
- Commission agencies (e.g., travel agencies, advertising agencies, insurance agencies, collection agencies, and manufacturers' representatives);
- Professional practices;
- Restaurants, lounges, taverns, and nightclubs;
- Personal services (e.g., hair salons, photographic studios, and shoe repair shops);
- Laundry and cleaning operations and routes (although the laundry and cleaning industry is one that also has large national operators);
- Service stations and automotive repair shops;
- Machine shops; and
- Funeral homes (an industry in the process of consolidation, however).

Different valuation approaches are used for smaller businesses for the following reasons:

- *Length of history.* Smaller businesses tend to have shorter track records, reducing emphasis on analyzing several years of historical data, often resulting in a capitalized single "normalized" year of earnings.
- *Key-person involvement.* Small companies are typically characterized by the personal involvement of their owners, increasing the emphasis placed on the analysis of extent or lack of continuity characteristics, including employment contracts and "noncompete" agreements.
- *Quality of financial statements.* Financial statements tend to be less reliable for smaller companies, requiring extensive analysis and adjustments or more emphasis on gross revenues or physical volume versus earnings and cash flow.
- *Compensation of owners.* The owners' compensation is often determined arbitrarily, requiring adjustments or focus on gross revenues.
- *Form of organization.* Many small companies are organized as sole proprietorships, partnerships, or S corporations, leading to a focus on earnings analyses on a pretax basis.
- *Comparable transaction data.* There is a lack of public comparables for derivation of market value parameters for smaller companies, often rendering direct market comparisons useless.
- *Cash versus terms.* Sales of companies are usually on terms other than cash, requiring adjustments to comparable sales data.
- *Assets versus stock sales.* Sales of companies are usually on an asset rather than a stock basis; this requires careful analysis of

what is included in comparable sales data in order to make the transactions comparable.

¶ 14.4 Market Factors That Affect Valuation Approaches

This section of the chapter deals with the market for purchases and sales of businesses and business interests as opposed to the markets for the goods and services offered by those businesses.

[1] Supply-and-Demand Conditions

The supply of and demand for business units in a particular industry will have a bearing on the valuation approaches taken.

The more the activity in ownership changes in the industry, the more the valuation approaches can use comparative transaction data to develop market value parameters. The classic example of the latter 1980s is the explosive surge of mergers and acquisitions in the banking industry, making data available on hundreds of transactions.

To the extent that buyers are actively driving up selling prices of certain types of businesses, valuation approaches should reflect such factors as synergies and control premiums as opposed to valuing the business strictly on the basis of an independent, stand-alone unit.

[2] Typical Terms of Sale and Types of Consideration Paid

Terms of sale and types of consideration paid may require considerable adjustment to convert transaction prices from face value to cash equivalent value or vice versa.

Interestingly, studies indicate that over 90 percent of all sales of small businesses through business brokers involve terms other than straight cash, almost always at interest rates below what it would cost buyers or sellers to borrow the same amount of money with comparable collateral if they could obtain financing in the market at all. Sales through investment bankers often result in the seller receiving stock in the buyer's company.

If consideration other than cash is received in either a comparable company transaction or the subject transaction, certain adjustments may be necessary to convert the face amount to a cash equivalent value.

[a] Notes or Contracts Receivable

Fixed-rate receivables should be converted to cash equivalent value by discounting the payment schedule at a market rate of interest for instruments of comparable risk.

[b] Stock

A seller may receive stock that falls into one of three categories:

1. Freely tradable stock in a public company, once received, is pretty close to cash unless the amount received relative to the amount normally traded is large enough that a blockage discount is indicated.
2. Sellers selling to public companies for stock usually get restricted stock (also sometimes referred to as "unregistered stock" or "letter stock"). This usually is worth less than freely tradable stock because of restrictions on transfer. It is not unusual for restricted stock to be worth as much as 35 percent less than its fully registered and freely tradable counterpart.
3. Stock in a privately held company would usually be discounted even further from a freely tradable public stock value equivalent because it is usually even more difficult to sell than are unregistered shares in a public company.

[c] Convertible Securities

The value of convertible preferred stock or convertible notes can be estimated by valuing the income stream just as one would value a fixed-income security and valuing the conversion feature just as one would value a warrant.

[d] Earnout Provisions

Earnouts are very hard to value but cannot be ignored when estimating the cash equivalent value of a deal. Perhaps the best approach is to make a best estimate of the earnout stream and discount it at a rate high enough to reflect the degree of risk. Many professional practices and personal service businesses are sold on an earnout basis in the sense that the price to be paid over a period of time is contingent on retention of existing clientele.

[3] Channels Through Which Industry Units Are Sold

In some industries, it is common for businesses to be sold directly between buyer and seller; in other industries, it is more common to see businesses sold through intermediaries, such as business brokers, merger and acquisition specialists, or investment bankers. Sales of automobile dealerships, for example, are almost always handled directly between the parties, while eating and drinking establishments are frequently sold through business brokers; larger manufacturers and chain retailers often are sold through investment bankers.

As far as valuation approaches are concerned, the channels through which businesses in the industry are typically sold has a bearing on the collection, interpretation, and extent of utilization of comparative transaction data.

¶ 14.5 Availability and Nature of Comparative Transaction Data

One of the biggest problems in implementing many desirable approaches to valuation is getting good market data on comparable company transactions. In some industries, there is plenty of comparable company transaction data; in others, there is little or none. The availability and quality of such data is a major factor in deciding what valuation approach to take in any given situation.

For convenience, comparable transaction data have been grouped into three categories:

1. Public market trading data;
2. Merger, acquisition, and divestiture data; and
3. Small private company sales data.

[1] Public Market Trading Data

In some industries, there are many public companies for which financial data and daily stock trading prices are readily available. Industries in which there are large numbers of public companies include the following:

- Banking and finance;
- Real estate investment trusts;
- Wholesale and distribution;
- Computer software, supplies, and services;
- Retail;
- Industrial and farm equipment and machinery;
- Drugs, medical supplies, and equipment;
- Food processing;
- Printing and publishing;
- Broadcasting; and
- Leisure and entertainment.

Using public market trading data, it is possible to collect market evidence on valuation parameters such as price/earnings ratios, price/cash flow ratios, price/revenues ratios, price/book value ratios, and dividend yields. It must be recognized, of course, that day-to-day transactions in the public market represent minority interests, which may require some adjustment to arrive at a control price for a company.

[2] Merger, Acquisition, and Divestiture Data

Several sources collect data on mergers, acquisitions, and divestitures; these data are generally limited to companies that are or have been public and larger private companies. In 1986, according to W.T. Grimm, the ten industries with the largest number of transactions reported were as follows (in order of number of transactions):

1. Banking and finance—415 transactions;
2. Miscellaneous services—235 transactions;
3. Computer software, supplies, and services—168 transactions;
4. Wholesale and distribution—160 transactions;
5. Retail—147 transactions;
6. Printing and publishing—130 transactions;
7. Drugs, medical supplies, and equipment—123 transactions;
8. Broadcasting—123 transactions;
9. Industrial and farm equipment and machinery—110 transactions; and
10. Food processing—101 transactions

[3] Small Private Company Sales Data

There are industries in which there are no public companies or very few. For example, automobile manufacturers prohibit their dealers from issuing public stock, and breweries similarly prohibit their distributors from issuing stock to the public. Other industries consist of companies that are too small or, for other reasons, would not have appeal to investors as public stocks.

There is no comprehensive central source for data on sales of small private companies. UBI, a business broker chain, maintains price/revenue ratios on its latest 1,000 sales of companies in 26 industries on line. Other business broker chains are considering maintaining similar data bases. In 1985, Willamette Management Associates started a business sale data base, but as of this writing, it has meaningful data on only a limited number of industries, including restaurants, drinking places, video rental and sales stores, accounting practices, and dental practices. Franchisers and manufacturers that use dealers and distributors usually have data on sales of companies but, typically, are reluctant to disclose this information. Trade associations can sometimes be helpful. The best source, in some cases, is a business broker who specializes in selling companies in a particular industry.

¶ 14.6 Industry Rule-of-Thumb Valuation Formulas

Many industries use long-cherished rules of thumb for valuing companies. Venture capitalist Thomas P. Murphy observed, "There seem to be norms for the worth of every imaginable business. My advice: Ignore them. Buying a business is too important for Kentucky windage."

The following are rules of thumb used to value companies in a few industries.

- *Funeral homes*—so many dollars per average annual complete burial service;
- *Oil jobberships and gas stations*—so many dollars for each average monthly or annual gallon delivered;
- *Grocery stores (in some areas)*—inventory plus so many weeks' gross sales (the multiple of gross sales is then assumed to be the value of the furniture and fixtures and so taken up on the books of the new owner);
- *Laundry, dry cleaning, linen supply, and uniform rental*—uncirculated inventory and other current assets plus so many weeks' gross receipts;
- *Accounting practices, property and casualty insurance agencies, and other professional practices and commission sales agencies*—current assets plus a year's gross revenues (or some fraction or multiple thereof);
- *Hotels, motels, and nursing homes*—so much per rental unit or per bed; and
- *Small specialty retailers*—assets plus a small percentage of one year's net income.

When an industry has a valuation rule of thumb, the appraiser should certainly take it into consideration, but he should not accept it at face value. Industry valuation rules of thumb tend to be fairly static and do not keep up with current industry and economic conditions. Also, the uniqueness of businesses generally precludes them from being valued properly by any sort of a formula applied en masse to companies in any industry.

In summary, there are many features associated with any particular industry that have a bearing on the choices of valuation approaches that will best serve in a particular situation.

15

MANUFACTURING

WALLACE F. FORBES[*]

			Page
¶ 15.1	Diversity Within the Manufacturing Industry and Manufacturing Valuations		15-2
	[1]	SIC Code Breakdown	15-2
	[2]	Defining What Is to Be Valued	15-3
		[a] Legal Structure	15-3
		[b] Type of Interest	15-3
		[c] Size of Interest	15-4
		[d] Rights or Restrictions	15-4
	[3]	Purpose of Valuation	15-5
	[4]	Revenue Ruling 59-60	15-5
¶ 15.2	Company Qualitative Analysis		15-6
	[1]	Product Line	15-6
	[2]	History and Organization	15-7
	[3]	Raw Materials	15-7
	[4]	Producing the Product	15-8
		[a] Work Force	15-8
		[b] Technology and Research and Development	15-9
	[5]	Marketing, Sales, and Distribution	15-9
	[6]	Other Factors	15-11
	[7]	Management	15-11
¶ 15.3	Company Financial Analysis		15-13
	[1]	Historical Income Statements	15-13
	[2]	Historical Balance Sheets	15-16
	[3]	Relating Income Statements to Balance Sheets	15-17
	[4]	Plans and Prospects	15-17
¶ 15.4	Industry Analysis		15-17
¶ 15.5	Valuation Approaches		15-22
	[1]	The Asset Approach	15-22

[*] WALLACE F. FORBES, CFA, CMC, is currently in private practice as a consultant. He is a retired principal of KPMG Peat Marwick and a founder of its Benchmark Valuation Consultants unit. The author has written numerous articles on valuation, which have appeared in such publications as *Harvard Business Review*, *Business Horizons*, *YPO Enterprise*, *Chief Executive*, and *Monthly Digest of Tax Articles*.

[2]	The Earnings (Discounted Cash Flow) Approach	15-23
[3]	The Market Approach	15-25
	[a] The Capitalization of Earnings	15-25
	[b] Market/Book Value Relationships	15-26
	[c] Dividend Returns	15-27
[4]	Other Valuation Approaches	15-27
[5]	Other Considerations	15-27

Manufacturers convert raw materials or unfinished products into finished products or those needing further processing. The industry classification "manufacturing," however, encompasses a wide variety of businesses. The characteristics of a steel producer are not analogous to those of a women's apparel manufacturer.

¶ 15.1 Diversity Within the Manufacturing Industry and Manufacturing Valuations

Because of the diversity in the manufacturing industry as well as the reasons for industry valuations, it becomes difficult to define the precise factors pertinent to valuing a specific manufacturing company. There are, however, certain basic considerations that have to be established before proceeding with the valuation of any manufacturing company as well as any other type of business organization.

[1] SIC Code Breakdown

To get some idea of how diverse the manufacturing industry is, it is worth taking a look at the Standard Industrial Classification (SIC) codes that fall under the heading of "manufacturing," as shown here:

- SIC Code 20—Food and kindred products
- SIC Code 21—Tobacco manufacturers
- SIC Code 22—Textile mill products
- SIC Code 23—Apparel and other textile products
- SIC Code 24—Lumber and wood products
- SIC Code 25—Furniture and fixtures
- SIC Code 26—Paper and allied products
- SIC Code 27—Printing and publishing
- SIC Code 28—Chemical and allied products
- SIC Code 29—Petroleum and coal products
- SIC Code 30—Rubber and miscellaneous plastic products
- SIC Code 31—Leather and leather products
- SIC Code 32—Stone, clay, and glass products
- SIC Code 33—Primary metal industries
- SIC Code 34—Fabricated metal products

- SIC Code 35—Machinery, except electrical
- SIC Code 36—Electrical and electronic equipment
- SIC Code 37—Transportations equipment
- SIC Code 38—Instruments and related products
- SIC Code 39—Miscellaneous manufacturing industries

From just a glance at these broad groupings within the manufacturing industry—without getting into the subgroups which, within the food category, include meat products, dairy products, preserved fruits and vegetables, grain mill products, bakery products, sugar and confectionery products, fats and oils, beverages, and more—it becomes clear that the simple fact of being classified as "manufacturers" does not give these companies much in common.

[2] Defining What Is to Be Valued

The varied interests to be valued also have to be defined and understood. Considerations that must be defined include the legal structure, the type of interest, the size of the interest, and the rights or restrictions that may be applicable.

[a] Legal Structure

An enterprise may be a C corporation, an S corporation, a partnership, or a proprietorship.

The legal structure of an enterprise has an impact upon its value because of factors such as the tax structure or exposure to personal liabilities that flow from the form of business organization. The C corporation and the S corporation, for example, give shareholders the protection of limited liability, but the former is a taxable entity in its own right, while the latter's profits or losses flow directly to the individual owner's personal income account, as do partnership interests and proprietorships. General partnerships and proprietorships, on the other hand, do not provide the personal protection of limiting any liabilities that may arise to the amount that can be met from the assets of the business enterprise itself.

[b] Type of Interest

The interest to be valued may be in the form of common stock, a general partnership interest, a limited partnership interest, preferred stock, a debt instrument, a convertible security, warrants, or options.

The values of common stock, warrants, options to purchase common stock, and general partnership interests are closely tied to the prospects of the issuing enterprise at the time of valuation. While such interests usually stand to appreciate the most if the enterprise is successful, they are also usually the first to suffer in times of adversity. On the other hand, preference rights to income or in liquidation may provide downside protection to limited partnership interests and preferred stock—but usually at the expense of limiting the upside appreciation potential. The value of debt instruments is directly connected to the enterprise's ability to meet interest requirements and repayment terms and the value of collateral that may be pledged, while the value of convertible securities is determined by the relative influences of the preference or equity features at the time of valuation. Clearly, however, the specific nature of the investment instrument will have a direct bearing on the values associated with it.

[c] Size of Interest

The size of an interest may represent 100% of the enterprise, a controlling interest in the enterprise, or a minority—or noncontrolling—interest in the enterprise.

The owner of 100% of an enterprise fully controls its destiny, from selection of its management to the product lines it will produce, and the general policies regarding merger, sale, or acquisition. For a business with promise, these are valuable rights that should be reflected in the amount that a willing buyer would pay for the company. A proportional share of all or most of the value associated with 100% ownership may also accrue to a controlling interest, depending upon the law in the state of incorporation (in some states ownership of 50.1% of an enterprise provides absolute control; in some states, a higher percentage is required).

The owner of a minority—or noncontrolling—interest in an enterprise cannot, by himself, change the policies of the enterprise, force its liquidation, or change its management. Therefore, these shares would naturally be accorded a lesser value than would shares that would transfer control to the buyer.

[d] Rights or Restrictions

The value of a particular security also depends upon whether it is a voting or a nonvoting interest; whether it is marketable; the nature of any restrictions on its sale or transfer; and other rights, obligations, or limitations that may apply.

Voting stock is more valuable than nonvoting stock if the stock represents control or the transfer of control in a specific situation, but the vote is not, in and of itself, a right of great consequence with respect to the value of minority shares. Marketability, on the other hand, has a very significant impact on value because the ability to find a ready buyer means that the owner has liquidity, while the owner who cannot immediately find a ready buyer cannot achieve immediate liquidity and may have to spend time and money to find such a buyer. Similarly, securities that are restricted by factors such as to whom they may be sold, when they may be sold, or by other factors are less valuable than securities that are not so restricted. There are also other specified rights, obligations, and limitations that may directly affect the value of securities.

[3] Purpose of Valuation

The need for a valuation may arise for many different reasons. When undertaking a valuation study, the purpose of the study must be specified because the answers will differ according to the purpose. A valuation for estate or gift tax purposes may differ from the valuation for a merger, a sale to a specific buyer, a buy-sell agreement, an employee stock ownership plan (ESOP), a right-of-appraisal statute, or a marital dissolution.

When doing an estate or gift tax valuation, you are dealing with a *theoretical* buyer and seller, while in the case of a merger or sale, you are dealing with a *specific* buyer and seller. The specific buyer may see certain synergistic advantages to making an acquisition that will positively affect its value to him, or the specific seller may have an urgent need to sell that will affect the price he is willing to accept. A buy-sell agreement may specify how value is to be determined. An ESOP will have "put" rights which provide significant elements of marketability that may not be available to other minority shareholders; while state laws or case law can directly affect valuation determinations under right-of-appraisal proceedings or in marital dissolutions.

[4] Revenue Ruling 59-60

In the discussion that follows, the assumption is that valuations of a manufacturing enterprise or an ownership interest in such an enterprise are done on a "going-concern" basis. Under Revenue Ruling 59-60, the IRS has provided a framework for valuing business enterprises and ownership interests in them for gift and estate tax purposes. These guidelines have been adapted for use in preparing valuations for a wide variety of business and legal purposes. For this discussion, Revenue Ruling 59-60's definition of "fair market value" is used.

> The price at which the property would change hands between a willing buyer and a willing seller when the former is not under any compulsion to buy and the latter is not under any compulsion to sell, both parties having reasonable knowledge of relevant facts.[1]

---

[1] Estate Tax Reg. § 20, 2031-1(b), Estate Tax Reg. 105 § 81.10; Gift Tax. Reg. § 25.2512-1, Gift Tax Reg. 108 § 86.19.

Court decisions have frequently added that the hypothetical buyer and seller are able and willing to trade and are well informed about the property and the market for such property.[2]

What is needed in dealing with any specific company is an identification and understanding of those elements important in determining the past and future prospects of that particular company and the manufacturing industry segment into which it fits. Many of those elements are peculiar to it as an industrial business; others are important in assessing its place within the broader economic and industry environment in which it operates.

The investigation of a company for valuation purposes means the systematic assessment of the business, financial, economic, and liquidity risks involved and the determination of an appropriate price to pay to achieve an adequate return for undertaking these risks.

¶ 15.2 Company Qualitative Analysis

A qualitative analysis of a company and its management means assessing the business risks and potential of that company. In order to do this, one must gain a good understanding not only of the company and its industry but the likely impact of the general economy on that company.

The function of a manufacturer is to take raw materials, produce a product from them through an organized process that involves a division of labor and the use of tools and machinery, and then to sell the products. This, therefore, suggests some areas that must be examined in the qualitative analysis process.

[1] Product Line

The company's principal lines of business need to be listed and grouped. The easiest way to group this data is by SIC codes. This initial breakdown should then be augmented by noting sales volume and profitability by product line to the extent that such information is available. The process of broadly defining the businesses in which the company is engaged provides a rational context from which almost all other elements for the analysis process take on meaning. A definition of the industry identifies the economic data to pursue and the competitors and bases of competition that apply. Knowing whether a company is in a single line of business or related lines that suggest dominating characteristics or a dependency on such factors as the construction cycle, defense expenditures, new births, utility expenditures,

---

[2] 1959-1 C.B. 287. Revenue Ruling 59-60 is reprinted as Appendix A at the end of this book.

or similar factors should provide the basis for determining pertinent avenues for further investigation. In addition, the basic identification process provides a perspective from which to look at past results as well as to view future prospects.

The business definition analysis should also include factors such as size, dependency on specific product lines, any vertical or horizontal integration that may exist, economies of scale, capital requirements, seasonality or cyclicality, and the life cycle of the product or products based on wear, technology, or other factors.

[2] History and Organization

Information about the history of a business not only helps in interpreting and understanding the business but can directly affect the valuation due to legal, tax, or other considerations. A start up company should not be viewed in the same way as a company with a long history of operation. Similarly, the rights with respect to selling a business differ for a 51% stockholder in a Delaware corporation and a 51% stockholder of a company incorporated in New York. In some states, certain business decisions must be approved by a majority of stockholders by class if there is more than one class of stock outstanding. Therefore, determining the date and state of incorporation and registration, the form of business organization and any changes in that form, together with an investigation of the company's bylaws and any rights or restrictions that may apply to the individual securities being valued is required.

Other factors, such as the details of prior mergers or acquisitions, prior bona fide offers to purchase, and any actual purchases or sales of the securities of the subject company are direct evidence of value at the time transactions or offers occurred. The history and makeup of the ownership and management of the company are among other elements that help put it in perspective for valuation purposes.

This list of factors is not all-inclusive but suggests the kinds of historic information that should be sought.

[3] Raw Materials

The raw materials needed for the manufacturer of a company's products is one of the company's most important distinguishing characteristics. It could be cotton for a textile manufacturer, iron ore for a steel manufacturer, flour for a bakery products producer, sheet metal for an automobile manufacturer, electronic components for a computer manufacturer. The most pertinent factors to consider in looking at the raw materials supply vary with the particular company being analyzed, but among these factors that should be reviewed are the location of the source of supply; the location of the production facilities; the control of the supply or the dependency on individual suppliers; competition among and the dependability of the suppliers; costs, cost trends, and the ability to hedge, if applicable; and the ability to substitute other raw materials.

The manufacturing company with ready access to the raw materials it needs, with many companies seeking to be its supplier, or with the ability to substitute other raw materials is clearly in a stronger position than are those without such advantages. Conversely, dependency upon a single supplier, limited availability of the raw materials needed, or high political risks associated with the source of supply suggest vulnerability to business interruptions or to uncontrollable pricing changes, such as those that occurred during the oil pricing shocks of the 1970s.

[4] Producing the Product

Type of manufacturing plant and production process are other distinguishing features of any manufacturing organization. When dealing with a so-called heavy industry producer—as, for example, a paper or steel manufacturer—factors such as plant location, size of facility needed to produce at an efficient level, potential for technological obsolescence, capacity utilization, lead time required to build new facilities, and capital requirements to build and maintain facilities are key factors to investigate as part of the analysis process. These factors are less important to a high-style garment manufacturer on Seventh Avenue, where capital equipment may consist of little more than cutting tables and sewing machines.

The kinds of factors to investigate when looking at plant and production processing include capital needs for plant and equipment; technological requirements; location; production cycle; and state of maintenance and repair.

[a] Work Force

The characteristics of the work force needed to carry out particular manufacturing functions and the relationship between the work force and management should be understood by the valuator. Among considerations to explore in this connection are the number of employees and where they are located, if there is more than one manufacturing facility; the availability of skills needed at the various locations; turnover; the average age of workers; whether the work force is unionized and, if so, what unions are involved and the status of the contracts; the history of the company's labor relations; and labor costs and the ability to control these costs through automation, training, or other approaches.

These factors vary in importance depending upon the type of manufacturer and the location of its facilities. Companies with militant unions and a high labor requirement in their manufacturing process may be riskier investments than are highly automated companies. The ability of management and the labor force to handle any needed changes in production methods or processes can also determine a company's competitive stance and, hence, future profitability. A dramatic example of a manufacturing industry whose labor problems exacerbated other competitive difficulties is the auto industry. Labor-management problems not only impeded needed changes but led to the consolidation of the domestic industry and had a strong impact on the rearrangement of international markets for the industry.

[b] Technology and Research and Development

Technology, research, and development—and the ability to finance such programs adequately—are factors of primary importance to high-tech companies, but of limited or marginal importance to fur-coat manufacturers or producers of plastic garbage cans. These factors can apply either to the products that the company is producing (in the case of a computer company) or to the methods of production (in the case of an electronic-chip manufacturer). Technology is a key requirement for success for some, research and development of new products for others. The production process can be a major element in cost control or product quality control for others. By comparison, these factors may have little importance for producers of commodity type products, like cement, where plant location, transportation costs, or other factors may be the primary determinants of competitive position.

[5] Marketing, Sales, and Distribution

Marketing, sales, and distribution characteristics and requirements vary widely from one type of manufacturer to another. Is the company selling capital goods or consumer products? Does it sell through its own organization, manufacturer's representatives, or retailers? Are the products of unlimited life and utility, like nuts and bolts, or are they perishable items, like foods with a limited shelf life? Are the products functional parts, like a spark plugs, or are they chips especially designed for a given manufacturer's needs? Does the market consist of other manufacturers or of consumers? The answers to these questions will dictate the type of marketing, distribution, or sales organization needed by a given manufacturer.

To develop an overall understanding of a manufacturing company's marketing and sales requirements, it is also necessary to understand the elements of competition that apply to its primary product lines. These elements vary dramatically by type of manufacturer, but the following are among the considerations that may be of greater or lesser consequence, depending upon the products being manufactured and the markets served:

- Price tends to be a dominant competitive consideration for many commodity-type products, such as bulk chemicals, many kinds of paper and allied products, unfinished metals, electronic and electrical products, and certain textile products. It is less of a consideration when product differentiation provides what may be an overriding advantage in the eyes of the customer.

- Quality and reputation are far more important than price as competitive factors for many manufacturers. The reputation for quality of foreign cars such as BMW, Mercedes, Volvo, and many Japanese cars has led to tremendous inroads in the domestic automobile market. Similarly, high-priced lines of foreign watches and perfumes are sought-after and have become status symbols for many buyers. Industrial customers also opt for quality or reliability of product as a primary basis for purchase for mechanical, electronic, or other components that affect their own products' reputation and reliability.

- Service can be a key determinant in buying decisions and may help to offset other factors, such as negative pricing differentials or technological lags. The service area of competition may include prompt delivery, which helps the customer hold inventory levels to a minimum; reliability as a source of supply; prompt servicing of equipment; or design and tailoring of products to customer needs. For example, vendors of original equipment to automobile manufacturers and many other types of mass producers of finished products are almost forced to compete on a service as well as a price basis. A classic example of a company that competes on a service basis is IBM, whose products have, at times, successfully competed with products that were more technologically advanced because of the company's reputation for reliable service.

- Style can be the most important competitive factor for some products, such as women's apparel, home furnishings, automobiles, and perfumes (where package design is a crucial element influencing consumer demand).

- Product differentiation may take many avenues in addition to considerations such as style, pricing, or service. Examples of strategies to promote product differentiation abound among consumer manufacturers of soaps, detergents, soft drinks, cigarettes, pain relievers, over-the-counter drug products, and motor oils, where hundreds of millions of dollars are spent on advertising and other promotion and marketing programs aimed at giving individual products distinction in the eyes of the buying public.

- Product protection can be derived from patents, licenses, secret formulas, technological advances, or even regulatory restrictions. This kind of protection can be a powerful stimulant to profits for as long as the protection lasts, as witnessed by the success of prescription drug companies with many new drug introductions and the success of Polaroid with its instant camera and Xerox in the early years of the copying industry.

[6] Other Factors

Other factors to be investigated by the valuator include the following:

- The ease or difficulty of entry into the business, based on its capital requirements or technology;
- The market share, which determines the pricing strategy, the ability to obtain shelf space, and other distribution advantages or disadvantages;
- The breadth of the product line, in terms of the price, size, color, and so on, because this serves as a means for obtaining or holding market share, improving costs, or spreading advertising or overhead expenditures;
- Vertical or horizontal integration and their effects on cost, reliability of supply, or distribution of products; and
- The extent of intraindustry competition and the ability to substitute one type of product for another (i.e., plastic for metal or textiles, glass fiber for copper wire, coal for oil, and so on).

[7] Management

The capability of a manufacturing company's management can be measured by its ability to purchase the needed raw materials at a reasonable cost and in sufficient supply; to produce the company's product line or lines efficiently; and to market, distribute, and sell the company's products in a manner that meets customer requirements and is cost-effective. In addition, the management of a manufacturer often requires greater breadth of financial management capability than may be true of many other kinds of companies in order to finance fairly large capital requirements for inventories of raw materials and work in process and accounts receivable (which may also have cyclical and/or seasonal patterns) as well as to finance substantial plant and equipment requirements.

Other areas of management capability that may need to be explored in making valuation judgments for some types of manufacturing companies are those dealing with research and development, technology and its application to product development as well as to the production process, and design and styling.

To look systematically at a company's management structure, it is helpful to prepare or have management provide an organization chart showing the functional breakdown of management, the reporting relationships, and the names and backgrounds of the individuals who fill key positions. Factors to consider in looking at management are the age and experience of the key members and the continuity of the management group. For the closely held manufacturing company, value is substantially affected if there is dependence on one or two key officers who may be responsible for multiple functions. The health and age of these individuals are primary concerns in evaluating the risks associated with dependency on them. These data, supplemented by further information with respect to their competence and the availability of backup management, should provide a useful profile and serve to point up areas of management vulnerability.

If the owners of a company are also its managers, the historic interrelationships of those involved and their individual or family goals need to be explored to evaluate the record to date and the future potential. The authority and the working relationship of the owners to each other, and to any successor generations, the levels of compensation paid, the perquisites used, the non-arm's length financial arrangements, and other evidence of nepotism are of concern. Another consideration when looking at a company whose owners are also its top managers is its ability to attract and keep managers who are *not* family members and who do not have ownership interests in the company.

Has current management dealt effectively with meeting the company's purchasing, production, marketing, financial, and other requirements over the years, both in absolute terms and relative to its competitors? What significant changes does it envision taking place within its industry, and how is it planning to take advantage of these changes or to defend itself against challenges that may evolve? The answers to these questions as they relate to those elements that have most significance for the individual manufacturing company provide the analyst with an insight into management's areas of strength and weakness.

While not an exhaustive list, the above are the types of factors pertinent in analyzing the strengths and weaknesses of individual manufacturers in order to give the analyst as good an understanding as possible of the business risks associated with the particular company.

The primary assessment of business risk rests, in turn, on the analyst's assessment of management and its ability to deal with the competitive environment in which the particular manufacturing company operates.

¶ 15.3 Company Financial Analysis

The financial analysis of a company is designed to help the analyst gauge the financial risks and liquidity associated with an investment in the company.

[1] Historical Income Statements

Historical income statements for a company in business over a period of years should be analyzed for at least five years prior to the valuation date or, in the case of cyclical companies, over one complete business cycle. If available, audited statements should be used for this purpose.

This analysis should concentrate on historical revenue patterns and sources of revenues, margins, cash flows, net income, and dividend payments. Nonrecurring items should be eliminated. Also, adjustments should be made if there are favorable purchases or sales with nonconsolidated affiliates or lease terms with affiliates that are not on a market basis, as may sometimes occur in privately owned businesses.

If the valuation date falls between annual statement dates, interim figures should be obtained, if at all possible, for the nearest available date prior to the valuation date and for the comparable earlier year period.

Analysis of historical results often indicates future potential and may also suggest areas for further questioning of management to explain past patterns or observed trends. The key elements to observe are the direction and magnitude of changes in revenue and expenses from year to year and the margins of the income statement from gross operating profits to net income before and after taxes. (See Tables 15-1 and 15-2 for examples of how to format these data for analytical purposes.)

If prior-year budgets are available, they should be compared to actual results in order to assess management's ability to forecast and achieve forecast results. This is important in assessing the risk that may attach to accepting current budgets and forecasts as part of the valuation process.

[Text continues on p. 15-16]

TABLE 15-1
XYZ MANUFACTURING COMPANY
COMPARATIVE INCOME STATEMENT DATA
($ Millions)

	19X1	19X2	19X3	19X4	19X5
Operating revenues	$ 90,662	$86,306	$111,645	$128,088	$136,238
Cost of goods sold, excluding depreciation	62,079	55,965	72,504	81,579	83,874
Gross profit before depreciation	$ 28,583	$30,341	$ 39,141	$ 46,509	$ 52,346
Other operating expenses before depreciation	28,217	27,362	33,618	38,295	48,140
Operating income before depreciation	$ 366	$ 2,979	$ 5,523	$ 8,214	$ 4,224
Depreciation in operating expenses	2,955	3,053	2,663	3,366	3,674
Operating income after depreciation	$ −2,589	$ −74	$ 2,860	$ 4,848	$ 550
Interest, net of interest capitalized	95	77	8	2	3
Other income (expense)—net	2,210	1,665	1,137	1,592	1,323
Income before income taxes	$ −474	$ 1,514	$ 3,989	$ 6,438	$ 1,870
Income taxes	−369	342	1,575	2,531	278
Minority interests	30	9	-0-	-0-	-0-
Equity in unconsolidated subsidiaries	-0-	-0-	-0-	-0-	-0-
Income before extraordinary items	$ −135	$ 1,163	$ 2,414	$ 3,097	$ 1,592
Supplementary Data					
Interest capitalized	$ -0-	$ -0-	$ -0-	$ -0-	$ -0-
Extraordinary items	-0-	-0-	-0-	-0-	-0-
Preferred dividends	-0-	-0-	-0-	-0-	-0-
Common dividends	-0-	-0-	-0-	-0-	348
Restated Data					
Operating revenues	90,662	86,306	111,645	128,088	136,238
Income before extraordinary items	−135	1,163	2,414	3,097	1,592
Depreciation and amortization restated	2,955	3,053	2,663	3,366	3,674
Interest expense plus income taxes restated	−274	419	1,583	2,533	281
Primary earnings per share	−0.96	8.35	17.31	28.03	11.47
Fully diluted earnings per share	−0.96	8.35	17.31	28.03	11.47
Valuation period data (XX/XX/XX-XX/XX/XX)					
Indicated dividend per common share ($)					2.50
Primary earnings per share—latest 12 months ($)					11.47
Diluted earnings per share—latest 12 months ($)					11.47

TABLE 15-2
XYZ MANUFACTURING COMPANY
COMPARATIVE INCOME STATEMENT
(Percentage of Operating Revenue[a])

	19X1	19X2	19X3	19X4	19X5
Operating revenues	100.0%	100.0%	100.0%	100.0%	100.0%
Cost of goods sold, excluding depreciation	68.5	64.8	64.9	63.7	61.6
Gross profit before depreciation	31.5%	35.2%	35.1%	36.3%	38.4%
Other operating expenses before depreciation	31.1	31.7	30.1	29.9	35.3
Operating income before depreciation	0.4%	3.5%	4.9%	6.4%	3.1%
Depreciation in operating expenses	3.3	3.5	2.4	2.6	2.7
Operating income after depreciation	−2.9%	−0.1%	2.6%	3.8%	0.4%
Interest, net of interest capitalized	0.1	0.1	0.0	0.0	0.0
Other income (expense)—net	2.4	1.9	1.0	1.2	1.0
Income before taxes	−0.5%	1.8%	3.6%	5.0%	1.4%
Income taxes	−0.4	0.4	1.4	2.0	0.2
Minority interests	0.0	0.0	0.0	0.0	0.0
Equity in unconsolidated subsidiaries	0.0	0.0	0.0	0.0	0.0
Income before extraordinary items	−0.1%	1.3%	2.2%	3.1%	1.2%
Supplementary data					
Extraordinary items	0.0%	0.0%	0.0%	0.0%	0.0%
Preferred dividends	0.0	0.0	0.0	0.0	0.0
Common dividends	0.0	0.0	0.0	0.0	0.3

[a] Percentages may not total due to rounding

[Text continues from p. 15-13]

[2] Historical Balance Sheets

Historical balance sheets covering the same time span as that of the income statements should be analyzed. The makeup of assets and liabilities over the period of time should be used to determine

- Whether liquidity is increasing or decreasing;
- Whether the company is increasing or decreasing its investment in fixed assets, which is particularly significant for a manufacturing company requiring a heavy component of plant and equipment;
- How the company's capitalization is changing in terms of debt/equity ratios; and
- The overall changes taking place in the financial structure of the company.

These factors are brought into perspective by looking at yardsticks such as quick assets (cash and short-term investments plus accounts receivable) versus current liabilities; current assets (quick assets plus inventories) versus current liabilities; and the makeup of the company's capital structure (current liabilities, long-term debt, other liabilities, preferred stock, and the book value of its common stock equity), as well as the changing relationships of these factors over the period being investigated.

Footnotes to the company's statements need to be reviewed to determine the accounting conventions used or the existence of off-balance-sheet assets (such as investments in other companies carried at cost), liabilities (such as future lease payments or pension plan obligations), other contingencies, and terms that apply to outstanding debt obligations. Similarly, the balance sheet analysis may reveal assets in excess of the needs of the business, such as marketable securities or real estate that could represent resources to be liquidated to finance future capital requirements or an added asset base to support higher levels of debt. If the company has more than one class of equity outstanding, the rights and obligations with each class must also be considered.

This type of balance-sheet analysis over a period of years should disclose any positive or negative trends or changes, which can be further explored to determine the reasons why they have occurred and as background for assessing the current and prospective financial well-being of the company. (See Tables 15-3 and 15-4 for examples of how to format historical balance-sheet information.)

[3] Relating Income Statements to Balance Sheets

Relating the income-statement analysis to the balance-sheet analysis gives information pertinent for judging how well the company has managed the capital employed. This is done by measuring asset turnover, return on total assets, return on the equity of the company, and the trends or changes in such returns over the historic period under investigation. While these returns need to be compared to the returns of other companies in the same industry to put them in perspective, they nevertheless provide a financial report card of management's stewardship and are of particular importance for manufacturing companies involved in capital-intensive industries. (See Table 15-5 for an example of how such data can be formatted for analytical purposes.)

[4] Plans and Prospects

Plans and prospects as represented by management at the valuation date are essential elements to factor into the valuation process. A review of the financial and operating history will help shed some light on how the company got to where it is and the future in which the willing buyer would be investing.

An understanding of the nature of a company's business and how it is managed forms the basis for inquiring of management how it intends to deal with the areas of risk and opportunity that may be uncovered. To the extent that management represents that changes will be made in management itself, in business lines, through expansion or contraction, new pricing tactics, changes in plant location or other investment programs, and so on, their plans must be tested for reasonableness by looking at past experience, assessing the reasonableness of future projections and the financial and managerial capacity to realize them. These tests of reasonableness should include reviewing past budgets or projections, if available, and comparing them to the actual results achieved; and assessing the company's competitive position within its industry segment or segments, its capacity to finance plant and working capital requirements; and the outlook for the company's product lines in relationship to the economy as a whole.

¶ 15.4 Industry Analysis

The preceding type of detailed analysis helps define as clearly as possible the various segments and subsegments of the manufacturing industry into which a company's product lines fall.

[Text continues on p. 15-21]

TABLE 15-3
XYZ MANUFACTURING COMPANY
COMPARATIVE BALANCE SHEET DATA
($ Millions)

	19X1	19X2	19X3	19X4	19X5
Assets					
Cash and short-term investments	$10,862	$15,936	$12,705	$ 9,747	$10,485
Accounts receivable	13,570	15,282	23,010	24,650	24,923
Quick assets	$24,432	$31,218	$35,715	$34,397	$35,408
Inventories	11,384	8,424	12,430	11,979	11,733
Other current assets	317	266	245	198	98
Total current assets	$36,133	$39,908	$48,390	$46,574	$47,239
Fixed assets—net	20,129	17,930	18,587	20,895	21,993
Intangibles	-0-	-0-	-0-	-0-	-0-
Other assets and investments	458	462	441	396	375
Total assets	$56,720	$58,300	$67,418	$67,865	$69,607
Liabilities and stockholders' equities					
Debt in current liabilities	$ 123	$ 113	$ -0-	$ -0-	$ -0-
Other current liabilities	9,249	10,257	17,030	13,188	13,899
Total current liabilities	$ 9,372	$10,370	$17,030	$13,188	$13,899
Long-term debt	834	23	-0-	-0-	-0-
Other long-term liabilities and minority interests	1,515	1,812	1,878	2,270	2,234
Preferred stock at liquidation value	-0-	-0-	-0-	-0-	-0-
Common stockholders' equity	44,999	46,095	48,510	52,407	53,474
Total liabilities and stockholders' equities	$56,720	$58,300	$67,418	$67,865	$69,607
Outstanding common shares at year-end[a]					138,240

[a] At 6/30

**TABLE 15-4
XYZ MANUFACTURING COMPANY
COMPARATIVE PERCENTAGE BALANCE SHEETS**
(Percentage of Total Assets[a])

	19X1	19X2	19X3	19X4	19X5
Assets					
Cash and short-term investments	19.2%	27.3%	18.8%	14.4%	15.1%
Accounts receivable	23.9	26.2	34.1	36.3	35.8
Quick assets	43.1%	53.5%	53.0%	50.7%	50.9%
Inventories	20.1	14.4	18.4	17.7	16.9
Other current assets	0.6	0.5	0.4	0.3	0.1
Total current assets	63.7%	68.5%	71.8%	68.6%	67.9%
Fixed assets—net	35.5	30.8	27.6	30.8	31.6
Intangibles	0.0	0.0	0.0	0.0	0.0
Other assets	0.8	0.8	0.7	0.6	0.5
Total assets	100.0%	100.0%	100.0%	100.0%	100.0%
Liabilities and stockholders' equities					
Debt in current liabilities	0.2%	0.2	0.0	0.0	0.0
Other current liabilities	16.3	17.6	25.3	19.4	20.0
Total current liabilities	16.5%	17.8%	25.3%	19.4%	20.0%
Long-term debt	1.5	0.0	0.0	0.0	0.0
Other long-term liabilities and minority interests	2.7	3.1	2.8	3.3	3.2
Preferred stock at liquidation value	0.0	0.0	0.0	0.0	0.0
Common stockholders' equity	79.3%	79.1	72.0	77.2	76.8
Total liabilities and stockholders' equities	100.0%	100.0%	100.0%	100.0%	100.0%

[a] Percentages may not total due to rounding

TABLE 15-5
XYZ MANUFACTURING COMPANY
PERCENTAGE[a] ANALYSIS OF RETURN ON YEAR-END ASSETS AND COMMON STOCKHOLDERS' EQUITY

	19X1	19X2	19X3	19X4	19X5
Operating revenues to total assets	159.8%	148.0%	165.6%	188.7%	195.7%
Times Gross profit margin before depreciation	31.5	35.2	35.1	36.3	38.4
Equals Gross profit before depreciation to total assets	50.4%	52.0%	58.1%	68.5%	75.2%
Less (as a percentage of total assets):					
Other operating expenses before depreciation	49.7	46.9	49.9	56.4	69.2
Depreciation in operating expenses	5.2	5.2	3.9	5.0	5.3
Equals Operating income as a percentage of total assets	−4.6%	−0.1%	4.2%	7.1%	0.8%
Plus (as a percentage of total assets)					
Other income (expense) net, before interest expense	3.9	2.9	1.7	2.3	1.9
Equals Return on total assets	−0.7%	2.7%	5.9%	9.5%	2.7%
Less (as a percentage of total assets):					
Interest expense, net of interest capitalized	0.2	0.1	0.0	0.0	0.0
Income taxes	−0.7	0.6	2.3	3.7	0.4
Minority interest	0.1	0.0	0.0	0.0	0.0
Equity in unconsolidated subsidiaries	0.0	0.0	0.0	0.0	0.0
Preferred dividends	0.0	0.0	0.0	0.0	0.0
Equals Income for common stockholders to total assets	−0.2%	2.0%	3.6%	5.8%	2.3%
Times Leverage (total assets to common stockholders' equity)	126.0	126.5	139.0	129.5	130.2
Equals Return on common stockholders' equity	−0.3%	2.5%	5.0%	7.5%	3.0%
Times Earnings retention rate	100.0%	100.0%	100.0%	100.0%	78.1%
Equals Internal rate of growth	−0.3%	2.5%	5.0%	7.5%	2.3%

[a] Percentages may not total due to rounding

[*Text continues from p. 15-17*]

The definition of the manufacturing segments in which the company operates also suggests the type of industry and economic data that need to be assembled and analyzed from both a historic and a prospective point of view. The pertinent information depends on the specific products involved and what economic and industry factors have had an impact on past results and will probably have an impact on future results. Examples of the industry and economic information that would be pertinent to investigate might include the following:

- Commodity prices for manufacturers dependent on raw materials such as oil, gas, coal, metal, grains, or other foodstuffs;
- Population trends by age group or in geographic regions served;
- Construction expenditures for those companies serving the building and related industries;
- Consumer incomes and expenditures for retailers and other manufacturers whose revenues are closely tied to such factors;
- Entry of new competitors and their types, origins, bases of competition—price, new products, new production methods, and so on—and how well they are financed;
- Technological changes and their potential effects on pricing, profits, market growth, and penetration;
- Inflationary trends and their potential effects on specific manufacturers, their suppliers, and their customers;
- Interest rate changes and their effects on the industry segment, its suppliers, and its customers;
- Business-cycle implications for companies tied to these cycles on a coincident, leading, or lagging basis; and
- Labor costs or labor supplies as they affect specific manufacturing segments.

There are a wide variety of sources from which to glean industry data that can help identify factors that may have particular pertinence to the industry being investigated. Such sources include general reference publications, such as Predicast's, *Sales & Marketing Management Magazine*, Standard & Poor's Industry Survey, the *Wall Street Journal* and *The New York Times*; on-line databases, such as Dialog Information Services, Inc.; and trade associations and governmental agencies and publications, such as the U.S. Industrial Outlook, the U.S. Statistical Abstract, and the Survey of Current Business.

Information drawn from such sources with respect to industry and economic factors that can affect the individual manufacturer gives the analyst a better understanding of the company's historic results and helps in formulating a reasoned judgment with respect to future expectations.

¶ 15.5 Valuation Approaches

There are three classic approaches to establishing the value of a business enterprise: (1) the asset approach; (2) the earnings approach (such as the discounted value of future earnings, cash flow, or dividend projections); and (3) the market approach (the comparative analysis of the subject company with publicly owned companies in similar lines of business).

[1] The Asset Approach

Valuing the assets in place is not a particularly helpful approach to establishing the "going-concern" value of most kinds of manufacturing concerns except to the extent that these assets are in excess of the operating needs of the company. Excess assets may take the form of real estate holdings beyond the needs of the company to carry on its business; cash or cash equivalents in excess of its operating requirements; investments; or other holdings not needed in the normal course of the company's business. To the degree that such assets exist and have not been accumulated with a specific purpose in mind, their value may add to the value that has been established on the basis of the company's ability to generate earnings. Otherwise, the assets held by a manufacturing company in the form of plant or equipment should be regarded merely as resources necessary to produce earnings; it is the valuation of these earnings that is the appropriate basis for establishing the company's "going-concern" value.

In manufacturing companies where resources are held as part of the integrated organization (such as paper companies holding timberlands or oil companies holding oil and gas properties), it may be necessary to determine fair market values for these resources as an added factor for consideration relative to the values that stem from the company's ability to produce earnings through its operations. The asset approach may also be used to establish a floor of value in situations where little or no profits are currently being generated from operations but where the company is expected to continue in business and has the financial capacity to do so. For most manufacturing companies, however, fair market value as a "going concern" is greatly dependent upon management's ability to use the resources at its command to produce earnings.

Note that the asset approach to valuation does not give explicit consideration to the adequacy of return on assets held versus returns available from alternative investments carrying similar risks.

Table 15-6 is a simplified example of how the asset approach to valuation may be viewed in comparison to book value.

TABLE 15-6

FAIR MARKET VALUE OF NET ASSETS
($000,000)

	Book Value	Fair Market Value
Current assets	$ 200	$ 250
Investments	500	0
Net fixed assets	1,000	1,900
Intangibles	150	0
Total assets	$1,850	$2,150
Less: Liabilities	1,250	1,250
Net asset value	$ 600	$ 900

[2] The Earnings (Discounted Cash Flow) Approach

The discounted cash flow (DCF) is the most common form of earnings approach to the valuation of business enterprises. Free cash flow equals the earnings of a company plus noncash charges less the cash requirements for capital investment or increased working capital. The DCF approach projects free cash flow over a period of years. A terminal value for the company (i.e., its value at the end of the projection period) is established. This terminal value can be determined by applying a multiple to projected cash flow or earnings for the final year of the period being projected or by taking a present value of an infinite stream of earnings, cash flow, or dividends after the end of the projection period and discounting this stream at a selected discount rate. Both the interim yearly free cash flow projections and the terminal value are then discounted to determine the present value of the projections. The valuator selects the discount factor based on his or her assessment of risks for realization of the results projected, or a prospective investor may use a minimum required rate of return on investment or hurdle rate as the discount factor.

A simple illustration of the DCF approach is presented in Table 15-7.

TABLE 15-7
FAIR MARKET VALUE BASED ON DISCOUNTED CASH FLOW
($000,000)

Year	Cash Flow	×	Discount Factor (20%)	=	Present Value
1	100		0.83		83
2	125		0.69		86
3	150		0.58		87
4	175		0.48		84
5	200		0.40		80
5	1,000[a]		0.40		400
					820

[a] Terminal value taken at 5 times the projected cash flow of $200,000 in the fifth year

This approach depends upon the selection of the three basic elements that lead to the valuation results calculated.

1. The rate of growth and the number of years over which to project growth of free cash flow
2. The determination of a terminal value at the end of the period over which year-to-year cash flows are projected
3. The discount rate to apply in bringing these projections back to a present value

Each of these elements dramatically affects the results derived from the mathematics applied to them.

This approach may be particularly open to error in dealing with manufacturing businesses that are highly cyclical or otherwise difficult to project with reasonable confidence on a near-term basis, much less on a longer-term basis. Also, this approach does not explicitly take into account current or historic earnings or the value of the assets of the company being valued.

The DCF approach does, however, provide a useful tool for buyers wanting to screen potential acquisitions to determine whether hurdle rates of return can be obtained from what are considered reasonable projections of future results. It is also one of the few tools that can be applied in valuing start up manufacturing enterprises where there is no operating history available. In general, this is an approach that is more applicable to control valuations than it is to minority-interest valuations.

[3] The Market Approach

The market approach to determining value depends upon the comparative analysis of the subject company with publicly owned companies in similar lines of business whose shares are actively traded. The financial performance of the subject company is compared to the performances of selected comparative companies.

The selection of companies to be used for comparative purposes will have a direct effect upon the values derived. A qualitative analysis of the subject company should turn up publicly traded direct competitors, if any. Further searches, using the SIC codes that apply to the subject company, should identify other public companies with significant representation within those code groupings. A systematic search for appropriate companies for comparative purposes should be made by setting up, in advance, the kinds of criteria to be considered. These may include maximum or minimum size, the proportion of business derived from specified SIC code categories, the geographic location of operations, the years of profitability prior to the valuation date, and minimum trading activity (the comparative companies' stocks must be listed in the Standard & Poor's *Stock Guide*, for example). It may, at times, be necessary to use a comparative not directly in the same line of business as the subject company. Such a company might be used, for example, because it is affected by similar economic factors or because its products are sold to much the same or similar customer groups. Whatever the selection process used, it must be reasonable and defensible and should include all comparatives turned up as part of the universe passing the selection screening process.

[a] The Capitalization of Earnings

After the comparatives are selected, a systematic analysis of their income statements and balance sheets over several prior years, usually five years, is made in the same manner as for the subject company. This data is then compared to the results for the subject company to see how its results compare to individual companies within the comparative group and to the group as a whole.

Results need to be examined over a period of years, not just the most recent year; interim results should also be reviewed on a year-to-year basis up to the valuation date if the valuation date falls much beyond the fiscal year end. It is desirable to get projections for the full year during which the valuation date falls and at least one year ahead for both the subject company and the companies being used for comparative purposes. When dealing with manufacturers that have a marked business cycle, the historic data should be examined over a full cycle.

Market prices for the public companies' common stocks are then compared to operating results. It is often helpful to look at earnings in relation to recent stock prices using five years' average earnings (and, in many instances, cash flows), three years' average earnings, most recent year earnings, most recent 12 months' earnings, and projected earnings. The valuator can then make judgments as to what price/earnings ratios over the periods investigated seem appropriate to apply to the earnings/or cash flow results of the subject company to derive several indicated prices. The valuator then weights the prices calculated to arrive at an appropriate price or range of prices based on the capitalization of earnings/or cash flows.

[b] Market/Book Value Relationships

The second approach to establishing value is to compare market price to the tangible book values of the companies in the comparative group. Frequently, the ratio of market price to book value shows, at least roughly, some parallel relationship to the return on equity that individual companies experienced versus other companies in the comparative group. It is therefore helpful to array the comparative companies with respect to their returns on common stock book value for the most recent year as well as on an average return basis for a period of prior years. This comparison helps in deciding what relationship of market price to tangible book value would exist if the subject company's stock were traded publicly. Table 15-8 is an example of one way in which the data can be developed for analytical purposes.

TABLE 15-8
XYZ COMPANY v. PUBLIC COMPANIES'
RETURN ON EQUITY AND MARKET PRICE TO
OTHER TANGIBLE BOOK VALUE
DURING THE VALUATION PERIOD
(in %)

Company	Return on Common Stockholders' Equity		Market Price to Tangible Book Value[a]
	Latest Year	5-Year Median	
A	21.5	14.9	330.4
B	19.7	19.7	356.8
C	18.5	18.5	231.6
D	12.0	14.1	201.9
E	10.8	18.8	177.2
XYZ	3.0	3.5	N.A.

[a] Average market price during the valuation period to latest year-end tangible book value

[c] Dividend Returns

A third approach to establishing value is to look at the dividends paid by the public companies in comparison with the dividend paid by the company under review. Frequently, a privately owned company does not pay dividends, and this factor may enter the valuation equation as a subjective influence rather than one derived from this statistical analysis process. The dividend approach is most useful in valuing minority interests.

These three approaches usually produce several different values. The analyst then determines how these values should be individually weighted in arriving at a conclusion as to what value or range of values apply to the stock of the subject company. This price or range of prices are those that would apply if the stock was, in fact, publicly traded in round minority lots in an actively traded public market. Any applicable discounts for lack of marketability or any premiums for control if control shares are being valued would not be reflected.

[4] Other Valuation Approaches

Other approaches to valuation may include the use of book value for making transactions. Book value would only be the same as fair market value by coincidence because it is derived from historic accounting for earnings and investment, not from a reflection of how the market would value a company or its securities at the date of valuation.

Another approach is through the application of a rule-of-thumb valuation formula. If such a formula exists within an industry and is used frequently without material alteration, it can be the basis for determining pricing for arm's-length transactions. However, such formulas need to be continually re-examined to determine their validity in reflecting the risks and returns associated with the type of enterprise to which they are applied. Manufacturing companies are less apt to be appropriately valued by formula than are certain types of service companies or professional practices, for example.

The valuator may decide to use more than one of the above valuation approaches to value a particular company. In that case, a decision has to be made on how to weight the varying indications of value.

[5] Other Considerations

The final determination of value for a manufacturing enterprise or an ownership interest in a manufacturing company is influenced by the same considerations that apply to other industries when dealing with such factors as premiums for control, discounts for lack of marketability, and appropriate consideration of the purpose for which the valuation study is being prepared: estate or gift tax purposes, an ESOP, a right-of-appraisal statute, a merger or acquisition, a marital dissolution, and so on. The application of these considerations in determining a final value is dealt with elsewhere in this text and should be referred to as appropriate.

16

SERVICE COMPANIES

Donald P. Jacobs and Charles H. Stryker[*]

		Page
¶ 16.1	What Is a Service Company?	16-2
¶ 16.2	When Are Valuations Needed?	16-3
	[1] Tax-Related Needs	16-3
	[2] ESOPs	16-4
	[3] Mergers and Acquisitions	16-4
	[4] Other Purposes	16-5
¶ 16.3	Information and Sources	16-6
¶ 16.4	Intangible Assets	16-7
	[1] Work Force	16-8
	[2] Customer Contracts	16-8
	[3] Software and Databases	16-8
	[4] Customer Base	16-9
	[5] Employment Contracts and Agreements Not to Compete	16-9
	[6] Trade Names	16-9
	[7] Other Intangibles	16-9
¶ 16.5	Financial Considerations	16-10
	[1] Cash vs. Accrual Accounting	16-10
	[2] Deferred Revenues	16-10
	[3] Working Capital	16-11
	[4] Other Financial Factors	16-11
¶ 16.6	Valuation Approaches	16-11
	[1] Majority vs. Minority Interests	16-12
	[2] Premises of Fair Market Value for Common Stock	16-12
	[3] Market Approach	16-13
	[4] Earnings Approach	16-18
	[5] Asset Approach	16-18
	[6] Rules of Thumb	16-20
¶ 16.7	Special Considerations	16-20
	[1] Hotels and Lodging	16-20
	[2] Personal Services	16-21

[*] DONALD P. JACOBS, CFA, ASA, CFP, MBA, is a manager at KPMG Peat Marwick in New York, New York. CHARLES H. STRYKER, CFA, MBA, is a senior manager at the same firm.

	[3]	Business Services	16-21
	[4]	Automotive Repair and Garage Services	16-21
	[5]	Motion Picture Services	16-21
	[6]	Amusement and Recreation Services	16-22
	[7]	Health Services	16-22
	[8]	Legal Services	16-22
	[9]	Educational Services	16-22
	[10]	Social Services	16-22
	[11]	Museums, Art Galleries, Botanical and Zoological Gardens	16-23
¶ 16.8		Summary	16-23

¶ 16.1 What Is a Service Company?

In the broadest sense, a service company is a company that provides a service, but many service organizations are not "companies" in the strictest sense of that word. They are frequently proprietorships, partnerships, or professional corporations. This chapter confines itself to a discussion of the services listed in the *Standard Industrial Classification (SIC) Manual*. They include a wide range of services that are divided into the following major categories:

- SIC Code 70—hotels, rooming houses, camps, and other lodging places
- SIC Code 72—personal services
- SIC Code 73—business services
- SIC Code 75—automotive repair, services, and garages
- SIC Code 76—miscellaneous repair services
- SIC Code 78—motion pictures
- SIC Code 79—amusement and recreation services, except motion pictures
- SIC Code 80—health services
- SIC Code 81—legal services
- SIC Code 82—educational services
- SIC Code 83—social services
- SIC Code 84—museums, art galleries, and botanical and zoological gardens
- SIC Code 86—members' organizations
- SIC Code 88—private households
- SIC Code 89—miscellaneous services

The diversity of services listed in the SIC *Manual* makes it necessary to examine each case on the basis of operating elements peculiar to the area of service being provided. In addition, service companies in general are people-dependent rather than capital-intensive. This must be taken into account in their valuations.

Many service firms, for example, are dependent upon an individual or a group of individuals with particular expertise or training. The service this person or group provides is also generally in response to a need unique to the client. Compensation, which may be an hourly fee—or a commission is paid directly to the individual person or group providing the service.

¶ 16.2 When Are Valuations Needed?

Valuations of closely held securities are required at various times during the life of an enterprise. In general, certain discernible events—the death of a shareholder, the desire to make a gift of shares to children or to sell shares to employees, the divorce of a shareholder, or the purchase of a business—may trigger the need for valuations. In addition, legal or contractual obligations—ESOPs (Employee Stock Ownership Plans), profit-sharing plans, and phantom stock plans—may require valuations at regular intervals.

[1] Tax-Related Needs

The IRS has issued a number of rulings relative to the valuation of closely held securities for tax purposes. The most important of these are the following[1]:

- 59-60[2]—Valuation methodology for estate and gift tax.
- 68-609[3]—Extension of applicability of Ruling 59-60 for all tax matters.
- 77-287[4]—Determination of lack of marketability discounts.
- 83-120[5]—Preferred stock valuations.

The most common situations requiring a valuation of closely held securities for tax purposes are estate taxes, gift taxes, charitable donations, estate planning, liquidations, reorganizations, purchase price allocations, income taxes, compensation stock or options, and net operating losses.

The prescribed methodology for use in tax matters is the comparative company approach described in Ruling 59-60. Quantitative and qualitative comparisons are made between the subject company and a

---

[1] Because of its significance, Revenue Ruling 59-60 is reprinted as Appendix A at the end of this book.
[2] 1959-1 C.B. 237.
[3] 1968-2 C.B. 327.
[4] 1977-2 C.B. 319.
[5] 1983-2 C.B. 170.

group of publicly traded companies engaging in a line of business similar to that of the subject company. Based upon these comparisons and the valuation of the comparative securities by the investing public (as evidenced by certain fundamental valuation factors such as price/earnings ratios, dividend yields, and market/tangible book value ratios), the valuator determines the value of the subject security as if it were traded in a free and active public market. Depending upon the circumstances, the valuator may add a premium for control for majority-interest valuations or may subtract a discount for lack of marketability for minority-interest valuations.

[2] ESOPs

The Tax Reform Act of 1986 requires that ESOPs (employee stock ownership plans) that consist of employer-issued closely held securities have independent annual appraisals of the securities fair market value by a person who customarily makes such appraisals. The IRS may question the valuations of ESOP securities because of the tax deductibility of ESOP contributions; the Department of Labor (DOL) may also question valuations in overseeing all employee benefit plans. ERISA[6] requires the DOL to issue ESOP valuation guidelines. As of this writing, the DOL has issued proposed guidelines for public comment. These guidelines have relied heavily upon the valuation framework of Revenue Ruling 59-60. They also provide additional guidance for ESOP valuations.[7]

[3] Mergers and Acquisitions

Valuations are often required for merger and acquisitions purposes. M&A valuation services may include pretransaction valuations, such as the determination of a selling or offering price; fairness opinions, relating to the terms of an offer in a takeover or a "going-private" transaction; determinations of exchange ratios for a merger as a shield for corporate directors; advisory opinions for the board of directors of a company subject to a tender offer; or inputs for or parts of a solvency opinion required by lending institutions desiring protection from bankruptcy or fraudulent-conveyance statutes in a leveraged buyout transaction. Ex-post (post-transaction) services may include valuations for allocation of purchase price, determination of net-operating-loss (NOL) carryforward limitations, or testimony under right-of-appraisal statutes. Generally, with notable exceptions, M&A valuations involve a majority or control premise of value.

---

[6] Employee Retirement Income Security Act of 1974, Pub. L. No. 93-406, 88 Stat. 829 (1974).

[7] 53 Fed. Reg. at 17632-17638 (May 17, 1988). DOL Pension and Welfare Benefits Administration Proposed Guidelines, 29 C.F.R. Pt. 2510.

These valuations must be tailored to the needs of the situation and may be required for a variety of reasons.

1. Federal tax purposes, where fair market value is the proper concept of value.
2. Federal securities law purposes.
3. Right-of-appraisal statutes, where fair value or fair cash value, depending upon the state of incorporation of the seller, is the proper concept of value.
4. Fraudulent conveyance or bankruptcy purposes, where fair salable value or fair value, depending upon the state of incorporation, is the proper concept of value.

Fair value and fair salable value are vague concepts that take on meaning only within the boundaries of a given state's legal code and case law. In addition, within a given state, these value concepts may continuously evolve. For years the proper determination of value under the right-of-appraisal statutes of Delaware was the Delaware Block Approach,[8] which gave consideration to values determined using a weighted average of an earnings approach, an asset approach, a market approach, and sometimes a dividend approach. The landmark case of *Weinberger v. UOP, Inc.*,[9] disregarded Delaware case law and accepted the use of a discounted-cash-flow approach to value. It is unwise, therefore, to make generalizations about concepts of value that may take on different meanings depending upon the venue of the court of jurisdiction.

[4] Other Purposes

Valuations may also be required for strategic planning, financial reporting, dissenting stockholder suits, damage suits, divorce cases, or foreign tax matters. While Revenue Ruling 59-60 provides a good valuation framework for any purpose, legal advisors should be consulted to determine the proper concept of value and the specific valuation methodology to be used in a given circumstance. With the exception of strategic planning studies and range-of-value studies, the litmus test of valuation is ultimately the court of jurisdiction. It is advisable, therefore, that valuations be performed with a view toward the possible presentation of testimony to support the conclusions of value arrived at in the applicable court of law.

---

[8] For an example of the Delaware Block Method approach, see Heller v. Munsingwear, Inc., 33 Del. Ch. 593, 98 A.2d 774 (1953).

[9] 457 A.2d 701 (Del. Super. Ct. 1983).

¶ 16.3 Information and Sources

The first and most important step in the valuation process is obtaining information about the subject company and its business environment. This can be done by interviewing key management personnel and advisors to the company and by going through the company's financial statements, important documents and agreements, industry and trade data and statistics, and other publicly available information. In general, the information obtained should include the following:

1. A specific definition of the property being valued and the purpose of the valuation;
2. Any legal documents and agreements having a bearing on value;
3. A descriptive history of the company;
4. A description of the current nature of the business and its operations, including (a) the services it provides, (b) key management and other personnel, (c) ownership of the company, and (d) its clients and markets;
5. Financial statements and other financial documents for at least the last five years and current interim financial statements;
6. Budgets or projections of management's expectations of future operating results and financial position;
7. Competition and markets; and
8. Management philosophy and business plans, including any expected significant future changes in the company and its business.

A clear definition of the property and the context in which it is being valued is necessary to assess the appropriate approaches and methodologies in determining its value. In "going-concern" valuations, property can be defined as ownership interests and related financial claims and investment vehicles, including common and preferred stock of a corporation, debt securities, options, and partnership interests. The property can represent the ownership of the entire business entity or a partial interest. The context and the jurisdiction in which the property is being valued may influence or dictate the valuation methodologies used.

Legal documents, including the company's charter and bylaws, shareholders' agreements, employment agreements, partnership agreements, loan agreements, and other important documents should be considered as they may define certain restrictions and limitations placed on the subject property.

All in all, a knowledge and understanding of the history, current status, and future outlook of the overall operation serve as the basis for determining the value of a subject property.

Because service companies are usually directly dependent upon the abilities, talents, and, in many cases, professional qualifications and expertise of individuals, it is of major importance for the valuator to gain an understanding of who the key individuals are; what special abilities, talents, experience, and training they possess; and how dependent the company is on them. Dependence on certain individuals, either for the provision of specific services or for the acquisition of clientele, is a major element to consider in the evaluation of risks.

The investigation in a service-company valuation should also include an assessment of the future of the market for the firm's services and the nature of the competition in that market. Service companies in the same line of business may be differentiated on the basis of the prices of the services they offer or other factors such as the availability and geographic proximity of their markets. The markets to which two firms' services are targeted may be the same, overlap, or be mutually exclusive. The geographic location of their markets may also help to differentiate firms providing a similar service. An understanding of a firm's competition and market will enable the valuator to assess trends and will provide insight into the present and future competitive risks and opportunities the firm may face.

A related consideration is the identification of the firm's clients and the extent of the firm's dependence on specific clients. Heavy reliance on a few major clients makes a firm more vulnerable to risk. Long-term, good relationships with its clients or long-term contracts, however, will lower this risk.

¶ 16.4 Intangible Assets

In general, the most important operating assets of a service company are intangible. When valuing a service company, therefore, the valuation expert must understand the nature and importance of intangibles. Different intangible assets take on different levels of importance depending upon the nature of the subject company's business. Intangible assets may also not be readily salable and may not, in fact, be severable from the company or its individual employees. It is impossible to anticipate all the intangibles that may be important in the valuation of a service company because, by its nature, each service company has unique characteristics. The broad types of intangibles that should be investigated, however, include the work force, customer contracts, software and databases, the customer base, employment contracts and any agreements not to compete, and trade names.

[1] Work Force

Companies spend large sums of money to find, keep, and train their personnel. Unlike all its other assets, a company's work force walks out the door at the end of the business day. For service industries requiring a high level of technical skill from their employees—such as engineering firms—the work force is the company's key asset. In order to determine the importance of the work force, the valuator must ascertain its technical skills, the educational background of the workers, training costs, labor availability, benefits, and historic turnover. In other instances, it is the sales force that is most important to a given service business. In this case, it is the quality of management, provisions for managerial succession, and the existence of key people that must be investigated.

[2] Customer Contracts

In general, the more favorable the terms of a customer contract and the longer the duration of the contract, the more valuable it is to a service company. Conversely, an unfavorable or short-term contract may be a negative factor or one of little value. The valuation expert should know the terms of key contracts, the ability of the supplier to perform in a manner consistent with these terms, the likelihood that the contract will be terminated, and the duration of the contract. For service companies whose business is conducted primarily according to contractual obligations, historic trends in contract terminations and new contracts should be investigated. Potentially valuable contracts include (1) design contracts with a branch of the armed services for major armaments, (2) mortgage servicing rights held by mortgage bankers, (3) long-term maintenance contracts for a power plant, (4) management contracts for real estate, and (5) hotel management agreements.

[3] Software and Databases

Proprietary software and databases may be used directly by a company—that is, to help it perform a service for its customers—or they may be licensed for a fee to customers who will use them for their own purposes. The value of software or databases is the income stream they generate or the cost savings they provide. Software can be an important asset to any service company involved with recordkeeping, internal reporting, and processing of data as well as for purveyors of software. Databases are important for service companies that specialize in providing information, such as data processing companies, credit information companies, and database companies. In analyzing the importance of software or databases, the valuation expert should inves-

[4] Customer Base

For service companies that do not have contractual relationships with their customers or have only short-term contracts, a key asset may be the customer base. Ongoing and repeat business with customers, even if not of a contractual nature, is extremely important to certain service businesses. Service business customers often do not want to terminate an ongoing relationship because of the cost involved in selecting a new supplier as well as the cost of familiarizing a supplier with individual requirements. The valuator should investigate the nature of and the historical termination experience of a company's customer relationships. Examples of services where customer base is an important asset include stockbrokers, advertising agencies, fuel oil suppliers, exterminators, accountants, attorneys, doctors, and architects and engineers.

[5] Employment Contracts and Agreements Not to Compete

As previously stated, many service companies are dependent upon the people who provide the services or who generate new business. Because personnel, unlike machinery and equipment, may walk out the door and join a competing firm or form a new firm, these companies are extremely vulnerable. Compensation policies, working environment, and fringe benefits may help keep key personnel. Many firms try to protect themselves from unwanted resignations and pilferage of customers by having key personnel sign employment contracts/or covenants not to compete. The existence of these types of agreements should be investigated and analyzed with respect to the benefits or degree of protection they provide the subject company.

[6] Trade Names

For many companies, trade names are key assets, particularly for companies where reputation for providing quality services is significant. Often a well-known and respected service firm will obtain new clients on the strength of its trade name alone. When the firm's name rather than its key people is associated with quality, there is less risk of a possible loss of business due to employee turnover.

[7] Other Intangibles

Industry-specific intangible assets should be analyzed where pertinent. Other intangibles that may have considerable value include favorable leaseholds, trademarks, technical drawings, customer lists, franchise agreements, television syndication rights, territorial rights, and film libraries.

Intangible assets are generally excluded from the balance sheet of service companies. The notable exception to this are companies who have purchased other companies and allocated a portion of the purchase price to specific intangible assets. Appraisers typically use three different approaches to value intangible assets: (1) the cost approach, (2) the income approach, or (3) the market approach. The existence of intangibles is usually reflected in above-average returns relative to a company's tangible book value.

¶ 16.5 Financial Considerations

Service companies are generally labor-intensive businesses and rarely require much in the way of capital equipment and physical inventories. Typically, the nature of income and expense flows and assets and liabilities differ from that of other types of concerns, such as manufacturing companies and retail establishments. The valuator must understand these financial differences when performing a valuation of a service company.

[1] Cash vs. Accrual Accounting

Often the valuation expert encounters a service company that prepares its financial statements on a cash accounting basis. Companies on a cash basis may have assets and liabilities not recorded on the company's balance sheet. Unrecorded or unbilled service time may be a significant asset for service organizations whose business involves the selling of professional time. Accrued vacation time payable may be a significant liability not recorded on the balance sheet. The valuation expert should thoroughly investigate the magnitude and significance of unrecorded and contingent balance sheet items.

[2] Deferred Revenues

Many professional service firms have a liability to perform services not yet rendered. Typically such firms require that their clients pay an up-front retainer as a matter of standard operating procedure. This type of liability, which is similar to the deferred subscription revenues of magazines, must be investigated for two reasons: first, it represents a liability of the firm and must be acknowledged; and, second, it may offer the firm the opportunity to invest funds between the time it receives the retainer and the time when the money must be paid to the provider of the service. The earnings from these investments can be a significant source of income for the firm. For example, insurance brokers typically invest the insurance premiums they receive for a period of time before they remit the payments to the insurance carriers.

[3] Working Capital

How a firm manages its working capital can be critically important to its success. Because many service firms have little or no fixed assets, it may be difficult to obtain longer-term financing without the personal guarantees of the principals. In analyzing a firm's working capital management, the valuation expert should look at the firm's current and quick ratio, aging of receivables, trends in average collection period, and the trend in number of days of payables, as well as working capital turnover.

[4] Other Financial Factors

The valuation expert should also take into consideration any lawsuits against the company, the significance and likelihood of any judgments against the firm, and possible exposure to future litigation. Malpractice and errors and omission insurance coverage should be investigated as to what protection they offer.

¶ 16.6 Valuation Approaches

When valuing the equity of a service organization, the valuation analyst must exercise care in the selection of approaches. Various approaches are available to value service organizations on a "going concern" basis. As in all valuations, there is a difference between the valuation of minority and majority interests.

Revenue Ruling 59-60 states the following about valuing service companies:

> In general, the appraiser will accord primary consideration to earnings when valuing stocks of companies which sell products or services to the public; conversely, in the investment or holding type of company, the appraiser may accord the greatest weight to the assets underlying the security to be valued.

All approaches to value can be categorized into the following three traditional approaches.

1. *Market approach.* This is based upon an analysis of comparable sales of equity interests of similar entities.
2. *Income approach.* This is based upon the present value of income to be received in the future or the "capitalization" of recurring income.

3. *Cost or asset approach.* This is a balance sheet approach to value resulting from the subtraction of the sum of the fair market values of all liabilities from the sum of the fair market values of all assets.

[1] Majority vs. Minority Interests

There is a difference between an interest in a company or entity where the rights of ownership enable the investor to control the affairs of the entity and a small interest in a company where the rights of ownership do not enable the holder to have any real influence over the company. The former is referred to as a majority or controlling interest and the latter a minority interest. In general, an investor holding a controlling interest is able to determine major corporate policies as well as direct the everyday operations of the company. While not all-encompassing, the following list provides examples of powers that accrue to someone holding a controlling interest but not to someone holding a minority interest:

- Determine dividend policy;
- Determine compensation levels, including own salary;
- Sell the company;
- Liquidate the company;
- Merge the company;
- Hire and fire management;
- Raise capital;
- Elect directors;
- Register shares with the SEC; and
- Amend the certificate of incorporation, charter, bylaws, and other documents.

The benefits accruing to a majority interest depend upon the size of the block of stock, the state of incorporation, and other legal and practical considerations. For example, a 51% shareholder can decide to liquidate a corporation domiciled in Delaware, but a holder of a New York State corporation must have at least two-thirds voting control in order to liquidate. The per-share fair market value of controlling interests generally greatly exceeds the per-share fair market value of noncontrolling interests because of the added benefits accruing to control shares.

[2] Premises of Fair Market Value for Common Stock

In general, there are three premises of fair market value for common stock:

1. *Enterprise value.* This is the value of the whole company. (It is often applicable on a proportional basis to a controlling interest.)
2. *Publicly traded minority value.* This is the value of minority interests if they were freely and actively traded in a public market.
3. *Privately held minority value.* This is publicly traded minority value less a discount for lack of marketability to reflect the fact that the subject shares do not enjoy a public market.

A premium for control is the difference between enterprise value per share and publicly traded minority value per share expressed as a percent of publicly traded minority value per share. For example, if freely traded value were $1 and enterprise value were $1.50, the premium for control would be 50%. A minority-interest discount is the same difference expressed as a percent of enterprise value. The minority interest discount in the above example is 33%. Different approaches to value yield an indication of enterprise value or as publicly traded minority value. The approach used, and whether or not the subject interest represents a majority or minority, dictates appropriate discounts or premiums to be taken in a given valuation assignment.

In general, these valuations rules apply:

1. A minority interest discount is appropriate to take when an enterprise value is used to determine publicly traded minority interest value.
2. A discount for lack of marketability from publicly traded minority value is generally appropriate for valuations of privately held minority interests.
3. A premium for control over publicly traded minority value is generally appropriate for valuations of controlling interests.

[3] Market Approach

Revenue Ruling 59-60 states that a fundamental factor to consider in performing a valuation of equity is as follows:

> The market price of stocks of corporations engaged in the same or a similar line of business having their stocks actively traded in a free and open market, either on an exchange or over-the-counter.

In implementing the market approach, quantitative and qualitative comparisons as to lines of business, financial performance, and financial conditions are made between the subject company and a group of publicly traded comparative companies. Care must be taken to ensure that the comparative companies have as many characteristics as possible in common with the subject company (e.g., line of business and size). Based upon the comparative analysis and the market valuation of the comparative companies (typically price/earnings ratios, price/cash flow ratios, dividend yields, and price/tangible book value ratios), the valuation expert selects appropriate capitalization rates to apply to the subject company's earnings, cash flow, dividends, book value, and so on. Revenue Ruling 59-60 presents an excellent review of the different factors to be considered. Capitalization rates chosen are based upon the risks associated with ownership of the subject entity.

Price/earnings and price/cash flow ratios can be applied to recurring earnings/cash flow from various time periods, for example, five-year average, three-year average, latest year, latest twelve months, and/or projected periods. In general, earnings for periods closest to the valuation date are generally given greater weight. Also, indicated values on an earnings or cash flow basis are given greater weight than those for dividends or tangible book value. For cyclical businesses, earnings measures based on three-year and five-year averages may be accorded more weight to reflect the average level of earnings during the cycle.

For service companies, price/revenue ratios should also be analyzed. Purchasers of service companies are more concerned about the recurring business of a service company and less concerned with the seller's cost structure as the buyer may be able to easily replace the seller's cost structure. The buyer may have favorable cost advantages vis-à-vis the seller reflecting such items as favorable lease terms, cheaper labor costs, and a greater reliance on capital equipment such as computers, and excess capacity.

Tables 16-1 through 16-6 present price/earnings ratios, price/projected earnings ratios, price/revenue ratios, market/tangible book value ratios, and dividend yields for a group of publicly traded advertising companies. According to the tables, the price/earnings ratios and the price/revenue ratios of the comparative companies were closely bunched together, whereas the dividend yields and market/tangible book values of the comparatives were greatly dispersed.

The market approach can be used to determine the publicly traded minority value of a service business by comparing the subject organization with a group of similar publicly traded minority interests. If warranted, a premium for control can be applied to determine enterprise value.

Enterprise value can also be obtained by pricing the subject business from the actual prices paid in acquisitions of entire companies that engage in similar lines of business to that of the subject organization.

[Text continues on p. 16-18]

TABLE 16-1
PUBLIC COMPANIES
PRICE/EARNINGS RATIOS BASED ON PRIMARY EARNINGS PER SHARE

	Fiscal Year-End	5-Year Average Earnings $	3-Year Average Earnings $	Latest Year's Earnings $	Latest 12-Months Earnings $	Date
Foote, Cone & Belding Company, Inc.	12/31	3.34	3.71	3.30	3.41	06/30/X1
Grey Advertising, Inc.	12/31	6.85	7.39	6.60	6.96	06/30/X1
Interpublic Group of Companies, Inc.	12/31	1.46	1.68	1.87	2.02	06/30/X1
Ogilvy Group, Inc.	12/31	1.67	1.95	1.90	1.87	06/30/X1
Omnicom Group, Inc.	12/31	0.99	0.86	−0.17	−0.28	06/30/X1
Saatchi & Saatchi Company, P.L.C.	09/30	0.72	1.02	1.35	1.52	06/30/X1

	Average Market Price[a] $	Price/Earnings Ratios Based on Above Earnings and Average Market Price[b] (Times)			
Foote, Cone & Belding Company, Inc.	61.38	18.4	16.5	18.6	18.0
Grey Advertising, Inc.	132.00	19.3	17.9	20.0	19.0
Interpublic Group of Companies, Inc.	40.50	27.7	24.1	21.7	20.0
Ogilvy Group, Inc.	36.63	22.0	18.8	19.3	19.6
Omnicom Group, Inc.	26.69	27.0	30.9	N/M	N/M
Saatchi & Saatchi Company P.L.C.	29.82	41.4	29.3	22.1	19.6
Median		24.5	21.5	20.9	19.6

[a] During valuation period of 09/10/X1-10/09/X1.
[b] Average earnings and price data are rounded; calculations for price/earnings ratios are based on actual numbers

TABLE 16-2
PUBLIC COMPANIES
PRICE/PROJECTED EARNINGS MULTIPLES

	19X1 $	19X2 $	19X4-X5 Average $
Foote, Cone & Belding Company, Inc.	3.80	4.95	7.10
Grey Advertising, Inc.	N/A	N/A	N/A
Interpublic Group of Companies, Inc.	2.15	2.48	4.30
Ogilvy Group, Inc.	2.10	2.44	3.45
Omnicom Group, Inc.	1.30	1.80	2.80
Saatchi & Saatchi Company, P.L.C.	2.05	2.34	3.70

	Average Market Price[a] $	Price/Projected Revenue Ratios[b] (Times)		
Foote, Cone & Belding Company, Inc.	61.38	16.2	12.4	8.6
Grey Advertising, Inc.	132.00	N/A	N/A	N/A
Interpublic Group of Companies, Inc.	40.50	18.8	16.3	9.4
Ogilvy Group, Inc.	36.63	17.4	15.0	10.6
Omnicom Group, Inc.	26.69	20.5	14.8	9.5
Saatchi & Saatchi Company, PLC	29.82	14.5	12.7	8.1
Median		17.4	14.8	9.4

[a] During valuation period of 09/10/X1-10/09/X1
[b] Average earnings and price data are rounded; calculations for price/earnings ratios are based on actual numbers

TABLE 16-3

PUBLIC COMPANIES
PRICE/REVENUE PER SHARE

	Fiscal Year-End	5-Year Average Revenues	3-Year Average Revenues	Latest Year's Revenues
		$	$	$
Foote, Cone & Belding Company, Inc.	12/31	71.74	75.68	78.47
Grey Advertising, Inc.	12/31	154.03	174.22	192.36
Interpublic Group of Companies, Inc.	12/31	31.06	32.79	37.10
Ogilvy Group, Inc.	12/31	31.06	34.77	39.42
Omnicom Group, Inc.	12/31	26.19	28.49	31.42
Saatchi & Saatchi Company, P.L.C.	09/30	N/A	N/A	N/A

	Average Market Price[a]	Price/Revenues Ratios Based on Above Revenues and Average Market Price[b]		
	$	(Times)		
Foote, Cone & Belding Company, Inc.	61.38	0.9	0.8	0.8
Grey Advertising, Inc.	132.00	0.9	0.8	0.7
Interpublic Group of Companies, Inc.	40.50	1.3	1.2	1.1
Ogilvy Group, Inc.	36.63	1.2	1.1	0.9
Omnicom Group, Inc.	26.69	1.0	0.9	0.8
Saatchi & Saatchi Company P.L.C.	29.82	N/A	N/A	N/A
Median		1.0	0.9	0.8

[a] During valuation period of 09/10/X1-10/09/X1.
[b] Average revenues and price data are rounded; calculations for price/revenue ratios are based on actual numbers

TABLE 16-4

PUBLIC COMPANIES
PRICE/PROJECTED REVENUE MULTIPLES

	19X1	19X2	19X4-X5 Average
	$	$	$
Foote, Cone & Belding Company, Inc.	83.35	93.00	111.10
Grey Advertising, Inc.	N/A	N/A	N/A
Interpublic Group of Companies, Inc.	40.55	45.15	66.65
Ogilvy Group, Inc.	49.30	53.20	66.45
Omnicom Group, Inc.	31.90	35.30	46.00
Saatchi & Saatchi Company, P.L.C.	23.30	25.95	43.85

	Average Market Price[a]	Price/Projected Earnings Ratios[b]		
	$	(Times)		
Foote, Cone & Belding Company, Inc.	61.38	0.7	0.7	0.6
Grey Advertising, Inc.	132.00	N/A	N/A	N/A
Interpublic Group of Companies, Inc.	40.50	1.0	0.9	0.6
Ogilvy Group, Inc.	36.63	0.7	0.7	0.6
Omnicom Group, Inc.	26.69	0.8	0.8	0.6
Saatchi & Saatchi Company, P.L.C.	29.82	1.3	1.1	0.7
Median		0.8	0.7	0.6

[a] During valuation period of 09/10/X1-10/09/X1
[b] Average revenues and price data are rounded; calculations for price/revenue ratios are based on actual numbers

TABLE 16-5

PUBLIC COMPANIES
RETURN ON EQUITY AND MARKET
PRICE/TANGIBLE BOOK VALUE DURING THE
VALUATION PERIOD

	Return on Common Stockholders' Equity		Market Price/ Tangible Book Value[a]
	Latest Year	5-Year Median	
	(Percent)		
Interpublic Group of Companies, Inc.	16.9	16.9	491.3
Ogilvy Group, Inc.	16.9	16.9	610.2
Grey Advertising, Inc.	12.1	16.9	229.6
Foote, Cone & Belding Company, Inc.	11.6	17.5	316.2
Omnicom Group, Inc.	−2.3	10.9	N/A
Saatchi & Saatchi Company, P.L.C.	NEG	15.2	N/A

[a] Average market price during the valuation period (09/01/$X$1-10/09/$X$1) to latest year-end tangible book value

TABLE 16-6

PUBLIC COMPANIES
DIVIDEND-PAYOUT RATIOS AND DIVIDEND YIELDS
DURING THE VALUATION PERIOD

	Dividend/Payout ratio		Dividend Yield[a]
	Latest Year	5-Year Median	
	(Percent)		
Foote, Cone & Belding Company, Inc.	64.3	55.4	3.6
Ogilvy Group, Inc.	40.7	40.2	2.3
Saatchi & Saatchi Company, P.L.C.	36.1	33.5	2.9
Interpublic Group of Companies, Inc.	31.9	32.6	1.7
Grey Advertising, Inc.	28.1	21.6	1.7
Omnicom Group, Inc.	NEG	66.3	3.7

[a] Based on indicated dividend rate and average market price during valuation period (09/01/$X$1-10/09/$X$1)

[Text continues from p. 16-14]

Again quantitative and qualitative comparisons would be made between the subject organization and the comparative companies in terms of earnings, cash flow, tangible book value, and revenue multiples. The problem with using this approach is that comparative sales of whole companies occurring close to the valuation date may not exist.

[4] Earnings Approach

There are two forms of approach to valuating earnings commonly used: (1) discounted cash flow (DCF) and (2) earnings capitalization.

The DCF approach is based upon the premise that the value of a business enterprise is equal to the net present value of its projected free cash flows. "Free cash flow" is defined as the amount of cash available to a company after all its operating expenses and investment needs, such as capital expenditures and incremental working capital, have been met. The approach can be applied on a debt-free basis (as if the company did not have any debt) to determine the fair market value of invested capital (equity and long-term debt). There are three components or steps used in the implementation of a DCF approach.

1. Preparation of a projection of free cash flow for a representative period;
2. Determination of the terminal value or selling price of the company at the end of the projection period;
3. Calculation and summation of the net present values of items 1 and 2, based on a market-derived discount rate giving consideration to the risk associated with the subject investment.

Tables 16-7 and 16-8 present a sample DCF calculation.

The capitalization of earnings approach involves the determination of the normalized recurring earnings power of the corporation. A required rate of return is obtained by reviewing the rates of return of alternative investments giving due consideration to the risk associated with investment in the subject company. Dividing the normalized earnings by the selected rate of return results in an indicated value.

[5] Asset Approach

The asset approach to value involves adjusting the subject company's latest available balance sheet to reflect the fair market values of all the assets and liabilities of the company. Off-balance sheet assets such as intangibles and off-balance sheet liabilities such as unfunded pension liabilities should be reflected on the adjusted balance sheet. Historically, the asset approach has primarily been used for valuations of service companies in cases where a company has been purchased and the purchase price was being allocated for tax and financial reporting purposes.

[Text continues on p. 16-20]

TABLE 16-7

ABC COMPANY
PROJECTED SALES, CASH FLOW, AND SELECTED KEY DATA
($ Millions)

	19X2	19X3	19X4	19X5	19X6	19X7
Sales	595.7	743.0	829.3	846.6	884.2	964.9
Cost of sales	516.3	647.3	722.1	732.1	763.9	835.2
Sales deductions (freight, duty)	4.7	5.2	5.8	5.9	6.2	6.8
Gross profit	74.7	90.5	101.4	108.6	114.1	122.9
Engineering and product development (50% in cost of sales)	7.2	7.2	7.6	8.4	8.1	8.8
Sales and marketing	38.2	40.1	44.0	47.5	50.5	54.5
Administration	21.2	22.0	22.8	23.6	25.5	27.5
Other expense	1.0	1.0	1.0	1.0	1.0	1.0
Profit before income tax	7.1	20.2	26.0	28.1	29.0	31.1
State and local tax	1.0	1.2	1.2	1.3	1.4	1.6
Federal minimum tax @ 3.4%	0.2	0.6	0.8	0.9	0.9	1.0
Net income	5.9	18.4	24.0	25.9	26.7	28.5
Capital expenditures	6.4	6.4	6.4	6.4	6.4	6.4
Working capital increase (decrease)	1.7	−7.4	11.3	2.1	4.6	1.3
Depreciation	5.6	5.8	6.0	6.1	6.2	6.3
Free cash flow	3.4	24.8	12.3	23.5	21.9	27.1

TABLE 16-8

ABC COMPANY
CALCULATION OF PRESENT VALUE
($ Millions)

	19X2	19X3	19X4	19X5	19X6	19X7
Free cash flow	3.4	24.8	12.3	23.5	21.9	27.1
Discount factor @ 13%	0.93897	0.82785	0.72988	0.64351	0.56735	0.50021
Net present value	3.2	20.5	8.9	15.1	12.4	13.6
Net present value 19X2–19X7						73.7
Terminal year's fully taxed earnings of 19.5 times 13				253.1		
Plus: 45% premium for control				113.9		
Total value of terminal year				367.0		
Discount factor @ 13%				0.48032		
Present value of terminal year						176.3
Indicated value						250.0

[Text continues from p. 16-18]

[6] Rules of Thumb

Valuation rules-of-thumb for certain service industries should be investigated. Examples of rules of thumb include the following:

1. A multiple of revenues for an insurance brokerage agency;
2. A price-per-subscriber for a health maintenance organization or for a cable television company; and
3. A price-per-bed for a hospital.

Valuation rules of thumb are really disguised earnings approaches to value where the buyer believes there is a reasonable rate of return on investment. Rules of thumb are more often used for asset purchases as opposed to equity sales because they do not give adequate consideration to balance sheet factors such as liquidity and debt levels nor do they give consideration to the business contacts of key people.

Rules of thumb should be employed with extreme caution. More often than not, they do not give reliable answers because they will not give adequate consideration to many factors that may have either a negative or positive impact on value. In addition, they are misleading and inaccurate with respect to minority interests since the yardstick used is based on the whole enterprise.

¶ 16.7 Special Considerations

Because the service field consists of a wide variety of firms, the valuator should recognize the unique characteristics of the type of service organization under investigation. Some of the key factors to consider in assessing the nature, the outlook, and the risks of different service firms and their environments are summarized next.

[1] Hotels and Lodging

Businesses engaged in hotel and lodging services derive revenues primarily from occupancy charges, food, and, in certain instances, gaming operations. The success of a hotel operation depends in large part upon the extent to which a hotel can maximize its occupancy rate. The occupancy rate is a function of several key factors including location, name recognition, seasonality, price of services, quality of services and facilities, and competition. For example, hotels in locations that attract many tourists, vacationers, business conferences, special events, and fairs are more likely to maximize occupancy than hotels in areas that don't. Of course, this depends upon the nature of competition that a hotel faces. Hotel chains that have high name recognition may also fare better than hotels not as recognized by the public. Seasonal factors may have an important effect on occupancy rates. For example, regions with warm climates attract travelers from cold winter climates. In addition, the valuator should consider the nature and diversity of hotel locations, the competition, outlook for growth in population, and other key demographic data. The valuator should also consider the potential value of the underlying properties, if owned.

[2] Personal Services

Personal services include laundry, barber, health club, porter, shoe repair, funeral, and numerous other personal services. Most such businesses rely to a large extent on the personal preferences of customers, as well as the location, expertise, quality, and price of those services. Most of these services are provided by small local firms which operate from one location. In such cases, lease terms and key people aspects of the business should be investigated.

[3] Business Services

Business services consist of a wide variety of functions offered to businesses, including advertising, consumer credit reporting, data processing, computer programming, research and development, valuation, and a host of other business services. The success of this type of business is dependent upon several factors including the reputation and track record of the firm as a whole and its key members, the price and quality of the services, reliability, timelessness, region, and seasonality. The size of these firms range from very small to very large.

[4] Automotive Repair and Garage Services

Automotive repair services derive revenues generally from fees for labor and parts. These businesses depend largely on several factors including affiliation with auto manufacturers, dealerships, insurance companies, and petroleum refiners, as well as location, price, and reliability of services

[5] Motion Picture Services

This category consists of movie theaters, producers, and distributors. Movie theaters generate revenues primarily from ticket sales, concessions, and advertising. The success of these operations depend upon various factors including the location or market, selection of movies, competition, seasonality, price, and the quality and comfort of the viewing facilities. In some cases, particularly for drive-in movie theaters, the underlying property may have significant value. Another key factor to consider is the growth in number of viewing screens.

[6] Amusement and Recreation Services

Amusement and recreation services include a wide variety of businesses including dance halls and studios, theatrical services, bowling and billiards, commercial sports, racing, golf courses, and amusement parks. These services derive revenues from various sources according to the type of service. The success of amusement and recreation services depends on several factors, including location, seasonality, popularity, quality, comfort, safety of facilities, and price.

[7] Health Services

Health services include private medical and dental practices, health maintenance organizations (HMO's), hospitals, nursing homes, and other medical programs. Depending on the type of organization, revenues are generally derived from fees for services, rates for occupancy, or flat subscription fees. The success of a health practice or organization is a function of many factors that include the quality, record, and reputation of health practitioners and organization, cost of services, extent of specialization, location, and condition and quality of facilities.

[8] Legal Services

Legal services include primarily law firms, which range from private law practices to major law firms. Revenues of such firms are derived largely from fees for legal services that are generally a function of the size, scope, risks, and outcome of cases. The degree of success of a firm depends primarily on the reputation and recognition of the practitioners and the firm itself, fees, extent of specialization, size, and location.

[9] Educational Services

Educational services include schools, colleges, universities, libraries, and information centers. These services derive funds primarily from tuitions and private and public funding. The success of these services depends upon various factors including the reputation of individuals and the institution itself, location, price, specialization, and the quality, size, and diversity of facilities.

[10] Social Services

Social services include individual and family social services, job training, child day care, residential care, and organizations that solicit funds for these and related services. These services derive funds from various sources including fees, private contributions, and government funding. The success of these types of services depends upon various factors, including reputation and location.

[11] Museums, Art Galleries, and Botanical and Zoological Gardens

Museums, art galleries, and similar services derive value from the collections they possess. As most such organizations are nonprofit, they derive revenues primarily from contributions and nominal fees in order to maintain an ongoing exhibition.

¶ 16.8 Summary

The key characteristics of most service organizations is a dependency on the people employed to deliver the services offered. The mix between capital and labor input varies widely from the hotel, hospital, or motion picture industries at one end of the spectrum to personal or professional service industries at the other. However, a major derivation of value in most instances is the ability to recruit, organize, and train a skilled work force to successfully market and deliver the services offered. The valuator of a service business, therefore, must focus attention on its people-related characteristics to a greater extent than when dealing with a manufacturing company, a distributor, or a raw materials producer where successful results depend more heavily on the organization and contribution of capital assets.

17

FINANCIAL INSTITUTIONS

JACK W. BERKA*

		Page
¶ 17.1	**Financial Institutions Industry**	17-3
	[1] Changes in the 1980s	17-4
	[a] Depository Institutions Deregulation and Monetary Control Act of 1980	17-4
	[b] Garn-St Germain Depository Institutions Act of 1982	17-4
	[c] Nonbank Banks	17-4
	[d] Growth in Secondary Loan Markets and Changing Capital Markets	17-4
	[e] Interstate Banking	17-5
	[f] The Tax Reform Act of 1986	17-5
	[g] Competitive Equality Banking Act of 1987	17-5
	[h] Hostile Takeovers	17-5
	[i] The Financial Institutions Reform, Recovery and Enforcement Act of 1989	17-5
	[j] Future Deregulation	17-5
¶ 17.2	**Savings and Loan Analysis**	17-6
	[1] Balance Sheet	17-6
	[a] Assets	17-6
	[b] Liabilities	17-10
	[c] Equity	17-10
	[2] Income Statement	17-10
	[a] Operating Income	17-10
	[b] Expenses	17-12
	[c] Nonoperating Income and Expenses	17-12
	[3] Financial Analysis	17-12
	[a] Size	17-15
	[b] Liquidity	17-15
	[c] Deposit Mix	17-18
	[d] Asset Mix	17-18

---

* JACK W. BERKA is senior vice president of Houlihan, Lokey, Howard & Zukin, Inc., a financial valuation and investment advisory firm headquartered in Los Angeles, California. He is also vice president of the firm's Financial Institutions Group and its Research Department. The author wishes to acknowledge the assistance of Jeffrey M. Botvinick and Andrew L. Berg in the preparation of this chapter.

	[e]	Capital Adequacy	17-20
	[f]	Profitability	17-20
	[g]	Interest Analysis	17-21
	[h]	Growth	17-21
[4]	Additional Analysis		17-21
[5]	Summary		17-22

¶ 17.3 **Commercial Bank Analysis** 17-22
    [1] Balance Sheet 17-22
        [a] Assets 17-22
        [b] Liabilities 17-23
    [2] Income Statement 17-26
    [3] Financial Analysis 17-27
        [a] Total Interest Expense/Average Earnings Assets 17-28
        [b] Total Interest Income/Average Earnings Assets 17-30
        [c] Earnings Asset Yield—Break-Even Yield 17-30
        [d] Total Interest Expense/Total Interest-Bearing Liabilities 17-30
        [e] Equity Capital + Capital Notes + Reserve for Loan Losses/Gross Loans .. 17-30
        [f] Loan Loss Provision/Average Gross Loans................................ 17-31
        [g] Net Charge-Offs/Average Gross Loans . 17-31
        [h] Nonperforming Loans/Average Loans .. 17-31
        [i] Loan Loss Provisions/Charge-Offs...... 17-31
    [4] Summary 17-32

¶ 17.4 **Other Valuation Considerations** 17-32
    [1] Off Balance Sheet Assets and Liabilities 17-33
    [2] Public Company Comparables 17-33
    [3] Control Premiums/Discounts for Minority Interest 17-33
    [4] Accounting Issues 17-33
    [5] Management Issues 17-34

¶ 17.5 **Summary** 17-34

    The valuation of financial institutions is, of course, the quantification of risk and return through techniques detailed throughout this book. However, the analysis of a financial institution relative to a manufacturing or service company is different due to its unique nature: a company comprised of *financial* assets and liabilities. The value of those financial assets and liabilities is derivative of the macroeconomic environment at large. Financial institutions are also an instrument of public policy and regulated by a myriad of overlapping regulatory agencies.

The purpose of this chapter is to present a general analytical framework for the analysis of financial institutions. The chapter is not intended to be all-inclusive, as the list of analytical considerations is situational and virtually endless. Rather, the chapter is intended to serve the reader as a framework to begin an analysis of a financial institution. While the focus is on savings and loans and commercial banks, the concepts presented are applicable to all types of financial institutions.

¶ 17.1 Financial Institutions Industry

The banking system in the United States evolved to facilitate the country's commerce and business by supplying credit and financing to businesses on a short-to-intermediate time horizon. Sources of funds were typically shorter-term deposits from businesses and individuals. As a result of the economic upheaval of the Depression, the activities of commercial banks were strictly regulated.

Savings and loan institutions were developed in the United States to supplement the financial services provided by the banking system. Savings and loans traditionally served middle- and working-class individuals who required safety of personal deposits on a slightly longer time horizon and access to mortgage funds. The thrift industry prospered into the 1970s with minimal risk by accepting deposits at regulated interest rates, slightly higher than that of commercial banks but nevertheless low rates, and lending to home buyers at predictably higher rates.

It is somewhat curious to note that while other industries pegged value as a function of earnings and cash flow, financial institutions pegged value to multiples of reported book value. In the highly regulated, relatively stable environment of the 1970s, the "rule-of-thumb" approach, using book value (or a multiple thereof) as a proxy for market value, appeared reasonable.

The regulated financial institution environment began to break down in the highly inflationary environment of the late 1970s. Disintermediation began as depositors responded by moving their funds to alternative unregulated financial investments for higher returns. As a result, financial institutions experienced a dramatic liquidity crisis. In addition, many commercial banks began withdrawing from the Federal Reserve System.

In response to the disintermediation of financial institution funds and the general policy of deregulation by the Reagan Administration, the financial institution industry was substantially deregulated in the

1980s. Other events also contributed to a dramatic change in the financial institution industry.

[1] Changes in the 1980s

Some restructuring of the financial institutions industry took place during the 1980s. Those changes are described in the following pages.

[a] Depository Institutions Deregulation and Monetary Control Act of 1980

The Depository Institutions Deregulation and Monetary Control Act of 1980 (DIDMCA) was the first major restructuring of the financial institutions industry since the Glass-Steagall Act of 1933. DIDMCA essentially deregulated the left-hand side of the balance sheet by phasing out interest rate ceilings on deposits. Financial institutions were now essentially free to compete for deposits.

[b] Garn-St Germain Depository Institutions Act of 1982

In response to the crisis in the thrift industry precipitated by the high interest rate environment of the early 1980s, whereby S&Ls were now paying market rates for deposits but were restricted essentially to mortgage lending, Garn-St Germain significantly expanded the lending and investment powers of thrifts. This had the effect of further blurring the distinctions between commercial banks and thrifts.

[c] Nonbank Banks

The 1980s also saw the emergence of unregulated "nonbank banks," such as Sears, Merrill Lynch, and American Express. As a bank is defined as an institution that accepts deposits *and* makes loans, nonbank banks skirted regulation by engaging in only one of these activities. Nonbank banks increased competition for financial services and further blurred the definition of and the distinctions between financial institutions.

[d] Growth in Secondary Loan Markets and Changing Capital Markets

As financial institution investment needs changed in response to the changing macroeconomic environment, many new securities developed. Included among these were mortgage-backed securities such as Collateralized Mortgage Obligations (CMOs); Real Estate Mortgage Investment Conduits (REMICs); and Stripped Mortgage Pass-Throughs (STRIPs). These securities comprised mortgage pools obtained from various savings and loans (S&Ls). The dynamic new securities provided an alternative strategy because S&Ls now had the option of originating and selling their loan portfolios versus originating and servicing their loan portfolios for their own accounts.

[e] Interstate Banking

De facto interstate banking evolved in the 1980s through regional compacts, franchising, and other methods. Competition increased, and the industry began a dramatic consolidation.

[f] The Tax Reform Act of 1986

The Tax Reform Act of 1986 (TRA '86) eliminated the interest expense deductibility associated with tax-exempt investments, reduced the bad debt reserve, and strengthened the alternative minimum tax. TRA '86 also put many financial institutions into an unfamiliar taxpaying position.

[g] Competitive Equality Banking Act of 1987

The Competitive Equality Banking Act of 1987 (CEBA) was intended to provide more uniformity of regulation between banks and thrifts. The act requires thrifts to effectively raise capital levels to the levels of their commercial bank counterparts.

[h] Hostile Takeovers

In March 1988 the Federal Reserve Board approved the hostile acquisition of Irving Trust Corporation by the Bank of New York. The approval reiterates the Board's position that it does not distinguish between hostile and friendly takeovers.

[i] The Financial Institutions Reform, Recovery and Enforcement Act of 1989

The Financial Institutions Reform, Recovery and Enforcement Act of 1989 (FIRREA) has established capital requirements for savings associations that must include leverage, tangible, and risk-based capital requirements that are no less stringent than the standards applicable to national banks.

[j] Future Deregulation

Proposed deregulation includes the imposition of risk-based capital requirements and the repeal of the Glass-Steagall Act. The implications of these proposed actions on financial institutions are profound.

This brief summary illustrates the profound change the financial institutions industry has undergone. Today's new environment of financial institutions has rendered rule-of-thumb approaches to valuation useless. Clearly, valuation has become more situational and complex. For example, a thrift making traditional mortgage loans using consumer deposits in a stable economic region may have significantly different valuation characteristics than a thrift making real estate loans and junk bond investments using brokered deposits.

Consequently, any valuation requires a thorough analysis of the financial institution's financial statements.

¶ 17.2 Savings and Loan Analysis

Our discussion of analytical frameworks for financial institutions starts with the savings and loan context. The reader should keep in mind, however, that the general concepts presented below are generally applicable, or can be adopted for the analysis of commercial banks.

The analysis of a savings and loan, like that of any company, requires a thorough understanding of the S&L's financial statements. From there, an analytical framework can be developed to assess important measures of the S&L's risk and return profile, critical to the valuation analysis.

[1] Balance Sheet

The balance sheet of a savings and loan, like the balance sheet of a nonfinancial corporation, displays the status of a company's assets, liabilities, and equity as of a given date. The nature and composition of the assets and liabilities, however, are very different from the typical manufacturing or service company. An understanding of the basic accounts which compose the S&L's financial statements is necessary to facilitate our analysis.

As shown in Table 17-1 on pages 17-8 and 17-9, the asset side of the balance sheet can be grouped into four major categories: cash and investments, loans, fixed assets, and other assets. As with the balance sheet of a nonfinancial corporation, the assets of an S&L are similarly listed from most liquid to least liquid.

[a] Assets

The cash account of a savings and loan generally includes the institution's currency and coin held in its vault, as well as other operating cash. An S&L will hold such cash to accommodate customers who may wish to exercise a deposit claim. Cash items in the process of collection from other financial institutions may make up yet another component of this account.

An additional element of the cash account includes accounts held with correspondent institutions and the Office of Thrift Supervision (OTS) (formerly the Federal Home Loan Bank Board) (FHLBB). Just as consumers have checking accounts with banks to aid in the acquisition of goods and services, S&Ls use and keep accounts with other financial institutions to facilitate their own transactions. Balances held with the FHLBB serve much the same function. In addition, these balances count as legal reserves for member institutions.

Investment securities are short-, intermediate-, and long-term investments in securities. Short-term securities provide liquidity to meet depositor withdrawals or loan demands. Intermediate and long-term securities provide a base of income for financial institutions. Table 17-1 shows investments in U.S. government securities in addition to "other investments."

The U.S. Treasury issues three primary types of securities: Treasury bills, Treasury notes, and Treasury bonds. An S&L will also hold these Treasury issues for supplementary income and liquidity. S&Ls will also hold "Agency" securities for the same reasons that they hold Treasury issues, with the added bonus of higher yields for issues of similar maturities.

Other securities can include certificates of deposit, commercial paper, and various corporate securities. Obligations of states and political subdivisions, which provide an added bonus of producing an income stream exempt from taxes, may also be included in this category. Junk bonds, a high-risk corporate security that came into acceptance in the early 1980s, also became a component of many S&Ls' investment portfolios.

The next category on the balance sheet depicts the loan portfolio, which typically comprises the largest segment of an S&L's assets. Net mortgage loans and contracts (mortgage-backed securities) typically constitute the largest portion of the loan portfolio. The portfolio may also contain some nonmortgage loans such as commercial loans and various consumer loans. Both mortgage and nonmortgage loans may be at fixed or variable rates. Variable or adjustable rate loans will allow the S&L to adjust the rate on these loans within limits and therefore reduce some of the risk associated with changing rates of interest.

The fixed asset account represents the book value of all office buildings, furniture and fixtures, and equipment, less depreciation.

Other assets is a catchall category for all assets not large enough to warrant a separate line item. Examples of other assets can be amounts due from other entities, income earned but not collected, and prepaid expenses.

There are, of course, other major asset items that are not contained in these asset categories. Many savings and loans have repossessed assets and real estate investments listed on their balance sheet. These accounts represent the book value, less depreciation, of all real estate and assets other than bank premises actually owned by the S&L.

[Text continues on p. 17-10]

TABLE 17-1
HOMETOWN SAVINGS AND LOAN ASSOCIATION
COMPARATIVE SUMMARY BALANCE SHEET

	19X8	19X7	19X6	19X5	19X4
Assets					
Cash, deposits and investment securites					
Cash and demand deposits	$ 14,044	$ 10,444	$ 2,145	$ 1,993	$ 1,522
U.S. government and agency securities	-0-	-0-	-0-	-0-	-0-
Other investments	127,849	66,843	59,168	49,143	46,714
Total cash, deposits and investment securities	$141,893	$ 77,287	$ 61,313	$ 51,136	$ 48,236
Net mortgage loans and contracts	$563,714	$417,688	$254,507	$222,453	$182,582
Other loans					
Commercial loans	11,375	7,859	2,887	1,623	1,034
Other nonmortgage loans	6,622	4,615	1,554	985	759
Net nonmortgage loans	$ 17,997	$ 12,474	$ 4,441	$ 2,608	$ 1,793
Repossessed assets	3,194	2,874	2,101	1,827	1,620
Real estate investments	31,532	23,674	21,372	17,061	16,382
Fixed assets	8,691	7,661	6,734	6,387	6,126
Other assets	146,863	126,738	96,722	80,758	74,734
Total assets	$913,884	$668,396	$447,190	$382,230	$331,473

TABLE 17-1
HOMETOWN SAVINGS AND LOAN ASSOCIATION
COMPARATIVE SUMMARY BALANCE SHEET *(continued)*

	19X8	19X7	19X6	19X5	19X4
Liabilities and stockholders' equity					
Deposits	$823,689	$553,296	$371,347	$315,875	$271,089
Borrowings					
FHLB advance	43,040	59,310	25,055	19,807	15,233
Other borrowings	8,305	11,749	11,665	10,349	9,105
Total borrowings	$ 51,345	$ 71,059	$ 36,720	$ 30,156	$ 24,338
Other liabilities	9,239	16,113	12,535	11,084	8,852
Total liabilities	$884,273	$640,468	$420,602	$357,115	$304,279
Stockholders' equity					
Common stock; paid-in capital	7,336	7,792	7,564	7,357	7,120
Retained earnings	22,275	20,136	19,024	17,758	20,074
Total stockholders' equity	$ 29,611	$ 27,928	$ 26,588	$ 25,115	$ 27,194
Total liabilities and stockholders' equity	$913,884	$668,396	$447,190	$382,230	$331,473

[Text continues from p. 17-7]

[b] Liabilities

Since deposits are the principal source of insured funds, they comprise the largest portion of an S&L's liabilities. The deposit category is composed of three primary forms of deposits: (1) fixed-maturity (time) deposits, (2) money-market deposits, and (3) passbook deposits.

Borrowings are funds obtained from various sources for use in meeting increased loan demand or depositor withdrawals. The primary source of such borrowings is the Federal Home Loan Bank (FHLB). Other forms of borrowed money come from the subject institution's own debt securities, from overdrawn amounts with other financial intermediaries, and from repurchase agreements.

Maturities on many of these investments are short; some borrowings are made overnight. These borrowings can also differ with respect to whether or not they are secured. A key factor affecting the cost of borrowing funds through these various instruments is the reserve requirement. If a bank is required to hold reserves against borrowed funds, the borrowing of such funds is increased.

Other liabilities is the category for all liability accounts not large enough to justify a separate line item. Amounts due to other entities and deferred tax credits are example of other liabilities.

[c] Equity

The final component of the balance sheet is shareholders' equity. The equity category usually includes common and preferred stock, surplus, and retained earnings. The surplus account is equivalent to the paid-in capital account of a nonfinancial corporation; it is not available for cash dividends and is sometimes increased by transfers from retained earnings for the purpose of increasing loan limits. Capital stock and surplus are recognized as permanent capital for the computation of an S&L's lending limit and for the calculation of regulatory capital requirements.

[2] Income Statement

The S&L's income statement contains a listing of all operating income and expense items.

[a] Operating Income

As shown in Table 17-2, assets are the primary source of operating income. Typically, interest and fees on loans compose the largest portion of operating income. Included in these amounts are all interest and discounts, both current and past due, along with fees and similar changes on loans. Also contained under this category may be portions of points charged on mortgage loans, renewal and past due charges, and commitment fees.

TABLE 17-2
HOMETOWN SAVINGS AND LOAN ASSOCIATION
COMPARATIVE SUMMARY INCOME STATEMENT

	19X8	19X7	19X6	19X5	19X4
Interest income					
Mortgage loans and contracts	$ 87,597	$ 79,446	$ 58,404	$ 38,066	$ 33,503
Mortgage-backed pass-through securities	89	80	72	36	27
Commercial loans	798	712	659	574	438
Consumer loans	732	632	671	612	491
Investments and deposits	10,508	9,185	8,840	8,365	7,572
Total interest income	$ 99,724	$ 90,055	$ 68,646	$ 47,653	$ 42,031
Fees on loans and leases	6,564	6,106	4,719	4,291	3,864
Other operating income	(2,432)	(2,831)	(1,906)	(1,863)	52
Total operating income	$103,856	$ 93,330	$ 71,459	$ 50,081	$ 45,947
Operating expenses	15,064	12,542	5,493	5,346	5,210
Cost of funds					
Interest on deposits, net	72,910	66,237	52,585	41,867	33,495
Interest on borrowed money	6,446	5,907	3,963	3,516	2,876
Less: Capitalized interest	(672)	(630)	(581)	(606)	(437)
Total cost of funds	$ 78,684	$ 71,514	$ 55,967	$ 44,877	$ 35,934
Operating income after cost of funds	$ 10,108	$ 9,274	$ 9,999	$ (142)	$ 4,803
Nonoperating income	6,836	4,290	3,316	3,108	2,986
Nonoperating expense	16,124	12,042	9,654	7,461	5,242
Income taxes (credit)	(1,319)	410	2,395	(2,179)	897
Net income	$ 2,139	$ 1,112	$ 1,266	($ 2,316)	$ 1,650

Another major source of income comes from an S&L's investment portfolio. Interest income is derived from the individual investments that the S&L holds in its portfolio.

Other operating income is a potpourri of various accounts, some of which may be exclusive to an individual savings and loan. Many of the more common accounts are service charges on deposit accounts and charges for safe deposit boxes. If the S&L involves itself with the sale of insurance policies or the servicing of mortgage loans originated by others, then the corresponding income accounts will be included in the other operating income category.

[b] Expenses

The largest portion of an S&L's expenses is its cost of funds, or, simply stated, the interest paid on its deposits and borrowed money. As a result of the various types of deposit accounts an S&L can offer, different rates of interest will be paid on them. Similarly, varying rates of interest will be paid on the diverse sources of an S&L's borrowed money. Analysis of the variability of these expenses will be discussed in the following section.

Operating expenses consist primarily of salaries, wages, pensions, and other benefits. Additional expenses found in this category can be furniture and equipment expenses, general overhead expenses, federal deposit insurance expense, and other general and administrative expenses that will be specific to an S&L's diverse operations.

[c] Nonoperating Income and Expenses

Nonoperating income and expenses are primarily those gains and losses associated with the foreclosed or repossessed property held by the S&L. These accounts are classified as "nonoperating" because they are not associated with the primary operation of an S&L—that is, the borrowing and lending of money.

[3] Financial Analysis

After a basic understanding of the financial statement is complete, the financial analysis can begin.

The financial statements submitted to the analyst provide a comparative historic look at the absolute levels of the various income statement and balance sheet accounts. While these absolute levels aid in the determination of trends, they are even more useful as inputs for making calculations of relative values. Relative values, such as those offered through a composition analysis, provide an indispensable perspective into an S&L's efficiency and profitability. For example, composition analysis of the income statement involves calculations of the percentage of various income and expense items to total operating income.

This distribution comparison should be made with those of previous years. A similar distribution is used for asset, liability, and equity accounts to total assets. Samples of "common-size" financial statements can be found in Tables 17-3 and 17-4.

TABLE 17-3

HOMETOWN SAVINGS AND LOAN ASSOCIATION
COMMON SIZE BALANCE SHEET

	19X8	19X7	19X6	19X5	19X4
Assets					
Cash, deposits, and investment securites					
Cash and demand deposits	1.5%	1.6%	0.5%	0.5%	0.5%
U.S. government and agency securities	0.0	0.0	0.0	0.0	0.0
Other investments	14.0	10.0	13.2	12.9	14.1
Total cash, deposits, and investment securities	15.5%	11.6%	13.7%	13.4%	14.6%
Net mortgage loans and contracts	61.7	62.5	56.9	58.2	55.1
Other loans					
Commercial loans	1.2	1.2	0.6	0.4	0.3
Other nonmortgage loans	0.7	0.7	0.3	0.3	0.2
Net nonmortgage loans	2.0%	1.9%	1.0%	0.7%	0.5%
Repossessed assets	0.3	0.4	0.5	0.5	0.5
Real estate investments	3.5	3.5	4.8	4.5	4.9
Fixed assets	1.0	1.1	1.5	1.7	1.8
Other assets	16.1	19.0	21.6	21.1	22.5
Total assets	100.0%	100.0%	100.0%	100.0%	100.0%
Liabilities and stockholders' equity					
Deposits	90.1%	82.8%	83.0%	82.6%	81.8%
Borrowings					
OTS advance	4.1	8.9	5.6	5.2	4.6
Other borrowings	0.9	1.8	2.6	2.7	2.7
Total borrowings	5.6%	10.6%	8.2%	7.9%	7.3%
Other liabilities	1.0	2.4	2.8	2.9	2.7
Total liabilities	96.8%	95.8%	94.1%	93.4%	91.8%
Stockholders' equity					
Common stock; paid-in capital	0.8	1.2	1.7	1.9	2.1
Retained earnings	2.4	3.0	4.3	4.6	6.1
Total stockholders' equity	3.2%	4.2%	5.9%	6.6%	8.2%
Total liabilities and stockholders' equity	100.0%	100.0%	100.0%	100.0%	100.0%

TABLE 17-4
HOMETOWN SAVINGS AND LOAN ASSOCIATION
COMMON-SIZE INCOME STATEMENT

	19X8	19X7	19X6	19X5	19X4
Interest income					
Mortgage loans and contracts	84.3%	85.1%	81.7%	76.0%	72.9%
Mortgage-backed pass-through securities	0.1	0.1	0.1	0.1	0.1
Commercial loans	0.8	0.8	0.9	1.1	1.0
Consumer loans	0.7	0.7	0.9	1.2	1.1
Investments and deposits	10.1	9.8	12.4	16.7	16.5
Total interest income	96.0%	96.5%	96.1%	95.2%	91.5%
Fees on loans and leases	6.3	6.5	6.6	8.6	8.4
Other operating income	(2.3)	(3.0)	(2.7)	(3.7)	0.1
Total operating income	100.0%	100.0%	100.0%	100.0%	100.0%
Operating expenses	14.5	13.4	7.7	10.7	11.3
Cost of funds					
Interest on deposits, net	70.2	71.0	73.6	83.6	72.9
Interest on borrowed money	6.2	6.3	5.5	7.0	6.3
Less: Capitalized interest	(0.6)	(0.7)	(0.8)	(1.0)	(1.0)
Total cost of funds	75.8%	76.6%	78.3%	89.6%	78.2%
Operating income after cost of funds	9.7%	9.9%	14.0%	(0.3%)	10.5%
Nonoperating income	6.6	4.6	4.6	6.2	6.5
Nonoperating expesne	15.5	12.9	13.5	14.9	11.4
Income taxes (credit)	(1.3%)	0.4%	3.4%	(4.4%)	2.0%
Net income	2.1%	1.2%	1.8%	(4.6%)	3.6%
Depreciation expense	0.5%	0.5%	0.7%	0.9%	0.9%

This analytical technique provides a simple and quick determinant of trends on both the balance sheet and income statement. Trend analysis is important because it may point to basic changes in the subject S&L's business. When analyzing trends, the analyst must look for disruptions from historic levels. When a deviation is established, the analyst must determine the cause and effect of the deviations.

Ratio analysis is an important means of stating the relationship between two numbers. To be useful, a ratio must represent a meaningful relationship, but use of ratios is not a substitute for the evaluation of the underlying data.

Ratios are guides that are useful in evaluating the financial position and operations of a company and in comparing them to previous years' data or to other institutions. On the following pages, ratio analysis is applied to eight analytical parameters: absolute size, liquidity, deposit mix, asset mix, capital adequacy, profitability, interest analysis, and growth. Table 17-5 displays a schedule of basic ratios. This is not a definitive list of ratios for an analysis but serves as a framework.

[a] Size

Size statistics allow a quick and easy way to rank the subject company with other savings and loans. Total assets is the most widely used indicator of S&L size; however, total deposits, total equity, and total operating income also measure the size of a financial institution. Size statistics also help determine if economies of scale have been attained. A financial institution with an asset size larger than $500 million may possess the capacity to perform services such as item and data processing for their own accounts.

[b] Liquidity

A savings and loan's liquidity is its ability to meet deposit withdrawals, maturing liabilities, and loan requests without delay. Liquidity requirements are also mandated by the various financial institution regulatory agencies. To meet potential demands for liquidity, S&Ls must maintain liquid assets or must rely on creating liquidity from borrowed funds.

Measuring liquidity risk is complex. If an S&L holds assets such as securities that can be sold to meet a need for funds, it may lower its liquidity risk. At the same time, holding liquid securities can limit returns since the S&L can earn higher yields on mortgage loans. Conversely, the S&L could borrow the money to maintain proper liquidity levels.

[Text continues on p. 17-18]

TABLE 17-5
HOMETOWN SAVINGS AND LOAN ASSOCIATION
COMPARATIVE FINANCIAL ANALYSIS

Statistics and Ratios	19X8	19X7	19X6	19X5	19X4
Size ($000s omitted)					
Total assets	$913,884	$668,396	$447,190	$382,230	$331,473
Total stockholder's equity	29,611	27,928	26,588	25,115	27,194
Total operating income	103,856	93,330	71,459	50,081	45,947
Net income	2,139	1,112	1,266	(2,316)	1,650
Liquidity ratios					
Cash and investment securities to total assets	15.5%	11.6%	13.7%	13.4%	14.6%
Total borrowing to total deposits	6.2	12.8	9.9	9.5	9.0
Deposit mix					
Fixed maturity deposits to total deposits	85.1%	85.5%	85.1%	86.0%	85.7%
Money market deposits to total deposits	8.7	8.4	8.3	8.1	7.9
Passbook deposits to total deposits	3.0	3.2	3.5	3.5	5.0
Asset mix					
Total mortgage loans to total assets	61.7%	62.5%	56.9%	58.2%	55.1%
Total nonmortgage loans to total assets	2.0	1.9	1.0	0.7	0.5
Loan mix					
Mortgage loans and mortgage-backed securities to total loans	96.9%	97.1%	98.3%	98.8%	99.0%
Federally guaranteed mortgages and mortgages on 1- to 4-family dwellings to total loans	32.2	31.9	32.0	33.0	32.8
Other mortgage loans to total loans	62.2	62.7	64.7	64.6	65.4
Fixed-rate mortgages to total loans	44.8	45.6	47.2	49.1	56.6
Adjustable-rate mortgages to total loans	35.5	34.9	32.1	30.5	29.6
Commercial loans to total loans	2.0	1.8	1.1	0.7	0.6
Consumer loans to total loans	0.9	0.9	0.8	0.3	0.0
Mortgage-based securities to total loans	2.5	2.5	1.6	1.2	0.8

TABLE 17-5
HOMETOWN SAVINGS AND LOAN ASSOCIATION
COMPARATIVE FINANCIAL ANALYSIS (continued)

Statistics and Ratios	19X8	19X7	19X6	19X5	19X4
Capital adequacy					
Stockholders' equity to total assets	3.2%	4.2%	5.9%	6.6%	8.2%
Profitability ratios					
Return on average assets	0.3%	0.2%	0.3%	(0.6%)	N/A
Return on average equity	7.4	4.1	4.9	(8.9)	N/A
Total interest income to total operating income	96.0	96.5	96.1	95.2	91.5
Fee income to total operating income	6.3	6.5	6.6	8.6	8.4
Other operating income to total operating income	(2.3)	(3.0)	(2.7)	(3.7)	0.1
Total operating expenses to total operating income	14.5	13.4	7.7	10.7	11.3
Cost of deposits to total operating income	70.2	71.0	73.6	83.6	72.9
Cost of borrowing to total operating income	6.2	6.3	5.5	7.0	6.3
Interest analysis					
Interest income to total average assets	12.6%	16.1%	16.6%	13.4%	*
Interest expense to total average assets	9.9	12.8	13.5	12.6	*
Net interest margin to total average assets	2.7	3.3	3.1	0.8	*
Growth statistics					
Annual deposit growth	48.9%	49.0%	17.6%	16.6%	N/A
Annual mortgage loan growth	45.0%	64.1%	14.4%	21.8%	N/A

N/A — Not available

[*Text continues from p. 17-15*]

As seen in the previous example, an S&L must be concerned with sustaining an appropriate level of liquidity. Too much liquidity sacrifices earnings. A lack of liquidity may impose borrowing requirements in an unknown interest rate environment, which in turn can increase costs and reduce earnings.

The two ratios used in a liquidity analysis are cash and investment securities to total assets and total borrowings to deposits, respectively. Both ratios are used as indicators of an S&L's degree of liquidity with the former serving as a measure of liquid assets to total assets and the latter as an expression of an S&L's dependence on borrowing to meet its liquidity needs.

[c] Deposit Mix

As mentioned earlier, deposits comprise the largest portion of an S&L's source of funds. The mix of deposit funds refers to the breakdown of money market, time, and passbook deposits. An analysis and breakdown of this mix is important because each deposit account has a separate cost and risk associated with it.

The ratios used in Table 17-5 merely define the percentage amount of the specific deposit account to total deposits. These ratios also help determine which type of account the S&L has been successful in attracting.

To help with the analysis of the deposit mix, it is important to note the unique characteristics of each deposit account. Time deposits are likely to be a high cost account, so a low percentage is usually favorable. Money market deposits carry a lower cost than fixed maturity deposits; however, interest paid on these accounts is highly variable since the S&L must pay market rates to attract them. Passbook accounts are the least costly and least volatile of all deposit accounts, so a high percentage is favorable.

[d] Asset Mix

Not all assets generate income. It is only the assets which generate income, known as earning assets, that provide a basis for analyzing the asset mix. These earning assets, principally composed of loans and investments, are the basis for most of an S&L's income stream.

The first step in analyzing the asset mix is to determine the percentage of earning assets that comprise total assets. This ratio can help the analyst differentiate income-earning from non-income-earning assets.

Earning assets can be broken down into individual components. The loan component can be reduced to the percentage of mortgage loans and nonmortgage loans to total earning assets, while the investment component can be reduced to its individual securities' percentage of total earning assets.

The analysis of the loan portfolio is important to determine the risks associated with the various loans and the income stream generated by them.

Mortgage loans usually comprise the largest portion of the entire loan portfolio. Mortgage loans are made on single-family residences, on income-producing property such as apartments and office buildings, and on special types of properties such as churches. These loans are permanent in nature and are secured by the underlying property. Because these loans are highly collateralized, they are thought of as the least risky of all the loans in the loan portfolio. Due to the secured nature of these loans, S&Ls typically carry a lower loan reserve when compared with a commercial bank.

Nonmortgage loans, while usually comprising the smallest portion of the loan portfolio, are far more risky than mortgage loans. Commercial loans, as well as consumer loans, may be secured or unsecured.

The risk and return characteristics of consumer loans differ significantly from those of commercial loans. The dollar amount of each individual consumer loan is small, which results in lower profit per dollar and less exposure to loss per loan.

Consumer loans also tend to be more uniform than commercial loans, which result in greater specialization of services associated with these loans. While the potential for profit from commercial loans is small, the potential for overall return can be large if loan-servicing is delivered at a low cost.

The investment portfolio must also be dissected. As mentioned previously, the investment portfolio contains securities which carry varying degrees of risk and return. These securities also provide a form of secondary liquidity so that if customers draw down deposits, these investments can be sold in the secondary market to meet deposit outflow.

Ratios should be used to determine the percentages of the components that comprise the total investment portfolio. Once the individual investments are isolated, the analyst should determine the risk of these securities. The analyst should be mindful of the basic elements of risk such as interest rate risk, credit risk, and marketability liquidity risk.

[e] Capital Adequacy

Capital ratios represent the primary technique of analyzing capital adequacy. Capital's primary function is to absorb losses, as well as to provide a base on which lending limits are established.

The primary ratio of measuring capital adequacy is equity to total assets. This ratio indicates the cushion available to absorb losses before depositors' funds become impaired.

Regulatory agencies have set a standard of 6% for this ratio.

Two additional ratios for measuring capital adequacy are equity to total liabilities and deferred gains (losses) to equity. The former measures the degree of leverage the institution has achieved, while the latter indicates the potential effect of deferred gains or losses on regulatory capital. The second ratio can be used to forecast a possible increase or decrease in capital as earnings are positively or negatively impacted.

[f] Profitability

Overall measures of performance, also known as profitability analysis, can be condensed into two basic ratios—return on assets (ROA) and return on equity (ROE). While many factors compose performance, ROA and ROE serve as primary targets for comparison within the industry. From a shareholder's point of view, ROA and ROE are two key measures of performance. Uninsured depositors (deposits with balances greater than $100,000) are concerned with safety and liquidity; thus ROA and ROE ratios are measures of equity increases for depositor protection. Regulators are also concerned with depositor safety and emphasize liquidity and capital adequacy. From the analyst's viewpoint, each of these interests must be given attention.

Further profitability analysis requires the examination of the major components of the various income and expense items. Table 17-4 displays the use of ratios to determine the percentage each income statement item has to total operating income. By the same token, non-operating income and expense should be made a percentage of total income.

Income derived from loans is accepted as the highest quality yet perhaps the riskiest. Fee income and income from investments are considered a lower quality stream of income. Since each income and expense item is unique in terms of returns and cost, the risk of each component should be taken into account. Analyzing the asset mix and deposit mix of the S&L will aid the analyst in this endeavor.

[g] Interest Analysis

Interest analysis helps the analyst determine the quality and yields of the S&L's earning assets. The ratios displayed in Table 17-5 provide the analyst with a sense of the quality of assets to the quality of deposits.

Yield analysis can be established with the use of ratios such as interest income to total loans and investments and interest income to total assets. These ratios indicate the interest rate generated on the S&L's earning assets. Yields attained through this analysis should be consistent with the riskiness of the underlying earning assets.

Interest-rate sensitivity can also be examined. Since S&Ls are operating in an uncertain economic environment, the analyst should know how a change in interest rates can affect the subject institution. The easiest way for the analyst to make this determination is to examine the rates of adjustable-rate loans to total loans.

[h] Growth

The growth statistic is yet another aid in the analysis of trends. The growth statistic typically measures the items located under the size statistic. Growth also provides the analyst with a quick understanding of the historic dynamics of the underlying institution.

[4] Additional Analysis

Once the basic financial analysis of an S&L has been accomplished, the analyst may wish to proceed with more intricate and perhaps quite qualitative forms of financial analysis. Examining scheduled items and branch efficiency are examples of such analysis.

S&Ls hold real estate for development, investment, or resale. S&Ls can also be the holder of repossessed or foreclosed property through default on a mortgage loan. Since real estate foreclosed and mortgage loans slow in collection can impact earnings, scheduled items must be examined. Scheduled items simply exhibit the collection problems that the S&L may be undergoing for a particular period. Since these accounts have impact on an S&L's current and future financial condition, they can be incorporated into the analysis.

An S&L's performance can also be measured in terms of branch efficiency. If an S&L has an efficient network of branches, then it can be assumed that economies of scale may have been reached. In other words, branches must maintain a certain level of deposit transaction volume to cover fixed costs and justify further expenditures and expensive computer systems to process transactions. To determine if an S&L

has achieved branch efficiency, a correlation of transaction volume to number of branches, cost of retail deposits and retail deposits to number of branches must be proven; as volume increases, costs decrease.

[5] Summary

The various general components of a financial analysis have been described. These components yield perspective to assist in the analyst's assignment of the risk/return profile of the subject institution. The statistics should not be analyzed in isolation; rather they are interactive. For example, a conclusion of strong profitability may be tempered by the knowledge that the primary profit source is income from junk bonds and a low provision for loan-loss reserve charge.

¶ 17.3 Commercial Bank Analysis

The preceding analytical framework for savings and loans can serve as a starting point for the analysis of commercial banks, with several important modifications. Banks differ from S&Ls in that banks are established to facilitate commerce. As such, the asset and liability composition of a bank is quite different from a thrift and requires a different analytical perspective.

[1] Balance Sheet

Table 17-6 on pages 17-24 and 17-25 illustrates a typical bank balance sheet. The assets and liabilities sections of that balance sheet are analyzed next.

[a] Assets

The liquidity requirements are different for a bank; thus, the liquid asset components of the bank's balance sheet is different (refer to Table 17-6). The liquid assets, again ranked in descending order of liquidity, include Fed Funds, which is excess cash lent to other banks, usually overnight.

A bank's loan portfolio is comprised of a variety of loans to businesses, consumers, other financial institutions, farmers, building contractors, real estate developers, and others seeking short-term financing. The loan portfolio may be grouped into categories on the balance sheet. The loan portfolio usually represents the least liquid and most risky group of assets on a bank's balance sheet.

Associated with the loan portfolio is unearned income and reserve for loan losses. Unearned income is income to be deferred in its accounting recognition. Reserve for loan losses is extremely important in bank analysis. This represents the bank's bad debt reserve. The reserve for loan losses is built up through charges to income (up to certain limits) and decreased by loan losses charged off. Net loans is simply gross loans less unearned income and reserve for loan losses.

[b] Liabilities

As Table 17-6 illustrates, the deposit composition of a bank includes demand deposits (including NOW accounts), savings deposits, and time deposits. Deposits usually serve as the least expensive form of borrowing for a bank. However, Table 17-6 also breaks out aggregate deposits of over $100,000 per account. This category can be riskier as depositors may withdraw these funds upon maturity.

Short-term borrowings include federal funds borrowed, repurchase agreements, commercial paper, and other short-term borrowings.

[Text continues on p. 17-26]

TABLE 17-6
HOMETOWN BANCORPORATION
COMPARATIVE SUMMARY BALANCE SHEET
($000s Omitted)

	19X8	19X7	19X6	19X5	19X4
Assets					
Cash and due from banks	$ 18,350	$ 23,320	$ 32,810	$ 18,010	$ 15,090
Interest-bearing deposits	16,690	15,660	19,370	12,930	36,060
Investments securities	122,500	123,310	136,600	26,480	25,970
Federal funds sold	50,000	30,000	24,000	27,000	29,000
Loans					
Commercial and financial	359,250	314,920	197,110	76,040	19,590
Real estate mortgage	42,770	21,180	17,550	12,390	6,890
Installment	20,100	18,890	19,590	18,890	12,170
Gross loans	$422,120	$354,990	$234,250	$107,320	$ 38,740
Less: Unearned income	2,550	2,130	2,550	2,400	2,100
Reserve for loan losses	3,480	3,010	1,370	640	200
Net loans	$416,090	$349,850	$230,330	$104,280	$ 36,440
Property and equipment	14,070	14,440	7,240	2,250	1,950
Deposit premium	5,930	6,130	6,860	-0-	-0-
Accrued interest receivable and other assets	10,650	8,660	10,290	3,010	2,730
Total assets	$654,280	$571,370	$467,500	$193,960	$147,200

TABLE 17-6
HOMETOWN BANCORPORATION
COMPARATIVE SUMMARY BALANCE SHEET
($000s Omitted) *(continued)*

	19X8	19X7	19X6	19X5	19X4
Liabilities and stockholders' equity					
Liabilities					
Deposits					
Demand deposits	$175,610	$188,410	$148,170	$86,630	$66,750
Savings deposits	151,660	194,250	187,040	45,050	35,480
Other time deposits	274,130	121,390	92,430	35,990	29,030
Total deposits	$601,400	$504,050	$427,640	$167,670	$131,260
Federal funds purchased	-0-	20,000	-0-	-0-	-0-
Accrued taxes and other expense	6,780	3,830	2,620	1,250	920
Subordinated note	4,500	4,500	-0-	-0-	-0-
Total liabilities	$612,680	$532,380	$430,260	$168,920	$132,180
Stockholders' equity					
Capital stock	17,960	17,960	17,960	16,940	7,960
Surplus	17,960	17,960	17,610	7,830	7,830
Retained earnings	5,680	3,070	1,670	270	(730)
Net stockholders' equity	$ 41,600	$ 38,990	$ 37,240	$ 25,040	$ 15,060
Total liabilities and stockholders' equity	$654,280	$571,370	$467,500	$193,960	$147,240

[2] Income Statement

Table 17-7 illustrates a typical bank income statement. In general, it is very similar to that of a thrift, with a few exceptions. Provision for loan losses increases the reserve for loan losses and decreases pretax income. Operating expenses for a bank may be very different from a thrift because, in general, banks have higher transactional volume.

TABLE 17-7

HOMETOWN BANCORPORATION
COMPARATIVE SUMMARY INCOME STATEMENT
($000s Omitted)

	19X8	19X7	19X6	19X5	19X4
Interest income					
Interest and fees on loans	$40,180	$32,060	$24,420	$10,270	$ 3,150
Interest on time deposits with banks	2,840	2,040	2,200	2,880	2,750
Interest on investment securities	9,760	14,420	11,080	2,770	1,490
Income on federal funds sold	2,290	2,830	3,830	1,100	3,610
Total interest income	$55,070	$51,350	$41,530	$17,020	$11,000
Total interest expense	22,550	21,530	16,410	5,570	3,420
Net interest income	$32,520	$29,820	$25,120	$11,450	$7,580
Provision for loan losses	1,450	2,370	1,600	570	250
Net interest income after loan loss provision	31,070	27,450	23,520	10,880	7,330
Other operating income	1,500	3,460	2,230	820	610
Other operating expenses:					
Salaries and related benefits	15,380	17,290	14,200	5,600	4,110
Occupancy expense	3,020	4,310	2,190	810	1,070
Other expenses	10,790	10,640	7,870	3,930	2,420
Total other operating expenses	$29,190	$32,240	$24,260	$10,340	$7,600
Gain on sale of securities	1,020	3,660	200	-0-	-0-
Pretax income	4,400	2,330	1,690	1,360	340
Income tax (benefit)	1,780	570	300	340	90
Net income (loss)	$ 2,620	$ 1,760	$ 1,390	$ 1,020	$ 250

Other operating income reflects income the bank receives from the services it provides. These typically include service charges on deposits, trust and investment advisor fees, and sales of real estate holdings. Other operating income is important in that it is noninterest rate sensitive.

Securities gains (losses) represent gains and losses from securities held in the bank's investment portfolio.

[3] Financial Analysis

The financial analysis for a bank is very similar to that of a thrift previously described. A trend analysis reveals changes in balance sheet and income statement accounts in absolute terms. A composition analysis (Tables 17-8 and 17-9) augments the trend analysis.

TABLE 17-8

HOMETOWN BANCORPORATION
COMPARATIVE SUMMARY BALANCE SHEET
($000s Omitted)

	19X8	19X7	19X6	19X5	19X4
Assets					
Cash and due from banks	2.8%	4.1%	7.0%	9.3%	10.2%
Interest-bearing deposits	2.6	2.7	4.1	6.7	24.5
Investment securities	18.7	21.6	29.2	13.7	17.6
Federal funds sold	7.6	5.3	5.1	13.9	19.7
Loans					
Commercial and financial	54.9	55.1	42.2	39.2	13.3
Real estate mortgage	6.5	3.7	3.8	6.4	4.7
Installment	3.1	3.3	4.2	9.7	8.3
Gross loans	64.5%	62.1%	50.1%	55.3%	26.3%
Less: Unearned income	0.4	0.4	0.5	1.2	1.4
Reserve for loan losses	0.5	0.5	0.3	0.3	0.1
Net loans	63.6%	61.2%	49.3%	53.8%	24.7%
Property and equipment	2.2	2.5	1.5	1.2	1.3
Deposit premium	0.9	1.1	1.5	0.0	0.0
Accrued interest receivable and other assets	1.6	1.5	2.2	1.6	1.9
Total assets	100.0%	100.0%	100.0%	100.0%	100.0%
Liabilities and stockholders' equity					
Liabilities					
Deposits					
Demand deposits	26.8%	33.0%	31.7%	44.7%	45.3%
Savings deposits	23.2	34.0	40.0	23.3	24.1
Other time deposits	41.9	21.2	19.8	18.6	19.7
Total deposits	91.9%	88.2%	91.5%	86.4%	89.1%
Federal funds purchased	0.0	3.5	0.0	0.0	0.0
Accrued taxes and other expenses	1.0	0.7	0.6	0.6	0.6
Subordinated note	0.7	0.8	0.0	0.0	0.0
Total liabilities	93.6%	93.2%	92.0%	87.1%	89.8%
Stockholders' equity					
Capital stock	2.7	3.1	3.8	8.7	5.4
Surplus	2.7	3.9	3.8	4.0	5.3
Retained earnings	0.9	0.5	0.4	0.1	−0.5
Net stockholders' equity	6.4%	6.8%	8.0%	12.9%	10.2%
Total liabilities and stockholders' equity	100.0%	100.0%	100.0%	100.0%	100.0%

TABLE 17-9

HOMETOWN BANCORPORATION
COMPARATIVE SUMMARY INCOME STATEMENT
($000s Omitted)

	19X8	19X7	19X6	19X5	19X4
Interest income					
Interest and fees on loans	73.0%	62.4%	58.8%	60.3%	28.6%
Interest on time deposits with banks	5.2	4.0	5.3	16.9	25.0
Interest on investment securities	17.7	28.1	26.7	16.3	13.5
Income on federal funds sold	4.2	5.5	9.2	6.5	32.8
Total interest income	100.0%	100.0%	100.0%	100.0%	100.0%
Total interest expense	40.9	41.9	39.5	32.7	31.1
Net interest income	59.1	58.1	60.5	67.3	68.9
Provision for loan losses	2.6	4.6	3.9	3.3	2.3
Net interest income after loan loss provision	56.4	53.5	56.6	63.9	66.6
Other operating income	2.7	6.7	5.4	4.8	5.5
Other operating expenses					
Salaries and related benefits	27.9	33.7	34.2	32.9	37.4
Occupancy expense	5.5	8.4	5.3	4.8	9.7
Other expenses	19.6	20.7	19.0	23.1	22.0
Total operating expenses	53.0	62.8	58.4	60.8	69.1
Gain on sale of securities	1.9	7.1	0.5	0.0	0.0
Pretax income	8.0	4.5	4.1	8.0	3.1
Income tax (benefit)	3.2	1.1	0.7	2.0	0.8
Net income (loss)	4.8%	3.4%	3.3%	6.0%	2.3%

The ratio analysis for a bank (Table 17-10) is again very similar to that used for a thrift. The ratio analysis attempts to measure various risk and return parameters such as size, liquidity, deposit mix, asset mix, capital adequacy, profitability, interest analysis, and growth. An analysis of the yield and earning characteristics of a bank's loan portfolio is important. Selected measures of yield analysis include the following.

[a] Total Interest Expense/Average Earnings Assets

This ratio calculates the yield that earnings assets must attain to cover the interest expenses generated by the liabilities that the bank holds. The yield that earnings assets must attain to meet interest expenses is called the break-even yield; the higher the yield, the higher the required return on the bank's earning assets to meet interest expenses.

TABLE 17-10
HOMETOWN SAVINGS AND LOAN ASSOCIATION
COMPARATIVE FINANCIAL ANALYSIS

Statistics and Ratios	19X8	19X7	19X6	19X5	19X4
Size ($000s omitted)					
Total assets	$654,280	$571,370	$467,500	$193,960	$147,240
Total stockholders' equity	41,600	38,990	37,240	25,040	15,060
Total operating income	56,570	54,810	43,760	17,840	11,610
Net income	2,620	1,760	1,390	1,020	250
Liquidity ratios					
Cash and investment securities to total assets	21.5%	25.7%	36.2%	22.9%	27.9%
Total borrowings to total deposits	70.2	70.4	54.8	64.0	29.5
Deposit mix					
Demand deposits to total deposits	29.2%	37.4%	34.6%	51.7%	50.9%
Savings deposits to total deposits	25.2	38.5	43.7	26.9	27.0
Other time deposits to total deposits	45.6	24.1	21.6	21.5	22.1
Asset mix					
Total mortgage loans to total assets	6.5%	3.7%	3.8%	6.4%	4.7%
Total nonmortgage loans to total assets	58.0	58.4	46.4	48.9	21.6
Capital					
Stockholders' equity to total assets	6.4%	6.8%	8.0%	12.9%	10.2%

[b] Total Interest Income/Average Earning Assets

This ratio measures the actual yield that the bank's earning assets generate. The yield generated is referred to as the earning asset yield.

[c] Earnings Asset Yield—Break-Even Yield

This relationship of the earnings assets yield less the breakeven yield provides analysts with the bank's net interest margin. This net interest margin indicates whether the bank is able to meet its interest-bearing-liabilities expenses with income from its interest-earning assets. In essence, the difference between these two yields provides the analyst with the margin of interest income over interest expense. A negative net-interest margin indicates that the bank is paying for interest expenses with noninterest income. Moreover, a negative net-income-interest margin indicates that the bank is riskier because it has no interest cushion against an adverse change in interest rates.

[d] Total Interest Expense/Total Interest-Bearing Liabilities

A bank's spread represents the difference between its assets' yield and its liabilities yield. The concept of spread differs slightly from that of the net-interest margin. While net-interest margin measures the difference between what assets are yielding and what they need to yield to break even, spread measures the relationship between the actual yield on a bank's assets and the actual yield that its liabilities are costing. A bank may have a positive spread and still not be able to meet its interest expenses. This is because spread provides the difference between yields but does not take into consideration the size of the assets and liabilities relative to one another. Therefore, when analyzing a bank's spread, it is important to look at the size of the assets and liabilities involved as well as their yields.

Other ratios of particular interest in the banking context include those that examine capital adequacy and the loan portfolio. Various measures of these factors include those discussed in the following sections.

[e] Equity Capital + Capital Notes + Reserve for Loan Losses/Gross Loans

This ratio demonstrates the bank's ability to absorb losses from its loan portfolio. By including the loan-loss reserve in the numerator and using gross loans for the denominator, the ability of the bank's management to accurately forecast reserve for loan losses is factored out. A ratio below one indicates that the bank does not have the ability to absorb losses from its loan portfolio.

[f] Loan Loss Provision/Average Gross Loans

This ratio provides an indication of management's perception of its loan portfolio. A high ratio may indicate that the bank's management has done a poor job selecting loans to fund and is now preparing for possible write-downs of these loans. A low ratio may indicate that management feels it has done a good job at selecting loans and does not anticipate large charge-offs. It is important to note that a low ratio, in and of itself, is not necessarily an indication of a healthy loan portfolio. A low ratio may also imply that management does not have the ability to foresee future loan problems. Conversely, a high ratio may be an indication that the bank's management may be too cautious in providing for bad loans at the cost of lowering income to shareholders.

[g] Net Charge-Offs/Average Gross Loans

This ratio compares actual loan charge-offs to average gross loans. When used in conjunction with the previous ratio, it is possible to see how well management has been able to anticipate loan losses. If this ratio is higher than the ratio of loan loss provisions to average gross loans, management has not adequately prepared for the charge-offs. On the other hand, if the ratio is lower than the loan-loss provisions to average gross loans ratio, the bank may have overprovided losses that did not occur. It should be noted that discrepancies between the two ratios does not imply bad management as long as the difference is not questionably large.

[h] Nonperforming Loans/Average Loans

Nonperforming loans are loans for which payments are overdue by ninety days or more. The reason for analyzing the ratio of nonperforming loans to average loans, in addition to the loan-loss provision to average gross loans, is that the provision for loan loss is an estimate of the percentage of nonperforming loans that are *expected* to be charged off, while nonperforming loans are not a subjective estimate but an objective number. Thus, a high ratio may indicate that management's ability to select a quality loan portfolio may be questionable.

[i] Loan Loss Provisions/Charge-Offs

This ratio provides an indication of management's ability to correctly foresee bad loans. A ratio above one implies that management anticipated more charge-offs than actually occurred, while a ratio below one indicates that management did not adequately prepare for the charge-offs. In either case, this is a very important ratio to look at from both a comparative and historical level. One needs to look at this ratio over a period of time to analyze trends in the ratio. A consistently high ratio indicates that management may be over-reserving at the expense of the shareholders.

[4] Summary

The analysis of commercial banks is very similar to that previously outlined in this chapter for thrifts. However, due to the different nature of banks, several important modifications need to be incorporated, as previously discussed.

¶ 17.4 Other Valuation Considerations

Basic financial analysis is the cornerstone of any financial institution valuation analysis, as shown in Table 17-11. There are, of course, many other considerations that are part of any valuation analysis. Many are generic to all types of companies and are examined elsewhere in this book. However, there are many valuation considerations unique to financial institutions.

TABLE 17-11

HOMETOWN BANCORPORATION
COMPARATIVE FINANCIAL ANALYSIS

Statistics and ratios	19X8	19X7	19X6	19X5	19X4
Profitability ratios					
Return on average assets	0.4%	0.3%	0.4%	0.6%	0.3%
Return on average equity	6.5	4.6	4.5	5.1	3.3
Total interest income to total operating income	97.3	93.7	94.9	95.4	94.7
Fee income to total operating income	71.0	58.5	55.8	57.6	27.1
Other operating income to total operating income	2.7	6.3	5.1	4.6	5.3
Total operating expenses to total operating income	91.5	98.1	92.9	89.2	94.9
Cost of borrowings to total operating income	39.9	39.3	37.5	31.2	29.5
Interest on earnings assets to total operating income	97.3	93.7	94.9	95.4	94.7
Interest analysis					
Interest income to total average assets	9.0%	9.0%	12.6%	10.0%	14.9%
Interest expense to total average assets	3.7	4.1	5.0	3.3	4.6
Net interest margin to total average assets	5.3	5.7	7.6	6.7	10.3
Growth statistics					
Annual deposit growth	19.3%	17.9%	155.0%	27.7%	N/A
Annual mortgage growth	101.9	20.7	41.6	79.8	N/A

[1] Off Balance Sheet Assets and Liabilities

These include standby letters of credit, loan commitments, foreign exchange contracts, interest rate or foreign currency swaps, financial futures and forward contracts, and certain loan sale programs. Many of these have very few reporting (disclosure) requirements.

[2] Public Company Comparables

Care should be taken in the selection of public company comparables. Those financial institutions selected should be similar in asset size and operate within the same geographic area to ensure comparability.

[3] Control Premiums/Discounts for Minority Interest

The consolidation of the financial institutions industry has profound implications on financial institution valuation. Specifically, control premiums (and their reciprocal, minority interest discounts) utilized should be based on an analysis of control premiums paid in the subject financial institution's geographic area.

Factors to consider include: applicable branching restrictions, if any; restrictions on out-of-state acquirors, if any; competition in the area from similar and dissimilar institutions; and knowledge of change of control applications and procedures.

[4] Accounting Issues

The Financial Accounting Standards Board (FASB) has issued several pronouncements that affect financial institution reporting. While not necessarily having economic effects on the financial institution, FASB does have reporting effects that must be recognized when conducting a valuation analysis.

> *FASB Statement No. 91*: "Accounting for Nonrefundable Fees and Costs Associated With Originating or Acquiring Loans and Initial Direct Costs or Leases" (issued December 15, 1988). FASB No. 91, in general, requires loan fees and origination costs to be amortized over the life of the loan through an adjustment to the loan's yield.
>
> *FASB Statement No. 96*: "Accounting for Income Taxes" (issued December 31, 1987). FASB requires a "liability" approach for the reporting of taxes. Deferred taxes are computed based on tax rates in effect for the periods in which "temporary differences" are expected to reverse. An annual adjustment of the deferred tax liability/asset is made through the income statement for any subsequent changes in enacted tax rate. FASB 96 could distort year-to-year comparisons in the valuation analysis.

FASB Technical Bulletin 87-3 (issued December 31, 1987). Addresses the accounting "problem" when servicing fee charged to a new borrower is significantly different from the prevailing "normal" servicing fee rates. Again, reported gain or loss on sale of assets may be "distorted" and/or not comparable to prior periods or comparable institutions.

[5] Management Issues

Any valuation of a financial institution must take into account the quality and effectiveness of management. The increasingly complex world of financial institutions requires a more sophisticated approach to management. A recent study by the Office of the Comptroller of the Currency concluded that, while 98 percent of the recent national bank failures were attributable to asset quality, 89 percent of the failures were attributable to management deficiency or director oversight. Specifically, the report found one or more of the following factors were present in a national bank failure:

- Uninformed or passive directors;
- Nonexistent or poorly followed loan policies;
- Inadequate controls or supervision of key officers;
- Inadequate systems for identifying problem loans;
- Domination of management by one individual;
- Nonexistent or poorly followed asset/liability management;
- Extremely aggressive, growth-minded management; and
- Insider abuse.

¶ 17.5 Summary

As previously discussed in this chapter and throughout this book, valuation is the quantification of risk and return. The initial step in that process is a financial analysis of the subject financial institution. As financial institutions are very different from manufacturing and service companies, a different analytical framework is required.

This chapter presented basic analytical frameworks to begin a financial analysis of savings and loans and commercial banks. The analysis started with a thorough understanding of the balance sheet and income statement. Then an analysis was developed, which included the following:

- Trend analysis;
- Composition analysis;
- Absolute size analysis;
- Liquidity analysis;

- Deposit mix;
- Asset mix;
- Profitability;
- Capital adequacy;
- Interest rate sensitivity; and
- Growth.

As valuation is situational, the frameworks presented in this chapter should be considered frameworks, to be modified by the analyst depending upon the facts and circumstances of the engagement.

18

INSURANCE COMPANIES AND INSURANCE AGENCIES

RUSSELL R. MILLER AND MARK S. LEFENFELD*

		Page
¶ 18.1	Valuing Insurance Companies	18-4
[1]	Reasons for Valuations	18-5
[a]	Mergers and Acquisitions	18-5
[b]	Long-Term Planning	18-5
[c]	Initial Public Offerings	18-5
[d]	Employee Stock Ownership Plans	18-5
[e]	Demutualization	18-6
[2]	Steps in the Valuation Process	18-6
[3]	Evaluation of Management Practices	18-6
[a]	Organizational Structure	18-7
[b]	Internal Controls System	18-7
[c]	Key Personnel and Functions	18-7
[d]	Recorded Financial Events	18-7
[e]	Sources of Anticipated Growth and Profit	18-8
[4]	Analysis of the Business	18-8
[a]	Business Mix and Products Offered	18-8
[b]	Forecasting Growth and Profit	18-8
[c]	Reinsurance Contracts and Reinsurers	18-8
	[i] Contracts Ceding Reinsurance	18-9
	[ii] Contracts of Assured Reinsurance	18-9
[d]	Underwriting Philosophies	18-10
[e]	Claims Department Procedures	18-10
[f]	Procedure for Estimating Incurred But Not Reported Losses	18-10
[g]	Determining Sufficiency of Loss Reserves	18-11

---

* RUSSELL R. MILLER, CPCU, MBA, is chairman of Russell Miller, Inc., a specialty investment banking and consultanting firm serving the insurance industry and headquartered in San Francisco. MARK S. LEFENFELD, MBA, JD, is a managing director of the same firm. Mr. Miller is the principal author of the merger and acquisition book, *Supergrowth*, and has authored numerous articles, speeches, and essays in the insurance field.

	[h]	Reviewing Company's Investment Policies	18-11
	[i]	Combined Ratio	18-11
	[j]	Responsiveness	18-12
	[k]	Competition	18-12
	[l]	Price Competitiveness	18-12
	[m]	Quality and Autonomy of Branch Office Network	18-12
	[n]	Geography	18-13
[5]	Financial Report Review		18-13
	[a]	GAAP Statements	18-13
		[i] Annual Reports	18-13
		[ii] Proxy Statement	18-16
		[iii] Form 10-K	18-16
		[iv] Quarterly Reports	18-17
		[v] Form 10-Q	18-17
		[vi] Supplemental Financial Information	18-17
		[vii] Loss and Loss Reserve Actuarial Report	18-18
		[viii] Industry Data	18-18
	[b]	Statutory Convention Statements	18-18
		[i] Balance Sheet	18-19
		[ii] Underwriting and Investment Income Exhibit	18-19
		[iii] Statement of Changes in Financial Position	18-20
		[iv] Additional Exhibits	18-20
		[v] General Interrogatories	18-20
		[vi] Notes to Financial Statements	18-20
		[vii] Supporting Schedules	18-20
[6]	Valuation Methods		18-21
	[a]	Adjusted Net Book Value Method	18-21
		[i] Appraisals	18-21
		[ii] Intangibles	18-22
		[iii] Valuing Licenses	18-22
		[iv] Valuing Reserves	18-23
		[v] Valuing Unearned Premium Account	18-23
		[vi] Federal Income Tax Effects	18-23
		[vii] Example	18-23
	[b]	Trading Market Method	18-24
		[i] Selecting Comparable Insurance Companies	18-24

INSURANCE COMPANIES/AGENCIES

	[ii] Adjusting Index	18-25
	[iii] Establishing Sustainable Pretax Income Level....................	18-25
	[iv] Determining Value	18-25
	[v] Example	18-26
[c]	Acquisition Value Method	18-26
	[i] Developing Index Ratio..........	18-26
	[ii] Segmenting Index	18-27
	[iii] Adjusting Index	18-27
	[iv] Determining Value	18-27
	[v] Example	18-28
[d]	Present Value of Future Profits: Method 1............................	18-28
	[i] Capitalizing Earnings	18-28
	[ii] Adjusting Capitalization Rate	18-29
	[iii] Using Risk-Free Rates	18-29
	[iv] Determining Value by Capitalization of Earnings........	18-29
	[v] Example	18-29
[e]	Present Value of Future Profits: Method 2............................	18-30
	[i] Value of Business in Force	18-31
	[ii] Value of New and Renewable Business	18-31
	[iii] Premium Growth Rate	18-31
	[iv] Renewal Rate	18-31
	[v] Loss and Loss Adjustment Expense Ratio...................	18-31
	[vi] Expense Ratio....................	18-32
	[vii] Loss Reserve Run-Out	18-32
	[viii] Current Earnings Rate on Investments	18-32
	[ix] Future Earnings Rate on Investments	18-32
	[x] Policyholder Surplus..............	18-32
	[xi] Alternative Assumptions	18-32
	[xii] Value Conclusions	18-32
	[xiii] Example	18-33
[f]	Summary of Methods and Required Factors	18-33
	[i] Adjusted Net Book Value Method	18-33
	[ii] Trading Market Method	18-33
	[iii] Acquisition Value Method	18-34

			[iv] Present Value of Future Profits Method	18-34
	[7]	Tax Reform Act of 1986		18-34
		[a]	Unearned Premium Reserve	18-34
		[b]	Recapture of Unearned Premium Reserve	18-35
		[c]	Dividends and Tax-Exempt Interest	18-35
		[d]	Loss Reserve Discounting	18-35
		[e]	Life Insurance Company Deduction	18-35
		[f]	Corporate Alternative Minimum Tax	18-36
		[g]	Impact of the Tax Reform Changes on Valuations	18-36
	[8]	Conclusion		18-36
¶ 18.2	Valuing Insurance Agencies			18-36
	[1]	Valuation Myths		18-37
		[a]	Commission Multiples	18-37
		[b]	Revenue Multiples	18-38
	[2]	Valuation Methods		18-38
		[a]	Public Company Method	18-39
			[i] Dilution of Earnings	18-40
			[ii] Discounting Shares	18-40
			[iii] Price/Earnings Multiple	18-40
			[iv] Working Capital Requirement	18-42
			[v] Tangible Net Worth	18-42
		[b]	Capitalization of Earnings Method	18-42
			[i] Minimum Risk Investments	18-43
			[ii] Additional Return Required	18-43
		[c]	Wasting Asset Method	18-43
			[i] Present Value Discount Rate	18-45
			[ii] Agency Growth	18-45
	[3]	Factors in a Valuation		18-46
		[a]	Income Statement Considerations	18-46
			[i] Pro Forma Adjustments	18-46
			[ii] Revenue and Expense Adjustments	18-46
		[b]	Balance Sheet Considerations	18-47
			[i] Tangible Net Worth	18-47
			[ii] A Public Company's Approach	18-47
			[iii] Amortization of Expirations	18-48
	[4]	Conclusion		18-50

¶ 18.1 Valuing Insurance Companies

The valuator of an insurance company has access to a variety of data and reports. This section describes the kinds of materials available to a valuator, the types of questions to ask management about the operations of the firm, and the components of the business or items in reports or statements to review and analyze when valuing an insurance company. Four valuation methods typically used are outlined, as are the sections of the Tax Reform Act of 1986 that directly affect insurance companies.

[1] Reasons for Valuations

There are many reasons for valuing an insurance company:

[a] Mergers and Acquisitions

A common reason for valuing an insurance company is for the purpose of a possible sale, merger, or acquisition. In the case of a sale, the seller wishes to gain an approximation of the value of the business before determining whether or not to bring the firm to the market. In a valuation for this purpose, a great deal of information is available to the valuator from the seller. Where a buyer wants to value a company, less information may be available on the company to be valued, as the seller may be unwilling to provide the buyer with much detail about the operations of the carrier (beyond certain financial data).

[b] Long-Term Planning

The management or directors of a company may, from time to time, request an outside valuation of the operation for the purposes of long-term planning and development of value for the policyholders or shareholders. If the company is not publicly held, certain significant information may not be available to the valuator, e.g., generally accepted accounting procedures (GAAP)-based financial statements and Securities and Exchange Commission (SEC) filings.

[c] Initial Public Offerings

Before a company is sold to the public through an initial public offering, the investment bankers managing the offering will value the company as a step in determining a price at which to offer stock to the public. The results of a valuation for this purpose may also affect the timing of the offering or the market in which the stock is made available for trade.

[d] Employee Stock Ownership Plans

To determine the amount of contributions to employee stock ownership plans (ESOPs), companies that have such plans must determine on a regular basis the value of the company. For companies that are not publicly owned and therefore have no ongoing determination of value, valuations performed periodically (typically annually) by outside experts are generally required.

[e] Demutualization

Insurance companies are owned either by the policyholders of the company (mutual companies) or by stockholders (stock companies). Frequently mutual companies convert to stock companies in a process of demutualization. This conversion is often driven by a need to raise cash through the offering of stock, either to the public in an initial public offering or to private investors. The process of demutualization requires a valuation of the carrier to determine a value for the company and a price at which to offer the stock.

[2] Steps in the Valuation Process

There are several steps in determining the value of an insurance company:

1. Evaluation of management practices, which typically includes a visit to the offices of the company;
2. Complete analysis of the segments of the business;
3. Complete analysis of the company's financial statements, both GAAP and statutory; and
4. Actual valuation, based on one or more commonly applied valuation methodologies.

Each of these steps builds on the step before. At each level, the valuator must use the information gathered and analyses performed in the earlier steps. The valuator should be integrally involved in this process, for the various methodologies assume that judgments will be made based on knowledge gained early in the review of the company being valued.

[3] Evaluation of Management Practices

The valuation process usually begins with a visit to the offices of the company. Prior to this visit, the valuator should gather the following information:

- Actuary's loss analysis for current year;
- Research on the current industry environment;
- A "valuation questionnaire," designed specifically for the company in question and completed by the management of the firm;
- Financial statements (GAAP and statutory) for at least five years; and
- The most recent insurance department triannual examination.

After reviewing the above information and performing a preliminary analysis of the data, the valuator should develop a set of questions and topics to cover with the management of the company during the on-site visit. When planning the visit, interviews and meetings should be arranged with the chief executive officer, the chief financial officer, and senior members of each of the company's major departments (i.e., Underwriting, Claims, Reinsurance, and Data Processing). During the visit the valuator should evaluate certain aspects of the company's operations in order to determine risk factors.

[a] Organizational Structure

Is it stable or unstable? Have there been any major reorganizations recently or are any planned? When was the last time the structure was internally reviewed and analyzed for redundant positions in light of technology changes? How many levels of management are there? What is the nature of the reporting structure?

[b] Internal Controls System

Examine in depth the control of the various functions that insurance companies perform, e.g., financial, underwriting, claims, reinsurance reporting and security review, electronic data processing, and regulatory compliance.

[c] Key Personnel and Functions

Look for responsibility and authority within importance functions. Review industry experience and company tenure of key people. Check for compatibility of abilities and responsibilities.

[d] Recorded Financial Events

Discuss the company's current financial position with the chief financial officer. (See later discussion of GAAP-based statements, SEC-mandated reports, and convention statements.) Discuss management's expectations and any prevailing trends. Ask questions regarding loss development and methods of calculating case reserves and incurred but not reported loss reserves. Find out how unearned premiums are recorded. Check tax calculations under the new tax laws, and review prior tax liabilities in light of these laws. Determine those revenue and expense items most significantly impacted by changes in premium and interest rates. Evaluate which product lines are market sensitive and to what extent.

[e] Sources of Anticipated Growth and Profit

If the company specializes in one or more product lines, what is the future of those areas? Are the industries growing or mature? Is there a limit to growth in the foreseeable future? Is the company considering refocusing? Can the firm develop additional marketing programs? Is the company producing business on a direct basis or through subproducers? Does it have any authorized managing general agents (MGAs)? If so, who are they, how are they controlled, what contracts exist? Review all contracts with MGAs.

After the on-site visit, the valuator should have adequate information to use in the next step of the valuation process.

[4] Analysis of the Business

The next step of the valuation process is the valuator's analysis of the business. A broad range of business characteristics, all of which are discussed next, must be assessed.

[a] Business Mix and Products Offered

Gather information on product lines, including loss ratios per line and percent of the total business for each line. Identify method of distribution for each line: number of agents, production per agent, agent commissions, and compensation mix. Do agents submit policies for approval or do they have underwriting authority? If agents are given that authority, how is it controlled and managed? What volume of business do agents write? Note trends, developments, and product line growth or decline over the past three-to-five year period. Give close examination to any assumed reinsurance contracts to which the carrier has committed.

[b] Forecasting Growth and Profit

Using the analysis developed of the current business mix and information gathered through interviews with the key personnel of the firm, project growth and future profits on a product line basis. Identify any expected dates of terminations of lines and reason for termination. (Allow for run-off in order not to distort the projections.) Note expected introduction dates of new products, which typically have lower loss ratios in their initial and early periods of writing. Typically, a forecast of the business is created in greater detail for the first few years, with broader assumptions used for later years.

[c] Reinsurance Contracts and Reinsurers

Insurance companies handle large risks by sharing (ceding) parts of the risk to other insurance or reinsurance companies. Similarly, companies assume parts of risks written by other insurance or reinsurance companies. The mechanism for sharing risks between insurance entities is known as *reinsurance*. When admitted reinsurance has been arranged for a line of business or a particular risk, deductions may be taken from the unearned premium and loss reserves on the income statement of the ceding company. At the same time, the carrier assuming the ceded portion of risk recognizes its proportion of the premiums received as income and its portion of the loss reserves as expense. The existence of a reinsurance contract does not change the primary liability of the ceding carrier to the original insured, for the ceding company is still the issuing carrier of the insurance policy.

The management of the company being evaluated should have established a system of internal accounting control over all reinsurance matters.

[i] Contracts Ceding Reinsurance

A ceding company should be able to document its evaluation of the financial stability and the capabilities of the company assuming the ceded business. This documentation should include a review of significant characteristics of the assuming company. These characteristics include financial results, retrocessional practices and experience, reputation, quality of owners and management, licensing authority, and adequacy of collateral.

[ii] Contracts of Assumed Reinsurance

A company assuming ceded business should be able to document its evaluation of the accuracy and the completeness of information submitted by the ceding company. This documentation should include a review of significant characteristics of the ceding company. These characteristics include financial results, motivation for seeking reinsurance contract, underwriting procedures, claims processing procedures, reserving procedures, and accounting controls for ceded reinsurance.

Be aware that the company being valued may follow all these guidelines and still make poor decisions selecting ceded reinsurers as well as deciding which reinsurance would be profitable to assume. As the firm is evaluated, thoroughly investigate the control systems and determine if the procedures are being carefully followed. Randomly review claims and underwriting files. Examine procedures followed before underwriting decisions are made. Check the reputation of the companies involved to judge whether the reinsurance recoverable is reasonably and realistically reported. Review reinsurance assumed contracts and files to satisfy oneself that this business is being adequately reported and represented by management.

[d] Underwriting Philosophies

Obtain information on underwriting philosophies and practices of management, past experience of the firm, and information on loss experience by product line. The company should have a database of loss information that will provide information on past experience and underwriting results. Loss ratios and trends should be studied. Review profitability by product line, by geography and, if the company appoints them, by MGAs as compared to regular offices of the company.

[e] Claims Department Procedures

Assess claims department procedures and philosophies regarding the handling, processing, investigating practices, reserving of reported claims, reserving for incurred but not reported (IBNR) claims, denial of claims, payment of claims, use of outside attorneys and claims adjusters, and risk management procedures to guard against "bad-faith" exposure. When a loss occurs and is reported, a case file should be established and an estimated reserve for its final defense or settlement of the case should be booked and properly recorded on the carrier's financial statements (case loss reserves). The valuator should analyze the historical development of past case loss reserves by examining the carrier's loss development experience as it relates to past claims that have been settled and closed. Were sufficient reserves set aside when the loss was initially reported? What percent of reserved funds was actually paid in settlement or did the reserve prove to be inadequate? Use the information developed from this analysis to project the expected future results of the current and opened case loss reserves.

[f] Procedure for Estimating Incurred But Not Reported Losses

At the close of any given financial period, management knows that some losses will have already occurred that have not yet been reported to the company. Theoretically, the company must set aside funds (reserves) to cover the eventual costs of those IBNR claims. Evaluate the historical development of the IBNR reserves. Were the formulas used to establish the reserves sufficient in assigning the proper ultimate cost to cover the claims eventually filed for losses during the period? Typically, the amount of IBNR reserves is carried over from one period to the next with the company just booking the change (increase or decrease) needed because of errors in judgment, adjustments based on new information, and new IBNR estimates for the current period. To project the sufficiency of IBNR reserves, one must first evaluate the history the firm's reserving practices and its development experience.

[g] Determining Sufficiency of Loss Reserves

Because of the relative arbitrariness of loss reserve levels, this area of the insurance company deserves close examination. However, unless a valuator uses an independent actuary, the valuation may have to be qualified based on the development of the loss reserves as reported by management. Either way, the valuator should get an indication from the reserve review and analysis as to the general sufficiency of current reserves. One way to confirm the reasonableness of reserves is to compare the subject carrier's experience with a similar company's experience. Any obvious or suspected insufficiency should be noted and used both as a possible pro forma adjustment to the firm's balance sheet for purposes of valuation and as part of the risk factor determination used in specific valuation methodologies.

[h] Reviewing Company's Investment Policies

Review the historic dependency of overall earnings on investment income. Are earnings becoming more or less dependent on this source? Evaluate procedures and practices. Analyze the company's internal control system as it relates to the approval of the selection of investments, recording results for financial statements, monitoring investments, and cash management. Consider the inherent risk or stability of the investment portfolio of the firm. Where is the majority of the firm's excess funds invested and what is the liquidity of those assets? How volatile are the investments? Has there been any trend toward investing in higher risk areas or those with less liquidity but perhaps higher yields? Are all investments approved for carrier investment? How is the portfolio managed and by whom? Examine investment income and the diversification of the portfolio among short-, medium-, and long-term investments. Medium- and long-term investment vehicles should be used only to the degree that maturities match expected future-loss payments.

[i] Combined Ratio

Of the total premiums charged by an insurance carrier, an expected portion is paid out in losses, another portion is paid out in expenses, and any funds remaining are considered profit. A quick method of evaluating the company's "reported" profitability is examining its combined ratio. This ratio is the sum of two operating ratios: the loss ratio and the expense ratio. The loss ratio is calculated by dividing losses incurred by premiums earned. The expense ratio is equal to expenses incurred divided by premiums written. If the combined ratio is greater than 100%, the company is not making an underwriting profit.

EXAMPLE 1: Company A has a loss ratio of 95.4% and an expense ratio of 106%. The combined ratio is therefore 106.0%. This means that for every $1.00 the company accepted in premiums, it incurred approximately $1.06 in losses and expenses.

If a company's combined ratio has been over 100% for a significant period of time, the valuator should examine more closely its underwriting policies and procedures, its loss experience, and its expense structure. A company's combined ratio should also be compared to the combined ratios of other comparable insurance companies to determine its experience to the industry.

[j] Responsiveness

How do the company's operations respond to underwriting or interest rate cycles? Are results highly correlated with these cycles and thus predictable, or does the firm perform contrary to expectations? What is the level of sensitivity or variability to the overall market?

[k] Competition

Who are the firm's competitors in each market and each product line? How comparable are their results? What marketing strategies differentiate the various carriers in each market? What areas of the business are expected to become more or less competitive in the future?

[l] Price Competitiveness

Examine the company's premium rates as compared to the rates of competing companies. Are the rates too high or low, or are they consistent with other companies? In what geographic areas are the rates competitive? Are noncompetitive rates in certain geographic areas an intentional part of more selective underwriting? Are the rates too low in too many areas, thereby exposing the company to disproportionately large claims experience in the future? How has price competition affected the firm's financial results?

[m] Quality and Autonomy of Branch Office Network

Examine the extent and scope of the branch offices of the carrier. How are the company's branch offices managed? What reporting information is available from the various offices? How are they reviewed? How does the management of the carrier decide whether to open additional offices or to close poorly performing ones?

[n] Geography

Is the firm's business concentrated in certain areas of the country or is it industry dependent? What is the impact of regional economies on the carrier's performance and operating results?

The analysis of all parts of the business should give the valuator an in-depth understanding of the operations of the carrier. This knowledge of the firm will play an important role in determining value.

[5] Financial Report Review

A thorough review and understanding of the company's financial information is crucial to the valuation. Obtain and analyze complete financial information for the prior five years and the current valuation year, both on a GAAP basis as well as a statutory basis. Income statement and balance sheet information is crucial.

[a] GAAP Statements

All publicly held firms, including insurance companies, must prepare one set of financial statements in accordance with GAAP. These statements are made available to the public in the form of corporate annual reports and in documents filed with the Securities and Exchange Commission (SEC).

[i] Annual Reports

Each year, publicly held firms prepare an annual report for shareholders. The annual report includes discussions about the firm's results over the past year, from financial results to management changes or marketing programs. This report informs the investor (or interested party) about the firm's business and activities. Annual reports are written by management and are intended to make the shareholders comfortable with the present and/or optimistic about the future. The annual report *must* include the following information:

- Income statement;
- Balance sheet;
- Statement of changes in financial position (sources and uses of cash);
- Statement of changes in shareholder's equity; and
- Notes to the financial statements.

Generally, publicly held firms present their financial statements on a consolidated basis. Often, in the notes to the financial statements, additional data is available regarding individual subsidiaries of the firm. The notes also give more detail to the basic financial statements of the company: description of significant accounting policies, detail on property, plant and equipment, specific maturities and values of short-term and long-term debt, transactions involving company stock, stock plans and pension funding, reconciliation of income taxes expensed and payable, and quarterly financial data. A prudent reviewer should examine those aspects of the annual report of an insurance company that are unique to insurance companies.

- ☐ *Management description of product lines.* Typically, the annual report includes lengthy descriptions of the product lines offered, e.g., personal lines, commercial, and accident and health. These sections cover the operating results by line, as well as marketing efforts and growth opportunities for each line.

- ☐ *Description of reinsurance arrangements.* The annual report should describe in detail the amounts of reinsurance ceded to other carriers as well as the amounts assumed for other carriers. This information is usually found in the Notes to the Financial Statements.

- ☐ *Unearned premium.* When a premium is paid by an insured to a carrier, a portion of the amount paid is recognized immediately as an earned premium. Typically, this is a pro rata amount that reflects the portion earned from the issue date of the policy to the time of the financial recording. The balance of the premium paid is credited to a liability account for an unearned premium. Over time (generally monthly), additional portions of the original premium are recognized as earned and are removed from the unearned premium account. Theoretically, at the expiration of the policy, the unearned premium account for that policy has a zero balance, indicating that the entire paid premium has been earned. If the policy were cancelled before the entire premium became earned, the amount still unearned would be refunded to the policyholder (less a penalty for midterm cancellation). For this reason, the unearned premium balance is carried as a liability on the books of the carrier.

- ☐ *Deferred policy acquisition costs.* GAAP theory maintains that revenues and expenses should be matched in the period when the revenue is recognized. Expenses associated with the production of insurance business cannot all be recognized in the period when the policy is written, as is the case in statutory accounting. For GAAP purposes, an asset called deferred policy acquisition costs, is established. These deferred costs are amortized over the period the premiums are recognized as revenue. This account should be reviewed to determine whether the costs are truly going to be future income, or whether they will be returned to the policyholder before they can be recognized as income.

☐ *Insurance reserve liabilities.* Reserve liabilities arise from case loss reserves (reserves established for losses reported and claims filed) and reserves for losses incurred but not reported. The amount booked as incurred losses on the income statement is the sum of the losses and loss adjustment expenses paid in the current period plus the change in case loss and IBNR reserves from the last period to the current period. An increase in reserves from one period to the next is expensed on the books and effectively decreases the policyholder surplus of the company. Therefore, if the company being valued has a steadily increasing reserve liability over a series of periods, the surplus in the company is just as steadily decreasing. This trend would have an adverse impact on the company, making the company more risky and less valuable.

☐ *Subsidiaries.* Insurance companies may have a variety of subsidiary companies. Typical subsidiaries include captive reinsurance companies and agency organizations. As part of the valuation of a company, any subsidiaries should be valued separately from the parent organization, as well as with the parent. The value of the whole group maybe higher than the sum of he values of the subsidiaries if the subsidiaries depend on the parent for a majority of their activities and revenues.

☐ *Auditor's opinion.* The annual report includes an auditor's opinion on the preparation of the statements presented in the report. This opinion is a *fairness opinion,* in which the accounting firm performing the audit states that it has examined the financial statements presented in the report and that the examination was made in accordance with generally accepted auditing standards. In order for the statements to meet SEC requirements, the auditors must conclude that the financial statements have been prepared in accordance with GAAP and present fairly the financial position of the firm. This is referred to as an unqualified opinion. Note, however, that the opinion only states that the financial position of the firm is presented fairly. This means that a prudent reviewer will have to independently decide whether the position itself is good or bad. The auditors only attest to the fairness of representation, without making value judgments about the firm's position, the company's management, or its current operating environment.

☐ *Qualified opinions.* The auditors may give a qualified opinion on the fairness of the representations for several reasons. One reason might be that the auditors found the firm had not been applying proper GAAP procedures as interpreted by the Financial Accounting Standards Board (FASB). Another possibility is that the reporting methodology was inconsistent from one period to the next. In these cases, the opinion may include a comment that the statements fairly present the financial position of the firm except for the area of disagreement. This kind of opinion should be a warning to investors and potential acquirers, as well as to valuators.

[ii] Proxy Statement

In addition to the annual report, publicly held firms prepare a proxy statement each year to be mailed to each shareholder. The proxy notifies the shareholder of the date, time, and place of the annual meeting and includes a description of any proposals that require the approval of the stockholders. For example, the board of directors of the company must be elected by the shareholders to serve specific terms as dictated by the firm's articles of incorporation. If the company wishes to appoint new board members, this request would be published in the proxy statement for shareholder review. Another example is a request to increase the authorized number of shares outstanding (typically pursuant to a stock split); this too must be approved by the shareholders. Proxies also discuss ownership of the company's securities, bonus compensation plans, pension plans, and activities of the board of directors. Any items that require shareholder approval must be fully presented and a proxy ballot included with the statement, so that any shareholder unable to attend the annual meeting of the corporation may vote (by proxy or absentee ballot) on the matters proposed.

For an insurance carrier, the proxy statement should be evaluated for any additional information it may contain about the management of the firm and the direction of the board wants to take with the company. Examine nominees for the board of directors. What are their backgrounds? What potential long-range interests do they have in the firm? How much knowledge do they have about the operations or management of an insurance carrier? Evaluate the status of the firm's pension or employee stock plans and any changes proposed; these may affect the ability of an outsider to take over the firm. In these days of "golden parachutes" and "poison pills," the proxy statement can be an invaluable clue to the direction the board is taking to protect its interests from outsiders, as most of these board-designed takeover defenses must be approved by the shareholders.

[iii] Form 10-K

Each year, publicly held firms must file Form 10-K with the SEC. This form is an extension of the annual report and provides additional information to the SEC and to interested investors/analysts about the firm's activities. This form must include the auditor's opinion on fairness of representation. Because the form may include some disclosures and detail not required in the annual reports, it should be reviewed in the valuation process in order to develop the most complete analysis of the firm's financial operations.

[iv] Quarterly Reports

Firms present, for the benefit of shareholders, brief quarterly reports that present an income statement for the quarter and a balance sheet as of the end of the quarter. Firms may include additional statements of financial position, notes to the financial statements and management discussions as deemed necessary by management. Typically, the data in these statements have not been audited and, therefore, there is no accountant's opinion. In a valuation, these reports may be useful because they attempt to represent the firm's standing at different times during the year. If the valuation is to take place as of a date other than the normal fiscal year end, the quarterly reports and filings (described below) will enable the valuator to create twelve-month "rolling" financial statements that can be used for comparisons to prior twelve-month periods. These reports make it possible for the valuation to be based on the most current information available about the firm.

[v] Form 10-Q

On a quarterly basis, firms file Form 10-Q with the SEC. This is similar in nature to the annual 10-K report and includes more detail for the SEC than firms give shareholders in the quarterly reports. An auditor's fairness opinion is not required for the filing of a 10-Q, but the firm's auditors usually review the filing in connection with regular auditing procedures. The 10-Q should be reviewed for the same reason as the 10-K: to gain a more complete picture of the firm with the most current information.

[vi] Supplemental Financial Information

Whenever possible, obtain additional financial information not necessarily included in the annual report or audited financial statements. In the case of firms whose quarterly or annual data is presented on a consolidated basis, a valuator should obtain financial statements for the individual subsidiaries. A careful review of the individual statements may uncover a cash flow problem in one subsidiary that may be masked when the cash from several subsidiaries is consolidated. If the valuation is of a consolidated group of companies, this is a particularly crucial part of the valuation. Request the consolidating worksheets that should show the individual companies and any intercompany adjustments and eliminations made during the period of a consolidating statement. Additional financial information may be obtained from the statutory convention statements filed with the insurance department of the carrier's state of domicile.

[vii] Loss and Loss Reserve Actuarial Report

Many state departments of insurance now require that a report on losses and loss reserves be filed annually. This report must be prepared by an actuary, either in house (usually for the larger carriers) or by an independent actuarial firm. The report is a complete and in-depth review of the firm's methodology of reserving for losses and the results of the application of the methodologies on past reserving. The report also includes an indication of the appropriateness of the methods used and the sufficiency of the reserves with respect to actuarial assumptions and expectations about the future of the business. The valuator should review this document as it relates to the adequacy of the company's reserves.

[viii] Industry Data

Some industrywide publications publish comparative data on insurance companies. One widely used reference is *Best's Insurance Reports*, which annually reports select financial and operational information on many insurance companies and assigns a rating ranging from A+ (superior) to C− (fair) to each of these companies. These resources can be used to compare the carrier being valued with similar carriers (by size, product lines, marketing efforts, or location). Trade journals and insurance publications are also valuable sources of industry data.

[b] Statutory Convention Statements

The various state departments of insurance require that each insurance carrier domiciled in the state file a quarterly and annual statement (convention statement) of the condition and affairs of the carrier. These statements are prepared by the management of the company and are not audited. Publicly held as well as privately held firms must file this statement, and for many privately held insurance carriers the statutory statements are the only financial statements available to the public. These convention forms are designed to present the financial condition of the firm for the specific interest of the policyholder, so that the policyholder may determine the stability of the company. The statutory reporting format is designed to show the policyholder the liquidation value of the company, which is generally lower than market value. For this reason, the statutory statements are somewhat different from GAAP financial statements, which consider the company as a going concern.

[i] Balance Sheet

The statement of the assets and liabilities on the statutory filing differs from GAAP reporting. First, treatment of allowable (admitted) assets is more conservative than the treatment of assets under GAAP. Certain assets of the company are classified as "nonadmitted assets" in the preparation of the statutory statements, and therefore are not included in the statutory calculation of the company's policyholder surplus. There is an exhibit in the statutory form that provides an analysis of all nonadmitted assets.

> *EXAMPLE 2*: Insurance company A has recorded premiums and agents' balances of $100,000 in its general ledger. This amount represents premiums receivable from producers which are still in the process of collection. The entire amount can be included in the GAAP statements as premiums receivable if management feels the accounts will eventually be collected in full. However, the rule for statutory reporting states that producers' balances that are over 90 days old (overdue) must be considered nonadmitted. The amount that is nonadmitted is excluded from the premiums receivable account in the statutory report.

A second difference between GAAP and statutory reporting is in the recognition of policy expenses. As discussed above, GAAP requires a matching of expenses with revenues, which leads to a deferred policy acquisition cost account on the asset side of the balance sheet. As the account is amortized over time, the expense amount is recognized on the income statement. Because the statutory reports are designed to show a more conservative view of the business, policy costs are recognized immediately and entirely as expenses when incurred, not over a period of time. Thus the statutory statement shows a lower profit and a lower surplus than the same period GAAP statement.

[ii] Underwriting and Investment Income Exhibit

This is a summary exhibit of the company's current period underwriting results. It is basically an income statement recorded according to statutory rules showing premiums earned less losses incurred, loss expenses incurred, and other underwriting expenses incurred. The exhibit also shows investment and other income, dividends paid to policyholders, federal and foreign taxes incurred, and a determination of statutory net income. This exhibit includes a detail of the changes in the capital and surplus account (comparable to the GAAP Statement of Changes in Shareholders' Equity).

[iii] Statement of Changes in Financial Position

This exhibit is basically the same as the Statement of Changes in Financial Position included in the Annual Report and 10-K filing. It details the funds provided by operations and the funds applied in operations and reconciles cash on hand and on deposit at the beginning and end of the year.

[iv] Additional Exhibits

In addition to the exhibit that analyzes nonadmitted assets, there are numerous tables presented in the statutories that detail the insurance operation. Several analyze underwriting and investments in greater depth than in the summary of underwriting and investment income: interest, dividends, and real estate income; capital gains and losses on investments; premiums earned and premiums in force; a summary of all premiums by line and premiums written; losses paid and incurred; unpaid losses and loss adjustment expenses; and underwriting/investment expenses. Statutory statements also include a reconciliation of ledger assets and an exhibit of premiums and losses by line.

[v] General Interrogatories

This section inquires about regulatory and statutory compliance and particularly compliance with the state department of insurance regulations. Several questions are of the yes/no variety, while others require brief answers. This section should be examined for any unusual answers.

[vi] Notes to Financial Statements

As is the case in the GAAP-prepared statements, there is provision in the statutories for additional relevant information. The issues covered by these notes include principle accounting methods used, discussion of federal income taxes, information concerning parent, subsidiaries and affiliates, and deferred compensation and retirement plans.

[vii] Supporting Schedules

Depending on the state, several supporting schedules may be required. These can include special deposits; other deposits; examination fees and expenses; five-year historical data; real estate owned, acquired or sold; long-term collateral loans in force, made, or discharged; long-term bonds, stocks, and preferred stocks owned, acquired, sold, redeemed, or disposed of during the year; short-term investments; ceded reinsurance; assumed reinsurance; loss development; loss expense development; losses by line; and premiums written by state.

In general, the financial reporting for insurance carriers is complex. Whenever possible, obtain both GAAP and statutory reports, and examine the differences between the two. Using both as references, the valuator should have a complete understanding of the financial situation of the firm.

[6] Valuation Methods

Four main methods are used in valuing insurance companies. Often, a valuator will use more than one methodology to establish a range of values for the company. Based on the valuator's view of the company being valued, the valuator's experience with similar companies and general knowledge of the industry, the valuator will then select a midpoint value that falls within the developed ranges. Some of the methods have more validity than others, depending on the given situation of the company and the information available to the valuator.

[a] Adjusted Net Book Value Method

The adjusted net book value method examines only asset and liability values (i.e., tangible net worth plus the value of licenses plus the excess value of reserves and unearned premiums over discounted reserves). Tangible net worth is the value of the balance sheet less any intangible items, such as goodwill. The adjustments to tangible net worth value may be negative, leading to a total value that is less than the adjusted tangible net worth; this could be the case if reserves are deemed to be inadequate. Some items that have a separate value may not be included on the balance sheet at the current market value; these additional values must be added to the book value. The process of adjusting book value is one of creating a pro forma balance sheet based on the adjusted values of the various items.

[i] Appraisals

The first step in adjusting the book value of the company is to appraise the stated balance sheet as the date of valuation. If the valuator is working only from the statutory reports, the balance sheet should be converted to a GAAP-basis balance sheet. Several items will need adjustment. First, analyze nonadmitted assets. As in the example cited above, agents balances that are over 90 days due must be excluded from the statutory balance sheet but would be included in a GAAP balance sheet. The amount of these overdue receivables may need to be adjusted to a value lower than face value to recognize uncollectibility of certain receivables. Other items in the balance sheet may require adjustments as well to convert the values from a liquidation-value appraisal to a market valuation. These may include property and equipment that are not liquid enough to be included in the statutory balance sheet but have market value so they meet the criteria for GAAP balance sheets.

[ii] Intangibles

Intangible assets such as goodwill should be removed from the balance sheet to develop the adjusted net book value. The account for deferred policy acquisition cost is also an intangible asset and should be removed since these costs have no realizable value. The adjustment to reduce the company's surplus recognizes the expenses related to policy acquisition costs as if such expenses had been recognized when incurred.

[iii] Valuing Licenses

Values should be assigned to state licenses as representative of the future value of the company if it were sold as a "shell company", i.e., no policies in force but with the license to write business in certain states. Shells have value to potential buyers that wish to enter the insurance industry or to expand their current operations to write business in additional states. This value may derive from the states having limited the number of insurers licensed or from the significant expense of obtaining a new license from the state. As a developed part of the business, the value of a license is not recognized as an asset until a company is sold and its buyer assigns some of the purchase price to licenses. This treatment is similar to the expensing of research and development costs or patent development costs in manufacturing companies. Ownership of state licenses and other intangibles is not capitalized on the balance sheets until sold to a third party. To appraise the value of these licenses, the valuator should research and document recent sales of licenses in similar states. From the history of transactions, an estimate should be developed to apply to each of the licenses owned by the company being valued. This is a pro forma adjustment that increases the assets of the company and thus the book value of the company.

[iv] Valuing Reserves

The valuator should use either the analyses developed in the initial steps of the valuation process or an actuarial report on loss reserves to value the reserves of the company. The analyses should result in a determination of the sufficiency of the reserves. If the valuator relies on reserves analyses developed by outside actuaries, such reliance should be noted as part of the valuation report. In either case, if the examination showed that the reserves as stated are insufficient to cover expected losses and loss expenses, then a pro forma adjustment should be made to remove the amount of deficiency from the company's surplus. This adjustment corrects for the expectation that a purchaser would need to contribute capital to fund under-reserved future losses.

[v] Valuing Unearned Premium Account

This step identifies a present value of future investment income flows that are not otherwise reflected on the balance sheet. To determine if that liability is appropriately stated or if too much premium has been recognized as earned, analyze the recent history of policy cancellations or terminations and premiums refunded. Determine how investment income, general expenses, and deferred acquisition costs will be allocated to the policies in force for which there are unearned premiums held as liabilities. Once a stream of profits is determined, discount the stream using a present value calculation, with a discount rate that reflects the appropriate risk level of the business. The discount rate that should be used must consider the risk of long-term investments adjusted for the unique risk level of this particular industry and specific company.

[vi] Federal Income Tax Effects

The stream of pretax profits that are determined to exist will generate additional taxes as the profits are realized. Many valuations take place on a pretax basis; however, the valuator may wish to further adjust the book value to recognize the future tax liability on the existing book of business.

[vii] Example

An evaluation of *XYZ* Insurance Company, Inc. yielded the figures shown in Table 18-1.

TABLE 18-1

XYZ INSURANCE COMPANY
FINANCIAL EVALUATION

Statutory reported surplus		$125,050,000
Plus:	Non-admitted assets	500,000
Less:	Write-down of assets (to market values)	(1,360,000)
	Remove deferred policy acquisition costs	(25,500,000)
Plus:	Present value of profits of current business	46,000,000
Less:	Reserve deficiency	(5,000,000)
Adjusted net book value		$139,690,000

Note that this method makes no provision for expected future profits from new business and business development. Only asset and liability values are considered.

[b] Trading Market Method

The trading market method relies on determination of value in relation to comparable publicly held insurance companies.

[i] Selecting Comparable Insurance Companies

Comparable insurance companies are those of a size similar to the company being valued, whose product lines and product mix are similar to the mix of the company being examined. The valuator may also wish to consider as comparable: similar marketing efforts, geography, capital resources, actual trading market, profitability and return characteristics, and size and position in the various markets. For example, if the company being valued writes 65% of its business in employee benefits coverages, a firm that writes only 10% employee benefits and the remaining 90% in workers' compensation coverages would not be considered comparable. The valuator should develop an index of price to earnings ratios and price to book value ratios for selected comparable companies. It would be more enlightening to track these ratios over a period of time (one to six years) to establish an index with some depth of information. By showing ratios over time, one can see the trends and the cycles of the business. This should help in selecting an appropriate multiple to apply to the company being valued.

EXAMPLE 3: The insurance companies selected as comparable have traded at prices of 15.5 times pretax earnings to 43.6 times pretax earnings over the last 7 years. The mean price/earnings ratio is 14.2. Graph the index over time; index levels on the Y-axis and time on the X-axis. If there is an evident cycle, the valuator should be able to predict a range where next year's price/earnings ratios should fall. The valuator should create a similar analysis for price to book value multiples.

[ii] Adjusting Index

The average price/earnings ratio thus developed should be discounted to reflect the relative attractiveness in the market of the company being valued. This is where the initial management analysis becomes useful. If the valuator concludes on the basis of the prior analyses performed that the company is more risky than the comparable firms, one would expect that, if publicly owned, it would trade at a lower-than-average multiple. The public has demonstrated its willingness to pay less for earnings that are less consistent or more unpredictable. Similarly, if the valuator believes that because of new programs or lines the firm would trade at a higher than average multiple, the valuator would adjust the index upward by adding a premium. This situation happens rarely.

[iii] Establishing Sustainable Pretax Income Level

To use the multiple of earnings methods, the valuation analyst must establish a level of sustainable earnings appropriate for the firm. Using a method that is comparable to adjusting the book value, the valuator should make adjustments to the income statement of the company to eliminate discretionary, nonrecurring and nonoperational items. These pro forma adjustments may include reducing officers' compensation to a level more in line with industry standards, adjusting automobile allowances to a more realistic level and eliminating contributions and donations as discretionary expenses. These adjustments should enable the valuator to establish a level of sustainable pretax earnings that would have been reported if the firm had been realistically operated as a publicly owned company.

[iv] Determining Value

Using the adjusted index as a basis, the valuator should then multiply the adjusted average price/pretax earnings by the company's sustainable pretax earnings, as developed above. Using the multiple of book value method, the adjusted average price/book value ratio is then multiplied by the company's adjusted book value. Remember to keep book values consistent: Book values of publicly owned firms will be GAAP-based values. If the valuation is based only on statutory reports, adjust the book value of the firm to a GAAP basis before determining value.

[v] Example

The evaluation of *ABC* Insurance Company, Inc. and several comparable companies yielded the figures shown in Table 18-2.

TABLE 18-2
ABC INSURANCE COMPANY
FINANCIAL EVALUATION

Average price earnings of comparable companies	12.5x
Less: Discount for risk: 20%	− 2.5x
Adjusted price/earnings multiple	10.0x
Pro forma sustainable pretax earnings	$2,500,000
Trading market value	$25,000,000

Note that this method only values the firm as a going concern and does not reflect liquidation or market values that would be realized if the firm were sold for liquidation.

[c] Acquisition Value Method

Acquisition value considers the universe of all acquisitions of property/casualty or life companies over the past several years. This method relies on published data regarding mergers and acquisitions as a basis for determining value. It is often a more helpful method of valuing a small insurance company than the trading market method since there are generally more transactions involving small insurance companies than there are comparable, publicly owned firms. The valuation "yardsticks" vary among the types of businesses, but most include the following: transaction values related to revenues and tangible net worth acquired; transaction values related to appropriate (statutory or GAAP) net worth; and specialty insurance company acquisition values.

[i] Developing Index Ratio

The valuator should develop an index ratio of purchase price to book value covering a historic time frame. This index will be applied to the company being valued. To create the index, published data on acquisitions should be researched. Sources of such information include the *Wall Street Journal*, insurance trade publications (e.g., *Best's Insurance Management Reports* and *Business Insurance* magazine), transaction databases (e.g., Securities Data Corporation Merger and Acquisition Data Base), and corporate annual reports; notes to financial statements generally give some details of acquisitions. The price/book value ratio for all acquisitions in the area of insurance carriers should then be computed. As in the trading market methodology, it is best to focus on transactions involving comparable companies. Note that these transactions may also include sales of insurance subsidiaries to/by other corporations. As with the trading market method, it helps to graph the multiples over time to see if acquisition multiples of book value rise and fall with the business cycle or if a trend can be predicted.

[ii] **Segmenting Index**

Depending on the availability of data, dividing the universe of transactions into groups makes for a better index. There are several ways of segmenting the data. First, deals can be distinguished by size of transaction. Second, they can be segregated by type of buyer (public or private). Additional groupings can be made by primary product lines or by any of the other qualifications used to determine comparable companies. By segmenting the data, the valuator can place the company being valued in the field of peer firms and thereby develop a better indication of value.

[iii] **Adjusting Index**

The valuator should adjust the average multiple to account for the specifics of the deal in question. What are the purchaser's objectives? How does the carrier fit in with the other businesses of the purchaser? Are the insurance lines complementary or competing? Will there be synergies with the existing business? How willing is the buyer to infuse capital and/or management into the deal? If the buyer a publicly owned firm or a private firm? Will a publicly owned firm pay more for this particular business than a private firm would or could pay? How profitable is the book of business when compared to those sold in prior deals? Are there intangible assets, such as goodwill, for which the buyer will pay a premium? What form of consideration will be paid to current owners of the company (cash or stock)? Asking these kinds of questions will narrow the range of multiples that the research will develop. A multiple should then be selected form within the range that reflects the valuator's judgment of the transaction at issue relative to the transactions defining the range.

[iv] **Determining Value**

In the trading market method, once the average sale multiple has been adjusted for the particular aspects of the transaction being considered and the company being valued, the book value of the company should be multiplied by the adjusted multiple to determine the value.

Consistency is necessary in the application of book values. If the research is based on GAAP book values in transactions, GAAP book values for the company being valued must be used as well. This means that if only statutory reports were originally used, the book value of the carrier must be converted to a GAAP-based book value.

[v] Example

The analysis of *PQR* Insurance Company and transactions involving comparable companies resulted in the figures shown in Table 18-3.

TABLE 18-3

PQR INSURANCE COMPANY
FINANCIAL EVALUATION

Average multiple of book value sold	1.70x
Less: Discount for risk: 20%	− 0.34
Adjusted multiple	1.36x
Pro forma GAAP book value for PQR	$5,300,000
Acquisition value	$7,208,000

A similar application of this method uses multiples of pretax earnings sold as a basis for determining an appropriate multiple.

The main difference between the acquisition value method and the trading market method is that the acquisition value method examines sales of entire companies, while the trading market method examines the current trading of the stock of companies among individual investors.

[d] Present Value of Future Profits: Method 1

Present value of future profits develops the value of the business as a going concern. Unlike the multiple methods, the present value method relies on estimates of future cash flows and the financial theory of present value. There are two generally accepted methods for determining value using the present value rule: capitalization of earnings and discounted cash flow.

[i] Capitalizing Earnings

This method is equivalent to the trading market method. To capitalize the sustainable earnings of the firm, begin with an established level of sustainable pretax earnings. The discount rate used for the capitalization is the rate of return investors would require from a comparable company. The acceptable rate of return is the inverse of the price-to-earnings ratios used in the valuation by the trading-market method. The discount rate therefore is equal to the price/earnings ratio of comparable companies.

[ii] Adjusting Capitalization Rate

The valuator will adjust the discount rate to reflect the additional risk of the company being valued.

EXAMPLE 4: The average pretax price/earnings ratio of the group of comparable firms is 11.9%. However, the valuator feels that because of the risk inherent in the company, outside investors would require a return that is twice as great as that for the average less risky publicly owned firm. Therefore, 23.8% would be used as the discount rate.

[iii] Using Risk-Free Rates

A similar method for determining the appropriate discount rate is to use a risk-free rate of return, which is the rate of return available on investments in government securities. Adjust this rate for the risk of the company being valued by adding a risk premium to the currently available risk-free rate. This would establish the rate at which investors would be induced to invest in this company, given its operations and inherent risk, rather than in "safe" government bonds.

EXAMPLE 5: The average risk-free rate currently available on government securities with maturities ranging from 10 to 20 years is 9.2%. For an investor to select the company being valued as an equally attractive investment alternative, the company would have to provide approximately twice the return of government bonds. Therefore, the appropriate discount rate to use is 18.4%.

[iv] Determining Value by Capitalization of Earnings

To determine value using this valuation method, divide the level of sustainable pretax earnings by the adjusted discount rate.

[v] Example

The analysis of *DCF* Insurance Company, Inc. developed the figures shown in Tables 18-4 and 18-5.

TABLE 18-4

DCF COMPANY
FINANCIAL EVALUATION

Pro forma sustainable pretax earnings	$1,500,000
Risk-free rate	9.4%
Risk premium	10.6%
Required rate of return	20.0%
Capitalization of earnings value	$7,500,000

TABLE 18-5

DCF COMPANY
FINANCIAL EVALUATION—
ALTERNATE FIGURES

Pro forma sustainable pretax earnings	$1,500,000
Average price earnings multiple	7.0%
Additional risk premium	13.0%
Required rate of return	20.0%
Capitalization of earnings value	$7,500,000

In Examples 4 and 5, two different risk premiums were used. This will often be the case, as the return on government securities will usually be less than the return on investments in the stock of comparable insurance companies. In either case, the valuator determines a required rate of return that would induce an investor to switch funds from a different investment into this company. The required premium may be different depending on where the funds are originally invested. All comparisons must be made on a consistent tax basis. (The above example uses pretax.) Generally, using pretax figures allows the elimination of the impact of taxes resulting from extraordinary or nonoperational events.

[e] Present Value of Future Profits: Method 2

The second present value method calculates value based on expected future profits under a variety of assumptions. There are three components to this method of valuation: the valuation of the business in force, the valuation of new and renewable business, and the valuation of the existing surplus.

[i] Value of Business in Force

This value is equal to the sum of the present value of investment income on current loss and loss adjustment expense reserves, plus the present value of investment income on unearned premium reserves, plus the equity in the unearned premium reserve. To make the present value calculation, an appropriate discount rate must be selected. The discount rate should equal the rate of return that the reserve funds would earn if it were invested from now until it ran out (due to claims). The present value is the amount remaining in each period, discounted at the appropriate rate to the present period. The firm's loss ratio when multiplied by the present value of the expected investment income on unearned premium reserves results in the value of this component of the business in force value component. This value is then added to the equity in the unearned premium reserve, which is the company's loss ratio multiplied by the unearned premium account.

[ii] Value of New and Renewable Business

This value component is equal to the sum of the present value of each year's first year underwriting profit or loss and the present value of each year's first year and future investment income on reserves and other cash flows; this assumes that losses, if any, are funded for all years and profits are paid out as earned. To determine the underwriting levels for future years, growth assumptions must be developed for each major income statement item. Using these assumptions one can project the future values of the various components of the operation. Typically, this approach is used to project the next five- to ten-year period. Several criteria for projecting assumptions are discussed below.

[iii] Premium Growth Rate

Based on the analysis of the business and the prospects for growth in the various lines, premium levels for future years can be projected on a product line basis.

[iv] Renewal Rate

The renewal rate assumed on existing business must be consistent with past and anticipated experience.

[v] Loss and Loss Adjustment Expense Ratio

These ratios have been used to value the equity in unearned premium reserves and the investment income on those reserves. For future business, the loss ratios can be adjusted for expectations of trends (higher or lower than historical ratios). Once these ratios have been adjusted for expected future losses, the adjusted ratios can be applied to the premiums as projected.

[vi] Expense Ratio

The firm's historical expense ratio may be adjusted to reflect new controls or commitments to expense levels. The adjusted ratio is applied to the premiums as projected.

[vii] Loss Reserve Run-Out

This rate is the amount of losses that are paid the first year of each accident year. The valuator may wish to adjust the historical rate.

[viii] Current Earnings Rate on Investments

The rate selected as an earnings rate on investments should represent a return that is attainable and sustainable throughout the period of the projections for the company's investment portfolio.

[ix] Future Earnings Rate on Investments

A pretax rate of return must be assumed on future investments. It is also sometimes assumed that the current portfolio is liquidated at market value and reinvested at current rates in appropriate maturities to match the expected loss requirements. This is necessary so that the going concern will have sufficient cash available in the future.

[x] Policyholder Surplus

The assumption above that the current portfolio be liquidated and reinvested may lead to an adjustment in the policyholder surplus. If the portfolio has been carried at the lower of cost or market, the market value may be higher and thus indicate a higher surplus.

[xi] Alternative Assumptions

This approach should use several combinations of assumptions, to reflect the sensitivity of operating results to the different potential business environments and cycles. Generally, projections are made under different scenarios; best, worst, and expected are typical.

[xii] Value Conclusions

This approach, with the various assumptions and scenarios, will result in several calculations of value. Using the knowledge of the company gained in the initial analysis of the firm coupled with the information gathered about comparable companies and about the business cycle in general, the valuator should select a scenario deemed appropriate for the future of the company being valued. The present value of the future business under those assumptions together with the present value of the business in force gives the total value of the company.

[xiii] Example

The analysis are projections of the business of *GHK* Insurance Company have the sets of present values shown in Table 18-6.

TABLE 18-6

GHK INSURANCE COMPANY
FINANCIAL EVALUATION AND PROJECTIONS

At 8% discount rate and 15% premium growth rate

Value of existing business	$ 6,478,000
Value of new and renewal business	12,000,000
Total present value	$18,478,000

At 8% discount rate and 10% premium growth rate

Value of existing business	$ 6,478,000
Value of new and renewal business	$ 9,500,000
Total present value	$15,978,000

In this case, the valuator may decide that the higher premiums growth rate is more appropriate for the firm and may therefore set a value of $18,000,000 for the company.

[f] Summary of Methods and Required Factors

Listed next are the essential components of each of the valuation methods:

[i] Adjusted Net Book Value Method

The essential components of the net book value method are:

- Statutory or GAAP-reported surplus;
- Adjustments to realistic market values;
- Present value of profits of current business; and
- Adjustment for reserve adequacy.

[ii] Trading Market Method

The essential components of the trading market method are:

- Price/earnings ratios of comparable companies;
- Reasonable adjustments to the average ratio; and

- Pro forma sustainable pretax income level.

[iii] Acquisition Value Method

The essential components of the acquisition value method are:

- Ratios of purchase price paid to book value acquired in recent transactions;
- Segmentation of the data into groups of comparable transactions;
- Reasonable adjustments to the average ratios; and
- Pro forma GAAP book value.

[iv] Present Value of Future Profits Method

The essential components of the future profits method are:

- Capitalization of earnings formula (including an appropriate capitalization (discount) rate and a pro forma sustainable pretax income level); and
- Present value of future profits formula (including present value of business in force and present value of new and renewable business, based on various assumptions regarding premium growth rates, renewal rates, loss and loss adjustment expense ratios, expense ratios, and current and future earnings rates on investments).

[7] Tax Reform Act of 1986

Several provisions of the Tax Reform Act of 1986 (TRA '86) affect both property/casualty and life/health insurance carriers. The purpose of these new rules is to increase overall the income taxes paid by insurance carriers, especially property/casualty carriers, despite the lowering of the maximum corporate tax rate. The general provisions of the code, of course, affect insurance companies just as other companies: the top corporate tax rate is reduced from 46% to 34% beginning July 1, 1987; capital gains will be taxed at the top corporate tax rate for ordinary income; the corporate dividend exclusion is reduced from 85% to 80%. However, certain sections of the code affect only insurance carriers. Following is a brief description of the major changes. For complete rules and information, consult the Internal Revenue Code of 1986.

[a] Unearned Premium Reserve

Property/casualty insurers now must include in taxable income 20% of the change in the unearned premium reserve. Congress, therefore, believed that this 20% approximates the costs of generating the policies. By only allowing a deduction from taxable income for 80% of the change, the code attempts to better match income with expenses.

[b] Recapture of Unearned Premium Reserve

The new law also provides for a transitional recapture of past reserves. It requires that 20% of the outstanding balance of the unearned premium reserve at the end of the last taxable year beginning prior to January 1, 1987 (this generally means the balance as of December 31, 1986) be included in income. This 20% will be included over six taxable years beginning after December 31, 1986.

[c] Dividends and Tax-Exempt Interest

A property/casualty company must now prorate a specified portion of its investment income by reducing the deduction for losses incurred by 15% of the sum of tax-exempt interest income and the deductible portion of dividends received during the taxable year. This proration rule generally applies to taxable years after December 31, 1986 and then only an interest and dividends received on investments acquired after August 1, 1986.

[d] Loss Reserve Discounting

Property/casualty firms must now use the concept of time value of money when taking a current deduction for future loss payments. The deduction for all unpaid losses is now limited to the increase in the amount of the discounted unpaid losses. This section of the code also applies to the loss reserves of accident and health claims, which in the past were not required to be discounted under life insurance rules. The amount of discounted, unpaid losses is computed each year for each line of business for each accident year by applying the new statutory pretax discounting rule. This amount is the present value of the carriers unpaid losses, computed using the undiscounted loss reserves (generally as reported in the statutory annual statement), an applicable rate of interest as determined by the Secretary of the Treasury, and the pattern of the payment of claims. The pattern is also determined by the Secretary of the Treasury for each line of business, or companies may irrevocably elect to use its own historical loss payment pattern.

[e] Life Insurance Company Deduction

Life insurance companies are no longer allowed a special life insurance company deduction equal to 20% of taxable income determined by excluding items attributable to noninsurance business.

[f] Corporate Alternative Minimum Tax

The corporate add-on minimum tax has been replaced with an alternative minimum tax for taxable years beginning after December 31, 1986. This provision of the law provides that a company's alternative minimum taxable income is equal to its regular taxable income, plus the taxpayer's tax preference items for the year, adjusted by computing certain items under special rules. This section of the code will likely increase the tax liability for small insurance companies.

There are many more and involved tax reform changes affecting insurance companies. It would be best for any company considering entering into a financial transaction to consult with its own tax accountant prior to meaningful negotiations.

[g] Impact of the Tax Reform Changes on Valuations

Several of the valuation method described previously are based on pretax earnings using financial statements (not tax returns) for data. However, the changes in the tax law mean that acquisition values or trading market values that are multiples of earnings reported under the former code may need to be discounted further before applying them to the company being valued. Because taxes paid affect cash flow, the multiples of earnings or book value may change significantly. As always, it is important to apply consistent standards when using any of the valuation. Any method that involves figures affected by the tax changes should be applied so as to create a consistency of values, either on a pretax or an after-tax basis, based on the former or the new code.

[8] Conclusion

The valuation of an insurance carrier is a complex and time-consuming process. However, there are experts available to assist with most of the steps in the valuation process: appraisers to help value tangible assets, actuaries to assist with analysis of reserves, accountants and financial analysts to evaluate financial statements, consultants to evaluate management and management reports. In all cases, the valuation should be based on a complete review and analysis of the business in question, the strategies that give rise to the business, and the methods by which the business is managed on a daily basis and on a reporting basis. Consistency in the application of method and thoughtfulness in the consideration of the company's relative risk are the keys to an appropriate valuation of an insurance carrier.

¶ 18.2 Valuing Insurance Agencies

Stated in simple terms, the fair market value of an agency is that reached through negotiation by a willing buyer and willing seller, where neither the buyer nor the seller is in a forced position and each has access to full information regarding the transaction. When will a buyer and a seller agree upon a value? Obviously, when both think they are getting more than they are giving. With cash deals, their difference in perception centers on the value of the agency. This same situation is present daily in the stock market. On a given day, the majority of a company's shareholders thinks the company is worth more than the market price and, therefore, chooses not to sell. The majority of nonshareholders thinks the value is below market price and chooses not to buy. The value of the stock on that day is determined by the willing buyers and sellers who agree upon a trading price. Stock prices, clearly, reflect purchases of small increments of a company. When the whole company sells, all stock is bought and this is often at a premium above the market price.

A company is worth exactly what someone else is willing to pay for it and no more. It is clear that the best valuation is done in the actual marketplace. The times when an expert valuation is needed are when there is a limited market (i.e., a closely-held agency), when the owner does not actually want to sell the agency, or when the seller is ready to go to market and needs a realistic expectation of value.

[1] Valuation Myths

Before discussing how an agency should be valued, let's dispel two common valuation myths.

[a] Commission Multiples

How many times have you heard someone say, "My agency is worth 1.5 times my annual commissions?" By contrast, do you often hear people say, "Stock X is worth 1.5 times annual sales?" Generally, the answer to the second question is no because stock prices are not necessarily reflective of sales. Remember that an agency is only worth what someone else will pay for it, just as a stock's value is determined by the market. Using an arbitrary "rule of thumb" to value your agency would likely result in something other than a true fair market value.

You've probably noticed that stocks tend to rise or fall immediately after an earnings announcement: prices rise after a higher-than-expected report and fall if earnings are lower than expected. In much the same way, the value of your agency is really based on earnings, not just commissions. It is easy to see that an agency with commissions of $500,000 and pretax earnings of $50,000 is worth more than another agency that also has commissions of $500,000 but has pretax earnings of only $25,000. Besides earnings, there are also more subtle questions to consider. For example, would you pay the same for two companies with the same commissions and earnings but where one has many accounts spread over several insurers, while the other has one account which represents over 50% of the book of business and the agency also has a poor loss ratio?

Other factors that can affect value include such things as agency management, competency of personnel, growth history, stability and broadness of market base, condition of accounts receivable, mix of business, special lines or areas of expertise, account size and concentration, location and geographic area of operations, and overall agency performance compared to the rest of the industry. Obviously, a simple commissions multiple cannot adequately account for all these factors.

[b] Revenue Multiples

Do revenue multiples work any better? To find out, look at the December 31 quoted stock market values expressed as a multiple of reported revenues for the three largest publicly held insurance brokers over a four-year period, as shown in Table 18-7.

TABLE 18-7

QUOTED STOCK MARKET VALUES AS MULTIPLES OF REVENUES

	1985	1986	1987	1988
Marsh & McLennan	2.18	2.45	1.75	1.79
Alexander & Alexander	1.31	0.96	0.63	0.79
Corroon & Black	2.08	1.77	1.38	1.25
Average	1.85	1.87	1.35	1.42

Source: Russell Miller, Inc., *Supergrowth Newsletter* (Jan.-Feb. 1989). Analysis is based on end-of-year quoted stock prices and reported revenues of each company.

It is quite noticeable that these values change over time. So why are private agencies still using a constant rule of thumb that was used ten years ago? It seems unreasonable for a private agency to expect to receive a 1.5 revenue multiple when the large and stable public brokers cannot consistently do so. Finally, why should the estimated 65,000 private agencies expect to have the same revenue multiple when the large brokers, a much more homogenous group, shown such a striking range?

[2] Valuation Methods

When attempting to define value, you must first decide what your viewpoint of value is. The only real measure of value is that a person can obtain for something on the market. The result is a fair market value.

☐ *Public company method.* Clearly, most owners do not intend to take their agencies to market but do want to have a feel for what the market price is. One way of valuing an agency is to adjust the income statement so that the agency looks as if it were run like a public company and then determine the most likely price that would be received if the agency were sold to/merged with a public broker. This method is referred to as the public company method of valuation because value is determined from the viewpoint of a public company.

☐ *Capitalization of earnings method.* A second way to view value is as an outside investor. This involves determining what rate of return an investor would require to assume the risk of putting money into a particular agency. This method requires examining returns available on other investments and evaluating the risk level of the agency. This second approach will be referred to as the capitalization of earnings method.

☐ *Wasting asset method.* The third valuation method is known as the wasting asset method. This method assumes that the real value of an agency is basically in its book of business of renewals. After all, the major asset of any agency *is* its book of business. Theoretically, the idea is to run the business "off the books." You must determine a time period for the run-off and assume that no new business is written. A present value calculation on the stream of income derived from the run-off, excluding any sales costs, will give a value for the particular book.

[a] Public Company Method

The main difficulty in valuing private agencies is that there is no easy way to determine, at any given time, what privately held stock is worth. There are, however, public companies whose stock is actively traded that can be used for comparison. Six such major public brokerages are Alexander & Alexander Services Inc., Corroon & Black Corporation, Crump Companies, Inc., Arthur J. Gallagher & Co., Frank B. Hall & Co. Inc., and Marsh & McLennan Companies, Inc.

The public company method of valuation uses information about these firms to determine the price that would be paid if the agency were to be acquired by or merged with a similar publicly-held company. This method is advantageous for two reasons.

First, inherent in a public company's value is how investors perceive the operations of a public brokerage that competes in the marketplace. This perception is expressed in the stock's price. Second, the six public brokers have been and still are major buyers of medium- and large-sized agencies and brokers. In acquiring private agencies, public brokers will normally not pay more for a stream-of-earnings than the current investors in the public company are paying for their own stream-of-earnings. In other words, the public company will not normally dilute its earnings.

A public company looking at acquiring a private company will generally ask itself two questions. First, they will want to know, "After the transaction, when the agency becomes a part of us, what kind of earnings are we going to derive from that agency?" The second question is, "How many shares of our stock must we give them for those earnings?" to help answer this second question, the public company determines how much each of their shares is currently earning? This figure is derived by dividing total after-tax earnings of the company by the number of shares outstanding. This number will give the company a base from which it can start to work.

[i] Dilution of Earnings

Before discussing the next step, let's go back to the subject of dilution in a little more detail. Most public companies will state that they do not want to dilute their stock. This means that if their stock is currently earning $3 per share after taxes and they are considering issuing some new shares, they will not want to issue them unless the new shares will also earn at least $3 per share after taxes. If the new stock were to earn only $2.50 per share, the overall effect of the issue would be dilutive. That is what dilution is all about, issuing new shares of stock that earn less than the old shares were earning and thus bringing down the average earnings of all the shares.

[ii] Discounting Shares

There is another issue involved here. A public company will almost never agree to a "parity" deal. This means that they will almost never give you a share of stock earning $3 for one of your shares also earning $3. They want an immediate enhancement of their earnings. Thus, they will likely say, "We will give you our share earning $3 for $3.30 worth of your earnings." This is called "discounting shares." Thus, the private company is contributing more to the public company's earnings per share than the public company will be earning in each of its own shares.

[iii] Price/Earnings Multiple

Another important concept involved is the price/earnings multiple. This is basically the number that public companies work with when discounting a seller's stock interest. The price/earnings multiple is computed by dividing the market price of a share by the earnings of that share. If we have a share of a public company that is earning $3 and determine that the share can be bought in the marketplace for $30, then the share has a price/earnings multiple of 10. That is, it is selling for 10 times its earnings.

Let's now see how these concepts relate to a specific valuation using the public company method. Assume that a public broker is interested in acquiring your agency but no one broker is currently negotiating such a purchase. To apply the public company method to your agency, an average of the price/earnings multiples of the six largest public brokers on the date of valuation should be obtained. Once this average is determined, it should be converted to a pretax multiple so the equation will be consistent. This can be done by multiplying the multiple by the quantity (1 - tax rate of broker).

Now you have a general pretax multiple to work with. However, a public company would generally not want to pay an amount equal to this full multiple times the private agency's earnings because a small private firm has many more inherent financial and operating risks than a large public broker. Because the agency's pro forma profits are based on a number of adjustments and assumptions, there is some risk that the agency will not be able to achieve the calculated level of pro forma profits. To make up for acquiring this risk and the other risks involved in agency management, the public broker discounts the price/earnings multiple. If the agency were not able to achieve the pro forma level of profits and the public company had not discounted the price/earnings multiple, dilution would occur. The risk of dilution and other operating risks generally translates into a 5-20 percent discount of the existing price/earnings multiple.

Table 18-8 gives an illustration of the public company method of valuation. As Table 18-8 illustrates, determination of value starts with pro forma pretax earnings. Next, because there is an assumption that no one public broker has made an offer for this agency, an average of several companies' price/earnings multiples is used. This average provides an approximate figure to work with in determining a value for the book of business. If a specific public company had made an offer to acquire the agency, the appropriate multiple to use would be the multiple of that specific public company. It is fairly obvious that the company is going to use its own multiple instead of the average when doing its own calculations.

The multiple is discounted for the reasons already mentioned. These include preventing dilution of earnings, accounting for the extra risk of assimilating a new operation, and reflecting the level of interest in acquisitions.

[iv] Working Capital Requirement

All valuation methods must account for the need of at least forty-five days' worth of working capital to generate the income stream that is the source of the value of the book of business. The working capital figure is removed from the value figure because the buyer expects the agency to be able to work on its own resources for forty-five days; the seller should not receive payment for that.

[v] Tangible Net Worth

Finally, the final figure of $2.5 million is only the value of the agency's earnings stream and not the full value of the agency. Full value would also include the value of the firm's tangible net worth, which is the difference between assets and liabilities less any intangible items.

TABLE 18-8

XYZ AGENCY
PUBLIC COMPANY METHOD

Pro forma pretax earnings of Rical Agency		$ 500,000
Public Broker	**Price/Earnings Multiple**	**Tax Rate**
ABC Company	10.5	40%
EFG Company	9.8	39%
XYZ Company	11.0	41%
Average multiple	10.4	
Average tax rate	40%	
Pretax average multiple	10.4 − 40% (10.4) = 6.24	
Discount rate	15%	
Discounted pretax multiple	6.24 − 15% (6.24) = 5.30	
Value of operations $500,000 × 5.30		$2,650,000
Less: 45 days working capital		(150,000)
Total		$2,500,000

[b] Capitalization of Earnings Method

The capitalization of earnings method establishes a rate of return that represents the average rate a prudent investor would require as a fair return on capital invested in the particular agency. The key element in this approach is in defining a "fair rate of return." Fair rate of return is made up of two components. The first is the return available on alternative minimum risk investments; the second is the additional return required for assuming the inherent risk existing in the specific insurance agency.

[i] Minimum Risk Investments

Minimum risk investments generally are defined as long-term treasury bonds and U.S. agency obligations, as well as AAA-rated corporate bonds. An investor could put money in these securities and receive a certain rate of return that carries virtually no risk. Because an insurance agency is clearly riskier than those minimum risk investments, the required rate of return on an investment in an agency would have to be higher. The buyer wants an extra return as compensation for exposure to risk.

[ii] Additional Return Required

The additional return required for investing in a specific agency is a function of the level of perceived risk in the agency. The higher the buyer perceives the risk to be, the higher the required rate of return. With the capitalization of earnings method, the pro forma pretax earnings are divided by the buyer's required rate of return. Table 18-9 shows an example using the capitalization of earnings method. As with the public company method, the value of the agency's tangible net worth must be added to the value of the business to arrive at total agency value.

[c] Wasting Asset Method

The third method of valuing an agency is to establish a value of the separate assets as they exist at a moment in time. The major asset in any agency is its expirations or renewals. This can be viewed as a 'wasting asset.' In other words, if no new accounts are produced, a certain percentage of accounts are lost each year even under the best of circumstances. Eventually there will be no accounts left in the book.

Most of the studies we have conducted as well as studies by universities, national brokers, and some regional firms seem to arrive at basically the same range of annual loss of business. This range is from 5% to 15% with the average between 7% and 12%.

TABLE 18-9

XYZ AGENCY
CAPITALIZATION OF EARNINGS METHOD

Pro forma pretax earnings of Rical Agency	$ 500,000
Rate of return on minimum risk investments (Rates as of valuation date)	10%
Additional rate of return (Based on agency risk)	12%
Total required rate of return for investing in Rical Agency	22%
Value of operations $500,000/22%	$2,272,727
Less: 45 days' working capital	(150,000)
Total	$2,122,727

The main idea behind this method is that the buyer of an agency is buying a book of business as of a certain day. Each year some of the existing accounts will be lost. Usually these accounts have been replaced by new accounts. However, once the agency is sold, any new accounts are due to the efforts of the new buyer, not the seller. Thus, in determining the value of the book of business, value is based on the earnings (exclusive of selling costs) of the actual business purchased by the buyer. Selling costs are excluded since no new business is being considered. The agency's expenses should only reflect the costs of servicing the existing accounts and not the costs of acquiring new accounts. Additional value is, however, given to the agency's ability to generate new business. This value is a function of new business written and the value determined for all existing accounts.

Table 18-10 shows how this method is calculated. Again, the value of the tangible net worth must be added to determine the total value of the agency.

TABLE 18-10

XYZ AGENCY
WASTING ASSET METHOD

Pro forma annual commissions	$2,500,000
Pro forma pretax profit	500,000
Plus: Selling expense	250,000
Pretax profit exclusive of selling expense	$ 750,000
Annual new business commissions	200,000
Annual attrition rate (lost commissions)	10%
Present value rate	18%
Value of operations	2,815,650
Less: 45 days' working capital	(150,000)
Total profit	$2,665,650

[i] Present Value Discount Rate

The present value of future earnings of the remaining accounts is used because a dollar today is worth more than a dollar a year from now. Also, the inherent risk of the agency requires that a discount be given to the buyer for assuming the risk that future earnings may not be realized. Thus, the present value discount rate is developed similarly to the required rate of return under the capitalization of earnings method and considers both the return on minimum risk investments and the inherent risk of the agency.

[ii] Agency Growth

A common question relating to this method is agency growth. The focus in the wasting asset method is on the existing book of business. Any growth that occurs will occur in the future and, arguably, is not, therefore, relevant to the valuation of existing accounts (i.e., any new business is a result of the buyer's efforts and assumption of risk and therefore the seller need not be compensated for it); however, the seller could argue that the buyer is being provided with the opportunity for future growth and so the seller should be compensated appropriately through additional value attending the going-concern nature of the business. The seller could further argue that to do otherwise would limit value to the present value of the earnings coming from the run-off of the existing accounts and that such value approximates liquidation value. On balance, sound logic mandates recognition of value for new business generation capacity.

[3] Factors in a Valuation

With the knowledge that agency worth is a function of earnings and on quantifiable factors, how is fair market value determined? As a guideline a prospective buyer must consider the following:

1. Prospect for sustainable earnings;
2. Risk factors;
3. Income statement;
4. Balance sheet; and
5. Methodologies for converting these factors into a single value.

Valuing an agency means considering everything because every detail can affect the value. At some point, however, achieving a more precise value may not justify the cost of endless investigation.

[a] Income Statement Considerations

Since value is primarily a function of earnings, the profit-generating capacity of the book of business has to be identified—the income statement.

[i] Pro Forma Adjustments

In a privately owned agency, identifying sustainable profitability requires that certain pro forma adjustments be made to expenses to reflect what the agency's revenues and expenses would be if the firm were run strictly for bottom-line profits by a nonownership management responsible to outside stockholders or owners. This requires adjustment of discretionary, nonrecurring, and nonoperational revenue and expense items.

[ii] Revenue and Expense Adjustments

Examples of items often adjusted are as follows:

- *Owner's compensation.* Owners generally receive a return on investment along with the amount for the actual job being performed. The return on the investment portion of compensation should be removed from the owner's compensation expense, thus adding the same amount to profit and leaving compensation only for the job performed. This adjustment results in the compensation expense reflecting only what would be paid to an outsider who has been hired to manage the business.
- *Asset sale revenues.* These are nonrecurring and should, therefore, be eliminated.
- *Personal travel and entertainment expenses.* These are not related to the ongoing business (i.e., they are nonoperational) and should, therefore, be eliminated.

☐ *Amortization expense of purchased intangibles.* Being a result of a purchase transaction, this expense is deemed nonoperational in nature and, therefore, appropriate for elimination.

Once all pro forma adjustments have been made, the calculated pretax profit of the agency will reflect a realistic and sustainable level of earnings for the agency and can serve as a basis for determining value.

[b] Balance Sheet Considerations

The balance sheet is also an important factor in determining value. All the valuation techniques discussed thus far have dealt primarily with the income statement. Now we will look at some balance sheet considerations.

[i] Tangible Net Worth

The first step in developing tangible net worth is to eliminate from the balance sheet all intangible assets and assets not related to the agency's business. There should also be a corresponding reduction in owner's equity. Assets such as goodwill are intangible assets that have no distinct or identifiable value to buyers. The theory for removing goodwill and other intangibles is that the income statement already includes the earnings generated from these assets. Hence, these assets will be fully recognized and valued by establishing the sustainable earnings stream of the agency. To leave goodwill and other intangibles on the balance sheet and then purchase them as assets would result in a double payment. After the intangibles have been removed, tangible net worth can be determined by subtracting total liabilities from total assets. This number is equal to the owners equity. Tangible net worth is basically the value that would be received if the agency were liquidated and all assets except the book of business were sold.

[ii] A Public Company's Approach

When a public company is looking to buy a private agency, it will want to compare its own balance sheet with that of the prospective seller. The idea is that the shares of stock the company will give away have assets behind them, as well as earning capabilities. The public company is likely to request that for every share of stock it gives you there be an amount of capital value on your balance sheet that is relatively comparable to the public company's.

One way a company may state this is to request a value equal to its own book value per share. For example, the buyer may request that there be $10 of excess book value per share. Therefore, if the seller were to receive 10,000 shares, the buyer will want $10 × 10,000 or

$100,000 in the seller's balance sheet over and above a zero balance base (assets − liabilities = 0).

Another approach might be for a buyer to request forty-five to sixty days' worth of working capital over and above the tangible net worth of the seller. The logic here is that working capital is essential to the production of earnings. The method here is to value the agency based upon earnings and then subtract forty-five to sixty days' working capital from value and add back any excess book value.

The main thrust of this whole issue is that the buyer does not want to put up the working capital for the new agency and will require instead that it be part of the deal. There is an inherent logic in this reasoning. If you visualize the selling agency as a machine to generate profit, a very important part of the machine is the oil and gas that make the machine run. The buyer is not really discounting the value of the seller's agency. If the buyer is a public company, it is saying, in essence, that the company trades in the marketplace at a certain multiple of earnings and that price includes approximately forty-five to sixty days' worth of working capital. Thus, the buyer is only asking that the seller contribute the same amount or to take that amount out of the sale price.

[iii] Amortization of Expirations

An issue closely related to the valuation of an agency that can play a major role in the negotiations of a sale price is that of the amortization of insurance expirations because a special opportunity may exist for a buyer to obtain a tax deduction for amortization of an agency's major asset—its expirations. While the Tax Reform Act of 1986 restricted the applicability of the amortization deduction, it is still available if the transaction is structured properly and is supported with adequate documentation. Generally, the required documentation is a report issued by an independent, qualified industry expert. The report should identify and segregate the value of the individual expirations purchased and establish their limited useful life. Obviously, such a study may be a prerequisite for negotiating a purchase price since the resulting deduction may be a material item in the economics of the transaction.

> ☐ *Separate assets.* Insurance expirations have been viewed as separate assets in the insurance industry for many years. It is commonplace for one agency to sell its expirations (and no other assets) to another agency, often for a substantial price. The fact that expirations are treated as a separate asset that may be purchased and sold is one of the strongest arguments

supporting the availability of an amortization deduction for purchased expirations.

The threshold problem faced by the taxpayer in attempting to amortize purchased expirations is to separate that asset from goodwill. In the most common case in which the taxpayer acquires all the assets of a going concern, an especially difficult burden of proof is needed in separating out the goodwill component from the whole which can be viewed as a "mass asset." Courts have often felt that no part of a mass asset may be amortized since the mass asset will generally remain the same.

☐ *IRS revenue ruling.* In the past, there has been confusion and debate as to whether expirations are part of goodwill, and, therefore, not able to be amortized, or if they are a separate asset with an identifiable useful life. In 1974, the Internal Revenue Service in Revenue Ruling 74-456[1] ruled that if an individual taxpayer could prove that expirations have a value separate and distinct from goodwill and that their useful life can be estimated with reasonable accuracy, then an amortization deduction is allowable. This ruling, however, does not prescribe or suggest any acceptable methodology for the taxpayer to use.

The few court cases since this ruling make it clear that the taxpayer must still sustain the burden of proof to obtain the deduction. The fundamental theme resulting from these cases is that if no effort is made by the taxpayer to segregate the expirations from goodwill in the purchase of an insurance business prior to the purchase, all the intangible assets are considered a mass asset. This was the result in the Chappelle Insurance Service, Inc. v. United States. If, however, sufficient efforts are made to segregate, value, and determine the useful life of the expirations, the taxpayer has a reasonable opportunity to prevail, as in the case of *Richard S. Miller & Sons, Inc. v. United States.*[2]

☐ *Allocation of purchase price.* It should be clear that it is necessary to allocate the purchase price of any agency among the different assets being purchased. This allocation is rarely challenged by the IRS because the buyer and seller generally have opposing interests in the classification of the assets for tax purposes. Thus, the allocation they arrive at can generally be presumed fair and reasonable.

---

[1] 1974-2 C.B. 65.
[2] 75-2 U.S.T.C. ¶ 9784 (Ct. Cl. 1975).

To sustain a deduction for amortization of insurance expirations, the taxpayer must produce evidence that accomplishes the following:

1. *Separates expirations from goodwill.* There are several ways a taxpayer may separate expirations from goodwill. As was mentioned, if the buyer and seller agree on an allocation the IRS will generally accept the value of the expirations. Also, by establishing separate values for all other intangibles, the value of expirations can be obtained as residual. If comparable sales of other expirations are considered, it may be possible to establish a value of those being purchased. Finally, a study can be made of each individual expiration to establish its value using valuation techniques applied by an expert.

It is generally recommended that you use more than one of these methods to support the value of the expiration. It may seem that the effort to list the each account is quite great, but this sort of study can help in achieving the next two requirements.

2. *Establishes that expirations have a limited useful life.* To establish that expirations have a limited useful life, the taxpayer should list all the accounts that are being purchased and prepare an attrition schedule showing the run-off in accounts each year.

3. *Establishes "with reasonable accuracy" the length of useful life in each particular case.* To determine what the useful life of the expirations is, the taxpayer should do a thorough historical analysis of each account to sustain the argument that a finite number of individual expirations was purchased. Insurance expirations follow a distribution that allows quite accurate projections to be made using statistical methods. As a result, the body of purchased expirations can be aged in a way that can be defended in court.

Although the process may seem long and complicated, the benefits of a successful defense of the deduction of amortization of purchased expirations is well worth pursuing. All that is required is good planning to guarantee that the burden of proof has been met.

[4] Conclusion

This section has discussed different ways of determining a fair market value for an insurance agency. Several things must be emphasized here. First, as mentioned earlier, the only real indicator of true market value is an actual selling price. However, the methods discussed can give you an approximate value when you do not want to take your agency to market or give you reasonable expectation of what it might bring when you do go to market.

Second, only under the greatest of coincidences will these or other acceptable methods arrive at the same value. Sometimes the results will be very close; other times they will vary widely. Generally, there are wide value variations for companies with low profitability. The lower the profitability, the greater the differences in calculated values. When doing an actual valuation, the results of some of the methods may be thrown out if it is determined that they clearly do not apply in the case of the agency being valued. This is where professional judgment comes into play.

Third, the values derived from the different methods are never averaged. It is up to the appraiser, based on all the facts, to arrive at a final conclusion as to fair market value. Remember that fair market value presumes that cash or the equivalent will be paid in full as of the valuation date. Actual prices will probably vary with the terms of payment. Generally, the longer it takes to be paid, the higher the price will be.

Finally, it is essential to realize that each agency has its own unique characteristics that must be considered in a valuation. Just as an agency owner suggests to clients that they use a professional to guide them in the complex aspects of insurance coverage, it is very important to have a skilled outside expert do the valuing of your agency. There are also many ways to structure a transaction, giving consideration to such things as tax consequences, estate planning, cash flows, depreciation of expirations, and so forth. For these reasons and for possible IRS scrutiny, it is recommended that you seek professional advice in structuring a sale or contingent transaction.

19

NATURAL RESOURCES

ALEX W. HOWARD[*]

		Page
¶ 19.1	Industry Orientation	19-2
	[1] Basic Valuation Principles	19-3
	[2] Practical Considerations	19-3
	[3] Companies Covered	19-3
¶ 19.2	Oil and Gas Companies	19-3
	[1] Ownership Forms	19-3
	[a] Corporations	19-4
	[b] Partnerships	19-4
	[c] Royalty Trusts	19-4
	[2] Financing Methods	19-4
	[a] Industry Deals	19-5
	[b] Drilling Partnerships	19-5
	[3] Operational Data	19-5
	[a] Reserve Production Profile	19-5
	[b] Reserve Changes and Causes	19-6
	[c] Lifting Costs	19-6
	[d] Finding Costs	19-6
	[e] Prospect Generation	19-6
	[f] Undeveloped Acreage	19-6
	[g] Drilling Record	19-6
	[h] Drilling Rigs	19-6
	[i] Government Regulation	19-7
	[j] Contracts	19-7
	[4] Taxation	19-7
	[5] Accounting	19-8
	[a] Methods	19-8
	[b] Adjusting for Comparability	19-9
	[6] Reserves	19-9
	[a] Petroleum Engineers' Reserve Analysis	19-9
	[i] Proved Reserves	19-10
	[ii] Probable and Possible Reserves	19-10
	[b] SEC Method	19-10

---

[*] ALEX W. HOWARD, CFA, is senior vice president at Lovett Underwood Neuhaus & Webb, Inc., an investment banking firm based in Houston, Texas. The author has spoken on and published numerous articles on financial valuation and mergers and acquisitions.

		[i] Pricing and Volumes	19-10
		[ii] Discount Rate	19-10
	[c]	Petroleum Engineer's Role	19-10
		[i] Reserve Quantities	19-11
		[ii] Pricing Scenarios	19-11
		[iii] Discount Rate	19-11
[7]	Considerations in Selecting Comparables		19-11
	[a]	Methods of Financing	19-11
	[b]	Ownership Form	19-12
		[i] Corporation	19-12
		[ii] Partnership	19-12
	[c]	Location of Reserves or Exploratory Activity	19-12
	[d]	Composition of Assets and Size	19-12
	[e]	Sources of Information	19-12
[8]	Valuation Methods		19-13
	[a]	Break-Up Value (Appraised Net Worth)	19-13
		[i] Reserves	19-13
		[ii] Undeveloped Leases	19-14
		[iii] Drilling Rigs, Well Service Assets, and Pipeline Assets	19-14
		[iv] Liabilities	19-14
	[b]	Financial and Operating Comparisons	19-14
		[i] Operating Data	19-14
		[ii] Financial Data	19-15
	[c]	Minority vs. Controlling Interests	19-15

¶ 19.3 **Coal Companies** 19-15
  [1] Influencing Factors 19-16
  [2] Valuation Methods 19-16
  [3] Taxation 19-16
¶ 19.4 **Timber Companies**................................ 19-17
  [1] Operating vs. Holding Companies 19-17
    [a] Operating Company 19-17
    [b] Holding Company 19-17
  [2] Partnerships 19-17
  [3] Taxation 19-18
¶ 19.5 **Other Extractive Industries** 19-18

¶ 19.1 Industry Orientation

The most predominant, frequently valued, and complex type of company in the natural resource industry is the oil and gas exploration and production company. The primary focus of this chapter will be on the specialized valuation techniques used for appraising this type of company.

[1] Basic Valuation Principles

The value of an individual financial asset is the present value of the future cash flow it generates. The value of a business entity is determined by its earning power, by its asset value, or by some combination of both. Valuators are quick to point out that these variables form the basis for any value and that no specialized industry orientation is needed to value a company or its securities properly. However, certain industries are distinctive due to a variety of factors, including the way they are financed, analyzed, and regulated. The valuation approach must be logical in light of the specific economics in an industry and the way risk and return are assessed by the industry players consummating transactions on a regular basis. The natural resource industry is among the industries with unique features affecting their analysis and method of valuation.

[2] Practical Considerations

It is necessary when analyzing natural resource companies to have at least a minimal understanding of reports engineering and to be able to converse intelligibly with management. Individual projects may be financed by a variety of methods that influence the risk of a company. In addition to financing methods, the different accounting methods available can make financial and operating comparability for oil and gas companies difficult to evaluate. Other factors relating to the specifics of natural resources are government regulation, taxation, and information sources.

[3] Companies Covered

The types of natural resource companies discussed in this chapter include oil and gas, coal, timber, and other extractive industries.

¶ 19.2 Oil and Gas Companies

Oil and gas entities, especially exploration and production companies, are as diverse in their ownership forms, financing methods, taxation, and analysis as almost any other industry an appraiser encounters.

[1] Ownership Forms

Oil and gas entities come in all shapes, sizes, and legal forms, some of which have become prominent only within the last few years. The three basic ownership forms are corporations, partnerships, and royalty trusts.

[a] Corporations

Integrated oil companies, both domestic and international, are normally operated in corporate form, as are most pipeline companies and exploration and production companies. Corporate form enables the entity to retain cash flow for building asset value.

[b] Partnerships

Partnerships have more than one use in the oil and gas universe. Public and private limited partnerships raise funds for drilling prospects, both exploratory and developmental. Income program partnerships acquire producing oil and gas properties. Master Limited Partnerships (MLPs) are a more recent innovation. Rather than being specific financing vehicles for the exploration and development of individual prospects, MLPs generally represent operating companies that choose to operate as publicly traded partnerships in order to distribute cash flow and avoid double taxation. Some exploration and production companies have converted to partnership form or spun off certain reserves into MLPs; pipeline companies also occasionally separated their oil and gas assets in this fashion in the hope of increasing shareholders' value by having the market recognize the value of their oil and gas assets.

[c] Royalty Trusts

Royalty trusts are publicly traded entities representing primarily overriding royalties or net profit interests in properties owned and operated by the sponsoring corporation that created the trust. Their tax treatment is more similar to partnerships than to corporations. Unlike corporations and MLPs, trusts are passive, nonoperating, self-liquidating entities.

[2] Financing Methods

Oil and gas operations are financed at various levels. In addition to financing at the corporate level through public and private offerings of debt and equity, drilling and completion activities may be financed through programs financed by institutional, individual, or industry partners. It is uncommon for an oil and gas company to explore without a partner or partners to share the risk. Bank borrowings, equity, or private and public debt are used to finance the company's portion of expenditures.

[a] Industry Deals

A company that has generated a prospect and secured acreage may bring in one or more partners on a standard industry "third for a quarter" deal, where others supply 100% of the financing for 75% of the profit, and maintain a 25% carried interest, called a "promote." The lessee of the prospect may also farm out this acreage to another oil company in exchange for some net profit interest in the future production.

[b] Drilling Partnerships

Due to investor interest in a risk/reward structure that made "big hits" possible and tax losses a sure thing, public and private drilling partnerships proliferated in the 1970s and early 1980s. Public programs registered with the Securities and Exchange Commission (SEC) usually had smaller unit sizes than private deals and more partners. These partnerships invested in drilling prospects sponsored by an oil and gas company, either exploratory, developmental, or a combination of both. When the economics of exploration and development began to deteriorate and tax rates declined, sponsors formed income programs to purchase developed oil and gas reserves, generating income with minimal focus on tax deductions.

The general structure of these partnerships has been either for the sponsor to promote the investors (e.g., investors put up 95% of the funds for 75% of the cash flow) or for the investors to give the sponsor a "reversionary interest" or "back in" after the limited partners had received some amount equal to or in excess of their original investment.

[3] Operational Data

The factors to be considered in the valuation of a company in the extractive industries, and especially the oil and gas industry, are significantly different from the factors to be considered in the valuation of the average manufacturing or service business.

[a] Reserve Production Profile

Developed properties should be reviewed according to area and drilling costs. Reserve production rates (proved reserves divided by production) can be used to determine the life of reserves. Distinguishing between proved developed and proved undeveloped reserves is important because proved undeveloped reserves have never produced and are thus clearly more speculative; they will also require additional capital to develop.

[b] Reserve Changes and Causes

Whether changes in reserve volumes result from new discoveries, extensions, or revisions affects the quality of existing reserve data. Extensive revisions signal past imprecision in estimating reserve quantities.

[c] Lifting Costs

Lifting costs indicate the potential profitability of existing reserves in the ground. These costs can be compared to industry standards or to the costs of other oil and gas companies.

[d] Finding Costs

Depending upon existing oil and gas prices, the viability of additional exploratory drilling can be assessed.

[e] Prospect Generation

Prospects may be generated by in-house staffs of exploration professionals, geologists, and landmen or by using consulting engineers and a geologist.

[f] Undeveloped Acreage

Acreage is expensive to carry and has a term that varies. There is a market for leases; usually, the company's land manager can help determine the value and potential of such acreage. This can be a significant asset and must be carefully reviewed. Leases are classified by state and by gross and net acres. Value depends on proximity to producing reservoirs, drilling experience, and remaining lease term.

[g] Drilling Record

A company's drilling record may be reviewed by looking at its success rate for exploratory and developmental drilling and comparing this to industry norms.

[h] Drilling Rigs

Depending on the current price and availability of drilling equipment and the method used to finance its purchase, rigs can either increase or decrease the value of a company. When drilling activity is high and the demand for equipment exceeds supply, as happened in the period from 1979 to 1981, rigs add value to an exploration company. Since then, their value has plummeted, and today, they may be worth only a small percentage of their book value.

[i] Government Regulation

Oil prices have been deregulated for a number of years, but there are still complicated regulations governing certain natural gas supplies. In most cases, the current pricing structure, due to the gas deliverability surplus, does not allow for achieving the maximum regulated price under the Natural Gas Policy Act (NGPA) of 1978 even for remaining regulated gas. Some states regulate production rates and developmental drilling. On July 26, 1989, the Natural Gas Wellhead Decontrol Act was signed into law. This Act allows for complete decontrol of natural gas prices by January 1, 1993, and a transition period between the enactment date and the total decontrol date for expiring and terminating contracts. For any oil and gas company, a complete description of existing regulations, both federal and state, can be found in "Item 1. Business" of Form 10-K.

[j] Contracts

Oil and gas are sold in the spot market at posted field prices that fluctuate with supply and demand. Due to the gas surplus, long-term contracts at fixed prices have been reduced in term and have become more flexible. Older "take or pay" contract prices have been reduced by "market-out" clauses that allow for reductions when prices fall. Many pipeline companies have settled such obligations with cash payments, or in some cases, have refused to take the gas despite contractual obligations. Under a recent Federal Energy Regulatory Commission (FERC) rule, pipelines have to serve as common carriers for producers selling gas directly to end users.

[4] Taxation

Working-interest owners of oil and gas property are exempt from the passive-loss rules of the Tax Reform Act of 1986 (TRA '86). Passive income and losses come from enterprises in which the taxpayer does little, if any, actual work. A working interest is generally one that is burdened with the cost of development and operation of an oil and gas property. A working-interest holder has more risk than a limited partner.

Corporations continue to be allowed deductions for intangible drilling costs (IDCs). Independent producers can write off 100% of their IDCs, while integrated producers can write off 70% and amortize the rest over five years. Limited partnerships or Subchapter "S" Corporations (corporations taxed like partnerships) that own working interests are subject to the passive-loss rules. For example, losses of MLPs can only be used to offset other passive income.

The large deferred income taxes of most oil and gas firms result from expensing drilling costs for tax purposes while capitalizing them for financial reporting. These taxes are reduced to differing degrees based upon the accounting method used to reflect the reduced corporate income tax rates. Some companies are hurt by the alternative minimum tax—which has increased preference items and is meant to stop corporations from reporting book income and paying no taxes—and by the repeal of the investment tax credit (ITC). The ITC was available for 15% to 25% of tangible drilling costs.

In addition, the industry maintains percentage depletion for independent producers, which allows depletion based on sales price instead of cost.

[5] Accounting

The Financial Accounting Standards Board (FASB) allows two possible method to determine profit and net worth. The SEC allows a third method in public company disclosures.

[a] Methods

The methods are (1) successful efforts, (2) full cost, and (3) reserve recognition. Accounting for oil and gas company results and understanding reported earnings and cash flow is an extremely difficult process, due primarily to the fact that companies can use different accounting methods. It is ironic that none of these methods directly address one major test of any oil and gas company's performance: where the value is being created by the company through increases in oil and gas reserves.

The oil industry has been debating the merits of the successful-efforts versus the full-cost method of accounting for more than 20 years. Smaller, independent exploration and production companies tend to use full-cost accounting, which favors aggressive drillers, since drilling costs can be capitalized or deferred into the future instead of being charged off against earnings. Earnings and balance sheets will be higher than they will under the alternative method because the expense of dry holes can be capitalized. The older successful efforts method, tends to give a more conservative picture of earnings when companies are drilling. Since the expenses of dry holes can be charged off against earnings as they occur, only the costs of successful wells are capitalized. This method tends to be used by larger producers.

Under the full-cost method, the capitalized cost of oil and gas reserves cannot be higher than the value of the reserves as reported under the SEC method of valuing reserves. The result of falling oil and gas prices in 1986 triggered that cap and forced some companies that were capitalizing dry holes to write down their capitalized pool. Some companies, including Tenneco, Inc., switched to the successful-efforts method, shifting the cost of the dry holes to prior years by restating results.

A number of years ago, the FASB tried to end full-cost accounting and force companies to write off dry holes, but the SEC overruled the board and let both methods continue. The SEC then implemented a third method, reserve-recognition accounting, to indicate whether companies were adding value to their reserves in greater amounts than they were depleting them through production. Due to the unreliability of reserve estimates, the method has not been accepted by the oil and gas industry, but companies can use it as a supplemental calculation.

The debate on appropriate accounting methods will surely continue. One thing is certain, though: the investor and other users of financial statements must be very careful when analyzing the results of oil and gas companies.

[b] Adjusting for Comparability

The following calculations will allow the valuator to compare cash flow from operations using full-cost and successful-efforts accounting methods.

Successful efforts method:
Net income after tax (*successful efforts*)
+ Depreciation, depletion, and amortization
+ Deferred taxes
= Cash flow from operations

Full cost method:
Exploration expenses
+ Dry-hole costs
+ Geological and geophysical costs
+ Lease acquisition
= Cash flow from operations (comparable to full cost)

[6] Reserves

Oil and gas reserves are, paradoxically, the key to evaluating oil and gas companies and, at the same time, very difficult to value.

[a] Petroleum Engineers' Reserve Analysis

A petroleum egineers' reserve analysis must cover a broad range of topics, including those described in the following pages.

[i] Proved Reserves

The classifications represent all proved reserves: proved developed production (PDP), proved developed nonproducing (PDNP), and proved undeveloped (PUD). Reserve definitions are published by the Society of Petroleum Evaluation Engineers.

Implicit in these reserve categories are the different levels of risk of the reliability of the quantities estimated. Producing reserves have clear production records and can be reasonably relied upon. Nonproducing reserves that have never produced or have limited histories are clearly more speculative, as are all PUDs that represent undrilled locations. In the current environment, nonproducing properties represent the potential for future additional reserves but not a large increment of value. As a result, reserve values may be risk adjusted, based on the reserve category.

[ii] Probable and Possible Reserves

These reserves, if computed, are pure speculation and do not deserve consideration as elements of specific value.

[b] SEC Method

All publicly traded oil and gas companies must indicate on Form 10-K, as a disclosure note, the value of their reserves based on a calculation required by the SEC.

[i] Pricing and Volumes

Current prices and costs are held constant, with escalations allowed only for contracts in force. The volumes are based on proved reserves only but include proved undeveloped categories. Capital costs to produce PUDs are included.

[ii] Discount Rate

The discount rate of 10 percent, required by the SEC, is applied to future net revenues of proved reserves based on unescalated prices and expenses, after deducting income taxes at the company's normal rate.

[c] Petroleum Engineer's Role

The function of petroleum engineers is more scientific than financial. As a result, an evaluator must learn how to use reserve reports and what data to rely upon. The credentials of the engineer retained must also be checked.

[i] Reserve Quantities

How much oil and gas is recoverable from a given well? Estimates of reserves are approximations at best and, at worst, are based on sketchy information where the history of the well or field is short or nonexistent.

[ii] Pricing Scenarios

The prices that oil and gas command are based on commodity pricing. Long-term contracts for gas are a thing of the past. The history of the late 1970s and early 1980s has taught us the dangers inherent in arbitrary escalations. The engineer's pricing scenario may be as flawed as anyone else's.

[iii] Discount Rate

This is a financial function and not an engineering question. Engineers discount future net revenues in a matrix of different rates. The appropriate rate must reflect the risk and return characteristics in the same way as any asset valued on an income stream. Future net revenues are after lease operating expenses (LOE), production taxes, windfall profits taxes (WPT), capital expenditures, and royalty payments.

The narrative part of the engineer's report should be reviewed as it assesses the reliability and risk inherent in the projections. The report should distinguish between the different reserve categories. The evaluator should understand the engineering method used. Proved reserve values based on volumetric analysis are riskier than those based on production history.

[7] Considerations in Selecting Comparables

Standard Industrial Classification (SIC) code 1311 is one of the largest SIC categories. Consequently, initial screening will yield a large group of companies for purposes of comparison. The following considerations can help narrow this group to a more appropriate and manageable size.

[a] Methods of Financing

Is company-financing provided by industry deals or by limited partnership? Although, historically, most companies have been financed with at least some limited partnerships, very few have been financed this way recently because the market has not been receptive to oil and gas deals.

[b] Ownership Form

Although cash flow is important when valuing oil and gas entities, asset value may have greater weight depending upon the form of ownership and size of the company.

[i] Corporation

The appraised net worth of a corporation is the primary benchmark in determining its value. The relationship of price to appraised net worth is based on a variety of factors, but the level of cash flow is one of the most important. The cash-flow multiple is important but generally secondary to the discount or premium to appraised net worth.

[ii] Partnership

Since partnerships pass a large percentage of their income to unit holders, cash-flow distributions are the major element of return to investors. The yield to investors is the predominant basis for value as opposed to appraised net worth.

[c] Location of Reserves or Exploratory Activity

The relevance of classifying companies depend upon the regulatory environment and the excitement associated with an exploratory drilling program in a potentially rewarding geological trend (e.g., deep Anadarko gas in early 1980).

[d] Composition of Assets and Size

The existence of other assets—marketable securities, drilling rigs, gas plants, and the percentage of oil versus gas reserves—must be considered in assessing comparability. Depending upon the environment at the valuation date, regulation, supply, demand, and pricing can vary between oil and gas.

[e] Sources of Information

Annual reports to shareholders, SEC disclosure documents (Forms 10-K and 10-Q), and published information sources, including John S. Herold, Inc. (Greenwich, CT), and brokerage company reports should be reviewed.

The quality and uniformity of the information in these reports varies greatly and should not necessarily be taken at face value. Due to the importance of net asset value, some uniform measure of net asset value is necessary. The underlying assumptions and computation methods should be studied because they might not be the same even when tabulated by the same source.

[8] Valuation Methods

The appropriateness of specific valuation methods is related to the type of entity being valued.

[a] Break-Up Value (Appraised Net Worth)

Break-Up value is the primary value indicator in the valuation of exploration and production companies. Integrated companies are more heavily influenced by cash flow. The company being valued may warrant a discount or premium to break up value depending upon a variety of factors, including the following:

- Net cash flow;
- Gross cash flow;
- Asset mix and quality;
- Industry and market conditions;
- Minority versus control value;
- Leverage;
- Management; and
- Reserve replacement.

In this method, the assets on the balance sheet are adjusted to fair market value, and liabilities other than certain deferred items are deducted at face value. This is not a liquidation value per se but more of a going-concern value, with assets at fair market value.

When valuing a minority interest, the desire is to determine break-up value on a consistent basis with comparable companies. If there are current John S. Herold, or brokerage company reports available for comparable companies, they should be consulted. Timing, treatment of various assets, and differences based on the source may not lead to consistent calculation. Consequently, it may be necessary to seek consistency by combining the different sources or by independently determining the values based on consistent application.

[i] Reserves

If the available sources are not consistent, reserves can be taken from the annual reports and Form 10-Ks on the SEC method. Such reserves can be "haircut" or discounted to reflect a higher required rate of return, if appropriate. This, of course, depends on the oil and gas industry environment at the time such determination is made. PUDs have less value than PDP reserves; consequently, the percentage of these reserves to the total should be an item of comparison.

[ii] Undeveloped Leases

Without an independent analysis, net book value (net of reserve for impairments) is a basis for comparability. The value of leases varies according to region, remaining lease term, and oil and gas industry conditions. Recently purchased acreage can be valued at cost, and the company's landman and management can help evaluate older leases.

[iii] Drilling Rigs, Well Service Assets, and Pipeline Assets

These assets are traditionally valued at multiples of average operating cash flow, operating assets, or multiples of revenues. Pipeline assets, generally including gas plants, are normally valued in the range of three to five times cash flow. Other well-service type assets, such as drilling rigs, workover rigs, compressors, and the like, tend to be valued at book value or less, although if write-downs have been inadequate, as reflected by very low levels of cash flow, a multiple of revenues may be more appropriate. Judgment and consistency must be applied because outside appraisals of equipment may not be cost effective.

[iv] Liabilities

While all debt categories should be deducted at face value, deferred taxes have traditionally been viewed as equity and not deducted. If it is clear that they are reversing, some decision must be made as to whether to deduct some portion or reflect the possibility of payment elsewhere in the valuation process (e.g., by increasing any discount from net asset value).

[b] Financial and Operating Comparisons

Based on the specific characteristics of an oil and gas company's operations, certain specific operating and financial ratios and data necessary for analysis and comparison should be computed. Some standard ratios based on accounting data are not very useful for these companies, due to the reporting options previously discussed.

[i] Operating Data

Operating data consist of the following:

- Reserve production ratio (reserves divided by production);
- Average prices received and exposure to price increases or decreases;
- Undeveloped acreage and cost per acre;
- Finding costs;
- Lifting costs; and

- Reserve changes (historical).

[ii] Financial Data

Financial data consist of the following:

- Net asset value composition (percentage of oil to gas);
- Leverage;
- Gross and net (discretionary) cash flow, including debt amortization and required capital expenditures;
- Net profit per unit (sales price less lifting costs); and
- General and administrative costs related to revenues.

[c] Minority vs. Controlling Interests

In both minority- and controlling-interest cases, discounts or premiums may be appropriate based on a review of comparable transactions. In a minority-interest valuation, using a consistently determined break-up value will provide strong quantitative evidence of value because the benchmark is similar for each company. In a controlling-interest valuation, the intrinsic net asset value should be determined based on more specific risk-adjusted asset values. This means trying to be specific, rather than merely consistent, as to asset values. In either way, conclusions on this basis should be checked by relating value to cash flow as a conformation of reasonableness. Ultimately, the 100% value of an independent oil and gas exploration and production company is equal to the fair market value of assets less liabilities adjusted up or down, depending upon net cash flow position.

In merger and acquisition valuation, cash flow should be modified for reductions in corporate overhead and lease operating expenses and, where appropriate, for savings achieved from the elimination of duplicate functions.

Many merger analyses include the price paid in terms of dollars per equivalent barrel of oil in the ground. In this analysis, the value of the transaction (both equity plus debt less other assets) is divided by the quantity of oil and gas. Gas is adjusted to equivalent barrels at the rate of 6 mcf (thousand cubic feet) per barrel of oil. This equivalence is based on the relative BTU content of oil versus gas. Because companies have different production rates, reserve lives, and lifting costs, this analysis has limited, if any, use as an economic or analytical tool.

¶ 19.3 Coal Companies

There are significant differences between oil and gas companies and coal and other extractive companies. Although some oil and gas reserves are long-lived, peak production generally exists for a relatively short period and then declines throughout the remainder of life. Very few, if any, "elephant" reservoirs remain to be discovered. Consequently, the primary thrust of oil and gas companies (especially exploration and production companies) is to find reserves to replace production. Coal is generally a long-lived resource, often sold under long-term contracts.

[1] Influencing Factors

For purposes of comparison and analysis, the following factors are relevant:

- *Type of coal*. Stream coal and metallurgical coal have different end users, price, preparation, and demand characteristics.
- *Contracts*. Much coal is sold under contract. Duration, cancellation clauses, and price adjustment factors should be studied.
- *Transportation*. Transportation costs are a substantial factor in competition and economic distribution capability.

From an analytical standpoint, the reserve production ratio, production costs per ton, and gross profit per ton should be reviewed.

[2] Valuation Methods

For minority-interest valuations, price/earnings ratios, dividends yields, and market price/book value rations are appropriate. Asset values are not normally available. For controlling-interest valuations, net asset value, discounted cash flow, and price/earnings ratios for comparable control transactions are appropriate.

[3] Taxation

TRA '86 includes the following provisions relating to hard minerals:

- *Exploration costs*. Under the straight-line method, 30% of corporate exploration and development costs are recovered over five years. Foreign mining costs can be recovered over a ten-year straight-line amortization schedule or, at the taxpayer's election, on a cost-depletable basis.
- *Depletion*. TRA '86 generally retains existing rules governing percentage depletion of hard minerals. However, for corporations, the reduction in excess coal and iron ore depletion is increased from 15%-20%.
- *Gains on mining interests*. TRA '86 requires recapture of all expensed mining exploration and development costs (to the extent not included in income upon reaching the producing

stage) plus depletion deductions that reduced the property's basis. The hard-mineral provisions generally are effective for costs or production after December 31, 1986.

¶ 19.4 Timber Companies

As in the case of all natural resource companies, asset quality and value is the key to the valuation of timber companies.

[1] Operating vs. Holding Companies

The analysis and evaluation of timber companies depends on whether the company is an operating forest products company or a holding vehicle for timber assets.

[a] Operating Company

Forest products companies are operating companies that add value to raw timber by producing a variety of products. Their value is looked upon more in terms of future cash flows than underlying asset values. Many brokerage firms publish estimates of the value of forest products companies' underlying assets, restated net worth, and the relationship of market price to appraised net worth (equity adjusted for the market value of assets). These companies sell at discounts, sometimes extreme discounts from that appraised net worth, especially on a minority-interest basis. The weighting of assets value increases in importance when a controlling interest is being valued.

[b] Holding Company

Holding companies are firms that hold timber assets and may have a sawmill but do not produce consumer or industrial products; they may even let others cut the timber for them. These firms tend to have relatively low cash flow and should be viewed as asset plays (i.e., they have values closely tied to the value of their underlying assets as opposed to cash flow). Consequently, value, even on a minority-interest basis, is based primarily on discounting from net asset value.

[2] Partnerships

As in the case of energy companies, forest products companies have discovered MLPs as a method of boosting the value of their own shares and as a takeover defense. As with the MLP units for the energy companies, these are valued on a yield basis, providing a combination of cash and tax benefits.

[3] Taxation

Under Section 631(a) of the Internal Revenue Code, timber companies were able to receive capital gains treatment on income generated from cutting timber that met the prescribed holding period. The new tax law conforms the capital gains treatment for individuals and corporations (i.e., there is no distinction between ordinary income and capital gains).

¶ 19.5 Other Extractive Industries

The leading "other extractive industries" include companies engaged in all types of mining, including gold, silver, and copper. Companies in this group are in a pure-commodity business characterized by spot market pricing and highly fluctuating prices. Changing technologies and industrial demand, worldwide supply-demand conditions, and, in some cases, speculative hedging control the prices.

It is difficult to postulate general rules for valuing companies engaged in these extractive industries, other than by exercising due diligence in assessing their potential for profitability based on the production costs and their operating and financial leverage.

20

PROFESSIONAL PRACTICES

RALPH ARNOLD AND SHANNON P. PRATT*

		Page
¶ 20.1	**Distinctive Characteristics**	20-2
	[1] Cash-Basis Accounting	20-3
	[2] Unaudited Financial Statements	20-3
	[3] Personal Nature	20-4
	[4] Intertwined Practice and Professional Goodwill	20-4
	[5] Comparative Transaction Data Dependent on Private Sources	20-5
¶ 20.2	**The Balance Sheet**	20-5
	[1] Accounts Receivable	20-5
	[a] Aging of Receivables	20-6
	[b] Actual Payment History	20-7
	[2] Work-in-Process Inventory	20-8
	[a] Fees Based on Time	20-8
	[b] Contingent Fees	20-8
	[3] Supplies	20-9
	[4] Prepaid Expenses	20-9
	[5] Equipment	20-9
	[6] Leasehold Improvements	20-10
	[7] Actual and Contingent Liabilities	20-10
	[a] Accounts Payable	20-10
	[b] Accrued Liabilities	20-11
	[c] Deferred Liabilities	20-11
	[d] Long-Term Debt	20-12
	[e] Lease Obligations	20-12
	[f] Contingent Liabilities	20-13
¶ 20.3	**Normalized Earnings**	20-13
	[1] Nonrecurring Income and Expenses	20-13
	[2] Extraneous Income and Expenses	20-13

---

* RALPH ARNOLD is senior valuation analyst at Willamette Management Associates, Inc. in Portland, Oregon. SHANNON P. PRATT, CFA, FASA, DBA, is president of Willamette Management Associates, Inc. in Portland, Oregon. Mr. Pratt has also written two books on business valuation: *Valuing a business: The Analysis and Appraisal of Closely Held Companies* (2d ed. 1989), and *Valuing Small Businesses and Professional Practices* (1986). This chapter was adapted from various chapters of *Valuing Small Businesses and Professional Practices*.

	[3]	Change in Outlook for Income and Expenses	20-14
¶ 20.4		**Practice Goodwill and Professional Goodwill**	20-14
	[1]	Practice Goodwill	20-14
	[2]	Professional Goodwill	20-14
¶ 20.5		**Elements of Goodwill in Purchases and Sales**	20-15
	[1]	Expected Future Earnings	20-15
	[2]	Level of Competition	20-16
	[3]	Referral Base	20-16
	[4]	Types of Patients and Clients	20-16
	[5]	Work Habits of the Practitioner	20-16
	[6]	Fee Schedules	20-17
	[7]	Practice Location	20-17
	[8]	Employees of the Practice	20-17
	[9]	Marketability of the Practice	20-18
¶ 20.6		**Elements of Goodwill in Divorce Valuations**	20-18
	[1]	Practitioner's Age and Health	20-19
	[2]	Demonstrated Past Earning Power	20-19
	[3]	Reputation for Judgment, Skill, and Knowledge	20-19
	[4]	Comparative Professional Success	20-19
	[5]	Nature and Duration of Practice	20-20
¶ 20.7		**Value of the Practice**	20-20
	[1]	Valuation Methods	20-20
		[a] Excess Earnings Method	20-21
		[i] Earnings Levels	20-21
		[ii] Capitalization Rates	20-22
		[b] Capitalization of Earnings Method	20-23
		[c] Multiple of Revenues Method	20-23
	[2]	Complete Value	20-24
¶ 20.8		**Summary**	20-24

Unlike other businesses in which many different events could necessitate a valuation, generally only two occurrences require an appraisal of a professional practice: the sale of the practice or an interest in the practice and the distribution of assets in a divorce.

Typically, the valuation of a professional practice is a two-step process. The first step is determination of the net tangible asset value and the second step is the determination of intangible asset value.

¶ 20.1 Distinctive Characteristics

Many valuation analysts consider professional practices to be in a completely different category than other equities. Although there are substantial differences between professional practices and other businesses, the basic characteristics of "what makes a business" characterize professional practices as well. For that reason, the basic tenets of business valuation are also used in professional practice valuation. The appraiser then needs to recognize the major differences between a professional practice and other types of businesses and how those differences influence the value of the practice.

[1] Cash-Basis Accounting

Businesses that report income only as it is received and expenses only as they are paid are said to be on a "cash basis of accounting." The "accrual basis of accounting" records revenues as they are earned and expenses as they are incurred. For example, accrual-basis balance sheets generally disclose amounts held in trade accounts receivable, even though they have not actually been received and expenses in trade accounts payable, even though they have not actually been paid. On the other hand, these line items usually do not appear in the balance sheets of businesses using the cash basis of accounting; they will be entered only after they are actually received or paid.

Generally accepted accounting principles hold that the accrual method accounting is more reliable in reporting the financial results of a business. However, the cash basis of accounting is not unusual for small businesses; almost all professional practices, large or small, use this method of accounting for tax purposes. Only a very small percentage of professional practices prepare financial statements using accrual accounting. This means that professional practice balance sheets will generally not disclose all assets and liabilities of the business at any one time. The income statement will not reflect the period's production, but only the collections received and expenses paid during the year. Because of the preponderance of cash-basis accounting in professional practices, most databases disclosing financial results of professional practices are strongly weighted with practices reporting cash-basis financial results.

[2] Unaudited Financial Statements

Very few professional practices have audited, or even reviewed, financial statements because of the nature of professional practices. Audited or reviewed statements are generally prepared for the information of nonparticipating owners or creditors of a company. Most professional organizations, such as the American Bar Association and the American Medical Association, forbid nonprofessionals or retired professionals from owning an equity interest in a professional practice, and professional practices ordinarily do not need large amounts of capital to operate. Consequently, most professional practices have no "outside" equity owners or creditors, thereby eliminating the need for audited and reviewed statements.

Audited and reviewed statements are more common in large professional practices with many owners because the owner/practitioners employ administrators to run the business end of the practice. Audited or reviewed financial statements may be prepared because of the size of the practice and because the practitioners are removed from the administration of the practice.

[3] Personal Nature

Professional practices are service businesses that depend on the people providing the service. Patients or clients generally work with one member of the professional staff, even of a very large practice, and develop a personal relationship with that practitioner. Of course, the importance of that relationship to the client's continued patronage differs in different types of professional practices. For example,, psychiatric services are based so heavily on the trust between psychiatrist and patient that the personal nature of the practice is extremely important to its value. On the other hand, although there is an element of trust built between an optometrist and patient, personal relationships are not extremely important compared to other factors that influence value (such as practice, location, number of eye prescriptions on file, and so forth).

[4] Intertwined Practice and Professional Goodwill

Goodwill value is the result of earnings associated with the professional practice, which, in turn, result from many different factors associated with both the practice and the practitioner. Generally, earnings resulting from the practice's location, capital structure, employees, advertising, and so forth produce what is called *practice goodwill*. On the other hand, earnings that result from the practitioner's individual skills, reputation, personality, and so forth produce a value usually referred to as *professional goodwill*. Unfortunately, it is easier to understand the distinction between practice and professional goodwill than to measure the value of each because they are intertwined. When starting a practice, the practitioner's individual reputation is of primary importance. However, as the practice grows and adds new practitioners, it tends to develop its own goodwill, while at the same time each practitioner develops personal goodwill. Generally, the smaller the practice, the more its goodwill value is professional, and the larger the practice, the more its goodwill is associated with the practice as a whole.

[5] Comparative Transaction Data Dependent on Private Sources

Often the best evidence of the value of a business is the market multiples of comparable publicly traded companies. However, because professional practices are not publicly traded there are not readily available public market multiples. Nevertheless, the appraiser cannot ignore valuation methods based on comparative transactions simply because there is no public data. The analyst must develop sources of information on private transactions. Obviously the information provided by such sources will never be as accurate or complete as information that can be gathered from public sources.

¶ 20.2 The Balance Sheet

As already mentioned, professional practices tend not to have audited or reviewed financial statements. Also, because so many professional practices are owned by a sole practitioner, the results of their operations may vary for personal reasons, rather than based on business decisions. For this reason, financial statement analysis and adjustment are extremely important in the valuation of professional practices. Although all asset, debt, income, and expense categories need to be analyzed, certain line item almost always deserve the analyst's attention.

[1] Accounts Receivable

The most valuable tangible asset of many practices is accounts receivable, representing a promise of a cash payment in a relatively short period of time. Moreover, the practitioner's efforts in generating this asset have already been expended other than the efforts required to collect the bill. Therefore, accounts receivable are generally considered a very liquid asset. However, accounts receivable are often not shown on the cash-basis balance sheets of professional practices. Therefore, it is necessary to determine the value of accounts receivable in order to include them in the value of the professional practice. Although there are several ways of keeping records of accounts receivable, gross receivables at any given date are easily determined from the day sheets or accounts receivable journals of most practices.

One category of accounts receivable that may be overlooked is those that have been turned over to a collection agency or attorney. Many times, when an account is assigned to collection, the amount assigned to collection is eliminated from the accounts receivable balance. Therefore, the analyst should be aware that accounts assigned for collection may have some (albeit little) value that is not reflected in the accounts receivable balances shown or calculated.

Having determined the gross value of the accounts receivable, the appraiser must adjust for uncollectible and slow-paying accounts. The two most common methods for estimating uncollectible accounts are as follows:

1. *Accounts receivable aging*—discounting the accounts on the basis of how long past due they are; and

2. *Actual payment history*—analyzing the payment trends of the specific practice and whether the trend is for more or fewer write-offs.

[a] **Aging of Receivables**

The appraiser needs either to acquire or to create an accounts receivable aging schedule showing the total accounts outstanding as of a particular time and how long since the account was billed. Thus, the schedule categorizes accounts as current, 30 days past due, 31-60 days past due, and so forth. This schedule indicates to the appraiser how diligently the practice has collected accounts in the past. Since older accounts are not as valuable as current receivables, the analyst usually discounts older receivables by a larger percentage than more current receivables. However, although this method generally gives a correct estimate of accounts receivable, certain caveats should make the appraiser cautious about using it to estimate uncollectible receivables:

- Some clients may have been slow to pay historically but do pay eventually.

- Some clients may have arranged to pay off their accounts over an extended period of time, and, even though their balance is shown as past due, their payments are actually current.

- A portion of some client's bills may be in dispute; when the disagreement is resolved, the undisputed portion will be paid (along with the disputed portion that the client agrees to pay).

- The amount due will be paid by a government agency or insurance carrier. Because all the paper work required to receive payment is not yet submitted, the payment may be past due when in fact it will be paid as soon as the practice fulfills its obligations.

Obviously, these types of accounts can be so prevalent that the entire method of estimating uncollectible accounts is rendered useless. However, even in these circumstances, the analyst still should have an aging of receivables to judge the collection efficiency of the practice.

[b] Actual Payment History

The second method of estimating the reserve for uncollectible accounts receivable analyzes the practice's individual collection history. This method compares accounts receivable written off during a period to the billings generated during the same period. The appraiser should request a schedule of the practice's charges and collections over a period of three to five years. This schedule would show the following information:

- Monthly patient charges;
- Monthly collections on accounts;
- Monthly debit adjustments to receivables (a debit adjustment adds to the value of total accounts receivable; generally, a debit adjustment occurs because a client or patient has overpaid on an account, causing a negative receivable balance for the patient; when the practitioner refunds the money, accounts receivable are debited to eliminate the negative balance);
- Monthly credit adjustments to receivables (a credit adjustment reduces the value of total accounts receivable; generally, a credit adjustment occurs when an account is determined not to be collectible and is written off); and
- Month-end accounts receivable balance for each month.

From these data, the charges, collections, and net adjustments can be totaled for the entire period examined and for each fiscal year. In this way, the appraiser determines the actual percentage of charges that are never collected and, by analyzing the trends for the fiscal years, can determine if the percentage of uncollectible accounts are increasing, declining, or remaining the same.

The problem with computing the percentage of historical net adjustments to billings is that if a significant number of clients pay immediately and are not billed for services, the total charges reflect not only accounts receivable but also cash transactions. Including these cash transactions in accounts receivable tends to artificially reduce the percentage of historical write-offs. Under these circumstances, the percentage of immediate cash payments on account should be considered in the calculation of historic write-offs.

Many practices "house-clean" their accounts at the end of a fiscal year, writing off the ones they consider uncollectible. The appraiser should be aware if a house-cleaning has occurred so that he does not overestimate uncollectible accounts receivable after the "house-cleaning" date.

Because accounts receivable can represent a significant value compared to other asset values of the practice, the appraiser needs to spend adequate time and effort to determine the gross value of the receivables, as well as the value of the net receivables. The amount of work involved cannot be adequately described in this chapter other than the general procedures that should be followed.

[2] Work-in-Process Inventory

Many professional practices, even those recording accounts receivable on their financial statements, have unrecorded assets for work that has been performed but not yet billed. Typically this asset, known as unbilled work in process, can be found in professional practices that bill for time spent or for which the fee is contingent on the successful outcome of efforts expended by the practice.

[a] Fees Based on Time

Accounting practices and many types of legal practices bill according to the amount of time spent on the client's case. There is generally a delay between when the time is actually spent on the case and the billing date. Therefore, billable services may not be billed (or included in accounts receivable) as of the valuation date, even though there is a client obligation to pay this amount. The appraiser should be aware of this characteristic. In such a case, time records generated between the latest billing prior to the valuation date and the valuation date should be obtained as well as an estimate of how much billable time is generally written off. This billable time may yet be adjusted and billed and then written off as uncollectible. Therefore, even after the value of the work in process has been determined, the analyst must subtract discounts for amounts never billed and amounts never collected from the gross value of the work-in-process inventory.

[b] Contingent Fees

Many legal practices (especially those involved in personal injury work) bill for their services only if the plaintiff receives money for damages. Often the appraiser of this type of practice finds a large contingent asset. Obviously, it is probably beyond the appraiser's capabilities to judge the likelihood of a successful settlement or award. If only a few cases involved this type of contingency, it is usually best for the appraiser not to value the asset but to recognize that it may have value and to recommend that the appraisal be adjusted for the results of the contingency upon its the ultimate resolution.

If, on the other hand, contingent fees represent such a large portion of the practice's assets that an appraisal would be meaningless without them, the appraiser must establish their value. If the practice has a history of contingent fee cases, the appraiser may use its historical averages. First an inventory of the hours spent on each contingency case currently pending is taken and an average hourly rate realized on past contingent cases that were resolved prior to the valuation date is calculated. Using these figures, the appraiser can apply the hourly rate realized on resolved contingent cases to hours on currently pending cases.[1]

[3] Supplies

Professional practices typically expense supplies as they are purchased, regardless of how long they may be on hand before being used. Therefore, at the valuation date there is almost always an inventory of supplies, whose value varies according to the type of professional practice. The office supplies of a CPA firm, for example, have a very small value compared to the inventory of glasses frames of an optometric practice.

If a practice does not have substantial value in its inventory, the appraiser can review the prior year's supplies purchases to estimate the value of supplies on hand; a detailed catalog of items in inventory is not needed. If there is to be a separate equipment appraisal, that appraiser might be requested to value the supplies as well. Regardless of the method of determining or estimating the value, the business appraiser ought to check the supplies on hand.

[4] Prepaid Expenses

Many types of expenses are prepaid, such as insurance, rent, dues and subscriptions, and other services. As of a particular date, these services are assets of the practice because they will be received in the future. Depending on the type of practice and the types of prepayments, these assets can be substantial. Consider, for example, a physician who pays the following year's malpractice premium of $50,000 on December 30. If the valuation date is December 31, the analyst must recognize the prepaid malpractice insurance as an asset equal in value to the amount paid by the physician one day earlier.

[5] Equipment

As was true of supplies, the amount and value of equipment necessary to operate a practice depends very much on the type of practice. A general dentistry practice generally has a large amount of equipment, and a psychiatric practice relatively little. If there is a large value in equipment, if it is very specialized, or if there are antiques among the practice's assets, the business appraiser should request an

---

[1] A more complete discussion of this method can be found in Arnold, "Putting a Value on Future Interests," *Family Advocate*, Summer 1984, at 32-36, 42.

appraisal of the equipment (or antiques) before completing the appraisal of the practice as a whole.

The equipment appraiser should be chosen carefully. A used equipment salesperson is sometimes engaged to value equipment instead of a qualified equipment appraiser, but there is an inherent bias in a salesperson. Generally, used equipment salespeople value equipment based upon what they would pay for it if they were to remove it from the premises and resell it. In other words, they provide a liquidation value for the equipment, not its in-place going concern value.

Even an equipment appraiser values the equipment, the financial appraiser also needs to examine it. Often equipment that is still being used in the practice has been fully depreciated and (incorrectly) removed from the financial records. If the appraiser relies solely on the equipment schedule in the financial statements, some fully depreciated but still valuable pieces of equipment could be missed in the appraisal.

[6] Leasehold Improvements

Another important asset is the leasehold improvements of the practice. During the appraiser's tour of the practice office, attention should be paid to the condition of the improvements—in other words, how well the office is packaged. If the leasehold improvements are in good condition, meet current styles, and have been fully depreciated on the books, a value needs to be placed on these improvements, giving consideration to the estimated time that the practice can remain in the facilities.

[7] Actual and Contingent Liabilities

The appraiser needs to consider not only items that add to the value of the practice, but also items that either reduce its value or reduce the proceeds that would be realized on its value.

[a] Accounts Payable

Since cash-basis account does not reflect bills that remain unpaid at the end of a period, the appraiser needs to calculate the value of bills payable at the valuation date. There are two basic methods for estimating accounts payable. The first requires examination of the practice's invoices and checks; the second is less accurate but provides a reasonable estimate of accounts payable with less voluminous field work.

Under the first method, the appraiser reviews all unpaid invoices at the valuation date. If field work is done substantially after the appraisal date, the appraiser should request all canceled checks written during a reasonable period of time after the valuation date, along with corresponding invoices. With this information, the appraiser can determine how much money the practice owed as of the appraisal date.

The second method is not as accurate but can give a reasonable estimate of payables at a particular date. The appraiser begins with the total expenses shown on the practice's income statement for the prior year. From that amount expenses that do not belong with accounts payable are subtracted—those payable immediately (such as salaries), those paid in advance (such as depreciation charges), and those shown as payables elsewhere (such as pension expense or payroll tax expense). The appraiser then considers the practice's regular bill-paying procedures, such as how often it pays and how long it holds the bills before paying them, to calculate the estimated accounts payable at the valuation date.

[b] Accrued Liabilities

Expenses allocated to a prior period but not yet due to be paid are called accrued expenses. A good example would be a promissory note that allowed for yearly interest payments each June 30. On December 31, even though payment is not due for another six months, interest expense has accrued for the first six months and should be reflected on the balance sheet as accrued interest payable. Other expenses that may to be accrued include salaries, bonuses, and taxes.

[c] Deferred Liabilities

These types of liabilities fall into three general categories: deferred revenues, deferred expenses, and deferred taxes.

Deferred revenues represent fees collected for services not yet performed. An obstetric practice is likely to have this kind of liability, even if it is not reflected on the balance sheet. Often, expectant parents pay the obstetrician in advance for the prenatal care and delivery of the child. Although the obstetrician may record these fees as income when received, a portion of them are actually for future services. Therefore, the appraiser needs to establish what percent of total fees are for future services and show this amount as deferred revenue (a liability account on the balance sheet), reducing owner's equity by an equal amount.

Deferred expenses are relatively unusual. One example might be deferred rent. A landlord may offer several months of free rent in return for a tenant's signing a long-term lease. This situation would warrant a liability account for deferred rent because the tenant could theoretically have negotiated a lease for the same period of time at a lower monthly rent without accepting the free rent, even though the total payments under each option would be equal. From an appraiser's viewpoint, the deferred rent expense is not necessarily an actual expense but is merely a balancing account for accounting purposes.

For this reason, it would normally be removed from the balance sheet, with an increase of a like amount to the owner's equity account.

Deferred taxes usually occur because of the difference in timing between recognition of income or expense for two different accounting systems for the same practice. For example, the practice may use straight-line depreciation on its own financial statements to reflect more accurately economic depreciation, but it might use accelerated depreciation on tax returns. The result of using these two procedures would be to show more income on the financial statements and less on the income tax returns. The amount of deferred income taxes on the financial statements is equal to the difference between the income taxes actually paid and what taxes would have been if based on the higher income as shown on the financial statements.

For the appraiser, the deferred taxes account may or may not reflect a true liability. If the practice rarely purchases new equipment, the depreciation for tax purposes will ultimately be less than for financial statement purposes, consequently showing more income on the tax returns than on the financial statements. In that case, the taxes actually paid in future years will be higher than taxes shown due on the financial statements, which means that the deferred taxes are an actual liability. In that case, the appraiser needs to recognize these deferred taxes as a debt that will ultimately need to be paid. On the other hand, if the practice continually buys new equipment, the financial statements could always show greater profits than the tax returns. In that case, the appraiser could conclude that deferred taxes will never be paid in the foreseeable future and could therefore remove them from the balance sheet liabilities.

[d] Long-Term Debt

In professional practices, the two most common reasons for long-term debt to be shown on the balance sheet are that the practice is financing the purchase of fixed assets or that a former practitioner is being bought out of the practice and the practice is making the payments. The appraiser should determine why the long-term debt occurred and get copies of the debt instruments.

[e] Lease Obligations

The appraiser should always obtain copies of all lease obligations of the practice. To know the future payments on all leases as well as terms of the leases for the practice's offices.

[f] Contingent Liabilities

Contingent liabilities are debts that may be incurred, depending on some future event. A good example would be a lawsuit against the practice not covered by insurance. Obviously, the appraiser needs to inquire about such potential liabilities.

¶ 20.3 Normalized Earnings

As in any operating business, the practice's expected future earnings are the most important factor in determining its value. Developing a "normalized earnings base" enables the appraiser to look at the practice's earnings as a potential buyer might. Normalized earnings use past earnings as a starting point, but they are adjusted to remove the effect of unusual events or accounting treatments. The appraiser's adjustments to earnings generally fall into three basic categories: nonrecurring income and expenses, extraneous income and expenses, and a change in outlook for income and expenses at the valuation date.

[1] Nonrecurring Income and Expenses

If certain income or expenses shown on the practice's financial statements were either extraordinary or the result of discontinued services, the appraiser must adjust past earnings to reflect current expectations based on current facts. Extraordinary income could come from a gain on the sale of assets outside the ordinary course of business or a large one-time contract. Other types of nonrecurring earnings include earnings from other practice locations that have been abandoned within the relevant accounting period(s) or income received from a service the practice no longer provides. Nonrecurring expenses might be associated with closing down the abandoned practice location, expenses associated with moving to a new practice location, or the large legal/accounting expenses associated with a tax audit. Obviously, many types of income and expenses fall into this category, which means that the appraiser needs to know the history of the practice as well as to analyze the financial statements for aberrations.

[2] Extraneous Income and Expenses

Aberrations in earnings can result from income included in the practice's income statements that is really not generated by the activities of the practice, or, alternatively, expenses that are not necessary to the operations of the practice. Extraneous income might include interest income; often, professional practices maintain investment accounts that are not necessary to the practice operations. In this case, the value of investments should be removed from the value of the practice, and, correspondingly, the income from these investments should be removed from the income stream of the practice. (If the investments are part of the property being valued, their value should be added to the value of the practice as an operating entity.) Extraneous expenses might include compensation or perquisites of the owner that are above what is necessary to the business operations. Many times extraneous expense or income takes the form of above- or below-market rental payments for the facility on a lease between the practice and the practitioner. Generally, rental expense needs to be adjusted to fair market value—that is, what unrelated parties would be likely to negotiate.

[3] Change in Outlook for Income and Expenses

Even if the nonrecurring income and expenses are removed and extraneous income and expenses eliminated, the resulting income figure still may not provide an accurate reflection of normalized earnings. As an example, if the appraiser learned that at the valuation date the physician engaged in family practice had just joined a health maintenance organization and fees were to be reduced by 25%, it would be necessary to adjust past earnings to reflect the new economic climate.

Obviously, normalized earnings can look quite different from any earnings previously reported. It should not alarm the analyst if they do, because, if the adjustments were made correctly, the normalized earnings will reflect more accurately the future earnings of the practice than will the past reported earnings of the practice.

¶ 20.4 Practice Goodwill and Professional Goodwill

In a professional practice, there are generally two types of goodwill: practice goodwill (sometimes referred to as business goodwill) and professional goodwill (sometimes referred to as personal goodwill). Practice goodwill is the goodwill associated with the entity as a whole while professional goodwill is associated with the individual.

[1] Practice Goodwill

Practice goodwill is specifically an asset of the practice entity and, therefore, is not really different from the goodwill held by any other business. Such elements as practice location, employment agreements with employees, client/patient lists, and so forth would be instrumental in developing and maintaining practice goodwill.

[2] Professional Goodwill

Although a professional practice does not possess personal goodwill, the practitioner(s) may have personal goodwill. A certain portion of the practitioner's clients or patients may be the result of personal reputation or a comfortable relationship, regardless of the professional practice; thus, professional goodwill generates earnings for the practice. If the practitioner were suddenly to leave the practice, much of the income generated from these personal clients and patients would probably leave as well.

The sale and transfer of professional goodwill is very difficult because it is so personal to the individual; however, there are methods by which a portion of this professional goodwill can be transferred into practice goodwill. The transfer of client trust and respect from seller to buyer requires the cooperation of both buyer and seller. Their efforts would include at least a letter of announcement from the seller to current clients, informing them that the buyer is taking over their cases and that the buyer has the qualifications and expertise to handle their needs. Another method to help transfer this personal goodwill would be to sell the practice to an associate after the associate has spent a period of time gradually taking on the client cases.

Nevertheless, it may be impossible to sell professional goodwill. Hospital-based as opposed to office-based physicians would find it very difficult to sell their professional goodwill. Also, practitioners who do not have regular clients or patients but who depend on referrals for one-time service, may have a difficult time selling their professional goodwill. Many state bar associations prohibit the sale of attorneys' goodwill, thereby nullifying its sale, even if it could be transferred.

¶ 20.5 Elements of Goodwill in Purchases and Sales

Goodwill is elusive and hard to define, generated by so many different factors and combinations of factors that it is impossible to list them all. If it is to have any value in the sale of a practice, goodwill must be transferable, and many elements of a professional practice can cause transferable goodwill to exist. Several factors dominant in determining the existence and value of practice and personal goodwill for professional practices are as follows.

[1] Expected Future Earnings

Like other business enterprises, one of the biggest factors contributing to goodwill value in a professional practice is the level of earnings. Although generally the higher the earnings, the more goodwill exists in the enterprise, an abundance of earnings does not inherently indicate an abundance of goodwill, nor does a dearth of earnings inherently indicate its lack. In judging the existence and value of goodwill based on the level of earnings, the appraiser should be sure to know the causes of the earnings level before concluding a value. High earnings may result from the professional's skills, reputation, and efficiencies or from working longer hours and seeing more clients per day.

Like goodwill itself, earnings do not occur by themselves, but because of other factors.

[2] Level of Competition

Because of the shortage of physicians in this country approximately twenty to thirty years ago, a physician who had met the educational requirements and received a license could hang up a shingle and begin seeing patients during the first week of practice. Because it was so easy to start a profitable medical practice, there was little market for their sale. Medical schools responded to the shortage by graduating more physicians, and the shortage was eliminated in most parts of the country, followed by an oversupply of physicians in many places.

It is not as easy to start a successful practice as it was at that time; in fact, it is economically infeasible in many areas. For that reason, established medical practices in some areas of the country are selling at prices more attractive to the seller (compared to several years ago), because new physicians are seeking to associate with established practices or to buy them outright. Obviously, as the demand for established practices has increased, so, too, has their value. In general, as competition increases in an area, the goodwill value of existing professional practices also increases.

[3] Referral Base

Since the sources of referrals are a key characteristic of a professional practice, it is natural that they should also have a profound effect on the value of goodwill. A practice whose referrals come from a large base of current patients and clients will generally have more goodwill value than one that relies on referrals from a relatively small client base or from other professionals.

[4] Types of Patients and Clients

The appraiser should know the types of clients who patronize the practice and why. Estimates should be made of how many are seen each day, how many new clients seek the practice's services for the first time during a time period and how many cease to do so, and whether the practice depends on any particular client or specific group of clients for a significant portion of its income. In general, the more diverse and numerous the client/patient base, the higher the goodwill value.

[5] Work Habits of the Practitioner

Business and practice owner/operators generally work long hours. However, some are willing to work longer hours than others. A practice that requires eighty hours a week of a practitioner's time will not be worth as much per dollar of income to a purchaser as one that requires only fifty hours per week. Different work habits also can affect the value. As an example, some dentists like to spend time with each patient, while others prefer to schedule several patients at a time and delegate more of the procedures to assistants. Obviously, a dentist of the more "personal" type considering purchasing a practice owned by one of the "mass production" type needs to consider how work habits will alter the earning capacity of that practice.

[6] Fee Schedules

The appraiser needs to understand the practice's fee schedule. Does it charge by procedure, time spent, or some other measure? How do this practitioner's fees compare with those of others of comparable qualifications? The appraiser should know how often the fee schedule is revised and the last time it was revised. The fee schedule can provide an index to the practitioner's skill and reputation. Also, if the fees are below community standards, there may be additional income that could be generated by the buyer if fees were raised.

[7] Practice Location

The location of a practice has a substantial impact on its value. Some areas are perceived to be more desirable than others. Both the community in which the practice is located and its exact location within that community are important. Factors that need to be considered with respect to the community include its size, growth, major industries, competition for the practice being valued, and the overall quality of living. The practice's location within the community needs to be evaluated in light of the areas prospects of contributing to the continued generation of practice income.

[8] Employees of the Practice

The employees of a professional practice can be very important to its value. They know the procedures, they know the clients, and the expense of training them has already been incurred. When patients come in for their first visit with the new practitioner, the familiar faces of the support personnel will help smooth the transition for the patients to the new practitioner. Particularly important are nonowner professionals employed by the practice. They may actually hold the goodwill of some clients, and if they chose to leave the practice, their clients might go with them. The appraiser should determine to what extent that is the case in the practice at hand. The buyer does not want to pay for goodwill value that is ultimately not the seller's to sell because it is owned by an employee. In such a situation, an employment contract and a covenant not to compete might be negotiated with the employee.

[9] Marketability of the Practice

The marketability of the practice depends on a number of factors, some of which have been discussed throughout this chapter. Demand for the type of practice for sale obviously affects its value. If there is a glut of accounting practices in the community, the value of those accounting practices tends to rise because it would be a difficult and lengthy process to establish a practice from scratch. On the other hand, extreme competition may cause the value of certain practices to drop, especially those practices that are not making an adequate return for the practitioner.

¶ 20.6 Elements of Goodwill in Divorce Valuations

Valuations for divorces are among the most common professional engagements the appraiser of professional practices encounters. Most of the states whose appellate courts have ruled on whether professional goodwill is a marital asset, subject to valuation and division, have held that it is indeed a marital asset and should be valued and accounted for in the division of property. Several states' appellate courts have ruled otherwise. The appraiser needs an understanding of the case law dealing with the valuation of professional practices in divorce for the state in which the practice being valued is located.

The elements that create goodwill discussed in the preceding section should be considered in valuing professional goodwill for divorce purposes. There are, however, other elements that need to be given consideration in divorce valuations. The various state courts have been helpful in establishing some fairly uniform guidelines that must be considered in appraising professional goodwill. The genesis of these factors is a California case, *Lopez v. Lopez*.[2] The Lopez decision is a good treatise on the valuation of professional goodwill for marital dissolutions. It has been widely quoted in many other states in supporting the establishment and value for professional goodwill in divorce cases.

One of the significant sections of the Lopez case deals with what elements the appraiser should consider before expressing an opinion of professional goodwill value. The factors it determined to be appropriate included the following.

As comprehensive as they seem, these factors have been the source of some confusion among appraisers, attorneys, and trial courts with respect to determining how they should be measured and reflected in the value of the practice.

---

[2] 38 Cal. App. 3d 93, 113 Cal. Rptr. 58 (1974).

[1] Practitioner's Age and Health

It is far easier to determine the practitioner's age and health than to know how these factors affect professional goodwill value. One close to retirement generally does not have a high professional goodwill value, even though historical earnings may have been good, because those earnings cannot be expected to continue very far into the future. Likewise, a practitioner approaching the end of high income years (for most practitioners, high income years fall between the ages of 45 to 55) would not have as much professional goodwill value as the practitioner at the beginning of high income years (everything else being equal). On the other hand, a fairly young practitioner who has only recently started practice would necessarily have a lower earning potential than the "average" practitioner; therefore, adjustments should be made before comparing those earnings to the average practitioner. Health is also important. If the professional will be limiting practice activities in the future because of poor health, the value of the professional goodwill will drop.

[2] Demonstrated Past Earning Power

Past earnings can be a good predictor of future earnings. Generally, five years of earnings need to be considered, including the trend in earnings. Ultimately, it may be decided that the latest three years, or even the last year, is more representative of expected earnings, but an earnings history is necessary to make that kind of judgment.

[3] Reputation for Judgment, Skill, and Knowledge

The practitioner's reputation for judgment, skill, and knowledge is one of the most abstract factors in the measurement of goodwill. After performing many professional practice valuations, the appraiser begins to get a "feel" for how these elements affect value, but it is difficult to quantify. The appraiser should request a copy of the practitioner's curriculum vitae and inquire about special certifications, articles written, classes taught, professional awards received, and professional society memberships. Any of these credits might help quantify these elements.

[4] Comparative Professional Success

"Success" is usually measured by earnings, but other factors, such as the number of patients seen, hours generally spent working, community standards of living, and so forth, must also be considered. It is very important to compare professionals with like professionals. If the appraiser is valuing the professional goodwill of an attorney practicing in the estate planning area, earnings and work habits should be compared with other attorneys practicing in the same area of law with the same experience, hours worked, and any other elements that lead to the generation of income.

[5] Nature and Duration of Practice

Up to this point, all the factors cited in the Lopez case have dealt with the personal attributes of the individual practitioner. However, the court recognized that the practice itself is a factor that must be considered when valuing goodwill. Therefore, the factors listed previously for purposes of sale are all important for divorce purposes also. Goodwill is built up over time, so the length of time the practice has been in existence will have a bearing on goodwill value. A long-established accounting firm will attract more and higher-paying clients than a new practice, which may rely primarily on tax return preparation fees. The following information about the practice needs to be investigated before a decision as to the value of professional goodwill can be made:

- Type of service offered;
- Type of clients served;
- Length of time at the current location;
- Length of time remaining on the lease and ability to renew the lease;
- How the fees are billed;
- Source of new clients;
- Individual practitioner's amount of production;
- Number of employees and their length of service;
- Economic and demographic information on the community where the practice is located;
- Number of other professionals in the community offering the same service of specialty; and
- Cost of setting up a new practice and the ability to attract new patients or clients to the practice.

¶ 20.7 Value of the Practice

There is no single correct method of valuing a professional practice, any more than there is a single correct method of valuing any asset. Over the years, many methods have been devised to appraise professional practices, most of them ultimately discarded as redundant, invalid, or too complex.

[1] Valuation Methods

Several methods, though, when properly used, have withstood the tests of time and reasonableness and are now the primary methods for valuating professional practices.

[a] Excess Earnings Method

The excess earnings method is derived from IRS Revenue Ruling 68-609. The method attempts to value the professional goodwill by considering appropriate returns on both tangible and intangible assets. The steps in the excess earnings method can be summarized as follows.

1. Determine a net tangible asset value for the practice.
2. Determine a normalized level of earnings.
3. Determine an appropriate percentage rate and return on the net tangible asset value. Multiply the net tangible asset value from step 1 by that rate to determine the amount of earnings attributable to the tangible assets.
4. Subtract the amount of earnings attributable to tangible assets (developed in step 3) from the normalized earnings (developed in step 2). The result of this step is called the "excess earnings," that is, the amount of earnings above a fair return on the net tangible asset value.
5. Determine an appropriate capitalization rate to apply to the excess earnings, which are presumably the earnings attributable to goodwill or other intangible assets, as opposed to tangible assets, and thus should be capitalized at a higher rate than the appropriate rate of return on tangible assets. Capitalize the excess earnings at that rate (that is, divide the amount of excess earnings developed in step 4 by the excess earnings capitalization rate).
6. Add the values of steps 1 and 5 to determine the total value of the practice, both tangible and intangible value.

The excess earnings method is used quite frequently in divorce proceedings—probably more so than in actual transactions.

[i] Earnings Levels

Generally, for a professional practice, total earnings are defined as all earnings available to the practitioner and are computed as follows.

- The net income of the practice, including salary and benefits to the practitioner;
- Plus nonrecurring expenses less nonrecurring income; and
- Plus excess expenses (expenses not related to the generation of practice income).

Unlike most equity valuations, no deduction is made for the value of the services of the owner/practitioner when calculating earnings. This is because professional practitioner earnings surveys are used to determine the normal earnings for the type of practice being valued, and these surveys include the compensation of the practitioner in the total earnings category.

Also, if the earnings survey used is of self-employed practitioners, step 3 shown in the excess earnings method above is generally not calculated (computing a return on tangible assets). The reason is that the earnings surveys of self-employed practitioners already include income that represents the return realized on the tangible assets of the practice. If such a survey is used and the subject practice's income level is reduced to reflect a return on net tangible asset value, in effect a double reduction in income has occurred because the survey's reported income also includes a return on net tangible asset values. Of course, if the earnings survey is of non-owner-employed practitioners, step 3 is an appropriate calculation, as the employed nonowner practitioner has no investment in the tangible assets.

[ii] **Capitalization Rates**

If the survey of practice earnings includes only nonowner employees, then two different capitalization rates need to be determined. The first is the rate applicable to the net tangible asset value (fair market value of the assets of the practice less the fair market value of the liabilities of the practice). This rate should at least reflect the cost of short-term borrowing on these assets plus a few points for a "real" return on these assets.

The second capitalization rate is for the excess earnings of the practice. As a rule, this rate (a division) runs from 100% to 20% (or a multiple of 1 to 5). Because the value of intangibles is highly volatile, the rate needs to reflect this risk (which is very large). Therefore, an average rate of 33% is usually the starting point, and it goes higher or lower depending on the various factors that determine the value of the professional goodwill. For example, if over 50% of a practice's patients come from one referral source, the risk of losing a substantial portion of income is great, and it follows that there is a large risk of losing all excess earnings. In this case, the capitalization rate would increase, causing the value of the professional goodwill to decrease.

The excess earnings method is used primarily in divorce valuations and less often in valuations for sales. It is helpful in establishing the value of just the professional goodwill, but it does not disclose the total rate of return that would be received for the tangible assets, practice goodwill, and professional goodwill combined. The capitalization of earnings method is a better method of determining the value of these assets.

[b] Capitalization of Earnings Method

This method values the entire practice, including tangible assets and practice and professional goodwill, in a lump sum. Instead of determining one capitalization rate for tangible assets and another for intangible assets, a single blended rate is established for all assets.

The choice of an earnings base to be capitalized has a significant impact on the choice of a capitalization rate. If earnings are defined as all earnings available to the practitioner before any owner/practitioner compensation, the capitalization rate will be much higher than if fair compensation to the owner/practitioner is removed from the earnings stream before it is capitalized. (A higher capitalization rate will produce a lower value, and a lower capitalization rate, a higher value.)

The capitalization rate is not the same as the required rate of return. The required rate of return is the average annual return expected over the term of holding the asset, and the capitalization rate is the rate by which to divide the current (or average past) earnings. Therefore, if the appraiser expects growth in future earnings, a capitalization rate less than the required rate of return would be chosen. For example, if the required rate of return is 20% (that is, the average annual return over the investment period) and long-term growth in earnings is expected to be 7.5% per year over a fairly long-time horizon, the capitalization rate (on current normalized earnings) will be closer to 12.5% (20% less 7.5%) than to the required rate of return of 20%.

[c] Multiple of Revenues Method

The multiple of revenues approach is one of the primary rules-of-thumb in many industries, primarily service industries. Because most professional practices provide a service, various rules-of-thumb are used to value professional practices. Revenue multiples are popular in appraising professional practices for several reasons.

- The method is simple to understand.
- Revenue are often easier to determine than the economic earnings of the practice.
- When looking for comparative transactions, sales price to revenues is often the only valuation ration that can be accurate calculated.

Revenue multiples are often used in setting prices for sales of professional practices. It is not wise to rely entirely upon them, however, because the specific practice may have certain positive and negative attributes that the multiple would not take into account. For example, if an accounting practice were appraised by the excess earnings method to be worth $100,000, the appraiser may want to check it against the industry standard rule-of-thumb revenue multiple. If the practice value seems out of line with the industry, the appraiser may have erred in calculating the value according to the excess earnings method (and would need to correct that error); alternatively, the particular practice may be so different (for example, having a different cost structure than is typical in the industry) that it does not fall into the standard revenue multiple range.

Although we have discussed three of the most commonly used methods of valuation, others are used and have gained acceptance in the appraisal community. These methods generally involve the measurement and valuation of cash flow, the likelihood of a diminution in goodwill value occurring over time, and analysis of prior transactions in the practice under appraisal.

[2] Complete Value

At the completion of any valuation, the appraiser needs to consider the complete value. Some thoroughly researched valuation reports, applying standard appraisal techniques, omit consideration of the complete value of the practice. For example, if the practice being valued was purchased three years earlier and the purchase price at that time was 100% of the prior year's revenues, it would not necessarily be proper to conclude that the practice today is worth 100% of its current revenues. The appraiser would need first to investigate the total transaction that took place three years ago. It may be that that transaction took place at a time when the practice had no debt, and that today the practice is highly leveraged. The complete value needs to recognize this fundamental difference.

¶ 20.8 Summary

Professional practices have several distinct characteristics that make them unique in appraisal practice, predominantly their accounting methods, their service orientation, and the fact that a substantial portion of their value lies in the skills of the practitioner. The appraiser needs to consider both the underlying net asset values of the practice and the goodwill value of the practice and/or practitioner.

The two classifications of goodwill are practice and professional goodwill. Practice goodwill is the same as business goodwill, but professional goodwill is a personal asset of the practitioner. For divorce purposes, various characteristics of the practitioner need to be taken into account to determine the existence and amount of professional goodwill. However, as is also true in valuations for sale, the nature and history of the practice must be considered in establishing the value of either practice or professional goodwill.

Although the valuation methods employed for professional practices are not completely different from the methods used in other equity valuations, the differences arise primarily because of the personal nature of the practice's intangible assets. It is not impossible to transfer this type of asset, but it is much more difficult than to transfer a tangible asset, and this difficulty needs to be recognized in the valuation process.

21

CANADIAN FINANCIAL VALUATION

RICHARD M. WISE*

		Page
¶ 21.1	**Statutes**	21-3
	[1] Income Tax Law	21-3
	[2] Company Law	21-5
	[3] Securities Regulation	21-6
	[4] Family Law	21-7
	[5] Expropriation Law	21-9
	[6] Bankruptcy Law	21-9
	[7] Competition Law	21-9
	[8] Employee Share Ownership Plans	21-11
¶ 21.2	**Commercial Transactions**	21-13
	[1] Acquisition, Sale, or Merger of a Business	21-13
	[a] Material Contracts/Agreements	21-16
	[b] Contingent and Other Liabilities	21-16
	[c] Economic and Political Climate	21-16
	[d] Taxation	21-16
	[2] Corporate Reorganizations	21-17
	[3] Fairness Opinions	21-18
	[4] Going Public	21-19
	[5] Going Private	21-19
	[a] Compulsory Acquisition Following Take-Over Bid	21-20
	[b] Oppression Remedy	21-20
	[c] Defining Fair Value	21-21
	[d] Valuation Approaches	21-22
	[e] Forcing-Out Premium	21-23
	[6] Partnership/Shareholder Buy-Sell Agreements	21-24
	[7] Employee Stock Option Plans	21-25
	[8] Allocation of Purchase Price	21-25
	[9] Related-Party Transfers	21-26
	[10] Financial Solvency Analyses	21-26

---

* RICHARD M. WISE, FCA, FCBV, ASA, is president of Richard Wise & Associates in Montreal, Canada.

		[11] Government Privatization	21-27
¶ 21.3		**Litigation Support**	21-27
	[1]	Litigious Issues	21-28
		[a] Income Tax	21-28
		[b] Going-Private Transactions	21-30
		[c] Minority Shareholder Oppression	21-32
		[d] Separation and Divorce	21-33
		[e] Expropriation—Business Disturbance, Loss of Goodwill	21-35
		[f] Breach of Contract	21-36
		[g] Torts	21-36
		[h] Personal Injury	21-37
		[i] Insurance Claims	21-38
	[2]	Arbitration	21-38
¶ 21.4		**Valuation Profession**	21-39
	[1]	The Canadian Institute of Chartered Business Valuators	21-39
	[2]	The Canadian Institute of Chartered Accountants	21-40
¶ 21.5		**Valuation Terms**	21-41
¶ 21.6		**Case Law and Regulatory Pronouncements and Practices**	21-41
	[1]	Leading Judicial Decisions	21-41
	[2]	Revenue Canada, Taxation	21-41
	[3]	Ontario Securities Commission	21-43
		[a] Ontario Policy Statement	21-45
		[b] Decisions Relating to Valuation	21-45
	[4]	British Columbia Securities Commission	21-47

Canadian business valuation practices are similar to those in the United States. There may, however, be differences as to emphasis or approach. These differences arise because of the background, training, and discipline of the valuator. For example, until the early 1980s, many public accounting firms in the U.S. were not involved in business and securities valuation; this was left to investment banking firms, CFAs (Certified Financial Analysts), and ASA (members of the American Society of Appraisers) although some CFAs and ASAs were also CPAs (Certified Public Accountants). Within the last half-dozen years or so, the major accounting firms in the United States, in particular the so-called "Big Eight" (until a number of mergers occurred that resulted in the "Big Five" or "Big Six"), developed or acquired business valuation departments and are now offering such services to their existing audit clients as well as to nonclients. In a number of instances, CPA firms purchased an independent firm of business valuators, which was then integrated into the former's practice, providing it with an instant business valuation capability.

In Canada, on the other hand, business valuations have traditionally been performed by public accounting firms, CAs (chartered accountants). The CICA (Canadian Institute of Chartered Accountants) is the Canadian counterpart of the AICPA (American Institute of Certified Public Accountants). Also, just as each state has its own CPA Institute under the overall umbrella of the AICPA, in Canada each of the ten provinces has a Provincial CA Institute. The Canadian counterpart of the business valuation discipline of the ASA (American Society of Appraisers) is the CICBV (Canadian Institute of Chartered Business Valuators), founded in 1971. Its membership and student enrollment comprise approximately 80% to 90% chartered accountants.

Other professionals also render business valuation services in Canada but the CICBV, like the ASA, is a professional society whose members have generally followed a prescribed program of studies, have successfully written uniform final examinations, and adhere to a strict code of ethics. Professionals who perform business valuation services in Canada but who are not accredited members of the CICBV generally include CAs and CFAs. CFAs are usually employed in the research or corporate finance department of a firm of investment dealers or stockbrokers.

¶ 21.1 Statutes

In Canada, a number of statutes refer to "value," which term is used in the respective context. For example, in income tax law (see below), the term "fair market value" is employed more than 400 times in the act. In company law and family law, for example, the term "value" appears in a number of different provisions. Accordingly, a number of statutes in Canada give rise to the requirement to arrive at value. Some examples are described below.

[1] Income Tax Law

Canada's federal income tax legislation is contained in the Income Tax Act, which is the counterpart of the U.S. Internal Revenue Code. While the term "fair market value" appears in numerous provisions, the statute does not define it. Such provisions normally relate to non-arm's-length transactions between corporations, their shareholders, or among family members, corporate reorganizations, transfer pricing, estate freezing, and so forth. Since the value determined impacts upon the base on which income tax is levied, there have been and there will continue to be numerous valuation disputes between taxpayers and revenue authorities.

The federal tax laws in Canada are administered and enforced by Revenue Canada, Taxation (the Department of National Revenue, Taxation Division), which is the Canadian counterpart of the Internal Revenue Service in the United States. The Minister of National Revenue, who is a member of the Canadian Cabinet and a member of Parliament, is the counterpart of the U.S. Commissioner of Internal Revenue. The Minister is also responsible for Canadian customs duties and excise taxes.

The types of areas in income tax legislation requiring a determination of fair market value and hence a potential for disagreement between the taxpayer and the Revenue Department and ultimate litigation include the following:

- Capital gains and losses;
- Benefits to shareholders;
- Benefits to employees;
- Employee stock option plans;
- Non-arm's-length transactions;
- Corporate reorganization—mergers, liquidations, and exchanges of shares;
- Transfer pricing;
- Gifting;
- Death of taxpayer;
- Change of use of property;
- Corporate and partnership rollovers (tax-deferred transfers);
- Allocation of proceeds/purchase price;
- Establishment of exit and entry values for business or investment interests on leaving or entering Canada;
- Measuring intangible value (e.g., goodwill, franchise, leasehold interest, license, and patents); and
- Deemed realizations.

Since valuation is not an exact science and since neither a definition nor a formula is contained in the income tax legislation, fair market value is based upon valuation theory, principles, and practices. Because the fair market value determined has a direct bearing on the amount of tax to be paid, this can be a highly litigious area. Notwithstanding the potential for dispute and even litigation, income tax valuations as a percentage of total valuations have decreased substantially for whatever reason. This means that the mix of types of business valuation services rendered in Canada has changed dramatically over the past ten years. Whereas valuation for income tax purposes used to account for more than two thirds to three quarters of a valuator's mandates in Canada, in 1989 less than 5% of valuation engagements were strictly for tax purposes. The emphasis has clearly changed from tax-related valuations to such areas as shareholder disputes (including the appraisal remedy), fairness opinions, mergers and acquisitions, family law, and the measurement of economic damages or business loss. In fact, the pure Canadian business valuation practice of ten years ago has evolved into a litigation-support practice.

Such change has prompted the CICA to publish a loose-leaf service entitled *Financial Litigation—Quantifying Business Damages and Values*,[1] written for business valuators, chartered accountants, and members of the legal profession as well as American CPAs and litigation attorneys.

[2] Company Law

Business valuations may be required in areas of company law for purposes of minority-shareholder appraisal rights, which are very similar to those in the United States.

In Canada, the types of corporate reorganizations or fundamental corporate changes that give rise to the appraisal rights afforded minority shareholders include the following:

- Amendment to a corporation's articles to alter or remove constraints on the issue or transfer of shares or to alter the business that the corporation may carry on;
- Amalgamation with a corporation other than a wholly owned subsidiary;
- Continuation of a corporation in another jurisdiction;
- Sale, lease, or exchange of all, or substantially all, of a corporation's assets; and
- Amendment to the articles derogating from the rights or conditions attached to the shares of a class or series having special rights or conditions.[2]

An appraisal right is also granted to minority shareholders whose shares are subject to compulsory acquisition under the takeover bid provisions of the Canada Business Corporations Act: If a takeover is

---

[1] R.M. Wise, *Financial Litigation—Quantifying Business Damages and Value* (1987).

[2] The corporate statutes of B.C., Alta., Sask., Man., Ont., N.S. and N.B. are basically identical to, and follow, § 190 of the Canada Business Corporations Act (S.C. 1974-75-76, c.33, as amended—CBCA. At the time of preparing this material, no corresponding provisions are to be found in the statutes of Que., P.E.I. or Nfld.

accepted by the holders of 90% of the target shares (other than shares held by the offeror), the offeror may acquire the remaining shares. A provision in the company law authorizing compulsory acquisition of less than 10% of the shares of a class outstanding following a takeover bid is to prevent oppression of the majority by the minority.[3]

Fair value opinions may also be required when there is minority shareholder oppression. A minority shareholder (i.e., a shareholder owning less than 50% of the voting shares) is protected by the company law statutes against prejudicial conduct of the majority. The oppression remedy is available when minority shareholders are unfairly treated by the majority. Under Section 241 of the CBCA, a shareholder may seek a remedy and apply to the court for an order that the majority or some other party acquire his/her shares or rectify the matters complained of, provided the court is satisfied with any of the following:

- Any act or omission of the corporation or any of its affiliates effects a result;
- The business or affairs of the corporation or any of its affiliates are or have been carried on or conducted in an oppressive or unfairly prejudicial manner; and
- The powers of the directors of the corporation on any of its affiliates are or have been exercised in a manner oppressive or unfairly prejudicial or that unfairly disregard the interests of any security holding, creditor, director, or officer.

Section 241(3) of the CBCA sets out the various and extensive powers of the court in such a situation.

[3] Securities Regulations

During the mid-1980s, many Canadian provinces enacted revisions to the business corporation statutes (i.e., the business corporations acts). Significant amendments have also been made to their respective securities acts. Policy statements have been issued by the securities commissions and stock exchanges as well.[4] The provinces have been enacting securities legislation on a more uniform basis across Canada, although Quebec is an exception in that it does not wish to merely follow but to pronounce based upon its own experience.

---

[3] Most provincial statutes contain analogous provisions relating to oppression of the minority (*e.g.*, § 247 of the Ont. Business Corporation Act).

[4] Baillie, in panel discussion, "Valuation Issues in Going-Private and in Takeover Bids," 5 J. Bus. Valuation 14 (July 1979) (The Canadian Inst. of Chartered Business Valuators).

The Province of Ontario has been a leader in this area and has continued to play the most active role. The provinces of British Columbia and, to a lesser extent, Quebec have also been active in enacting legislation and formulating policies that address the new or novel types of transactions that give rise to possible areas of concern.

While there have been a number of amendments throughout the legislation, the following comments focus strictly on those matters of prime importance to Canadian business and securities valuators. As noted above, since the Ontario and British Columbia Securities Commissions have been the most active in this regard, the following comments summarize the respective practices and policies in these provinces.

[4] Family Law

In Canada, each province has its own divorce legislation. From a valuation point of view, the rules can differ from province to province, as shown in Table 21-1.

TABLE 21-1

CANADIAN FINANCIAL VALUATION
FACTORS FOR FAMILY LAW

Province	Valuation Basis	Valuation Date
Newfoundland	Nonspecified	None
Prince Edward Island	Nonspecified	None
Nova Scotia	Nonspecified	None
New Brunswick	Nonspecified	None
Quebec	Market value	Earliest of specified events
Ontario	Value	Earliest of specified events
Manitoba	Fair market value	Date of last cohabitation
Saskatchewan	Fair market value	Date of application or adjudication
Alberta	Nonspecified	None
British Columbia	Nonspecified	None

Other provinces may be reforming the legislation to be more along the lines of Ontario.

Most significant from a valuation point of view is the legislation in the provinces of Ontario, Saskatchewan, and British Columbia. This provides for an equalization of the net family property of each spouse, i.e., the increase in the value of each spouse's property since marriage. In the Province of Ontario, the FLA (Family Law Act of 1986), which came into force on March 1, 1986, provided an entire new system for the division of property in the event of a marriage breakdown or upon the death of a spouse. For business valuators, accountants, and lawyers in the Province of Ontario, the act provides a wide array of potential litigation issues, in particular, valuation-related issues. Many CA firms and business valuation firms have already assigned some of their professional staff to specialize in this area and to sharpen their skills in the field of litigation support.

Under the new Ontario law, the distinction between family and nonfamily assets has been replaced with a "deferred community of property system." All property interests are currently subject to equal division between the spouses through an "equalization" payment. Hence, when there is either a marriage breakdown or the death of a spouse, the value of the net family property of each spouse is to be shared equally. The FLA defines NFP ("net family property") in Section 4 as the value of all property owned by a spouse on the "valuation date."

Apart from planning and consulting with respect to prenuptial agreements, marriage contracts, shareholders' buy/sell agreements, and so forth, business valuators may be engaged to determine the NFP of one or both spouses. This raises important valuation issues such as the interpretation of the term "value" as used in Section 4 of the FLA. Is it "fair market value," "fair value," "market value," "value to the owner," or "value in use"? Also, valuation issues such as whether a discount for income taxes should be factored into the calculation of corporate share value (e.g., in respect to recaptured depreciation, capital gains, distribution of corporate surplus) are paramount. The Ontario courts have been addressing such issues, and the decisions have varied. A number are currently before the Court of Appeal. For example, in the *Rawluk v. Rawluk* decision of 1986, Justice Walsh commented as follows:

> While the Act speaks of value, it contains no definition of that term nor, indeed, guidelines of any kind to assist in the determination of its meaning other than the provision contained in Section 4 that when value is required to be calculated as of a given date, it shall be calculated as of the close of business on that date. Absent any statutory direction, "value" must then be determined on the peculiar facts and circumstances as they are found and developed on the evidence in each individual case. While this approach does not lead to uniformity and predictability of result, it does recognize the individuality inherent in each marriage and case and permit the flexibility so often necessary to insure an equitable result.[5]

---

[5] 550 R.2d 704, 3 R.F.L.3d 113 (Ont. H.C.J. 1986).

One area of contention deals with compensation to a spouse in respect to his/her contribution to the other spouse's earning a degree and/or obtaining a professional license. This is a matter also addressed by the United States divorce courts. Is a degree or a license family property and, if so, how it is to be valued? In such matters, the valuator must liaise closely with the attorney.

[5] Expropriation Law

Each of the provinces has legislation that provides for compensation to a party whose property was expropriated or whose business was being conducted on expropriated land, whether in leased or owned premises. Where a province, municipality, or other authority expropriates property, the affected party may make a claim under the relevant provincial statute. Business valuation input may be required on either side to quantify the loss of future profits, any disturbance damages, loss of goodwill and, in a case where the business moves to a new location, duplicate operating costs. If a settlement cannot be reached, valuation evidence would be brought before a compensation board or expropriation tribunal.

[6] Bankruptcy Law

The Canadian Bankruptcy Act uses the term "value" in the context of a security creditor being required under certain circumstances to value the security held. "Value" is not defined. The services of a business valuator may be required for purposes of determining whether the debtor is solvent or insolvent or whether the realization of business assets (including the sale of a business as a going concern) by a trustee and bankruptcy is improvident.

The Bankruptcy Act defines "insolvency" as any of the following: (1) inability to meet obligations as they generally become due; (2) ceasing to pay current obligations as they generally become due; and (3) having a net asset position in aggregate that is not "at fair valuation" sufficient or if disposed of at a fairly conducted sale under legal process would not be sufficient to enable payment of all legal obligations due and accruing due.

[7] Competition Law

In June 1986 the Canadian Parliament enacted the Competition Act, which renames and amends the Combined Investigation Act. The purposes of this act are (1) to maintain and encourage competition in Canada to promote the efficiency and adaptability of the Canadian economy; (2) to assist Canadian participation in world markets so that small- and medium-sized enterprises are able to participate in the economy; and (3) to provide consumers with competitive prices and product choices. The legislation applies to each of these types of transactions:

- Merger;
- Acquisition of assets in Canada of an operating business;
- Acquisition of voting shares of a corporation carrying on an operating business or controlling a corporation that carries on an operating business;
- Amalgamation of two or more corporations where at least one carries on an operating business or controls a corporation carrying on an operating business; and
- Combination of two or more persons carrying on a business otherwise than through a corporation.

For example, the Competition Tribunal, which replaces the former Restrictive Trade Practices Commission, may find that a merger or a proposed merger is likely to prevent or lessen competition substantially. In the case of a merger that has been completed, it may dissolve the merger, dispose of assets, or take other action. In the case of a proposed merger, the Tribunal may direct that the merger not be proceeded with, in whole or in part.

Under Part VIII of the Competition Act (Sections 80 to 96), persons proposing to acquire assets of shares or to amalgamate or combine must notify the Director of Investigation and Research of the proposed transaction and provide specific information (required under Section 92 or 93) prior to completing the transaction. However, this requirement applies only where the parties thereto, together with their affiliates, meet either of these conditions:

1. Have assets in Canada that exceed $400 million in aggregate value;
2. Have gross revenues from sales in, from, or into Canada that exceed $400 million in aggregate.

(The foregoing and following amounts are expressed in Canadian dollars.) Asset acquisitions are included only if the assets are in Canada and the aggregate value of the assets acquired or the gross revenues generated in Canada from such assets exceed $35 million.

Share acquisitions requiring pre-notification include those in which the corporation, or a corporation controlled by it, carries on business and the aggregate value of its assets in Canada (other than shares that it or another controlled corporation owns) exceeds $35 million or the gross revenue from sales in Canada generated from such assets exceed $35 million per annum.

Additional rules have been enacted that relate to public companies.

Amalgamations must also be reported where the aggregate value of the assets owned by the continuing corporation, or corporations controlled by that corporation subsequent to the amalgamation, exceeds $70 million or where the gross revenue from sales in or from Canada generated from such assets exceeds $70 million.

If there is a proposal to combine to carry on business otherwise than through a corporation, the Director must be notified if one or more of the persons intends to contribute assets that form part of an operating business carried on or controlled by that person and if the aggregate value of the assets in Canada that relate to the combination or gross revenue from sales in or from Canada generated from such assets exceeds $35 million.

Regulation 4(1) provides that for the purpose of Sections 81 and 82 of the Competition Act deductions are to be made in respect of the following items in determining the aggregate value of assets:

- Amounts representing duplication arising from transactions between affiliates;
- Amounts representing duplication arising from an ownership interest of one person in another person, whether or not those persons were affiliated; and
- Amounts provided for the depreciation or diminution of the value.

Regulation 4(2) prohibits the deduction of liabilities or encumbrances in arriving at value, and Regulation 5(2) requires the deduction of any amounts that represent duplication arising from transactions between affiliates. Regulations 6 to 14 contain various rules relating to determining the values of the aggregate assets, adjustments to such values, and gross sales revenues.

Whether the director of Investigation and Research and the parties will always agree on the value of the assets in Canada for purposes of the provisions of Part VIII is doubtful. As valuation-related areas of contention will no doubt surface, business valuators will be faced with some challenging accounting and valuation issues.

[8] Employee Share Ownership Plans

The Province of Ontario has established an incentive program to encourage employees of small- and medium-sized corporations to purchase newly issued shares of their employer company. The law, effective as of January 1, 1987, is contained in the Employee Share Ownership Plan Act. It provides that companies incorporated in Canada that pay at least 75% of their salaries and wages in the Province of Ontario and whose gross revenue or total assets, together with the gross revenue or total assets of associated corporations do not exceed $50 million in the previous taxation year, may apply to register an employee stock ownership plan (ESOP). Once a corporation's gross revenue and total assets, together with the gross revenue and total assets of associated corporations, exceed $75 million the corporation is no longer eligible.

The mandatory provisions to be contained in an Ontario ESOP include the following:

- The offering of newly issued voting shares to all eligible employees;
- A method of share valuation that applies to all common shares of the corporation;
- Providing terms for the purchase, sale, transfer, or redemption of the shares;
- Providing financial information and advice on the Securities Act to employees; and
- The appointment of an independent administrator for the plan who will retain the shares purchased by the employee for two years as well as amounts to be repaid to the Treasurer of Ontario from the proceeds of any sale during the two-year period (where the employee had been in receipt of a grant from the Ontario government).

Full-time or part-time employees resident in the Province of Ontario who have worked for their employer for at least six months may apply for a grant after they purchase and fully pay for the newly issued shares unless the employee already owns, or the employee is related to any person who already owns, 10% or more of any class of shares in the employer corporation. The purchase of the shares must result in new capital being paid into the employer corporation; no grant will be paid by the government where an employee uses the proceeds from the sale of the previously owned shares to purchase new shares.

Various rules are contained in the act. For example, Paragraph 3(2)(b) provides that the "total assets of a corporation" are equal to the sum of these values:

- The total assets as disclosed in the financial statements of the corporation for that taxation year prepared in accordance with generally accepted accounting principles; and
- The amount by which the value of any asset of a corporation has been written down and deducted from its income or undivided profits where such amount is not deductible in the calcu-

lation of its taxable income for the current and all prior taxation years under Part I of the Income Tax Act (Canada).

Ontario is the only province to date that has enacted ESOP legislation. Because of the significant incentives offered to both companies and employees of the ESOP, other provinces are expected to provide similar rules.

The United States's experience with ESOPs will provide guidance as to a number of common areas in the valuation of such securities.

¶ 21.2 Commercial Transactions

Quite apart from statutory or regulatory reasons for determining value, there are a number of day-to-day open market transactions in the commercial world where valuation is required. Parties to a material transaction are well advised to not only seek legal and accounting advice but valuation-related input. Canada, being so similar to the United States with respect to commercial transactions, has always had the need for valuation input when it comes to establishing price/value. Some types of transactions where the need for a valuation is obvious are outlined next.

[1] Acquisition, Sale, or Merger of a Business

Typically, where independent professional valuations are sought by a purchaser or vendor of a business or business interest, the business valuator provides judgment, experience, and skill in arriving at a price or a range of prices for purposes of negotiations between the parties. Canadian business valuators may also be requested to prepare a report quantifying the potential synergies resulting from the purchase or merger. This is done in conjunction with input from management, engineers (where appropriate), market surveys, etc. Such services may be provided to the purchaser and/or vendor of the business for purposes of calculating the premium in respect of the synergies or economies of scale anticipated from the corporate combination.

As the various methods used in valuing a business are described elsewhere in this book, the following outlines the more important valuation issues as well as the types of professional services that the Canadian business valuator would provide to a United States or other foreign investor acquiring or buying a Canadian business. (The comments assume that if an acquisition of a controlling interest is contemplated, it would be a "friendly" and not a "hostile" takeover and that all relevant information would be made readily available to the Canadian valuator.)

The analysis, methodology, and conclusions will vary depending on whether the business interest being acquired by the foreign investor is (1) a public company, (2) a private, closely held corporation, or (3) a partnership or joint venture. Whichever type of entity is being valued, if less than 100% is to be acquired, important valuation and fiscal issues may surface, depending upon whether such interest represents control or a minority position. The following matters must therefore be addressed by the Canadian valuator:

- Whether a premium or discount should be applied to the ratable share value of the business interest;
- If a controlling interest is to be valued, the degree of control (e.g., 51% or 66 2/3% or 90%) since the various voting percentages will afford different rights under the Canadian corporate law;
- The possible synergies or economies of scale that may ensue to the foreign purchaser through business combination;
- How the repatriation of profits of the Canadian enterprise will be taxed; and
- Whether the transaction may be subject to the provisions of the Investment Canada Act.

In Canada, financial statement disclosure requirements of generally accepted accounting principles (GAAP) have, for a number of years, been ahead of the requirements set out in federal or provincial company law. Accordingly, a number of Canadian provinces require that financial statements be prepared in accordance with GAAP in their company legislation.

As a general rule, every company incorporated in Canada is required to produce annual financial statements with comparative figures for the previous year, comprising a balance sheet, income statement, statement of retained earnings, and statement of changes in financial position. Where appropriate, there must also be explanatory notes to the financial statements. Because a critical aspect of the business valuation involves a detailed review and analysis of the financial statements, there are significant advantages in retaining the professional services of a Canadian business valuator, who is also likely to be a Chartered Accountant, to interpret these statements.

The following are some examples where Canadian rules depart from those in the United States:

- In some foreign jurisdictions, research and development costs must be expensed as they are incurred. The Canadian rules permit deferral of development costs where certain criteria as to recoverability are met; otherwise, they must be expensed as incurred.

- In connection with foreign currency translation, Canadian GAAP require that gains and losses arising from the translation of long-term monetary items and monetary items with fixed or determinable lives are to be deferred and amortized to income during the remaining life of them. In some other countries, these gains and losses are included in or deducted from income when realized.
- Canadian GAAP require the cost of an asset or an expense to be reduced by any related investment tax credits. Some other countries allow, as an alternative, a reduction of the company's income tax expense.
- Non-interest-bearing receivables or payables are not required to be adjusted on the balance sheet under Canadian GAAP. Accounting practices in some other countries require adjustment, even where the receivable or payable bears interest, but at other than prevailing market rates.
- Canadian GAAP permit the capitalization of interest costs incurred during the period of construction of major property, plant, and equipment, although there is no mandatory requirement.

There are, as well, a number of other differences between GAAP in Canada and those in other countries; hence, it would be advantageous, indeed prudent, for a United States or other non-resident purchaser to retain the services of a Canadian business valuator who can interpret and draw meaningful conclusions from the financial statements of the Canadian acquisition candidate.

Finally, interpreting and evaluating the company's own projections also plays a key role. Accordingly, it is important that the Canadian valuator review and assess the reasonableness and reliability of such forecasts or projections both in the light of the company's historical track record as well as the future conditions expected to prevail. The CICA (Canadian Institute of Chartered Accountants) like its counterpart in the United States, the AICPA, has set high standards as to the extent to which its members may report upon projections; all assumptions and calculations are required to undergo rigorous scrutiny. (The Technical Research Committee of the Union Europeen des Experts Comptables, Economiques et Financiers (U.E.C.)—a group based in Germany—has codified valuation procedures to be followed in the European Economic Community, requiring, for example, that forecasts be projected out for eight years. However, as commendable a development as this is, Canadian and United States valuation procedures, which are not codified, have total flexibility.)

The input of a Canadian business valuator would be particularly useful with respect to the following.

[a] Material Contracts/Agreements

Since all major agreements to which a company is party have a bearing on the future operations of the business (leases, labor union agreements, supply contracts, sales contracts, franchises, and license agreements), a review of the financial aspects of such contracts in the light of prevailing Canadian business and market conditions is essential.

[b] Contingent and Other Liabilities

Particularly if shares are being acquired, it is essential to attempt to evaluate the risk relating to contingencies, spending lawsuits, income tax assessments, the status of deferred taxes, the degree to which assets have been encumbered, and so forth. To the extent that a company has received government grants, the valuator's analysis must consider whether, under what conditions, and to what extent government grants are to be repaid by the company in the future. On the other hand, there may be the possibility of government grants and other incentives to the business; these may come from Canadian federal, provincial, or municipal authorities.

[c] Economic and Political Climate

Economic and monetary conditions (including currency fluctuations), political climate, competitive environment, international trade, regulatory controls, condition of and future prospects for the industry, and a number of other external factors will impact upon the future of the Canadian business. These factors establish the environment, marketplace, and climate in which the acquired business will be operating. Even though Canada is one of the most stable countries in the world, regard must also be paid to how foreign capital would be treated.

[d] Taxation

Canadian taxation is also important for valuation purposes, in that the United States or other non-resident investor looks either to the ultimate repatriation of the Canadian business' profits or to reinvesting the profits in Canada. The income tax aspects would be considered on two distinct levels: (1) the Canadian corporate tax on the profits generated by the Canadian business operation and (2) the taxes exigible on the cross-border flow of after-tax corporate profits, say by way of dividends. Accordingly, corporate income tax considerations, such as the ability of the company to deduct from taxable income "capital cost allowance" (depreciation for tax purposes), may be a material factor in determining future net earnings and cash flow. Regard must also be given to withholding taxes on dividends, management fees, and royalties to the non-resident investor, pursuant not only to Canadian tax laws but also to the provisions contained in the income tax treaty between Canada and country of the foreign investor. Generally, Canada's new treaties closely follow the provisions of the OECD (Organization for Economic Cooperation and Development) model treaty.

Other considerations include those relating to the effects to purchaser and vendor of acquiring the Canadian business on the basis of either its assets or its shares. Since income taxes can differ materially under either alternative, the ultimate price paid for the business will be different. It should be noted, however, that Canadian tax laws do not require an allocation of purchase price among various categories of assets if a share transaction occurs. In another area requiring attention, the CA or Canadian business valuator may also be able to provide assistance in addressing (and overcoming, if appropriate) considerations presented by the Investment Canada Act.

The terms "control" and "value" as used by Investment Canada require proper interpretation for purposes of determining whether the Canadian company is subject to "review." There may also be many different types of legislation—both on a federal and provincial level—relating to the business being acquired depending on the particular industry (banking, broadcasting, mining, life insurance, airlines); in these situations, the Canadian valuator would be familiar with regulations affecting the Canadian company and its shareholders. This is a key area in that the rights and conditions attaching to the shares being acquired by the non-resident are governed by the relevant corporate law (e.g., Canada Business Corporations Act or a similar provincial statute) as well as the company's articles of incorporation, by-laws, shareholders' agreements, and so forth. These have a direct bearing upon the value of the business interest being acquired by the nonresident.

Economic and political trends, as they relate to the future prospects of the company, are also important. It is advantageous to reap the benefits of local experience with an understanding of such trends rather than to rely upon, for example, newspaper reports describing events in a particular geographic area in Canada.

Knowledge of comparable transactions of interests in similar types of businesses is extremely useful in assessing value; it may be that the Canadian valuator is familiar with negotiations concerning the purchase/sale of a similar type of business.

[2] Corporate Reorganizations

As in the United States, there are various corporate reorganizations that take place for commercial purposes. These include recapitalizations, the winding up of a subsidiary company into its parent, the sale by a corporation of its operating assets into an affiliated company, and so forth. For financial, fiscal, and various corporate purposes, business valuations are required with respect to the issued shares of the companies involved and/or of the goodwill and other intangible values belonging to any of the affected businesses.

[3] Fairness Opinions

Where there are minority shareholders of a corporation that is either participating in a major transaction with a related party (i.e., a transaction not at arm's length) or where there may be fundamental corporate changes, an opinion from an independent professional is generally requested. In Canada, there is no prohibition with respect to the company's auditor performing the valuation. In the United States, the auditor would not qualify as being "independent" for purposes of a fairness opinion to the minority shareholders. In fact, the Canadian auditors of a Canadian subsidiary of a United States parent company, whose shares were listed on the New York Stock Exchange, were precluded by the Securities Exchange Commission (SEC) from expressing an independent valuation opinion in the United States. In the request by the Canadian company's auditors to the SEC, reference was made to the position of the Ontario Securities Commission (OSC), the most active provincial securities commission in Canada, noting that the OSC generally permits the company's auditors to express a fairness opinion. Notwithstanding the reference to the Ontario "precedent," the SEC refused to recognize an opinion expressed by the Canadian auditors as to the value of the shares of its audit client.

In a 1978 address, the former chairman of the OSC, in discussing whether the Commission should accept valuations from investment dealers (as opposed to public accounting firms or independent valuation firms), stated the following:

> There has been a concern expressed with the investment dealer approach. First, there is not the same historic emphasis on independence, the same degree of necessity for independence to do your job properly on an on-going basis. Second, the investment dealers rely very heavily on the market and their inclination is to say, the purpose of the market is to set a price.[6]

In Canada, therefore, while the auditor may be acceptable for purposes of expressing a fairness opinion, the investment dealer (although capable and competent) may not always be viewed as possessing independence. For example, the investment dealer in Canada is the firm that underwrites various issues or participates in various private place-

---

[6] See *supra* note 4.

ment offerings as well as public issues and has an on-going relationship with the client, who pays fees based upon the dollar value of the issue. Nonetheless, investment dealers in Canada have expressed and continue to express opinions as to (1) the fair value of certain securities and (2) whether the transaction is fair and reasonable from a financial point of view.

[4] Going Public

Canadian private companies that wish to go public, i.e., have a class of shares listed on a securities exchange, often retain the services of an independent business valuator to obtain an objective view of the value of the company "en bloc." While it is through negotiations with the investment dealer who will determine the optimum price of the issue, it is prudent for the principal shareholder of the company to seek an independent opinion. In the majority of cases where a valuation is requested, it is performed by the business valuation department of the auditing firm. The investment dealer sponsoring or underwriting the issue nonetheless also performs its own valuation, but more from a market point of view.

[5] Going Private

The Canada Business Corporations Act (CBCA) and most provincial company law statutes grant a shareholder the right to dissent where the corporation resolves to effect certain major, or fundamental, corporate changes. These changes include reorganizations that have, or intend to have, the effect of terminating the interest in the corporation of any [common] shareholder without his/her consent and without substituting common shares of equivalent value in the corporation, an affiliate, or a successor to the business. The comments and statutory references that follow relate to the appraisal rights under the CBCA and those provincial company law statutes that contain basically identical provisions.

The types of fundamental corporate changes giving rise to an appraisal right have been outlined earlier in this chapter. A "going private" (squeeze-out) transaction usually involves one of the above fundamental changes. The CBCA grants a minority shareholder an appraisal right: If the minority shareholder refuses to participate in such a fundamental change, he/she may sell his/her shares to the corporation for "fair value." If the shareholder and the corporation fail to agree on the value of the shares to be purchased, either party may apply to the court to fix a "fair value."[7] An appraiser (often a

---

[7] A number of articles have been written on going private (minority shareholder squeeze-outs). *See, e.g.,* Wise, "Determining 'Fair Value' Under the Appraisal and

Chartered Accountant) may, at the court's discretion, assist in the fixing of value.

Perhaps the simplest description of the appraisal remedy is that described by the court in the celebrated *Domglas* decision[8]:

> By the 'appraisal remedy' proper is usually meant the statutory right granted to minority shareholders, even where 'oppression' as such is not in issue, to oblige either the majority or the corporation to purchase the share of those minority shareholders who dissent from some basic change imposed by the majority. That purchase is at an appraised value effected by an independent outside instrumentality; be it an appraiser, a valuator, a referee, or a panel of such persons . . .; or by a court directly, with or without the assistance of a court appointed expert.

[a] Compulsory Acquisition Following Take-Over Bid

An appraisal right is also granted to minority shareholders whose shares are subject to compulsory acquisition under the take-over bid provisions in Section 199 of the CBCA, which provides that if a takeover is accepted by the holders of 90% of the target shares (other than shares held by the offeror), the offeror may acquire the remaining shares. A provision in the company law authorizing compulsory acquisition of less than 10% of the shares of a class outstanding following a takeover bid is to prevent oppression of the majority by the minority.

[b] Oppression Remedy

A minority shareholder is also granted a right under Section 241 of the CBCA to have his/her shares acquired by either the corporation or the majority shareholder, if it has been established that the corporation or its directors have acted in a manner oppressive or unfairly prejudicial to him/her. (The types of fundamental changes listed earlier are not, in and of themselves, oppressive and are contemplated by Section 190, not Section 241.)

Under Section 234, a shareholder may apply to the court for an order that the majority acquire the minority shares if the court is satisfied of any of the following:

- Any act or omission of the corporation or any of its affiliates' effects a result, or

---

Oppression Remedies—A Valuator's Perspective," in 3 *Corporate Structure, Finance and Operations* 105-149 (L. Sarno ed. 1984).

[8] [1980] C.S. 925, 13 B.L.R. 135, *aff'd* [1982] C.A. 377, 22 B.L.R. 121, 138 D.L.R. 3d 521 (Que. C.A.). The various powers the Court has in such a situation are set out in Section 241(3).

- The business or affairs of the corporation or any of its affiliates are or have been carried on or conducted in a manner, or
- The powers of the directors of the corporation or any of its affiliates are or have been exercised in a manner,

that is oppressive or unfairly prejudicial to or that unfairly disregards the interests of any security holder, creditor, director, or officer, the court may make an order to rectify the matters complained of.[9]

Finally, it should be noted that the provisions for an order by the court for the purchase of the minority's shares in cases of oppression do not refer to "fair value"; they provide a remedy related to the right to dissent. This point was recognized in an important valuation case dealing with the oppression remedy, *Montel v. Groupe de Consultants P.G.L., Inc. et al.*[10] Justice Rothman stated:

> The value requested by Petitioners [under Section 241 of the CBCA] is essentially the same as the value provided under Section 190 of the Act to be paid to dissenting shareholders. . . .
>
> I can see no reason why the valuation should be any less just and equitable in the case of a shareholder who has been expelled or oppressed under Section 241 than it would be for a dissenting shareholder under Section 184.
>
> I would therefore value these shares on the basis of their fair value.

[c] Defining "Fair Value"

In determining fair value for purposes of an appraisal right, it must be emphasized that the value term employed in the relevant appraisal statutes such as the CBCA is *"fair value."* For example, the Income Tax Act employs the term "fair market value." The Alberta Expropriations Act[11] employs both "market value" and "value to the owner."

On the other hand, "fair" in "fair value" qualifies "value" not the "market." For purposes of Canadian corporate law, it means "just and equitable." In the *Domglas* case, (for tax purposes as well as investment purposes) the fair market value of a small minority shareholding was $14 per share (quoted stock market price); the "fair value" of this same shareholding under the appraisal remedy was held to be $36.

Since the concept of the appraisal remedy in favor of dissenting shareholders had its origin in the United States, Canadian courts

---

[9] RSC 1980, c. E-16.
[10] No. 500-05-004409-817 (unreported decision of the Que. Super. Ct., July 4, 1983) (Rothman, J.).
[11] S.Q. 1978, c.37, *as amended.*

sought guidance from the American cases[12] as to the interpretation and determination of "fair value." However, as a result of the *Domglas* decision, there is now an important Canadian judicial authority as to the meaning and determination of "fair value." In *Domglas*, a case involving a company going private, it was necessary for the Court to determine the "fair value" of the dissenting minority's shares. The types of valuation issues considered by the Court were similar to those in the United States. In fact, because of the long history of United States case law with respect to going-private transactions, the Canadian Court examined now only Canadian case law[13] dealing with "fair value," it also examined very carefully the U.S. jurisprudence. In fact, the Court even reviewed Professor Bonbright's treatise, *Valuation of Property*,[14] long considered a leading authority on business valuation. As a result, in cases subsequent to *Domglas*, the Courts have not had to look much further,[15] although other issues have since surfaced in subsequent decisions, which are by no means as learned and scholarly as the *Domglas* decision.[16]

[d] Valuation Approaches

The Canadian Courts recognize four possible approaches in valuing the shares of a corporation for purposes of an appraisal right.

1. Market price (in the case of a public company);
2. Assets approach;
3. Earnings ("investment value") approach; or
4. Some combination of the above.

As in the United States, the most common approach recognized by the courts is the earnings ("investment value") approach. It is not very often that a combination of approaches is adopted, nor is the use of the so-called "Delaware Block" method. In Canada usually one approach (being the most appropriate one) is adopted rather than weighing each of the approaches as has sometimes been the case in the United States.

---

[12] *E.g.*, American Gen. Corp. v. Camp et al., 190 A. 225 (Md. Ct. App. 1937); Roessler v. Security Sav. & Loan Co., 72 N.E.2d 259 (Ohio 1947); Warren v. Baltimore Transit Co., 154 A.2d 796 (Md. Ct. App. 1959); Woodward v. Quigley, 133 N.W.2d 38, *modified on rehearing*, 136 N.W.2d 280 (Iowa 1965); Southdown v. McGinnis et al., 510 P.2d 636 (Nev. 1973); Libby, McNeill & Libby, 406 A.2d 54 (Me. Super. Ct.), *rev'd* Sup. Jud. Ct. of Me. (1979).

[13] *Re* Wall & Redekop Corp. et al., (1975), 50 D.L.R.3d 733; Diligenti v. RWMD Operations Kelowna, Ltd. et al. (No. 2), [1977] 4 B.C.L.R. 134; *Re* VSC Holdings, Ltd. et al., [1978] W.W.R. 559; Neonex Int'l Limited v. Kolasa et al., [1978] 3 B.L.R. 1 (B.C.S.C.).

[14] 2 J.C. Bonbright, *The Valuation of Property* (1937).

[15] Les Investissements Mont-Soleil Inc. v. National Drug Limited, [1982] C.S. 716 (Que. S.C.); Montel v. Groupe de Consultants P.G.L., Inc. et al., at 500-05-004409-817.

[16] *See, e.g.*, Brant v. KeepRite (unreported).

- Appraisal Remedy (for fundamental corporate changes/going private).

    The provisions of Section 190(3) of the CBCA provide that "fair value" is to be determined as of the close of business on the day before the adoption of the act or order which it is dissented from. Any appreciation or depreciation in anticipation of the vote upon the corporate resolution resulting in the appraisal remedy may be a factor in arriving at fair value. Therefore any foreseeable future value, having regard to the "fundamental change" itself, is to attach to the minority shares.

- Oppression Remedy
    (a) Any adverse effects from the oppression itself must not be considered in preparing a valuation.[17]
    (b) Goodwill must be included among the corporation's assets. This point is important, since a minority shareholder seeking fair value for his/her shares may be faced with the argument that goodwill should not be included because the majority shareholder was responsible for most of the company's business (i.e., the [personal] goodwill belonged to him/her). Canadian courts have referred to a United States decision that addressed this issue,[18] where the Court held that "the goodwill of a business carried on by a corporation belongs to the corporation alone." In another decision, the valuator's report was successfully attacked because no consideration was given to goodwill.[19]

[e] Forcing-Out Premium

Generally, prior to *Domglas*, "fair value" was essentially ratable fair market value (or ratable intrinsic value) with no minority discount: the minority were given their "proportionate share." That excluded both minority discounts *and* forcing-out premiums. In *Domglas*, however, the Court took the law a long step farther by importing a notion of subjective fairness. It rules in effect, that (1) "intrinsic value" is not "fair value" but rather "fair market value without the application of a minority discount" and (2) "fair value" is fair market value (without

---

[17] *Re* National Building Maintenance, Ltd., [1971] 1 W.W.R. 8, aff'd [1972] 5 W.W.R. 410 (B.C.C.A.).

[18] Brown v. Allied Corrugated Box Co., 154 Cal. Rptr. 170, 91 Cal. App. 3d 477 (1979).

[19] Bexley v. Dunning, [1976] 4 W.W.R. 446 (B.C.S.C.).

the application of a minority discount) *increased, however, by a "forcing-out premium":*

> In cases of the "squeeze-out" of the dissenting shareholders, which is equivalent to the expropriation, "fair value" goes beyond the concept of "intrinsic value", in that the former must include a premium for forcible taking, and is not subject to a minority discount.
>
> In this Court's opinion, in a "squeeze-out" situation, as exists in the case at Bar, the absence of a discount in valuing a minority holding, and the increment or premium for forcible taking, are the essence of the distinction between "fair value" and "fair market value."[20]

The Court in *Domglas* added onto the full ratable value of the minority shares a forcing-out premium of 20% (over and above ratable "en bloc" fair market value). Such premium was to recognize the expropriation nature of the squeeze-out. The Court also held that "fair value" must always be greater than "fair market value." The Judge commented as follows:

> The payment by the Petitioner [Domglas] of 'a fair value', even if more than the 'intrinsic value' of the shares, is the price that must be paid by it for the privilege of effecting the amalgamation over the protest of the Dissenting Shareholders, who in effect are being ousted from the corporation.

In effect, the Court held that if dissenting minority shareholders are to be frozen out of the corporation, they should be entitled to be paid at least the ratable value of their shares—possibly at a premium.

[6] Partnership/Shareholder Buy-Sell Agreements

Buy/sell agreements are commonly used in Canada by shareholders in closely held corporations. Such provisions typically ensure a market for the shares, an appropriate price for the departing shareholder's interest, a manner in which the continuing shareholders may acquire such interest, and protection as to ownership without outside interference. Sometimes only the minority shareholders are subject to the buy/sell agreement whereas the controlling shareholder is not. Numerous articles have been written on the subject, which set out the circumstances and mechanisms by which the continuing shareholders of the company may acquire the shares of the terminating shareholder. These articles, which have been published in Canadian journals, out-

---

[20] [1980] C.S at 925, 13 B.L.R. at 135, 233.

line the particular types of events or circumstances that trigger the buy-sell provisions in a shareholders' agreement (e.g., death, mental or physical disability, retirement, dismissal, dissension among the shareholders) and describe the types of mechanisms for establishing the price to be paid for the terminating shareholder's shares when the specified event is triggered.[21]

The traditional methods for determining price in Canadian buy/sell agreements are the following:

- Fixed price agreed to in advance and updated periodically;
- Price determined by an independent third party such as the auditor of the company (or an arbitrator);
- Price arrived at by consensus among the parties;
- Price established by formula;
- Price determined by a "shot-gun" (put/call) clause; and
- Price established by a "right of first refusal."

Apart from the value term employed, there is no single approach to establishing a price under a buy/sell agreement that meets all situations and entirely satisfies both the vendor and the purchaser(s). Each of these alternatives has its distinct advantages and disadvantages; the price-setting mechanism will depend upon the nature of the specified event.

[7] Employee Stock Option Plans

Over and above the requirements for value determination under the Income Tax Act, a number of employee incentive plans that provide for the acquisition of shares by the employee at specified points in time require fair market value determinations.

[8] Allocation of Purchase Price

Where assets rather than shares are being transacted, Canadian income tax law requires there to be a reasonable allocation of the total price to the various categories of assets. Such allocation has, of course, an effect on both the purchaser and vendor. The types of considerations are similar to those in the United States. Such allocation is also required for business, commercial, and accounting purposes. However, unlike the requirement in the United States where the purchase of a

---

[21] *See, e.g.*, Wise, *Some Valuation Concerns in Buy-Sell Agreements*, C.A Mag., The Canadian Institute of Chartered Accountants (Toronto: Feb. 1985), p. 52 and Wise, *Valuation Aspects of Shareholders' Buy-Sell Agreements*, 1984 *Conference Reports*, Proceedings of the Thirty-Sixth Conference of The Canadian Tax Found. (Toronto: The Canadian Tax Found., 1984).

corporation's issued shares requires an allocation of the purchase price among the corporation's assets, Canada has no such requirement. That is, the acquisition of shares is simply that, and there is no necessity of allocating the price paid for the shares to the various assets of the acquiree corporation. Of course, where a corporation purchases the shares of a company that becomes the former's subsidiary, upon consolidation there is a calculation of the excess of the purchase price over the book value of the acquiree's net assets. This is referred to as "goodwill on consolidation," "unallocated cost of acquisition," or some other similar term for financial statement (balance sheet) presentation.

[9] Related-Party Transfers

In addition to the requirements under income tax legislation,[22] transactions between or among related parties require fair market value determination. Such a requirement could arise, for example, where two sister companies controlled by a common parent transact with each other. To the extent that the respective minority shareholders of each corporation are different, there will be an advantage to one company's minority with a corresponding disadvantage to the other company's minority if the transaction is at other than fair market value. Independent valuations are thus obtained to ensure that the price is fair and reasonable. Such an opinion would, of course, be considered a "fairness" opinion.

[10] Financial Solvency Analyses

Opinions are sought from business valuators with respect to the ongoing financial viability of a corporation's business for a number of various reasons. For example, there continues to be a substantial amount of litigation in Canada when a bank has not given adequate time to its customer to repay the loan or even refinance. Under such situations where the bank has called its loan without having given proper notice and has sent in a receiver, receiver-manager, or agent, the bank has been sued for damages resulting from illegal "trespass and conversion." In such cases, business valuators may be retained by the plaintiff company and/or the defendant bank (1) to establish whether the business was viable as a going concern and (2) to quantify the damages, if any, resulting from such trespass and conversion.

Where the courts have found that the creditor, lender, or financial institution has been guilty of not allowing sufficient time for the customer to repay or refinance, damages have been awarded equal to the

---

[22] Under the provisions of Income Tax Act, § 69, which are similar to those in I.R.C. § 482.

fair market value of the business immediately before foreclosure. The leading cases in Canada on this matter are listed in Table 21-2.

TABLE 21-2
LEADING CANADIAN CASES IN FINANCIAL SOLVENCY ANALYSIS

- Ronald Elwyn Lister, Ltd. et al. v. Dunlop Canada Ltd., [1985] 52 O.R.2d 88; 9. O.A.C. 39 (C.A.)
- Mister Broadloom Corp. (1968), Ltd. v. Bank of Montreal et al., [1983] 44 O.R.2d 368 (C.A.).
- Kavcar Inv. Weiss et al. v. Aetna Factors, Ltd., File No. 9074/80 (Ont. Sup. Ct., released Apr. 11, 1986) (unreported).
- McLachlan v. Canadian Imperial Bank of Commerce, Henfrey & Co., Ltd. et al., [1987] 13 B.C.L.R.2d 300.
- National Bank of Canada v. Houle (Que. C.A., released July 10, 1987) (unreported)

Evidence is provided by professional business valuators respectively representing the plaintiff company and the defendant bank or creditor, which could be a supplier. The type of evidence given relates not only to the value of the business as a going concern but also whether the business was viable and would have survived as a going concern, as determined immediately prior to the alleged illegal act.

[11] Government Privatization

The federal government through its agencies and crown corporations, as well as some of the provincial governments, may decide from time to time to "privatize" certain agencies or crown corporations. For example, there has been much talk of privatizing the government-owned airline, Air Canada. Independent valuation opinions are required in connection with such types of transactions for both commercial and fairness purposes.

¶ 21.3 Litigation Support

In Canada, particularly since the capital gains tax was introduced in the 1971 Tax Reform, the measurement of fair market value became increasingly in demand. However, by the late 1970s, Canadian practitioners were being retained in cases where "quantum"—not just "value" *per se*—was required in financial litigation. For example, commercial and civil litigation lawyers would require an independent professional opinion in quantum-related disputes such as damages, lost profits, adverse effect, lost opportunity, loss of goodwill, and so forth. In cases where "value" was the subject of the litigation, it most likely referred to minority shareholder appraisal rights in a going-private transaction or a takeover bid or where there was shareholder oppression.

Hence, the direction of litigation-related engagements had shifted dramatically—away from the typical taxation and capital gains issues to non-tax-related commercial, corporate, and business disputes.

[1] Litigious Issues

In financial litigation, valuation evidence is often at the heart of the quantum assessment. In assessing economic damages, a plaintiff's loss of profits is one of the "heads of damages" that must be quantified and business valuators are typically retained in such areas. Some of the litigation areas are outlined below.

[a] Income Tax

Canadian income tax legislation gives rise to a number of contentious areas where valuation matters may result in litigation. These types of areas are listed in Section 1(a). The typical tax litigation relates to non-arm's-length or related-party transfers of business interests, whether for purposes of an estate freeze, a corporate reorganization, or a gifting arrangement. As in the United States, the issues that often result in litigation include (1) whether or not a minority discount is appropriate and, if so, how much of a discount; (2) whether a going-concern approach or a liquidation approach, for example, should be adopted; and (3) the "valuation day" ("V-Day") value of shares and other properties in order to determine the cost basis at the beginning of the period when capital gains became taxable in Canada, i.e., January 1, 1972. From that date on, any capital gains or losses are recognized for Canadian income tax purposes. Valuation day is December 31, 1971 for all properties other than Canadian publicly traded shares; in this latter case, valuation day is December 22, 1971.

Canadian taxpayers and their advisors have been arguing for higher valuation day values to have a higher cost base ("adjusted cost base") from which a gain or loss could be measured, whereas, on the other hand, Revenue Canada would often arrive at a lower V-Day value. Similarly, in non-arm's-length transactions or in gifting, valuation disputes arise with respect to the deemed fair market value at the time of the transaction. Often, in these types of (current) transactions, the taxpayer seeks low values and Revenue Canada seeks high values—quite the opposite of what is sought for V-Day!

Other litigious issues relate to non-arm's-length transfers under the provisions of Section 69 of the Canadian Income Tax Act, which are similar to the provisions contained in Section 482 of the U.S. Internal Revenue Code. The major difference between the Canadian and American provisions is that the former do not permit a corresponding adjustment on the books of the other transacting party. For example, if property having a fair market value of $10,000 is transferred by taxpayer *A* to a related party, *B*, for $3,000, Section 69 of the Income Tax Act deems taxpayer *A* to have received the full $10,000. However, no corresponding adjustment is permitted on the books of taxpayer *B*, with the result that *B*'s cost base is only $3,000 (the amount actually paid to *A*). In effect, the $7,000 differential is subject to double taxation (by including it in *A*'s accounts notwithstanding that *A* received only $3,000 and by denying *B* a step-up for the $7,000 after same amount has been added back to *A* under Section 69. It is understood that Section 482 of the U.S. Code, on the other hand, permits a corresponding adjustment by the other party. Accordingly, the Canadian rules subject such a transaction to a penalty, thereby serving as a deterrent to transfer-pricing at other than fair market value.

For such reasons, price/adjustment clauses or escalation clauses are included in purchase/sale contracts between non-arm's-length parties. Notwithstanding the inclusion of such clauses, a reasonable attempt must still be made to establish fair market value to avoid Revenue Canada's invoking Section 69. (Revenue Canada has issued pronouncements in this respect in one of its "interpretation Bulletins.")

Again with regard to V-Day valuations, there has been some interesting Canadian tax litigation involving the V-Day value of publicly traded shares held by a taxpayer since the end of 1971 and subsequently disposed of. In the case of publicly traded Canadian securities, Revenue Canada has prescribed values for purposes of determining the V-Day value of the shares in question. Basically, the values prescribed are the quoted stock market prices at the end of December 1971.[23] However, because the law states that the fair market value of publicly traded securities held at V-Day is the greater of (1) the prescribed (i.e., quoted) price and (2) the fair market value "otherwise determined,"[24] a taxpayer with a shareholding in a family corporation publicly issued will attempt to establish a V-Day value for his/her shares in excess of the quoted stock market price, on the basis that such shareholding is part of a family control group and, hence, the stock market price is not appropriate. For numerous reasons, a departure from stock market price may in any event be justified.

---

[23] More precisely, in the case of public company shares, the V-Day is December 22, 1971.

[24] Income Tax Application Rules § 126(11) (1971). For a detailed discussion of these issues, see Wise, "The V-Day Value of Publicly Traded Shares," Canadian Tax J. 253 (Mar-Apr. 1980).

[b] Going-Private Transactions

In Canada the federal statute, the Canada Business Corporations Act, and most of the provinces grant minority shareholders the right to have their shares valued where a corporation reorganizes in such a manner as to have or intend to have the effect of compelling a minority shareholder of the company to terminate his/her interest therein ("fundamental corporate changes"). A number of the statutes also contain provisions granting to minority shareholders the right to have their shares valued when the shares are subject to compulsory acquisition under take-over bid provisions.

Until early 1979, all of the appraisal statutes and those proposed in the Canadian jurisdictions (with the exception of the Province of British Columbia) provides that, in determining "fair value" for purposes of a fundamental change, any increase or decrease in value reasonably attributable to the anticipated adoption of the resolution should be excluded. The philosophy was that, since the minority shareholder would no longer be a shareholder after the "squeeze-out," the value of the shares after he/she was gone would be irrelevant. This was obviously unfair, since it denied the minority shareholder the ability to participate in the company's future value taking into account the reorganization itself. In 1979, Section 184(3) of the CBCA was amended so that any appreciation or depreciation in anticipation of the vote upon the corporate resolution resulting in the squeeze-out would be a factor in the determination of fair value.

The CBCA and those provincial statutes that grant a similar appraisal remedy provide that if the dissentient and the corporation fail to agree on the value of the shares to be purchased, either party may apply to the court to fix a value for the shares. The statutes imposed upon the court the responsibility to determine a "fair value." One or more valuators may, at the court's discretion, assist in the fixing of value.

The courts in both Canada and the United States have dealt with the meaning of the expression "fair value" as it applies to the appraisal remedy; this term is not defined in any of the Canadian company law statutes. It is noted that in the United States certain statutes provide for an appraisal and payment of the "value," "fair value," or "fair cash value"; others provide for an appraisal and the payment of the "market value" or "full-market value."

Since the concept of the appraisal remedy in favor of dissenting shareholders has its origin in the United States, Canadian courts—and indeed the valuation profession—have looked to American jurisprudence as a guide to the interpretation and determination of "fair value." However, as a result of the Canadian decision *Re Domglas Inc.*, there is now an important precedent and authority relevant in the determination and meaning of "fair value" for purposes of both the appraisal and oppression remedies. In this important decision, Justice Greenberg of the Quebec Superior Court reviewed the case law that had emerged from the American courts. He also examined the reported British Columbia cases dealing with "fair value" under the terms of the British Columbia corporate statute. Having considered the relevant United States and British Columbia jurisprudence, Justice Greenberg considered, *inter alia*, three further valuation issues in reviewing the approach to be adopted in arriving at "fair value."

1. Whether the dissenters' shares (minority) should be subject to a minority discount in arriving at "fair value";
2. Whether the use of hindsight or retrospective evidence should be admitted; and
3. Whether a "forcing-out" premium should be paid to the dissentients.

While it appears obvious that a minority discount should not be applied in arriving at "fair value," it is worth noting the *Domglas* court's position on the limited use of hindsight as well as a forcing-out premium.

Justice Greenberg noted, in *Re Domglas, Inc.*, as follows:

[T]he 1978 projections are very useful; and the reasonableness may properly be measured against the yardstick of 1978 actual results. Hence, evidence of such actual results is both relevant and admissible for such purpose. The Petitioners' objections to that evidence are accordingly hereby dismissed.

In concluding that the reasonableness of the 1978 projections may properly be measured against the yardstick of 1978 actual results, the *Domglas* court reviewed certain jurisprudence and referred to, among other things, the well-known *Couzens* (Ford Motor Company) case decided by the U.S. Board of Tax Appeals.[25]

In summary, it appears that the Canadian courts will restrict the use of hind-sight evidence to test the reasonableness or the validity of assumptions and projections made and actually existing as of the valuation date. New facts introduced, i.e., facts or trends that came into existence or took place subsequent to the valuation date, will not be admitted.

In *Domglas*, the court also adopted the position that "fair value" is fair market value without the application of a minority discount and

---

[25] Couzens v. Comm'r, 11 B.T.A. 1040.

increased by a "forcing-out premium." Justice Greenberg stated as follows:

> In cases of the "squeeze-out" of the dissenting shareholders, which is equivalent to an expropriation, "fair value" goes beyond the concept of "intrinsic value", in that the former must include a premium for forcible taking, and is not subject to a minority discount.
>
> In this Court's opinion, in a "squeeze-out" situation, as exists in the case at Bar, the absence of a discount in valuing a minority holding, and the increment or premium for forcible taking, are the essence of the distinction between "fair market value" and "fair value".

The *Domglas* court therefore added onto the full ratable value of the minority shares a forcing-out premium of 20%.

It is beyond the scope of this commentary to address the numerous other issues that have been dealt with by the Canadian courts subsequent to the *Domglas* decision.

[c] Minority Shareholder Oppression

Canadian company law statutes also provide an "oppression remedy" in favor of minority shareholders in Section 241 of the Canada Business Corporations Act as well as a number of the provincial statutes. Essentially, if a corporation or its directors act in a manner oppressive or unfair to a shareholder, the court may order the corporation or the majority shareholder to acquire his/her securities. There are no statutory rules, guidelines, or criteria established for valuing the shares where these provisions apply. While the statutes refer specifically to "fair value" where there are fundamental changes as in going-private transactions, there is no reference to the price to be paid an oppressed minority shareholder. For example, Section 241(3)(f) of the CBCA, which provides for an order by the court for the purchase of the minority's shares, does not specifically refer to "fair value." It provides a remedy related to the right to dissent, which is provided in Section 184; Section 184(3) refers to "fair value." This can be seen from the comments of the court in *Montel v. Groupe de Consultants PGL Inc. (supra)*, a case dealing with the oppression remedy under Section 241 of the CBCA.

> The value requested by Petitioners is essentially the same as the value provided under Section 184 of the Act to be paid to dissenting shareholders in cases where a corporation resolves to amend its articles in certain respects or amalgamate with another corporation, etc. While Section 184 clearly does not apply to the pres-

ent dispute, the analogy of valuation at "fair value" is a perfectly sound one. . . .

I can see no reason why the valuation should be any less just and equitable in the case of a shareholder who has been expelled or oppressed under Section 243 than it would be for a dissenting shareholder under Section 184.

I would therefore value the shares on the basis of their *fair value*. [Emphasis added.]

[d] Separation and Divorce

Similar to the United States, Canada has a high divorce rate. A number of situations require the determination of the value of family property for purposes of quantifying the payment(s) from one spouse to the other. In the provinces of Ontario, Saskatchewan, and British Columbia, an equalization payment is required from the spouse having the greater value of net family property. Valuation issues arise with respect to the determination of the value of the property of each spouse as well as the ability of a spouse to provide alimentary support to the other. The business valuator therefore gives evidence not only in respect of valuation issues but also with respect to the actual income-earning capacity of, say, the husband notwithstanding what his income tax return may show. For example, the husband may own all the issued shares of a holding company ("Holdco") which, in turn, controls an active operating company ("Opco"). Notwithstanding that the husband may draw, say, $30,000 a year from Holdco, which would be reflected on his income tax return, Holdco may be receiving another $200,000 per annum by way of dividends or management fees from Opco. In providing evidence, the valuator will explain to the court that the "notional" income that the husband has access to is not merely $30,000 but rather an amount well in excess thereof. Furthermore, to the extent that there are personal expenses being paid on the husband's behalf by Opco, the pre-tax and after-tax value thereof is included in the analysis of husband's ability to pay. (Such personal expenses would typically include automobile charges, entertainment, travel, non-productive persons on the payroll.)

In separation and divorce, the types of valuation issues that surface most often relate to minority discounts, lack of marketability, whether contingent tax[26] and liquidation costs should be considered in determining share values, the effect of shareholders' buy-sell agree-

---

[26] For a detailed discussion of valuing shares where there are contingent taxes, *see* Wise, "The Valuation of Preferred Shares Issued on a Section 85 Rollover," 32 Canadian Tax J. 239 (Mar.-Apr. 1984). *See also* Wise, "Ontario's Divorce Courts Bring New Issues to Light," C.A. Mag. 57 (Dec. 1987).

ments on share values, etc. Nonshare valuation issues relate to pension benefits, university degrees, professional licenses, etc.

In 1986 Ontario enacted the Family Law Act (FLA). This significant new legislation resulted not only in an avalanche of assignments for business valuation and Chartered Accountants but a significant amount of litigation. As a result, numerous decisions have been handed down by the Ontario courts touching, or indeed focusing, upon business valuation and related issues. The greatest number of, and most visible, cases addressing valuation issues, therefore, are those emanating from the Ontario courts (the Unified Family Court, the High Court of Justice, and the Supreme Court of Ontario).

Since the value term employed in the FLA is "value," the first issue that must be considered by the valuator and counsel for whom he/she is working is whether this means "fair market value," "fair value," "value to the owner," or some other value term. While, fair market value may be what is generally intended, this is not necessarily so as evidenced by some of the decisions recently being handed down by the Ontario courts.

It is also to be noted that in many situations, two notional valuations are required: one as of the "valuation date" (the earliest of the date of separation, divorce, or the day before the death of one spouse) and the other being the date of the marriage—very much as we have had with respect to valuations under the Income Tax Act: a current valuation at the date of the deemed disposition and an earlier one at "valuation day."

In summary, while the Canadian Income Tax Act employs the term "fair market value" and the Canada Business Corporations Act employs the term "fair value," the FLA uses the term "value" (Section 4). The courts have had to consider the context in which value is to be determined, having regard in each case to the particular circumstances.

In *Dibbley v. Dibbley*[27] the court accepted "fair market value" as being same as "value." However, *Rawluk v. Rawluk*,[28] Justice Walsh contemplated that bases other than "fair market value" may also be appropriate. In *Corless v. Corless*,[29] a case which related to the valuation of the husband's law practice, Steinberg J. (Mr. Justice Steinberg) rejected the "value in use" approach and took the "exchange value" as being appropriate, i.e., he adopted a market value approach. In this decision, the court held that if the asset could be exchanged legally, it had no value pursuant to Section 4 of the FLA. As regards the market, the court held that the exchange value would be what the husband's

---

[27] [1987] 5 R.F.L.3d 381 (Ont. H.J.C.).
[28] [1986] 2 R.F.L.3d 113, 55 O.R.2d 704 (Ont. H.J.C.).
[29] [1987] 5 R.F.L.3d 256, 58 O.R.2d 19 (Ont. U.F.C.).

partners would pay to him on his voluntary withdrawal from the law practice, reflecting any noncompetition arrangements.

In an unreported decision handed down by Mr. Justice Jean Marquis in April 1987, the Quebec Superior Court concluded, in the case of a successful going concern, that the book value of the husband's company had nothing to do with fair market value for purposes of establishing his net worth. Furthermore, the fact that for tax purposes the revenue authorities had a few years earlier agreed to book value as a basis to reach a settlement as to contested share values of the same private corporation also had nothing to do with fair market value. A negotiated settlement for tax purposes should not prejudice the determination of the true fair market value.

Following the federal tax reform that came into effect in Canada in 1972, there were a large number of cases addressing a host of valuation issues such as control, minority discounts, use of hindsight, special purchase premiums, capitalization rates, methodology, expert witness, etc. These decisions emanated from the Tax Court of Canada (formerly the Tax Review Board), the Federal Court—Trial Division, and the Federal Court of Appeal. A number of valuation issues were considered and adjudicated by these courts. Major changes were also made to the company law of British Columbia in 1974. These were followed by amendments to the federal legislation in the Canada Business Corporations Act and the provincial legislation in the various provinces' statutes in 1975 and subsequent years. Since then, the courts have been addressing other valuation issues, particularly those relating to the determination of "fair value."[30]

Numerous fair value issues have been arising in connection with a corporation's going private, the oppression of minority shareholders by the majority, or a takeover bid followed by a compulsory acquisition (of minority shares).

[e] Expropriation—Business Disturbance, Loss of Goodwill

The relevant provisions from a valuation and litigation support point-of-view that are contained in the various expropriation statutes relate to compensation to the party whose property or business has been expropriated. Issues such as the loss of goodwill, disturbance damages, duplicate operating costs, etc. are often the subject of dispute as to the quantum theory.

In the case of small businesses, an important issue that frequently surfaces is whether, in the operations of a store carrying on as a "one-

---

[30] See Wise, "The CA's Role in Valuation: An Inside-Out Perspective," C.A Mag. 28 (Sept. 1984); Wise, "Fair Value for Dissenting Shareholders," CA Mag. 52 (June 1987).

man business," a deduction should be made for imputed management salaries. In an important Canadian expropriation case dealing with this issue, *Plouffe v. City of Ottawa*,[31] the Land Compensation Board concluded that no deduction should be made:

> This [annual] net income represented earnings to the claimant from the efforts of himself and his family and provided a living for them. As a saleable proposition, however, the grocery store was operating at a loss on the basis of the accountant's standard practice of including a management salary and clerical wage in the operating expenses of the business in consequence of which the business had no saleable goodwill. The Board relies on a line of decisions of the Lands Tribunal of England and finds that in the circumstances of this case a deduction should not be made for the value of the claimant's and his family's services in the grocery store.

[f] Breach of Contract

Business valuators are called upon to provide services in the following types of cases:

- Sales cases in which is it necessary to establish either the purchaser's lost profits or the vendor's lost profits;
- Breach-of-warranty cases (either express or implied warranty);
- Negligence; and
- Other types of contracts, including: (1) contracts to render services, (2) exclusive agency contracts, (3) covenants not to compete, (4) leases, (5) construction contracts, (6) manufacturing contracts, and (7) contracts to provide loans.

In such cases, the business valuator works closely with the attorney and is given guidance as to what is required for court. The valuator is called upon to express his/her opinion as to the loss of net profits due to the breach of contract as well as, if appropriate, the loss of goodwill. In these types of issues, the business valuator's report will usually be quite detailed and will contain appropriate graphics to assist in explaining to the court various trends and so forth.

[g] Torts

Business valuators are also called upon to provide professional services in cases where there is a breach of a defendant's obligation that does not arise from a contract. Such types of cases generally include the following:

---

[31] [1973] 4 L.C.R. 37.

- Negligence;
- Intentional torts; and
- Strict liability in torts.

The first category, negligence, includes cases involving personal injury and property damage. Intentional torts include fraud, interference with a contract, business interference, defamation, nuisance, and unfair competition. Strict liability in tort is generally limited to physical harm to a user or consumer caused by the product of the vendor.

Because the numbers of cases involving tort causes of action have increased substantially in Canada, the role of the business valuator has increased significantly. There has been a dramatic rise in the numbers of claims for lost profits and other economic or pecuniary damages. In these types of cases, the business valuator is also called upon to provide evidence as to factual causation. In analyzing the cause of lost profits, the Canadian valuator acting as an expert determines what would have happened had the conduct of the defendant not occurred.

As business valuation techniques become more sophisticated and with the increasing assistance of computers, Canadian business valuators use techniques such as regression analysis (e.g., to quantify lost profits in a damage claim). A predictive trend would be established based on historical (pre-damage) data and the trend would then be applied to post-damage data to estimate what the revenues would have been had the damage not occurred. The pre-damage data could relate to the subject business or, if appropriate, one that closely parallels (i.e., is a model for) the subject business.

[h] Personal Injury

In Canada, business valuators play a key role in quantifying damages resulting from personal injury. The types of damages that are determined by the business valuator working closely with the attorney often include the following:

- Loss of future earnings;
- Loss of household services;
- Loss of financial support; and
- Loss of parental guidance.

The valuator must also address the issue as to whether inflation should be taken into account when arriving at "special damages" (which include hospital, medical, and loss of salary/wages up to the date of the judgment).

Some of the more important Canadian cases on personal injury are shown in Table 21-3.

TABLE 21-3

LEADING CANADIAN CASES ON PERSONAL INJURY

- Andrews v. Grand & Toy Alberta Ltd., [1983] D.L.R.3d 452, [1978] 1 W.W.R. 577, [1978] 2 S.C.R. 229
- Borland v. Mutterbach (1985), 23 D.L.R.4th 664 (Ont. C.A.), *rev'g* [1984] 15 D.L.R.4th 486 (Ont. H.C.)
- Thornton v. Board of School of Trustees of School District No. 57 (Prince George), [1978] 2 S.C.R. 267
- Arnold v. Teno, [1978] 2 S.C.R. 287, 1983 D.L.R.3d 609.
- Lindal v. Lindal, 19 C.C.L.T. 1 (S.C.C.)

As regards the income tax implications of damage awards, Revenue Canada, taxation has issued, on May 8, 1987, Interpretation Bulletin No. IT-365R2 entitled "Damages, Settlements and Similar Receipts."

[i] Insurance Claims

Canadian business valuators also provide services to either the claimant company or the insurer with respect to insurance for loss of business, physical assets, and so forth. The measurement of lost profits involves the same types of analyses as for calculating the earnings value of a business. The valuator may also be required to opine on whether, say in the case of a fire or a flood, damages to the factory should be calculated on the basis of a piecemeal liquidation of the machinery and equipment or on the basis of an "en bloc" going concern. In this connection, the valuator will determine whether the company immediately before the damage was viable as a going concern or whether the business was worth more on liquidation. If the latter were applicable, the valuator must consider whether installation costs, engineering costs, etc. should be totally written off.

[2] Arbitration

The business valuator may be appointed as an arbitrator in connection with a valuation dispute (which could include the interpretation of a value term contained in a shareholders' agreement, for example) or, alternatively, could be appointed the arbitrator by two other arbitrators, each acting for an adverse party. The third alternative would be for the valuator to be appointed by one side, the other side appointing another valuator, and the two valuators mutually agreeing on a third.

There is a body called the Arbitrators Institute of Canada, Inc. to which a number of business valuators belong. That Institute sets high standards with respect to the arbitration process and issues periodic publications relating to, or summarizing, various arbitration matters and so forth. In 1988 a designation C.Arb. will be given to members who have met certain criteria and standards.

¶ 21.4 Valuation Profession

As in the United States, the valuation profession is divided essentially between business and securities valuators on the one hand and real estate and equipment appraisers on the other. Because business and securities valuation has typically been performed by the public accounting profession for a number of years, it is not too often that business valuators and tangible-asset appraisers operate under the same roof. That is, it is rare for the accounting firms or independent business valuation firms to also provide real estate or equipment appraisals. In Canada there is no overall appraisal society, such as the American Society of Appraisers in the United States, which is a multi-disciplinary professional society. While there are in Canada appraisers of works of art, jewelry, and so forth, appraisers of these types of assets are few and far between.

[1] The Canadian Institute of Chartered Business Valuators

In Canada, the professional body whose members carry out the practice of business and securities valuation is the CICBV (Canadian Institute of Chartered Business Valuators), which was initially formed in 1971 as the Canadian Association of Business Valuators. The CICBV was established for the purpose of encouraging the development of a high level of competence in the field of business valuation.

To be an accredited member of the CICBV, an applicant must satisfy all of these requirements:

- He/she has successfully completed the Institute's program of studies (essentially a three-year correspondence course with the University of Toronto).
- He/she has had either two years of full-time experience, or part-time experience that is the equivalent of two years of full-time experience, in the valuation of business interests of various classes.
- He/she provides the Membership Committee with a signed recommendation of a Member (who has reviewed the valuation experience of such applicant) that such applicant be accepted as a Member of the Institute and the attestation of such member as to the applicant's valuation experience.
- He/she has successfully written the following uniform final entrance examinations which are held in two parts (three hours each) (1) a single- and multisubject questions examination and (2) a comprehensive case examination.

Members must also adhere to the Institute's Code of Ethics.

Most members (and candidates) of the CICBV are Chartered Accountants in public practice. As noted earlier, business valuation in Canada has historically been performed by Chartered Accountants, although Certified Financial Analysts employed by investment dealers perform such services but more with respect to the public equity markets and companies going public, public companies reorganizing or going private, etc.

The courses that candidates are required to complete to meet the education prerequisite of the CICBV are as follows:

- Valuation I and II;
- Special Topics;
- Taxation in Business Valuation;
- Law and Valuation; and
- Litigation.

[2] The Canadian Institute of Chartered Accountants

Because of the important role played by Canadian Chartered Accountants in the field of business valuation, both from a practice point of view as well as in the activities of the CICBV, some background information about Chartered Accountants is worthwhile.

In Canada, the history of the accounting profession descends directly from Scottish and English practices. The first group of professional accountants in the Western world was established in Scotland in 1854. In 1880, the Association of Accountants was formed in Montreal, and in 1883 the Institute of Chartered Accountants of Ontario was established. In May 1902, an Act incorporating the Dominion Association of Chartered Accountants received Royal assent. In 1949, the name was changed to its current name, The Canadian Institute of Chartered Accountants. All provincial institutes' members are automatically members of the CICA.

The CICA operates very much like the American Institute of Certified Public Accountants, with numerous committees, various publications, and a strong code of ethics. It is a participant in the International Congress of Accountants as well as the Inter-American Accounting Conference.

Recognizing the importance and growth of the field of business valuation in Canada and the fact that during the past two decades (particularly as a result of the introduction of capital gains in the Canadian income tax system in 1972), the CICA's official publication, *CA Magazine*, has a bimonthly column entitled "Business Valuation."

¶ 21.5 Valuation Terms

Various valuation terms, such as those noted below, are essentially defined in Canada in a manner similar to that in the United States:

1. Fair market value;
2. Market value;
3. Fair value;
4. Book value;
5. Adjusted book value;
6. Replacement value;
7. Value to the owner;
8. Intrinsic value;
9. Liquidation value;
10. Value in use; and
11. Retention value.

Since, at the time of writing this chapter, the Business Valuation Committee of the American Society of Appraisers has been in the process of re-examining the definitions of the various value- and valuation-related terms, it is not considered appropriate to comment any further except to state that, in general and in principle, the valuation terms in both countries are basically the same. Any differences may arise simply because of semantics.

¶ 21.6 Case Law and Regulatory Pronouncements and Practices

[1] Leading Judicial Decisions

While the Canadian courts at both the federal and provincial levels continue to hear valuation-related issues, there are a number of cases that the valuation profession considers as precedent setting. The topics in Table 21-4 have been considered by the various courts over the years.

[2] Revenue Canada, Taxation

On a periodic basis Revenue Canada, Taxation releases pronouncements as to its official attitude with respect to various taxation matters. These publications include "Interpretation Bulletins," which outline Revenue Canada's interpretation of specific sections of the Income Tax Act and "Information circulars," which address administrative and procedural matters. Revenue Canada, similar to the IRS's Revenue Rulings, also issues certain income tax rulings that it selects for publication. The Revenue Canada tax rulings contain disguised summaries of certain advance income tax rulings, the subject matter of which may be of relatively widespread interest.

TABLE 21-4
PRECEDENT-SETTING CASES IN CANADA

- ☐ **Fair market value**
  - Untermyer v. Attorney General of British Columbia, [1929] S.C.R. 84, [1929] 1 D.L.R. 315
  - Henderson v. MNR; Bank of New York v. MNR, [1973] C.T.C. 636, 73 D.T.C. 5471

- ☐ **Fair value—going private**
  - Re Douglas, Inc. [1980] C.S. 925, 13 B.L.R. 135, aff'd [1982] C.A. 377, 22 B.L.R. 121, 138 D.L.R.3d 521 (Que. C.A.)
  - Johnston v. West Fraser Timber Co. Ltd., [1982] 19 B.L.R. 193 (B.C.S.C.), [1982] 17 B.L.R. 16 (B.C.S.C.).
  - Neonex International Ltd. v. Kolasa, [1978] 84 D.L.R.3d 446, [1978] 2 W.W.R. 593, 3 D.L.R. 1
  - Cyprus Anvil Mining Corp. v. Dickson [1982] 20 B.L.R. 21

- ☐ **Theory of blockage**
  - Untermeyer v. Attorney General of B.C., *supra*

- ☐ **Escrowed shares**
  - W.L. Falconer v. MNR, 59 D.T.C. 622, 61 D.T.C. 1176, 62 D.T.C. 1247

- ☐ **Minority discounts**
  - A.R. Levitt v. MNR, 76 D.T.C 1047
  - Diligenti v. RWMD Operations Kelowna, Ltd. [1977] 4 B.C.L.R. 134
  - Moynihan v. MNR., 62 D.T.C. 64

- ☐ **Restrictions on shares**
  - Estate of A.W. Beaument v. MNR, 69 D.T.C. 5016, 70 D.T.C. 6130 (S.C.C.)
  - Estate of J.J. West v Minister of Finance of British Columbia, 76 C.T.C. 313

- ☐ **Personal goodwill**
  - J. Young v. MNR, 65 C.T.C. 242

- ☐ **Admissibility of hindsight**
  - E. Littler, Sr. v. The Queen, 76 D.T.C. 6210, 78 D.T.C 6179
  - National Syst. of Banking of Alberta v. The Queen, 78 D.T.C. 6019; 80 D.T.C. 6178
  - Re Domglas, Inc., *supra*

- ☐ **Leasehold interest**
  - Saskatoon Drug and Stationery Co. v. The Queen, 75 D.T.C. 103, 78 D.T.C. 6396

- ☐ **Valuation of publicly listed shares (for tax purposes)**
  - National Sys. of Banking of Alberta v. The Queen, 78 D.T.C. 6018 (F.C.T.D.), 80 D.T.C 6178 (F.C.A.)

- ☐ **Expert witness**
  - H.P. Connor v. The Queen, 78 D.T.C. 6497 (F.C.T.D.)
  - D & H Friedman, v. MNR, [1978] C.T.C. 2809; 78 D.T.C. 1599
  - W.R. Brunelle v. MNR, 77 D.T.C. 326

- ☐ **Special purchaser**
  - Dominion Metal & Refining Works v. The Queen, 83 D.T.C. 322 (T.R.B.)
  - E. Littler, Sr. v. The Queen, 76 D.T.C. 6210; 78 D.T.C. 6179
  - Lakehouse Enterprises, Ltd. v. MNR, 83 D.T.C. 388

- ☐ **Allocation of sales price**
  - Saskatoon Drug and Stationery Co. v. The Queen, *supra*

- ☐ **Capitalization rates**
  - A. Yager v. The Queen, 85 D.T.C. 5413 (F.C.T.D.)
  - Re Domglas, Inc. *supra*
  - Neonex International Ltd. v. Kolasa, [1978] 84 D.L.R.3d 446; [1978] 2 W.W.R. 593, 3 D.L.R. 1

- ☐ **Price adjustment clause (escalation clause)**
  - Guilder News Co., v. MNR, 73 D.T.C 6146, 73 D.T.C. 5048

- ☐ **Family control**
  - E. Littler, Sr. v. The Queen, *supra*

Of the numerous information circulars that Revenue Canada has issued, one is directly on the subject of business valuation: Information Circular 89-3.[32]

However, in practical terms, there are substantially fewer tax-related situations requiring business valuations. Most valuations relate to determining the "valuation day" value of capital property, including shares and business interests. Although "valuation day" for capital gains purposes is nearly 20 years ago, it nonetheless is still important in Canada because capital gains tax is based on the increase in the gain from valuation day on (with respect to property owned continuously since the end of 1971).

[3] Ontario Securities Commission

The relevant law is contained in the Securities Act and the Regulations made under the Act. Regard must also be paid to the Ontario Business Corporations Act, the provisions of which are essentially analogous to those of the federal statute, the Canada Business Corporations Act.

An insider circular bid, or a circular bid where the offeror anticipates that a going-private transaction will follow the takeover bid, must contain a summary of a formal valuation of the acquiree as well as an outline of any previous valuation of the acquiree prepared within the prior twenty-four months; this must include a description of the source and circumstances under which it was prepared (Regulation 163(2)). There are three exceptions:

1. If the offeror establishes to the Director's satisfaction that the offeror lacks access to information enabling the insider to prepare the valuation;
2. If the Director of the Commission gives written consent to any waiver or variation in the valuation requirement; and
3. If there is an application by an interested party or a waiver of the valuation requirement because the disclosure of information to the acquiree's shareholders would "cause a detriment" to the acquiree or the shareholders outweighing the benefit of the information to prospective recipients.

The insider engages an investment dealer or public accounting firm to prepare a formal valuation "based upon techniques that are appropriate in the circumstances, after considering going-concern or liquidation assumption or both, together with other relevant assumptions [such] that [the valuation] arrives at an opinion as to a value or

---

[32] *Policy Statement on Business Equity Valuation*, Information Circular 89-3 (Aug. 25, 1989).

range of values for the participating securities based upon such analysis without any downward adjustments to reflect the fact the participating securities do not form part of a controlling interest" (Regulation 163(1)).

The valuation must be prepared not more than 120 days prior to the date of the takeover bid, and it must contain appropriate adjustments for material intervening events (Regulation 163(4)). A summary of a formal valuation of more than 120 days may be used "if it is accompanied by a letter addressed to the directors of the [acquiree] confirming that the valuer has no reasonable grounds to believe any intervening event has materially affected the value or range of values determined in such valuation, or if there has been such an event, describing it and stating the resulting change in the value or range of values in the valuation" (Regulation 163(5)).

A "prior valuation" is defined as an "existing independent appraisal or valuation or any material non-independent appraisal or valuation in respect to any issuer, its material assets or its securities" (Regulation 163(1)). Accordingly, the circular must include disclosure of any independent valuation or any "material" non-independent (e.g., if prepared by the corporation itself) valuation.

The insider circular must state that a copy of the valuation will be sent to any registered target shareholder upon payment of a charge that is sufficient to cover printing and postage (Form 32, Item 14). The valuation (and any letter of confirmation where it is more than 120 days old, as noted above) must be filed along with the filing of the circular, except where the Director of the Commission otherwise permits.

It should be noted that the circular referred to above is either a takeover bid circular in respect of an insider bid, a takeover bid circular where it is anticipated by the offeror that a going-private transaction will follow the takeover bid, or an issuer bid circular.

Going-private transactions are regulated under Section 189 of the Ontario Business Corporations Act and Policy 9.1 of the Ontario Securities Commission's Policy Statements. Corporations intending to go private (i.e., to squeeze out the minority) and where the transaction is not to be preceded by a takeover bid or issuer bid are subject to the rules set out in Policy 9.1. The above-noted rules set out in Regulation 163 apply in Policy 9.1.

The information circular sent to shareholders with respect to the going-private transaction must comply with most of the disclosure rules outlined above in connection with the issuer bid circular.

[a] Ontario Policy Statement

Policy 9.1, entitled "Going-Private Transactions, Issuer Bids and Insider Bids," sets out the valuation requirements. It should be noted that the Commission may exempt the valuation requirement in a going-private transaction where there is a minimal minority position and the cost to the issuer would be undue in the circumstances.

Ontario's Policy Statement employs various terms as defined in the Securities Act and the Regulations thereunder. In the Policy Statement, "valuation procedures" are defined as meaning the following:

a) A summary of the valuation should be included in the material sent to security holders in connection with the transaction. Copies of the complete valuation should be available for inspection and the material provided to security holders should indicate that a copy of the valuation will be sent to any registered holder upon request for a nominal charge sufficient to cover printing and postage. Where the Director is of the opinion that disclosure of information in the valuation would cause a detriment to the issuer or its security holders that would outweigh the benefit of the information to the prospective recipients, the Director may permit the omission of the information from the copies to be so made available.
b) The summary of the valuation to be included in the material should disclose the basis of computation, the scope of review, the relevant factors and their values and key assumptions on which the valuation is based. The summary of the valuation should also disclose the extent to which any advantage to a personal or company continuing as a security holder after completion of the transaction has been considered in the valuation.
c) The valuation shall be at a date not more than 120 days prior to the date of the transaction and shall contain appropriate adjustments for material intervening events. Where a valuation at a date more than 120 days prior to the date of the transaction is available it may, if accepted by the Director, satisfy the valuation requirement if the summary of the valuation is accompanied by a letter addressed to the security holders confirming the valuation and confirming that the valuer, after making due investigation, has no reasonable ground to believe that any intervening event has materially affected the value or range of values determined in such valuation or, if there has been such an event, describing it and stating the resultant change in the value or range of values in the valuation.

[b] Decisions Relating to Valuation

As regards the exemption for valuation, as noted above, Paragraph 5 of the section on Interpretations states that a valuation is not required where the Director of the Commission is satisfied of any of the following:

a) The price offered was arrived at in an arm's length transaction or negotiation whereby control of the issuer has changed or will change hands within one year prior to the transaction, and two directors, on behalf of the board of directors, and two senior officers certify that no prior event in the affairs of the issuer undisclosed at the time of the initial transaction or negotiation had occurred which is disclosed could reasonably be expected to have affected the price arrived at in the arm's length transaction or negotiation and that no intervening event in the affairs of the issuer has occurred which could reasonably be expected to increase materially the value of the issuer. Examples of such transactions include a take-over bid or a private agreement resulting in a change of control of the issuer. The Director may determine that arm's length transactions for less than a control block (for example, an arm's length purchase by the controlling security holder of a sizeable block of the minority held securities) will qualify for this exception from the valuation requirement. Evidence will probably be required that the selling security holder in such an instance had such knowledge of the issuer that other than purely market considerations would likely have been considered in arriving at the price. The reason for insisting generally upon a transaction involving a control block if it is to displace the valuation requirement in a subsequent transaction is that, typically, an offeror who seeks to acquire control of an issuer will have considered underlying values, as will the selling security holder; in a transaction for less than control, purely market considerations or financial considerations peculiar to the selling security holder are much more likely to have constituted the decisive factors;

b) The price offered is not less than fair value of the securities concerned, based on factors which are appropriate in the circumstances; or

c) After the bid those security holders who decline the offer will have available a market to dispose of their securities that is not materially less liquid than prior to the bid. Where an issuer wishes to rely upon this exception, the Director should be provided with an opinion from a registered dealer with respect to the liquidity of the market in the securities both before and after the proposed bid and, if the securities of the issuer are listed, a letter from The Toronto Stock Exchange or other stock exchange where the securities are listed indicating the concurrence of such exchange.

[4] British Columbia Securities Commission

Legislation and rules relating to business valuation are contained in the British Columbia Securities Act and the Regulations thereunder. As with the Province of Ontario, the British Columbia Securities Commission has issued a Local Policy Statement 3-04 entitled "Guidelines for Technical Reports on Non-Natural Resources, Properties and Program Proposals Which are the Subject of Funding on Prospectuses and Other Statements of Material Facts Submitted for Receipting by the Superintendent of Brokers," effective February 1, 1987. This Local Policy Statement is to be read in conjunction with Section 8.0 of Local Policy Statement 3-07 and with Section 45(1) of the Securities Act.

Rather than filing a prospectus and listing shares on the stock exchange, a number of Canadian and American companies wishing to go public have used a publicly traded "shell" company listed on the Vancouver Stock Exchange, of which there is an abundant supply. This is often accomplished by an exchange of shares, resulting in the business of the private operating company being "rolled" into the public shell.

Since the proposed transaction would require full, true, and plain disclosure about the property (e.g., the business) being acquired, a technical report may be required which may include "where fair market value may not be readily determined," a valuation of assets, which the issuer has acquired or plans to acquire.

A technical report must be submitted when any one or a combination of the following conditions apply (Section 2.6):

- The issuer plans to acquire an entity which is not a going-concern entity as defined in Local Policy 3-07.
- The project which is the subject of the funding involves the launching by an entity of a new product or service or an entry into a new field by such entity.
- A fair market value of a property acquired cannot be determined objectively by comparison with prices of similar acquisitions carried out free of duress, and therefore a valuation process involving some assessment or estimates of earnings performance or the application of some other generally recognized valuation technique is required. Where a prospectus offering of an unlisted issuer is involved, this condition is likely to obtain whenever the escrowing of share consideration is prompted under Section 8.1.2 of Local Policy 3-07. Where an offering by way of statement of material facts is involved, this condition will obtain whenever the fair market value cannot be determined as noted above, in which case any shares to be issued or other consideration to be paid will be required to be made on an earn-out basis.

Where assets have been acquired by the issuer for valuable consideration, the technical report must be met on the reasonableness of adequacy of the valuation techniques used in arriving at a valuation for such assets. The report should also comment if an asset is deemed to have no value or indeterminate value.

In practical terms, the technical report will be prepared by engineers, marketing consultants, or others with experience and expertise in relation to the subject business. Only with such information can the valuator begin to assess the future prospects of that business and even then with some difficulty as many new emerging companies being rolled into these public shells do not have much of a history or track record (even though there may appear to be good potential).

Local Policy Statement 3-07 entitled "Policy Guidelines Respecting Consideration to Vendors of Property and the Issuance of Escrow and Free-Trading Shares" contains certain rules with respect to valuation. Section 5.5 provides that "the employment of a going-concern value rather than a book value for shares will be considered where appropriate." Section 8.1.2 provides as follows:

1) Where a property is not a going-concern and an estimate of earnings performance of such property is so highly speculative as to be not meaningful, it is not appropriate to seek a valuation of the property to substantial share consideration. The Commission proposes to continue the practice followed in 1986 of permitting issuance of escrow shares. . . .
2) Consideration other than within the limits in (1) above can be considered where a valuation is prepared supported by the following attributes:
   a) There is some sales earnings history;
   b) An extensive market analysis has been carried out, and
   c) The risks associated with a limited track record has been accounted for through the application of significant discount rates.

Such valuation should be submitted in conjunction with a technical report prepared in accordance with Local Policy Statement 3-04. The valuation should be prepared in accordance with generally accepted valuation techniques and *preferably by a registered member of The Canadian Institute of Chartered Business Valuators*. [Emphasis added.]

For purposes of the Local Policy, a going-concern issuer means an issuer that over the past five years has experienced three years of profitable operation or is otherwise considered by the Commission to be a going-concern issuer.

Finally, Section 2.3.3 of National Policy 2-B requires that an acceptable technical report must contain a statement that discounted cash flow values of reserves reported therein may not necessarily constitute the fair market value of such reserves.

In effect, and for practical purposes, what the B.C. Securities Commission and the Vancouver Stock Exchange are attempting to ensure is that promoters cannot simply roll into a publicly traded shell company a private business in return for shares of the transferee and immediately turn around and sell such publicly traded shares on the stock market. Accordingly, attempts to protect the public are made through independent valuations, earn-out clauses attaching to escrow agreements, and other types of control; these are overseen by the Superintendent of the Vancouver Stock Exchange. For example, Local Policy Statement 3-07 contains a Schedule "C" entitled "Earn-out Formula for Use in Schedule 'D' of Local Policy Statement 3-07," containing an example of terms of release from escrow to be followed by issuers. (The formula essentially relates to cash flow.)

APPENDIX A

REVENUE RULING 59-60

PART III.—GROSS ESTATE

SECTION 2031.—DEFINITION OF GROSS ESTATE
26 CFR 20.2031-2: Valuation of stocks and bonds. Rev. Rul. 59-60
(Also Section 2512.)
(Also Part II, Sections 811(k), 1005, Regulations 105, Section 81.10.)

In valuing the stock of closely held corporations, or the stock of corporations where market quotations are not available, all other available financial data, as well as all relevant factors affecting the fair market value must be considered for estate tax and gift tax purposes. No general formula may be given that is applicable to the many different valuation situations arising in the valuation of such stock. However, the general approach, methods, and factors which must be considered in valuing such securities are outlined.

Revenue Ruling 54-77, C.B. 1954-1, 187, superseded.

SECTION 1. PURPOSE.

The purpose of this Revenue Ruling is to outline and review in general the approach, methods and factors to be considered in valuing shares of the capital stock of closely held corporations for estate tax and gift tax purposes. The methods discussed herein will apply likewise to the valuation of corporate stocks on which market quotations are either unavailable or are of such scarcity that they do not reflect the fair market value.

SEC. 2. BACKGROUND AND DEFINITIONS.

.01 All valuations must be made in accordance with the applicable provisions of the Internal Revenue Code of 1954 and the Federal Estate Tax and Gift Tax Regulations. Sections 2031(a), 2032 and 2512(a) of the 1954 Code (sections 811 and 1005 of the 1939 Code) require that the property to be included in the gross estate, or made the subject of a gift, shall be taxed on the basis of the value of the property at the time of death of the decedent, the alternate date if so elected, or the date of gift.

.02 Section 20.2031-1(b) of the Estate Tax Regulations (section 81.10 of the Estate Tax Regulations 105) and section 25.2512-1 of the Gift Tax Regulations (section 86.19 of Gift Tax Regulations 108) define fair market value, in effect, as the price at which the property would change hands between a willing buyer and a willing seller when the former is not under any compulsion to buy and the latter is not under any compulsion to sell, both parties having reasonable knowledge of relevant facts. Court decisions frequently state in addition that the hypothetical buyer and seller are assumed to be able, as well as willing, to trade and to be well informed about the property and concerning the market for such property.

.03 Closely held corporations are those corporations the shares of which are owned by a relatively limited number of stockholders. Often the entire stock issue is held by one family. The result of this situation is that little, if any, trading in the shares takes place. There is, therefore, no established market for the stock and such sales as occur at irregular intervals seldom reflect all of the elements of a representative transaction as defined by the term "fair market value."

SEC. 3. APPROACH TO VALUATION

.01 A determination of fair market value, being a question of fact, will depend upon the circumstances in each case. No formula can be devised that will be generally applicable to the multitude of different valuation issues arising in estate and gift tax cases. Often, an appraiser will find wide differences of opinion as to the fair market value of a particular stock. In resolving such differences, he should maintain a reasonable attitude in recognition of the fact that valuation is not an exact science. A sound valuation will be based upon all the relevant facts, but the elements of common sense, informed judgment and reasonableness must enter into the process of weighing those facts and determining their aggregate significance.

.02 The fair market value of specific shares of stock will vary as general economic conditions change from "normal" to "boom" or "depression," that is, according to the degree of optimism or pessimism with which the investing public regards the future at the required date of appraisal. Uncertainty as to the stability or continuity of the future income from a property decreases its value by increasing the risk of loss of earnings and value in the future. The value of shares of stock of a company with very uncertain future prospects is highly speculative. The appraiser must exercise his judgment as to the degree of risk attaching to the business of the corporation which issued the stock, but that judgment must be related to all of the other factors affecting value.

.03 Valuation of securities is, in essence, a prophesy as to the future and must be based on facts available at the required date of appraisal. As a generalization, the prices of stocks which are traded in volume in a free and active market by informed persons best reflect the consensus of the investing public as to what the future holds for the corporations and industries represented. When a stock is closely held, is traded infrequently, or is traded in an erratic market, some other measure of value must be used. In many instances, the next best measure may be found in the prices at which the stocks of companies engaged in the same or a similar line of business are selling in a free and open market.

SEC. 4. FACTORS TO CONSIDER.

.01 It is advisable to emphasize that in the valuation of the stock of closely held corporations or the stock of corporations where market quotations are either lacking or too scarce to be recognized, all available financial data, as well as all relevant factors affecting the fair market value, should be considered. The following factors, although not all-inclusive are fundamental and require careful analysis in each case:

(a) The nature of the business and the history of the enterprise from its inception.

(b) The economic outlook in general and the condition and outlook of the specific industry in particular.

(c) The book value of the stock and the financial condition of the business.

(d) The earning capacity of the company.

(e) The dividend-paying capacity.

(f) Whether or not the enterprise has goodwill or other intangible value.

(g) Sales of the stock and the size of the block of stock to be valued.

(h) The market price of stocks of corporations engaged in the same or a similar line of business having their stocks actively traded in a free and open market, either on an exchange or over-the-counter.

.02 The following is a brief discussion of each of the foregoing factors:

(a) The history of a corporate enterprise will show its past stability or instability, its growth or lack of growth, the diversity or lack of diversity of its operations, and other facts needed to form an opinion of the degree of risk involved in the business. For an enterprise which changed its form of organization but carried on the same or closely similar operations of its predecessor, the history of the former enterprise should be considered. The detail to be considered should increase with approach to the required date of appraisal, since recent events are of greatest help in predicting the future; but a study of gross and net income, and of dividends covering a long prior period, is highly desirable. The history to be studied should include, but need not be limited to, the nature of the business, its products or services, its operating and investment assets, capital structure, plant facilities, sales records and management, all of which should be considered as of the date of the appraisal, with due regard for recent significant changes. Events of the past that are unlikely to recur in the future should be discounted, since value has a close relation to future expectancy.

(b) A sound appraisal of a closely held stock must consider current and prospective economic conditions as of the date of appraisal, both in the national economy and in the industry or industries with which the corporation is allied. It is important to know that the company is more or less successful than its competitors in the same industry, or that it is maintaining a stable position with respect to competitors. Equal or even greater significance may attach to the ability of the industry with which the company is allied to compete with other industries. Prospective competition which has not been a factor in prior years should be given careful attention. For example, high profits due to the novelty of its product and the lack of competition often lead to increasing competition. The public's appraisal of the future prospects of competitive industries or of competitors within an industry may be indicated by price trends in the markets for commodities and for securities. The loss of the manager of a so-called "one-man" business may have a depressing effect upon the value of the stock of such business, particularly if there is a lack of trained personnel capable of succeeding to the management of the enterprise. In valuing the stock of this type of business, therefore, the effect of the loss of the manager on the future expectancy of the business, and the absence of management-succession potentialities are pertinent factors to be taken into consideration. On the other hand, there may be factors which offset, in whole or in part, the loss of the manager's services. For instance, the nature of the business and of its assets may be such that they will not be impaired by the loss of the manager. Furthermore, the loss may be adequately covered by life insurance, or competent management might be employed on the basis of the consideration paid for the former manager's services. These, or other offsetting factors, if found to exist, should be carefully weighed against the loss of the manager's services in valuing the stock of the enterprise.

(c) Balance sheets should be obtained, preferably in the form of comparative annual statements for two or more years immediately preceding the date of appraisal, together with a balance sheet at the end of the month preceding that date, if corporate accounting will permit. Any balance sheet descriptions that are not self-explanatory, and balance sheet items comprehending diverse assets or liabilities, should be clarified in essential detail by supporting supplemental schedules. These statements usually will disclose to the appraiser (1) liquid position (ratio of current assets to current liabilities); (2) gross and net book value of principal classes of fixed assets; (3) working capital; (4) long-term indebtedness; (5) capital structure; and (6) net worth. Consideration also should be given to any assets not essential to the operation of the business, such as investments in securities, real estate, etc. In general, such nonoperating assets will command a lower rate of return than do the operating assets, although in exceptional cases the reverse may be true. In computing the book value per share of stock, assets of the investment type should be revalued on the basis of their market price and the book value adjusted accordingly. Comparison of the company's balance sheets over several years may reveal, among other facts, such developments as the acquisition of additional production facilities or subsidiary companies, improvement in financial position, and details as to recapitalizations and other changes in the capital structure of the corporation. If the corporation has more than one class of stock outstanding, the charter or certificate of incorporation should be examined to ascertain the explicit rights and privileges of the various stock issues including: (1) voting powers, (2) preference as to dividends, and (3) preference as to assets in the event of liquidation.

(d) Detailed profit-and-loss statements should be obtained and considered for a representative period immediately prior to the required date of appraisal, preferably five or more years. Such statements should show (1) gross income by principal items; (2) principal deductions from gross income including major prior items of operating expenses, interest and other expense on each item of long-term debt, depreciation and depletion if such deductions are made, officers' salaries, in total if they appear to be reasonable or in detail if they seem to be excessive, contributions (whether or not deductible for tax purposes) that the nature of its business and its community position require the corporation to make, and taxes by principal items, including income and excess profits taxes; (3) net income available for dividends; (4) rates and amounts of dividends paid on each class of stock; (5) remaining amount carried to surplus; and (6) adjustments to, and reconciliation with, surplus as stated on the balance sheet. With profit and loss statements of this character available, the appraiser should be able to separate recurrent from nonrecurrent items of income and expense, to distinguish between operating income and investment income, and to ascertain whether or not any line of business in which the company is engaged is operated consistently at a loss and might be abandoned with benefit to the company. The percentage of earnings retained for business expansion should be noted when dividend-paying capacity is considered. Potential future income is a major factor in many valuations of closely-held stocks, and all information concerning past income which will be helpful in predicting the future should be secured. Prior earnings records usually are the most reliable guide as to the future expectancy, but resort to arbitrary five-or-ten-year averages without regard to current trends or future prospects will not produce a realistic valuation. If, for instance, a record of progressively increasing or decreasing net income is found, then greater weight may be accorded the most recent years' profits in estimating earning power. It will be helpful, in judging risk and the extent to which a business is a marginal operator, to consider deductions from income and net income in terms of percentage of sales. Major categories of cost and expense to be so analyzed include the consumption of raw materials and supplies in the case of manufacturers, processors and fabricators; the cost of purchased merchandise in the case of merchants; utility services; insurance; taxes; depletion or depreciation; and interest.

(e) Primary consideration should be given to the dividend-paying capacity of the company rather than to dividends actually paid in the past. Recognition must be given to the necessity of retaining a reasonable portion of profits in a company to meet competition. Dividend-paying capacity is a factor that must be considered in an appraisal, but dividends actually paid in the past may not have any relation to dividend-paying capacity. Specifically, the dividends paid by a closely held family company may be measured by the income needs of the stockholders or by their desire to avoid taxes on dividend receipts, instead of by the ability of the company to pay dividends. Where an actual or effective controlling interest in a corporation is to be valued, the dividend factor is not a material element, since the payment of such dividends is discretionary with the controlling stockholders. The individual or group in control can substitute salaries and bonuses for dividends, thus reducing net income and understating the dividend-paying capacity of the company. It follows, therefore, that dividends are less reliable criteria of fair market value than other applicable factors.

(f) In the final analysis, goodwill is based upon earning capacity. The presence of goodwill and its value, therefore, rests upon the excess of net earnings over and above a fair return on the net tangible assets. While the element of goodwill may be based primarily on earnings, such factors as the prestige and renown of the business, the ownership of a trade or brand name, and a record of successful operation over a prolonged period in a particular locality, also may furnish support for the inclusion of intangible value. In some instances it may not be possible to make a separate appraisal of the tangible and intangible assets of the business. The enterprise has a value as an entity. Whatever intangible value there is, which is supportable by the facts, may be measured by the amount by which the appraised value of the tangible assets exceeds the net book value of such assets.

(g) Sales of stock of a closely held corporation should be carefully investigated to determine whether they represent transactions at arm's length. Forced or distress sales do not ordinarily reflect fair market value nor do isolated sales in small amounts necessarily control as the measure of value. This is especially true in the valuation of a controlling interest in a corporation. Since, in the case of closely held stocks, no prevailing market prices are available, there is no basis for making an adjustment for blockage. It follows, therefore, that such stocks should be valued upon a consideration of all the evidence affecting the fair market value. The size of the block of stock itself is a relevant factor to be considered. Although it is true that a minority interest in an unlisted corporation's stock is more difficult to sell than a similar block of listed stock, it is equally true that control of a corporation, either actual or in effect, representing as it does an added element of value may justify a higher value for a specific block of stock.

(h) Section 2031(b) of the Code states, in effect, that in valuing unlisted securities the value of stock or securities of corporations engaged in the same or a similar line of business which are listed on an exchange should be taken into consideration along with all other factors. An important consideration is that the corporations to be used for comparisons have capital stocks which are actively traded by the public. In accordance with section 2031(b) of the Code, stocks listed on an exchange are to be considered first. However, if sufficient comparable companies whose stocks are listed on an exchange cannot be found, other comparable companies which have stocks actively traded in on the over-the-counter market also may be used. The essential factor is that whether the stocks are sold on an exchange or over-the-counter there is evidence of an active, free public market for the stock as of the valuation date. In selecting corporations for comparative purposes, care should be taken to use only comparable companies. Although the only restrictive requirement as to comparable corporations specified in the statute is that their lines of business be the same or similar, yet it is obvious that consideration must be given to other relevant factors in order that the most valid comparison possible will be obtained. For illustration, a corporation having one or more issues of preferred stock, bonds or debentures in addition to its common stock should not be considered to be directly comparable to one having only common stock outstanding. In like manner, a company with a declining business and decreasing markets is not comparable to one with a record of current progress and market expansion.

Sec. 5. Weight To Be Accorded Various Factors.

The valuation of closely held corporate stock entails the consideration of all relevant factors as stated in section 4. Depending upon the circumstances in each case, certain factors may carry more weight than others because of the nature of the company's business. To illustrate:

(a) Earnings may be the most important criterion of value in some cases whereas asset value will receive primary consideration in others. In general, the appraiser will accord primary consideration to earnings when valuing stocks of companies which sell products or services to the public; conversely, in the investment or holding type of company, the appraiser may accord the greatest weight to the assets underlying the security to be valued.

(b) The value of the stock of a closely held investment or real estate holding company, whether or not family owned, is closely related to the value of the assets underlying the stock. For companies of this type the appraiser should determine the fair market values of the assets of the company. Operating expenses of such a company and the cost of liquidating it, if any, merit consideration when appraising the relative values of the stock and the underlying assets. The market values of the underlying assets give due weight to potential earnings and dividends of the particular items of property underlying the stock, capitalized at rates deemed proper by the investing public at the date of appraisal. A current appraisal by the investing public should be superior to the retrospective opinion of an individual. For these reasons, adjusted net worth should be accorded greater weight in valuing the stock of a closely held investment or real estate holding company, whether or not family owned, than any of the other customary yardsticks of appraisal, such as earnings and dividend paying capacity.

Sec. 6. Capitalization Rates.

In the application of certain fundamental valuation factors, such as earnings and dividends, it is necessary to capitalize the average or current results at some appropriate rate. A determination of the proper capitalization rate presents one of the most difficult problems in valuation. That there is no ready or simple solution will become apparent by a cursory check of the rates of return and dividend yields in terms of the selling prices of corporate shares listed on the major exchanges of the country. Wide variations will be found even for companies in the same industry. Moreover, the ratio will fluctuate from year to year depending upon economic conditions. Thus, no standard tables of capitalization rates applicable to closely held corporations can be formulated. Among the more important factors to be taken into consideration in deciding upon a capitalization rate in a particular case are: (1) the nature of the business; (2) the risk involved; and (3) the stability or irregularity of earnings.

SEC. 7. AVERAGE OF FACTORS.

Because valuations cannot be made on the basis of a prescribed formula, there is no means whereby the various applicable factors in a particular case can be assigned mathematical weights in deriving the fair market value. For this reason, no useful purpose is served by taking an average of several factors (for example, book value, capitalized earnings and capitalized dividends) and basing the valuation on the result. Such a process excludes active consideration of other pertinent factors, and the end result cannot be supported by a realistic application of the significant facts in the case except by mere chance.

SEC. 8. RESTRICTIVE AGREEMENTS.

Frequently, in the valuation of closely held stock for estate and gift tax purposes, it will be found that the stock is subject to an agreement restricting its sale or transfer. Where shares of stock were acquired by a decedent subject to an option reserved by the issuing corporation to repurchase at a certain price, the option price is usually accepted as the fair market value for estate tax purposes. See Rev. Rul. 54-76, C.B. 1954-1, 194. However, in such case the option price is not determinative of fair market value for gift tax purposes. Where the option, or buy and sell agreement, is the result of voluntary action by the stockholders and is binding during the life as well as at the death of the stockholders, such agreement may or may not, depending upon the circumstances of each case, fix the value for estate tax purposes. However, such agreement is a factor to be considered, with other relevant factors, in determining fair market value. Where the stockholder is free to dispose of his shares during life and the option is to become effective only upon his death, the fair market value is not limited to the option price. It is always necessary to consider the relationship of the parties, the relative number of shares held by the decedent, and other material facts, to determine whether the agreement represents a bonafide business arrangement or is a device to pass the decedent's shares to the natural objects of his bounty for less than an adequate and full consideration in money or money's worth. In this connection see Rev. Rul. 157 C.B. 1953-2, 255, and Rev. Rul. 189, C.B. 1953-2,294.

SEC. 9. EFFECT ON OTHER DOCUMENTS.

Revenue Ruling 54-77, C.B. 1954-1, 187, is hereby superseded.

BIBLIOGRAPHY

SHANNON P. PRATT*

	Page
General Valuation Issues	B-1
Articles	B-1
Books and Services	B-12
Dissenting-Stockholders' Actions	B-17
Articles	B-17
Goodwill and Other Intangibles	B-20
Articles	B-20
Marketability and Minority Interests	B-21
Articles	B-23
Mergers and Acquisitions	B-27
Articles	B-27
Books and Services	B-29

General Valuation Issues

Articles

Abruster, Steve and Polo Merguzhis, "Thinking of Selling Your Business." *Busines Puerto Rico* (May/June 1988), pp.12-14.

Albo, Wayne P. "Special Purchasers." *Journal of Business Valuation*, 1987 (Proceedings of the First Joint Institute of Chartered Business Valuators and The American Society of Appraisers, October 1986), pp. 139-61.

Alderman, David. "Evaluating a Company's Management Team." *Journal of Business Valuation*, 1987 (Proceedings of the First Joint Institute of Chartered Business Valuators and The American Society of Appraisers. October 1986), pp. 129-37.

Alvarez, Edward M. "The Deductibility of Reasonable Compensation in the Close Corporation." *Santa Clara Lawyer* 11 (1971), pp. 20-36.

Arneson, George S. "Accounting for Inflation in Valuing Closely Held Companies." *Taxes* (June 1981), pp. 391-98.

---

* SHANNON P. PRATT CFA, FASA, DBA, is president of Willamette Management Associates, Inc. in Portland, Oregon. The author has also written several books and articles on business valuation, all of which are included in this bibliography.

Arneson, George S. "Dividend Paying Capacity Has Little or No Relevance in Valuing Closely Held Corporations." *Taxes* (April 1981), pp. 251-57.

Bakken, John E. "Professional Negligence and Liability of the Appraiser." *Journal of Business Valuation*, 1987 (Proceedings of the First Joint Institute of Chartered Business Valuators and The American Society of Appraisers. October 1986), pp. 257-64.

Banks, Warren E. "Measuring the Value of Corporate Stock." *California Western Law Review* 11 (Fall 1974), pp. 1-59.

Banks, Warren E. "The Accounting Balance Sheet as a Guide to Stock Value." *Detroit College of Law Review* (1978), pp. 241-59.

Bannen, John T. "Valuation of Closely Held Corporations." *Wisconsin Bar Bulletin* (February 1982), pp. 15-17, 53.

Barenbaum, Lester. "Utilizing the Gordon Model: Discounting Net Income vs. Available Cash Flow." *Journal of Business Valuation*, 1987 (Proceedings of the First Joint Institute of Chartered Business Valuators and The American Society of Appraisers. October 1986), pp. 119-27.

Barenbaum, Lester, and Thomas F. Monahan. "Revenue Ruling 59-60: Valuation Theory and Practice in Conflict." *ASA Valuation* (December 1984), pp. 2-7.

Bielinski, Daniel W. "The ERI Equity Risk Premium Selection Method." *Business Valuation Review* (September 1987), pp. 124-27.

Bielinski, Daniel W. "The 'Debt-Free' ('Financing Neutral') Discounted Cash Flow: Capital Structure Assumptions." *Business Valuation Review* (December 1988), pp. 163-168.

Black, Fischer. "A Simple Discounting Rule." *Financial Management* (Summer 1988), pp. 7-11.

Blair, Vernon A. "Valuation Terms and Concepts: Canadian vs. U.S." *Journal of Business Valuation*, 1987 (Proceedings of the First Joint Institute of Chartered Business Valuators and The American Society of Appraisers, October 1986), pp. 7-15.

Bonqvitz, Sheldon M. "Impact of the TRA Repeal of *General Utilities*." *Journal of Taxation* (December 1986), pp. 388-97.

Brinig, Brian P., and Michael W. Prairie. "Expert Testimony: The Business Appraiser as a Valuation Expert Witness." *Business Valuation News* (March 1985), p. 8.

Brock, Thomas. "More on Capitalization Rates." *ASA Valuation* (June 1986), pp. 68-71. Also in *Business Valuation News* (December 1985), pp. 5-8.

Brown, Ralph J., and Dennis A. Johnson. "Inflation Valuation and the Discount Rate." *Appraisal Journal* (October 1980), pp. 549-55.

Butala, John H., Jr. "Valuation of Closely Held Corporations." Philip E. Heckerling Institute on Estate Planning, University of Miami Law Center, 1973, pp. 1400-34.

Cantor, Gilbert M. "New Warnings on Stock Valuation." *Journal of the American Society of CLU* (May 1985), pp. 60-63.

Carn, Neil; Joseph Rabianski; and James D. Vernor. "Trial Techniques of Expert Witnesses." *Real Estate Review* (Spring 1986), pp. 66-74.

Casey, Cornelius J., and Norman J. Bartczak. "Cash Flow—It's Not the Bottom Line." *Harvard Business Review* (July-August 1984), pp. 61-66.

"Compilation and Review of Financial Statements." American Institute of Certified Public Accountants, Accounting and Review Services Committee. *Statement on Standards for Accounting and Review Services, No. 1* (1979).

Cooper, Glen. "How Much Is Your Business Worth?" *Business* (September-October 1984), pp. 50-54.

Craig, Darryl; Glenn Johnson; and Maurice Joy. "Accounting Methods and P/E Ratios." *Financial Analysts Journal* (March-April 1987), pp. 41-45.

Cushing, James E., Jr. "The Valuation of a Close Corporation: Glimpses of Objectivity in an Inflationary Period." *Loyola University of Chicago Law Journal* 13 (Fall 1981), pp. 107-33.

Czumak, Michael. "The Appraiser Goes to Court." *ASA Valuation* (June 1988), pp. 34-40.

Dickerson, F. Gregg. "The Appraisal of Public Utilities and Railroads for Ad Valorem Taxation: Application of the Unit Rule." *Property Tax Journal* (June 1988), pp. 145-55.

Dietrich, William C. "A Risk Premium/Growth Model to Determine the Earnings Multiple." *Business Valuation News* (March 1986), pp. 10-17.

Diskin, Barry A., Patrick F. Maroney, and Frank A. Vickory. "Appraisers' Perspective on Industry Regulation: Is It Time?" *Appraisal Journal* (July 1987), pp. 378-93.

Donias, Claire H. "Valuation Terms and Concepts: Canadian vs. U.S." *Journal of Business Valuation*, 1987 (Proceedings of the First Joint Institute of Chartered Business Valuators and The American Society of Appraisers, October 1986), pp. 1-5.

Donohue, Matthew J. "Closely Held Stock Valuation—In Support of General Guidelines and in Defense of the Courts." *Taxes* (June 1982), pp. 455-58.

Drymalski, Raymond, Jr. "Valuation of Stock of a Subchapter S Corporation—a New Form of Business Organization." *Illinois Bar Journal* (April 1968), pp. 672-89.

Faris, John P.; Walter R. Holman; and Patrick A. Martinelli. "Valuing the Closely Held Business." *Mergers & Acquisitions* (Fall 1983), pp. 53-59.

Feakins, Nicholas L. "Relevance of Financial Analysis to Standard Appraisal Methodology." *Business Valuation Review* (September 1987), pp. 105-15.

Fearon, Richard H., and Mitchell R. Julis. "The Role of Modern Finance in Bankruptcy Reorganizations." *Temple Law Quarterly* 56, no. 1 (1983), pp. 1-48.

Feinberg, Andrew. "What's It Worth?" *Venture* (January 1988), pp. 27-31.

Field, Irving M. "A Review of the Principles of Valuation." *ASA Valuation* (June 1986), pp. 2-10.

Fishbein, Mark. "Valuation—An Ozymandian Task." *Corporate Finance* (July 1988), pp. 37-39.

Fishman, Jay E. "The Alternate Market Comparison Approach In Valuing Closely Held Enterprises." *FAIR$HARE* (October 1988), pp. 7-8.

Fishman, Jay E. "The 'Key Man' Concept in Business Valuation upon Divorce." *FAIR$HARE* (June 1982), pp. 3-4.

Fishman, Jay E. "The Problem with Rules of Thumb in the Valuation of Closely Held Entities." *FAIR$HARE* (December 1984), pp. 13-15.

Forbes, Wallace F. "Putting a Value on a Closely Held Company." *Family Advocate* (Summer 1984), pp. 28-30.

Fortang, Chaim J., and Thomas Moers Mayer. "Valuation in Bankruptcy." *UCLA Law Review* 32 (1985), pp. 1061-1132.

Fox, Jeffery D. "Closely Held Business Valuations: The Uninformed Use of the 'Excess Earnings/Formula' Method." *Taxes* (November 1982), pp. 832-36.

Garland, Gary D. "The Impact of New Sec. 1060 on Purchase Price Allocations." *Tax Adviser* (November 1987), pp. 793-99.

Gilbert, Gregory A. "Price/Sales Ratios." *Business Valuation News* (June 1986), pp. 7-15.

Goff, Gary A. "Fair Market Value: A Primer for Texas Legal Practice." *Texas Tech Law Review* 15 (May 1984), pp. 637-71.

Goldberg, Daniel S. "Fair Market Value in the Tax Law: Replacement Value or Liquidation Value." *Texas Law Review* 60 (May 1982), pp. 833-73.

Goodman, Barry R. "Valuing Investment Limited Partnerships." *Business Valuation News* (September 1986), pp. 8-15.

Goodman, Wolfe D. "Development in Valuation Principles, As Reflected in Some Recent Judicial Decisions." *Journal of Business Valuation*. 1987 (Proceedings of the First Joint Business Valuation Conference of The Canadian Institute of Chartered Business Valuators and The American Society of Appraisers, October 1986), pp. 17-29.

Goodwin, Michael W. "Use and Misuse of the Income Approach." *Property Tax Journal* (June 1986), pp. 85-96.

Gordon, Myron J., and Paul J. Halpern. "Cost of Capital for a Division of a Firm." *Journal of Finance* (September 1974), pp. 1153-63.

Graham, Gale. "Use 'Equivalency': Keep Your Friendly Lender Solvent." *The Real Estate Appraiser and Analyst* (Winter 1985), pp. 19-22.

Gray, Gerald. "When Is Fair Market Value Unfair?" *ASA Valuation* (June 1984), pp. 2-7.

Haynsworth, Harry J., IV. "Valuation of Business Interests.'" *Mercer Law Review* 33 (Winter 1982), pp. 457-517.

Heaton, Hal. "A Reply to 'Use and Misuse of the Income Approach.'" *Property Tax Journal* (June 1988), pp. 199-209.

Howard, J. "What's It Worth to You?" *Inc.* (July 1982), pp. 75-80.

Howe, Rex C., and Lee A. Kamp. "Appraisers as Expert Witnesses Before the IRS." *The Real Estate Appraiser and Analyst* (Summer 1984), pp. 52-55.

Jacobs, Bruce I., and Kenneth N. Levy. "On the Value of 'Value.'" *Financial Analysts Journal* (July/August 1988), pp. 47-62.

Janata, Jerrold F. "Appraisals—Use to Determine Fair Market Value in Tax-Oriented Partnerships and Other Transactions." New

York University Institute on Federal Taxation, 1985, pp. 57.1-57.37.

Jensen, Herbert L. "Valuing Actively Traded Securities Involves More Than Researching Daily Price Quotations." *Taxation for Accountants* (July 1976), pp. 36-40.

Johnson, Linda L., and Loucks, Christine. "The Effect of Certification and Licensure on Appraisers and Users of Appraisals." *Appraisal Journal* (October 1988), pp. 548-55.

Johnson, Lyle R.; Eli Shapiro; and Joseph O'Meara, Jr. "Valuation of Closely-Held Stock for Federal Tax Purposes: Approach to an Objective Method." *Pennsylvania Law Review* 166 (1951), pp. 166-95.

Jones, D.A. "Update on Valuation Issues and Policies." *Journal of Business Valuation*, 1979 (Proceedings of the Fourth Biennial Conference of the Canadian Association of Business Valuators, October 1978), pp. 121-36.

Jones, Jeffrey. "The Spouse Loses Out if *Rathmell* Stands." *ASA Valuation* (June 1988), pp. 60-65.

Joyce, Allyn A. "Valuation of Nonpublic Companies." In *Accountants' Handbook*, 6th ed. (1981), pp. 38.1-38.28.

King, Alfred M. "Fair Value Reporting." *Management Accounting* (March 1985), pp. 25-30.

Kingston, John P.R. "Damages—Lost Profits." *Journal of Business Valuation*, 1987 (Proceedings of the First Joint Institute of Chartered Business Valuators and The American Society of Appraisers, October 1986), pp. 111-18.

Kinsman, Michael D., and Bruce Samuelson. "Personal Financial Statements: Key Thorny Issues for CPAs: Closely Held Businesses, Trust Interests, Estimated Taxes." *Journal of Accountancy* (September 1987), pp. 138-48.

Klein, Ronald. "The Role of the Expert in Divorce Valuation." *FAIR$HARE* (May 1986), pp. 3-6.

Kurzman, Stephen A. "How to Value a Closely Held Busines." *Practical Accountant* (May 1988), pp. 64-74.

Landsman, Stephen A. "Handling the Control Problems When Close Corporation Stock Is Transferred in a Divorce." *Taxation for Accountants* (July 1983), pp. 26-31.

Largay, James A., III, and Clyde P. Stickney. "Cash Flows, Ratio Analysis and the W.T. Grant Company Bankruptcy." *Financial Analysts Journal* (July-August 1980), pp. 51-54.

Lembke, Valdean C. "Determination of Reporting Basis for Long-Term Intercorporate Investment." *Mergers and Acquisitions* (Fall 1979), pp. 14-17.

Leung, T.S. Tony. "Myths about Capitalization Rate and Risk Premium." *Business Valuation News* (March 1986), pp. 6-10.

Leung, T.S. Tony. "Tax Reform Act of 1986: Considerations for Business Valuations." *Business Valuation Review* (June 1987), pp. 60-63.

Leung, T.S. Tony. "Understanding Fair Market Value." *Business Valuation News* (December 1982), pp. 4-6.

Litzenberger, Robert H., and Krishna Ramaswamy. "The Effect of Personal Taxes and Dividends on Capital Asset Prices." *Journal of Financial Economics* (June 1979), pp. 163-95.

Lokey, O. Kit, and Richard Masson. "Evaluating the Closely Held Business." *Management Review* (July 1987), pp. 45-47.

Longenecker, Ruth R. "A Practical Guide to Valuation of Closely Held Stock." *Trusts & Estates* (January 1983), pp. 32-41.

Looney, Steve R. "Using LIFO to Value Costs under the Completed Contract Method: A Tale of Two Accounting Methods." *Tax Lawyer* (Winter 1986), pp. 235-83.

Loudon, Colin H., and John M. Davison. "The Law of Damages—A Valuator's Perspective." *Journal of Business Valuation*, 1987 (Proceedings of the First Joint Business Valuation Conference of The Canadian Institute of Chartered Business Valuators and The American Society of Appraisers, October 1986), pp. 97-110.

Lusht, Kenneth M. "Most Probable Selling Price." *Appraisal Journal* (July 1983), pp. 346-54.

Maughan, G.B. "The Defence of Professional Liability Claims against Valuators in Canada." *Journal of Business Valuation*, 1987 (Proceedings of the First Joint Business Valuation Conference of the First Canadian Institute of Chartered Business Valuators and The American Society of Appraisers, October 1986), pp. 251-55.

McDaniel, William R. "Sinking Fund Preferred Stock." *Journal of the Financial Management Association* 13, no. 1 (Spring 1984), pp. 45-52.

McMullin, Scott G. "Discount Rate Selection." *Business Valuation News* (September 1986), pp. 16-19.

Meyers, Robert M. "United States Experience in Valuating Closely-Held Corporations." *Journal of Business Valuation*, 1983 (Proceedings of the Sixth Biennial Conference of the Canadian Association of Business Valuators, November 1982), pp. 195-207.

Miller, Neil. "Selecting Expert Witnesses With Litigation Savvy." *National Law Journal* (October 24, 1988), p. 44.

Miller, Paul B.W. "The New Pension Accounting (Part 1): If Pensions Weren't Broke, How Come the FASB Fixed 'Em?" *Journal of Accountancy* (January 1987), pp. 90-108.

Miller, Paul B.W. "The New Pension Accounting (Part 2): Putting It Into Practice." *Journal of Accountancy* (February 1987) pp. 86-94.

Mills, Steven R. "Making 'Cents' of the Tax Law." *Business Age* (November/December 1988), pp. 6-11, 64.

Mollica, Anthony F. "Evaluating the Stock of a Closely Held Corporation." *Case & Comment* (January 1982), pp. 12-15.

Moskowitz, Jerald I. "What's Your Business Worth?" *Management Accounting* (March 1988), pp. 30-34.

Nevers, Thomas J. "Capitalization Rates." *Business Valuation News* (June 1985), pp. 3-6.

Newton, Grant W., and James J. Ward, Jr. "Valuation of a Business in Bankruptcy." *CPA Journal* (August 1976), pp. 26-32.

Office of the Chief Economist. "The Effects of Dual-Class-Recapitalizations on the Wealth of Shareholders." Securities and Exchange Commission. June 1, 1987, pp. 1-34.

Oliver, Robert P. "Moving Beyond the Real Estate Appraisal: Valuing Fractional Interests in Closely Held Real Estate Companies." *Business Valuation News* (June 1986), pp. 16-19.

Parker, George G.C., and Samuel S. Stewart, Jr. "Risk and Investment Performance." *Financial Analysts Journal* (May-June 1974), pp. 49+.

Patterson, R., and W. Albo. "What's It Worth? Business Valuations and the Banker (Canada)." *Canadian Banker* (June 1984), pp. 18-23.

Paulsen, James Walter. "Closely Held Corporations in the Wake of *Vallone*: Enhancement of Stock Value by Community, Time, Talent, and Labor." *Baylor Law Review* 35 (1983), pp. 47-96.

Pratt, Shannon P. "A Note on Developing a Capitalization Rate Using the Capital Asset Pricing Model." *Business Valuation News* (March 1985), p. 24.

Pratt, Shannon P. "Closely Held Company Valuation Techniques Differ by Size and Purpose of Appraisal." Parts I and II. *The Oregon Certified Public Accountant* (January-February 1986).

Pratt, Shannon P. "Developing the Valuation Model—Comparisons, Approaches, and Sources." *Journal of Business Valuation* (Proceedings of the Seventh Biennial Conference of the Canadian Association of Business Valuators, 1985), pp. 7-18.

Pratt, Shannon P. "Rates of Return as an Influence on Value." New York University Proceedings of the Third Annual Institute on State and Local Taxation and Conference on Property Taxation (1985), pp. 21.1-21.15.

Pratt, Shannon P. "The Opinion of the College on Defining Standards of Value." *ASA Valuation* (June 1989), pp. 65-72.

Pratt, Shannon P. "The State of the Art of the Business Appraisal Profession." *ASA Valuation* (January 1989), pp. 8-14.

Pratt, Shannon P. "Understanding Capitalization Rates." *ASA Valuation* (June 1986), pp. 12-29.

Pratt, Shannon P. "Valuing a Practice: Choosing the Right Capitalization Rates." *CA Magazine* (April 1987), pp. 49-52.

Pratt, Shannon P. and Ralph Arnold. "Placing a Value on Your Professional Practice" (Part One). *Lawyer/Manager* (May/June 1989), pp. 42-48.

Pratt, Shannon P. and Ralph Arnold. "Specific Methods for Determing the Value of Your Law Practice," (Part Two). *Lawyer/Manage* (July/August 1989), pp. 41-49.

Pratt, Shannon P., and Philip M. Smith. "Valuing Stock Options, with Applications to Closely Held Companies." *Journal of Business Valuation*, 1987 (Proceedings of the First Joint Business Valuation Conference of The Canadian Institute of Chartered Business Valuators and The American Society of Appraisers, October 1986), pp. 227-49.

Rappaport, Alfred. "Converting Merger Benefits to Shareholder Value." *Mergers & Acquisitions* (March-April 1987), pp. 49-55.

Rappaport, Alfred. "Do You Know the Value of Your Company?" *Mergers and Acquisitions* (Spring 1979), pp. 12-21.

Reiff, Wallace W., and Arthur E. Gimmy. "Assigning Values to Management Contracts." *Mergers & Acquisitions* (January-February 1986), pp. 77-81.

Reilly, Raymond R. "Business Valuation Using the Stock and Debt Method." *ASA Valuation* (December 1984), pp. 28-34.

Reilly, Robert F. "The Measure of Economic Obsolescence." *ASA Valuation* (January 1989), pp. 34-48.

Rennie, Richard; Jack G. Vico; and George T. Murphy. "Factors in the Determination of the Valuation of Private Business Interests." *Osgood Hall Law Journal* (June 1982), pp. 261-73.

Roll, Richard, and Stephen A. Ross. "An Empirical Investigation of the Arbitrage Pricing Theory." *Journal of Finance* 35 (December 1980), pp. 1073-1103.

Rosen, Arthur R.; Joan S. Faber; and Jeffrey Tutnauer. "The Effect of Federal Tax Reform and Accounting Changes on the Valuation of Utilities." *Property Tax Journal* (June 1988), pp. 181-98.

Rosenbloom, Arthur H. "How to Determine the Value of a Business: A Case Study." *Practical Accountant* (March 1983), pp. 28-34.

Rubinstein, William S., and Nancy R. London. "Sales and Leasebacks: Some Valuation Problems." *Tax Lawyer* (Spring 1984), pp. 481-507.

Sammons, Donna. "Evaluating the Valuators." *Inc.* (May 1983), pp. 186-88.

Shackelford, Aaron L. "Valuation of 'S' Corporations." *Business Valuation Review* (December 1988), pp. 159-72.

Schilt, James H. "A Rational Approach to Capitalization Rates for Discontinuing the Future Income Stream of a Closely Held Company." *Financial Planner* (January 1982), pp. 56-57.

Schilt, James H. "A Review of the Standard Methods of Evaluating Closely Held Companies." *ASA Valuation* (November 1981), pp. 2-9.

Schilt, James H. "A Short Essay on Intrinsic Value." *Business Valuation News* (March 1984), pp. 23-26.

Schilt, James H. "An Objection to the Excess Earnings Method of Business Appraisal." *Taxes* (February 1980), pp. 123-26.

Schilt, James H. "Appraisal under California Corporations Code Section 2000." *Business Law News* (State Bar of California, Summer 1985). Also in *Business Valuation News* (December 1985), pp. 9-16.

Schilt, James H. "Appraising the Close Corporation, *Lotz, Hewitson* and *Ronald* Not Withstanding." *Business Valuation Review* (December 1986), pp. 25-34. Also in *Business Law News* (State Bar of California, Summer 1986).

Schilt, James H. "Challenging Standard Business Appraisal Methods." *Business Valuation News* (December 1984), pp. 4-14. Also in *Business Law News* (State Bar of California, Winter 1985), and *ASA Valuation* (June 1985), pp. 2-10.

Schilt, James H. "Pitfalls in the Valuation of Closely Held Companies." *Trusts & Estates* (June 1980), pp. 44-47.

Schilt, James H. "Selection of Capitalization Rates for Valuing a Closely Held Business." *Business Law News* (Spring 1982), pp. 35-37.

Schmehl, John W. "How Liquidations and S Elections May Avoid the Impact of TRA '86." *Journal of Taxation* (July 1987), pp. 30-38.

Schneider, Willys H., and Sarah G. Austrian. "Widespread Changes for Corporations in 1987 Act." *Journal of Taxation* (April 1988), pp. 196-202.

Schreier, W.T., and O. Maurice Joy. "Judicial Valuation of 'Close' Corporation Stock: Alice in Wonderland Revisited." *Oklahoma Law Review* 31 (Fall 1978), pp. 853-85.

Siegel, Joel G. "The 'Quality of Earnings' Concept—a Survey." *Financial Analysts Journal* (March-April 1982), pp. 60-68.

Sherwood, Arthur M. "Family Businesses Breed Conflict." *Trust & Estates* (February 1989), pp. 30-36.

Singleton, Margaret. "What's It Worth to You?" *Inc.* (September 1986), pp. 113-14.

Sirmans, C.F.; G. Stacy Sirmans; and Ben T. Beasley: "Income Property Valuation and the Use of Market Extracted Overall Capitalization Rates. *The Real Estate Appraiser and Analyst* (Summer 1986), pp. 64-68.

Stockdale, John J. "Comparison of Publicly-Held Companies with Closely-Held Business Entities." *Business Valuation Review* (December 1986), pp. 3-11.

Tannenbaum, Jeffery A., and Udayan Gupta. "Bidding for Small Companies Is Slowing." *Wall Street Journal* (December 16, 1988), p. B-1.

"The Use of Appraisals in SEC Documents." *University of Pennsylvania Law Review* (November 1973), pp. 138-61.

Thompson, Donald J., IV. "Sources of Systematic Risk in Common Stock." *Journal of Business* (April 1976), pp. 173-88.

Thompson, Mark S. and Jeb Brooks. "Focusing on the Wide Range of Investment Partnerships." *Trusts & Estates* (November 1988), pp. 27-35.

Thompson, Mark S. "How to Value Real Estate Limited Partnership Interests." *Trusts & Estates* (December 1984), pp. 35-41.

Thompson, Mark S. "Valuing Interests in Real Estate Partnerships." *Real Estate Review* (Winter 1987), pp. 36-40.

Treanor, Richard B., and Jack Johnson. "Valuation of Community Property Minority Interests Reflect Judicial Inconsistencies." *Journal of Taxation* (June 1980), pp. 356-60.

"Valuing a Closely-Held Business: What a Buyer Will Pay." *Small Business Report* (November 1986), pp. 30-35.

Vinso, Joseph D., and Burton H. Marcus. "Valuing the Closely Held Company: The Implications of the *Hewitson* Case." *Business Valuation News* (June 1985), pp. 7-10.

Walker, Donna J., and Curtis R. Kimball. "Business Valuations: What Are They Worth to You?" *Business Age* (November/December 1988), pp. 54-58.

Weberman, Bernard H. "Current Approaches to Findings of Overvaluations in Tax Shelter Cases." *Journal of Taxation of Investments* (Winter 1986), pp. 99-127.

Weiss, Arthur A. "S Election Can Mitigate Effect of *General Utilities* Repeal." *Journal of Taxation* (December 1986), pp. 414-16.

Weiss, Stuart. "Business Appraising: Beware of Amateur Hour." Business Week (February 9, 1987), p. 74.

Wilcox, Jarred W. "The P/B-ROE Valuation Model." *Financial Analysts Journal* (January-February 1984), pp. 58-66.

Wise, Richard M., ed. "More Laws—More Valuations." *CA Magazine* (October 1987), pp. 52-57.

Wise, Richard M. "Valuing Business For Foreign Investors." *CA Magazine* (May 1987), pp. 89-94.

Yaney, J.P.; D.G. Seamans; and J.D. Crawford, Jr. "Going-Concern Value: An Elusive Intangible Asset That Can Upset Allocations in Business Transfers." *Taxation for Lawyers* (May-June 1985), pp. 366-70.

Books and Services

Appraisal of Utilities and Railroad Property for Ad Valorem Taxation. Seventeenth Annual Program Proceedings of the Public Utilities Workshop. Wichita Kan.: Wichita State University, 1987. (Program proceedings are published annually from 1971 to present.)

Babcock, Henry A. *Appraisal Principles and Procedures*. Washington, D.C.: American Society of Appraisers, 1980.

Baron, Paul B. *When You Buy or Sell a Company*. Meriden, Conn." The Center for Business Information, Inc., 1983.

Bernstein, Leopold A. *Financial Statement Analysis: Theory, Application and Interpretation*. 4th ed. Homewood, Ill.: Richard D. Irwin, 1989.

Bienenstock, Martin J. *Bankruptcy Reorganization*. New York: Practicing Law Institute, 1987.

Bierman, Harold, Jr., and Seymour Smidt. *The Capital Budgeting Decision: Economic Analysis of Investment Projects*. 6th ed. New York: Macmillan, 1984.

Blackman, Irving L. *The Valuation of Privately Held Businesses*. Chicago: Probus Publishing, 1986.

Bonbright, James C. *The Valuation of Property*, vols. 1 and 2. Charlottesville, Va.: The Miche Company, 1965 (reprint of 1937 ed.).

Borden, Arthur M. *Going Private*. New York: Law Journal Seminars Press, 1986.

Brown, Ronald L., ed. *Valuing Professional Practices and Licenses: A Guide for the Matrimonial Practitioner*. Clifton, N.J.: Prentice Hall Law & Business, 1987.

Burke, Frank M., Jr. *Valuation and Valuation Planning for Closely Held Businesses*. Englewood Cliffs, N.J.: Prentice-Hall, 1981.

Cohen, Jerome B.; Edward D. Zinbarg; and Arthur Zeikel. *Investment Analysis and Portfolio Management*. 4th ed. Homewood, Ill.: Richard D. Irwin, 1982.

Cottle, Sidney; Roger F. Murray; and Frank E. Block. *Graham and Dodd's Security Analysis*. 5th ed. New York: McGraw-Hill, 1988.

Crandall, Arthur L. *Valuing Businesses and Professional Practices with Revenues under $20 million*. New York: American Institute of Certified Public Accountants, 1988.

Desmond, Glenn M., and Richard E. Kelley. *Business Valuation Handbook*. Los Angeles, Calif.: Valuation Press, 1980.

Desmond, Glenn M., and John Marcello. *Handbook of Small Business Valuation Formulas*. Los Angeles, Calif.: Valuation Press, 1987.

Dewing, Arthur Stone. *The Financial Policy of Corporations*. 5th ed. vols. 1 and 2. New York: Ronald Press, 1953.

Diamond, Stephen C. *Leveraged Buyouts*. Homewood, Ill.: Dow Jones-Irwin, 1985.

Directory of Wall Street Research. Rye, NY: Nelson Publications (annual service).

Dunn, Robert L. *Recovery of Damages for Lost Profits.* 3rd ed. Kentfield, Calf.: Lawpress Corporation, 1987.

Fisher, Irving. *The Theory of Interest.* New York: Macmillan, 1930 (Reprinted Augustus M. Kelley, 1961.)

Fisher, Kenneth L. *Super Stocks.* Homewood, Ill.: Dow Jones-Irwin, 1984.

Foster, Henry H., Jr., and Ronald L. Brown, eds. *Contemporary Matrimonial Law Issues: A Guide to Divorce Economics and Practice.* New York: Law & Business, Inc./Harcourt Brace Jovanovich. 1985.

Fuller, Russell J. *Capital Asset Pricing Theories: Evolution and New Frontiers.* Charlottesville, Va.: The Financial Analysts Research Foundation. 1981.

Goldberg, Barth H. *Valuation of Divorce Assets.* St. Paul, Minn.: West Publishing, 1984.

Goldstein, Arnold S. *The Complete Guide to Buying and Selling a Business.* New York: New American Library, 1983.

Graham, Benjamin; David L. Dodd; and Sidney Cottle. *Security Analysts: Principles and Techniques* 4th ed. New York: McGraw-Hill, 1962.

Grimes, John Alden, and William Horace Craigue. *Principles of Valuation* New York: Prentice-Hall, 1928.

Gurney, Roland. *Share Valuation Manual.* Brookfield, Vt.: Gower Publishing Company, 1987.

Hagendorf, Stanley. *1989 Tax Guide for Buying and Selling a Business.* 7th ed. Englewood Cliffs, N.J.: Prentice-Hall, 1989.

Hampton, John J. *Financial Decision making: Concepts, Problems, and Cases* 3rd ed. Reston, Va.: Reston Publishing, 1983.

Handbook of Basic Economic Statistics. Washington, D.C.: Economic Statistics Bureau (annual service with monthly supplements).

Harfax Guide to Industry Special Issues. Cambridge: Harfax, 1984.

Ibbotson, Roger G., and Gary P. Brinson. *Investment Markets: Gaining the Performance Advantage.* New York: McGraw-Hill, 1987.

Krahmer, Johannes R. *Valuation of Shares of Closely Held Corporations.* Washington, D.C.: Tax Management Inc., 1985 (Estates, Gifts, and Trusts, 221-2d T.M.).

Kramer, Yale. *Valuing a Closely Held Business*, Accountant's Workbook Series. New York: Matthew Bender, 1987.

Lane, Marc J. *Purchase and Sale of Small Businesses: Tax and Legal Aspects*. New York: John Wiley & Sons, 1985.

Levine, Sumner N., ed. *The Financial Analyst's Handbook*, 2nd ed. Homewood, Ill.: Dow Jones-Irwin, 1988.

Lipper, Arthur, III. *Venture's Guide to Investing in Private Companies*. Homewood, Ill.: Dow Jones-Irwin, 1984.

Martin, Thomas J., and Mark R. Gustafson. *Valuing Your Business*. New York: Holt, Rinehart & Winston, 1980.

McCarthy, George D., and Robert E. Healy. *Valuing a Company: Practices and Procedures*. New York: John Wiley & Sons, 1971.

Mergerstat Review. Chicago: Merrill Lynch Business Brokerage and Valuation, Inc. (annual service).

Miles, Raymond C. *Basic Business Appraisal*. New York: John Wiley & Sons, 1984.

Moody's Bank & Finance Manual. New York: Moody's Investors Service (semiweekly with annual cumulation).

Moody's Industrial Manual. New York: Moody's Investors Services (semiweekly with annual cumulation).

Moody's OTC Industrial Manual. New York: Moody's Investors Service (weekly with annual cumulation).

Moody's Public Utility Manual. New York: Moody's Investors Service (semiweekly with annual cumulation).

Moody's Transportation Manual. New York: Moody's Investors Service (semiweekly with annual cumulation).

Ness, Theodore, and William F. Indoe. *Tax Planning for Disposition of Business Interests*. Boston: Warren, Gorham & Lamont, 1985.

O'Neal, F. Hodge, and Robert B. Thompson. *O'Neal's Close Corporations*, 3rd ed., vols. 1 and 2. Wilmette, Ill.: Callaghan & Company, 1958, 1963, 1965-1987.

O'Neal, F. Hodge, and Robert B. Thompson. *O'Neal's Oppression of Minority Shareholders*. 2nd ed., vols. 1 and 2. Wilmette, Ill.: Callaghan & Company, 1975-1985.

Poynter, Daniel F. *The Expert Witness Handbook: Tips and Techniques for the Litigation Consultant*. Santa Barbara, Cal.: Para Publishing, 1987.

Pratt, Shannon P., ed. *Readings in Business Valuation.* Washington, D.C.: American Society of Appraisers Educational Foundation, 1986.

Pratt, Shannon P. "Valuation of Closely Held Businesses," in Whitman, Robert (Ed.), *Estate Planning and Administration Service*, ch. F-90, pp. F90-1–F90-37. New York: Warren, Gorham, & Lamont, 1989.

Pratt, Shannon P. *Valuing a Business: The Analysis and Appraisal of Closely Held Companies*, 2nd ed. Homewood, IL: Dow Jones-Irwin, 1989.

Pratt, Shannon P. *Valuing Property Management Companies* (A Study). Chicago: Institute of Real Estate Management Foundation, 1988.

Pratt Shannon P. *Valuing Small Businesses and Professional Practices.* Homewood, Ill.: Dow Jones-Irwin, 1986.

Predicasts F & S Index. Cleveland: Predicasts (weekly, monthly, and annual cumulations).

Reilly, Frank M. *Investment Analysis and Portfolio Management*, 2nd ed. Hinsdale, Ill.: Dryden Press, 1985.

Securities and Exchange Commission, *Directory of Companies Required to File Reports with the Securities and Exchange Commission.* Washington, D.C.: U.S. Government Printing Office (annual service).

Schnepper, Jeff A. *The Professional Handbook of Business Valuation.* Reading, Mass.: Addison-Wesley Publishing, 1982.

Shank, Steven J., and Richard K. Olson. *Practical Divorce Valuation and Financial Analysis.* Eau Claire, Wis.: Professional Education Systems, Inc., 1986.

Siegel, Joel G. *How to Analyze Businesses, Financial Statements, and the Quality of Earnings.* Englewood Cliffs, N.J.: Prentice-Hall, 1982.

Smith, Gordon V. *Corporate Valuation: A Business and Professional Guide.* New York: John Wiley & Sons, 1988.

Smith, Gordon V., and Russell L. Parr. *Valuation of Intellectual Property and Intangible Assets.* New York: John Wiley & Sons, 1989.

Sokoloff, Kiril, ed. *The Paine Webber Handbook of Stock and Bond Analysis.* New York: McGraw-Hill, 1979.

Speedy, Squire L. *Financial Appraisal.* Wellington, New Zealand: New Zealand Institute of Valuers, 1982.

Standard & Poor's Analyst's Handbook. New York: Standard & Poor's Corporation, Inc. (annual service).

Standard & Poor's Industry Surveys. New York: Standard & Poor's Corporation, Inc. (quarterly and annual service).

Standard & Poor's Register of Corporations, Directors and Executives. New York: Standard & Poor's Corporation (annual service).

Standard & Poor's Statistical Service. New York: Standard & Poor's Corporation, Inc. (monthly service).

The Value Line Investment Survey. New York: Value Line, Inc. (weekly service).

U.S. Department of Commerce. *Handbook of Economic Statistics.* Washington, D.C.: National Technical Information Service, 1984.

Williams, John Burr. *The Theory of Investment Value.* Cambridge, Mass.: Harvard University Press, 1938. (Reprinted in Amsterdam by North Holland Publishing, 1956.)

Dissenting-Stockholders' Actions

Articles

"Achieving Fairness in Corporate Cash Mergers: *Weinberger v. UOP.*" *Connecticut Law Review* 16 (Fall 1983), pp. 95-119.

Allred, William S. "Corporate Law—Chipping Away at the Delaware Block: A Critique of the Delaware Block Approach to the Valuation of Dissenter's Shares in Appraisal Proceedings." *Western New England Law Review* 8 (Spring 1986), pp. 191-227.

Banks, Warren E. "A Selective Inquiry into Judicial Stock Valuation." *Indiana Law Review* 6 (1972), pp. 19-44.

Birk, David R. "Shareholders' Appraisal Process: Need for Reform." *New York State Bar Journal* (June 1979), pp. 274-77, 314-21.

Booth, Richard A. "The New Law of Freeze-Out Mergers." *Missouri Law Review* 49 (1984), pp. 517-69.

Brudney, Victor. "Standards of Fairness and the Limits of Preferred Stock Modifications." *Rutgers Law Review* 26 (1973), pp. 445-87.

Brudney, Victor, and Marvin A. Chirelstein. "Fair Shares in Corporate Mergers and Takeovers." *Harvard Law Review* 88 (December 1974), pp. 297-346.

Chazen, Leonard. "Fairness from a Financial Point of View in Acquisitions of Public Companies: Is 'Third-Party Sale Value' the

Appropriate Standard?" *Business Lawyer* (July 1981), pp. 1439-81.

Cohen, Shlomo. "*Bell v. Kirby Lumber Corp.*: Ascertaining 'Fair Value' under the Delaware Appraisal Statute." *Columbia Law Review* 81 (March 1981), pp. 426-40.

Coleman, Joseph M. "The Appraisal Remedy in Corporate Freeze-Outs: Questions of Valuation and Exclusivity." *Southwestern Law Journal* 38 (1984), pp. 775-98.

Dennis, Roger J. "Valuing the Firm and the Development of Delaware Corporate Law." *Rutgers Law Journal* 17 (Fall 1985), pp. 1-49.

Deutsch, Jan G. "The Mysteries of Corporate Law: A Response to Brudney and Chirelstein." *Yale Law Journal* 88 (1978), pp. 235-41.

Easterbrook, Frank H., and Daniel R. Fischel. "Corporate Control Transactions." *Yale Law Journal* 91 (1982), pp. 698-737.

Gray, Gerald. "When Is Fair Market Value Unfair?" *ASA Valuation* (June 1984), pp. 2-7.

Haight, Carol B. "The Standard of Care Required of an Investment Banker to Minority Shareholders in a Cash-Out Merger: *Weinberger v. UOP, Inc.,*" *Investment Banker* 8 (1983), pp. 98-121.

Herzel, Leo, and Jesse A. Finklestein. "Fairness: Majority vs. Minority." *National Law Journal* (July 16, 1984), pp. 15-19.

Hobart, Geoffrey A. "Delaware Improves Its Treatment of Freezeout Mergers: *Weinberger v. UOP, Inc.*" *Boston College Law Review* 25 (May 1984), pp. 685-723.

Hotchkiss, David L. "Corporations—Fair Value for Dissenting Shareholders under the Pennsylvania Appraisal Statute." *Dickinson Law Review* 78 (Spring 1974), pp. 582-96.

Johnson, W.A. "Dissenter Shareholder Valuations: A Study of Cases and References." *Business Valuation Review* (March 1988), pp. 9-17.

Kanda, Hideki, and Saul Levmore. "The Appraisal Remedy and the Goals of Corporate Law." *UCLA Law Review* 32 (Fall 1985), pp. 429-73.

Lorne, Simon M. "A Reappraisal of Fair Shares in Controlled Mergers." *University of Pennsylvania Law Review* 126 (May 1978), pp. 955-88.

McLean, John T. "Minority Shareholders and Cashout Mergers: The Delaware Court Offers Plaintiffs Greater Protection and a Procedural Dilemma—*Weinberger v. UOP, Inc.*" *Washington Law Review* 59 (1983), pp. 119-40.

Mirvis, Theodore N. "Two-Tier Pricing: Some Appraisal and 'Entire Fairness' Valuation Issues." *Business Lawyer* (February 1983), pp. 485-501.

Nathan, Charles M., and K.L. Shapiro. "Legal Standard of Fairness of Merger Terms under Delaware Law." *Delaware Journal of Corporate Law* 2 (1977), pp. 44-64.

Payson, Robert K., and Gregory A. Inskip. "*Weinberger v. UOP, Inc.*: Its Practical Significance in the Planning and Defense of Cash-Out Mergers." *Delaware Journal of Corporate Law* 8 (1983), pp. 83-97.

Prickett, William, and Michael Hanrahan. "*Weinberger v. UOP*: Delaware's Effort to Preserve a Level Playing Field for Cash-Out Mergers." *Delaware Journal of Corporate Law* 8 (1983), pp. 59-82.

Rams, Edwin M. "Judicial Valuation of Dissenting Shareholder Interests." *Lincoln Law Review* 8 (1973), pp. 74-89.

Roberts, William M. "The Status of Minority Shareholders' Remedies for Oppression after *Santa Fe* and *Singer* and the Question of 'Reasonable Investment Expectation' Valuation." *Delaware Journal of Corporate Law* 6 (1981), pp. 16-53.

Rogers, J. Steven. "The Dissenting Shareholder's Appraisal Remedy." *Oklahoma Law Review* 30 (Summer 1977), pp. 629-43.

Schaefer, Elmer J. "The Fallacy of Weighting Asset Value and Earnings Value in the Appraisal of Corporate Stock." *Southern California Law Review* 55 (July 1982), pp. 1031-96.

Schilt, James H. "*Weinberger v. UOP, Inc.*: Challenge for the Business Appraiser." *Trusts & Estates* (August 1984), pp. 87-90.

Seligman, Joel G. "Reappraising the Appraisal Remedy." *George Washington Law Review* 52 (May 1984), pp. 829-71.

Steinberg, Marc I., and Evalyn Lindahl. "The New Law of Squeeze-Out Mergers." *Washington University Law Quarterly* 62 (Fall 1984), pp. 352-414.

Thompson, Robert B. "Squeeze-Out Mergers and the 'New' Appraisal Remedy." *Washington University Law Quarterly* 62 (1984), pp. 415-34.

Tinio, Ferdinand S. "Valuation of Stock of Dissenting Stockholders in Case of Consolidation or Merger of Corporation, Sale of Its

Assets, or the Like." 48 A.L.R. 3d 430 (1973, Supplements 1979, 1986).

"Valuation of Dissenter's Stock under Appraisal Statutes." *Harvard Law Review* 30 (May 1966) pp. 1453-74.

Van Nuis, Rosalie P. "Delaware's Solution to the Problem of the Minority Stockholders in a Cash-Out Merger—*Weinberger v. UOP, Inc.*" *Northern Kentucky Law Review* 11 (1984), pp. 575-611.

Ward, David A. "The Appraisal Remedy." *Journal of Business Valuation*, 1983 (Proceedings of the Sixth Biennial Conference of the Canadian Association of Business Valuators, November 1982), pp. 117-32.

Ward Rodman, Jr., and John G. Day. "Finding Fair Value: The Delaware Block Method Revisited." *Journal of Business Valuation*, 1987 (Proceedings of the First Joint Business Valuation Conference of The Canadian Institute of Chartered Business Valuators and The American Society of Appraisers, October 1986), pp. 87-96.

Weiss, Elliott J. "Balancing Interests in Cash-Out Mergers: The Promise of *Weinberger v. UOP, Inc.*" *Delaware Journal of Corporate Law* 3 (1983), pp. 1-58.

Weston, Mark G. "Delaware's Appraisal Statute: The Court's Artificial Ceiling on Asset Valuation Weighting." *Notre Dame Law Review* 58 (December 1982), pp. 410-28.

Wise, Richard M. " 'Fair Value' and the Appraisal Remedy." *Journal of Business Valuation*, 1987 (Proceedings of the First Joint Business Valuation Conference of The Canadian Institute of Chartered Business Valuators and The American Society of Appraisers, October 1986), pp. 77-86.

Wise, Richard M. "Fair Value for Dissenting Shareholders." *CA Magazine* (June 1987), pp.52-54.

Goodwill and Other Intangibles

Articles

Ackerman, Alan T. "Just Compensation for Condemnation of Going Concern Value." *ASA Valuation* (June 1986), pp. 42-55.

Adams, Fred M. "Professional Goodwill as Community Property: How Should Idaho Rule?" *Idaho Law Review* 14 (Spring 1978), pp. 473-91.

Arnold, Ralph. "Putting a Value on Future Interests." *Family Advocate* (Summer 1984), pp. 32-36, 42.

Baker, Glenn A. "Goodwill, Going Concern Become Harder to Avoid." *Mergers & Acquisitions* (Summer 1984), pp. 58-62.

Bergman, Gregory M. "Valuation of Goodwill." *Los Angeles Bar Journal* (August 1977), pp. 87-98.

Berland, Lawrence J. "Partnership Interest Valued as Going Concern." *CPA Journal* (February 1988), p. 104.

Blaine, David S. "Valuation of Goodwill and Going Concern Value." *Mergers & Acquisitions* (Spring 1979), pp. 4-11.

Blum, Marc P. "Valuing Intangibles: What Are the Choices for Valuing Professional Sports Teams?" *Journal of Taxation* (November 1976), pp. 286-88.

Boehm, Ted. " 'Hoskold's Formula' for the Valuation of Intangibles." *Capital University Law Review* 10 (Winter 1980), pp. 297-307.

Davis, Michael E. "Valuation of Professional Goodwill upon Marital Dissolution." *Southwestern University Law Review* 7 (Spring 1975), pp. 186-205.

Doernberg, Richard U., and Thomas D. Hall. "The Tax Treatment of Going-Concern Value." *George Washington Law Review* 52, no. 3 (March 1984), pp. 353-94.

Dostart, Thomas J. "Professional Education as a Divisible Asset in Marriage Dissolutions." *Iowa Law Review* 64 (March 1979), pp. 705-21.

Fejer, Douglas, K. "Missouri Supreme Court States Preference for Market Approach When Valuing Professional Goodwill." *Business Valuation Review* (December 1988), pp. 150-54.

Florio, Nicholas, and Frank J. LaGreca. "Valuing Amortizable Intangible Assets: Are They Being Wasted?" *Tax Adviser* (September 1986), pp. 544-49.

Ganier, Patricia K. "Treatment of Goodwill: Allocating a Lump Sum Purchase Price among Mixed Assets of a Going Business." *Journal of Corporate Taxation* (Summer 1980), pp. 111-36.

"Going Concern Value Can Exist Even without Goodwill." *Taxation for Lawyers* (January-February 1977), pp. 229-30.

"Going Concern Value Rather Than Liquidation Value Utilized in Valuing Partnership Interests for Estate Tax Purposes." *Journal of American Society of CLU & ChFC* (January 1988), p. 14.

Gomes, Glenn M. "Excess Earnings, Competitive Advantage, and Goodwill Value." *Journal of Small Business Management* (July 1988), pp. 22-31.

"Goodwill." 5 *American Jurisprudence Proof of Facts* 505 (1960, Supplement 1979).

"Goodwill." 38 *American Jurisprudence* 2d 911 (1968, Supplement 1979).

"Goodwill." 38 *Corpus Juris Secundum* 948 (1943, Supplement 1979).

Gross, Paul H. "Establishing Fair Market Value of Intangible Assets." *Journal of Business Valuation* 4 (July 1977), pp. 5-17.

Hauserman, Nancy R., and Carol Fethke. "Valuation of a Homemaker's Services." *Trial Lawyer's Guide* (Fall 1978), pp. 249-66.

Henszey, Benjamin N. "Going Concern Value after *Concord Control, Inc.*" *Taxes* (November 1983), pp. 699-705.

Hocker, Jerry W. "Methods of Valuing Intangibles in Leveraged Buyouts." *Journal of Buyouts & Acquisitions* (August-September 1984), pp. 33-37.

King, Roger T. "The Valuation of Goodwill: An Approach for the Appraiser." *Appraisal Review Journal* (Summer 1984), pp. 77-79.

Locke, Dennis H. "A Systematic Approach to Patent Valuation." *Business Valuation News* (September 1986), pp. 23-27.

McMullin, Scott G. "The Valuation of Patents." *Business Valuation News* (September 1983), pp. 5-13.

Osborne, Kent L. "Recent Decision Invalidates Second Tier Allocation and Favors Residual Method for Valuing Goodwill and Going Concern Value—A Note." *Business Valuation News* (June 1985), pp. 11-13.

Paulsen, Jon. "Measuring Rods for Intangible Assets." *Mergers & Acquisitions* (Spring 1984), pp. 45-49.

Pinnell, Robert E. "Divorce after Professional School: Education and Future Earning Capacity May Be Marital Property." *Missouri Law Review* 44 (Spring 1979), pp. 329-40.

Projector, Murray. "Valuation of Retirement Benefits in Marriage Dissolutions." *Los Angeles Bar Bulletin* 50 (April 1975), pp. 229-38.

Reilly, Robert F. "The Valuation of Intangible Assets." *ASA Valuation* (June 1988), pp. 16-25.

Rosenstein, Barnard Lapointe Pierre. "The Valuation of Intangibles: Legal and Tax Aspects." *Journal of Business Valuation*, 1983

(Proceedings of the Sixth Biennial Conference of the Canadian Association of Business Valuators, November 1982), pp. 67-84.

Schilt, James H. "Goodwill and Excess Earnings." *Business Law News* (Winter 1982), pp. 18-20.

Schnee, Edward J., and Barney R. Cargile. "Going Concern Value—A New Intangible?" *Tax Adviser* (July 1984), pp. 386-92.

Shipley, W.E. "Accountability for Good Will on Dissolution of Partnership." 65 A.L.R.2d 521 (1959, Supplements 1978, 1979).

Udinsky, Jerald H. "The Microeconomics of Goodwill with an Application to Law." *Business Valuation News* (June 1983), pp. 3-10.

Udinsky, Jerald H. "Putting a Value on Goodwill." *Family Advocate* (Fall 1986), pp. 37-40.

Vinso, Joseph D. "Excess Earnings Estimation of Intangibles—a Note." *Business Valuation News* (December 1984), pp. 15-17.

Vinso, Joseph D. "Valuing Professional Goodwill: The *Slivka* Case Revisited." *Business Valuation Review* (December 1987), pp. 156-63.

Wiener, Hilton M. "Going Concern Value: Goodwill by Any Other Name?" *Tax Lawyer* (Fall 1979), pp. 183-97.

"Your Practice: You Need to Know Right Now What It's Worth." *Medical Economics* (October 24, 1988), pp. 77-89.

Marketability and Minority Interests

Articles

Amihud, Yakov, and Haim Mandelson. "Liquidity and Stock Returns." *Financial Analysts Journal* (May-June 1986), pp. 43+.

Arneson, George S. "Minority Discounts beyond Fifty Percent Can Be Supported." *Taxes* (February 1981), pp. 97-102.

Arneson, George S. "Nonmarketability Discounts Should Exceed Fifty Percent." *Taxes* (January 1981), pp. 25-31.

Arneson, George S. "The Case for No Majority-Control Premium." *Taxes* (March 1981), pp. 190-93.

Austin, Douglas V., and Michael J. Jackson. "Tender Offer Update." *Mergers & Acquisitions* (updated article appears annually).

Bolten, Steven E. "Discounts for Stocks of Closely Held Corporations." *Trusts & Estates* (December 1984), pp. 22-23.

Coolidge, H. Calvin. "Discount for Minority Interest: Rev. Rul. 79-7's Denial of Discount Is Erroneous." *Illinois Bar Journal* 68 (July 1980), pp. 744-49.

Coolidge, H. Calvin. "Fixing Value of Minority Interest in a Business; Actual Sales Suggest Discount as High as 70%." *Estate Planning* (Spring 1975), pp. 138-40.

"Cost of Flotation of Registered Issues, 1971-72." Washington, D.C.: Securities and Exchange Commission, 1974.

Cummins, J.R.; M.S. Weinberg; and D.M. Roth. "Current Attitudes towards Estate Tax Discounts for Restricted Securities and Underwriting Fees." *Estate Planning* (September 1983), pp. 276-81.

Dant, Thomas W., Jr. "Courts Increasing Amount of Discount for a Minority Interest in a Business." *Journal of Taxation* (August 1975), pp. 104-9.

"Discounts Involved in Purchases of Common Stock (1966-1969)." *Institutional Investor Study Report of the Securities and Exchange Commission*. H.R. Doc. No. 64, Part 5, 92d Cong., 1st Sess. (1971), pp. 2444-56.

Emory, John D. "The Value of Marketability as Illustrated in Initial Public Offerings of Common Stock: January 1985 through June 1986." *Business Valuation Review* (December 1986) pp. 12-14.

Emory, John D. "The Value of Marketability as Illustrated by Initial Public Offerings of Common Stock: January 1980 through June 1981." *Business Valuation Review* (September 1985), pp. 21-24.

Featherston, Thomas M., Jr., and William R. Trail. "Enhanced Value of Closely-Held Stock, Community or Separate: Closer to a Solution." *Texas Bar Journal* 47 (February 1984), pp. 128-44.

Gampel, Peter. "Recent Thoughts When Valuing a Minority Interest in a Closely Held Company." *Business Valuation Review* (June 1987), pp. 64-85.

Gauthier, Andre P. "Valuation of Minority Shares of Publicly Held Companies." *Journal of Business Valuation*, 1981 (Proceedings of the Fifth Biennial Conference of the Canadian Association of Business Valuators, October 1980), pp. 201-22.

Gelman, Milton. "An Economist-Financial Analyst's Approach to Valuing Stock of a Closely-Held Company." *Journal of Taxation* (June 1972), pp. 353-54.

Harper, John S., Jr., and Peter J. Lindquist. "Quantitative Support for Large Minority Discounts in Closely Held Corporations." *The Appraisal Journal* (April 1983), pp. 270-77.

Johnson, Richard D., and George A. Racette. "Discounts on Letter Stock Do Not Appear to Be a Good Base on Which to Estimate Discounts for Lack of Marketability on Closely Held Stock." *Taxes* (August 1981), pp. 574-81.

Lease, Ronald C.; John J. McConnell; and Wayne H. Mikkelson. "The Market Value of Control in Publicly-Traded Corporations." *Journal of Financial Economics* 11 (1983), pp. 439-71.

Lease, Ronald C.; John J. McConnell; and Wayne H. Mikkelson. "The Market Value of Differential Voting Rights in Closely Held Corporations." *Journal of Business* (October 1984), pp. 443-67.

Lipkin, Laurence. "The Theory of Minority Discount in Regard to ESOP Shares of Closely-Held Corporations." *ASA Valuation* (November 1980), pp. 130-34.

Lyons, Robert P., and Michael J. Wilczynski. "Discounting Intrinsic Value." *Trusts & Estates* (February 1989), pp. 22-27.

Lyons, William P., and Martin J. Whitman. "Valuing Closely-Held Corporations and Publicly-Traded Securities with Limited Marketability: Approaches to Allowable Discounts from Gross Values." *Business Lawyer* (July 1978), pp. 2213-29.

Maher, J. Michael. "An Objective Measure for a Discount for a Minority Interest and a Premium for a Controlling Interest." *Taxes* (July 1979), pp. 449-54.

Maher, J. Michael. "Application of Key Man Discount in the Valuation of Closely-Held Businesses." *Taxes* (June 1977), pp. 377-80.

Maher, J. Michael. "Discounts for Lack of Marketability for Closely Held Business Interests." *Taxes* (September 1976), pp. 562-71.

Maxson, Page. "Layered Discounts: When Are They Appropriate?" *Business Valuation Review* (December 1988), pp. 155-58.

Moore, Philip. "Valuation Revisited." *Trusts & Estates* (February 1987), pp. 40-52.

Moreland, E.R. "The Control Value of Noncontrolling Shares." *Review of Taxation of Individuals* 8 (Fall 1984), pp. 291-348.

Moroney, Robert E. "Most Courts Overvalue Closely Held Stocks." *Taxes* (March 1973), pp. 144-54.

Moroney, Robert E. "Why 25 Percent Discount for Nonmarketability in One Valuation, 100 Percent in Another?" *Taxes* (May 1977), pp. 316-20.

Much, Paul J., and Rima N. Krisst. "Paying a Premium for Control." *The Tax Times* (Prentice-Hall), Vol. 1, No. 9 (May 1987).

Obstler, David M. "The Investment Company Discount: *Estate of Folks* and Beyond." *Taxes* (January 1983), pp. 47-50.

Penn, Thomas A. "Premiums: What Do They Really Measure?" *Mergers & Acquisitions* (Fall 1981), pp. 30-34.

Pratt, Shannon P. "Valuing a Minority Interest in a Closely Held Company." *Practical Accountant* (June 1986), pp. 60-68.

Solberg, Thomas A. "Valuing Restricted Securities: What Factors Do the Courts and the Service Look For?" *Journal of Taxation* (September 1979), pp. 150-54.

"Survey Shows Trend toward Larger Minority Discounts." *Estate Planning* (September 1983), pp. 281-82.

Trieschmann, James S., E.J. Leverett, and Peter J. Shedd. 'Valuating Common Stock for Minority Stock and ESOPs in Closely Held Corporations." *Business Horizons* (March/April 1988), pp. 63-69.

Trout, Robert R. "Estimation of the Discount Associated with the Transfer of Restricted Securities." *Taxes* (June 1977), pp. 381-85.

"Valuation of Corporate Stock for Purposes of Succession, Inheritance, or Estate Tax, as Affected by Quantity Involved." 23 *A.L.R.* 2d 775 (1952, Supplements 1970, 1979).

"Valuing Closely Held Stock: Control Premiums and Minority Discounts." *Emory Law Journal* 31 (Winter 1982), pp. 139-99.

Vaughan, Jack M.; Chris B. Parsons; and Thomas J. Featherston, Jr. "Valuation of Community Property Interests in Closely Held Stock: The Minority Interest Discount Controversy Continues." *Community Property Journal* (Winter 1982), pp. 3-14.

Vincent, Gordon S. "*Estate of Bright* and *Propstra*: Rejection of Family Attribution in Estate Valuation." *Virginia Tax Review* 2 (April 1982), pp. 357-69.

Wiley, Thomas W. "Valuing Large Holdings of Publicly-Traded Stock: The 'Blockage' Problem." Philip E. Heckerling Institute on Estate Planning, University of Miami Law Center, 1974, pp. 800-819.

Mergers and Acquisitions

Articles

Alberts, William W., and James M. McTaggart. "The Short-Term Earnings per Share Standard for Evaluating Prospective Acquisitions." *Mergers & Acquisitions* (Winter 1978), pp. 4-18.

Anderson, Charles M. "1 + 1 = 3." *Management Accounting* (April 1987), pp. 28-31.

Asquith, Paul. "Merger Bids, Uncertainty, and Stockholder Returns." *Journal of Financial Economics* 11 (1983), pp. 51-83.

Asquith, Paul; Robert F. Bruner; and David W. Mullins, Jr. "The Gains to Bidding Firms from Merger." *Journal of Financial Economics* 11 (1983), pp. 121-39.

Bierman, Harold, Jr. "Valuing an Acquisition." *Financial Executive* (July 1980), pp. 20-23.

Blaising, James S., and John R. Gasiorowski. "Beyond Tire-Kicking: The Appraiser's New M & A Role." *Mergers & Acquisitions* (Summer 1983), pp. 34-40.

Bradley, James W., and Donald H. Korn. "Bargains in Valuation Disparities: Corporate Acquirer versus Passive Investor." *Sloan Management Review* 20 (Winter 1979), pp. 51-64.

Brown, Paul B., and John A. Byrne. "Let's Do a Deal." *Business Week* (April 18, 1986), p. 265.

Brudney, Victor. "Efficient Markets and Fair Values in Parent Subsidiary Mergers." *Journal of Corporation Law* (Fall 1978), pp. 63-86.

Brudney, Victor, and Marvin A. Chirelstein. "Fair Shares in Corporate Mergers & Takeovers." *Harvard Law Review* (December 1974), pp. 297-346.

Chambers, John C., and Satinder K. Mullick. "Determining the Acquisition Value of a Company." *Management Accounting* (April 1970), pp. 24-31, 39.

Chazen, Leonard. "Fairness from a Financial Point of View in Acquisitions of Public Companies: Is 'Third-Party Sale Value' the Appropriate Standard?" *Business Lawyer* (July 1981), pp. 1439-81.

Chirelstein, Marvin A.; Ernest J. Sargeant; and Martin Liptin. " 'Fairness' in Mergers between Parents and Partly-Owned Subsidiaries." New York: Practising Law Institute, Institute on Securities Regulation, 1977, pp. 273-308.

Einhorn, Stephen. "Notes on the Decision to Keep or to Sell a Small Business." *Mergers & Acquisitions* (Summer 1977), pp. 29-31.

Faber, Peter L. "Acquisitions and Liquidations Involving S Corporations after Tax Reform." *Practical Accountant* (September 1987), pp. 98-114.

Faris, John R.; Walter R. Holman; and Patrick A. Martinelli. "Valuing the Closely Held Business." *Mergers and Acquisitions* (Fall 1983), pp. 53-59.

Fiflis, Ted J. "Accounting for Mergers, Acquisitions and Investments in a Nutshell." *Business Lawyer* (November 1981), pp. 89-140.

Ginsburg, Martin D. "Special Topics in the Acquisitions Area." *San Diego Law Review* 22 (1985), pp. 159-69.

Gooch, Lawrence B., and Roger J. Grabowski. "Advanced Valuation Methods in Mergers and Acquisitions." *Mergers & Acquisitions* (Summer 1976), pp. 15-29.

Heath, John, Jr. "Appraisal Processes in Mergers and Acquisitions." *Mergers & Acquisitions* (Fall 1974), pp. 4-21.

Levinton, Howard, and Robert A. Snyder, Jr. "Negotiating Strategies When a Client Wants to Sell a Closely Held Corporation." *Taxation for Lawyers* (January-February 1986), pp. 204-11.

Loomis, Carol J. "LBOs Are Taking Their Lumps." *Fortune* (December 7, 1987), pp. 63-68.

Lorne, Simon M. "A Reappraisal of Fair Shares in Controlled Mergers." *University of Pennsylvania Law Review* 126 (May 1978), pp. 955-88.

Mullaney, Michael D., and Richard W. Bailine. "Corporate Acquisitions after the Tax Reform Act of 1986." *Tax Adviser* (April 1987), pp. 212-25.

Penn, Thomas A. "Premiums: What Do They Really Measure?" *Mergers & Acquisitions* (Fall 1981), pp. 30-34.

Rappaport, Alfred. "Financial Analysis for Mergers and Acquisitions." *Mergers & Acquisitions* (Winter 1976), pp. 18-36.

Reilly, Robert F. "Pricing an Acquisition: A 15-Step Methodology:" *Mergers & Acquisitions* (Summer 1979), pp. 14-31.

Ritchey, James S. "Acquisition Valuation: DCF Can Be Misleading." *Management Accounting* (January 1983), pp. 24-28.

Roche, James M.; Lonn W. Myers; and Daniel M. Sucker. "Price Allocation on Acquisitions and Basis Step-Up: Tilting at Windmills?" *Taxes* (December 1987), pp. 833-45.

Rock, Milton L., and Martin Sikora. "Accounting for Merger Mania." *Management Accounting* (April 1987), pp. 20-27.

Rosenbloom, Arthur H., and Alex W. Howard. "Bootstrap' Acquisitions and How to Value Them." *Mergers & Acquisitions* (Winter 1977), pp. 18-26.

Saffer, Brian H. "Touching All Bases in Setting Merger Prices." *Mergers & Acquisitions* (Fall 1984), pp. 42-48.

Schipper, Katherine, and Rex Thompson. "Evidence on the Capitalized Value of Merger Activity for Acquiring Firms." *Journal of Financial Economics* 11 (1983), pp. 85-119.

Vernick, Mitchell F. "Business Value Lending in a Leveraged Acquisition." *Mergers & Acquisitions* (November-December 1987), pp. 73-77.

Whitmarsh, Duane R. "How to Investigate a Potential Acquisition." *Practical Accountant* (June 1981), pp. 37-43.

Books and Services

Acquisition/Divesture Weekly Report. Santa Barbara: Quality Services, Inc. (weekly service).

Bank Mergers & Acquisitions. New York: Curran & Roemer, Inc. (monthly service).

Douglas, F. Gordon. *How to Profitably Sell or Buy a Company or Business.* New York: Van Nostrand-Reinhold, 1981.

Grimm, W.T. & Company. *Mergerstat Review.* Chicago: W.T. Grimm & Company (annual service).

Jenkins, James W. *Mergers and Acquisitions: A Financial Approach*, 2nd ed. New York: American Management Association, 1986.

Jurek, Walter. *Merger & Acquisition Sourcebook*, vols. 1 and 2. Santa Barbara, Calif.: Quality Services Company, annual.

Lee, Steven J., and Robert P. Colman, eds., *Handbook of Mergers, Acquisitions and Buyouts.* Englewood Cliffs, N.J.: Prentice-Hall, 1985.

Lorne, Simon M. *Acquisitions and Mergers: Negotiated and Contested Transactions.* New York: Clark Boardman Company, Ltd., 1986.

Marren, Joseph H. *Mergers and Acquisitions: Will You Overpay?* Homewood, Ill: Dow Jones-Irwin, 1985.

Mergers & Acquisitions Sourcebook. Santa Barbara: Quality Services Company (annual service).

Mergers & Acquisitions. Philadelphia: Information for Industry (quarterly service).

Morris, Joseph M. *Acquisitions, Divestitures, and Corporate Joint Ventures*. New York: John Wiley & Sons, 1984.

Pritchett, Price. *Making Mergers Work: A Guide to Managing Mergers and Acquisitions*. Homewood, Ill.: Dow Jones-Irwin, 1987.

Pritchett, Price. *After the Merger: Managing the Shockwaves*. Homewood, Ill.: Dow Jones-Irwin, 1985.

Rock, Milton R., ed. *The Mergers & Acquisitions Handbook*. New York: McGraw-Hill, 1987.

Scharf, Charles A.; Edward E. Shea; and George C. Beck. *Acquisitions, Mergers, Sales, Buyouts and Takeovers: A Handbook with Forms*. 3rd ed. Englewood Cliffs, N.J.: Prentice-Hall, 1985.

Smith, William K. *Handbook of Strategic Growth through Mergers and Acquisitions*. Englewood Cliffs, N.J.: Prentice-Hall, 1985.

TABLE OF CASES

[References are to paragraphs (¶).]

A

Albrecht v. Herald Co. .... 9.4[1][d] n.83
Allegheny Airlines, Inc., Feldman v. .... 9.4[2][d] n.95; 9.4[2][f]
Allen v. Toledo .... 9.4[2][a]
Allied Corrogated Box Co., Brown v. .... 21.2[5][d] n.18
American Gen. Corp. v. Camp et al. .... 21.2[5][c] n.12
American Metal Climax, Inc., Kohn v. .... 3.4[1][c] n.45
A.R. Levitt v. MNR .... 21.6[2]
Arneson, Arneson v. .... 11.2[1] n.2; 11.4[1] n.11
Arneson v. Arneson ...... 11.2[1] n.2; 11.4[1] n.11
Asbury, Marriage of .... 11.7[3][c]
Atlantic States Constr., Inc. v. Beavers ...... 9.3[1][b]; 9.3[1][g]
Attorney Gen. of B.C., Untermeyer v. .... 21.6[2]
Aufmuth, Marriage of ...... 11.5[1][a] n.22
A.W. Beaumont, Estate of v. MNR .... 21.6[2]
A. Yager v. The Queen ...... 21.6[2]

B

Bade, Endicott Johnson Corp. v. .... 9.3[1][e]
Bader v. United States 1.5
Baltimore Transit Co., Warren v. .... 21.2[5][c] n.12
Banc One v. Comm'r 1.5
Bank of N.Y. v. MNR .... 21.6[2]
Baragry, Marriage of .... 11.8[4]
Barnert, Marriage of ...... 11.3[2][b]; 11.11[1]
Barriteau, District of Columbia v. .... 9.4[2][f]
Battye, Tri-Continental Corp. v. .... 9.3[1][a]; 9.3[1][a] n.13
Beardstown Pearl Button Co. v. Oswald .... 9.3[1][a] n.12
Beatty, Robbins v. .... 9.3[1][b]
Beaulieu v. Elliott .... 9.4[2][f]
Beavers, Atlantic States Constr., Inc. v. .... 9.3[1][b]; 9.3[1][g]
Beebe v. Pacific Realty Trust .... 3.4[1][c]
Beech Aircraft Corp., Fontana Aviation, Inc. v. .... 9.4[1][d] n.78
Behrens, Marriage of .... 11.13[1]
Bell v. Ellis .... 1.1[1] n.4
Berge v. International Harvester Co. .. 9.4[1][b] n.68; 9.4[1][c] n.74
Berish, Berish v. .... 11.10[1]
Berish v. Berish .... 11.10[1]
Bexley v. Dunning .... 21.2[5][d] n.19
Bigelow v. RKO Radio Pictures, Inc. .... 9.4[1][c] n.72
Bolubasz, Kaczkowski v. .... 9.4[2][f]
Borodinsky, Borodinsky v. .. 11.10[1] n.54; 11.13[1]
Borodinsky v. Borodinsky .... 11.10[1] n.54; 11.13[1]
Brant v. KeepRite .... 21.2[5][c] n.16
Brigden, Marriage of .... 11.13[1] n.67
Bright, Estate of v. United States .... App. 8-1
Brown v. Allied Corrogated Box Co. .... 21.2[5][d] n.18
Buffalo Tool & Die Mfg. Co. v. Comm'r 1.5
Butler v. New Keystone Copper Co. .... 9.3[1][a] n.12
Butler v. United States ...... 9.4[2][d] n.92

C

California Steel & Tube v. Kaiser Steel Corp. .... 9.2[2][e]
Camp et al., American Gen. Corp. v. .... 21.2[5][c] n.12
Canal Barge Co., Hamilton v. .... 9.4[2][d] n.95
Canavin v. Pacific Southwest Airlines .... 9.4[2][e]
Care Corp., Treadway Cos. v. .... 3.2[1]
Carr v. Carr-O'Brien Co. ..... 9.3[2][c] n.61
Carr-O'Brien Co., Carr v. .. 9.3[2][c] n.61
Cartwright, United States v. .... App. 8-1

[References are to paragraphs (¶).]

Cavalier Oil Corp. v. William J. Harnett .... 9.3[1][g] n.42
Central R.R. Co. of N.J., Scalise v. .... 9.4[2][e] n.103
Central Trust Co. v. United States 1.5
Central Zone Property Corp., Eisenberg v. .... 9.3[1][a] n.12
Chapman Value Mfg. Co., Hacker Pipe & Supply Co. v. .... 9.4[1][c] n.73
Charles S. Foltz et al. v. U.S. News & World Rep. et al. 1.5
Chesapeake & Ohio R.R. v. Kelley .... 9.4[2][f] n.104
Chicago Corp. v. Munds .... 9.3[1][a] n.12
City of Ottowa, Plouffe v. .... 21.3[1][e]
Clark, Marriage of ...... 11.5[2] n.28
Comm'r, Banc One v. 1.5
Comm'r, Buffalo Tool & Die Mfg. Co. v. 1.5
Comm'r, Concord Control v. 1.5
Comm'r, Couzens v. .. 1.5; 21.3[1][b] n.25
Comm'r, Hooker Indus., Inc. v. .... App. 8-1
Comm'r, Kirkpatrick, Estate of v. 1.5
Comm'r, Little, Estate of v. 1.5
Comm'r, Mark S. Gallo, Estate of v. 1.5
Comm'r, Messing v. 1.5
Comm'r, Northern Trust Co. v. .. 1.5
Comm'r, Oakley J. Hall, Estate of v. 1.5
Comm'r, Parker v. 1.5
Concord Control v. Comm'r 1.5
Contemporary Mission, Inc. v. Famous Music Corp. .... 9.4[1][c] n.75
Continental Baking Co. v. Old Homestead Bread Co. .... 9.4[1][d]; 9.4[1][d] n.81
Continental Oil Co., Fraier v. .... 9.2[2][f] n.9
Corless, Corless v. .... 21.3[1][d]
Corless v. Corless .... 21.3[1][d]
Couzens v. Comm'r .... 1.5; 21.3[1][b] n.25

Cox, Santee Oil Co., Inc. v. .... 9.3[1][b]
Crandall & Godley Co., Godley v. .... 9.3[2][a]
Credit Mgrs. Ass'n of So. Cal. v. Federal Co. .... 13.1[1]
Cruttwell v. Lye .... 1.1[1] n.2
Culver v. Slater Boat Co. .. 9.4[2][d]
Cunningham, Donovan v. .. App. 8-1
Cyprus Anvil Mining Corp. v. Dickson .... 21.6[2]

D

David J. Greene & Co. v. Dunhill Int'l .... 9.3[1][e] n.31
Dean, Dean v. .... 11.4[3][a]
Dean v. Dean .... 11.4[3][a]
D & H Friedman v. MNR .... 21.6[2]
Dibbley, Dibbley v. .... 21.3[1][d]
Dibbley v. Dibbley .... 21.3[1][d]
Dickson, Cyprus Anvil Mining Corp. v. .... 21.6[2]
Diligenti v. RWMD Operations Kelowna, Ltd. et al. (No. 2) .... 9.3[1][g]; 21.2[5][c] n.13; 21.6[2]
District of Columbia v. Barriteau .... 9.4[2][f]
Doca v. Marina Mercante Nicaraquense S.A. ...... 9.4[2][d]; 9.4[2][d] n.97; 9.4[2][f]
Domglas, Inc. v. Jarislowsky, Fraser & Co. .... 9.3[1][g]; 21.2[5][a]; 21.2[5][c]; 21.2[5][e]; 21.3[1][b]; 21.6[2]
Dominion Metal & Refining Works v. The Queen .... 21.6[2]
Donovan v. Cunningham .... App. 8-1
Douglas, Inc., Re .... 21.6[2]
Dugan, Dugan v. .. 11.12[1]; 11.12[3] n.63
Dugan v. Dugan .... 11.12[1]; 11.12[3] n.63
Dunhill Int'l, David J. Greene & Co. v. .... 9.3[1][e] n.31
Dunning, Bexley v. .. 21.2[5][d] n.19

E

E. Littler, Sr. v. The Queen .. 21.6[2]

TABLE OF CASES

[References are to paragraphs (¶).]

Eastman Kodak Co. v. Southern
 Photo Materials Co. ...... 9.4[1][c]
 n.73
Eisenberg v. Central Zone Property
 Corp. .... 9.3[1][a] n.12
Elliott, Beaulieu v. .... 9.4[2][f]
Ellis, Bell v. .... 1.1[1] n.4
Endicott Johnson Corp.
 v. Bade .... 9.3[1][e]
Epstein, Marriage of .... 11.5[2] n.28

F

Famous Music Corp., Contemporary
 Mission, Inc. v. ...... 9.4[1][c] n.75
Farmington Dowel Prods. Co. v.
 Forster Mfg. Co. .... 9.4[1][d];
 9.4[1][d] n.82
Federal Co., Credit Mgrs. Ass'n of S.
 Cal. v. .... 13.1[1]
Feldman v. Allegheny Airlines,
 Inc. .... 9.4[2][d] n.95; 9.4[2][f]
Fenton, Marriage of .... 11.12[4]
Fitzpatrick, Whittemore v. 1.5
Fleischer v. Gift Pax, Inc. .. 9.3[1][g]
Fonstein, Marriage of .... 11.5[2];
 11.5[2] n.28
Fontana Aviation, Inc. v. Beech
 Aircraft Corp. ...... 9.4[1][d] n.78
Forster Mfg. Co., Farmington Dowel
 Prods. Co. v. ...9.4[1][d]; 9.4[1][d]
 n.82
Fortier, Marriage of .... 11.4[2]
Foster, Marriage of ...... 11.2[1] n.1;
 11.3[2][b]
Fraier v. Continental Oil
 Co. .... 9.2[2][f] n.9

G

Gamble-Skogmo, Inc., Gerstle v.
 .... 3.4[1][a] n.37; 3.4[1][d] n.46
Geffen v. Moss .... 11.12[2] n.62
General Elec. Co., Ohio Valley Elec.
 Corp. v. .... 9.4[1][d] n.77
Gerstle v. Gamble-Skogmo,
 Inc. .. 3.4[1][a] n.37; 3.4[1][d] n.46
Gift Pax, Inc., Fleischer v. .. 9.3[1][g]
Gleneagles Inv. Co., United States
 v. .... 13.1[1]; 13.1[1] n.2
Godley v. Crandall & Godley
 Co. .... 9.3[2][a]
Gold Coast Selection Trust, Ltd. v.
 Humphrey .... 9.3[1][e]

Golden, Golden v. .... 11.7[3][a] n.35
Golden v. Golden .... 11.7[3][a] n.35
Green v. Santa Fe Indus.,
 Inc. .... 3.5[1] n.51
Group de Consultants PGL, Inc. et
 al., Montel v. .... 21.2[5][b];
 21.2[5][c] n.15; 21.3[1][c]
Guilder News Co. v. MNR.... 21.6[2]

H

Hacker Pipe & Supply Co. v.
 Chapman Value Mfg. Co.
 .... 9.4[1][c] n.73
Hamilton v. Canal Barge
 Co. .... 9.4[2][d] n.95
Hanson Trust PLC v. SCM
 Corp. .... 3.2[1]; 3.2[1] n.12
Hargrave, Marriage of .... 11.4[4]
Hawaiian Oke & Liquors, Ltd., Joseph
 Seagram & Sons, Inc. v. .. 9.2[2][e]
Heller v. Munsingwear, Inc. .. 16.2[3]
 n.8
Henderson v. MNR .... 21.6[2]
Herald Co., Albrecht v. .... 9.4[1][d]
 n.83
Hewitson, Marriage of........ 11.2[2];
 11.3[2][a] n.7; 11.4[3][a]; 11.4[3][b]
H.F. Ahmanson & Co., Jones
 v. .... 3.3[1]
Hooker Indus., Inc. v.
 Comm'r .... App. 8-1
House, Marriage of .... 11.7[2][c]
Howing v. Nationwide Corp. .. 3.5[1]
H.P. Connor v. The Queen.... 21.6[2]
Huffines, Norte & Co. v. .... 3.4[1][c]
Humphrey, Gold Coast Selection
 Trust, Ltd. v. .... 9.3[1][e]
Hutton, Johns Hopkins Univ.
 v. .... 9.3[3]

I

Imperato, Marriage of...... 11.7[4][c];
 11.8[2]
Inland Steel Co., Lebold
 v. .... 9.3[2][c] n.60
International Harvester Co., Berge
 v. .... 9.4[1][b] n.68; 9.4[1][c] n.74
Ithaca Trust Co. v. United
 States 1.5

[References are to paragraphs (¶).]

J

Jarislowsky, Fraser & Co., Domglas v. .... 9.3[1][g];
21.2[5][a]; 21.2[5][c]; 21.2[5][e]; 21.3[1][b]; 21.6[2]
Jasper Blackburn Co., Riba v. .... 9.4[2][e] n.100
J.J. West, Est. of v. Minister of Fin. of B.C. .... 21.6[2]
Johns Hopkins Univ. v. Hutton .... 9.3[3] n.66
Johnson v. Penrod Drilling Co. ...... 9.4[2][d]; 9.4[2][e] n.101
Johnson v. Serra ...... 9.4[2][e] n.100
Johnston v. West Fraser Timber Co. .... 21.6[2]
Jones v. H.F. Ahmanson & Co. .... 3.3[1]
Joseph v. Shell Oil Co. ...... 3.3[1]; 3.3[2] n.32; 3.4[1][b]; 3.4[1][c]; 3.4[1][c] n.43
Joseph E. Seagram & Sons, Inc. v. Hawaiian Oke & Liquors, Ltd. .... 9.2[2][e]
J. Young v. MNR............ 21.6[2]

K

Kaczkowski v. Bolubasz...... 9.4[2][f]
Kaiser Steel Corp., California Steel & Tube v. .... 9.2[2][e]
KeepRite, Brant v. .... 21.2[5][c] n.16
Kelley, Chesapeake & Ohio R.R. v. .... 9.4[2][f] n.104
Kimball Laundry v. United States 1.5
King, Marriage of .... 11.8[3][a]; 11.8[3][b]; 11.10[2] n.55
Kirkpatrick, Estate of v. Comm'r................. 1.5
Kohn v. American Metal Climax, Inc. .... 3.4[1][c] n.45
Kolasa et al., Neonex Int'l, Ltd. v. .... 21.2[5][c] n.13; 21.6[2]
Koppleman, Marriage of .... 11.10[1]
Kuffed v. Seaside Oil Co. .. 9.4[1][d] n.79

L

Lakehouse Enterprises, Ltd. v. MNR .... 21.6[2]
Lavene, Lavene v. ...... 11.3[2][a] n.7
Lavene v. Lavene ...... 11.3[2][a] n.7
Lebold v. Inland Steel Co. .. 9.3[2][c] n.60
Leipelt, Norfolk & Western R.R. Co. v. .... 9.4[2][e] n.103
Les Investissements Mont-Soleil, Inc. v. National Drug, Ltd. .. 21.2[5][c] n.15
Libby, McNeill & Libby .... 9.3[1][e]; 21.2[5][c] n.12
Liff et al. v. Schildkrout .... 9.4[2][a] n.87
Little, Est. of v. Comm'r 1.5
Lopez, Lopez v. 20.6
Lopez v. Lopez 20.6
Lopez, Marriage of .. 11.2[3]; 11.12[1]
Lotz, Marriage of .... 11.4[3][a]; 11.7[4][b] n.38
Lye, Cruttwell v. .... 1.1[1] n.2
Lynch v. Vickers.............. 3.5[2]

M

MacAndrews & Forbes Holdings, Inc., Revlon v. .... 3.2[2]
MacMillan, Mill's Acquisition Co. v. .... 3.2[2] n.17
Magnavox Co., Singer v. ...... 3.3[1]; 9.3[1][c]
Marina Mercante Nicaraquense, S.A., Doca v. .. 9.4[2][d]; 9[4][2][d] n.97; 9.4[2][f]
Mark S. Gallo, Estate of v. Comm'r..................... 1.5
Marx, Marriage of .... 11.7[2][b]
McDonnell Douglas Corp., Rodriguez v. .... 9.4[2][e] n.103
McGinnis et al., Southdown v. .... 21.2[5][c] n.12
Messing v. Comm'r............. 1.5
Metropolitan Nat'l Bank v. St. Louis Post-Dispatch Co. ...... 1.1[1] n.5

TABLE OF CASES

[References are to paragraphs (¶).]

Millington v. Southeastern Elevator Co. .... 9.4[2][a] n.87
Mills Acquisition Co. v. MacMillan .... 3.2[2] n.17
Minister of Fin. of B.C., J.J. West, Estate of v. .... 21.6[2]
MNR, A.R. Levitt v. .... 21.6[2]
MNR, A.W. Beaumont, Est. of v. .... 21.6[2]
MNR, Bank of N.Y. v. ...... 21.6[2]
MNR, D & H. Friedman v. .. 21.6[2]
MNR, Guilder News Co. v. .. 21.6[2]
MNR, Henderson v. .... 21.6[2]
MNR, J. Young v. .... 21.6[2]
MNR, Lakehouse Enterprises v. .... 21.6[2]
MNR, Moynihan v. .... 21.6[2]
MNR, W.L. Falconer v. ...... 21.6[2]
MNR, W.R. Brunelle v. ...... 21.6[2]
Montel v. Groupe de Consultants PGL, Inc. et al. .... 21.2[5][b]; 21.2[5][c] n.15; 21.3[1][c]
Moss, Geffen v. .... 11.12[2] n.62
Moynihan v. MNR .... 21.6[2]
Munds, Chicago Corp. v. .... 9.3[1][a] n.12
Munguia, Marriage of .... 11.4[5]
Munsingwear, Inc., Heller v. .... 16.2[3] n.8

N

National Bldg. Maintence, Ltd., Re .... 21.2[5][d] n.17
National Drug, Ltd., Les Investissements Mont-Soliel, Inc. v. .... 21.2[5][c] n.15
National Sys. of Banking of Alberta v. The Queen .... 21.6[2]
Nationwide Corp., Howing v. .... 3.5[1]
Neonex Int'l, Ltd. v. Kolasa et al. ...... 21.2[5][c] n.13; 21.6[2]
New Keystone Copper Co., Butler v. .... 9.3[1][a] n 12
New York Cent. R.R. Co., Raines v. .... 9.4[2][e] n.103
Norfolk & Western R.R. Co. v. Leipelt .... 9.4[2][e] n.103
Norte & Co. v. Huffines .... 3.4[1][c]
Northern Trust Co. v. Comm'r 1.5

O

Oakley J. Hall, Est. of v. Comm'r 1.5
O'Brien, O'Brien v. .... 11.12[5] n.65
O'Brien v. O'Brien ...... 11.12[5] n.65
Ohio Valley Elec. Corp. v. General Elec. Co. .... 9.4[1][d] n.77
Old Homestead Bread Co., Continental Baking Co. v. .... 9.4[1][d]; 9.4[1][d] n.81
Oswald, Beardstown Pearl Button Co. v. .... 9.3[1][a] n.12
Oxford Paper Co. v. United States................... 1.5 n.48

P

Pacific Realty Trust, Beebe v. .... 3.4[1][c]
Pacific Southwest Airlines, Canavin v. .... 9.4[2][e]
Page, Page v. .... 9.3[2][a]
Page v. Page .... 9.3[2][a]
Parker v. Comm'r 1.5
Paterson Parchment Paper Co., Story Parchment Co. v. .... 9.4[1][c] n.71
Penrod Drilling Co., Johnson v. .... 9.4[2][d]; 9.4[2][e] n.101
Pereira, Pereira v. .... 11.9[1]
Pereira v. Pereira .... 11.9[1]
Plouffe v. City of Ottawa .. 21.3[1][e]
Plourd v. Southern Pac. Transp. Co. .... 9.4[2][e] n.103
Popp, Marriage of .... 11.10[1]
Priddis, Marriage of .... 11.10[1]

Q

Quigley, Woodward v. ...... 9.3[1][g]; 9.3[2][a]; 21.2[5][c] n.12

R

Raines v. New York Cent. R.R. Co. .... 9.4[2][e] n.103
Rawluk, Rawluk v. .... 21.1[4]; 21.3[1][d]
Rawluk v. Rawluk .... 21.1[4]; 21.3[1][d]
Revlon v. MacAndrews & Forbes Holdings, Inc. .... 3.2[2]

Riba v. Jasper Blackburn Co. .... 9.4[2][e] n.100
Richard S. Miller & Sons, Inc. v. United States .... 18.2[3][b][iii]
Richter v. United States 1.5
Rifkind, Marriage of ...... 11.6[2][b]
Ripley Int'l, Ltd. .... 9.3[1][f]
Rives, Marriage of .... 11.11[2]
RKO Radio Pictures, Inc., Bigelow v. .... 9.4[1][c] n.72
Robbins v. Beatty .... 9.3[1][b]
Rodriguez v. McDonnell Douglas Corp. .... 9.4[2][e] n.103
Roessler v. Security Sav. & Loan Co. ...... 9.3[1][b]; 21.2[5][c] n.12
Roger, Strong v. 1.5
Rosan, Marriage of .... 11.5[1][a] n.22
RWMD Operations Kelowna, Ltd. et al. (No. 2), Diligenti v. .... 9.3[1][g]; 21.2[5][c] n.13; 21.6[2]

S

Santa Fe Indus., Inc., Green v. .... 3.5[1] n.51
Santee Oil Co. v. Cox ...... 9.3[1][b]
Saskatoon Drug & Stationery Co. v. The Queen .... 21.6[2]
Scalise v. Central R.R. Co. of N.J. .... 9.4[2][e] n.103
Schildkrout, Liff et al. v. .... 9.4[2][a] n.87
SCM Corp., Hanson Trust PLC v. .... 3.2[1]; 3.2[1] n.12
Seaside Oil Co., Kuffed v. .. 9.4[1][d] n.79
Security Sav. & Loan Co., Roessler v. .... 9.3[1][b]; 21.2[5][c] n.12
Seltzer, Estate of .... 11.5[1][b]
Serra, Johnson v. .... 9.4[2][e] n.100
Shell Oil Co., Joseph v. ...... 3.3[1]; 3.3[3] n.32; 3.4[1][b]; 3.4[1][c]; 3.4[1][c] n.43
Shelton, Marriage of .... 11.13[2] n.71
Singer v. Magnavox Co. ...... 3.3[1]; 9.3[1][c]
Skinner v. Smith ...... 9.3[1][a] n.12
Slater Boat Co., Culver v. .. 9.4[2][d]
Slater, Marriage of .... 11.5[1][a]

Smith, Marriage of .... 11.7[3][a] n.36; 11.12[1]; 11.13[2] n.70
Smith, Skinner v. ...... 9.3[1][a] n.12
Smith v. Van Gorkom .... 3.2[1]; 3.4 n.33; 3.5[2]; 9.3[1][c] n.26
Southdown v. McGinnis et al. .... 21.2[5][c] n.12
Southeastern Elevator Co., Millington v. .... 9.4[2][a] n.87
Southern Pac. Transp. Co., Plourd v. .... 9.4[2][e] n.103
Southern Photo Materials Co., Eastman Kodak Co. v. .... 9.4[1][c] n.73
St. Louis Post-Dispatch Co., Metropolitan Nat'l Bank v. .... 1.1[1] n.5
Stallcup, Marriage of .... 11.10[1]
Stern, Stern v. .... 11.5[1][a]; 11.5[2]; 11.7[2] n.31
Stern v. Stern ...... 11.5[1][a]; 11.5[2]; 11.7[2] n.31
Strong v. Roger 1.5
Story Parchment Co. v. Paterson Parchment Paper Co. .... 9.4[1][c] n.71

T

Tabor Court Realty Corp., United States v. .... 13.1[2]
The Queen, A. Yager v. ...... 21.6[2]
The Queen, Dominion Metal & Refining Works v. .... 21.6[2]
The Queen, E. Littler, Sr. v. .... 21.6[2]
The Queen, H.P. Connor v. .. 21.6[2]
The Queen, National Sys. of Banking of Alberta v. .... 21.6[2]
The Queen, Saskatoon Drug & Stationery Co. v. .... 21.6[2]
Toledo, Allen v. .... 9.4[2][a]
Treadway Cos. v. Care Corp. .. 3.2[1]
Tri-Continental Corp. v. Battye ...... 9.3[1][a]; 9.3[1][a] n.13

U

United States, Bader v. 1.5

TABLE OF CASES

[References are to paragraphs (¶).]

United States, Bright, Est. of
v. .... App. 8-1
United States, Butler v. .... 9.4[2][d]
n.92
United States v.
Cartwright .... App. 8-1
United States, Central Trust Co.
v. 1.5
United States, Ithaca Trust Co.
v. 1.5
United States, Kimball Laundry
v. 1.5
United States, Oxford Paper Co.
v. 1.5 n.48
United States, Richard S. Miller &
Sons, Inc. v. .... 18.2[3][b][iii]
United States, Richter v. 1.5
United States v. Gleneagles Inv. Co.
v. .... 13.1[1]; 1.3[1] n.2
United States v. Tabor Court Realty
Corp. .... 13.1[1]
Untermeyer v. Attorney Gen. of
B.C. .... 21.6[2]
UOP, Inc., Weinberger v. 1.5;
3.2[2]; 3.3[1] n.20; 3.3[2]; 3.3[3];
3.4[1][b]; 3.4[2]; 9.3[1][c]; 9.3[1][c]
n.22; 9.3[1][d]; 9.3[1][e]; 9.3[1][f];
9.3[1][h]; 16.2[3]
U.S. News & World Rep. et al.,
Charles S. Foltz et al. v. 1.5

V

VanCamp v. VanCamp .. 11.9[2] n.47

VanCamp, VanCamp v. ...... 11.9[2]
n.47
Van Gorkom, Smith v. ...... 3.2[1];
3.4 n.33; 3.5[2]; 9.3[1][c] n.26
Vickers, Lynch v. .... 3.5[2]
VSC Holdings, Ltd. et al.,
Re .... 21.2[5][e] n.13

W

Wall & Redekup Corp. et al.,
Re .... 21.2[5][c] n.13
Warren v. Baltimore Transit
Co. .... 21.2[5][c] n.12
Webb, Marriage of .... 11.4[4]
Weinberger v. UOP, Inc. 1.5;
3.2[2]; 3.3[1] n.20; 3.3[2]; 3.3[3];
3.4[1][b]; 3.4[2]; 9.3[1][c]; 9.3[1][c]
n.22; 9.3[1][d]; 9.3[1][e]; 9.3[1][f];
9.3[1][h]; 16.2[3]
West Fraser Timber Co., Johnston
v. ....21.6[2]
Whittemore v. Fitzpatrick 1.5
William J. Harnett, Cavalier Oil Corp.
v. .... 9.3[1][g] n.42
W.L. Falconer v. MNR ...... 21.6[2]
Woodward v. Quigley ...... 9.3[1][g];
9.3[2][a]; 21.2[5][c] n.12
Woodworth v. Woodworth .. 11.12[5]
n.65
Woodworth, Woodworth
v. .... 11.12[5] n.65
W.R. Brunelle v. MNR ...... 21.6[2]

INDEX

[References are to paragraphs (¶).]

A

Absolute control, defined 2.2
Accountants
   letter of solvency .... 13.1[2]
Accounting method .... 16.5[1]
   See also specific accounting method; Valuation on method
   oil and gas companies ... 19.2[5][a]; 19.2[5][b]
   professional practices .... 20.1[1]
   specialized industries ...... 14.3[11]
Accounts receivable
   aging schedule .... 4.2[3][b]
   professional practices ..... 11.12[4]; 20.2[1]
   aging of .... 20.2; 20.2[1][a]
   payment history .. 20.2; 20.2[1][b]
   turnover ratio .... 2.6[6]
   valuation upon marital
     dissolution .... 11.7[2]; 11.7[2][a]; 11.7[2][b]; 11.7[2][c]; 20.2[1]
Accrual accounting
   service company .... 16.5[1]
Acid test ratio .... 2.6[4]; 4.2[1][b]
Acquisitions
   See also Mergers and acquisitions
   comparative data .... 14.5[2]
   insurance company ..... 18.1[1][a]; 18.1p[5][a][i]
   service company .... 16.2[3]
Acquisition value method of valuation .... 18.1[6][c]
Activity ratio .... 4.2[3]
   average collection period
     ratio .... 4.2[3][b]
   defined .... 4.2[3]
   fixed-assets turnover
     ratio .... 4.2[3][c]
   inventory turnover ratio ... 4.2[3][a]
   total assets turnover
     ratio .... 4.2[3][d]
   working capital turnover
     ratio .... 4.2[3][d]
Actuary's loss analysis .... 18.1[3]; 18.1[5][a][vii]
Adjusted net book value valuation method .... 18.1[6][a]

Administrative law
   defined .... 9.1[2][b]
Agreements not to compete
   service company .... 16.4[5]
Alimony
   valuation upon marital
     dissolution .... 11.7[2][b]
Answer
   defined .... 9.1[3][b]
   role of valuation expert .... 9.1[3][b]
Antitrust violations
   litigation *re* .... 9.1[1]
Appraisal
   See also Appraisal rights
   defined 2.2
   familiarity with business ..... 2.4[1]
   licensing of appraisers 1.6
   purpose of .... 1.1[3]
Appraisal firms
   Canadian .... 21.2[2]; 21.3
   evolution of 1.2
   licensing of 1.6
Appraisal report
   See Valuation report
Appraisal rights,
   shareholders' .... 3.2[2]; 9.3[1][a]
APT .... 2.9[4]
Arbitrage pricing theory .... 2.9[4]
Arbitration
   Canadian law .... 21.3[2]
Asset approach to valuation
   manufacturing firm .... 15.5[1]
   service firm .... 16.4[7]; 16.6[5]
Asset management ratio .... 2.6[5]; 2.6[6]; 2.6[7]
Assets
   See also Intangible assets; Tangible assets
   collateralization of .... 7.3[3]; 7.5[2][c]
   combined highest and best
     use..................... 10.1[1]
   database as .... 16.4[3]
   determination of what is to be
     valued.................. 15.1[2]
   ease of entry into industry .. 14.3[5]
   financial institution
     commercial banks ..... 17.3[1][a]

[*References are to paragraphs (¶).*]

Assets *(cont.)*
  financial institution *(cont.)*
    S & Ls ..... 17.1[1][a]; 17.1[3][d]
    intangible .... 11[6]; 10.1[1][b];
      10.1[3]; 16.4; 16.4[1]–16.4[7];
      18.1[6][a][ii]
    manufacturing company .... 15.5[1]
    marketability .... 15.1[2][d]
    non-real-estate .... 14.3[2][d]
    proceeds from liquidation
      of .... 7.3[3]
    professional license as ..... 11.12[5]
    protection of .... 7.3[3]
    securitization of .... 7.3[3]
    service company .... 16.6[5]
    software as .... 16.4[3]
    solvency analysis .... 13.2[2][a];
      13.3[2][a]–13.3[2][h]
  valuation approach
    equipment .... 14.3[2][d]
    financial assets .... 14.3[2][a]
    fixtures .... 14.3[2][d]
    furniture .... 14.3[2][d]
    inventory .... 14.3[2][b]
    machinery .... 14.3[2][d]
    natural resources ...... 14.3[2][e]
    real estate .... 14.3[2][c]
  valuation upon marital
    dissolution 11.7
    education .... 11.12[5]
    license .... 11.12[5]
    professional practice 11.12;
      11.12[1]–11.12[4]
Auditor's opinion
  insurance company .... 18.1[5][a][i]
Average collection period
  ratio .... 2.6[6]; 4.2[3][b]

B

Balance sheet
  See also Off balance sheet items
    adjustments to .... 2.6[11]
    analysis of .... 2.5[3]
    examination of .... 2.5[3]; 2.6[2]
    financial ratios .... 2.6[3]
    insurance agency .... 18.2[3][b]
    insurance company ... 18.1[5][a][i];
      18.1[5][b][i]; 18.1[6][a][i]
    professional practices 20.2
Balance sheet test ...... 13.2; 13.2[2]
    assets .... 13.2[2][a]
    case study .... 13.3[2][a]–13.3[2][h]
    contingent liabilities ...... 13.2[2][c]
    interest-bearing debt ..... 13.2[2][b]

Banking
  See also Financial institutions
    interstate .... 17.1[1][e]
    nonbanks .... 17.1[1][c]
Bankruptcy
  bondholder's rights 7.1
  Canadian law .... 21.1[6]
  fair and equitable test ..... 3.1[1][b]
  indication of constructive
    fraud 13.1
**Before-and-after method of calculating
  lost profits** .... 9.4[1][d]
Benefit stream .... 7.5[4]
  determination of .... 2.9[1]
Board of directors
  See Directors
Bonds 7.1
  as fixed-income security 7.1
  bondholder's right to force
    bankruptcy 7.1
  cash flow 7.1; 7.2
  convertible bonds .... 7.5[4]
  interest preference .. 7.1; 7.2; 7.3[2]
  junk bonds .... 5.2[3]
  risk factor .... 5.2[3]
  tax treatment of 7.1
  treasury bonds .... 5.2[3]
  vs. preferred stock 7.1
  zero-coupon bonds .... 5.2[3]
Book value
  adjusted .... 6.7[5]; 6.8[5]
  defined .... 2.1[6]
Breach of contract
  in Canada .... 21.3[1][f]
  litigation *re* .... 9.1[1]
**Break-up valuation
  method** .... 19.2[8][a]
Buildup method .... 2.9[4]
Business appraisal
  See Appraisal
Business assets
  See Assets
Business continuity .... 14.3[8]
Business judgment rule .... 3.2[1]
Business losses
  See Damages; Recovery of damages
Business, organization of 2.5
  importance of capitalization .. 1.1[3]
  valuation of .... 1.1[3]
Business owner
  bookkeeping policies ...... 14.3[10]

INDEX

[References are to paragraphs (¶).]

disbursement policies ...... 14.3[10]
nonmonetary benefits ...... 14.3[10]
personal involvement .... 14.3[9]
Business risk
  See Risk to investor
Business start-ups
  See Start-ups
Business valuation
  See Marital dissolution; Valuation
Business valuation expert
  See Valuation expert
**But for profits, computation
  of** .... 9.4[1]; 9.4[1][b]
Buy-sell agreements
  Canadian .... 21.2[6]
  marital dissolution
    valuations ..... 11.5[1];11.5[1][c];
              11.5[1][d]

C

Call options
  See Call provisions
Call provisions .... 7.3[4][a]; 7.5[1]
  convertible bonds .... 7.5[4]
  impact on bond price .... 7.5[3]
  impact on preferred stock.... 7.5[3]
Canadian valuation
  acquisitions .... 21.2[1]
    compulsory .... 21.2[5][a]
  appraisal remedy .... 21.2[5][d]
  bankruptcy law............ 21.1[6]
  buy-sell agreements .... 21.2[6]
  company law.............. 21.1[2]
  competition law .... 21.1[7]
  corporate reorganization .... 21.2[2]
  definitions of terms 21.5
  employee share ownership
    plans................... 21.1[8]
  expropriation law .... 21.1[5]
  fairness .... 21.2[3]; 21.2[5][c]
  family law ...... 21.1[4]; 21.3[1][d]
  financial solvency analysis .. 21.2[9]
  forcing-out premium .... 21.2[5][e];
                    21.3[1][b]
  going private .... 21.2[5]; 21.6[3]
  going public............... 21.2[4]
  goodwill .... 21.3[1][e]
  income tax law ..... 21.1[1]; 21.6[2]
  litigation..... 21.1[1]; 21.2[10]; 21.3
  merger .... 21.2[1]
  oppression remedy ...... 21.2[5][b];
              21.2[5][d]; 21.3[1][c]
  prior valuation defined ..... 21.6[3]
  privatization .... 21.2[11]

purchase price, allocation
  of..................... 21.2[8]
related-party transfers ...... 21.2[9]
sale .... 21.2[1]
securities regulation ....21.1[3];
              21.6[3]; 21.6[4]
valuation approaches ..... 21.2[5][d]
**Capital asset pricing method
  (CAPM)** .... 2.9[4]; 5.2[6]; 6.8[4]
  in liquidation....... 10.3[2]; 10.3[5]
Capital markets .... 17.1[1][d]
Capital ratios .... 17.2[3][e]
Capital structure
  changes in
    cost of debt .... 5.2[7]
    cost of equity .... 5.2[7]
    WACC .... 5.2[7]
  fixed-income securities
    tax treatment of 7.1
    valuation of 7.1
  impact on fixed income
    securities .... 7.4[1]; 7.5[2][b]
Capitalization of dividends ..... 6.7[2];
              6.8[3][d]
Capitalization of earnings
  manufacturing firm ...... 15.5[3][a]
  service firm .... 16.6[4]
  valuation method .... 18.2[2];
              18.2[2][b]; 20.7[1][b]
Capitalization rates .... 1.1[4];
              18.1[6][d][i]–18.1[6][d][iv]
  cash flow, defined .... 5.1[1][c]
  company-specific factors ... 5.1[3][c]
  computation of rates .... 5.1[2];
              5.1[2][a]; 5.1[2][b]
  defined 2.9
  discount rates compared ..... 5.2[2]
  EBDIT .... 5.1[1][f]
  EBIT .... 5.1[1][f]
  industry-specific factors.... 5.1[3][b]
  price/cash flow multiple ... 5.1[1][f]
  price/debt-free cash flow
    multiple .... 5.1[1][e]
  price/debt-free earnings
    multiple .... 5.1[1][d]
  price/future earnings
    multiple .... 5.1[1][b]
  price/net book value
    multiple .... 5.1[1][g]
  price/revenue multiple ....5.1[1][h]
  variations in
    company-specific
      factors .... 5.1[3][c]

[*References are to paragraphs (¶).*]

Capitalization rates *(cont.)*
variations in *(cont.)*
  general economic
    conditions .... 5.1[3][a]
  industry-specific
    factors .... 5.1[3][b]
CAPM
See Capital asset pricing method (CAPM)
Case law
  Canadian .... 21.6[2]
  defined .... 9.1[2][c]
  relationship to valuation ... 9.1[2][c]
  researching .... 9.1[2][c]
Cash accounting
  service company .... 16.5[1]
Cash contribution
  nonleveraged ESPO .... 8.3[1][b]
Cash flow 10.3
See also Discounted cash flow
  defined .... 5.1[1][c]
  discounted
    manufacturing firm ...... 15.5[2]
    service firm .... 16.6[4]
  fixed-income securities......... 7.2
  future
    discounted .... 6.8[4]
    price/cash flow ratio ...... 5.1[1][c]
Cash flow test .... 13.2; 13.2[3]
  case study .... 13.3[3]
Cash ratio .... 4.1[1][c]
Client records .... 11.6[2][a]
Closely held business
  definitions of value.... 2.1[1]–2.1[7]
  description of assets.......... 2.2
  financial statements
    reliance on by expert
      witness .... 9.2[2][g]
  valuation date 2.3
Coal companies
  contracts .... 19.3[1]
  taxation
    depletion .... 19.3[3]
    exploration costs......... 19.3[3]
    gains on mining
      interests .... 19.3[3]
  transportation .... 19.3[1]
  type of coal .... 19.3; 19.3[1]
  valuation .... 19.3[2]
Collateralization
  fixed-income securities........7.3[3]; 7.5[2][c]
Combined highest and best use of assets .... 10.1[1]

Combined ratio
  insurance company ...... 18.1[4][i]
Commercial banks 17.1
See also Financial institutions
  accounting issues .... 17.4[1]
  balance sheet
    assets
      Fed funds .... 17.3[1][a]
      loan portfolio .... 17.3[1][a]
      reserve for loan
        losses .... 17.3[1][a]
    liabilities
      demand deposits..... 17.3[1][b]
      short-term
        borrowings .... 17.3[1][b]
  financial analysis........... 17.3[3]
  income statements .... 17.3[2]
  management issues......... 17.4[5]
Commodity industry, defined .. 14.3[6]
Common equity securities
See also Common stock
  valuation on liquidation ...... 10.1; 10.4[2]
  discount rate .... 10.3; 10.3[1]–10.3[5]
  impact of shareholder
    taxation .... 10.4[6]
  minority interests .... 10.4[5]
  value of assets
    intangible assets .... 10.4[3]
    vs. value of stock .... 10.4[1]
Common-size statements 2.6
Common stock
See also Stock
  purchase of by leveraged
    ESOP .... 8.3[2][a]
  valuation of .... 14.4[2][b]
    manufacturing
      company .... 15.1[2][d]
    service company .... 16.6[1]; 16.6[2]
Common valuation litigation ... 9.1[1]
Company-specific risk
See also Risk to investor
  fixed-income securities......7.2; 7.4
  measurement of .... 7.5[4]
  nature of capital
    structure .... 7.4[1]
  variability of operations ... 7.4[2]
Comparative industry ratios ...... 4.7; 6.8[1]; 6.8[2]

INDEX

[References are to paragraphs (¶).]

Comparative transaction data ... 14.5
Complaint
   definition of .... 9.1[3][a]
   filing of .... 9.1[3][a]
   role of valuation expert .... 9.1[3][a]
Compulsion value
   in marital dissolution .... 11.2[3]
Confidentiality .... 11.6[2]; 11.6[2][a];
                                11.6[2][b]
Conflict of interest
   appraised company vs. valuation
     expert .... 9.2[2][c]
Consideration paid for
   business .... 14.4[2]
Constructive fraud
   See also Leveraged transactions
   debtor's financial condition, test
     of 13.1
   defined 13.1
   lender's penalties 13.1
   solvency analysis 13.2
   steps to fraudulent conveyance
     judgment 13.1
Consultant
   vs. valuation expert .... 9.2[2][a]
Contingent fees
   See also Contingent payments
   professional practices ..... 20.2[2][b]
Contingent liabilities
   balance sheet test .... 13.2[2][c]
   professional practices .... 20.2[7]
   solvency analysis and ..... 13.2[2][c]
Contingent payments
   See also Contingent fees
   ESOP independent and ...... 8.6[3]
Contract, breach of
   See Breach of contract
Control premium .... 2.11; 8.6[2]
Controlling interest premium 2.11;
                            6.9[1]; 6.10[2]
Conversion premium .... 8.3[2][a]
Convertible bond .... 7.5[4]
   callability .... 7.5[1]
   debt component .... 7.5[1]
   equity component .... 7.5[1]
Convertible preferred stock
   purchase by leveraged
     ESOP .... 8.3[2][a]
Convertible securities
   See also Convertible bond;
     Convertible preferred stock
   valuation of .... 14.4[2][c]

Copyrights .... 1.1[6]
Corporate alternative minimum tax
   insurance company ...... 18.1[7][f]
Corporate bonds
   risk factors .... 5.2[3]
Corporation
   dissolution of
     liquidation vs. .... 9.3[2][a]
     litigation *re* .... 9.1[1]; 9.3[2]
     valuation date .... 9.3[2][d]
     valuation upon .... 9.3[2][a];
                                  9.3[2][c]
     voluntary vs.
       involuntary .... 9.3[2][b]
   oil and gas companies ... 19.2[1][a];
                             19.2[7][b][i]
   reorganization of
     Canadian companies ..... 21.2[2]
   state statutes *re* expert
     witnesses .... 3.1[2]
Cost approach to valuation
   See Asset approach to valuation
Cost of debt .... 2.9[3];5.2[6]
   changing capital structure ... 5.2[7]
Cost of equity .... 2.9[3]; 5.2[6]
   arbitrage pricing theory ..... 2.9[4]
   buildup method .... 2.9[4]
   CAPM .... 2.9[4]
   used to discount equity
     flows .... 5.2[6]
   yield-plus-growth method .... 2.9[4]
Cost valuation methods 2.10
   excess earnings approach ... 2.10[2]
   underlying asset approach .. 2.10[1]
Current ratio .... 2.6[4]; 4.1[1][b]
Current yield .... 7.5[1]
Customer base
   service company .... 16.4[4]
Customer contracts
   service company .... 16.4[2]

D

Damages
   See also Recovery of damages
   defined .... 9.1[3][f]
   expert testimony as factor in
     calculating .... 9.4[2][d]
   legal theory .... 9.4[1][c]
   personal injury cases ..... 9.4[2][a];
                                  9.4[2][c]

[References are to paragraphs (¶).]

Damages *(cont.)*
   quantification of ... 9.4[1]; 9.4[1][b]
      elements of value .... 9.4[1][b]
      methodology .... 9.4[1][b]
      valuation of entity ...... 9.4[1][b]
   recovery of .... 9.1[1]; 9.4[1]pd[
   time span used for
      calculation .... 9.4[1][b]
   vs. valuation .... 9.4[1][b]
   wrongful death cases .... 9.4[2];
      9.4[2][a]; 9.4[2][b]; 9.4[2][d]
Database
   service company asset ...... 16.4[3]
Days of inventory ratio .... 2.6[5]
Debt/equity ratio .... 2.6[8]
Debt-free cash flow .... 6.7[4]
Debt management ratios .... 2.6[8]
   debt/equity .... 2.6[8]
   times interest earned .... 2.6[8]
   total debt/total assets ...... 2.6[8]
Deferred insurance policy acquisition costs .... 18.1[5][a][i]
Deferred revenue .... 16.5[2]
Delaware block method of valuation .... 1.5; 9.3[1][e]; 16.2[3]; 21.2[5][d]
Demutualization .... 18.1[1][e]
Depreciation expenses
   examination of .... 2.5[2]
Depreciation replacement cost .... 14.3[2][d]
Deregulation of financial institutions .... 17.1[1][j]
Dilution
   defined .... 12.1[5][a]
Directors
   as auctioneers .... 3.2[2]
   business judgment rule ...... 3.2[1]
   duties owed to stockholders 3.2
Disclosure requirements
   fairness
      federal .... 3.5[1]
      state .... 3.5[2]
   going private .... 3.5[1]
Discount rate .... 5.2; 6.7[4]
   See also Discounts
   adjusting for risk ..... 5.2[5]; 5.2[6]
   capitalization rate
      compared................ 5.2[2]
   debt instruments and .... 5.2[3]
   defined 2.9
   determination of .... 5.2[3]
   fixed adjusted discount rate .... 9.4[2][f]
   growth projections .... 5.2[2]
   initial public offering ..... 12.3[1][a]
   oil and gas .... 19.2[7][a][iii]
   on liquidation
      choice of .... 10.3; 10.3[4]
      lack of marketability ... 10.4[5][d]
      minority-issue discount .... 10.4[5][b]
      vs. operating company's rate .... 10.3[1]
   present value and .... 5.2[1]
   stated yields vs. .... 5.2[4]
   total offset method .... 9.4[2][f]
   variable adjusted rate discount .... 9.4[2][f]
Discounted cash flow 10.3
   manufacturing firm .... 15.5[2]
   risk to investor .... 7.5[1]
   service firm .... 16.6[4]
   value in IPOs .... 12.3[1][a]
Discounts
   See also Discount rate
   lack of marketability ... 2.11; 6.9[3]; 10.4[5][b]
   loss reserves
      insurance company .... 18.1[7][d]
   minority interest .... 2.11; 6.9[2]; 6.10[1]; 9.3[1][g]; 10.4[5][b]
Discovery
   depositions .... 9.1[3][c]
   interrogatories .... 9.1[3][c]
   requests for production of documents .... 9.1[3][c]
   role of valuation expert
      defense .... 9.1[3][c]
      prosecution .... 9.1[3][c]
Dissolution
   See also Corporation; Partnership
   liquidation vs. .... 9.3[2][a]
   voluntary vs. involuntary .. 9.3[2][b]
Divesture
   comparative data .... 14.5[2]
Dividends
   excess .... 7.5[4]
   fair market value and .... 6.7[2]
   fixed-income securities .... 7.3[2]
   insurance agency .... 18.1[7][c]

INDEX

[References are to paragraphs (¶).]

insurance company ...... 18.1[7][c]
manufacturing firms..... 15.5[3][c];
   16.4[7]; 16.6
Divorce
   See Marital dissolution
DLOM .... 2.11; 6.9[3]
Drilling partnerships .... 19.2[3][b]
   See also Oil and gas companies
Due diligence
   in solvency analysis .... 13.2[1]
DuPont system 4.4
Duration of security
   See Holding period
Duty of fairness 3.1

E

Early redemption options ...... 7.5[1]
Earnings
   capitalization of ...... 1.1[3]; 1.1[4]
   dilution of
      insurance agency .... 18.2[2][a][i]
   organization of .... 1.1[3]
Earnings approach to valuation
   manufacturing firm .... 15.5[2]
   service firm ... 16.6; 16.6[4]; 16.4[7]
Earnings before depreciation, interest,
   and taxes (EBDIT) .... 2.6[8];
      4.2[2][b]; 5.1[1][f]; 6[7][1]
   price/EBDIT ratio .... 6.8[3][c]
Earnings before interest and taxes
   (EBIT) ...... 2.6[8]; 5.1[1][f]; 6.7[1]
   price/EBIT ratio .... 6.8[3][c]
Earnings capitalization
   See Capitalization of earnings
Earnout provisions .... 14.4[2][d]
EBDIT
   See Earnings before depreciation,
      interest, and taxes (EBDIT)
EBIT
   See Earnings before interest and
      taxes (EBIT)
Economic overview ..... 2.4[2]; 6.5[2]
Education, professional
   as marital asset .... 11.12[5]
Employee stock ownership plans
   (ESOPs)...... 3.1[1]; 6.9[3]; 6.10[2]
   adequate consideration
      control premiums .... 8.6[2]
      fair market value ..... 8.6[1]; 8.7
      marketability of
         securities .... 8.6[2]

proposed regulations ... 8.2; App.
   8–1
report requirements 8.8
Canadian law ...... 21.2[7]; 21.2[8]
contingent payments .... 8.6[3]
defined 8.1
economic benefits 8.4
fiduciary
   employer's duty as in
      valuation 1.5
   independence of .... 8.6[3]
financial adviser
   documentation of opinion.... 8.8
   fairness of opinion 8.9
   independence of .... 8.6[3]
   insurance companies ..... 18.1[1][d]
levels of fair market value 6.9
leveraged ESOPs .... 8.3[2]
   effect on value per
      share ... 8.3[2][a]; 8.3[2][b]; 8.5
   per-share valuation ..... 8.3[2][c]
   stock purchases........ 8.3[2][a];
      8.3[2][b]
   vs. nonleveraged ESOPs ... 8.3[2]
multi-investor equity allocation
   issues .... 8.5; 8.5[1]
nonleveraged ESOPs .... 8.3[1]
   cash contributions ...... 8.3[1][a]
   form of stock
      contributions......... 8.3[1][a]
   vs. leveraged ESOPs ...... 8.3[2]
parties involved in the
   determination of fairness .. 3.1[2]
put rights .... 8.6[2]
quantification of benefits 8.4
tax benefits 8.1
valuation of ...... 8.3[2][c]; 8.4; 8.5;
   8.5[1]
   service company .... 16.2[2]
Employment contract
   service company .... 16.4[5]
Enterprise value .... 2.11; 8.6[2]
   defined .... 2.1[7]
Entire fairness .... 3.3[1]; 9.3[1][c]
Equipment
   professional practices....... 20.2[5]
   valuation approach....... 14.3[2][d]
   valuation upon marital
      dissolution .... 11.7[1]
Equipment trusts ..... 7.3[3]; 7.5[2][c]
Equity allocation issues, multi-
   investor............... 8.5; 8.5[1]

FINANCIAL VALUATION   I-8

[References are to paragraphs (¶).]

Equity valuation
See also Financial statement analysis
classificaiton of business
   activities .... 2.4[1]
   SIC codes .... 2.4[1]
competition .... 2.4[2]
customer base .... 2.4[1]
economic and industry
   research .... 2.4[2]
evolution of company .... 2.4[1]
financial data
   review of .... 2.4[1]
general economic analysis.... 2.4[2]
history of business .... 2.4[1]
management structure .... 2.4[1]
nature of business........... 2.4[1]
other external factors........ 2.4[1]
physical plant .... 2.4[1]
Revenue Ruling 59-60......... 2.4
sources of supply .... 2.4[1]

ESOPs
See Employee stock ownership plans (ESOPs)

Excess dividends............... 7.5[4]

Excess earnings valuation
method .... 2.10[2]; 20.7[1][a]

Excess interest .... 7.5[4]

Exchangeable preferred stock .... 7.3[4][b]

Expense accounts
professional practices balance
   sheet .... 20.2[3]; 20.2[4]
review of .... 2.5[2]

Expense ratio .... 18.1[6][d][vi]

Expert opinion 3.4
See also Valuation expert
bankruptcy .... 3.1[1][b]
business judgment rule ...... 3.2[1]
factor in calculation of lost
   earnings .... 9.4[2][d]
liability of .... 3.4[2]
marital dissolution cases .... 11.4[1];
          11.5[1][d]; 11.7[2][a]
state corporation statutes .... 3.1[2]
weight given to .... 3.4[1]

Expert witness
See Expert opinion; Valuation expert

Extractive industries
See also specific industry
coal companies 19.3
oil and gas companies 19.2
other .... 19.4[5]
timber companies 19.4

F

Fair and equitable test ...... 3.1[1][b]
Fair cash value ....21.3[1][b]
Fair market value............ 1.1[2]
Canadian law ....21.1; 21.1[1];
    21.2[3]; 21.3[1][b]; 21.3[1][d]
controlling .... 6.9[1]
defined .... 2.1[2]
dividends paid and .... 6.7[2]
entire fairness .... 9.3[1][c]
ESOP transactions .... 8.6[1]
   date of appraisal............ 8.7
fairness of transaction 3.1
marital dissolution .... 11.2[1]
mergers and acquisitions... 3.1[1][a]
minority interest .... 6.9[2]
Revenue Ruling 59-60...... 15.1[4]
service company .... 16.6[2]
   acquisition .... 16.2[3]
   merger .... 16.2[3]
unmarketable interest .... 6.9[3]
vs. fair value .... 9.3[1][b]

Fair price
defined .... 3.3[2]
going-concern transaction .... 3.3[3]
procedure in determining .... 3.3[3]

Fair rate of return
valuation of, insurance
   agency .... 18.2[2][b]

Fair salable value
service company .... 16.2[2]

Fair value
See also Fair market value
Canadian law ... 21.2[5]; 21.2[5][c];
    21.2[5][e]; 21.3[1][b]; 21.3[1][c]
determination of .... 9.3[1][e]
entire fairness .... 9.3[1][c]
in liquidation............ 10.4[5][c]
service company .... 16.2[3]
tangible asset liquidation value vs.
   going-concern liquidation
   value .... 9.3[2][a]
vs. fair market value ...... 9.3[1][b]

Fairness of transaction
determination of
   parties involved .... 3.1[2]

INDEX

[References are to paragraphs (¶).]

disclosure requirements
  federal .... 3.5[1]
  state .... 3.5[2]
entire fairness .... 3.3[1]
expert opinion 3.4
fair market value vs. 3.1
fair price .... 3.3[3]
  defined .... 3.3[2]
good faith and entire
  fairness .... 3.3[1]
inclusion of fair market
  value .... 3.3[2]
mergers and acquisitions ... 3.1[1][a]
procedural fairness .... 3.3[3]
Fed funds .... 17.3[1][a]
Federal income tax
See Taxation
Federal Rules of Civil Procedure
use in valuation ... 9.1[2][d]; 9.1[3]
Federal Rules of Evidence
use in valuation ... 9.1[2][d]; 9.1[3]
Fiduciary
employer's duty as 1.5
independence of
  ESOP .... 8.6[3]
Financial adviser
ESOP .... 8.6[3]
Financial analysis
See Financial statement analysis;
Solvency analysis
Financial and operating valuation comparisons .... 19.2[8][b]
Financial institutions
See also Commercial banks; Savings
and loan (S & L) institutions
capital markets .... 17.1[1][d]
commercial banks ... 17.3[1]–17.3[5]
current legal trends ..... 17.1[1][a];
  17.1[1][b]; 17.1[1][f]; 17.1[1][g];
  17.1[1][i]; 17.1[1][j]
hostile takeovers .... 17.1[1][h]
interstate banking .... 17.1[1][c]
nonbanks .... 17.1[1][c]
S & Ls .... 17.2[1]–17.2[5]
secondary loan markets ... 17.1[1][d]
Financial leverage 4.5
Financial leverage ratio .... 2.6[8]
Financial ratios
activity ratios .... 4.2[3]
asset management ratios
  accounts receivable turnover
    ratio .... 2.6[6]

inventory turnover ratio ... 2.6[5]
total assets utilization
  ratio .... 2.6[7]
debt management ratios
  debt/equity ratio .... 2.6[8]
times interest earned
  ratio .... 2.6[8]
total debt/total assets
  ratio .... 2.6[8]
evaluation of .... 4.2[5]
leverage ratios .... 4.2[2]
limitations on analysis of 4.9
liquidity ratios .... 4.2[1]
  current ratio .... 2.6[4]
  quick ratio .... 2.6[4]
profitability ratios
  net profit margin ratio .... 2.6[9]
  return on assets ratio ...... 2.6[9]
  return on equity ratio ..... 2.6[9]
Financial risk
See Risk to investor
Financial solvency analysis
See Solvency analysis
Financial statement analysis ... 2.4[1];
  2.5; 2.6; 6.6
See also Balance sheet; Income
statement; Solvency analysis;
Statement of Changes in
Financial Condition
adjustments to ..... 2.6[10]; 2.6[11];
  2.6[12]; 2.6[13]
Canadian .... 21.2[10]
expert testimony *re* .... 9.2[2][g]
importance of tax returns .... 2.5[1]
insurance company ... 18.1[5][a][i];
  18.1[2]; 18.1[3]
manufacturing
  firms .... 15.3[1]–15.3[4]
professional practices .... 20.1[2]
ratio analysis 4.1
S & Ls .... 17.1[3]
  ratio analysis .... 17.1[3]
  trend analysis .... 17.1[3]
**Fixed adjusted discount
rate** .... 9.4[2][f]
Fixed-assets turnover ratio ... 4.2[3][c]
Fixed charges
defined .... 4.2[2][d]
**Fixed-charges coverage
ratio** .... 4.2[2][d]
Fixed fees
ESOP independence and ..... 8.6[3]

[References are to paragraphs (¶).]

Fixed-income securities 7.1
  bonds 7.1
  cash flows .... 7.2; 7.4[1]
  company-specific risk.......... 7.2
  issue-specific risk 7.2; 7.3
    dividend protection .... 7.3[2]
    duration .... 7.3[1]
    interest protection .... 7.3[2]
  preferred stock 7.1
  valuation of 7.2
Fixtures
  valuation of .... 14.3[2][d]
Forcing-out premium ...... 21.2[5][e];
                               21.3[1][b]
Forest product companies
  See Timber companies
Form 10–K
  insurance companies .. 18.1[5][a][iii]
  oil and gas companies ... 19.2[6][b];
                  19.2[7][e]; 19.2[8][a][i]
Form 10–Q
  insurance companies .. 18.1[5][a][v]
  oil and gas companies .... 19.2[7][e]
Franchises
  value of .... 1.1[6]
Fraudulent conveyance .... 16.2[3]
  judgment 13.1
  leveraged transactions 13.1
Full and fair disclosure
  See Disclosure requirements
**Full cost and accounting valuation
  method** .... 19.2[5][a]; 19.2[5][b]
Full market value .... 21.3[1][b]
Funds flow statement
  examination of .... 2.5[4]
  insurance company ... 18.1[5][a][i];
                            18.1[5][b][iii]
Funeral expenses
  recoverability of .... 9.4[2][a];
                               9.4[2][b]
Furniture
  valuation method .... 14.3[2][d]
  upon marital dissolution .. 11.7[1]
Future earnings
  See also Inflation; Lost earnings
  discounting .... 9.4[2][f]
    fixed adjusted discount
      rate .... 9.4[2][f]
    total offset method ...... 9.4[2][f]
    variable adjusted rate discount
      rate .... 9.4[2][f]
  present value of .... 18.1[6][d];
                               18.1[6][e]
  professional practices.. 20.3; 20.5[1]
  projection of .... 9.4[2][d]
Future profits
  See Future earnings

G

GAAP statements
  Canadian law .... 21.2[1]
  insurance policies .... 18.1[5][a];
                             18.1[5][a][i]
General economic overview .... 2.4[2];
                                 6.5[2]
General Utilities doctrine .. 10.1[3][a];
                                 10.2[2]
Going-concern liquidation .... 9.3[2][a]
Going-concern value ..... 1.5; 15.1[4]
  defined .... 2.1[4]
  discounted cash flow 10.3
  vs. costs .... 10.1[3][a]
  vs. gross liquidation
    proceeds .... 10.1[3][a]; 10.1[3][b]
  vs. net liquidation
    value .... 10.1[3][a]; 10.1[3][b]
  vs. present worth .... 10.1[3][b]
  vs. taxes .... 10.1[3][a]; 10.4[6]
Going private .... 3.1[1][a]
  Canadian law ... 21.1[5]; 21.2[5][c];
                        21.3[1][b]; 21.6[3]
  disclosure requirements...... 3.5[1]
  LBO vs. .... 3.1[1][a]
  SEC rule .... 3.5[1]
Going public
  Canadian law .... 21.2[4]
Good faith and entire fairness .. 3.3[1]
Goodwill
  defined .... 1.1[1]
  loss of..................... 1.1[5]
    formula for determining ... 1.1[5]
    in Canada .... 21.3[1][e]
  valuation of .... 1.1[1]
    insurance agency ... 18.2[3][b][iii]
    insurance
      company .... 18.1[6][a][ii]
    outside bankruptcy ..... 9.3[2][a]
    corporate
      dissolution .... 9.3[2][c]
    partnership
      dissolution .... 9.3[2][c]
    professional practice

[References are to paragraphs (¶).]

marital dissolution . . . . . 11.7[3];
11.8[3][d]; 11.12[3]; 20.1[4]; 20.4;
20.4[1]; 20.4[2]; 20.5; 20.6
marital separation . . . . . 11.7[3];
11.8[3][d]
**Gordon dividend valuation
method** . . . . 2.9[2]
Gross liquidation proceeds . . . . 10.1[2]
vs. going-concern value . . 10.2[3][a];
10.1[3][b]
**Gross profit margin/sales
ratio** . . . . 4.2[4][a]
Growth vs. risk 5.1

H

Holding period
fixed-income securities . . . . 7.3[2]
relationship to issue-specific
risk . . . . 7.3[1]

I

IDCs
See Intangible drilling costs (IDCs)
Income approach to valuation
See Earnings approach to valuation
Income statement
adjustments to . . . . 2.10[12]
analysis of . . . . 2.5[2]
categories . . . . 2.5[2]
examination of . . . . 2.5[2]; 2.6[1]
financial ratios . . . . 2.6[3]
insurance agency . . . . 18.2[3][a]
insurance company . . . . 18.1[5][a][i]
Income valuation method 2.9
benefit stream . . . . 2.9[1]
capitalization rate
defined 2.9
common measures of benefits
cash flow . . . . 2.9[1]
EBDIT . . . . 2.9[1]
EBIT . . . . 2.9[1]
net cash flow . . . . 2.9[1]
discount rate
defined 2.9
Gordon dividend valuation
model . . . . 2.9[?]
risk to investor . . . . 2.9[3]
time horizon used . . . . 2.9[2]
Increased costs
recovery of damages for . . . 9.4[1][d]

**Index
ratio** . . . . . 18.1[6][c][i]–18.1[6][c][iii]
Industry analysis . . . . . . 2.4[2]; 6.5[2];
6.6[3]; 6.8[1]; 6.8[2]; 15.4
Industry rates of return 4.6
Inflation
See also Future earnings; Lost
earnings
adjustment for future income
taxes . . . . 9.4[2][e]
factor in calculation of lost
earnings . . . . 9.4[2][d]
evidentiary approach . . . . 9.4[2][d]
middle-ground
approach . . . . 9.4[2][e]
traditional approach . . . . 9.4[2][e]
Initial public offering (IPO)
comparison to comparable
firm . . . . 12.3[2][b]–12.3[2][d]
discount rate . . . . 12.3[1][a]
discounted present value of
expected future cash
flow . . . . 12.3[1][a]
financing . . . . 12.1[2]
insurance companies . . . . . 18.1[1][c]
price/book value ratio . . . . 12.3[2][b]
price/earnings ratio . . . . . 12.3[1][a];
12.3[1][b]; 12.3[2]; 12.3[2][a];
12.3[2][b]
limitations on . . . . 12.3[2][e]
price/sales ratio . . . . 12.3[2][b]
risk factor . . . . 12.1[1]
ROI . . . . 12.1[2]
analysis of . . . . 12.1[5]
premoney vs. postmoney
valuations . . . . 12.1[5][b]
taxation . . . . 12.3[1][a]
Insurance agency 18.2
See also Insurance company
acquisition by public
company . . . . 18.2[3][b][iii]
agency's growth as valuation
factor . . . . 18.2[2][c][ii]
amortization of
intangibles . . . . 18.2[3][a][ii]
asset sale revenues . . . . 18.2[3][a][ii]
balance sheet . . . . 18.2[3][a]
commission multiples . . . . 18.2[1][a]
income statement . . . . 18.2[3][b]
insurance expirations
allocation of purchase
price . . . . 18.2[3][b][iii]

[References are to paragraphs (¶).]

Insurance agency *(cont.)*
  insurance expirations *(cont.)*
    goodwill . . . . 18.2[3][b][iii]
    Revenue Ruling
      74–456 . . . . 18.2[3][b][iii]
    separate assets . . . . . . 18.2[3][b][iii]
    useful life . . . . 18.2[3][b][iii]
  owner's
    compensation . . . . . . 18.2[3][a][ii]
  revenue multiples . . . . 18.2[1][b]
  tangible net worth . . . . . 18.2[3][b][i]
  travel and entertainment
    expenses . . . . 18.2[3][a][ii]
  valuation methods
    capitalization of
      earnings . . . . 18.2[2][b]
    public company . . . . 18.2[2][a]
    wasting asset . . . . 18.2[2][c]
Insurance claims
  Canadian law . . . . 21.3[1][i]
  litigation *re* . . . . 9.1[1]
Insurance company 18.1
  See also Insurance agency
  branch office network . . . 18.1[4][m]
  business
    evaluation of . . . . 18.1[4]
  claims department
    procedures . . . . 18.1[4][e]
  competition . . . 18.1[4][k]; 18.1[4][l];
                      18.1[5][a][iii]
  corporate alternative minimum
    tax . . . . 18.1[7][f]
  dividends . . . . 18.1[7][c]
  financial analysis . . . . . . 18.1; 18.1[5]
    annual reports . . . . 18.1[5][a][i]
    deferred policy
      acquisitions . . . . 18.1[5][a][i]
    GAAP statements . . . . . 18.1[5][a]
    Form 10–K . . . . 18.1[5][a][iii]
    Form 10–Q . . . . 18.1[5][a][v]
    product lines . . . . 18.1[5][a][i]
    proxy statements . . . 18.1[5][a][ii]
    reinsurance . . . . 18.1[4][c];
                        18.1[5][a][i]
    subsidiaries . . . . 18.1[5][a][i]
    unearned
      premiums . . . . 18.1[5][a][i];
              18.1[7][a]; 18.1[7][b]
  intangibles . . . . 18.1[6][a][ii]
  investment policies . . . . 18.1[4][h]
  life insurance company
    deduction . . . . 18.1[7][e]

  loss reserves . . . . 18.1[4][g];
    18.1[5][a][i]; 18.1[5][a][vii];
                        18.1[7][d]
  management
    evaluation of . . . . 18.1[3]
  statutory convention
    statements . . . . 18.1[5][b]
  tax-exempt interest . . . . 18.1[7][c]
  Tax Report Act, effect of . . . 18.1[7]
  unreported losses . . . . 18.1[4][f]
  valuation methods
    acquisition value . . . . . . 18.1[6][c];
                     18.1[6][f][iii]
    adjusted net book
      value . . . . 18.1[6][a]; 18.1[6][f][i]
    present value of future
      profits . . . . 18.1[6][d]; 18.1[6][e];
                    18.1[6][f][iv]
    trading market
      valuation . . . . 18.1[6][b];
                      18.1[6][f][ii]
Intangible assets
  service company 16.4;
                    16.4[1]–16.4[7]
  valuation . . . . . 1.1[6]; 18.1[6][[a][ii]
  upon liquidation . . . . . . 10.1[1][b];
                          10.1[3]
**Intangible drilling costs
(IDCs)** . . . . 19.2[4]
Intentional fraud
  See also Leveraged buyout (LBO)
    transactions
  defined 13.1
  lender's penalties 13.1
Interest
  bonds . . . . 7.1; 7.2; 7.3[2]
  controlling . . . . 6.9[1]
  excess . . . . 7.5[4]
  fixed-income securities . . . . . . 7.3[2]
  insurance company . . . . . . 18.1[7][c]
  minority . . . . 6.9[2]
  preferred stock preference 7.1;
                    7.2; 7.3[2]
  unmarketable . . . . 6.9[3]
Interest analysis
  S & Ls . . . . 17.2[3][g]
Interest-bearing debt . . . . 13.2[2][b]
Interest expense . . . . 2.5[2]

INDEX

[References are to paragraphs (¶).]

Intrinsic value
  defined .... 2.1[3]
  in marital dissolution .... 11.2[2]
Inventory valuation
  approach .... 14.3[2][b]
Inventory turnover ratio .... 2.6[5];
                                        4.2[3][a]
Investigaion of target business ... 6.3
Investment value
  See Intrinsic value
Investor
  See Risk of investment; Risk to investor
Investor ratios 5.1
IPO
  See Initial public offering (IPO)
IRS guides to valuation .... 1.1[3]
IRS valuation manuals .... 1.1[3]
Issue-specific risk 7.2; 7.3
  See also Risk to investor
  fixed-income securities
    asset protection .... 7.3[3]
    corporate protection ...... 7.3[4]
    dividend and interest
      protection .... 7.3[2]
    holding period .... 7.3[1]

J

Judge, role of
  defined .... 9.1[3][g]
Judicial process .... 9.1[3]
  discovery .... 9.1[3][c]
  judge, role of .... 9.1[3][g]
  jury, role of .... 9.1[3][g]
  motions .... 9.1[3][d]
  pleadings .... 9.1[3][a]; 9.1[3][b]
  pretrial hearing .... 9.1[3][e]
  requests for admission ..... 9.1[3][d]
  stipulations .... 9.1[3][d]
  trial .... 9.1[3][f]
  verdict .... 9.1[3][h]
Junk bonds .... 5.2[3]
Jury, role of
  defined .... 9.1[3][g]

L

Lack of marketability
  discount for on
    liquidation .... 10.4[5][d]

LBO
  See Leveraged buyout (LBO) transactions
Letter of solvency .... 13.1[2]
Leverage ratios .... 4.2[2]
  defined .... 4.2[2]
  fixed-charges covering
    ratio .... 4.2[2][d]
  times interest earned
    ratio .... 4.2[2][c]
  total debt/total assets
    ratio .... 4.2[2][a]
  total interest-bearing debt/equity
    ratio .... 4.2[2][b]
Leveraged buyouts (LBOs)
  See Leveraged buyout (LBO) transactions
Leveraged ESOPs .... 8.3[2]
  equity allocation
    investors vs. noninvestors .. 8.5[1]
    stock purchases .... 8.3[2][a];
                                      8.3[2][b]
    effect on value per
      share ... 8.3[2][a]; 8.3[2][b]; 8.5
    mirror loans .... 8.3[2][a]
    tax advantages .... 8.3[2]
    vs. nonleveraged ESOP ...... 8.5[2]
Leveraged buyout (LBO) transactions
  See also Constructive fraud
  changes in capital structure .. 5.2[7]
  constructive fraud 13.1
  ESOPs .... 16.2[3]
  going private vs. .... 3.1[1][a]
  intentional fraud 13.1
  SEC rule .... 3.5[1]
  solvency analysis ... 13.2[1]–13.2[4]
    case study 13.3
  solvency letter .... 13.1[2]
Liability
  defined .... 9.1[3][f]
  on professional practice's balance
    sheet .... 20.2[7][b]–20.2[7][g]
Licenses
  insurance company ... 18.1[6][a][iii]
  professional
    marital asset .... 11.12[5]
Life insurance company
  deduction .... 18.1[7][e]
Lifting costs .... 19.2[3][c]
Limited partnerships
  See also Partnerships
  oil and gas companies .... 19.2[1][b]

[*References are to paragraphs (¶).*]

Liquidation
  combined highest and best use of
    assets .... 10.1[1]
    intangible assets .... 10.1[1][b]
  vs. continued
    operations .. 10.1[1][a]; 10.3[5];
      10.4[4]
  complete.................. 10.2[1]
  dissolution vs. .... 9.3[2][a]
  going-concern liquidation .. 9.3[2][a]
  gross proceeds of .... 10.1[2]
  reduction to net liquidation
    value..... 10.1[3][a]; 10.1[3][b]
  partial................... 10.2[2]
  risks
    business risk .... 10.3[2]
    financial risk .... 10.3[2]
    stock liquidity risk....... 10.3[2]
  tangible asset liquidation... 9.3[2][a]
  valuation upon 10.3
    assets vs. stock ... 10.4[1]; 10.4[2]
    defined .... 2.1[5]
    discount for lack of
      marketability........ 10.4[5][d]
    ESOPs .... 8.6[2]
    fairness............... 10.4[5][c]
    intangible assets .... 10.4[3]
    minority interests
      minority interest
        discount............ 10.4[5][b]

Liquidity
  commercial banks....... 17.3[1][a];
    17.3[3]
  risk, generally .... 2.9[3]
  S & Ls .... 17.1[3][b]
  stock liquidity risk .... 10.3[2]

Liquidity ratios................. 2.6[4]
  acid test ratio ..... 2.6[4]; 4.1[1][b]
  cash ratio............... 4.1[1][c]
  current ratio .... 2.6[4]; 4.2[1][a]
  defined .... 4.2[1]
  quick ratio............... 4.1[1][b]

Litigation
  See also Judicial process
  Canadian law 21.3
    arbitration .... 21.3[2]
    breach of contract ..... 21.3[3][f]
    case law .... 21.6[1]; 21.6[2]
    expropriation.......... 21.3[3][d]
    going-private
      transactions.......... 21.3[1][b]
    insurance claims .... 21.3[1][i]
    marital disputes .... 9.1[1];
      21.3[1][d]
    minority shareholder
      oppression .... 21.3[1][c]
    personal injury ....21.3[1][h]
    solvency .... 21.2[10]
    taxation ...... 21.1[1]; 21.3[1][a]
    torts ....21.3[1][g]
  common causes of .... 9.1[1]
  expert witness testimony....... 9.1;
    9.2[2]; 9.2[2][i]
  judicial process ..... 9.1[3]–9.1[3][h]
  preparation of
    case.......... 9.1[2][a]–9.1[2][d]
  valuation expert
    sample retainer
      agreement ..... 9.2[2][e]; App.
      9–2

Loans
  valuation upon marital
    dissolution .... 11.7[4]

**Loss adjustment expense
  ratio** .... 18.1[6][e][v]

Loss expense ratio ...... 18.1[6][e][v]

Loss reserves
  insurance company ...... 18.1[4][g]
  discounting .... 18.1[7][d]

Lost earnings
  See also Future earnings; Inflation;
    Lost profits
  future earnings .... 9.4[2][d]
  inflation, adjustment for ... 9.4[2][d]
  personal injury cases
    cure of impairment ..... 9.4[2][c]
    extent of impairment .... 9.4[2][c]
  productivity, adjustment
    for.................... 9.4[2][d]
  recoverability of .... 9.4[2][a]
  wrongful death cases ...... 9.4[2][d]

Lost profits
  See also Lost earnings
  computation of .... 9.4[1]; 9.4[1][b]
  before-and-after
    method............... 9.4[1][d]
  market-share method.... 9.4[1][d]
  yardstick method .... 9.4[1][d]
  recovery of damages ...... 9.4[1][d]

M

Machinery
  valuation of............. 14.3[2][d]

[*References are to paragraphs (¶).*]

Manufacturing firm
  distribution .... 15.2[5]
  financial analysis.... 15.3[1]–15.3[4]
  industry analysis............. 15.4
  management .... 15.2[7]
  marketing.................. 15.2[5]
  product line................ 15.2[1]
  production .... 15.2[4]
  raw materials .... 15.2[3]
  research and
    development .... 15.2[4][b]
  sales .... 15.2[5]
  SIC Code breakdown ...... 15.1[1]
  technology .... 15.2[4][a]
  valuation .... 15.5[1]–15.1[5]
    asset approach .... 15.5[1]
    discounted cash flow
      approach .... 15.5[2]
    market approach .... 15.5[3]
Marital dissolution
  See also Marital separation
  apportionment of property 11.9
    corporate stock .... 11.13[1]
    court determination of ... 11.9[3]
    fair return on separate capital
      method............... 11.9[1]
    premarital 11.9
    reasonable compensation
      method............... 11.9[2]
  business valuation and........ 11.1
    buy-sell agreements ...... 11.5[1];
        11.5[1][c]; 11.5[1][d]
    components of value 11.7
    formulas for
      determining........... 11.3[2];
        11.3[2][a]–11.3[2][c]
    judicial attitudes towards ... 11.4;
        11.4[1]–11.4[5]
  Canadian law ... 21.1[4]; 21.3[1][d]
  control of business during
    action .... 11.11; 11.13[2]
  definition of value
    compulsion value .... 11.2[3]
    investment value......... 11.2[2]
    market value .... 11.2[1]
  education .... 11.12[5]
  goodwill .... 11.12[3]; 20.6
  price/earnings ratio ...... 11.4[3][a]
  privacy restrictions....... 11.6[2][d]
  professional practices........ 11.12;
    11.12[1]–11.12[4]
    licenses .... 11.12[5]
  role of valuation expert..... 11.4[1];
    11.4[5]
  stock-for-stock
    transactions .... 11.4[3][b]
  tax liabilities .... 11.5[2]
    accounts receivable .... 11.7[2][a]
    unreported income .... 11.6[1]
  valuation date ...... 11.10; 11.10[1];
    11.10[2]
Marital separation
  See also Marital dissolution
  Canadian law .... 21.3[1][d]
  date of separation............ 11.8
  defined .... 11.8[4]
  postseparation earnings ..... 11.8[2];
    11.8[3][a]–11.8[3][d]
  treatment of earnings....... 11.8[1]
  valuation date .... 11.10[2]
  valuation of loans to
    shareholders .... 11.7[4]
Market risk premium .... 2.9[4]
**Market-share method of calculating
  lost profits** .... 9.4[1][d]
Market/book value
  manufacturing firm ...... 15.5[3][b]
**Market comparison valuation
  methods** 2.8
  comparative company
    search .... 2.8[1]
  market information .... 2.8[3]
  valuation ratios............. 2.8[2]
Market price/net book value ... 6.7[3]
Market value
  See Fair market value
Market valuation method
  manufacturing firms
    capitalization of
      earnings .... 15.5[3][a]
    dividend returns ...... 15.5[3][c];
      16.4[7]; 16.6
    market/book value..... 15.5[3][b]
  service company .... 16.6[3]
Marketability of asset....... 15.1[2][d]
  lack of .... 2.11; 6.9[3]; 10.1[1]
  discount for upon
    liquidation .... 10.4[5][d]
  ESOPs .... 8.6[2]
Medical expenses
  recoverability of .... 9.4[2][a];
    9.4[2][b]

[References are to paragraphs (¶).]

Mergers and acquisitions
 Canadian law ...... 21.1[7]; 21.2[1]
 comparative data .... 14.5[2]
 concept of fair market value ... 3.1; 3.1[1][a]
 concept of fairness .... 3.1; 3.1[1][a]
 insurance company ...... 18.1[1][a]
 searches .... 2.8[3]
 service company .... 16.2[3]
Method of valuation
 See Valuation method
Mezzanine investors .... 12.1[1]
 Minimum-risk investments
 defined .... 18.2[2][b][i]
Minority discounts .... 2.11; 6.9[2]; 6.10[1]; 9.3[1][g]
 in liquidation............. 10.4[5][b]
Mirror loans .... 8.3[2][a]
Miscellaneous expenses
 examination of .... 2.5[2]
Mortgages
 collateralization of .... 7.3[3]; 7.5[2][c]
Motion
 defined .... 9.1[3][d]
Multi-investor equity allocation
 issues .... 8.5; 8.5[1]
Multiple of cash flow-price/cash flow ratio .... 6.8[3][b]
Multiple of earnings .... 6.7[1]
 See also Price/cash flow ratio; Price/earnings ratio
Multiple of revenues valuation method .... 20.7[1][c]

N

Natural resources
 See also Extractive industries
 valuation .... 14.3[2][e]
Net book value .... 5.1[1][g]
Net liquidation value .... 10.1[3]
 vs. going concern value.. 10.1[3][a]; 10.1[3][b]
Net profit margin ratio .... 2.6[9]
Nonbanks.................. 17.1[1][c]
Nonleveraged ESOPs .... 8.3[1]
 cash contributions .... 8.3[1][b]
 impact on value .... 8.3[1][b]
 purpose of .... 8.3[1][b]
 defined .... 8.3[1]
 stock contributions

 form of .... 8.3[1][a]
 tax benefits .... 8.3[1][a]
 vs. leveraged ESOPs .... 8.3[2]
Nonmarketable minority interests .... 9.3[1][g]
Nonoperating income vs. operating income .... 2.5[2]
Non-real estate fixed assets .... 14.3[2][d]
Nonrecurring expenses .... 2.5[2]

O

Off balance sheet items....... 14.2[3]
 commercial banks.......... 17.4[1]
 service company .... 16.6[5]
Oil and gas companies
 See also Extractive industries
 accounting methods
  full cost .... 19.2[5][a]; 19.2[5][b]
  reserve recognition.... 19.2[5][a]; 19.2[5][b]
  successful efforts...... 19.2[5][a]; 19.2[5][b]
 contracts
  market-out clauses ..... 19.2[3][j]
  take or pay .... 19.2[3][j]
 corporations ... 19.2[1][a]; 19.2[7][i]
 discount rate .... 19.2[7][a][iii]
 drilling rigs .... 19.2[3][h]; 19.2[8][a][iii]
 financing.................. 19.2[2]
 finding costs .... 19.2[3][d[
 government regulation.... 19.2[3][i]
 leases .... 19.2[3][f]
  undeveloped .... 19.2[8][a][ii]
 lifting costs .... 19.2[3][c]
 partnerships.. 19.2[1][b]; 19.2[3][b]; 19.2[7][b][ii]
 petroleum engineers
  reserve analysis........ 19.2[6][a]
  role of................. 19.2[6][c]
 Petroleum Engineers' Reserve Analysis .... 19.2[6][a]
 pipeline assets .... 19.2[8][a][iii]
 reserves................. 19.2[8][a][i]
  location .... 19.2[7][c]
  production .. 19.2[3][a]; 19.2[3][b]
 royalty trusts............. 19.2[1][c]
 taxation of .... 19.2[4]
 valuation methods
  break-up value .... 19.2[8][a]

INDEX

[References are to paragraphs (¶).]

financial and operating
   comparisons .... 19.2[8][b]
minority vs. controlling
   interests .... 19.2[8][c]
well-service assets ..... 19.2[8][a][iii]
Oil and gas leases .... 19.2[3][f]
**Operating income vs. nonoperating
income** .... 2.5[2]
Operational control
   defined 2.2
Opportunity cost .... 2.9[3]
Oppression remedy .... 21.2[5][b];
   21.2[5][d]; 21.3[1][c]
Over-the-counter companies .... 2.8[1]

P

Partnerships
   drilling partnerships ...... 19.2[2][b]
   liquidation vs.
     dissolution .... 9.2[3][a]
   litigation *re* .... 9.1[1]; 9.3[2]
   oil and gas partnerships .. 19.2[2][b]
   timber companies .... 19.4[2]
   valuation date .... 9.3[2][d]
   valuation upon
     dissolution .... 9.3[2][a]; 9.3[2][c]
   voluntary vs. involuntary .. 9.3[2][b]
Patents .... 1.1[6]
   infringement actions ...... 9.4[1][a]
Patient records .... 11.6[2][a]
Personal injury actions
   Canadian law .... 21.3[1][h]
   expert witnesses .... 9.4[2]
   litigation *re* .... 9.1[1]
   recoverable damages
     lost earnings .. 9.4[2][a]; 9.4[2][c]
**Petroleum Engineers' Reserve
Analysis** .... 19.2[6][a]
Pleadings
   defined .... 9.1[3][a]; 9.1[3][b]
   role of valuation expert ... 9.1[3][a];
   9.1[3][b]
Preferred stock
   as fixed-income security 7.1
   callability .... 2.3[4][a]
   cash flow 7.1; 7.2
   convertible
     purchase by leveraged
       ESOP .... 8.3[2][a]
   exchangeability .... 7.3[4][b]
   interest preference .. 7.1; 7.2; 7.3[2]
   tax treatment 7.1
   vs. bonds 7.1
Premarital property
   apportionment of 11.9
Premium above control ...... 9.3[1][5]
Premiums
   above control .... 9.3[1][g]
   control .... 2.11; 8.6[2]
   controlling interest ..... 2.11; 6.9[1];
   6.10[2]
   conversion .... 8.3[2][a]
   forcing-out .... 21.2[5][e]
   market risk .... 2.9[4]; 5.2[3]
   unearned
     insurance agency ...... 18.1[7][b]
     insurance company .. 18.1[5][a][i]
Present value ..... 5.2[1]; 18.2[2][c][i]
**Present value discount
rate** .... 18.2[2][c][i]
**Present value of future
profits** .... 18.1[6][d]; 18.1[6][e]
Present worth
   in liquidation
     vs. going-concern
       value .... 10.1[3][a]
Pretrial conference .... 9.1[3][e]
Pretrial discovery
   See Discovery
Pretrial hearing .... 9.1[3][e]
Pretrial order .... 9.1[3][e]
Price/book ratio .... 2.8[2]; 12.3[2][b]
Price/cash flow multiple ..... 5.1[1][c]
   cash flow, defined .... 5.1[1][c]
Price/ cash flow ratio .... 2.8[2];
   6.8[3][b]
**Price/debt-free cash flow
multiple** .... 5.1[1][e]
**Price/debt-free earnings
multiple** .... 5.1[1][d]
Price/dividend ratio .... 2.8[2]
Price/earnings multiple 5.1;
   5.1[1][a]
   earnings defined .... 5.1[1][a]
Price/earnings ratio .. 2.8[2]; 6.8[3][b]
   insurance agency
     valuation .... 18.2[2][a][iii]
   insurance company
     valuation .... 18.1[6][b][i];
   18.1[6][b][ii]
   IPOs .... 12.3[1][a]; 12.3[1][b];
   12.3[2]; 12.3[2][a]; 12.3[2][b]

FINANCIAL VALUATION   I-18

[*References are to paragraphs (¶).*]

Price/earnings ratio *(cont.)*
  IPOs *(cont.)*
    limitations on .... 12.3[2][e]
    marital dissolution
      cases .... 11.4[3][a]
Price/EBDIT ratio .... 6.8[3][c]
Price/EBIT ratio .... 6.8[3][c]
Price/future earnings
  multiple .... 5.1[1][b]
Price/net book value
  multiple .... 5.1[1][g]; 6.8[3][d]
Price/revenue multiple ...... 5.1[1][h]
Price/sales ratio .... 12.3[2][b]
Private companies
  sales data .... 14.5[3]
Private placements
  defined 12.4
  financing................... 12.1
  floor of value............ 12.4[1][b]
  performance vs.
    promise .... 12.4[2][a]
  return on investment .... 12.1[2]
    analysis of .... 12.1[5]
    percentage required by
      investors............ 12.4[1][a]
    premoney vs. postmoney
      valuation ... 12.1[5][b]; 12.4[2]
  risk factor .... 12.1[1]; 12.4[1][e]
Procedural fairness .... 3.3[3]
Product liability actions ..... 9.4[1][a]
Professional appraisal associations
  Canadian .... 21.4[1]; 21.4[2]
  evolution of 1.6
  licensing of 1.6
Professional practice
  accounting for............. 20.1[1]
  as asset.... 11.12; 11.12[1]–11.12[4]
    education .... 11.12[5]
    licenses .... 11.12[5]
  competition .... 20.5[2]; 20.5[3]
  defined 20.1
  fee schedule .... 20.5[6]
  financial statements .... 20.1[2]
  goodwill .... 11.12[3]; 20.5; 20.6
    practice goodwill ... 20.1[4]; 20.4;
                            20.4[2]
    professional goodwill ..... 20.1[4];
                        20.4; 20.4[1]
  normalized earnings.......... 20.3
  service company
    designation .... 20.1[3]
  valuation methods

    capitalization of
      earnings .... 20.7[1][b]
    excess earnings .... 20.7[1][a]
    multiple of revenues ... 20.7[1][c]
  valuation upon marital
    dissolution 20.6
Profit margin/sales ratio .... 4.2[4][b]
Profitability analysis
  savings and loans .... 17.2[3][f]
Profitability ratios .... 4.2[2]
  defined .... 4.2[4]
  gross profit margin/sales
    ratio .... 4.2[4][a]
  net profit margin .... 2.6[9]
  profit margin/sales ratio ... 4.2[4][b]
  return on assets ratio........ 2.6[9];
                          4.2[4][c]
  return on equity .... 2.6[9]
  return on net worth
    ratio .... 4.2[4][d]
Property
  See Real property
Proximate cause
  defined .... 9.1[3][f]
Proxy statement
  insurance company ... 18.1[5][a][ii]
Public company valuation
  method .... 18.2[2]; 18.2[2][a]
  dilution of earnings .... 18.2[2][a][i]
  lack of parity......... 18.2[2][a][ii]
  price/earnings
    multiple .... 18.2[2][a][iii]
Public market trading data ... 14.5[1]
Put rights..................... 6.1
  ESOP termination .... 8.6[2]

Q

Quick ratio .... 2.6[4]; 4.1[1][b]

R

Rate of return (ROR) ...... 2.9[4]; 4.6;
                          5.2–5.2[5]
Ratio analysis 4.1
  See also DuPont system; Financial
    ratios; Trend analysis
  commercial banks.......... 17.3[3]
  importance of .... 2.6[3]
  limitations on 4.9

INDEX

[References are to paragraphs (¶).]

S & Ls .... 17.1[3]
Real estate
  oil and gas leases .... 19.2[3][f]
  valuation approach .... 14.3[2][c]
  valuation upon marital
    dissolution .... 11.7[1]
Reasonable capital test .. 13.2; 13.2[4]
  case study .... 13.3[4][a]–13.3[4][c]
Recovery of damages
  See also Damages
  future earnings .. 9.4[2][d]; 9.4[2][f]
  future expenses .. 9.4[2][a]; 9.4[2][b]
  increased costs .... 9.4[1][d]
  loss of going-concern
    value .... 9.4[1][d]
  lost earnings .... 9.4[2][a]; 9.4[2][c];
    9.4[2][d]
  lost profits .... 9.4[1][d]
  before-and-after method of
    calculation .... 9.4[1][d]
  market-share method of
    calculation .... 9.4[1][d]
  yardstick method of
    calculation .... 9.4[1][d]
  medical expenses .... 9.4[2][a];
    9.4[2][b]
Regulatory environment ...... 14.3[4]
Regulatory law
  defined .... 9.1[2][b]
  oil and gas companies .... 19.2[3][i]
Reinsurance contracts .... 18.21[4][c];
  18.1[5][a][i]
Reinsurers .... 18.1[4][c]
Related-party transfers
  Canadian law .... 21.2[9]
Request for admission of
  evidence .... 9.1[3][d]
Request for production of
  documents .... 9.1[3][c]
Reserve production, oil and
  gas .... 19.2[3][a]; 19.2[3][b]
Reserve recognition accounting
  method .... 19.2[5][a]; 19.2[5][b]
Return on assets (ROA) .... 2.6[9]
Return on equity (ROE) .... 2.6[9]
Return on investment (ROI)
  analysis of .... 12.1[5]
  dilution .... 12.5[1][a]
  start-up businesses
    percentage required by
      investors............ 12.2[1][a]
Return on net worth ratio ... 4.2[4][d]

Return on total assets ratio .. 4.2[4][c]
Revenue Ruling 59-60 .... 1.3; 1.3
  n.16; 2.1[2]; 2.1[2] n.2; 2.4; 15.1[4];
  App. A
Risk-adjusted discount rate .... 5.2[5];
  5.2[6]; 7.5[4]
Risk-free rate .... 2.9[4]
Risk premium
  defined .... 5.2[3]
Risk to investor .... 2.9[3]
  See also Capitalization rates;
    Discount rates
  business risk .... 2.9[3]
  call options .... 7.5[1]
  company-specific risk 7.2; 7.4
  corporate bonds .... 5.2[3]
  current yield .... 7.5[1]
  discounted cash flow
    approach .... 7.5[1]
  early redemption options .... 7.5[1]
  financial risk .... 2.9[3]
  growth vs. risk 5.1
  impact on liquidation ...... 10.3[2]
  IPOs .... 12.1[1]; 12.3[1][e]
  issue-specific risk 7.2; 7.3
  measurement of .... 7.5[1]; 7.5[4]
  valuation of ..... 7.5[2]; 7.5[2][a];
    7.5[2][b]
  junk bonds .... 5.2[3]
  liquidity
    risk factor .... 2.9[3]
    S & Ls .... 17.1[3][b]
  off balance sheet factors .... 14.3[3]
  private placements .... 12.1[1];
    12.4[1][3]
  start-up businesses .... 12.1[1];
    12.1[1][e]
  treasury securities........... 5.2[3]
ROA
  See Return on assets (ROA)
ROE
  See Return on equity (ROE)
ROI
  See Return on investment (ROI)
ROR
  See Rate of return (ROR)
Royalty trusts .... 19.2[1][c]
Rules of Civil Procedure ... 9.1[2][d];
  9.1[3]
Rules of Evidence ... 9.1[2][d]; 9.1[3]

FINANCIAL VALUATION   I-20

[References are to paragraphs (¶).]

S

Sales
  analysis of growth of
    decline .... 2.5[2]

S & Ls
  See Savings and loan (S & L)
    institutions

Savings and loan (S & L)
  institutions.................. 17.1
  See also Financial institutions
  asset mix .... 17.2[3][c]
  balance sheet .... 17.1[1]
    assets .... 17.1[1][a]
      cash accounts .... 17.1[1][a]
      fixed assets.......... 17.1[1][a]
      investment
        securities .... 17.1[1][a]
      loan portfolio .... 17.1[1][a]
      other assets .... 17.1[1][a]
    equity .... 17.1[1][c]
    liabilities.............. 17.1[1][b]
      borrowed funds ..... 17.1[1][b]
      deposits .... 17.1[1][b]
      other liabilities ...... 17.1[1][b]
  branch office efficiency ..... 17.2[4]
  capital ratios .... 17.2[3][e]
  collection problems .... 17.2[4]
  deposit mix .... 17.2[3][c]
  income statement .... 17.1[2]
    expenses .... 17.1[2][b]
    nonoperating
      expenses .... 17.1[2][c]
    nonoperating income ... 17.1[2][c]
    operating income ...... 17.1[2][a]
      fees and other
        interest .... 17.1[2][a]
      other operating
        income .... 17.1[2][a]
  interest analysis .... 17.2[3][g]
  profitability analysis ...... 17.2[3][f]

SEC
  See Securities and Exchange
    Commission (SEC)

Secondary loan markets .... 17.1[1][d]

Securities and Exchange Commission (SEC)
  source of comparative data...2.4[1]; 2.8[1]; 2.8[3]

Security analysis 4.8
  Canadian law .... 21.1[3]

Separate assets .... 18.2[3][b][iii]

Separation
  See Marital separation

Service company
  accounting methods .... 16.5[1]
  acquisitions .... 16.2[3]
  deferred revenues .... 16.5[2]
  ESOPs .... 16.2[2]
  mergers................... 16.2[3]
  professional practice as ..... 20.1[3]
  SIC code classification........ 16.1
  sources of information........ 16.3
  valuation methods
    asset .... 16.6; 16.6[5]
    earnings .... 16.6; 16.6[4]
    market .... 16.6; 16.6[3]; 16.4[7]
    working capital .... 16.5[3]

Shareholder
  See also Stockholder
  appraisal rights .... 9.3[1][a]
  dissenting shareholder
    actions .... 9.1[1]
    burden of proof .... 9.3[1][d]
    control .... 9.3[1][g]
    fairness of action ...... 9.3[1][b]; 9.3[1][c]
    minority interest
      discounts .... 9.3[1][g]
    nonmarketable minority
      interest .... 9.3[1][g]
    postmerger effects....... 9.3[1][f]
    premium above
      control .... 9.3[1][g]
    role of valuation expert.... 9.3[1]
  minority shareholder
    Canadian .. 21.2[5][b]; 21.1[5][d]; 21.3[1][c]
  taxation of
    upon liquidation ...... 10.1[3][a]; 10.4[6]
  valuation methods .... 9.3[1][e]
  valuation of loans to
    upon marital separation .. 11.7[4]

SIC code
  See Standard Industrial
    Classification (SIC) System

Single-period benefit .... 2.9[1]

Software
  service company asset ...... 16.4[2]

Solvency analysis
  balance sheet test ..... 13.2; 13.2[2]
  Canadian law .... 21.2[10]

[References are to paragraphs (¶).]

case study 13.3
cash flow test 13.2
due diligence
   cost structure .... 13.2[1]
   financial flexibility .... 13.2[1]
   recession behavior .... 13.2[1]
Solvency letter .... 13.1[2]
Standard Industrial Classification (SIC) Manual .... 14.2[1]
Standard Industrial Classification (SIC) System ... 2.4[1]; 2.8[1]; 2.8[3]
   classifications .... 14.1[1]; 14.2[3][a]
   manufacturing companies .... 15.1[1]
   oil and gas companies .... 19.2[7]
   service companies 16.1
   limitations .... 14.2[3]
   usefulness .... 14.1[2]
Start-up businesses
   financing .... 12.1[1]
   risk factor .... 12.1[1]; 12.1[1][e]
   ROI .... 12.1[2]
   analysis of .... 12.1[5]
   percentage required by investors .... 12.2[1][a]
   premoney vs. postmoney valuation .... 12.1[5][a]
   valuation of .... 12.2[1]–12.2[2]
State tax returns
   examination of .... 2.5[1]; 2.5[2]
Statement of changes in financial position
   examination of .... 2.4[4]
   insurance company ... 18.1[5][a][i]; 18.1[5][b][iii]
Statement of changes in shareholder's equity .... 18.1[5][a][i]
Statutory law
   defined .... 9.1[2][a]
   relationship to valuation ... 9.1[2][a]
Stipulation
   defined .... 9.1[3][d]
Stock
   See also Common stock; Preferred stock
   cash flow 7.2
   common stock
   manufacturing company .... 15.1[2][d]
   purchase by leveraged ESOP .... 8.3[2][a]
   service company .... 16.6[1]; 16.6[2]
   valuation .... 14.4[2][b]
   contribution of by nonleveraged ESOP .... 8.3[1][a]
   discounting shares
   insurance agency ... 18.2[2][a][ii]
   disposition of in marital dissolution .... 11.13[1]
   preferred stock .... 7.1; 8.3[2][ii]
   purchase by ESOP .... 8.3[2][a]; 8.3[2][b]
Stock-for-stock transactions
   marital dissolution cases .... 11.4[3][b]
Stockholder
   See also Shareholder
   appraisal rights ..... 3.2[2]; 9.3[1][a]
   duties owed by directors 3.2
Stockholder's equity .... 5.1[1][g]
Subsidiaries
   insurance companies ... 18.1[5][a][i]
Successful efforts accounting method .... 19.2[5][a]; 19.2[5][b]

T

Tangible asset liquidation .... 9.3[2][a]
Tangible net worth ...... 18.2[2][a][v]
   insurance agency valuation balance sheet considerations ..... 18.2[3][b][i]
   public company method .... 18.2[2][a][v]
Tangible property
   valuation upon marital dissolution .... 11.7[1]
Taxation, federal
   See also State tax returns
   advantages of leveraged ESOP .... 8.3[2]
   Canadian law ... 21.1[1]; 21.3[1][a]
   coal companies .... 19.3[3]
   inflation adjustment for .... 9.4[2][e]
   insurance company .. 18.1[6][a][vi]; 18.1[6][b][iii]
   effect of valuation on .... 18.1[6][a][vi]
   IPOs .... 12.3[1][a]

[*References are to paragraphs (¶).*]

Taxation, federal *(cont.)*
liquidation
    effect on
        shareholders .... 10.1[3][a];
        10.4[6]
    oil and gas companies ...... 19.2[4]
    sales of business upon marital
        dissolution .... 11.5[2]
        accounts receivable .... 11.7[2][a]
        unreported income .... 11.6[1]
    service companies .... 16.2[1]
    tax returns
        examination of ..... 2.5[1]; 2.5[2]
    timber companies .... 19.3[4]
    upon liquidation
        shareholder .... 10.4[6]
    vs. going-concern
        value .... 10.1[3][a]
Terms of sale of business ..... 14.4[2]
Thrift institution
    See Savings and loan (S & L)
    institutions
Timber companies
    holding company .... 19.4[1][b]
    operating company .... 19.4[1][a]
    partnerships .... 19.4[2]
    taxation of .... 19.4[3]
Times interest earned ratio .... 2.6[8];
    4.2[2][c]
Tort actions
    Canadian law .... 21.3[1][g]
    litigation *re* .... 9.1[1]
Total assets turnover ratio ... 4.2[3][e]
Total assets utilization ratio ... 2.6[7]
Total debt/total assets ratio .... 2.6[8];
    4.2[2][a]
Total interest-bearing debt/equity
    ratio .... 4.2[2][b]
Trademarks .... 1.1[6]
    infringement actions ...... 9.4[1][a]
Trade names .... 16.4[6]
Trade secrets .... 11.6[2][a]
Trading market valuation
    method .... 18.1[6][b]
Treasury securities .... 5.2[3]
Trend analysis 4.3
    commercial banks .... 17.3[3]
    S & Ls .... 17.1[3]
Trial
    focus of .... 9.1[3][f]
    role of valuation expert .... 9.1[3][f]

U

Underlying asset valuation
    method .... 2.10[1]
Underwriters .... 18.1[4][d];
    18.1[5][b][ii]
Unearned premium reserve
    recapture of ... 18.1[7][a]; 18.1[7][b]
Unreported income
    marital dissolution .... 11.6[1]
Utilization ratios .... 2.6[5]

V

Valuation
    See also Financial institutions;
        Manufacturing companies;
        Marital dissolution; Insurance
        agency; Insurance company;
        Litigation; Service companies;
        Value; Valuation date; Valuation
        expert; Valuation method;
        Valuation report
    business continuity as
        factor .... 14.3[8]
    Canadian law .... 21.6[3]
    case study 6.4–6.10
    combined highest and best
        use .... 10.1[1]
    common elements in ...... 9.3[1][e]
    competition as factor .... 14.3[6];
    14.3[7]
        availability of data 14.5
    depreciation as a factor .. 14.3[2][c];
    14.3[2][d]
    determining assets to be
        valued .... 15.1[2]
    dissenting shareholder's right
        to .... 9.3[1][a]
    ease of entry into industry .. 14.3[5]
    fair market value .... 1.1[2]
    financial institution
        commercial
            banks .... 17.3[1]–17.3[4]
        comparables .... 17.4[1]
        off balance sheet items ... 17.4[1]
        S & Ls .... 17.2[1]–17.2[5]
    goodwill .... 1.1[1]; 1.1[5]
    industry characteristics
        affecting 14.3
    insurance agencies 18.2

INDEX

[References are to paragraphs (¶).]

insurance companies 18.1; 18.2
intangible assets .. 1.1[6]; 10.1[1][b]
IPOs .. 12.1; 12.3; 12.3[1]–12.3[2][f]
IRS guides and manuals 1.3
manufacturing
   companies 15.1–15.5
market factors affecting 14.4
minority issue discounts ... 9.3[1][g]
nonmarketable minority
   interests .... 9.3[1][g]
off balance sheet factors .... 14.3[3]
owner's input ..... 14.3[9]; 14.3[10]
postmerger effects .... 9.3[1][f]
premium above control .... 9.3[1][g]
private placements 12.1; 12.4;
                 12.4[1]–12.4[3]
purpose of .... 15.1[3]
regulatory environment ..... 14.3[4]
service companies 16.1–16.8
small business vs. larger
   business .... 14.3[12]
start-ups 12.1; 12.2;
                 12.2[1]–12.2[2]
upon marital dissolution
   accounts
      receivable .... 11.7[2]–11.7[2][c]
   alimony .... 11.7[2][b]
   goodwill .... 11.7[2][c]
   hard assets .... 11.7[1]
   loans to shareholders ... 11.7[2][d]
   special issues
      confidentiality .... 11.6[2]
      unreported income ..... 11.6[1]
vs. damage
   determination .... 9.3[1][b]
   elements of value .... 9.4[1][b]
   entity to be valued ...... 9.4[1][b]
   valuation method .... 9.4[1][b]
Valuation analysis 6.8
Valuation date 2.3
   Canadian ..... 21.3[1][a]; 21.3[1][d]
   corporate dissolution ...... 9.3[2][d]
   fraud action .... 9.3[3]
   marital dissolution 11.10;
                11.10[1]; 11.10[2]
   partnership dissolution .... 9.3[2][d]
Valuation expert
   See also Expert opinion; Valuation
     report
   Canadian ..... 21.2[1][a]–21.2[1][d]
   conflicts of interest .... 9.2[2][c]
   discovery

depositions .... 9.1[3][c]; 9.2[2][i];
                     9.2[3][c]
   interrogatories .... 9.1[3][c]
   requests for production of
     documents .... 9.1[3][c]
favorable personal
   attributes .... 9.2[1][a]
   impression of judge ..... 9.1[3][g]
   impression of jury ...... 9.1[3][h]
   professionalism .... 9.2[1][b];
                     9.2[2][b]
insurance agency ..... 18.2[3][b][iii]
motions .... 9.2[3][d]
opinion of
   factor in calculating
     damages .... 9.4[2][d]
petroleum engineer .... 19.2[6][c]
professional appraisal
   associations .. 1.6; 21.4[1]; 21.4[2]
professional
   practices .... 20.5[4]–20.5[9];
                      20.7[2]
requests for admission ..... 9.1[3][d]
service company .... 16.4[7]
stipulations .... 9.1[3][d]
testimony 9.1
   hearsay .... 9.2[2][f]
   preparation for .... 9.2[2][h];
                     9.2[3][b]
   pretrial hearing .... 9.1[3][e]
   trial .... 9.1[3][f]; 9.2[3][d]
   use of valuation report .. 9.2[3][b]
understanding of
   capital intensity 14.3
   financial assets .... 14.3[2][a]
   fraudulent conveyances 13.1
   industry characteristics 14.3
   inventory .... 14.3[2][b]
   natural resources ...... 14.3[2][e]
   non-real estate assets ... 14.3[2][d]
   real estate .... 14.3[2][c]
vs. consultant .... 9.2[2][a]
Valuation litigation
   See Litigation
Valuation methods 2.7; 6.7;
                   6.7[1]–6.7[6]
   Canadian
     assets .... 21.2[5][d]
     earnings .... 21.2[5][d]
     market price .... 21.2[5][d]

FINANCIAL VALUATION I-24

[References are to paragraphs (¶).]

Valuation methods *(cont.)*
  capitalization of earnings,
    generally .... 1.1[3]; 1.1[4]
  coal companies .... 19.3[2]
  financial institutions
    commercial
      banks .... 17.3[1]–17.3[4]
    comparables .... 17.4[1]
    off balance sheet items ... 17.4[1]
    S & Ls .... 17.2[1]–17.2[5]
    generally 14.1; 14.6
  insurance agencies
    capitalization of
      earnings .... 18.2[2][b]
    public company
      method .... 18.2[2][a]
    wasting assets .... 18.2[2][c]
  insurance companies
    acquisition value ...... 18.1[6][c];
                    18.1[6][f][iii]
    adjusted net book
      value .... 18.1[6][a]
    present value of future
      profits .... 18.1[6][d]; 18.1[6][e];
                    18.1[6][f][iv]
    trading market .... 18.1[6][b]
  manufacturing firms
    asset .... 15.5[1]
    discounted cash flow ..... 15.5[2]
    market .... 15.5[3]
    other .... 15.5[4]
  marital dissolution
    apportionment of
      property .. 11.9; 11.9[1]–11.9[3]
    components of value 11.7
    compulsion value .... 11.2[3]
    investment value .... 11.2[2]
    market value .... 11.2[1]
  oil and gas companies
    break-up value .... 19.2[8][a]
    financial and operating
      comparisons .... 19.2[8][b]
    minority vs. controlling
      interests .... 19.2[8][c]
  professional practices
    capitalization of
      earnings .... 20.1[5]
    comparative transaction
      data .... 20.1[5]
    excess earnings .... 20.7[1][a]
    multiple of revenues ... 20.7[1][c]
    reconciliation of .... 6.10[1]

  service companies
    asset .... 16.6[5]
    fair market value vs. common
      stock .... 16.6[2]
    earnings .... 16.6[4]
    majority vs. minority
      interests .... 16.6[1]
    market .... 16.6[3]
    special considerations 16.7
  timber companies 19.4
Valuation ratios .... 2.8[2]
Valuation report .... 2.4[1]; 3.4
  form of .... 9.2[3][a]
  use of in preparation for testi-
    mony deposition .... 9.2[3][b]
    trial .... 9.2[3][b]
Value
  book value .... 2.1[6]
  defined 2.1
  enterprise value .... 2.1[7]
  fair market value .... 2.1[1]
  fair value .... 2.1[2]
  going-concern value .... 2.1[4]
  intrinsic value .... 2.1[3]
  investment value .... 2.1[3]
  liquidation value .... 2.1[5]
Value in use
  defined .... 2.10[2]
Variable adjusted rate
  discount .... 9.4[2][f]
Variability of operations .... 7.4[2]
Varied interests to be valued
  defined .... 15.1[2]
Venture capital .... 12.1[1]
Verdict
  defined .... 9.1[3][h]

W

WACC
  See Weighted average cost of capital
    (WACC)
Wasting asset valuation
  method .... 18.2[2]; 18.2[2][c]
Weighted average cost of capital
  (WACC) .... 5.2[6]; 5.2[7]; 6.8[4]
Weighted average method of valuation
  See Delaware block method of
    valuation
Work-in-process inventory
  professional practices .... 20.2[2]

[References are to paragraphs (¶).]

Work-life expectancy
  projection of .... 9.4[2][d]
Working capital .... 16.5[3];
                                     18.2[2][a][iv]
Working capital turnover
  ratio .... 4.2[3][d]
Wrongful death
  compensible damages ...... 9.4[2][a]
    funeral expenses .... 9.4[2][a];
                                    9.4[2][b]
    lost earnings .... 9.4[2][d]
    medical expenses ...... 9.4[2][a];
                                    9.4[2][b]
  expert opinion .... 9.4[2]
  litigation *re* .... 9.1[1]

Y

Yardstick method of calculating lost
  profits .... 9.4[1][d]
Yield-plus growth valuation
  method .... 2.9[4]

Z

Zero-coupon securities .... 5.2[3]